There is a road, steep and thorny, beset with perils of every kind—but yet a road: and it leads to the Heart of the Universe. I can tell you how to find Those who will show you the secret gateway that leads inward only. . . . For those who win onwards, there is reward past all telling: the power to bless and save humanity. For those who fail, there are other lives in which success may come.

HELENA PETROVNA BLAVATSKY
(discovered in her desk after her death
on May 8, 1891)

THE GUPTA VIDYA

THE PILGRIMAGE OF HUMANITY

THE GUPTA VIDYA

THE GUPTA VIDYA

VOLUME III

THE PILGRIMAGE OF HUMANITY

RAGHAVAN NARASIMHAN IYER

Tr

Theosophy Trust Books

Norfolk, VA

The Gupta Vidya
Volume III
The Pilgrimage of Humanity

by Raghavan Narasimhan Iyer

Library of Congress Control Number: 2019908542
ISBN: 978-1-7334650-2-1
10 9 8 7 6 5 4 3 2 1

Publisher's Cataloging-In-Publication Data
(Prepared by The Donohue Group, Inc.)

Names: Iyer, Raghavan, 1930-1995, author.
Title: The Gupta Vidya. Volume III, The pilgrimage of humanity /
Raghavan Narasimhan Iyer.
Other Titles: Pilgrimage of humanity
Description: First edition. | Norfolk, VA : Theosophy Trust Books, 2020.
| Previously published in Hermes, 1975-1989. | Includes bibliographical
references and index.
Identifiers: ISBN 9781733465021 | ISBN 9781733465045 (ebook)
Subjects: LCSH: Theosophy. | Spiritual life. | Reincarnation. | Pilgrims
and pilgrimages. | Enlightenment--Religious aspects. | Human evolution--
Religious aspects.
Classification: LCC BP565.I97 G863 2020 (print) | LCC BP565.I97
(ebook) | DDC 299.934--dc23

Theosophy Trust Books
Norfolk, VA

First edition: June 20, 2020

Published and printed in the United States of America

Articles from *Hermes* may be found at https://www.theosophytrust.org

ACKNOWLEDGEMENTS

[Editor's note: the introductory materials were intended for all three volumes, and are reproduced in each volume for the reader's convenience.]

The arcane teachings in these three volumes on the Gupta Vidya were, almost entirely, delivered orally from 1949 to 1989 in India, England, Canada and the United States. The talks and answers to questions were taped and transcribed, edited and published in the journal *Hermes* (1975 - 1989), Concord Grove Press, 1407 Chapala Street, Santa Barbara. I am deeply grateful to all those who generously helped in the task of taping, transcribing, preliminary editing, proofing, composing and formatting, copy editing and printing.

I am especially indebted to Pico Iyer for his patient and superb editing, and to Elton Hall and Kirk Gradin for transferring them from the Verityper format to that of my own computer, whilst I alone am responsible for all errors and deficiencies in this work. Whatever is of value in these volumes I owe to the writings of H.P. Blavatsky, W.Q. Judge, D.K. Mavalankar, Claude St. Martin, Bhavani Shankar, Robert Crosbie and Krishna Prem, and to my Spiritual Teachers—Ramana Maharshi, B.P. Wadia, D.S. Sharma, Sarvepalli Radhakrishnan, S. Subramaniya Aiyer, Thangammal Gopalaswami Iyer, K. Swaminathan, Krishna Shastri, my parents L. Narasimhan and Lakshmi N. Iyer, and my wife Nandini.

I have also enormously benefitted over half a century from memorable conversations with honest agnostics and humane gnostics alike—Dr. J.N. Chubb of Elphinstone College, T.D. Weldon (my main Oxford Tutor), Dr. R.H. Thouless, Maude Hoffman, Hans Christofel, Christmas Humphreys, Claude Houghton, Clifford Bax, Gilbert Murray, Victor Gollancz, H.S.L. Polak, Friedrich Plank, Rabbi Rosen, Dr. John Smythies, James Laver, Lord Bertrand Russell, Bhikshu Sangharakshita, H.D. Lewis, Stephen Spender, Arne Naess, Arnold Toynbee, Julian

Huxley, David Astor, Rev. Michael Scott, Sir William Deakin, David Footman, James Joll, H.H. Price, Sir Alfred Ayer, Sir Patrick Strawson, Patrick Corbett, Geoffrey Hudson, John Plamenatz, Richard Crossman, Sir Isaiah Berlin, Guy Wint, Albert West, Pyarelal Nair, Lord Pethick-Lawrence, Viscount and Bronwen Astor, Vinoba Bhave, Fosco Maraini, Sir Richard Livingstone, Dr. Roberto Assigioli, the monk Sangye Tenzin, the Ashanti Chief in Ghana, Danilo Dolci, Bratako Ateko, Kudjo Mawudeku, Robert Hutchins, Herbert Schneider, Paul Wienpahl, Bishop James Pike, Caesar Chavez, Ian Stevenson, Svetoslav Roerich, Tenzin Gyatso (the 14th Dalai Lama), Periyavar (the late Kanchi Shankaracharya, 1894 - 1994), and Tangye Tenzin, the wise Abbot of Sera Je Monastery (Shigatze and Bylakuppe, Mysore).

This three-volume work on the *Gupta Vidya* is gratefully dedicated to The Venerable Lohan ("The Great Sacrifice"), The Maha Chohan (Arghyanath, the "Lord of Libations"), Agatsya Muni ("the Regent of Aryavarta"), Mahatma M. (Rishi Vishvamitra) and Mahatma K.H. ("Pitaguru"). They called it forth and for Them it was recorded.

March 10, 1995   R. N. I.

SHRI RAGHAVAN N. IYER

(March 10, 1930 – June 20, 1995)

He drew a circle that shut me out —
Heretic, rebel, a thing to flout.
But Love and I had the wit to win:
We drew a circle that took him in!

Edwin Markham

The spiritually penetrating essays in these three volumes were set forth for the expressed purpose of shedding the pristine light of universal Theosophy on the path of spiritual self-regeneration in the service of humanity. The Theosophical philosophy is predicated on the ageless truth that divine wisdom exists, and, most significantly, that wise beings exist who dynamically embody it in world history; that sages and seers still grace the globe and that they continually oversee the spiritual, mental, and physical evolution of man and nature. The secret Society of Sages that guides human progress periodically sends forth one of their own to sound afresh the Divine Philosophy and exemplify the spiritual life in all its richness and mystery. Such an enlightened spiritual teacher articulates eternal but forgotten truths in ingenious ways, adopting modalities that inspire the mind, release soul perception, and cut through the froth of history and the miasma of an age.

Shri Raghavan N. Iyer was a man of immense magnanimity and deep spiritual and intellectual genius. Born in Madras, India in 1930, he matriculated at the University of Bombay at the precocious age of fourteen and received his bachelor's degree in economics at age eighteen. Two years later he received the Chancellor's Gold Medal, earned his master's degree in Advanced Economics, and was selected as the Rhodes Scholar from India to Oxford University. At Oxford, he excelled in his academic studies and avidly participated in Oxford's rich social, political, and cultural life. During his undergraduate years, he eagerly joined a number of Oxford University clubs and societies. He was apparently so well-liked and respected that, in time, he was elected president of several prominent student organizations: the Oxford Social Studies Association, the Voltaire Society, and the Plotinus Society (which he also founded). His broader social sympathies and para-political concerns were served by joining and eventually becoming president of the Oxford University Peace Association and the Oxford Majlis Society (a debating society of Oxford students from South Asia that took up political issues). In 1954, he became president of the prestigious Oxford Union—perhaps the premiere debating society of his time. (Debates were usually spontaneous, witty, and packed full of appropriate references to recognizable historical figures in literature, politics, and society.) At year's end, he earned first-class honors in Philosophy, Politics, and Economics and later was awarded his master and doctorate degrees in Political Theory.

Shri Raghavan was an outstanding teacher of philosophy and politics throughout his public life. He assumed the mantle of teaching at the age of eighteen when he was appointed Fellow and Lecturer in Economics at Elphinstone College, University of Bombay. In 1956, he was appointed an Oxford don, giving tutorials in moral and political philosophy. In addition to teaching at Oxford, he lectured throughout Europe, America, and Africa, e.g., the University of Oslo in Norway (1958), the College of Europe in Belgium (1962), Erasmus Seminar in the Netherlands (1962), the University of Chicago in America (1963), and the University of Ghana in Legon (1964). His profound insights, sparkling intellectual clarity, mastery of different conceptual languages, and his infectious enthusiasm inspired thousands of students on different continents and earned him the deep respect of his contemporaries.

After accepting a professorship at the University of California (Santa Barbara) in 1965, he taught classes and seminars in political philosophy until his retirement at the age of fifty-six. His introductory classes and graduate seminars were legendary for their philosophical depth, theoretical openness, and visionary richness. His class topics were innovative and they attracted the curious, the committed, the idealist, the political realist, and the culturally disenfranchised. The most inspiring (and exacting) undergraduate courses were always enrolled to the maximum and lectures frequently ended with spontaneous standing ovations from the students. Those classes included: "Parapolitics and the City of Man", "Anarchist Thought", "Plato and the Polis", "The Dialectic from Plato to Marx", "Politics and Literature", "American Radicalism", and "The American Dream and the City of Man". His lectures were full of wit as well as wisdom and they unfailingly inspired students to cultivate an abiding confidence in themselves as learners and to become viable contributors to the emerging City of Man. His formal lectures and innumerable informal gatherings affected generations of students who later contributed to diverse fields of work, worship, and humanitarian service.

In addition to his vast and varied gifts as a teacher, Shri Raghavan Iyer was a devoted consultant and lecturer to various world organizations committed to some form of universal human betterment. While an Oxford don, he became a member of the Executive Committee for the World Association of World Federalists (The Hague) and likewise became a consultant and lecturer for the Friends International Centre (Kranj, Yugoslavia). In a similar spirit of rendering service, he became a consultant to OXFAM and accepted the temporary post of Director of Studies, UNESCO Conference on "Mutual Understanding Between the Orient and the Occident". He was also a member of The Club of Rome, The Reform Club, and The World Futures Studies Federation. In later years he became a contributing member of the Task Force appointed by U.S. President Jimmy Carter to develop "The Global 2000 Report for the President"—a call for Promethean initiatives to meet the most compelling needs of an emerging global civilization.

Over the arc of his extraordinary life, Shri Raghavan wrote numerous articles in diverse fields of thought as well as authored and edited many works that point toward an emerging global consciousness—replete with multiple challenges and stirring prospects. In 1965, he edited *The Glass Curtain between Asia and Europe.* This compilation of essays by internationally reputed historians contained a fascinating dialogue between Shri Raghavan and the world's most eminent historian at the time, Arnold Toynbee. They mutually explored Shri Raghavan's thesis that there exists an obscuring "glass curtain" between Asia and Europe that needs to be recognized and dealt with before there can be true intellectual and cultural understanding between East and West.

His most well-known and prominent books are *The Moral and Political Thought of Mahatma Gandhi* (1973) and *Parapolitics — Toward the City of Man* (1977). Each of these remarkable pioneering works is accessible to both the profound thinker and the serious inquirer, the erudite scholar and the dedicated student, the earnest seeker and the committed practitioner. Later, in 1983, he edited an extraordinary collection of spiritually inspiring readings entitled *The Jewel in the Lotus* — aptly characterized by Professor K. Swaminathan, a noted compiler of Gandhi's collected writings, as "a Universal Bible". In addition, Shri Raghavan edited and wrote luminous introductions for numerous sacred texts, including Hindu, Buddhist, Jain, Jewish, Christian, and Sufi teachings.

The deeper replenishing current of Shri Raghavan's life, however, flowed from the empyrean springs of *Theosophia*. He became a Theosophist at age ten when his father first took him to the United Lodge of Theosophists in Bombay. In time, he was introduced to the profound writings of H.P. Blavatsky and W.Q. Judge. Not long after entering the orbit of the Theosophical Movement, he made a sacred resolve to serve the Lodge of Mahatmas and increasingly assumed responsibility for forwarding the impulse of the worldwide Theosophical Cause of promoting universal brotherhood. For the rest of his life, all his efforts in the academic, social, political, and religious arenas were infused by his wholehearted devotion to the service of the Brotherhood of Bodhisattvas and to the enlightenment of the human race. This deeper, ever-present golden thread of meaning that wove together all his worldly activities became more apparent when he emigrated to America.

In 1965, Shri Raghavan moved with his wife and son to Santa Barbara, California. (His wife, Nandini, a brilliant Oxford don who received a First in Philosophy, Politics, and Economics at Oxford, went on to teach in both the Philosophy and Religious Studies departments at the University of California, Santa Barbara until her retirement. Pico, their only child, was born in Oxford in 1957. He later graduated from Oxford University and became a contributing writer to *Time* magazine and is now a noted author of international standing.) Once settled in California, Shri Raghavan and Nandini founded the United Lodge of Theosophists, Santa Barbara. Beginning informally in October of 1966, the Lodge grew from fourteen initial students to over a hundred active associates. Soon after its inaugural meeting on February 18, 1969 (the death anniversary of Shri Krishna), Lodge members were invited to give talks and, in time, to co-lead Theosophy School classes for the young. In addition to evolving various modalities of giving and receiving Theosophical instruction, Shri Raghavan and Nandini founded several ancillary institutions that further served the global aims of the worldwide Theosophical Movement.

One such ancillary institution is the Institute of World Culture in Santa Barbara. On July 4, 1976—the bicentennial of the American Declaration of Independence—Shri Raghavan and Nandini co-initiated this educational non-profit organization. Its "Declaration of Interdependence" elucidates ten aims that are the visionary basis of all its intellectually and culturally enlightening programs and activities. The Institute of World Culture regularly hosts engaging seminars, forums, lectures, study circles, and film series. There is a wholesome blending of spiritual, intellectual, ethical, and cultural themes for focused thought and extensive discussion. The Institute has proved to be a culturally "consciousness expanding" experience for many and has, in its own way, contributed to a deeper appreciation of the often unsuspected power of classical and renaissance cultures to provide illuminating perspectives on a host of contemporary national and global issues.

As a forward-looking extension of his sacred obligation to serve the Theosophical Movement, Shri Raghavan founded, edited, and wrote for the golden journal *Hermes* (1975 – 1989). This wide-ranging spiritual journal was dedicated to the pristine sounding of Brahma Vach and to the spiritual regeneration of humanity. The profound articles found in *Hermes* span the spectrum of human thought from the metaphysical to the mystical, the ethical to the psychological, the spiritual to the material, the mythical to the historical. They convincingly reveal the subtle Theosophical foundations of all religions, philosophies, and sciences. They ingeniously address the chronic problems of the age and provide much needed "correctives to consciousness" in an age that tilts away from soul-saving and revitalizing ideals.

As repeatedly witnessed by close students, Shri Raghavan spoke at many different levels and freely interacted with each and all—regardless of race, creed, or condition. He exemplified—for the sake of the future—a multitude of Aquarian modalities and qualities. He was, in one sense, very Hindu: a true Brahmin—spiritual, cultured, brilliant, full of the graces that immediately remind one of ancient India and of golden ages long past. He was also very English: confident, highly educated, extremely literate, and at ease with statesmen, scientists, educators, and royalty. He was also very American: a true and fearless rebel, innovative, resourceful, visionary, and the eternal friend of the common man. But, beyond all this, he was in a much deeper sense the Universal Man, original, *sui generis* and timeless. His sympathies were always compassionately inclusive and his repeated emphasis—from first to last—was to "draw the larger circle" through universality of thought, the richness of imagination, the therapeutics of speech, and the magic of selfless action.

The wide-ranging arcane teachings in all three of these volumes were transcriptions of talks given between 1949 to 1989 in India, England, and the United States and were carefully edited by Shri Raghavan shortly before his death. When meditated upon and skillfully applied to the realm of self-chosen duties, they purify the mind, cleanse the heart, and give birth to men and women committed to creatively contributing to the universal civilization of tomorrow.

CONTENTS

Appendices

AUM

To contemplate these things is the privilege of the gods, and to do so is also the aspiration of the immortal soul of man generally, though only in a few cases is such aspiration realized.

PLATO

INTRODUCTION

GUPTA VIDYA *is like an ancient Banyan tree. Some come to sit in its shade, while others come to exchange words and seek friends. Still others come to pick fruit. Nature is generous.*

Some come to sit in the presence of teachers to receive instruction in the mighty power of real meditation, to secure help in self-examination. All are welcome.

The antiquity and enormity of the tree are beyond the capacity of any person in any period of history to enclose in a definition or formulation.

Great Teachers point beyond themselves to that which is beyond formulation, which is ineffable and indefinable. They seek to make alive and to make real for every man the priceless boon of learning truth.

RAGHAVAN N. IYER

THE GUPTA VIDYA

The universe is even as a great temple.
CLAUDE DE ST. MARTIN

The central truths of Gupta Vidya are not derived from any ancient or modern sect but represent the accumulated wisdom of the ages, the unrecorded inheritance of humanity. Its vast scheme of cosmic and human evolution furnishes all true seekers with the symbolic alphabet necessary to interpret their recurrent visions as well as the universal framework and metaphysical vocabulary, drawn from many mystics and seers, which enable them to communicate their own intuitive perceptions. All authentic mystical writings are enriched by the alchemical flavour of theosophical thought. Gupta Vidya is an integrated system of fundamental verities taught by initiates and adepts across millennia. It is the *Philosophia Perennis*, the philosophy of human perfectibility, the science of spirituality and the religion of responsibility. It is the primeval fount of myriad religious systems as well as the hidden essence and esoteric wisdom of each. Its cosmology is known as *Brahma Vidya* and its noetic psychology is known as *Atma Vidya*. Man, an immortal monad, has been able to preserve this sacred heritage through the sacrificial efforts of enlightened and compassionate individuals, or Bodhisattvas, who constitute an ancient Brotherhood. They quietly assist in the ethical evolution and spiritual development of the whole of humanity. Gupta Vidya is Divine Wisdom, transmitted and verified over aeons by the sages who belong to this secret Brotherhood.

The supreme presupposition of Gupta Vidya is an eternal substance-principle postulated as the ineffable Ground of all being. It is called a substance-principle because it becomes increasingly substantial and differentiated on the plane of manifestation, while it essentially remains a homogeneous principle in abstract space and eternal duration. The perceived universe is a complex mirroring of this Unknown Source, all finite conceptions of which are necessarily incomplete. It is the Absolute Negation of all that exists. It is Be-ness or *Sat*, the Secondless Reality, the No-thing of ancient philosophy, the 'Boundless Lir', the Unknown Beginning of Celtic cosmogony. Compared with It, all manifestation is no more than an impermanent illusion or *maya*, a kaleidoscopic medium through which the one Reality shows itself in a series of reflections. Spirit and matter are the two facets of this indivisible principle which only seem to be separate during a vast period of cosmic manifestation. They radiate from this transcendent source, yet are not causally related to It, since neither quality nor mode may properly be ascribed to It. They appear periodically on the objective plane as the opposite poles of this Reality yet they are not inherently separate, but mutually coexist as spirit-matter. In manifestation this substratum differentiates itself into seven planes of increasing density, reaching towards the region of sense data. Everywhere the root essence of homogeneous substance is the same, transforming itself by minute degrees from the most ethereal to the most gross.

The seven planes of manifestation may be seen as condensations of rarefied matter and also as living streams of intelligences — primordial rays proceeding from an invisible Spiritual Sun. All modes of activity in the Universe are internally guided by powers and potencies arrayed in an almost endless series of hierarchies, each with its exact function and precise scope of action. They are called Dhyan Chohans in Tibetan cosmogony and bear many other titles in the rich panoply of religious traditions — Angels, Devas, Dhyani Buddhas, Gods, Elohim, etc. All these are transmitting agents of cosmic Law (*ṛta*) which guides the evolution of each atom on every plane in space, the hierarchies varying enormously in their respective degrees of creative consciousness and monadic intelligence. As an aggregate, this immense host of forces forms the manifesting Verbum of an unmanifest Presence, constituting simultaneously the active Mind of the cosmos and its immutable Law. The idea of myriad hierarchies of intelligences animating visible Nature is a vital key to understanding all true mysticism. Many flashes of intuitive perception reveal multitudes of radiant beings elaborating the interior architecture of matter. Great mystics show a reverential recognition of the Logos or Verbum, the Army of the Voice, operating behind the screen of surface events as the noumenal cause of natural phenomena. This involves deciphering the signs of these intelligent forces by following the traces of their effects. The natural world bears the signatures of a divine archetypal world. With proper keys to archaic symbolism, the true seeker can read these signatures and recover the lost knowledge which would restore a primeval state of gnosis equivalent to that of the Gods. The letters composing the Sanskrit language are the phenomenal expressions of these finer forces, and by understanding them one could discover the root vibration, the ineffable Word, reverberating throughout the sentient world of visible Nature.

The arcane teaching concerning the Great Chain of Being in the supernatural realm continually reappears in human history as the inexhaustible fountain-head of aesthetic expression, heroic action and mystic illumination. The diverse expressions of creativity in the arts, religion and philosophy stem from this common unseen source, and the search for its origin is the hallowed mission of many a mystic and artist. The problem of tracing particulars to universals is as crucial to art as to psychology. The sevenfold classification of man's inner constitution corresponds to seven cosmic planes of being. Man is truly a microcosm and miniature copy of the macrocosm. Like the macrocosm, the individual is divine in essence, a direct radiation from the central Spiritual Sun. As pure spirit, every human being needs the vestures through which life may be experienced on differentiated planes of existence, so that one can become fully conscious of individual immortality and one's indissoluble identity with the whole. Every person is a complete reflection of the universe, revealing oneself to oneself by means of seven differentiations. In one's deepest self, the individual is *Atman*, the universal spirit which is mirrored in the luminous soul or *Buddhi*.

The light of *Buddhi* is focussed through *Manas* or impersonal intellect, the source of human individuation. These three together constitute the imperishable fire in man, the immortal Triad that undertakes an immense pilgrimage through successive incarnations to emerge as an effortlessly self-conscious agent of the divine will, the Light of the Logos, Brahma Vach.

Below this overbrooding Triad is the volatile quaternary of principles drawn from the lower planes of cosmic matter: they are *kama*, the force of blind passion and chaotic desire shared by man with animal life; *prana*, the life-current energizing the whirling atoms on the objective plane of existence; the astral paradigmatic body (*linga sharira*), the original form around which the physical molecules shape themselves, and hence the model for the physical frame (*sthula sharira*). This quaternary of principles is evanescent and changeable, established for man's use at the time of incarnation and dissolved at death into its primary constituents on their corresponding planes. The real man, the higher Triad, recedes from the physical plane to await the next incarnation. The function of each of these sheaths differs from one individual to another according to the level of spiritual development of the incarnated soul. The astral body of the Adept is of a much higher degree of resilience and purity than that of the average man. In visionaries and mystics, the sheaths intervening between the spiritual man and the brain-mind are sufficiently transparent so that they can receive communications from the overbrooding Triad in a relatively lucid manner. Man is a compound being simultaneously experiencing two worlds, inner and outer. Each person's present life experience is but a minute portion of what was witnessed by the immortal individuality in previous incarnations. Thus if men and women assiduously search within themselves, they can recover a vast heritage of knowledge spanning aeons. These memories are locked in mansions of the soul which only ardent desire and strong discipline can penetrate.

Memory is integral to consciousness and since all matter is alive and conscious, all beings from cells to deities have memory of some type. In man, memory is generally divided into four categories: physical memory, remembrance, recollection and reminiscence. In remembrance, an idea impinges upon the mind from the past by free association; in recollection, the mind deliberately searches it out. Reminiscence, however, is of another order altogether. Called 'soul-memory', it links every human being to previous lives and assures each that he or she will live again. In principle, any man or woman may recover the knowledge gained in previous incarnations and maintain continuity with the *sutratman*, the thread-soul, the eternal witness to every incarnation. There are also types of memory which are indistinguishable from prophecy, since the more one progresses towards homogeneous and rarefied planes of existence, the more past, present and future collapse into eternal duration, within the boundless perspective of which an entire cycle of manifestation may be surveyed. Such was the level of insight reached by the great seers or rishis who recorded their findings in the Vedas and other great scriptures, thus transmitting the ancient *Gupta Vidya* or 'the Secret Doctrine', fitly taken as the title of H.P. Blavatsky's monumental modern exposition of theosophical thought. Some mystics have penetrated deeply into the realms of reminiscence, bringing back the fruits of knowledge in previous lives. Greater still is the ability to enter into former and more spiritual epochs of humanity and to make those visions come alive for those who had lost all but a faint intuition of a larger sense of self.

The source and destiny of the soul's inward life fundamentally involve the entire scope of evolution. Coeval with the manifestation of the seven worlds of the cosmic plenum is the re-emergence of beings who assume once more the evolutionary pilgrimage after an immense period of rest. The emanation of matter and spirit into the objective plane of existence is but half the cycle. Its return brings all beings and forms to the bosom of absolute darkness. The period of manifestation covering trillions of years is called a *manvantara* and the corresponding period of rest, called *pralaya*, lasts for an equal duration. They are the Days and Nights of Brahmā, which were reckoned with meticulous precision by the ancient Aryans. The whole span of the *manvantara* is governed by the law of periodicity which regulates rates of activity on all planes of being. This is sometimes spoken of as 'the Great Breath' which preserves the cosmos. The essence of life is motion, growth and expansion of awareness in every atom. Each atom is at its core a monad, an expression of the highest self *(Atman)* and its vesture is the spiritual soul *(Buddhi)*. Prior to the monad's emergence in the human family, it undergoes aeons of experience in the lower kingdoms of nature, developing by natural impulse (metempsychosis) until the latent thinking faculty of *Manas* is awakened by the sacrificial efforts of beings who have risen far above the human state in *manvantaras* past. They kindle the spark of self-consciousness, making the unconscious monad a true man *(Manushya)*, capable of thought, reflection and deliberate action. The soul embarks upon a long cycle of incarnations in human form to prepare itself for entry into still greater planes of existence.

The evolutionary tide on earth is regulated by the unerring hand of cyclic law. Man passes through a series of Rounds and Races which allows him to assimilate the knowledge of every plane of existence, from the most ethereal to the most material. Man's planetary evolution describes a spiral passing from spirit into matter and returning to spirit again with a wholly self-conscious mastery of the process. Each Round is a major evolutionary period lasting many millions of years. Each Race in turn witnesses the rise and fall of continents, civilizations and nations. An earlier Race than our own, the Lemurian, lived in an idyllic Golden Age, an epoch ruled by natural religion, universal fraternity, and spontaneous devotion to spiritual teachers. Many of the myths regarding an era of childlike purity and unsullied trust in humanity's early flowering preserve the flavour of this period. As man evolved more material vestures, *kama* or passion tainted his power of thought and inflamed his irrational tendencies. The nightmare tales of Atlantean sorcerers are the heavy heirloom of contemporary humanity. The destruction of Atlantis ushered in the Aryan race of our own epoch. The Indian sages who inaugurated this period are among the torchbearers for the humanity of our time. Intuitive mystics recognize the sacred role of ancient India as mother and preserver of the spiritual heritage of present humanity. The classical Indian scriptures resonate with the authentic voice of the Verbum, uncorrupted by time and human ignorance.

Pertinent to historical insight is the doctrine of the *yugas*, the cycle of four epochs through which every Race passes, the Golden, Silver, Bronze and Iron Ages. The *yugas* indicate a broad sweep of karmic activity at any point in the life of an individual or collection of individuals. The entire globe may not be undergoing the same age simultaneously nor may any one individual be necessarily in the same epoch as his social milieu. According to Hindu calculations, *Kali Yuga* began over 5,090 years ago and will last altogether for a total of 432,000 years. This dark age is characterized by widespread confusion of roles, inversion of ethical values and enormous suffering owing to spiritual blindness. Many have celebrated the myth of the Golden Age as extolling the plenitude of man's creative potential. The doctrine of the *yugas* is not deterministic. It merely suggests the relative levels of consciousness which most human beings tend to hold in common. Thus a Golden Age vibration can be inserted into an Iron Age to ameliorate the collective predicament of mankind. The Golden Age surrounded human beings as a primordial state of divine consciousness, but their own pride and ignorance precluded its recovery. In the wonder of childhood, in archaic myths, in the sporadic illuminations of great artists and in mystical visions, one may discern shimmering glimpses of the Golden Age of universal *eros*, the rightful original estate of humanity.

The progress of humanity in harmony with cyclic law is facilitated by a mature grasp of karma and rebirth. These twin doctrines of responsibility and hope unravel many of the riddles of life and Nature. They show that every person's life and character are the outcome of previous lives and thought patterns, that each one is his or her own judge and executioner, and that all rise or fall strictly by their own merits and misdeeds. Nothing is left to chance or accident in life but everything is under the governance of a universal law of ethical causation. Man is essentially a thinker, and all thoughts initiate causes that generate suffering or bliss. The immortal Triad endures the mistakes and follies of the turbulent quaternary until such time as it can assume its rightful stature and act freely in consonance with cosmic order and natural law. As man is constantly projecting a series of thoughts and images, individual responsibility is irrevocable. Each person is the centre of any disturbance of universal harmony and the ripples of effects must return to him. Thus the law of karma or justice signifies moral interdependence and human solidarity.

Karma must not be seen as a providential means of divine retribution but rather as a universal current touching those who bear the burden of its effects. This has been called the law of spiritual gravitation. The entire scope of man's affairs — his environment, friends, family, employment and the like — are all dictated by the needs of the soul. Karma works on the soul's behalf to provide those opportunities for knowledge and experience which would aid its progress. This concept could be expanded so as to encompass all connections with other human beings of even the most casual kind, seeing them as karmically ordained not for one's own progress but for the sake of those who struggle with the dire limitations of ignorance, poverty or despair. A deeply moving account of this trial is given in *The Hero in Man*, wherein, while walking among the wretched outcasts of Dublin, the author, George William Russell ('A.E.'), rejoices in the conviction that the benevolence he feels for each benighted soul will forge a spiritual bond through which he may help them in the future. Karma means a summons to the path of action and duty. As one cannot separate one's own karma from that of one's fellow-men, one may determine to devote one's life to the remission of the karmic burden of others.

At death the true Self or immortal Triad casts off the physical and astral bodies and is released from the thraldom of passions and desires. Its natural tropism to gravitate upwards allows it to enter the rarefied plane of consciousness where its thoughts are carried to culmination, clothed in a finer body suited to that sublime existence. This state, *devachan,* is a period of rest and assimilation between lives and the basis of the popular mythology of heaven. On the other hand, the lower quaternary languishes after death in *kamaloka,* the origin of theological dogmas concerning hell and purgatory. There it dissolves by degrees back into its primary elements at a rate determined by the cohesion given them by the narcissistic personality during life on earth. Inflamed passions and poisonous thoughts sustained for long periods of time endow this entity with a vivid, vicarious and ghoulish existence. This plane of consciousness, termed 'the Astral Light' by Eliphas Lévi, is intimately connected with the lives and thoughts of most of mankind. It is the vast slag-heap of Nature into which all selfish and evil thoughts are poured and then rebound back to pollute and contaminate human life on earth. This plane of carnalized thought tends to perpetuate the horrors of the Iron Age and condemn humanity to a state of spiritual darkness.

The crucial difference between individuals lies in whether they are enslaved by the Astral Light (the region of psyche) or whether they are capable of rising above it to a calm awareness of the wisdom and compassion latent in their higher nature, the realm of nous. Beyond the region of psychic action lies the pristine sphere of noetic awareness called *Akasha,* from which empyrean individuals could derive the inspiration needed to go forth and inaugurate a Golden Age by laying down the foundations of a regenerated civilization. Sages, past and present, saluted as Men of the Word *(Brahma Vach),* have accomplished the arduous transformation of their own natures, overcoming every vice and limitation and perfecting themselves in noetic ideation and sacrificial action. Mahatmas or Hierophants and Bodhisattvas renounce everything for the sake of suffering humanity. Solitary mystics on the ancient Bodhisattva path of service salute them as gurus, guides and preceptors and acknowledge their invisible presence as the *Guruparampara,* the sacred lineage behind their own modest labours for mankind. These wise beings are the noble trustees of the *Philosophia Perennis* and the compassionate teachers of the whole human family. The mystical pilgrimage of mankind is an authentic reflection of their ageless wisdom.

THE PILGRIMAGE
OF HUMANITY

THE REBIRTH OF HUMANITY

We are only in the Fourth Round, and it is in the Fifth that the full development of Manas, as a direct ray from the Universal MAHAT — a ray unimpeded by matter — will be finally reached. Nevertheless, as every sub-race and nation have their cycles and stages of developmental evolution repeated on a smaller scale, it must be the more so in the case of a Root-Race. Our race then has, as a Root-race, crossed the equatorial line and is cycling onward on the Spiritual side; but some of our sub-races still find themselves on the shadowy descending arc of their respective national cycles; while others again — the oldest — having crossed their crucial point, which alone decides whether a race, a nation, or a tribe will live or perish, are at the apex of spiritual development as sub-races.

The Secret Doctrine, ii 301

Ranging from the minutest circles of daily life to the massive arcs of cosmic evolution, the spiralling progress of spiritual humanity has successive phases and synchronous aspects, marked by critical turns and decisive epochs. There are fateful times of birth and death, of transfiguration and rebirth, for individuals as well as civilizations. The majestic beating of the karmic heart of the cosmos resonates within the breast of every intrepid pilgrim-soul so that none is exempt from the challenge of the hour nor impervious to the clarion call of the Mahabharatan "war between the living and the dead." Days and hours are marked by moments of going forth (*pravritti*) and going within (*nivritti*), whilst decades and centuries have their own coded rhythms of activity and rest. In a universe of inexorable law and ceaseless transformation, no two moments in the life of any being are exactly alike. Similarly, in the lifetimes of races the accumulated karma of the past converges with the archetypal logic of cycles to precipitate climacteric moments.

At the present historical moment there is a rapid descent of *Dharmakshetra* into *Kurukshetra* and an awesome re-enactment, before the soul's eye, of the titanic struggle between Kronos and Zeus. To serve the Mahatmas, and through them all of humanity, is the most meaningful and precious privilege open to any person. The readiness to serve is helped by the fusion of an altruistic motive with skill in timely action. These may be gestated through deep meditation on behalf of the good of all beings and an authentic renunciation of earthly concerns for the sake of the many who are lost. One must lay one's heart open to the present plight of millions of souls who are wandering adrift and are much afflicted by the psychological terror prophesied in Tibet. Not even affording the visible reference of an external cataclysm, this psychological convulsion is needed for the transformation of the humanity of the past into the humanity of the future.

The ramifications of this crucial transition were anticipated and provided for by the Brotherhood of Bodhisattvas. The Avataric descent of the Seventh Impulsion into the moral chaos consequent upon two World Wars and the world weariness of the present epoch marks the culmination of a seven hundred-year cycle extending back to Tsong-Kha-Pa. Whilst this may be more than can be encompassed in the cribbed and cabined conceptions of mortals, it is scarcely an instant in the eyes of those who ever reside on the plane of Shamballa. Sages are fully aware that the voluntary descent of a spiritual Teacher into Myalba merely provides the outward illusion of passage through various phases of earthly life, using but a small portion of an essentially unmanifest Self. Impervious to containment by form, the true being of the Avatar abides in timeless duration, always honouring the One without a second, *Tad ekam*, that which as the central Spiritual Sun is the single source of all that lives and breathes throughout the seven kingdoms of nature, and of all that is lit up at any level of reflected intelligence from the tiniest atom to the mightiest star in this vast cosmos which extends far beyond the solar system and this earth.

One with the unmanifest Logos, Dakshinamurti remains poised at the threshold of the realm of boundless Light, the mathematical circle dividing infinity from finitude, and reposes as *achutya* — unfallen. As H.P. Blavatsky declared:

> The first lesson taught in Esoteric philosophy is that the incognizable Cause does not put forth evolution, whether consciously or unconsciously, but only exhibits periodically *different aspects of itself* to the perception of *finite* Minds.
>
> *The Secret Doctrine*, ii 487

In the *Bhagavad Gita,* Krishna disclosed that he incarnates on earth periodically for the preservation of the just, the destruction of the wicked and the establishment of righteousness. In Hindu iconography Narayana holds the conch shell, symbolizing his ability to rock the earth through sound, the potency of the Logos as *Shabdabrahman,* the Soundless Sound of the indestructible *Akshara* behind and beyond and within all the spaces of "the AUM throughout eternal ages". This clarion call has gone out to heroic souls incarnated in the last half century for the solemn purpose of gathering together those spread out across the globe who readily recognize the immense danger to humanity from itself, the spiritual danger of self-destruction. It is a summons to halt the desecration of the sacred soil of the good earth upon which all human beings must find their common ground, regardless of race, sex, religion, creed, atheistic philosophy, indifferentism, or any set of beliefs and values. Regardless of whatsoever labels and idiosyncracies of form, all human beings are sharers of the *Nur* of Allah, the Light that lighteth up every soul that cometh into the world, that Light which is beyond Darkness itself. It is the One Light which has been known by diverse names amongst the many forgotten peoples of our globe over millions and millions of years, in civilizations long buried under deserts and mountains or slipped beneath the sea before existing continents emerged. Infinitely resplendent in eternal duration, it is the Light which was transmitted over eighteen million years ago when the *Manas* of humanity was lit up by divine beings of one lip, one race, one mind, one heart, seers of whom the Vedas speak.

> The mysteries of Heaven and Earth, revealed to the Third Race by their celestial teachers in the days of their purity, became a great focus of light, the rays from which became necessarily weakened as they were diffused and shed upon an uncongenial, because too material soil.
>
> *Ibid.,* ii 281

Truly God is one, but manifold are its names. As the *Q'uran* teaches, there are as many ways to God as there are children of the breaths of men. Tragically, as mankind became progressively enwrapped in the illusion of material existence, its eyes and ears dimmed, though the light within remained inviolate. Outside the circle of ever vigilant custodians of the Mysteries, the arcane teaching of the universal sound and light of the Logos was obscured, distorted and lost. Today those who call themselves Muslims, Christians, Jews, Hindus, Jains, Sikhs, Buddhists or Zoroastrians, men and women of every sect and nation throughout every continent of the globe, are bereft of the lost Word, *Shabdabrahman.* Although lost, it has yet been fervently sought by many more millions in our time than ever before in recorded history or even in earlier epochs of antiquity shrouded in myth and mist. The unseen tablets of nature, which are a vast reservoir of enigmatic glyphs and symbols and eternal verities, record the unknown strivings of innumerable human beings, groping in their gloom, sometimes with shame but often with nothing else to support them than the pathos of their search. It is a search to find one's way back home, out of exile from the kingdom of God, the land of the midnight sun.

In order to gather together the afflicted, the Divine Cowherd summons all awakened souls, wherever and however disguised, through the sounding of the mighty conch. Independent of all modes of external communication, and relying upon the oldest mode of communication known to the Ancient of Days — controlled transference of benevolent thought and ineffable sound — the call is heard by scattered volunteers "in the fierce strife between the living and the dead." As with Jacob's ladder in his dream, heaven and earth are reunited, even if momentarily. In this manner, over the coming years the world will move through the darkness, yet mysteriously, step by step, faltering and failing yet persisting, it will move towards that moment when Anno Domini has ceased to be, and a new era will dawn with a new name. There will then be no U.S.A. but a new Republic of Conscience which will take its place in the community of mankind which would have come of age and declared itself as one family.

This is a grand prospect for which there can be inherently no empirical or merely rational proof. Yet it may be tested by any intuitive individual who is courageous enough to pour his or her deepest unspoken feelings, unarticulated dreams and unexpressed inner agony into the alchemical crucible of spiritual striving on behalf of others. It is a tryst that such souls make with destiny, but also with the grandchildren of persons yet unborn. It is a tryst with the humanity of the future, and with the full promise of the Aquarian Age which dawned on the nineteenth of June, 1902, ninety-three years ago, with mathematical precision. This has an exact relationship to that moment five thousand and ninety-seven years ago, in 3102 B.C., when Krishna, having witnessed the outcome of the Mahabharatan war between the greedy Kauravas and the foolish Pandavas, was able to end his seeming life on earth and withdraw from the terrestrial scene. Thus standing apart from this universe, into which he never really enters, he creates therein his *mayavi rupas* through the mighty magic of *prakriti*, the seminal potency of mystic thought in the eternal life of self-ideation. Again and again, under different names, it is the same being behind every divine incarnation, whether past or future.

As Dakshinamurti, the Initiator of Initiates, he is seated immovable above Mount Kailas, in mystic meditation since over eighteen million years ago from the time when there was no Mount Kailas and no Himalayas as presently understood. Coming down through all the subsequent recorded and unrecorded eras, he carries forth in unbroken continuity the onward spiritual current which is the irresistible, unconquerable, ineluctable forward march of humanity. He is Shiva-Mahadeva, reborn as the four Kumaras in the successive races of humanity, and that still more mysterious and solitary Being alluded to in the secret teachings.

> *The inner man of the first * * * only changes his body*
> *from time to time; he is ever the same, knowing neither rest*
> *nor Nirvana, spurning Devachan and remaining constantly*
> *on Earth for the salvation of mankind.*
>   *The Secret Doctrine,* ii 281

Attuned to the rhythms of the cosmic ocean of Divine Thought, he is the still motionless centre in its depths around which revolve, like myriad mathematical points in spinning circles, the scattered hosts of humanity. Amidst the larger and larger circles of ripples upon ripples, waves upon waves, all souls are citizens of that universe which is much vaster than the disordered kingdom which, as earthlings, they may seem to inherit but to which they have no claim except as members of a single family.

This mystic vision can only be fleetingly glimpsed and partially understood by beginning to ask sincere if faulty, searching if somewhat confused, questions. Herein lies the starting-point of the dialectical method taught by Krishna in the fourth chapter of the *Gita*. The sacred teaching of the kingly science was originally given by Krishna to Vivasvat, who in turn imparted it to Manu. Then Vaivaswat Manu taught it to Ikshvaku, who stands for all the regal Initiates of forgotten antiquity in the golden ages of myth and fable. Thus the vigilant preservers and magnanimous rulers of this world, without abdicating from their essential state of Mahatmic wisdom, assumed the guise of visible corporeality to descend on earth and reign upon it as King-Hierophants and

Divine Instructors of the humanity then incarnated upon the globe. It is this self-same eternal wisdom that Krishna gives unto Arjuna, an unhappy warrior, not for his own sake, especially when he was not entirely ready to assimilate the Teaching, but for the sake of his work in the world and his help in concluding the Mahabharatan war.

In the great summation of the eighteenth chapter of the *Gita*, Krishna reveals secrets upon secrets, wrapped in each other in seemingly unending layers, like a Chinese treasure. Every time a secret is revealed, there is more and yet more, because in the end one is speaking of that which is part of the secret of every human soul in its repeated strivings and recurrent lives upon earth. Amidst the chaos and obscuration of misplayed roles, faded memories and fragmented consciousness, coupled with the fatigue of mental confusion, there is also the power of persistence, the *sutratman* and its *connatus* which enables every person to breathe from day to day and through each night. In deep sleep, as in profound meditation and the intervals between incarnations, the immortal soul enters into the orbit of the midnight sun and emerges out of the muddle of mundane life and mangled dreams. There it discerns the melody of the flute of Krishna, the music of the spheres, and the hidden magic of the ages which, when heard self-consciously, frees the soul from the fatuous burden of self-imposed delusions. It is the priceless prerogative of every Arjuna in our time to seek once more the pristine wisdom, the sovereign purifier, through unremitting search, through fearless questions, through grateful devotion and selfless service.

Surveying the wreckage of this century in bewilderment and dismay, many have sought an understanding of events in the oft-quoted, though little understood, remarks of H.P. Blavatsky concerning the role of the New World in the evolution of the races of humanity. Too many have submitted to the delusion, to the strange idea, that spiritual evolution is possible only for a few. The idea that any single people out of the globe's teeming millions, selected at random and fed on the fat of the land, weighted down by the gifts of blind fortune, should be preferred by Krishna must be firmly repudiated. No instrument of the real work of the Lodge of Mahatmas can ever be permitted to become the refuge of the few, the chosen avenue for the exclusive salvation or cloistered comfort of any élite. Now, thanks to many benefactors and blessings in disguise, Americans are being made to slow down to the point where they may hear some of the echoes of what the pilgrim fathers heard when they landed in Plymouth over three centuries ago. In a way which could not have been known clearly to them, their setting out upon a long and difficult sea voyage was reminiscent of far more ancient voyages of seed-pilgrims across the waters of floods guided by Manu. These pilgrims to the New World had set out after having formed a compact with each other, which was a pure act of faith in themselves and in the future and in whatever their God had to offer them. This was one of many precious moments in the long and unwritten history of this mighty continent, whose vastness extends from the Arctic Circle to the Straits of Magellan, encompassing great rivers, the Grand Canyon, and awesome ranges of mountains girdling a third of the globe.

There is much more in the civilizations and peoples of pre-Columbian history than can ever be garnered through perfunctory reading of post-Columbian events. The brief journey of Columbus from Spain to the Caribbean, in search of India, but resulting in the rediscovery of America, could foretell little of the future birth in these lands of old Hindus from the India of a million years ago. It could convey few hints of the far-flung variety of spiritual strivings that would occur on the American continent, or of the enormous blasphemy, pride and temerity of inscribing the Third Eye upon the dollar bill. Yet somewhere, past all the humbug of petty educators, pompous bureaucrats and self-serving politicians, an impartial witness can only feel a genuine empathy with the series of lonely men carrying a strenuous burden of leadership in the emerging American republics.

Men such as Lincoln defined the ideal of action "with malice towards none and charity for all" and spoke for all mankind in affirming that "government of the people, by the people, and for the people, shall not perish from the earth." Much earlier, a perceptive person like President Everett of Harvard could clearly see that the death of Jefferson and Adams on the fourth of July in 1826 was an event that had nothing to do with the destiny of one nation alone, but rather with the whole of humanity. Alas, it now seems paradoxical to some Americans that few people have honoured Jefferson as highly as Ho Chi Minh, and it is a mark of the myopia of educated Americans that they could not honour Eisenhower as much as the humble villagers of India who came in millions to greet this self-effacing soldier. Humanity recognizes its own, just as many Americans during the thirties saw in Gandhi the enduring re-enactment which was once seen in Christ. This is a very different world from that of seventy years ago, and it is still changing rapidly. America is now much less imposing, fortunately for all, than it was threatening to be after the Second World War. Through omission and commission, through misspent and lost opportunities, as well as outright misdeeds, more lives have been lost since World War II owing to the U.S.A. than during World War II, more lives lost than even those due to the Soviet Union, with its barbaric despotism but its immense potential for good.

This is a curious world in which there are few major actors or authentic mandates, but in which there are millions of awakened human souls who are like unto sad-eyed veterans of history, but who are also coolly waiting to strike when the iron is hot so that the City of Man, now like an embryo hidden in the dark, like Venus before the dawn, will make its timely descent. Thanks to the ineffable grace of *Daiviprakriti*, which alone can act as a midwife to the rebirth of humanity, there could suddenly emerge a successful sequel to the aborted birth of the United Nations in 1945, so that the world may find itself and retrace its pathways to a more honourable prospect than anything cogitated since that time. The teeming lands and rich resources of the earth, like the seeds of the spiritual harvest of mankind, do not belong to any single tribe and cannot be handed on by any legal system of inheritance. Just as some governments and groups have already done more to protect the environments of the earth than individuals alone could accomplish, so too will future networks and agencies initiate efforts to pool natural and human resources, the seeds and skills that creative pioneers may bring to fruition in the age of microelectronics, so that the whole world could move into a new era of global solidarity. It will be an era of self-conscious interdependence, promoting the global discovery of the richness and immensity of the potentials in the human brain, matching the vast imaginative potentials for creative longings in the human heart.

This daunting prospect is no less magnanimous than the mandate and the vision of the Brotherhood of Mahatmas and Bodhisattvas, who stand in relation to drifting mortals as they are in relation to the black beetle, in T.H. Huxley's telling metaphor. Mahatmas are always present in the orbit of the Avatar and his true disciples on earth. They ever move in their invisible forms and are known by infallible signs. This is an arena wherein there is no room for delusion or pretence. It may well be that the Bodhisattvas are recognized only by a few, but this does not alter the fact that they are sometimes more numerous as shining witnesses to the critical events of history than the visible and volatile participants. It is high time that creedal religion catches up with contemporary science, which already knows that in every supposed physical object there is only a mere one-quadrillionth part that is, even by any stretch of the imagination, capable of being called matter. All the rest is empty space, the Akashic empyrean of Adepts, gods and elementals.

The multitudinous sense-perceptions of human beings, as Heraclitus recognized, are liars. Eyes and ears are bad witnesses for the human soul unless one looks with the awakened eye and hears with humble and receptive eardrums that are tuned to the proper vibrations, the music of the Hierophants, the great Compassionaters, the true lovers and friends and servers, but also the fathers and elder brothers, of the entire human race. It is in their name that the Avatar speaks, as no divine incarnation can be separated from the Logoic host which is with and behind the

Magus-Teacher. At this critical point in cosmic evolution, after more than eighteen million years, when the human race has already passed the mid-point and is approaching a climactic phase, it is only He who was present at the beginning and who will prevail at the end who can redeem humanity. Whilst the Logos *in esse* is outside the solar system, it is only through its accredited and self-authenticated agency in the world that it performs its Paracletic function, which was sensed both by those around Buddha and Christ as well as by those like the blind king in the presence of Krishna. Already, even those who can see but dimly can discern the grim fate that awaits those minute minorities which perversely block the way to the welfare of the vast majority of mankind.

The earth must go back to the ultimate democracy of the immense majority, and no one can be excluded. All men and women, in the far corners of the earth, as well as in the first land of the common man, must inwardly pledge themselves to work for their spiritual ancestors and also for their unseen descendants who will constitute the humanity of the future. This is the original meaning and future promise of the American Dream, which has little to do with the institutionalized gains of the past two centuries, but is vitally relevant to the embryonic world civilization to be founded upon a brave declaration of human solidarity and global interdependence. Whereas Thomas Paine once welcomed mysterious messengers of thought, and later statesmen ascribed their intimations of the ever-expanding American Dream to the inspiration of God, the time has come when all true promptings of theophilanthropists must be consecrated to the Brotherhood of Bodhisattvas, the Society of Sages, the Benefactors of mankind.

Just as the global rebirth of humanity mirrors the archetypal birth of humanity in the Third Root Race, so too the authentic spiritual renewal of every human being reflects and resonates with the wider cycle of the race. Prior to physical birth each monad has had the meta-psychological experience of being catapulted into what the Orphics called the tomb of the soul, but also that which the Ionians regarded as the temple of the human body. And whilst every baby enters the world voicing the AUM, each with a unique accent and intonation, it is given to very few to end their lives with the sacred Sound. This is the difference which human life makes, with its saga of fantasy and forgetfulness. What one sensed in one's pristine innocence at the moment of birth and which is witnessed through the enigmatic sounding of the Word becomes wholly obscured by the time of death unless one has deliberately and self-consciously sought out the path leading to spiritual rebirth. Through the complex processes of karmic precipitation and conscious and unconscious exercise of the powers of choice, each human being differentiates from others, self-selecting his or her own destiny. To minimize the dangers to the soul and to maximize the continuity of spiritual self-consciousness between the commencement and close of incarnation, one must learn to look back and forwards over the entire span of a lifetime, breaking it up into successive septenary cycles and their sub-phases. All cycles participate in birth, in adolescence, in slow and painful maturation, in the shedding of illusions, and in a sort of death or disintegration leading to new beginnings. In some portions of the globe the wheel revolves so rapidly that most human beings have been through many lives within one lifetime, and though this poignant fact is little understood by other persons, even those who experience it acutely do not think through its implications.

One cannot really comprehend such primal verities without silent contemplation. As Krishna hinted in the *Uttara Gita*, every time one opens one's mouth, the astral shadow is lengthened. In the demanding discipline of preparation for spiritual rebirth, there are very few who could hope to match or even approach the example of the Kanchipuram Shankaracharya, who perfected his *svadharma* over the past half century, provided sagely counsel to myriad devotees, and then retreated under a vow of silence. There is evidently a Himalayan difference between mighty Men of Meditation and the motley host of deluded mortals called fools by Puck in *A Midsummer Night's Dream*. Nevertheless, the folly of mortals is largely a protected illusion. If a human being knew from the age of seven everything that was going to happen in his or her life from that moment to the time of death, life would be intolerably difficult. Similarly, if one knew exactly what tortures one had committed or connived at in the time of the Inquisition or elsewhere in the history of the world — and there is no portion of the globe which has not witnessed terrible misdeeds — it would be very hard to avoid being overwhelmed by such knowledge. Every human being has at times, like Pilate, opted out of responsibilities upon the unrecorded scenes of history. Whilst all, like Ivan in Dostoevsky's *The Brothers Karamazov*, would like to think of themselves as holding to the principle that it is never justifiable to harm even a single child, each person bears the heavy burden of karmic debts, every one of which will have to be repaid in full before the irreversible attainment of conscious immortality is feasible.

To begin to raise such questions about oneself is to realize that they cannot be answered in the utilitarian calculus of the age of commerce, which is the only crude morality of the market-place. Many people simply refuse to be priced, bought and sold or even appraised, in terms of market values or competitive criteria, especially in a time of spurious inflation. One has indeed to find out what is one's own true value. One must gain an inward recognition of the elusive truth of the axiom, "To thine own self be true . . . and thou canst not then be false to any man." Looking at the whole of one's life in terms of what one feels is the truest thing about oneself, one must search out the deepest, most abiding hope that one holds, apart from all fantasy myths. For most human beings, this hope is much the same. It is the hope to conclude one's life without being a nuisance or hindrance to others. It is the wish to finish one's life without harming other human beings, but making some small contribution to the sum-total of good, so that at the moment of death one may look back over life and feel that one has lived the best one knew how.

Broadly, too many human beings torture themselves with an appalling amount of useless guilt, owing to their utter lack of knowledge of the mathematics of the soul. Just as it is useless and unconstructive to become guilty or evasive about one's checkbook balance, because the figures do not lie and the facts cannot be denied, it is equally fruitless and destructive to become immersed in guilt-fantasies with regard to one's whole life. Even a little knowledge of the relevance of simple mathematics to the realm of meta-psychology can save one from recurring though needless despair. Every attempt to blot out awareness of responsibility for karma through giving way to emotional reactions obscures the impersonal continuity of one's real existence and is an insult to the divine origin of one's self-consciousness.

> In each of us that golden thread of continuous life — periodically broken into active and passive cycles of sensuous existence on Earth, and super-sensuous in Devachan — *is* from the beginning of our appearance upon this earth. It is the *Sutratma,* the luminous thread of immortal *impersonal* monadship, on which our earthly lives or evanescent *Egos* are strung as so many beads — according to the beautiful expression of Vedantic philosophy... Without this principle — the emanation of the very essence of the pure divine principle *Mahat* (Intelligence), which radiates direct from the *Divine mind* — we would be surely no better than animals.
>
> The Secret Doctrine, ii 513

In order to insert one's own efforts to recover this Mahatic awareness into the regeneration of humanity by the Mahatmas and the Avatar, one must learn to work first with the cycles of the seasons of nature. The period of fourteen days beginning with the winter solstice and culminating on the fourth of January, which is sacred to Hermes-Budha, may be used as a period of *tapas* for the sake of generating calm and sacrificial resolves. The precious time between January and March may be spent in quiet inward gestation of the seeds of the coming year. Care needs to be taken if one is to avoid excess and idle excitement at the time of the vernal equinox and deceptive dreams about the carefree, indolent summer. From March until June there is an inevitable and necessary descent into manifestation, but if the summer solstice is to find one prepared for the season of flourishing, one must not give way to the extravagances of anticipation and memory. If one observes this solstice with one's resolves intact, then one is in a good position to maintain inward continuity, free from wastefulness and fatigue, until the onset of autumn. Then arriving at the autumnal equinox, not having accumulated a series of debts and liabilities owing to lost opportunities and forgotten resolves, one will be able to maintain the critical detachment needed to participate in the season of withdrawal and regeneration, culminating in the return of the winter solstice.

By setting oneself realistic goals and working with the rhythms of nature, it is possible over a period of seven years to nurture within oneself the seedlings of the virtues — "the nurslings of immortality" — needed to become a true servant of the Servants of Humanity. Owing to the dual nature assumed by *Mahat* when it manifests and falls into matter as self-consciousness, it is necessary to correct for the terrestrial attractions of the moon of the mind if one would recover the illumination of the solar power of understanding. As Longfellow said, one may hit the mark by aiming a little bit above the mark because every arrow feels the earth's gravity. One must allow for the sagging or declination of the curve, but whilst one allows for it, one must not hesitate to resolve with inner strength and cool confidence. Spiritual rebirth initially means being born again with new eyes and with the ability to see each successive year and cycle as truly new. This noetic perspective can be gained only by linking each year or cycle with its predecessors, not in detail but in essence. And infallibly, if one is able to live consciously and self-consciously throughout the cycles and seasons of life, one will be able to use the thread of continuity at the moment of death. *Sutratma-Buddhi* thus becomes *Manas-Sutratman*, and both arise through the fiery, Fohatic energy of the *Mahat-Atman*.

Those who are serious about engaging in spiritual self-regeneration in the service of others could begin with the simplest assumption: death is inevitable but the moment of death is uncertain. This is in no wise a morbid or gloomy assumption, for death always comes as a deliverer and a friend to the immortal soul. If one can remotely resonate to the words of Krishna and feel in the invisible heart the ceaseless vibration of one's essential immortality, then one will understand that being born is like putting on clothes and dying is like taking them off. At this point in human evolution it is too late to indulge in body identification along with its consequent denial of the ubiquity of death and suffering for mortal vestures. It is a mark of spiritual maturity to recognize that human life involves risk and pain. Were it otherwise, it could hold no promise. Even if one is not yet prepared for the Himalayan heights of spiritual mountain climbing, nonetheless, one may begin to discern and hearken to the light of daring that burns in the heart. Whatever one's mode of self-measurement, that measure should be in favour of what is strong, what is true, what is noble and what is beautiful in oneself. All the Avatars concur in the strength of affirmation that the spirit is willing, even though the flesh is weak. Unlike the preachers of discouragement who emphasize the element of weakness in the flesh, the true prophets of the divine destiny of mankind place the stress upon the willingness of the spirit.

In this difficult time of collective death and regeneration, signified by the entry of Uranus into Scorpio, the whole host of Bodhisattvas bears witness to the Avataric message that this is a propitious time of opportunity for all souls to protect, to nurture and fructify the seeds of futurity that sleep deep beneath the astral soil of the earth. It is a time of silent burgeoning growth, and there is a supple softness and mellowness in the astral light as at the dawn of Venus. It is also a time rather like the crimson sunset because it is the twilight hour for the devouring demons of recorded history. It is the sacred hour of the dawn of the humanity of the future in which there will be neither East nor West, neither North nor South, neither black nor brown nor white nor yellow. Though all this will not materialize in eighteen years of Mahabharatan struggles, the time has surely come for the sacred reaffirmation of true learning, of the supernal light of the transcendent Logos, such that myriad souls may rekindle the divine spark of creativity and compassion (Agni-Soma) and seek the hidden cornerstone of the City of Man.

THE AQUARIAN TIDE

Let us prepare, and let us study Truth in all its aspects, trying not to ignore any of them, if we do not wish, when the hour will have struck, to fall into the abyss of the unknown. It is useless to rely on chance, and to await the approaching intellectual and psychic crisis with indifference if not with total incredulity, saying to oneself that if worse comes to worst, the tide will carry us quite naturally to the shore; for there is a strong likelihood of the tide stranding but a corpse! The battle will be fierce, in any case, between brutal materialism and blind fanaticism on the one hand, and on the other philosophy and mysticism — that more or less thick veil of the Eternal Truth.

It is not materialism that will have the upper hand.

La Revue Theosophique　　　　　　　　　H.P. BLAVATSKY
March 1889

According to the ancient maxim of Protagoras, "Man is the measure of all things; of things that are, that they are; of things that are not, that they are not." However interpreted, this evidently implies that every individual and collective crisis is a crisis of self-concept, self-reference and identity. It further implies that every response to a crisis is shaped and prefigured by factors within human nature. At root, one's ontological estimate of humanity and one's cosmological calculation of the position of man relative to Nature will determine one's capacity to respond creatively in any situation. It should be common sense that the expression of wisdom in human life cannot exceed the sum-total allotted to man by Nature. Nonetheless, the measure of human wisdom postulated by any human being or culture may be seriously defective or needlessly self-constrained. As practical self-knowledge inevitably involves self-reference, the human being who gives short measure to humanity will not be able to draw upon the full potential of human nature. The individual who seeks to integrate the Logoic principle of cosmos with the essential being of man in Nature can remain inwardly open to the whole measure of wisdom attainable by man. It is a paradox of human self-consciousness that Nature will always negate vanity, though it cannot negate despair without human assistance.

This asymmetry in human consciousness, with its awesome implications for pessimism and optimism, arises out of the basic distinction between the evolutionary and involutionary arcs of manifestation. The upward progress of humanity along the evolutionary arc ascending towards self-conscious realization of Spirit depends decisively upon human initiative. It is part of the tragedy of the modern age that, offered the Promethean fire of wisdom, it has chosen instead to bind itself into servitude to Zeus with the gilded chains of kamamanasic desire. Offered the call of the Christos, capable of resurrecting Lazarus from the dead, the western world adopted instead the self-mutilating worship of the cross of matter. Like Procrustes caught in his own clumsy contrivance, for nearly two millennia the West has suffered spiritual deprivation through its self-imposed idolatry of psychic materialism. Since the fourteenth century, the Great Lodge of Mahatmas has sustained a cyclic effort to ameliorate this anguished condition. The culmination of this effort, adjusting the entire range of human principles, was planned to coincide with the Avataric impulse accompanying the Aquarian Age and profoundly affecting the future races of humanity.

Thirteen years before the beginning of the Aquarian Age, in an essay entitled "The New Cycle", addressed in French to a European audience, H.P. Blavatsky powerfully spelt out the choices open to the West. By the latter decades of the nineteenth century, certain divisions of society and thought had already become acute. Millions were caught up either in the spiritual materialism of orthodox religion, or the soulless materialism of mechanistic science. Throughout the seventies and eighties of the Victorian era, a tremendous debate had blown up around human evolution, with science and religion drawing up lines on opposite sides. Going beyond the closed terms of this dilettantish debate,

H.P. Blavatsky drew attention to what had already been noticed by a variety of writers, especially in Russia; namely, what she called the death-struggle between brutal materialism and blind fanaticism on the one side, and philosophy and mysticism on the other. This fierce battle, she affirmed, would be the crucial issue of the twentieth century, and, she prophesied:

> Everyone fanatically clinging to an idea isolating him from the universal axiom — 'There is no Religion higher than Truth' — will find himself separated like a rotten plank from the new ark called Humanity. Tossed by the waves, chased by the winds, buffeted by this element so terrible because unknown, he will soon find himself swallowed up.
>
> *Ibid.*

H.P. Blavatsky was actually sounding a grave and compassionate warning that those souls unable to enter the current of the future would be discarded by Nature. In the 1890's, and increasingly throughout the twentieth century, the growing perception of this fateful choice has instilled a tremendous fear in a despairing element within the human race. Instead of discovering brave and powerful responses to the challenge of the future, that minuscule percentage of the human race which is terrified, for karmic reasons, that it has no future, has developed literature and thought, a full-blown psychology of doom. Through the power of the printed word, and later the electronic media, and with the aid of pathological art and pessimistic fiction, this vociferous minority managed to transfer its psychological ailments to vast numbers of human beings. Entire societies have become caught up in this pathology — in Vienna before the First World War, and even more acutely after the war; in France before the Second World War, and especially during the war and after; and in pre-Nazi Germany. The pathology converged in England during the late 1930's in a literature of bitter disenchantment. It appeared in Russia, particularly during the early days of the Stalinist era, in pessimistic poems and novels, to be somewhat eclipsed by a more heroic stance in the later 1940's and 1950's. It has reappeared in England in recent decades, and it has been a constant problem in post-war America. Like the deadly emanations of the *upas* tree, it spreads its contagion wherever hapless individuals are neither self-inoculated through spiritual resolve nor actually immune through the protection of vital ethical traditions.

Through many forms of scholarship and literature, and a system of semi-institutionalized opinions and manipulated media, a modern system of negative thought-control fosters and diffuses a sense of hopelessness and helplessness. This entire phenomenon in fact represents the death-throes of those elaborate structures of psychology and philosophy rooted in the ideas of ontological scarcity and bourgeois materialism. The present manifestation is a long shadow cast by the seventeenth century where the power of the Catholic Church, particularly on the Continent, cramped those philosophers who sought to celebrate the human spirit. In trying to comprehend human nature, thinkers of the seventeenth century were unable to remove themselves from an obsession with original sin. As this notion became secularized and disguised through sociology and psychology, it came to pervade the intellectual life of the nineteenth century. And as an unsolicited and unsuspected term of debate, it crept into the twentieth century in every field of thought affected by theories of behavioural conditioning. In every case, it shrinks the conception of Nature and of human nature. But, ultimately, all such stultifying and self-crippling conceptions of man are doomed. Parasitic and vampiric, their borrowed and vicarious life may continue for a while, but they will become increasingly irrelevant to the human condition.

Already, millions are tired of nihilists and misanthropes and are stimulated instead by the positive urges of their own sporadic intuitions of the Divine. This is especially true in America, where mass belief is rarely registered by the media, which bases its claims upon limited surveys and the pronouncements of self-appointed experts who speak gibberish while presuming to represent the

American spirit. Indeed, throughout the world, human beings refuse to be trapped within negativism. H.P. Blavatsky spoke of the time "when the flame of modern materialism, artificial and cold, will be extinguished for lack of fuel." The evidence of this can be seen in the decaying heart of the cities which were once the centres of civilization. In Paris and London, New York and Los Angeles, materialistic entrepreneurs and purveyors of the doctrine of inescapable selfishness are finding it difficult to find living human fuel to sustain the structures of human confinement. Their children simply will not go along. They would rather do almost anything else. Like Ahab bound to the sounding whale, the materialist is fast becoming lonely and hopeless, though at times angry and desperate.

It is not easy for the human soul to shake off the yoke of materialism, for even with a strong conviction in the immortal soul, one may unknowingly retain mental habits that are materialistic. Any concern for spiritual progress for oneself must, therefore, be rooted out and dispelled as a pernicious form of a spiritual materialism. Any tendency to identify with the physical body, or act for the sake of oneself as a separative entity in order to gain spiritual gifts and advantages, is incompatible with conscious life in spirit, as opposed to matter. To conceive truly of the *Atman* and *Atma-Buddhi,* the light of the Universal Spirit and the Divine Self, one must shun all separative thinking. It is to this contrast of the living and the dead within human nature that H.P. Blavatsky referred when she wrote:

> The Spirit of Truth is at this moment moving upon the face of these black waters, and, separating them, forces them to yield their spiritual treasures. This spirit is a force that cannot be either checked or stopped. Those who recognize it and feel that this is the supreme moment of their salvation, will be carried by it beyond the illusions of the great astral serpent.
>
> *Ibid.*

Those who are vitalized by the vigorous current of spiritual energy can enjoy states of consciousness and peak experiences that transcend the personality. Freed from the thraldom and tension of self-concern, they will become happy that other human beings exist, thrilled that there are babies on earth, and convinced that where there is a larger view, there is always hope.

Owing to the relentless pressure of the age, it is more and more necessary to abjure separative thinking and join the larger perspective of the majority of mankind. The intensity of the struggle happily compels individuals to choose. Those who pretend to remain indifferent to the prospects of the future only doom themselves to the "arid wastes of matter . . . to vegetate there through a long series of lives, content henceforth with feverish hallucinations instead of spiritual perceptions, with passions instead of love, with the rind instead of the fruit." Unless they scorn selfish assumptions, they will come to resemble the squirrel on its ceaselessly revolving wheel, whirling round and round chewing the nut of nihilism. But once spiritual starvation and material satiety move them to forget self, they will recognize the necessity of an intellectual and moral reform. The privilege of beginning this fundamental reform within oneself, and working for its fulfilment on behalf of other human beings, is extended by the Brotherhood of Bodhisattvas to every true friend of the human race.

> This reform cannot be accomplished except through Theosophy and, let us say it, Occultism, or the wisdom of the East. Many are the paths leading to it, but Wisdom is forever one. Artists foresee it, those who suffer dream of it, the pure in spirit know it. Those who work for others cannot remain blind before its reality even though they do not always know it by name. It is only the light-headed and empty-minded, the selfish and vain drones deafened by the sound of their own buzzing, who can ignore this high ideal.
>
> *Ibid.*

Whilst many have dreamt of ideal wisdom, some actually know it. They know it in their bones and in their blood; they have tested and tasted it; they have found that it works, and made it the basis of their thought and their lives. In the best cases, they have made it the basis of their unlimited devotion to the interests of others, and in the unselfishness of their service they have become invulnerable and indifferent towards the world and its evanescent opinions.

This is a very high state indeed. But in contemplating it, one should not fall prey to self-recrimination and recurring doubt. To do so would only reaffirm the contagious materialism that one wishes to leave behind. It does not matter at what level a human being approaches Divine Wisdom. Even if one can embody only one percent of the ideal, one must hold fast to the conviction that what is real in oneself and can be realized in practice is the only element that truly counts. This alone must be taken as the focus of one's concentration. Whilst it is always possible at any given time to say that one can only do so much, and no more, it is also always possible to enjoy and contemplate the ideal in meditation. The ideal can, and must, be separated from the limitations of incarnated existence. Thus, two different types of development emerge. First of all, one is intensifying through devotion to the ideal the architectonics of one's thought with regard to the ideal. This will be elaborated in *devachan* after death in the celestial condition of dreams of goodwill and creativity which can cut grooves in the *karana sharira*, the causal body, and affect lives to come. At the same time, one may recognize in other aspects of the vestures, particularly in the *linga sharira* or astral form, that one is unfortunately enslaved by many habits.

Under the karmic curve of the present life, one cannot enormously increase one's power of concentration however much one tries, because one lacks the strength to resist negative forces. Therefore, whilst maximizing development within the present lifetime, individuals must also recognize how little they can do and consequently how modest and honest they must be in the day to day walk of life. By understanding this dual process affecting both the present life and future lives, one can awaken a balanced courage and a spirit of unconditionality in one's commitment to an ideal.

> To take the first step on this ideal path requires a perfectly pure motive; no frivolous thought must be allowed to divert our eyes from the goal; no hesitation, no doubt must fetter our feet. Yet, there are men and women perfectly capable of all this, and whose only desire is to live under the aegis of their Divine Nature. Let these, at least, have the courage to live this life and not to hide it from the sight of others! No one's opinion could ever be above the rulings of our own conscience, so, let that conscience, arrived at its highest development, be our guide in all our common daily tasks. As to our inner life, let us concentrate all our attention on our chosen Ideal, and let us ever look *beyond* without ever casting a glance at the mud at our feet.
>
> *Ibid.*

It may be natural enough and even nutritionally sound for children to eat a little dirt, but it is unnatural and unhealthy for adults to savour the mentally negative or psychically muddy. They must rather train themselves always to look beyond, towards the stars and towards the future. By gazing towards the radiant though distant summit of enlightenment, they can keep their heads above the waters of chaos. By learning to float, by learning to tread water, they can begin to swim, and even to deal with the shifting tides of the psychic nature. Under karma, these forces work differently for different people. Some can concentrate on that which is universal and impersonal for long periods of time; others find that they cannot do so for more than a few minutes at a time. Again, the length of meaningful meditation is less important than the authenticity of the attempt. The more one can calmly accept the limits of one's abilities, the more those limits will expand. Here as everywhere the greater one's application the greater one's results.

And like many physical habits, these mental exercises must be established at an early age. What is easy for the young is not so easy for the old. If one acquires healthy mental habits whilst young one should be grateful for the auspicious karma. If one does not recognize the need for a mental reform until later in life, again, one should be grateful for the recognition itself, as for the counsel required to carry out the reform. One must desire reform, and having embarked upon it, persevere with courage. One must become a true friend of oneself and strive without guilt, enjoying progress, without falling into the anxious traps that began with 'original sin'. Like Job, one must learn that one's burden is neither greater nor less than one can bear, and thus become receptive to every form of good.

As Pythagoras taught, spiritual courage arises out of the conviction that the race of men is immortal. From the soil of its lunar beginnings to its ultimate dwelling-place beyond the stars, humanity follows the cyclic path of transformation wherein each element of human nature is transmuted into a self-conscious aspect of Divine Wisdom. The acquisition and unfoldment of knowledge of these elements in man and in Nature is an essential component of the collective spiritual progress of the race. The vivifying ideal of wisdom itself is inconceivable apart from the practical acquisition of knowledge, and the perfection of human nature is thus impossible where the mind-principle is either degraded or defamed. It is the peculiar demerit of materialism enforced through the dogma of original sin that it attempts to accomplish both these negative ends at once. Thus in the last century, H.P. Blavatsky had to oppose materialism in both religion and science. Owing to concretized conceptions of progress connected with a unilinear view of history and a short-sighted enthusiasm about technological change, it was very difficult in the latter part of the nineteenth century to challenge a prevailing blind faith in science. Nonetheless, H.P. Blavatsky prophetically anticipated the demise of this faith, which would take place in Europe because of the First World War. She also anticipated and stimulated a series of revolutionary scientific changes in the early decades of the Aquarian Age. Since then, even at a popular level, people have begun to assimilate something of quantum theory and theories of light, much that was implicit in the work of Einstein, Eddington and the early biologists. They have come to see that most of the nineteenth century categories of science are obsolete and irrelevant. This perception was already common in Europe in the 1920's and 1930's, but was considerably slower in coming to America, which is perhaps the last colonial country left on earth and usually moves about thirty years behind Europe in acknowledging significant shifts in thought.

After the Second World War, America tended to nurture an adolescent glorification of technology, but even this was challenged in the 1960's, and most thinking individuals discovered that they could not return to their earlier blind faith in technology. Unfortunately, this has produced an actual obstacle to understanding how the fruits of contemporary science and technology, for example micro-electronics, can be used to extend the effectiveness of human potential. Attitudes in America, unlike those in Sweden or Japan, are often polarized by mass society. Science and technology are met with a sluggish indifference or an incapacity to understand how they may be put to constructive use. Through the powerful blandishments of economics, however, there has recently been an enormous increase in the numbers of people seeking training in the use of computers, so much so that the facilities of educational institutions have been sorely taxed.

What is important and unusual in these developments is that people have set aside their former blind faith and begun to learn whatever skills are needed to put science and technology to use. Instead of reinforcing and reinvigorating outmoded conceptions of science, many have now learnt how to use the media to acquire information about cosmology and astronomy, about the earth and the oceans, about the body and the brain. Suddenly Americans, like Russians over the past thirty or forty years, have become more aware of the spiritual implications of science. They have begun to understand that the best science forces a rethinking of one's view of human nature, human potential, and the place of man in the cosmos. Once the spirituality of advanced science is recognized, there can be no return to a merely materialistic interest in technology. Men and women are now concerned with the creative noetic uses of scientific knowledge, and also with the raising of scientific questions that go to the heart of human existence. The largest questions in science always prompt honest disagreement and ultimately a ready recognition of ignorance.

Today, as was not true of the nineteenth century, enough is known in every field of science to recognize that what is known is a minute fragment of what is possible to know; leading scientists distinguish themselves in their fields only by admitting that they know next to nothing about fundamentals. Physiologists cannot penetrate all the miracles of the human brain. The finest physicists admit that almost nothing is known about the ultimate nature of matter. The best astronomers readily allow that they know little of the depths of outer space. The foremost biologists remain modestly silent before the mysteries of embryology. All of this is consonant with the vital keynote of the Aquarian Age, and extremely hopeful for the future of humanity. It is to this keynote that H.P. Blavatsky made reference when she declared:

> . . . you Occultists, Kabalists, and Theosophists, you know well that a word as old as the world, though new to you, has been sounded at the beginning of this cycle . . . you know that a note, never before heard by the men of the present era, has just been sounded, and that a new kind of thought has arisen, fostered by the evolutionary forces. This thought differs from all that has ever been produced in the 19th Century; yet it is identical with what was the keynote and the keystone of every century, especially the last one: 'Absolute Freedom of Human Thought.'
>
> *Ibid.*

As more and more people become aware of what the best minds of every age have always known — that they have hardly touched the threshold of the unknown — they will, paradoxically, be thrown back upon themselves. The willingness of people to become self-dependent is an important sign of the inception of the Aquarian Age. It is becoming progressively more difficult to convince people through statistical polls that what several million people think is necessarily true. Many individuals now prefer to think for themselves. As the antiquated machinery of thought-control breaks down, individuals are now discovering within themselves a willingness to exercise their own faculties. As they discover the challenge of true self-reliance, they become less blindly acquiescent to narrow scientific or religious dogmatism. With every increment of mental, moral and spiritual freedom gained, grand vistas of human possibility are opened before them. Even though the average human being uses much less than ten percent of the brain's potential, and even less of the heart's, the tide has begun to turn. Even though many still live like spiritual paupers, well below their potential means, they have begun to recognize their possibilities and the need for initiative in improving the human condition. Relinquishing the mummeries of the past, they have begun to understand that only through developing the natural powers of concentration and spiritual attention can they enrich their collective future. Through the joy and the beauty, the dignity and the self-respect, that come from self-discipline, they can alchemically quicken their creative faculties and thereby tap the potential energies of the higher mind and heart. Thus, following the small old path depicted in every religious tradition and intimated in every authentic myth, each good and true human soul may discern the spiritual possibilities of the Aquarian Age and stay abreast of the vanguard of humanity.

AQUARIAN CIVILIZATION

*Our races . . . have sprung from divine races, by
whatever name they are called. . . . Every nation has either
the* seven *and* ten *Rishis-Manus and Prajaptis. . . . One and
all have been derived from the primitive Dhyan-Chohans of
the Esoteric doctrine, or the 'Builders' of the Stanzas. From
Manu, Thot-Hermes, Oannes-Dagon, and Edris-Enoch, down
to Plato and Panadores, all tell us of seven divine Dynasties,
of seven Lemurian, and seven Atlantean divisions of the
Earth; of the seven primitive and dual gods who descend from
their celestial abode and reign on Earth, teaching mankind
Astronomy, Architecture, and all the other sciences that have
come down to us. These Beings appear first as 'gods' and
Creators; then they merge in nascent man, to finally emerge
as 'divine-Kings and Rulers'. . . . There were five Hermes —
or rather one, who appeared — as some Manus and Rishis
did — in several different characters. . . . But under
whichever of these characters, he is always credited with
having transferred all the sciences from* latent to active
potency, i.e., *with having been the first to teach magic to
Egypt and to Greece, before the days of* Magna Graecia, *and
when the Greeks were not even Hellenes.*
The Secret Doctrine, ii 365-367

To take the entire subject of cosmic hierarchies at the human
level to its sublime heights, one must start with the
momentous recognition that many of the 'gods' of the
ancient theogonies belonged to the First Race of humanity.
Human beings in that First Race were gods or *devas*, and in the
Second Race they were demi-gods — celestial spirits still too
ethereal to occupy the human form that was being gestated by
the lunar Pitris. Then, in the Third Race, with the lighting-up of
Manas and the incarnation of the *Manasaputras* into human form,
humanity underwent an evolution which passed through several

stages. Beginning with the androgynous and bisexual, it proceeded through the protracted dual-sexed epoch of the human race. There was the legendary era of great heroes and giants. The seven divine dynasties were thereafter to be found in the Third Race and again in the Fourth Race, the Lemurian and Atlantean periods. Instructing humanity in diverse arts and sciences, they laid the primeval foundations of human culture and civilization around the globe.

Within this broad framework, the extraordinarily evocative power of the name and presence of Hermes is especially relevant to the 1975 Cycle and to the civilization of the future. Hermes is a generic name, associated with potent thought, and linked to Mercury-Buddha — a Dhyani — as well as with multiple incarnations in the history of humanity. As the god Hermes-Thot, he is the pristine archetype of Initiators in ancient Egypt, where he was reverenced as Hermes Trismegistus, a name applying to an entire lineage of Initiators. This solar line of spiritual Teachers can be traced back to Shiva as Dakshinamurti, the Initiator of Initiates. The hoary tradition which holds that Hermes taught all sciences to the nascent Mediterranean civilization suggests that he instructed those ready for divine theurgy. The arcane sciences transferred by Hermes from latent to active potency collectively constitute divine *gnosis*, a precise and comprehensive knowledge of the complex laws governing the seven kingdoms of Nature. These laws encompass the planes of matter, both visible and invisible, the planes from which noumenal prototypes become precipitated or projected into the phenomenal realm. Science in its essence is concerned with primary causes and is rooted in a mature apprehension of noetic consciousness. This is the true and noble meaning of science, *vidya* in the old sense, which was mysteriously intimated by the Mahatmas to European civilization in the seventeenth and eighteenth centuries to counteract the corruption of creedal religion.

Modern science is a recent flower, emerging sporadically after the Renaissance, and, in particular, after Giordano Bruno's activities in Germany and his historic visit to Oxford. The Royal Society

was founded by heretical and courageous clergymen, men like the
Warden of Wadham, who recognized that Aristotelian
scholasticism was throttling the growth of human thought, that
theology had become nothing more than a corrosive word-game.
Together with bold patrons in the discreetly pagan aristocracy,
these pioneering heretics founded a small club in London which
they called the Royal Society. It was concerned from the beginning
with the systematic support of all earnest experimental
investigation into the natural world. In this, its purest sense, early
modern science is one of the minor contributions of the
Brotherhood of Bodhisattvas to the post-Renaissance world. Yet,
in the context of the ancient meaning of science, it is a limited
thing indeed, shadowy and modest. Originally, 'science' referred
to a system of laws capable of application by human consciousness
to what later came to be cherished by a few reticent brotherhoods
as true magic or divine wisdom. Magic is an exact and definite
knowledge of the noumenal laws of invisible Nature. Through
the proper use of that carefully transmitted knowledge, one can
affect the rates of growth and primary structures of energy on the
Akashic and astral planes, and so affect conditions and
combinations on the physical plane. Modern science, through its
neglect of the primacy of consciousness, can hardly approach such
a universal synthesis, fusing meta-geometry, meta-biology and
meta-psychology.

In the ancient and archetypal view of noetic magic, there is
a summoning from latency to active potency of arcane knowledge
that was originally impressed in the imperishable soul-memory
of all humanity. Going all the way back to the middle of the Third
Root Race, when self-consciousness had been attained, human
beings were in astral vestures that were capable of effortless and
benevolent use of the spiritual senses. Human beings, therefore,
through their intuitive knowledge of the correlations of sound,
colour and number, were able to communicate effortlessly. In that
Golden Age, shrouded in the myths and mists of antiquity, they
showed spontaneous reverence to Magus-Teachers, Hierophant-
Adepts moving openly among human beings, teaching in fabled

"concord groves" all over the earth. Seated under banyan trees (varieties of *ficus religiosa*), they bestowed divine wisdom upon those who were ready to learn. In that idyllic time the vast human inheritance of spiritual wisdom and scientific magic was assimilated into the *karana sharira*, the permanent vesture of the monad. It is in that inmost vesture, which is the container of all soul-memories, that the original wisdom and theurgy of humanity lie latent to this day.

It is suggestive and significant that contemporary physicists, like Roger Jones, have come to see that a great deal of what is known in particle physics and quantum mechanics points to a necessary transcendence of conventional space and time. This is strikingly reminiscent of the recondite concept of the *karana sharira*. A few intuitive scientists find the idea of such a causal field or morphogenetic matrix intensely meaningful because it intimates modes of action that are independent of many of the restrictions that hold in ordinary space and time. Because it allows for what would appear from a physical standpoint to be simultaneous transmission, it suggests the operation of laws very different from those applicable to the objective-seeming world of disparate material entities. Hence, it may have application or relevance to some of the energy fields and the "broken symmetry" that pertain to fundamental particles. Considered in relation to noetic consciousness and benevolent magic, the significance of the *karana sharira* is that it is the ground of the latent knowledge called to active potency by Hermes.

Hermes is the paradigm of the oldest sacred tradition, going back a million years ago to India *(Bharata Dwipa)*. There, among the Initiates, the basis was laid in all the Mystery Schools for the manasic development of the seminal civilizations of the Fifth Race. When the most creative minds of the Aquarian Age gain a sufficient knowledge of Sanskrit, they will come to see that all latter-day sciences are but pale and poor fragments compared with the systematic ontology and epistemology of *Brahma Vidya*, *Theosophia* or *Dzyan*. With reference to astronomy, to physics, physiology and to chemistry, to the mathematical and geometrical sciences, even to mechanics, transmission devices and aerial transport, the lost knowledge of the ancients was overwhelming. Some of this knowledge, still accessible through scattered texts, is being slowly recovered today by remarkable young scholars like David Pingree, who has dedicated his life to the translation of available Sanskrit texts in astronomy. This is only one small field within a vast body of information, but by the end of the century many such texts should be accessible to those who can effectively use them.

The foreshortened view of the emergence and growth of civilization which has characterized the last two hundred years is rooted in a habit of mind extending back over a period of some two thousand years, but nonetheless a minor incident in human evolution. Historians tend to focus upon the material aspects of civilization and cultures, to become obsessed with power and violence; yet since a nation's spiritual decline accompanies its material ascent, such a truncated approach can only distort the truth and mislead the unwary. Any attempt to account for this messianic history of recent millennia must begin fundamentally with a recognition that many human souls were badly scarred in decadent Atlantis, and, having lost the Third Eye, were left merely with an external sense of power connected to a crude conception of energy which still mesmerizes them through awe of tangible bigness and gross strength.

This is reminiscent of Plato's memorable reference to the contest between the Gods and the Giants. Whilst such events go back far beyond even the declining period of Egyptian dynasties, it does not, after all, characterize the entire million-year history of the Fifth Root Race. Certainly, such a shrunken perspective does little or no justice to the more than eighteen million years of human existence on this globe, or to the immeasurable reservoir of soul-memories garnered in the earliest golden ages. Every major culture reflects, to some degree, these finest and persistent intuitions in human beings. That is what gives many people a kind of reverence, however confused, before the Native Americans and other so-called 'primitive' peoples. Even if many of these cultures have lost their spiritual knowledge, and so have fallen to the mercy of inferior races, these same Monads may yet recover and re-enact their wisdom in future civilizations.

This process has recurred again and again. It was played out before the days of Magna Graecia in events that were encapsulated by Herodotus in his brief work, *Euterpe.* Therein he acknowledged the debt of gratitude that the Greeks owed to the grand Egyptian civilization which preceded it. This is even more explicit in Plato, who made Socrates speak of Solon, and the great Egyptian teachers of Sais, next to whom the Greeks were as little children. Yet whilst the reverence of Herodotus for predecessors was genuine, and expressed with almost religious awe, he also wrote that more familiar kind of historical narrative through which he is known as the "Father of History". In an often overlooked passage, he commended the Persians for their exemplary bravery and sense of truth, which, he said, were lacking among the Greeks. The courage to tell the truth and stand by it, the sense of the sacredness of a man's word of honour — these, he thought, were virtues that the Greeks could learn from the ancient Persians.

At the same time, however, Herodotus, in dealing with the Persian legal system, began to generate some of the snobbery that long prevailed among Athenians when they contemplated their *polis* and its democratic institutions. Through dramatized contrasts with the corrupt despotism of Persian institutions, Herodotus managed to compress, and devalue, the scope and successive phases of Persian civilization. In virtually every subsequent account of the supposed history of ancient civilizations, this same compression is found compounded. It arises because of decadence and the disappearance from active human memory of the greatest epochs of antiquity. This has led to the extraordinary and confusing conclusion that all the collective knowledge of the human race can somehow be made readily available to the common man. Some even insist that the less one knows, the more one has a right to demand all and sundry information.

This puny standpoint is seriously threatened by the fact that the seminal periods of human evolution are hidden and secret, and yet span millions of years which are inaccessible except through initiation. The profoundest truths were never written about in popular chronicles. They were available only in glyphs and symbols, in monuments, in secret libraries in central Asia and elsewhere. They were not for the eyes of curious crowds. In any event, even ordinary people in more mature cultures have a natural reticence about spiritual wisdom. Just as, in old age, those beset by a sense of failure, a fear of death and a feeling of audience deprivation seek refuge in reminiscence, so too cultures grow infatuated with telling their inflated history only after they have begun to decay. They become compulsively autobiographical, repeatedly retelling their life story. The truly creative, mindful of the enormous potency of mathematical and spiritual knowledge, are careful to protect that knowledge. They will make it available to those who can use it constructively; but they will keep it away from those who may abuse it, delude others and harm themselves.

Seen from this perspective, one can begin to appreciate the sense in which much of modern science is based upon the half-baked occult secrets of the semi-esoteric groups that persisted from the days of the early Church Fathers to the Renaissance. Whilst it may come as a surprise to post-colonial Europeans, it is still held by the Ashanti elders that had they been more careful with their accumulated wisdom, modern science and medicine could have avoided their premature and amoral growth. What such wise elders knew, and what was intuited by Pauwels and Bergier — the authors of *The Morning of the Magicians* — is that what is presently extolled as modern science is significantly based upon the scattered and leaked secrets of medieval and ancient classical knowledge.

The disappearance of alchemy and the authentic occult arts is inseparable from the karmic record of those souls who were not capable of handling theurgic teaching and practical knowledge in relation to the various secret sciences. But something of that tradition remained in the Platonic Academy, which lasted for nine hundred years, among the early Muslims in Cordoba, and through them, among their pupils in Italy and France. At about the same time, out of small beginnings in a few houses the University of Oxford was born. All these communities struggled towards an understanding of the seven sciences, the *trivium* and *quadrivium*. Respect for these sciences is the origin of what were once sacred terms — bachelor of arts and master of arts. These were degrees going back to old initiations, carrying memories of earlier times. Then they became attached to universities which, since the twelfth century, have helped to bring knowledge to thousands of people who would otherwise have had no access to it. Until Wycliffe, for example, no one who was poor or ignorant of Latin could read the Bible.

This breaking down of the closed circle connected with knowledge in general, and sacred texts in particular, is not yet complete. It is thus a vital part of the present climactic Cycle: over the coming decades Sanskrit and Greek will be simplified and taught so that anyone may acquire them. Languages will be rescued from the grammarians. For so-called experts, who have never penetrated the inner meanings of ancient texts, nonetheless manage to discourage the spiritual enquirer from learning the language. At a certain level, this renaissance in ancient languages will be part of the Hermetic work of the 1975 Cycle.

To understand the work of Hermes at a more fundamental level in relation to civilization, one must begin to generate a conception of the cosmic hierarchies in Nature and in Man which unites the spiritual with the physical, and both of these with the moral and the political. This fundamental recognition of the relationship of the celestial and the terrestrial must be forged through a living link in the psychological realm. That link is Man. Only through the rediscovery within human nature of all orders of being from the gods to the elementals can there be a recovery of the continuity of the Great Chain of Being from the highest to the lowest. All hierarchies — from the Dhyanis through the *danavas* and *daityas*, to the *devas* or gods, the *devatas* and elementals — are represented within the individual human being. The five middle principles of human nature, leaving out of consideration the *Atman* and the physical body, are the direct gift and transmitted essence of the sixfold Dhyani Buddhas. That is why even *kama manas* is in essence sacred. It is lent to human beings to show them how to connect and how to discriminate.

If this is difficult to perceive, it is because all of these intermediate principles have been polluted, all have been abused on behalf of the shadowy self, of egotism and separatism. Human beings of the past, like little children in the present, showed an innate confidence that comes from knowing oneself as a ray of the Divine. They recognized themselves as immortal souls, centres of consciousness capable of expansion and contraction, of diffusion and concentration. Thus they could regard the body as an instrument, to be used by the soul as a horse by its rider. The mind is a necessary and useful tool of the soul, but it must be regularly cleansed. A person who senses this does not identify with his clothes in the spiritual and philosophical sense. Instead, he is always turned inward through meditation, and upward through aspiration; he is forever rising heavenward towards the invisible cosmos. It becomes natural for him to start with the cosmic and come down to the human, to descend from *Hiranyagarbha* — the luminous golden egg of Brahmā — to the recognition of one's own egg, from *Mahat,* or cosmic mind, to *Manas,* his small share in cosmic ideation. Descending from the universal to the particular is essential to the Hermetic method.

Modernity, by contrast, stands on its head, tries to move upward, and thus severs off the umbilical connection between man and cosmos. This approach, antithetical to the spiritual nature of man, had to be corrected by the Copernican revolution, which clarified the relation of the earth and the sun. But while the contemporaries of Copernicus thought they were discovering new truths, they were, in fact, only recovering the ancient laws of Pythagorean wisdom. If a sense of the right relationship of heaven and earth is to be restored, the sort of reorientation and recentering that has taken place in astronomy must take place psychologically and metaphysically. This can be attempted in many ways. Ordinary people could, for example, develop skill in consulting the *I-Ching.* They would not be able to use it for precise prediction, for that mysterious science requires a great deal of reverence. But by simply considering the *I-Ching*, they will be reminded that there are seasons, and continuous connections between heaven and earth.

A recognition of the correspondences between the celestial and terrestrial is the beginning of wisdom. The fear of God is not the beginning of wisdom. Wisdom is attainable only through love of the gods and recognition of their immanence within the human temple. The realization of human nature as a living psychological link between the celestial and the terrestrial will come about only through meditation and contemplation in the highest sense. Through the awakening of Buddhic feeling, one may feel close to the stars and to the galaxy. But one will also feel close to that which corresponds to *Akasha* within the astral brain and spiritual heart, and also within the *karana sharira*. Without this therapeutic and creative feeling, true learning and science can never progress. A few pioneers have recognized that for three centuries now science has been a mutilated victim of methodological dogmatism. This has led to a mechanistic reductionism, often trumpeted only because people are not good at mathematics. When they are lacking in mathematics in the highest sense, they become addicted to the habit of tinkering with jars and lamps. Owing to the delusion that has shadowed the diffusion of science, the tremendous integrity of the highest mathematical method has been inaccessible to the majority of practitioners, who have become like Shaw's barbarians. They resemble the civilized savage, who, upon switching on the light, thinks he knows about electricity.

Fortunately, this adolescent state of science is coming to an end. Yet although many people now recognize that science must deal with consciousness, most scientists are still encumbered by a philosophically narrow view of sense-data, sense-experience and inductive logic. As a result, pioneering researchers who want to elevate consciousness have difficulty in doing so. They must meditate, consult maps of consciousness, employ philosophical criteria, if they are to make any genuine progress. In the Aquarian academies of the future, they will have to submit themselves to certain rigorous tests. They will have to prove that they have the powers, not just of concentration, but also of directing consciousness towards universally constructive connections and correlations. This will involve both analogy and correspondence, intuition and mathematics; it will draw upon meta-sciences as yet only dimly formulated. In general, what is required is a conception of mind correlated with a conception of matter, both of which exist on many levels. Different planes of matter corresponding to different states of mind are richly interconnected with each other in different sets and subsets, systems and subsystems, as well as supersystems. All of this has application to the arrangement of atoms and molecules, but also to what lies beyond what are presently called atomic and subatomic particles. These are but ghostly shadows of the invisible atoms in which inheres the eternal motion of the *Atman* and which may be spoken of as the *Atma-Buddhi-Manas* of the atom.

Science will not truly advance unless it goes beyond the mere analysis of physical matter, the mundane tricks which for a while bewitched hordes of ex-peasants coming out of villages. It was advantageous to have a little vulgar technology in the age of the automobile, the steam engine and the electric motor. It was comforting to share in a collective sense of automatic progress. But that time is over. The present aim must be to transcend the mere classification of matter which characterizes, for example, most of modern medicine, and instead to determine critical and relevant factors through theoretical and experiential knowledge of general and universal laws. This capacity must extend not only over the realm of physical phenomena, but also over psychological and moral life, and the social and political realms of human existence. Ultimately, this capacity will derive from strong foundations in spiritual self-awareness that can only be laid through a fundamental inner change. One might say this decisive change will require not merely framing the Hippocratic Oath but directly experiencing a reverence for life and truth. Early in the century such a spirit blessed the scientific academies of Germany, Switzerland and England.

Since 1914, however, much of this has been lost in the tumultuous rush after more technology and mere techniques. That is why the shining example of Mahatma Gandhi is so important to everyone who is authentically concerned with the disinterested pursuit of pure truth, while secure in its indifference to worldly concerns. The celestial was joined to the terrestrial in the West in certain monastic and intellectual communities, but since that connection was lost, to recover it requires something far more fundamental — a discriminating knowledge of metaphysics strong enough to broaden all one's categories and to deepen one's insights.

The radical regeneration of civilization and the restoration of a golden age can ultimately only be understood in relation to the descent of the gods. The golden age is eternally associated with Shiva-Saturn and the hosts of the Kumaras, whilst its terrestrial incarnation is inseparable from the incarnation of divine dynasties and king-hierophants. Thus, Thot-Hermes was the secretary of King Saturn presiding over the pre-dynastic Golden Age. Plato, in *The Statesman*, speaks of the Golden Age as a time of universal well-being wherein all basic needs were fulfilled. This dream continually recurs in myth and literature, for example, in the vision of Gonzalo in *The Tempest*. But it is more than a dream. It is a recollection of reality. It refers not just to the Third Root Race, but also to certain recurring moments in human evolution. The time of Rama, a million years ago, was the last great Golden Age. It was possible then for Divine Instructors to move openly among ordinary human beings. As kingship was sacred, rulers in that age could exemplify benevolent magic, exercising a just and compassionate custodianship over their close-knit communities. In the age of Shiva-Saturn, the cooperative hierarchies of human relationships mirrored the cosmic hierarchies of invisible Nature.

However, as Plato recognized in *The Statesman*, once the Age of Zeus began, it was no longer possible for Divine Instructors to come openly into the world. Here Plato is referring to the beginning of Kali Yuga five thousand one hundred eight years ago. It is a familiar characteristic of the Iron Age that human beings must rely on rules to restrain their weaknesses and vices. But it is also well known that all rules can be manipulated and that in rule-governed systems oligarchy and inequality work continuously. The pervasive recognition that rule-governed societies are only dim reflections of some higher ideal is itself evidence that one cannot extinguish from the human heart an innate sense of devotion to true Teachers, Gurus and ethical leaders. One of the crucial contributions of the 1975 Cycle has been to awaken soul-memories in many peoples around the world. This had to be done before the beginning of the present Cycle, because no one can benefit from it until he or she has first been shown how to learn and to respect Teachers. Because all of this was significantly accomplished before 1975, many people are now more open and willing to function in environments that are precursors of the secular monasteries of the future, spiritual centres profoundly hospitable to learning and to oral instruction by true Teachers.

This was wisely anticipated by Damodar K. Mavalankar in the nineteenth century, who understood that the Theosophical Movement has essentially one object and no other. As a natural logician, Mavalankar knew that what he understood, others would also understand, namely, that if Mahatmas and Adepts can move freely among human beings, any one of them can solve myriads of persisting problems among myriads of responsive human beings. One need only open the door to the free movement of such enlightened beings. This could not have been attempted during the last Cycle; if anything it was retarded, first by ignorant misuse of the Teachings, and later by abject cowardice. The lifeless thought-forms, crippled images and paranoid vestiges of the past millenia must be bypassed through the progressive initiation of the Aquarian *sanghas,* the academies and the lodges of the future. As this Pythagorean fusion attains fruition during the next century, there will around the globe be widespread hospitality to the wisdom and necessity of acceptance of the Guruparampara chain. There will be a willingness to learn, which can draw upon the natural reciprocity and self-validating strength of the relationship between teacher and taught. Like a deep and loving relationship between a parent and a child, this cannot be manipulated by a third party. Its reciprocity arises within the unique context of a particular karmic field, and points to the timeless ideal of the Guru-chela relationship.

This universal Aquarian diffusion of the true ideal of spiritual science and lifelong learning will enable human beings to awaken a vibrant sense of universal justice, universal compassion and universal concord. It will enable people to learn anew how to think, how to speak and how to contribute fearlessly yet appropriately to the collective fund of human wisdom: how to evoke benevolent spirits. If one employs harsh words, or even gentle words in a harsh manner, one will attract negative elementals. These, over time, accumulate, blocking the capacity to question or to formulate truths. But, by purifying words, speech and the aura around words and by cleansing one's motivation, one's tone of voice and one's movements, one can reorient oneself and so draw finer elementals into one's sphere. Through this elevation of the orbit of one's consciousness, one may become more benevolent and more magnanimous, while at the same time learning to use potent knowledge with more deliberation, courage and compassion.

The regeneration of global civilization through such a tapping of the inward spiritual resources of humanity is the enigmatic Hermetic and Avataric function exemplified by Hermes-Thot. It is the sacred function central to every Mystery School in recorded and unrecorded history. It goes back directly to Dakshinamurti, the Initiator of Initiates, and it has never been absent from the earth. It has been self-evidently crucial when the beginnings of civilizations were laid in different parts of the world. To make it now a vital part of a universal outlook in the dawning Aquarian Age, where there is more freedom from competitiveness and more openness to universal truths, could lead to a new kind of soul-etiquette. Founded upon the principle of drawing the larger circle, there could be the elaboration of a new code of relationship between human beings which would be more hospitable to the profoundly paradigmatic teachings of the

Upanishad, "Sit down near me and let me whisper in your ear." This is the ancient Platonic-Upanishadic method, born with the human race, perpetually nourishing it, and recognized by the noblest precursors of the Aquarian Age.

AQUARIAN HARMONY

'Our old writers said that Vach *is of four kinds ...*
para, pasyanti, madhyama, vaikhari *(a statement found
in the Rig-Veda and the Upanishads). ... Vaikhari-Vach is
what we utter.' It is sound,* speech, *that again which
becomes comprehensive and objective to one of our physical
senses and may be brought under the laws of perception.
Hence: 'Every kind of* Vaikhari-Vach *exists in its*
Madhyama ... Pasyanti *and ultimately in its* Para
form. ... The reason why this Pranava *is called Vach is this,
that these four principles of the great Kosmos correspond to
these four forms of Vach. ... The whole Kosmos in its objective
form is* Vaikhari *Vach; the light of the Logos is the*
madhyama *form; and the* Logos *itself the* pasyanti *form;
while Parabrahmam is the* para *(beyond the* noumenon *of
all* Noumena) *aspect of that Vach.'*

The Secret Doctrine, i 432

Harmony is the central idea in Aquarian thought.
Compassionate sacrifice and intelligent suffering are the
necessary means to an understanding of harmony; their
eventual fruition is noetic self-knowledge. Spiritual growth is
epitomized by the image of the silent, ceaseless construction of
the Temple of Truth, precipitated in its crystalline splendour by
meditative action out of the Akashic waters of life. True spiritual
will, the conscious direction of energy by intelligent ideation and
self-conscious volition, is the supreme criterion and sovereign
talisman of Aquarian humanity. Opposed to this vision are the
irrational and involuntary forces of blind desire, the persistent and
obscuring veil cast over human perception and action through
lives of thoughtless involvement with the grosser fields of material
nature. Aquarians can readily grasp this problem, but they are few
and far between. The therapeutic Aquarian standpoint depends
upon a fundamental appreciation, through meditation, of the

metaphysical structure of all reality and Nature, of God and Man.

The idea of cosmic harmony and human solidarity is as old as the Vedas and is vital to every authentic spiritual tradition. Long before the Christian era, at the time of Confucius and Buddha, when the basis for civilization was being laid in different parts of the world, Pythagoras required all his diligent pupils to study arithmetic, geometry, astronomy and music. Musical harmony was considered one of the four branches of mathematics, a reflection of the deeper nature of spiritual harmony. At some instinctive level, all human beings recognise the difference between harmonious and disharmonious movement. In one of the first human rites of initiation, learning to walk, it is necessary to learn, to assimilate and to embody some understanding of the relationship between harmony and self-direction. The art of physical movement is analogous to the mystical process of treading the spiritual Path. Pythagoras said that he could understand the inward nature of a human being by watching the way he or she walked, because he comprehended the continuous embodiment of universal harmony which extends from the highest to the lowest in Nature and Man.

> Pythagoras esteemed the Deity (the Logos) to be the *centre of unity* and 'Source of Harmony.' We say this Deity was the *Logos,* not the MONAD that dwelleth in Solitude and Silence, because Pythagoras taught that UNITY being indivisible is *no number.* . . . The Pythagoreans asserted that the doctrine of Numbers — the chief of all in Esotericism — had been revealed to man by the celestial deities; that the world had been called forth out of Chaos by Sound or Harmony, and constructed according to the principles of musical proportion; that the seven planets which rule the destiny of mortals have a harmonious motion 'and intervals corresponding to musical diastemes, rendering various sounds, so perfectly consonant, that they produce the sweetest melody, which is inaudible to us, only by reason of the greatness of the sound, which our ears are incapable of receiving.'   *Ibid.,* i 433

To rise above a merely instinctual awareness of harmony and

to become a more receptive agent and instrument of cosmic harmony, one must apprehend the idea in reference to the mind and the heart and understand too the rhythms of the invisible vestures. One must reflect upon what it means, first of all, to see oneself as a source of harmony, a Logoic being, capable of centering oneself in consciousness at that point in abstract space which is indivisible, unconnected with any form. This point is a focus of concentration, and also a point from which there can be diffused in every direction, as in a sphere, radii reaching out with deliberation and benevolence towards every life-atom. Whether putting on one's clothes, or eating food, or sitting down, one is always dealing with life-atoms. How grateful and gentle is one towards everything that one has the privilege of touching and using? To increase benevolence one must locate oneself correctly through meditation, heightening awareness from a central point of harmony. In the Bhagavad Gita, Krishna instructs Arjuna to take the point between the eyes as his starting-point in coming to see himself as a centre of harmony. A being is not his eyes, his ears, his mouth, his head, not any of his organs nor his entire body. But he can be the mystical point between the eyes.

This meditative exercise to see oneself as a monadic point should be complemented by an effort to see what is at the core of every relationship with other human beings. What gratitude does one owe one's father, who initiated one's physical incarnation by providing not only one's bone structure but also the seminal essence out of which the body was formed? What reverence does one owe to one's mother, who gave not only the flesh and soft tissue of the body, but also the egg itself from which was born the embryo that was gestated for seven months in the womb and then protected for two more months before being delivered? What does one owe one's spouse and children in the present lifetime and one's former spouses and children in all one's former lives? What is crucial in one's relationship to one's friends and neighbours and their families who constitute the community one lives in, and what is at the core of one's relationships in one's sphere of work?

All such questions highlight the crux of one's *dharma*, that which upholds a human being, linking him or her to the entire fabric of human life. If human beings would only begin to centre themselves through meditation, reflection and preparation, they would realize the great privilege of entering the world. One must prepare oneself inwardly before using one's eyes, if one would see other human beings reverentially as points of light. If one is going to speak compassionately, not compulsively, one must consider before speaking how one's words may be relevant or beneficial to another. "Please" or "Thank you" must be said sincerely, not automatically; favours must be asked kindly, not imperiously. By coming to see life in terms of the primary facts of birth and death, one may learn to act with deliberation and noetic discernment, like an orderly in a hospital who, though always very busy, does not mind being overlooked. By a smile, by a word or by silent exemplification alone, one may remain centered as a monadic point, giving off therapeutic vibrations to all.

Seen in this way, life can be extraordinarily beautiful and simple. Life seems difficult only because so much comes in the way of understanding oneself as a source of harmony. Human beings are continually concerned with the boundaries between themselves as individuals, yet those boundaries exist only in the realm of ephemeral forms, and therefore provide no stable basis for self-centering. Without deep meditation and fundamental metaphysics, it is impossible to learn anything significant about centering oneself in consciousness. Thus, thousands of people who use those terms loosely are looking for disciples and not finding any who will stay with them. That is because they never stayed with anything themselves; they have hence not centered themselves in their own consciousness. Like the dilettantes Plato warned against in his portrayal of democracy, they have no internal sense of priority or proportion, and hence no spiritual will. Yet there exists today an increasing number of Aquarian pioneers, like the scattered droplets presaging the monsoon, who have begun in earnest the difficult task of gradually centering themselves in the Verbum — *Brahma Vach*.

By removing what is excessive and by refining a sense of what is essential, they are learning to radiate benevolence and intelligence. They are learning the constructive use and dissemination of thought, feeling and will-energy. They have become self-consciously engaged in the transformation of the energy-field of the entire earth, that grand project which is the task of the Aquarian Age. The forces of harmony will be progressively strengthened, whilst disharmony will become nothing but a dialectical opportunity for growth. As the Aquarian Age unfolds, there will be a continuous increase in human awareness, a deepening of privacy. Each human being will become more of a solitary person of silence and meditation. In mature Aquarian culture, what is said and done will be meaningful and thoughtful, deliberate and discerning, but rendered with ease, sweetness and even beauty.

Clearly, the transformation from Piscean to Aquarian civilization poses an extraordinary challenge. Yet the resources available to any human being who wishes to assist this transformation are tremendous. The internal reservoirs of Akashic energy and ideation potentially available to the aspiring human soul are virtually infinite. To tap them self-consciously and thereby to contribute to the civilization of the future requires an understanding of metaphysics grounded in meditation as well as a moral self-discipline enlightened by at least some preliminary understanding of the arcane teachings about cosmic hierarchies. The greatest conceptual barrier to a practical increase in the sense of human solidarity is the mistaken notion that human beings must do something to unify the world. It is an ultimate and irreducible metaphysical fact that the world is already one. All beings are one, and all Being is One. Since all beings are one in a primordial invisible state, the true task is to mirror that unity on the lower, manifested planes of differentiated thought and action. This is impossible without first reaching towards that invisible unity, and hence Pythagoras taught his disciples to be extremely humble about That which is No Number. That is not zero, a place-holder in the number continuum. It is, rather, the source of dynamic harmony that lies behind all the spheres and circles of the metaphysical and physical universes. The key to the harmony and Akashic continuity of the One and the many lies concealed within the mystery of the zero and the point.

To convey this to the modern age, the great Rishi, masquerading as H.P. Blavatsky, set forth before the world the ancient *Stanzas of Dzyan*. During the nineteenth century, the Sixth Century Impulsion in the septenary series initiated by Tsong-Kha-Pa, the term *'Brahma Vidya'* was often used as an equivalent to *Theosophia*. Whilst *Brahma Vidya* refers to the sacred science, spiritual knowledge has not, over a hundred years, been put to intensive use by very many individuals. In that sense, the Theosophical Movement was once again a comparative failure. As it had failed over two thousand years ago in the time of Jesus, it failed again and again throughout the six impulsions of recent centuries. It failed especially, dramatically and poignantly, in the eighteenth century, despite an extremely powerful infusion. It gained a partial success on the secular, social and political planes, but the true import and teaching of the Enlightenment was subverted. "Liberty, equality and fraternity" did not come about in the true spiritual sense in which it was envisaged by the great Adepts of the eighteenth century.

In the 1975 Cycle, no quarter is given either to spiritual pretensions or to paranoid empiricism. The clutter and lumber of the past, whether pseudo-Theosophical, pseudo-religious, pseudo-scientific or pseudo-political, are being wiped out, so that human beings must endure severe testing before they can return to the timeless basics of living. They are being forced to ask themselves what it means to be a human being and how one uses sound and speech. Given the course of human evolution over the last five million years, a situation must be created in which the word 'human' cannot any more be applied in the future tense to someone who misuses sound and speech. Nothing can be done about the right use of speech on the plane of appearances without getting to the root of the problem on the plane of thought. There must be a restoration of the Mysteries and an elimination of the worldly worship of secondary and tertiary emanations through religious systems and mindless rituals. New rules must be created for speech, and new criteria must be created for silence, so that meditation can become more widespread and constructive. It must be brought home that *Dzyan* means self-reform through meditation, and that maturity is nothing more than mastery over the power of speech.

For these reasons, *Brahma Vidya* in the 1975 Cycle has been supplanted by the term '*Brahma Vach*', as a synonym for *Theosophia*. The aim is to get to the root of that which is beyond even the pre-cosmic sidereal gods. Whether it is called the Logos or *Vach* or *Brahma Vach*, it is the primordial latent sound and light in *Parabrahm*. That latent sound and light in *Parabrahm* is *Para Vach*, and that *Para Vach* is beyond both manifestation and non-manifestation. It is the Great Breath beyond the cosmos that vitalizes root matter, the eternally self-existent vibration of eternal motion. It transcends the distinction between *Mahamanvantara* and *Mahapralaya*, and even the creative vibratory light of the *sandhya* at the dawn of differentiation. In the dawn of manifestation that light exists in its most virginal, luminous and noumenal potential state. Its latency becomes meditated upon and thus draws upon the ideational energy of the Logos. This is *Pashyanti Vach*, coexistent with the Logos and inseparable from its own highest self-awareness. *Para Vach* is like a ray from the primordial ever-darkness of *Parabrahm*, flowing out of the pre-cosmic sources of all as *Kalagni*, dark spiritual fire. It is misleading to think of it as actually emerging from *Parabrahm*, because it is always the ever-concealed potency in *Parabrahm*. There is a stirring within that eternal state from which arises the awareness of latent light and sound, which becomes *Pashyanti Vach*, yielding the Logos, Brahmā, Ishwara, Sanat — the Ancient of Ancients. Simultaneous with the emergence of the androgyne Logos is the emergence of its feminine counterpart which is Vach.

Vach thus refers in its *para* form to that which is absolutely latent light and sound. Vach also refers to Brahmā, who, as the Logos, is Vach, whilst Vach as the consort of Brahmā is the light of the Logos — *Daiviprakriti* — which is Vach in its *madhyama* form. In other words, given latent light and sound, and given ideation upon that latent light and sound, that ideation is expressed in a most pristine form in the dawn of manifestation. It is like the dawn of Venus on the terrestrial plane; physically, there is darkness, but a most noumenal light is irradiated on earth. Cats have a psychic awareness of this and wish to be outside at that time; even the glow-worm enjoys the light before dawn. Human beings should understand the analogy between terrestrial dawn-light and the noumenal and causal light of the invisible Sun. On the plane of *Buddhi-Manas* intellectual light is consubstantial with the essential light-energy of *Suddhasattva*, the substance of the gods. In this sense, Vach, as the consort of Brahmā and the Light of the Logos, is also the mother of the gods. She is Sarasvati, the goddess of wisdom and beauty, and Aditi, out of whose noumenal form emanate the seven primordial rays, each of which carries a luminous vesture.

The substance of these vestures is not matter in any sense that can be understood by terrestrial criteria, but rather rays so luminous and radiant that they are called the sons of *Daiviprakriti*. These sons are preconditions to a cosmos, and it is from these primordial seven that there is a rapid multiplication in sevens and fourteens, in tens and twelves, producing *en masse* the array of the hierarchies. It is these in turn that produce the objective manifested universe, or *Vaikhari Vach*. Thus, H.P. Blavatsky speaks of Vach as

> the most mysterious of all the Brahmanical goddesses, she who is termed 'the *melodious* cow who milked forth sustenance and water' (the Earth with all her mystic powers); and again she 'who yields us nourishment and sustenance' (physical Earth). *Isis* is also mystic Nature and also Earth; and her cow's horns identify her with Vach. The latter, after having been recognised in her highest form as *para*, becomes at the lower or material

end of creation — *Vaikhari.* Hence she is mystic, though physical, Nature, with all her magic ways and properties.

Ibid., i 434

The conception of Vach as mystic Nature points to the continuity of the entire field linking *Para* to *Vaikhari Vach.* The two opposite poles, the one beyond all manifestation and the other representing the maximum degree of differentiation, the most transcendental and the most immanent, are held together by *Akasha.* It is a supersensuous, fiery, fluidic ether surrounding the earth and the solar system, but also pervading the brain, the heart and the entire human body, which is largely composed of water and empty space.

'Waters' and 'water' stand as the symbol for Akasa, the 'primordial Ocean of Space,' on which Narayana, the self-born Spirit, moves; reclining on that *which is its progeny....* 'Water is the body of Nara'; thus we have heard the name of water explained. Since Brahmā rests on the water, therefore he is termed 'Narayana'.... 'Pure, Purusha created the waters pure...' at the same time Water is the third principle in material Kosmos, and the third in the realm of the Spiritual: *Spirit* of Fire, Flame, Akasa, Ether, Water, Air, Earth, are the cosmic, sidereal, psychic, spiritual and mystic principles, *pre-eminently occult,* in every *plane* of being. 'Gods, Demons, Pitris and men,' are the four orders of beings to whom the term Ambhamsi is applied (in the Vedas it is a synonym of gods): because they are all the product of WATERS (mystically), of the Akasic Ocean, and of the Third principle in nature.

Ibid., i 458

Akasha-Vach is mystic Nature pervading the entire cosmos. It is the celestial virgin and Alkahest of the alchemists, the 'Virgin Mother' of the magician. It is the mother of love, mercy and charity, as well as the waters of grace which can only be tapped by true meditation, total benevolence and selflessness. That is why it is only possible to gain self-knowledge through selfless love. A mother blessed with pure love can, just by a glance, avert impending danger to her child. Through the power of pure love, the mother and child become one, experiencing *Akasha*. This notion of two identities fusing is neither simple in itself nor vague. Although it may be readily observed in the animal kingdom, it cannot be understood through terms like 'instinct'. Crude notions such as 'mother instinct' are worse than useless. In seeking to understand *Akasha*, it is best not to speak. The less one analyses, the better. Too many people analyse too much instead of living and learning from the simplest aspects of life.

Mystic Nature is extremely close to everyone. It flows in and through the human form. This can be seen as soon as one investigates the pressure points in one's hands and feet, gently and lovingly, but also with firmness and courage. Suddenly one will discover that there are many knots throughout the body, causing people to fall ill. The same lesson may be learnt by treating objects gently, using *Brahma Vach* in daily life when washing dishes or walking, when putting on clothes, or touching any object. If one does not learn harmonious and gentle action in the sphere of daily duties, which are the *ABCs* of *Theosophia*, one will never become even remotely able to understand the Mysteries. Above all, one must learn harmony in speech, for sound is the leading attribute of *Akasha-Vach*. When an Adept sees the aura around a human being who has not yet entered the Mysteries, the Adept is interested only in whether that human being will learn before death the *ABCs* of life. Has the person learnt how to be humble, how to learn, how to apologize, how to mentally prostrate before elders and teachers? The degree to which a human being has learnt generosity and gratitude during life will infallibly determine his or her state of consciousness at the moment of death.

If the basics have been learnt in this lifetime, then karma will be kind in the next. The person will find birth in a family where the parents are not much moved by likes and dislikes, and raise their children accordingly. Such parents will give their children few options, and they will also probably be impoverished peasants.

The child will have no option but to learn the only arts that its parents have to teach — farming, carpentry, housekeeping. For the fortunate soul life does not consist of menus; there is only one thing to eat. In such an environment the soul can perfect the lesson of the *ABCs* and advance towards self-knowledge. Many people are terrified that they are not learning the *ABCs*, that they are merely repeating formulae and not really learning, and this is indeed a widespread and dangerous condition. But instead of exacerbating it through futile fears, they can begin letting go of the tight, knotting egotistical grip they have on themselves, can begin to renounce the psychic claustrophobia that imprisons them. Many lifetimes may pass before they can hear the Akashic sounds of the mystic heights or before they can feel the flow of the *Akasha* within the heart and brain.

Such persons can still look up at the sky and have their vision healed by it. They can still appreciate the light of the dawn and have their hearts renewed by it. They can still sit quietly in the twilight and sense in the sounds of Nature its uninterrupted harmony as day recedes into night. They can behold the midnight sky, thrilling to the sight of stars more numberless than human beings, and gain an inward sense of the spaciousness of the cosmos. Seeing the sky as the great purifier of consciousness, they may touch the veil of mystic Nature as the container of all things *in potentia*. Using the great Teachings in these ways, they may prepare themselves for preliminary exercises in meditation and lay the seeds for the discipline of silence which is ultimately consummated in the full perception and self-conscious embodiment of universal harmony by the sovereign Adept. Every honest effort to follow this alchemical path is irrevocably a step towards the noonday Sun of Aquarian enlightenment.

AQUARIAN THERAPY

To suffer woes which Hope thinks infinite;
To forgive wrongs darker than death or night;
To defy Power, which seems omnipotent;
To love, and hear; to hope till Hope creates
From its own wreck the thing it contemplates;
Neither to change, nor falter, nor repent;
This, like thy glory, Titan, is to be
Good, great and joyous, beautiful and free;
This is alone Life, Joy, Empire, and Victory.
                                    PERCY BYSSHE SHELLEY

In the Aquarian Age the mental fire of devotion and sacrifice means purgation, and no substitute will serve. Human beings may seek authentic confidence in their own divine destiny — out of pain through experience, by sifting, by meditation, by mistakes and learning from them. In time they can therapeutically release within themselves that mental breath and spiritual fire where they always feel benevolent towards all, but where that benevolence is backed by depth of thought directed by a precise, luminous intelligence. This great challenge is partly what W.Q. Judge meant when he prophesied that the time will come when powers will be needed and pretensions will go for naught. It is a strange advantage that now there are so many swamis, lamas and gurus of every kind, on almost every street corner, because once and for all people will have to go behind and beyond labels, externals, forms, names, claims and containers of all kinds. They will have to discover the life-giving stream of wisdom that becomes a self-sustaining current, fertilizing the soil of the mind, and giving birth to creative ideas and beneficent impulses. They will have to learn to direct the power to act in new ways, with willing cooperation in a context larger than themselves, and on behalf of a vision that is only dimly sensed. This is what Shelley suggested by pointing to the star,

> The loftiest star of unascended heaven,
> Pinnacled dim in the intense inane.

'Inane' in ordinary language means 'foolish', 'idiotic', 'chaotic', 'meaningless', and 'incoherent', but 'inane' in the archaic language of spiritual alchemy refers to something beyond primordial chaos. It is the original ground of creativity in the whole of nature, latent in the unmanifest realm. It is also specifically called a liquid fire, the word *aqua* being an alchemical term. Therefore, the idea of Aquarius the Water-Bringer, even at the simplest level — bringing water to a parched soil, to thirsty human beings, and connected with rain coming down from heaven — has timeless beauty to it. Everyone knows how sweet the earth smells after a generous shower of rain. Each can appreciate that it is universal and innate to feel a natural gratitude when one's thirst is slaked by a glass of water extended by a brother. But these are mere reflections on the physical plane of something metaphysically quintessential. The ancient Egyptians depicted Aquarius as a serpent coiled in a spiral around a jar containing liquid fire. This image has reference to those who can tap the highest sources of primordial energy in invisible Nature, and channel it, bring it down and apply it, as in the restoration of sap in a piece of desiccated wood by applying resin from a pine tree. They are able to do as much revitalizing as is allowed by forms that are, alas, nearly dead.

The sacred metaphor of fire is profound, whether applied to the fire of enthusiasm, the fire of devotion, the fire of intelligence, the fire of creativity, the fire that warms, the fire that glows, or to the fire that makes one see beyond to That — TAT. Anybody who has sat by a log fire and watched it for a long time has seen something extraordinary. Behind the leaping flames there is an invisible colour. What is seen on the outside is golden yellow but inside there is actually an electric blue. Through such analogies one begins to get more and more to the core of the hidden source of creativity in human beings. More significantly, the Great Teachers of Gupta Vidya hint that the noumenon of the Three-in-One — the inmost invisible Triad in every human being and the source of all thought, will and feeling — itself has an invisible central point in *Akasha,* the noumenon which is the very essence of spiritual fire.

If one is going to learn to kindle this fire, one has to make a beginning somewhere. Consider a person who is fortunate not to have much to unlearn and whose mind was not contaminated, either because the person did not take seriously pseudo-education, or sifted it all and started to think originally. Such a person does not need to make claims to know, but can get excited about a great idea, and can incarnate it by continually dwelling upon it. The idea of aspiration, the idea of harmony, the idea of solidarity in its deepest sense — any of the ideas that are the living germs of Aquarian therapeutics — can be put to use and made to light a fire. By intensely dwelling upon such an idea, a person can actually ignite a small spark which will be sustained by regular return to the thought, looking at it in different ways — from north, south, east and west, above and below, at least from six points of view — without becoming entranced by any false crystallization or rigid formulation. Through returning again and again to the main idea, a person can, in time, light up a radiant centre in the human constitution which may serve as a hooking point from which the person can go deeper and come closer to the noumenal. This can also be done in the realm of action. Sometimes one experiences an immense exhilaration from doing one thing crisply and cleanly, even if it be only taking a bath or sitting down to perform something very simple. To do it crisply, honestly and noetically brings about a perceptible release of silent self-respect.

Spiritual will has to do with true self-esteem, moral firmness and continuity of consciousness. If a person begins without self-esteem — because the person is mauled, extremely weak-willed, or is weighted down by the recurrent karma of incompletion and passively expects it to continue throughout life — the person will complete nothing. Everything seems fraught with failure. But suppose such a person is truly honest and still says, "There is some one thing on the basis of which I can respect myself. I can do it. It is the best I know." Such a person, as Kierkegaard suggested in *Purity of Heart*, can one-pointedly will the good. Through the very attempt — not the planning, the anticipation, the calculation, and the anxiety, but just in the simple release of the will in the single act — the person can also come in time to light up the spark of self-confidence by acting in the name of something greater than the shrunken self.

The ideal way and the greatest mode of doing this, going back to the Golden Age of infant humanity in the presence of Divine Teachers, is devotion. This is the Gem of *Bodhi*, the hidden flame in the heart. When the mind is polluted, when the will is perverted, there is still somewhere a small spark of decency in the human heart. If its inaudible vibration were totally destroyed, the person would perish. Months before a person dies this silent sound ceases, the constant pulsation of the spiritual heart known in Sanskrit as the *Anahata*, the indestructible centre. There is a deathless core to the heart of every human being. There is a ceaseless if unheeded hope. Therefore anyone can respond to Shelley's vision in *Prometheus Unbound*. Despite all the most negative evidence, one can still go on. This is why even a tormented person who is about to take his life one day can still get up and make another effort, even if it seems wholly futile.

Instead of merely showing devotion fitfully and fearfully, which is like running away from the divine temple, one must seek it positively, nurturing the finest, the truest, the most valid feelings in one's own heart. One must not make devotion conditional, saying, "I will only give where I can be sure that the other person is going to give back." One should not even think in this way. One must experience the thrill of giving so much that it is impossible to expect anyone else to give anything like the same in return. The outpouring of love and joy cannot be manifest on the external plane, for when it is real it is as constant as breathing. Such is the inaudible hum, the unspoken mantram of the indestructible heart. A person who constantly cherishes this with true humility can effortlessly adopt the mental posture of unostentatious prostration. One of the most beautiful postures that the human body can ever assume is bending low and prostrating on the floor. It is also extremely relaxing and regenerative, in the teaching of Raja Yoga. A person who can assume this as a mental posture in relation to a vast ideal that is relevant to the whole of humanity can begin to perfect mental devotion to what is at the heart of the human heritage — devotion to all the Mahatmas, Bodhisattvas, Krishnas, Buddhas and Christs that ever existed in millions of years, exceeding the possibility of reckoning or measure, beyond the shifting boundaries of recorded history.

If a person can light up that deep devotion and focus it in one direction, serving one's *Ishtaguru* or chosen Teacher, and can totally concentrate with undivided, unbroken, uninterrupted love, loyalty and obedience, there is then the absolute assurance of fanning the flame in the heart. However dark the world appears to be, however heavy one's suffering seems, however confusing the karma of the times, the secret flame ever strengthens itself. Ever reaching upward, it helps *Manas* to salute the *Atman* and to become one-pointed in seeking the *Atman* without expectation. Then as surely as there is a law of periodicity that cannot be confined to the trivial timetable of the ignorant personal self which does not know the vaster cycles or the previous lives of its indwelling monad or what is at the very core of its own being, invariably and infallibly the strength of that impulse will prepare one for that perfectly right moment when the *Atman* through *Buddhi* can initiate and instruct. The *Atma-Buddhi* is the Guru. It speaks to the soul as the inner voice of the *daimon,* the voice of the Master, who is the invisible escort. That is the sovereign experience of true initiation.

A constant flame, enabling one to come to ever-higher levels of purification, the ceaseless self-purgation that is a prelude to total self-transformation, can be lit from small beginnings. Such endeavours must be sifted, honed down to a fine authenticity, and not even whispered to a single living person. But at the same time the line of life's meditation must not be forgotten by oneself. That is difficult. Maintained steadily and with continuity of consciousness, sincere efforts will lead from what, at one level, is the spark of simple devotion to an unknown object, to that deeper fire of inward devotion of the whole of one's sense of being in a manifest form, and then to the invisible prototype that is the Guru. This is signified by the higher line in the symbol of Aquarius. It is the vibration of universal consciousness, *Mahabuddhi*, which is always capable of being mirrored in the fleeting moment. It is also capable of dissolving the inverted and perverted image of itself formed in the waters of astral chaos out of conflicting feelings, ideas and wills. These can all be displaced and transcended by the deathless vibration of supreme devotion in the indestructible heart.

There is always that in a human being which says, "If I can only find that one real thing, it can cut through a great deal of the froth and darkness in my life." Even though people say this, do they really mean it? Are they in earnest? Or do they merely say it at one moment and forget it the next? To mean it, to maintain it in the mind and to make it the driving purpose of one's entire life is, doubtless, a daunting task. Just as individuals begin by self-definition to know that they can create this fire and sustain it through the darkness of minor pralayas, all human beings will have to admit that they must themselves start again, admitting that they do not know, but can still learn humbly, how to put two sticks together and light a fire. No one need be driven mad by the jackal voices of the jungle which is the crematorium of the psychic corpses of the sad failures in human evolution.

To start again means one must cure the fundamental alienation of the self so pervasive in urban society. When the mind is misused and mutilated, the whole of one's being cannot cooperate with that treacherous mind, and devotion seems to be impossible. When the mind is further alienated by constant association with a crippling self-image, one's condition is terrible. One is trapped by a sense not only of past failure but of permanent failure; a sense not only of how one once erred, but also of how one is irredeemably unworthy of one's innate destiny. In this condition one never really knows whether one was not up to it because of not giving oneself a chance in that mathematics class when one was a child of ten, or because of troubles at home, or because of that gossip next door who was interfering so much. One really does not know. But the fear that one can never accomplish anything real is too tragic. People even fear that they could never for the rest of this life put their minds to concentrate on a simple primer of geometry. Human beings fall prey to these fears because of the pressing pace of change and inexorable karmic precipitation, because of the tremendous sorting out that is going on, involving the collective karma of those who have failed spiritually as well as the karma of those who have misused and perverted the mind in the name of great ideas. They have done it in the name of the Church with the horrors of the Inquisition. They have done it in the name of the State with wars involving the innocent and unborn. They have done it in the pursuit of knowledge. When the karma of misuse is so heavy that there is an ever-growing fear, many neither know what is the root-cause nor sense the possibility of any cure.

This alienation of the mind is very real. It is most poignant in industrial society at this time. But even now there are people in many other parts of the world who are grateful to have the opportunity to sit by an electric light and enjoy the use of a tattered pamphlet. They are thrilled, when living far out in the wilds, to borrow a book or to have somebody send one to them, and to read it, enjoy it, and use it. There are awakened masses all over the globe. In Russia and Japan today, there is a greater *per capita* enjoyment of books than ever before in recorded history. This is happening all over the world. If it is not the same story everywhere, it is because of the changing karmic balances of peoples. Wherever there is a terrible mutilation of the mind, and a consequent anger, a crippling sense of self-alienation, there is the rush of the lemmings, as well as the desperate desire for a simple solution, a fervent wish to cop out altogether from their responsibilities.

When the mind is stretched only by bribe and threat (and more by threat than by bribe), and merely on behalf of restrictive and narrow ideas, then all the most insecure and frustrated souls, all the preachers without pulpits, the self-tormented teachers from past lives and all parts of the globe, grasp every chance to show pretension and fake wisdom in Kali Yuga, as the ancient *Vishnu Purana* prophesied. Even when such pseudo-teachers get their pulpit and their opportunity, they do not really believe in anything or in themselves. As this gets worse, year by year, they are constrained to concede to themselves that they do not really have anything to teach or exemplify, though they perfect the art of outward pretense. Thus all the vicious circles of antagonistic counterclaims multiply between the different sects of those who do not believe in themselves. Shelley wrote with poignant and powerful imagery about what happens to the mind when it is so totally immobilized, so wholly corrupted, so vampirical, that it becomes poisonous unto itself as well as to others. Why is such self-destructive manipulation doomed to disappear? The reason is that one cannot take an immortal soul that has journeyed much longer than is dreamt of by the boldest genealogists of the age of man, and expect such a being to swallow the rubbish of reductionism of every sort.

Human beings need ideas large enough to accommodate their sense of readiness for the future. This means that the only way to overcome self-alienation is by attunement to the Universal Mind through the contemplation of universal ideas. Because the personal mind has become flaccid, especially when it considers noble ideas enshrined in the platitudes of the past, it is liable to cling to mere externals. It must penetrate behind the visible forms to the formless ideas. Then it is meaningful to say, "I do not know," because each idea presupposes a larger idea which in turn ontologically presupposes one which is still more profound. There is an expanding transcendence of existing conceptions of space, time, motion and identity. The more one realizes this, the more genuine is the recognition that one does not know and the greater the possibility of developing the desire to persist, to function freely within a realm of pure anti-entropic thought which is completely potential, for which contemporary languages do not have any words. Sometimes from a Sanskrit root, a Greek term, or even an English word, one can extract a deeper meaning that was lost in the course of time. This is true of the word 'devotion.' It is true of most terms when traced back to their origin. There is a beautiful core to the word 'devotion,' from *de votum*, 'to dedicate by a vow.' As with any important word that has been used for a very long time, it has acquired accretions of meaning and limitations of usage. One has to take a stand somewhere in reference to the inbred tendency to identify the meanings of words ostensively or by rigid definitions, to become fixated on the conventional trappings of language. To start using the mind constructively and freeing it from habitual grooves is going to be difficult and at times extremely painful. It requires at least the level of minimal attention needed for training the lower mind, but which one did not give because it was demanded at too high a price by institutional reward and penalty.

All of this points to the unavoidable suffering caused by persisting errors through repeated mis-identification. Imagine persons who misused the gift of walking by kicking other beings. They might well have several lives without the use of legs. The terrible need and desire to walk and move is there, but they are crippled and bewildered. They need to wear out the karmic causes of their condition through that suffering, which is incomprehensible to *kama-manas*. Understanding such causes in terms of possible past misuse can bring them to a point where they will, when they regain the power of locomotion, never misuse it again. They will not dream of using it to kick another human being. They will not use it carelessly and impulsively. What is true in reference to legs is also true in regard to the eyes and to every human organ. Above all, it is true in reference to the mind, which is an invisible organ corresponding to the tongue, to the divine prerogative of speech, and to the power of conceptualization. When imagination is polluted, the mind goes awry. When imagination becomes sterile, the mind becomes paralyzed, and all it can do is to adapt and be imitative. Reductionists, puzzled by any glimmerings of something more to the power of the mind, try to freeze the situation by stating a restrictive theory, holding that the mind can only be adaptive, thereby engendering imitativeness.

The human mind, however, is original. It is self-reproductive. Patanjali says it is capable of two lines of self-reproductive thought. One of these is bound up with memory images, associations, and with likes and dislikes. It is possible to halt this compulsive self-reproductive chain of mere reactive thinking and get to a condition of balance — *nirodha* — if one persists in trying always to bring the mind back to one idea, holding oneself steady, exactly as people would do if they had partially lost the use of their legs and had to re-educate their muscles in a therapeutic ward. This must be done with the brain and the thinking faculties. Then a stage can come where another kind of self-reproductive power begins to be exercised by the mind, where it can maintain in a self-sustaining manner a level of thinking that is more universal and constructive, which is capable of a great deal of diversification, fertilization and replication. Then, when this flow is itself brought to a smooth and controlled pace, it is possible to move to a further stage where one can see oneself from outside, and remain disengaged from the uninterrupted steady flow of higher mental awareness.

Even though it must eventually come to a halt and meanwhile be diagnosed correctly at this point of history, the misuse of the mind is very old. It goes back many lives, to the time when the mind was enormously powerful and was employed on behalf of personal status and power. Every time one hears some person say, "I want to do this because I want to be famous," it is a sign that he is burdened by a fear of failure from the past. If such a person comes into contact with Gupta Vidya and still thinks in these ways, the resultant condition is tragic. There is an incredible misplacement and displacement of human energy. What a price to pay when one is young to over-compensate for little hurts and petty slights to the personal self, which needs to be refined into an invulnerable if imperfect instrument for the immortal individuality. People nonetheless get into false and exaggerated attitudes when they want to use the mind, with its limited powers, for some ignoble purpose that involves the illusory security of the personal self. History has now come to a point where, with the abuse of print and the enormity of empty pontification, Nature is insisting that there be a halt to wastage and misuse. People can go on cutting trees to make paper. Society can go on mass-producing people who think they have something to teach, but the game of deception is speedily coming to an end. Frustrated and over-wrought teachers do not have credibility with themselves. They do not know how to win the trust of their students, even amongst captive audiences. They are exhausted by their mutual rivalry and they will feel increasingly alienated and miserable. This is the cumulative precipitation of a long process of religious and secular exploitation.

The mind is a glorious gift. In its true function as a means of reflective self-conscious thought, *svasamvedana*, it is the greatest gift of the human being. Plato warned his hearers never to be so naïve as to think that any pleasure can ever have any meaning to the heart if the mind and imagination are not involved. To recover the true power of self-consciousness requires a tougher discipline and a larger perspective than can be encompassed by the personal self. It requires *dianoia* based upon Aquarian axioms and involves, above all, a new posture of humility. It is crucial to train human beings in contemporary culture to say, and to enjoy saying, "I do not know." This had become easy for many people at other times and in other places. In a highly competitive society, however, people are encouraged to claim to know when they do not. To acknowledge ignorance is very painful, but that pain is necessary for the restoration of psychological health. It is one of the tasks of the present time to give people the release and strength of saying, "I do not know, but I wish to know." First they have to say, "I do not know," and then they have to learn to practise it, however painful it is, until they burst through the pseudo-image of false knowledge. Then they have to say, "I do not know, but I want to know. I really want to know." They have to hunger for knowledge. This is required for the readjustment of the *psyche* and the awakening of *nous*.

They have to want to know out of devotion to some great purpose for its own sake, which is very difficult to understand in the context of corrupt instrumentalism. They have to want to know for the sake of some larger good, and hence they must think of a larger good in the context of which they have no position of privileged access. This is the ultimate Aquarian paradox. One does not really know what the larger good is, yet one is asked to think about it. This is superb discipline for the human soul. Keep thinking about the good of others, the good of all. One may not know what it is, but keep thinking, practising *dianoia*. Above all, in the process of doing so, one must totally negate any concern for oneself in the future. Through this practice or *abhyasa*, the lower line of the Aquarian glyph, the serpent of self that has got coiled in the wrong way, is being stretched and brought back to a condition where it can be subdued. Paradoxically, when one has totally forgotten any concern for one's own future, then one's true purpose as a soul, one's deeper destiny, will speak as the voice of the spiritual heart. It is the destiny of the divine prototype of every human being who has become alienated, like the estranged face in *The Hound of Heaven* of Francis Thompson. Self-alienation is caused by the wearing of the false mask of which Shelley speaks —the loathsome mask of the personal self. The divine prototype will not reveal the hidden purpose of this incarnation until the loathsome mask is seen for what it is and stripped away, layer by layer.

The purgation of self-crucifixion is painful and protracted until one can fully prepare the ground and find the true self amidst the darkness and agony of not knowing whether one's life has any point. But each will know in time, in a way that is unique and inimitable, and through myriad intimations. Existentially, in the very act of doing something for others, one learns to say readily and simply, "I do not know what is going on in the world. I do not know the future course of history. Above all, I certainly do not know what is unfolding in the Aquarian Age. This means that whenever I hear otherwise, I will turn a deaf ear, without being rude to the individuals concerned." This is hard. Those who can go through such self-chosen mental asceticism will come to a point where they will be able to serve others in simple ways, sharing a vision that is grander than ever could be told to them. They could find themselves sufficiently to know at that beautiful moment when death comes as a deliverer and a friend, "My life had meaning and purpose. I have not lived in vain."

Those who sense the significance of being on the threshold of a New Age will cherish the practice of meditation, of self-study, of listening, learning, and preparing themselves cheerfully and ceaselessly. They must be willing to test themselves, out of self-respect, by prescribing their own daily discipline to follow for a week. Even reduced to this short period, it is very tough for too many. But if even a few persons can follow through for a week, there is a chance that they will do something worthwhile in their lives. Typically, given the widespread fragmentation of consciousness, most people are not going to be able to do this for seven days, much less for successive weeks and months between the solstices and the equinoxes. But they have to keep trying, week by week, testing themselves. "Can I take one thought and can I maintain it as a vibration in my mind and heart for a week?" This is a strain. It will not be immediately possible. The worst will be that one will not even know that one has forgotten. But, giving oneself a chance week after week, a point comes where one must succeed. There can be no respect for oneself if it cannot be cultivated when one's faculties are relatively healthy and when one has received so much from the teachings of the Mahatmas and the abundance of Nature. The very thing that is difficult has to be attempted. Where the entire educational system in a hedonistic culture is encouraging the weak to take what is easy and avoid what is hard, courageous souls should take the hardest test — to maintain one essential idea every day throughout the week.

If a person can really do this, then that person can carry something into the next week, can work with the cycles of the seasons, the solstices, the equinoxes. But, above all, that person will so significantly change the ratios in the astral vehicle that the result will show itself on the physical plane to those who know. Every true aspirant will be recognized and receive unseen help. Who are those who know? Simply those who have mastered this very practice. Anyone who does not even understand the nature of what has to be done is certainly hoping for something which is impossible — some sort of vicarious atonement, some kind of messianic salvation. The latest form of it is the collectivization of the whole of human consciousness, put in terms of evolutionary progress, which is automatically going to become enlightened. Human consciousness is going to do nothing automatically and never has done anything automatically or suddenly in millions of years. In this way the central problem is fudged. It is foolish to imagine that somehow automatically enlightenment will descend in a secular or spiritual garb. All of this is of the past, a ghost of the Piscean Age. Enlightenment can only be reached by thought and effort based upon a sense of individual and personal insignificance. It requires withholding judgment while cheerfully persisting, trying to get to the very core of meaning in every situation and thinking through one's sense of self until it really hurts. It is like squeezing an orange until the pips squeak. Think until the brain is ready to burst. Feel until the heart cries out. Do not stop short. Get to the root. Persist and come out of it a stronger person, regenerated through *tapas*. Then follow the great injunction of the Upanishad: "Awake, arise, seek the Great Ones, *and learn.*" The Rishis assumed that unless you did all of these you could not begin to understand the meaning of the Law.

Spiritual life is the paradigm of learning. Its reflections are all the other forms of learning, but these reflections no longer reflect. To recover the primordial sense of learning that is coeval with breathing requires a total break with existing thought-forms and habits of speech. They are the modes of the past. The one thing that many people rightly sense is that they may be left out of the current and the cycle of the future. But this cannot be safeguarded against by any external means. The only way to enter into that fast-moving and invisible stream, which will become a mighty river in the future, is by becoming capable, through voluntary self-training, of activating the unmanifest potency of the universe — the liquid fire that springs from deep devotion to universal good, and by reaching out to the whole of the human race, including the unborn who are always far more numerous than those who are presently incarnated.

This is a formidable task. But any person, by self-training in the art of using Aquarian axioms, can enter the evolutionary stream which will eventually produce minds as pellucid as crystal and hearts which are wisely benevolent. Luminous with the intelligence of the universe, they shall have done with the pseudo-dramas of the past. They will recognize the beauty and dignity of being like a grain of sand at birth and death, assigning no false valuation to the pseudo-entity called the personality, which is merely a logical construction. Recognizing links at all levels between the atomic and the infinite, they will dispense with the fairy story of name and form, which was born at a certain time, died at a certain time, and achieved this and did not achieve that. Completely wiping it out is a mark of maturity. The currency of thought and language will radically have to change. Individuals will have to stand apart from many of the patterns which have become raucously agitated precisely because they are obsolete. The personality becomes most active when it is threatened. Something like this has happened collectively. This is inescapable and irreversible, and wholly to be welcomed from the mature standpoint of soul-evolution.

The most significant hope for the future may well be that people have no authentic way of celebrating festivals, no credible thoughts about the destiny of the world, no clear ideas about what they are going to do this year or next year. The voiding of all shallow expectations is extremely therapeutic. When people practise this sufficiently, they will learn to flow with the current of the whole. What can be seen in terms of law or of many levels of consciousness can also be seen quite simply as flowing like a small stream that must of necessity empty itself into the ocean. One may flow with the vaster forces of history, of humanity, and of the cosmos. When individuals forget themselves, then, paradoxically, they discover themselves. When they consider themselves as irrelevant, they become relevant. When they see themselves as unimportant, they become important. This is the mode of self-definition and the pedigree of the twice-born on the threshold of the epoch of Universal Enlightenment, the Aquarian Age, which has entered its second degree and moves steadily towards its millennial culmination.

AQUARIAN SPIRITUALITY

*It is argued that the Universal Evolution, otherwise, the
gradual development of species in all the kingdoms of nature,
works by uniform laws. This is admitted, and the law enforced
far more strictly in Esoteric than in modern Science. But we
are told also, that it is equally a law that 'development works
from the less to the more perfect, and from the simpler to the
more complicated, by incessant changes, small in themselves,
but constantly accumulating in the required direction.'
. . . Esoteric Science agrees with it but adds that this law
applies only to what is known to it as the* Primary
Creation — *the evolution of worlds from primordial atoms,
and the* pre-primordial ATOM, *at the first differentiation
of the former; and that during the period of cyclic evolution
in space and time, this law is limited and works only in the
lower kingdoms. . . . As the Hindu philosophy very justly
teaches, the* 'Aniyamsam Aniyasam,' *can be known only
through false notions. It is the 'many' that proceed from the*
ONE — *the living spiritual germs or centres of forces —
each in a septenary form, which first generate, and then give
the* PRIMARY IMPULSE *to the law of evolution and gradual
slow development.*

The Secret Doctrine, ii 731-732

Viewed from the impersonal standpoint of collective Karma
and cyclic evolution, Nature suffers fools not unkindly but
with compassion. Nature will not indefinitely indulge or
underwrite human folly, for as Cicero observed, time destroys the
speculations of man whilst it confirms the judgement of Nature.
Through cyclic opportunities, Nature actually affords individuals
innumerable occasions for the clarification and purification of
perception and intention. If human judgement and design are to
have adequate leverage on Nature, they must have as their stable
fulcrum an intuitive apprehension of law. At the most

fundamental level, human judgement and natural law alike stand upon a common ground, a single transcendental source of Being. It is only by rejecting all dualisms, mediaeval or modern, and by refusing to absolutize polarities that the designs of men and the differentiations of Nature may be brought into self-conscious harmony. In Gupta Vidya, there is no cleavage between the aim of Self-knowledge (Atma Vidya) and the practical ideal of helping Nature and working on with her *(Ahimsa Yagna)*. To the perfected will of the *yogin* of Time's circle *(Kalachakra)*, Nature is the ally, pupil and servant. Fully comprehending that man is the key to the lock of Nature, the wise *yogin* finds no intrinsic tension been obeisance to the judgement of Nature in Time and obedience to Shiva, the good gardener of Nature in Eternity.

This philosophic fusion of science and religion, of *vidya* and *dharma*, is essential to the structure of the Aquarian civilization of the future and enshrined in the axiom that there is no religion higher than Truth. In accordance with this evolutionary programme and in tune with the Avataric vibration of the age, the Brotherhood of Bodhisattvas has actively sought to dispel the delusive dichotomy between science and religion. Krishna conveyed the beautiful synthesis of *jnana* and *bhakti* in his classic portrait of the Self-governed Sage in the *Bhagavad Gita*. Spiritual teachers have repeatedly warned against the degrading effects upon the mind-principle of ahankaric greed and atavistic fear working through materialism and superstition. From the therapeutic standpoint of the ancient Rishis, the murky ferment of the twentieth century is not to be viewed as a creative tension between two viable cultures, the one religious and traditional, the other modern and scientific. Rather, it is to be seen as the ignorant and schizophrenic clash of two largely moribund inversions of authentic culture. Neither secular religion, with its crude demonolatry and selfish salvationism, nor materialistic science, with its cowardly conformity and slavish hedonism, still less the mutual recriminations and denunciations of one by the other, can offer human beings an assured basis for fulfilment and growth. Just as two wrongs do not make a right, no compound of these costly inversions can rectify the malaise of modern civilization. Neither fight nor flight nor unholy alliance can correct the deficiencies of two waning schemes of thought that do little justice to Man or Nature.

In order to participate freely in the regenerative, not the destructive, tendencies of the Aquarian Age, one must recognize that true religion and science do not need to be rescued from contemporary chaos by messianic crusaders. On the contrary, creative individuals must learn to cultivate moral courage and cool magnanimity so that they may plumb the depths of pure science and true religion within themselves. This cannot be done without assuming some degree of responsibility for the intense karmic precipitations during the present period of rapid transition. Without self-confidence based upon inviolable integrity, the bewildered individual will regrettably fall prey to the contagion of despairing diagnoses, sanctimonious effusions and evasive rationalizations offered by self-appointed pundits and critics alike. No shallow conceit, cynical or complacent, can substitute for the mental discernment and spiritual strength required of pathfinders in the Aquarian Age. Rather than sitting in idle judgement upon contemporary history and humanity, wise individuals will seek to insert themselves into the tremendous rethinking initiated by scattered pioneers in regard to the essential core of Man and Nature and the vital relationship between them. If through earnestness, simplicity and *dianoia* one can radically revise one's conception of Nature and Man, then one may powerfully assist that silent revolution and subtle healing taking place today behind the clutter of competing slogans and chaotic events.

As individuals increasingly recognize that the faults which bedevil them lie in themselves and not in the stars, they will progressively discern the Aquarian design woven in the heavens. Through the religion of renunciation of the personal self and the science of Buddhic correlation, one can begin the difficult ascent in consciousness towards comprehension of the mysteries of heaven and earth.

As above, so below. Sidereal phenomena, and the behaviour of the celestial bodies in the heavens, were taken as a model, and the plan was carried out below, on earth. Thus, space, in its abstract sense, was called 'the realm of divine knowledge', and by the *Chaldees* or Initiates *Ab Soo*, the habitat . . . of knowledge, because it is in space that dwell the intelligent Powers which *invisibly* rule the Universe.

The Secret Doctrine, ii 502

Conceptions of space have varied significantly over the centuries, depending largely upon cognate conceptions of time, matter and energy. The arcane conception of space as at once an infinite void and an invisible plenum, replete with intelligence, offers a profound challenge not only to post-Einsteinian science but also to post-Gandhian religion. It demands an entirely fresh view of causality and consciousness, of activity and time. From the standpoint of contemporary physics, any object, including the human form, is almost entirely empty space devoid of anything that might be considered matter. Even without studying particle physics, perceptive individuals are prepared to accept that if they could visualize what an X-ray would show, they would find that only about one quadrillionth of any object is constituted of a few particles and that all the rest is seemingly empty space. Similarly, if they could visualize what various detectors operating over the visible and invisible spectrum reveal, they would find that every point in space is the intersection of myriad vibrating fields of energy. Again, if one were prepared to penetrate beneath the surface of personal and collective habits and institutions, through the discerning power of the disciplined conscience and awakened intuition, one would find an array of Monadic individuals suspended like stars in the boundless void of the unmanifest. To the resonant heart, this immense void would reveal itself as alive at every point with the vibration of the Great Breath in its complex rhythmic differentiations. Through such reflection one may recognize that the seeming solidity of things is mayavic. Their surfaces and contours as they appear to the physical senses and the perception of the psyche are enormously deceptive and strangely confining. By using the mind's eye one can come to see that what is seemingly full is void and that what is seemingly void is extremely full of Atma-Buddhi-Manasic or noumenal aspects of invisible atoms.

The term 'atom' itself conveys a wide range of meanings in ancient philosophy, including that connotation which has indelibly impressed itself upon the consciousness of the twentieth century. The Greek root of the term 'atom' literally means 'uncuttable', 'indivisible' or 'individual' and corresponds to the Sanskrit term *anu*. In its most metaphysical sense *anu* is the *Aniyamsam Aniyasam,* the smallest of the small, which is also the greatest of the great, equivalent to SPACE and a pointer to *Parabrahm.* In another sense, *anu* is the absolute Motion or eternal vibration of the Great Breath differentiated in the primordial manifested ATOM, equivalent to Brahmā. Neither in the pregenetic or primogenetic states is *anu* subject to multiplication or division. The first plurality of atoms arose with the pristine differentiation of the sevenfold *Dhyani*-energies in the *Mahatattwa* creation, which was in turn followed by further hierarchies of atoms in the succeeding two creations. The meanings of the term 'atom' as applied to the first three creations refer to spiritual and formless realities, including the use of the term to designate Atma-Buddhic monads. Beginning with the fourth, or *mukhya,* creation, sometimes called the *primary creation* because it is the first of a series of four creations connected with material form, the term 'atom' has a new series of meanings pertaining to the germinal centres of the elemental, mineral, plant and animal kingdoms. The term 'atom' used in the customary physical sense applies to the extreme degree of differentiation in this series. Just as the infinite points of differentiated spaces are inseparable from the One Point that is the indivisible sum total of boundless Space, the living atoms of every plane are indivisible from *anu* — the ONE LIFE — and all resound to the fiery vibration of its eternal Motion.

To grasp the noetic significance of the existence of atoms, it is helpful to compare the atom with the molecule. The term 'molecule' literally means 'that which is ponderable or massive', and refers in chemistry to the smallest unit of a substance displaying fixed chemical properties. Typically, molecules are complex compound entities produced and altered through processes of action and reaction. From the standpoint of meta-chemistry, atomic energies derive from the indivisible unity of the One Life, whilst molecular actions stem from the interplay of vital though secondary emanations. The same facts viewed from the standpoint of meta-psychology lead to the distinction between the noetic action of *Buddhi-Manas*, which draws upon the light of the one indivisible *Atman*, and the psychic action of the lower *Manas*, which is inherently restricted by the polarities of the *kama* principle to residual effects upon the composite mortal vestures. In essence, the difference between atoms and molecules, between noetic and psychic action, is the difference between seeing from within without and seeing only from outside. Hence, people often come closest to the core of things when they shut their sense-organs, which is where concentration and meditation begin.

By withdrawing, closing the eyes, closing the mouth, shutting the ears, by turning off the tumult of the mayavic kaleidoscope of the phenomenal world, one can draw within and enter into what initially seems like chaotic darkness. By persisting, one becomes more familiar with what may be called the photosphere surrounding every human being, the field of light-energies that operates beneath the visible world of form. As one becomes more sensitive to these indwelling energies, one can begin to apprehend that there are vast arrays of intelligent powers which invisibly rule the universe. What people ordinarily call intelligence is only the most superficial and limited aspect of a single distributed intelligence, working through cosmic hierarchies, and originating in a common transcendental source.

Something of the sacred potency and designing power of divine intelligence was broadly familiar to people in the nineteenth century, though in a distorted form due to the inversions of sectarian religion. Given that the impersonal nature of that intelligence can only be comprehended through the noetic faculties consubstantial with that intelligence, it is scarcely surprising that H.P. Blavatsky took such care to provide accounts of cosmogenesis and anthropogenesis free from any taint of the notion of an anthropomorphic creator. It is also suggestive, given the transcendental and *arupa* nature of the intelligence within cyclic evolution, that she so firmly repudiated the materialist conception of a blind, chemically-driven evolution. What was perhaps not so clear in the nineteenth century was her profound reason for pointing to the essential distinction between the atomic and molecular character of noetic and psychic action.

Humanity now finds itself at a fortunate moment; much of what is happening in the sciences is reminiscent of what was once called Hermetic wisdom. If one reads any first-rate book on the frontiers of science, one is at times encountering the threshold of Gupta Vidya. As H.P. Blavatsky prophesied, physics and chemistry have begun to penetrate the realm of atomic vibrations underlying the gross physical design of objects, and have partially revealed the complex matrix of differentiations of the ATOM, as they apply to the lowest planes. Whilst these sciences have not yet moved closer towards the metaphysically indivisible ATOM, they have clearly demonstrated that all physical structure is the superficial derivative of more fundamental differentiations. Although much of the systematic elaboration of these scientific insights has taken place since the commencement of the Aquarian Age in 1902, the critical moves were already made between 1895 and 1902, when there was a crucial intersection of cycles involving the close of the first five thousand years of Kali Yuga and the six-hundred-year cycle inaugurated by Tsong-Kha-Pa, as well as the zodiacal transition.

Towards the close of the nineteenth century, chemistry and physics found themselves up against myriad dead ends. Drawing upon Dalton's hypothesis of units of chemical type distinguishable by weight called atoms (1803), and Avogadro's hypothesis that standard volumes of gases of different compounds contain equal numbers of molecules (1811), chemistry was engaged in filling in the periodic table of the elements proposed by Mendeleev

(1869). Having mastered the arts of ballistics and bridge-building, physics was winding down the practical elaboration of Oersted's discovery of the relation between electricity and magnetism (1819), and its elegant mathematical formulation in the electromagnetic field theory of light-waves developed by Maxwell (1861). Late in the century a noted lecturer even assured the British Association that physics was a closed and completed field, and that young men ought to go elsewhere to find challenging careers. All of this changed abruptly in 1895, when Roentgen discovered an entirely unaccountable type of radiant energy, the enigmatic X-rays. In 1896 Becquerel was able to localize this internal fire of matter to the substance uranium, which was then called 'radioactive'. Following some researches of Crookes, Thomson discovered the 'electron' in 1897, the unit charge of electricity, a genuine fohatic entity on the physical plane. In 1898, the same year that the Curies discovered the existence and radioactivity of radium, Rutherford was able to identify two of the fohatic messengers of radioactivity — alpha particles and beta particles — the latter turning out to be identical with Thomson's electrons. In 1899 the Curies made the fateful discovery that radioactivity could be artificially induced. Pursuing quite different lines of thought, Planck proposed in 1900 that all physical change takes place via discrete units or quanta of action. In 1902 Rutherford and Soddy developed the modern alchemical hypothesis that radioactivity was both the result and the cause of the transmutation of atoms from one chemical element to another.

Drawing upon these critical discoveries and insights, the entire face of the sciences has been transformed in the first decades of the Aquarian Age, and the new alchemists have had more than a little impact upon society. In 1905 an unknown Swiss patent clerk wrote a series of articles synthesizing the discoveries of the time with such remarkable breadth, clarity and force that his name has become virtually synonymous with the atomic age. Within twelve months Albert Einstein demonstrated several revolutionary propositions.

First of all, he showed that all electromagnetic radiations, including light, were composed of packets or quanta of energy, or 'photons', thus resolving the nineteenth century wave-particle debate about the nature of light. This proposal corresponds to the principle that *Buddhi*, the light of the *Atman*, is both indiscrete in relation to the eternal motion of the Great Breath and discrete in relation to the mayavic field of vibratory Monadic emanations.

Secondly, he showed that physical energy and mass are mutually equivalent and interconvertible through a parametric matrix defined by the velocity of physical light. This corresponds to the occult axiom that spirit and matter constitute a double stream starting from the neutral centre of Being as *Daiviprakriti*, the Light of the Logos.

Thirdly, he showed that all physical measurements of distance, speed and time undertaken by observers moving relative to each other are transformed through a parametric conversion matrix defined by the velocity of physical light when passing from the frame of reference of one observer to that of another. This proposal, which put to rest the search for a crude material aether by joining light to the metric foundations of all physical phenomena, has its occult correspondence in the triadic unity of pre-cosmic Space, Motion and Duration on the plane of *Aether-Akasha*, mirrored in all relations and phenomena on the lower planes.

Fourthly, he showed the equivalence of the long-observed Brownian motion of small particles with a set of statistical laws of motion of molecules and atoms he derived from thermodynamics, thus developing the basis of the first empirical confirmation of the physical existence of atoms and molecules. This proposal, ending the nineteenth century career of atoms and molecules as merely rationalistic entified abstractions, has occult correspondences to the principles of distributive and collective Karma.

Since 1905 there has been a virtual explosion in the sciences, as successive dimensions and orders of microcosmic and macrocosmic nature have been explored. In 1911 Rutherford discovered the nuclear structure of physical atoms, in 1913 Bohr proposed the quantum theory governing that structure, and in

1913 and 1914, respectively, Soddy and Moseley re-wrote the periodic table of the elements in terms of modern atomic theory, thus resuscitating the entire field of chemistry. In 1915 Einstein himself proposed an as yet controversial, and only partially elaborated or confirmed, theoretical synthesis of space, duration, motion and force. This line of enquiry, if perfected, would correspond to the occult correlation of the differentiations of Fohat as it "scatters the Atoms" on the plane of *Aether-Akasha*. In 1927 Heisenberg formulated the 'uncertainty principle' concerning the limits of observation of location and motion, a principle which is gradually compelling scientists to include consciousness in their theories of atomic and subatomic physical nature. By 1953 the labours of many biochemists culminated in the work of Crick and Watson, revealing the double helix of DNA, thus joining atomic and molecular theory to the design of living forms.

Whilst the dawn of the Aquarian Age is as yet far from witnessing the emergence of a complete scientific theory integrating the One Life and the primordial ATOM with myriad lives and atoms on seven planes, it has certainly relinquished the stolid, compartmentalized conceptions of the late Piscean Age. People have now become far more aware that the invisible universe is an extremely intelligent universe; someone well trained in contemporary science is much more aware of the spiritual than those caught up in sectarian religion. Sectarians are often weak in theory owing to their weak wills in practice, and often are merely in search of alibis. But those who deeply ponder upon the cosmos with the aid of physics, biology and chemistry, and who show some philosophical or metaphysical imagination, can readily accommodate the idea that behind the sloganistic term 'vibes' is an exact knowledge governed by precise laws. Given this holistic standpoint, what is the necessary connection between directing these forces and that true obedience to Nature envisaged by the Gupta Vidya? This question became ominous and acute for human society on January 22, 1939, because on that day the uranium atom was split by Hahn and Strassman. Significantly, on the same day in 1561 Francis Bacon, one of the forefathers of modern science, was born.

Bacon's vital insight that "Knowledge is power" echoed the ancient Eastern view that knowledge can liberate men. This perspective made possible the enormous adventure of modern science and the correlative spread of universal education. Before Bacon, despite Renaissance affirmations of the dignity of man, few people were able to read or write. Even the Bible was a closed book to human beings who lacked sufficient knowledge of the language to appreciate religious texts. In the Elizabethan Age, at the turn of the sixteenth century, people had to look to Nature for learning; hence the Shakespearean affirmation that there are "books in the running brooks, sermons in stones," and hence, too, his reference to "the book and volume of my brain." Like the Renaissance, Shakespeare recognized the old Pythagorean and Hermetic conception of man as a microcosm of the macrocosm. If one studies the Elizabethan world, especially in E.M. Tillyard's enthralling book, one finds an extraordinary collection of reincarnated Pythagoreans inhabiting and regenerating a society in which it was the most natural thing to draw from the many great metaphors of the Mahatmic Sage of Samos.

Troilus and Cressida, in one of the most inspired passages Shakespeare ever penned, portrays the Pythagorean conception of cosmic hierarchies and their continual relevance to human society. Speaking of the precise degree and placement of everything in Nature, Ulysses affirms that each thing has a function, which stands in relation to that which is above it, that which is beyond it, that which is below it, and that which is beside it.

> The heavens themselves, the planets, and this centre
> Observe degree, priority, and place,
> Insisture, course, proportion, season, form,
> Office, and custom, in all line of order;
> And therefore is the glorious planet Sol
> In noble eminence enthron'd and spher'd
> Amidst the other; whose med'cinable eye
> Corrects the ill aspects of planets evil,
> And posts, like the commandment of a king,

> Sans check to good and bad. But when the planets
> In evil mixture to disorder wander,
> What plagues and what portents, what mutiny!
> What raging of the sea, shaking of earth!
> Commotion in the winds! frights, changes, horrors,
> Divert and crack, rend and deracinate
> The unity and married calm of states
> Quite from their fixture! O, when degree is shak'd,
> Which is the ladder of all high designs,
> The enterprise is sick. How could communities,
> Degrees in schools, and brotherhoods in cities,
> Peaceful commerce from dividable shores,
> The primogenitive and due of birth,
> Prerogative of age, crowns, sceptres, laurels,
> But by degree, stand in authentic place?
>   *Troilus and Cressida*, Act I, Scene iii

This was also the time of the great seafaring adventurers of Europe, with rich memories of Marco Polo's fascinating stories about customs and cultures prevalent in different parts of the Eastern world. It was truly a period of considerable excitement and curiosity about the cultures of humanity and the vast unknown potential and mystery of Nature itself. By the seventeenth century the alchemical and Rosicrucian traditions of mysticism and magic had laid the basis for what is now called modern technology, with its manifold implications in the social, economic and political arenas. The leading scientists of the nineteenth century showed a keen interest in patterns in Nature, and in the connections between them. For it is only by making connections between otherwise isolated and disparate events, and by discerning patterns, that synthesized conceptions of natural order may be developed. Creative individuals tend to think in terms of wholes, in terms of integrated and patterned arrangements of parts. Such holistic thinking is important to painters and poets and spontaneous amongst little children. But it is also central to the acquisition of that knowledge of Nature which, Bacon declared, is equivalent to power. Because the capacity to discern the patterns of Nature is the prerequisite for enlisting the forces of Nature on behalf of human designs, there is an inevitable moral component in every acquisition and use of knowledge. Bacon, a mysterious man, acknowledged this when he said, "We cannot command Nature except by obeying her."

In effect he showed a concern that there was already a certain presumption towards Nature which would later turn out to be exceedingly costly. Men were seeing Nature in terms of the outmoded conceptions of the Christian church, going back to Augustine and Aquinas, as something dead, inert and wholly apart from the soul. By the eighteenth century, many associated Nature with the chaotic wilderness, and displayed a cultural preference for horticultural hybrids, hothouse growths and elaborate gardens designed by man. It is true that there can be a great beauty in gardens, particularly those of Chinese and Japanese design, wherein beauty and tranquillity are created by the simplest arrangement of stones and plants. Yet, this need not involve despising Nature. And if people in the eighteenth century came to dislike the wilderness because they were frightened by the ghosts and goblins they encountered on the Yorkshire moors, this can hardly excuse the terrible exploitation and desecration of Nature in the nineteenth and twentieth centuries in support of industrialism and technology. This is precisely the hubris of Thrasymachus, in *The Republic* of Plato, criticized by Socrates as showing an inferior intelligence and character, a missing sense of proportion, and an ultimately self-divisive and self-destructive vanity. This Atlantean obsession with the will to dominate completely inverts the principles of proportion, degree and design that govern the evolution of the organic vestures which human beings presently inhabit.

If human beings would prove themselves worthy of the divine apprehension and intelligence within themselves, they must learn to design not merely gardens, but societies and cultures which observe and obey divine proportion and degree. They must learn to awaken and apply the noetic intuitive faculty to the arrangement and rearrangement of communities considering the relationships of individuals not only with each other, but also with empty space. By synthesizing their awakening Buddhic intelligence with the universal intelligence of the One Life, they must learn to cherish the intimations of infinite possibilities contained within the minutest elements of space. Following the Pythagorean conception of the ether as some sort of fluidic substance involved in vortical motion and filled with whirling bubble-like spheres equivalent to atoms, they must come to see that the mathematical laws governing the arrangement of atoms in living forms are the expression of Divine Thought mirroring unmanifest Harmony or *Rta*.

It is not possible to perceive a seemingly opaque world of form as a transparent and luminous manifestation of the One Life without arousing the noetic faculty. Furthermore, it is not possible to awaken the noetic faculty without learning to command the elements of the kingdoms below the fourth plane and without gaining joyous obedience to the Divine Will. It is this combination of self-command and self-obedience which Socrates characterized as *sophrosyne*, the self-government of the soul by its superior element coupled with the consent of the inferior element. It is also the basis of preparation for discipleship and entry into the Path leading towards Initiation. It is also equivalent to the Gandhian conception of *swaraj* or self-rule based upon *swadeshi* or self-reliance, which is sought by the devotee of *satya* in his experiments with truth on behalf of universal welfare or *Lokasangraha*.

If only because human beings have now learnt that there is enough physical energy present in a toothpick to produce twenty-five million kilowatt-hours of electricity, they have reached a point in evolution where they must gain *swaraj* through experiments in the use of soul-force and moral power if they are not to forfeit the divine estate of being truly human. Gandhi's soul-force is equivalent to the atomic noetic force of *Buddhi*, and his idea of moral power is equivalent to the psychic or molecular force of *prana*, moral perception and vital energy. Gandhi demonstrated and taught the possibility of noetic force using psychic force on behalf of human brotherhood and universal welfare. As more and more people come to see that selfishness, invariably rooted in the dissociation of human vital energy from its origins in the Great Breath, is inevitably suicidal, they also begin to recognize that it is only through noetic self-command that there can be genuine self-respect. If they are perceptive, they will readily recognize that the perils and crises of the atomic age are a physical parable of a meta-psychological crisis. As the current of the Aquarian Age compels people to turn inward, the idea is spreading that it is not merely by changing the external environment, or by protesting what other people are doing, that a genuine improvement can be gained in collective human life. As Gandhi taught, the peril of our time arises from the abuse, misuse and neglect of soul-force. In Pythagorean terms, the evolutionary degree, and hence the authentic basis of self-respect, for each soul is to be found in the totality of its intentional relations with the entirety of Nature, both manifest and unmanifest.

The science of spirituality and the religion of responsibility are rooted in the metaphysics of the universe, and therefore have the complete support of cosmic will and design. Hence *The Voice of the Silence* instructs all those who would set themselves upon a secure foundation: "Give up thy life, if thou would'st live." Without a total renunciation of what one hitherto called living — which is really drifting in some sort of psychic daydream — one cannot cultivate the heightened spiritual attention and awareness needed for adequate participation in the Aquarian civilization of the future. The Gupta Vidya affirms that it is possible for human beings to cooperate with the invisible world self-consciously and to find meaning and dignity through obedience to the Law of Karma, obedience to the Will of the Spirit, obeisance to the Divine Order, obedience to the Logos in the cosmos and the God in man. The test of integrity in this inward search is effortless lightness and joyous control.

In the Aquarian communities and secular monastic ashrams of the future, it will be possible by design to have both free play and also continuous recognition of the evolving patterns and possibilities of Nature. Emancipation from the tyranny of habit and the conscious insertion of spiritual will into one's life will enable men and women to take full advantage of the invisible elements within space, within their own rooms, their brains, their hearts, but also throughout the entire plenum of Nature. As they gain a sense of themselves as trustees of a mysterious set of living vestures composed of visible and invisible atoms and nourished by Nature's generous gift of the life-giving waters of wisdom, then, through gratitude, individuals will become more humane, and more worthy of the Aquarian design of *Civitas Humanum*, the City of Man.

THE AQUARIAN ELIXIR

> SOMA *is the moon astronomically; but in mystical phraseology, it is also the name of the sacred beverage drunk by the Brahmins and the Initiates during their mysteries and sacrificial rites. The 'Soma' plant is the* asclepias acida, *which yields a juice from which that mystic beverage, the* Soma *drink, is made. Alone the descendants of the Rishis, the Agnihotri (the fire priests) of the great mysteries knew all its powers. But the real property of the* true *Soma was (and is) to make a new* man *of the Initiate, after he is* reborn, *namely once that he begins to live in his* astral *body . . . for, his spiritual nature overcoming the physical, he would soon snap it off and part even from that etherealized form.*
>
> The Secret Doctrine, ii 498-499

In order to tap the vast potential of soul-wisdom in any single epoch of human evolution, it is vital to retain a reverential standpoint towards the known and the unknown, as well as towards That which is inherently Unknowable. At all times human beings seem to be surrounded by clusters of familiar objects and inexplicable events. Yet, with a minimal degree of introspection, individuals may discern that their mundane experience is largely conditioned by habitual states of consciousness. If they remain sensitive to the ebb and flow of the tides of earthly existence, yet aware of the strange illusion of temporal succession, they may ardently seek to reach beyond conventional norms of logic and morality so as to establish a firm foundation for cognition and conduct. Within the limits of every epoch, individuals foster an ideal image of themselves and formulate diverse strategies for the attainment of goals in different sectors of human life. Depending upon the clarity and care with which the ideal of excellence is pursued, it can exercise a civilizing influence upon individuals, cultures and societies. Whilst much of human striving and motivation may be comprehended within the scope of dominant civilizations and their goals, a more fundamental perspective is needed to understand the rise and fall of long-lived cultures.

The intuitive seeker of Gupta Vidya turns to the cryptic teaching of cyclic evolution, suspended between the impenetrable mystery of *Parabrahm* and the pivotal laws of karma and reincarnation. Affirming the immeasurable ontological abundance of TAT in the infinitudes of space and the triple hypostases of the *Atman* as the universal basis of harmonious manifestation, Gupta Vidya portrays cyclic evolution as encompassing incremental degrees of self-knowledge and self-regeneration, and at the same time affording illimitable refinement in the noetic apprehension of cosmic order and justice. In practice this means that the elements of mystery and discipline — wisdom and method, symbolized by the Tibetan bell and *dorje* — are correlative components of human growth and experience. No single testament of wisdom can embrace the exhaustless potential of TAT. And yet, not even a glimmering of spiritual insight is without value in the pursuit of universal good. Each successive phase of manifest existence, whether of individual Monads or of the entire human race, is new and unprecedented in a Heraclitean sense. Yet, every unfolding moment epitomizes the vast sum-total of the past, is replete with the rich potential of the future, and evanescently bubbles upon the infinite ocean of eternity.

When probing the meaning and significance of the Aquarian Age or any of the major and minor cycles of human evolution, it is helpful to retain a sense of mystery as well as an undaunted resolve to sift essential insights gleaned through an alert Manasic intelligence, whilst shedding vested illusions. The potential mystery pervading the present epoch is archetypally represented by *soma*, and the formative forces of the emerging cosmopolis may be glimpsed through contemplating the zodiacal transition from the Piscean to the Aquarian Age. *Soma* is the arcane symbol of initiation. The zodiacal ages indicate the alchemical transmutation of the meta-psychological elements underlying formative change. If initiation is to be understood as individuation through the universalization of consciousness, it must also be retained intact with increasing continuity of consciousness through the etherealization and specialization of the vestures needed for effective incarnation.

The alchemical significance of these interrelated processes was suggested by H.P. Blavatsky in her gnostic interpretation of the cosmogonic myths of Chaldea, Egypt, Greece and, above all, India. Each points to the physico-chemical principle of primordial creation:

> The first revelation of the Supreme Cause in its triple manifestation of spirit, force, and matter; the divine *correlation*, at its starting-point of evolution, allegorized as the marriage of *fire* and water, products of electrifying spirit, union of the male active principle with the female passive element, which become the parents of their tellurian child, cosmic matter, the *prima materia*, whose spirit is ether, the ASTRAL LIGHT!
>
> *Isis Unveiled,* i 156

Shiva, as Dakshinamurti, the Hierophant of Hierophants, descends from the empyrean in a pillar of fire, and remains aloof and invulnerable like the world-mountain Meru, an allegorical representation of primal cosmogony.

> Within the mysterious recesses of the mountain — the matrix of the universe — the gods (powers) prepare the atomic germs of organic life, and at the same time the life-drink, which, when tasted, awakens in man-matter the man *spirit*. The *soma*, the sacrificial drink of the Hindus, is that sacred beverage. For, at the creation of the *prima materia*, while the grossest portions of it were used for the physical embryo-world, the more divine essence of it pervaded the universe, invisibly permeating and enclosing within its ethereal waves the newly-born infant, developing and stimulating it to activity as it slowly evolved out of the eternal chaos.
>
> *Isis Unveiled,* i 157

Like the swans who separate milk from water, seekers of Gupta Vidya must learn to distil the divine *Akashic* essence out of the matrix of organic elements. The process of distillation takes place within the alembic of noetic consciousness and the secret sanctuary in the temple of the human form, not in any terrestrial location.

A genuine understanding of the awakening of the "man spirit" could begin with a calm consideration of the extraordinary commencement of human activity on this globe over eighteen million years ago. At the time of the initial lighting up of Manasic self-consciousness, there was an awakening of the potent fires of self-knowledge in all human beings. This sacred heritage has enabled the immortal soul to maintain intact its sutratmic thread throughout myriads of lives upon earth. It is the continuity of this spiritual thread that enables individuals to learn and recollect in any lifetime. None of the facile theories of behavioural conditioning or social imitation can account for the elusive mystery inherent in the infant's learning of a language. Still less can they satisfactorily explain xenoglossy. Many little children spontaneously speak ancient and forgotten tongues, including those which are not even found in exhaustive glossaries of modern languages.

Dr. Ian Stevenson, in his fascinating study of xenoglossy, has investigated a number of such cases, including that of a child in New York who spoke a language which simply could not be readily identified, but which, on detailed investigation, was found to be a long unspoken tongue from Central Asia. Similarly, in other studies concerning what often seem to be the nonsensical sounds of babies, it has been shown that what looked like nonsense had a definite meaning. Not only are there significant patterns in the sounds made by infants all over the world, but there are also recurrent features in a wide variety of children's games, which often seem simple, but are often more complex than adult sports. The significance of all such evidence for a universal grammar independent of cultures is sharpened by consideration of the work of Noam Chomsky in philosophic linguistics. Chomsky has effectively shown that there is no sound evidence to suggest that in learning the alphabet children are actually being conditioned from the outside. Rather, it seems as if there is a kind of innate response to sounds on the part of infants. The learning of language essentially provides a telling example of how children bring back memories from other lives. More broadly, all knowledge is recollection in a Socratic sense. In alchemical terms, the signature of language is found in the Soul, and the sigils are learnt in childhood.

The relationship between sutratmic continuity and present learning is likely to remain obscure unless one is ready to probe deeply into the simplest things of life. For example, whilst it may seem easy to learn to walk, anyone who has ever made the effort to teach a cat or dog to walk on two legs would soon discover that it is exceedingly difficult. Circus trainers are able to get four-legged animals to walk like two-legged human beings for short lengths of time. With proper stimuli they can produce predictable responses. But these patterned responses are quite different from the intrinsic Manasic ability of children to hold their heads and spines erect and to be able to function as self-moving beings. The Socratic conception of the *psuche* as a self-moving agent, together with the Platonic idea of *nous* as the matter-moving mind, points to the initiatory potential inherent within every human being. Whenever an individual makes a new beginning, initiating a considered line of activity during a day, a week, a month or a year, such a commencement could signify the start of a new phase of learning. Whether one takes as the starting-point of such an endeavour one's birthday or any other cyclic reference-point in life, one is recognizing the permanent possibility for all individuals of making fresh ventures into the unknown. Ordinarily, human beings are protected by not knowing too much about their previous lives or knowing too much even about the immediate future of this one. Since individuals learn to live in ignorance of the unknown, and at the same time venture on the basis of what they do know, clearly there is an indestructible element in every immortal soul which enables a human being again and again to make a fresh start. This permanent element is not simply the *Atma-Buddhi* or Divine Monad, but also the distilled and assimilated wisdom of past lives gathered in the *sutratman*, the repository of the fragrant aroma of past learning.

If every human being brings this precious inheritance of prior efforts towards individuation into the present life, and if all have passed through several initiations in distant lives, what relevance does this have to the onset of the Aquarian Age? Commencing on June 19, 1902, and having completed its first degree, the Aquarian Age has already brought about an unprecedented heightening of self-consciousness, and it holds a tremendous potential for the future. Something of the fundamental significance of the Aquarian Age can be glimpsed by recollecting that the year 1902 was not unconnected with the increasing concern to fly in the air. In the nineteenth century, on the other hand, the ocean was the common term of reference for many people in regard to travel, exploration and geopolitics. If people in the last century took many of their analogies and metaphors from the nautical world, this was because they had such an impressive collection of imposing sailing ships and modern steamships. In Greenwich and in Plymouth, from Cathay to Cape Horn, the romance and excitement of the pioneering exploration of the world's oceans fired the imagination of adults and children alike. Beginning in the sixteenth century, the rapid expansion of sea trade lay at the basis of the commercial and cultural growth of European civilization. By the close of the Victorian Age, the idea of a maritime civilization had become crystallized in the minds of such writers as Mahan and Fisher and consolidated the image of a globe governed by sea power. The construction of large ocean liners capable of sailing thousands of miles at considerable rates of speed provided ordinary people with basic metaphors concerning the conduct of life. The exacting skills needed in navigation received an attention reminiscent of older conceptions in literature and myth, viewing man as the captain of his soul. Yet now, in the twentieth century, with the vast elaboration upon what the Wright Brothers began, there is a fundamentally new outlook that has emerged with reference to the atmosphere surrounding the earth.

Even early in the century, artists and visionaries were stimulated by grand, if sometimes fanciful, conceptions of what the implications of flight could mean to human beings in general. By the time of the First World War, shrewd politicians like Winston Churchill perceived with almost prophetic clarity the significant change in the balance of power brought about by the airplane and the appalling dangers that this new capacity could unleash. For most people, despite pioneering efforts by individuals and businesses, it was not until after the Second World War that they were able on a large scale to travel by air. Then suddenly they experienced what otherwise could only have been done by climbing mountains — they gained some sense of what it is like at different elevations. In the past few decades this upward ascent has passed beyond the proximate atmosphere of the earth, reaching into the empyrean of space. Tapping the theoretical insights of a few and drawing upon the cooperative labours of specialized teams of scientists and engineers, a small coterie of intrepid individuals has travelled into space and brought back beautiful images of the earth as a shining gem suspended in the void. Spacecraft with intricate instruments have ventured towards Mercury, Venus, Mars, Jupiter and Saturn, linked to earth only by the finest etheric threads of electrical impulse, and returning copious information regarding long-recognized globes in our solar system.

Broadly, the Aquarian Age is typified by the concept of vertical ascent, whereas during the nineteenth century and before, the idea of horizontal movement was far more prevalent. This is not to minimize the importance of the great circumnavigations of the globe conducted in the maritime era, nor to discount the considerable knowledge gained by daring explorers and naturalists in regard to diverse forms of life. At their best, the nineteenth century naturalists discovered valuable principles of continuity in living form and developed significant intuitions into the geometry of dynamic growth. But now, in the twentieth century, principally because of air travel, people are much more conscious of the enormous relevance of factors such as altitude and atmosphere in relation to the elevation of consciousness. Through the beneficent invention of pressurized cabins, vast numbers of people have had the opportunity to observe that the earth does not seem the same when seen from an airplane as it does when seen on the plains.

All of this merely suggests that there has been a vital change taking place in human consciousness progressively over the last eighty years. From a merely empirical standpoint the entry of human beings into the airy regions is conclusive of nothing. From the standpoint of the Gupta Vidya, however, these outward changes are emblematic of the shift in the fundamental perspective of human experience. The nature and significance of this change cannot be comprehended through conventional and pseudo-rationalistic schemes of popular astrology. Caught up in erratic frameworks and outdated calculations, most astrologers are no more aware of the true meaning of the Aquarian Age than the average person. Few, if any, have deeply reflected upon the precession of the equinoxes, or upon the essential differences between the Taurean, Piscean and Aquarian Ages. Nonetheless, an increasingly large number of individuals have begun to sense a new awakening of human consciousness. Whether they interpret this from a purely personal standpoint, or connect it to some form of secular or sectarian millennial thinking, they can discern that a fundamental change is taking place in the global atmosphere of human life. Some who are sensitive see this in terms of a subtle beauty and alteration in the atmosphere of the earth itself, whilst those who are more perceptive detect a similar change in the atmosphere that surrounds each human being. In general, there is a growing recognition and widespread acknowledgement of a fresh opportunity for human souls at the present time of metamorphosis. Such glimmerings provide an array of opportunities which bring with them fresh avenues for awakening and growth.

Philosophically, all awakening is self-awakening. Self-consciousness represents an extraordinary privilege as well as a burden. It is a privilege because it brings with it the ability to choose, and through choices to comprehend connections between causes and consequences. It is a burden because it also brings with it the obligation to act in harmony with one's most fundamental perceptions. It is not possible to prove oneself worthy of the privilege of self-awakening through fulfillment of obligations and commitments without strengthening a practical sense of self-transcendence through contemplation and meditation. Whilst the Aquarian Age has already seen a surfeit of schemes for meditation which appeal to the suggestibility and gullibility of people who think that they can get something for nothing, the authentic and therapeutic teaching with regard to the true nature of contemplation is now available to more human beings than ever before. In their essentials, meditation and contemplation are neither episodic nor dependent upon any technique. Rather, they require the unremitting watchfulness of the mind and heart for the sake of restoration of purity of consciousness.

It is only through purity of thought, word and deed that the inexpressible yearning of the inner man for the infinite can find the fulfillment of its aspiration. It is only through the perfected continuity of the will, incessantly striving towards the highest ideal of divine manhood, that spiritual awakening through meditation can take place. There can be no increment of individuation or continuity of consciousness through any form of passivity. To give focus to aspiration, as *The Voice of the Silence* teaches, the mind needs breadth and depth and points to draw it towards the Diamond Soul. For example, one could take the Four Golden Links — Universal Unity and Causation, Human Solidarity, Karma and Reincarnation — as axiomatic starting-points for meditation. Beginning with an intellectual comprehension of these universal axioms, and deriving deductive inferences regarding particulars, a preliminary grasp of the true aim of meditation must be gained. Then, having worked out some tentative conception of the scheme of causes and effects to be comprehended, it is possible to pass inductively and intuitively from a contemplation of the known phenomena of the world of effects to the as yet unknown causes in the noumenal and unmanifest realm. Thus constructing and using a Jacob's Ladder of ideation, an individual can insert himself or herself into the evolutionary programme and explore the opportunities that it offers to the entire globe. It is the prospect and promise of this inward ascent in consciousness that so many people dimly feel, and which makes them sense the privilege of being alive at a critical moment in human evolution.

This inward ascent towards self-awakening consciousness is inconceivable apart from the acquisition of freedom of movement in and through the vestures. To move the centre of one's consciousness from a plane of relatively gross effects to a relatively subtle plane of causes implies a gradual transfer from a more gross to a more ethereal body. To learn to live in the physical world, but not be of it, is in effect to begin to live in the purified astral body. This means that anyone who genuinely begins to participate in a life of meditation and contemplation becomes, in an anticipatory mode, a partaker of *soma*. As H.P. Blavatsky suggested:

> The partaker of *Soma* finds himself both linked to his external body, and yet away from it in his spiritual form. The latter, freed from the former, soars for the time being in the ethereal higher regions, becoming virtually 'as one of the gods,' and yet preserving in his physical brain the memory of what he sees and learns. Plainly speaking, *Soma* is the fruit of the Tree of Knowledge forbidden by the jealous Elohim to Adam and Eve or *Yah-ve*, 'lest Man should become as one of us'.
>
> *The Secret Doctrine*, ii 499

All human beings sense at times that the physical body cannot be seen merely as something restricted to the familiar plane of sense-perceptions. Though many may not be much aware of what is going on within the body, and though they may not understand too much about the blood and the cells, about the empty chambers of the brain and the heart, most do recognize that by the simple act of breathing it is possible to direct the physical body. Anyone who has engaged in extreme physical exertion and discipline over a period of seven years, perhaps as a runner or a dancer, will have experienced a distinct alteration in the range and rhythms of consciousness. Though this may be intolerably arduous for most people, almost every person is somewhat aware of the tangible ways in which the use of the physical body impinges upon his or her perception of the world. Every point in the physical form, each life-atom, is shot through and through with reflected *Mahabuddhi*, the latent power of self-consciousness.

The entire cosmos is intensely alive and there is intelligence in every point of space. There is not a single speck of space which is not ensouled by the light of universal intelligence. In the kingdoms below man this intelligence works without the self-conscious direction associated with the human kingdom. Thus, in those kingdoms, intelligence works precisely because of the cosmic hierarchies which act collectively and not individually. The world below the mineral kingdom is therefore understood as a realm of elementals, of *devas* and *devatas*, wherein there are myriads upon myriads of entities, hosts of life-atoms which work in perfect concert. Just as when human beings attend a concert and hear a majestic symphony, and come together to participate in the music, in a similar manner there is a complex symphonic harmonizing of nature in all its kingdoms. Whether one considers fire, air, earth or water, there is a continual expression of the intricate intelligence of nature. Some people have a child-like interest in sea shells and pine-cones, in seeds and acorns, because they can recognize in them the complex and mysterious intelligence of living Nature, which fills every point in the cosmos with burgeoning life and creativity.

Universal intelligence has attained a high degree of self-awareness in human beings. It is indeed possible for the human mind through meditation to gain eventually that degree of development, intimated in *The Voice of the Silence*, where one can slay one's lunar form at will. It is possible to gain continuity of consciousness through the night and through the three states of consciousness — *jagrat, swapna* and *sushupti.* One can gain an inkling of the *turiya* state of spiritual freedom from captivity to the three *gunas* — *sattva, rajas* and *tamas.* It is thus possible to alter the polarity of the *linga sharira,* the astral form. This is done by breaking up the clusters of elementals impressed with grosser or weaker types of life-energies and given a particular colouring and a certain tonality over a lifetime of habits. In order to cease from drifting as a victim and creature of habit, and in order to be able to rearrange the life-atoms of the subtle vestures, one must engage in an intimate and practical study of the astral body. Because the astral form is sevenfold, it is helpful to do this in terms of the number 7. Over a week of seven days, over seven weeks, over seven months or seven years, one could attempt to make some discoveries about the relative proportions of *sattva, rajas* and *tamas* in the life-atoms of the vestures. And, because there are four elements, excluding the synthesizing ether, it is also pertinent to consider the four quarters of the day, the four phases of the moon, and the four seasons of the year.

When one really begins to undertake such a study, it gradually becomes possible to comprehend the extraordinary relevance of the injunction to gain the power to slay the lunar form at will. Many enigmatic statements in *The Voice of the Silence* are practical instructions to the Lanoo which also could be taken as guidance for ethical experiments in the laboratory of the human temple. By treating the body as a temple and also as a laboratory for the making of judicious experiments through the powers of ideation and imagination, much can be discovered in reference to the different principles. In this way one can, from small beginnings, venture towards the sort of exacting discipline which ultimately leads to the complete awakening of conscious immortality during incarnated existence.

Those who would master meditation and contemplation and enter into the Path that leads towards initiation must ponder the profound meaning of the War in Heaven, the relentless strife between the sons of God and the sons of the Shadow of the Fourth and Fifth Races. This war must not be viewed as some distant event in the earlier stages of human evolution, but rather should be seen as a karmic heirloom, a living memory, affecting the spiritual striving of every human being on earth. It is to the *asuras* that spiritual humanity owes its most fundamental allegiance. They were born from the breath — *Asu* — of Brahmā-Prajāpati. It is only through the perverse inversion perpetrated by the enemies of Divine Wisdom that they came to be called *a-suras* or no-gods. In the oldest portions of the *Rig Veda* the *asuras* are the spiritual and the divine ancestors of Manasic humanity.

> They are the sons of the primeval Creative Breath at the beginning of every new Maha Kalpa, or Manvantara; in the same rank as the Angels who had remained 'faithful'. These *were the allies of Soma* (the parent of the *Esoteric Wisdom)* as against *Brihaspati* (representing ritualistic or *ceremonial* worship). Evidently they have been degraded in Space and Time into opposing powers or demons by the ceremonialists, on account of their rebellion against hypocrisy, sham-worship, and the dead-letter form.
>
> *The Secret Doctrine*, ii 500-501

In the present age, though popular opinion may not readily credit the fact, the allies of Brihaspati persist as the enemies of the allies of *soma*. The proponents of superstition, ceremonialism, hypocrisy and sham await the unwary pilgrim who is too weak-willed, vain or sentimentally naïve to acknowledge his or her own complacent ignorance of the occult world. Wallowing in the mire of seemingly self-devised exoteric ritual, he or she who does not know what it is to live in the world, and yet not be of the world, is incapable of guarding Self against self. No matter what pill or potion, fad or fancy, trick or technique, is taken up to mimic the realities of spiritual wisdom, the result is inevitably unconscious enslavement and voluntary degradation. That is why those who have learnt the painful truth regarding the pertinacity of the exoteric or thaumaturgic tendency in human nature, and have begun in earnest the entirely inward work of theurgy, of purifying their motive and volition, remain reticent before such sacred conceptions as *soma*, initiation, the Third Eye and *Kriyashakti*.

Like humble apprentices in a spiritual environmental protection agency, they would rather work to purify their own emanations than risk polluting the astral atmosphere in which others must breathe. With patience, they can learn to penetrate the external skin of the earth and the palpable skin that covers all objects, discovering how to make a vital difference to states of consciousness through noetic control over ideation and imagination. This is much harder and takes more time and thought than any simple scheme of social amelioration aimed at quick results. But, if one is not afraid of spiritual mountain climbing, even though one's dharma may keep one at a great distance from legendary mountains, then one is willing to get ready one's mental and moral equipment, and also to plant patiently the nourishing seed-ideas that are generously available in the abundant storehouse of Gupta Vidya. By making preliminary experiments with altruistic breathing and abstract meditation, one could begin to see how to work consciously not only with the seasons but also with the days of the week and the different times of the day.

This is the beginning of the path of selfless service and inward ascent towards the realm of Divine Wisdom open to all human beings in the Aquarian Age. It is also the small old path followed by every true ascetic of every age, and presided over by Shiva, the mighty Yogin, the paragon of all the Adepts and the foremost ruler of the divine dynasties, the patron of the Mysteries in the Fifth Root Race. It is the path of unconditional realization of the *Paramatman* and the elixir of *soma*, and the divine discipline taught by Krishna to a long lineage of hierophants and faithful devotees. The *soma* of the Vedas and the Brahmanas was aptly associated with thunder and electricity, purification and speed, brilliance and fertility. *Soma* fills heaven and earth with rays like the sun, dispels darkness, invigorates and impregnates thought and action, heals the sick, stimulates the voice, and exhilarates every limb. *Soma* is the maker of seers, the generator of hymns, the protector of prayer and the soul of sacrifice. Even in the dawn of the Aquarian Age, some forerunners may be entitled to exclaim: "We have drunk *Soma*, we have become immortal, we have entered into light, we have known the gods."

THE HEALING OF SOULS

The whole essence of truth cannot be transmitted from mouth to ear. *Nor can any pen describe it, not even that of the recording Angel, unless man finds the answer in the sanctuary of his own heart, in the innermost depths of his divine intuitions. It is the great* SEVENTH MYSTERY *of Creation, the first and the last; and those who read St. John's Apocalypse may find its shadow lurking under the* seventh seal.

The Secret Doctrine, ii 516

Self-exiled from the spiritual sanctuary at its core and perversely deaf to the divine promptings of intuition, mankind in our time has enacted a protracted melodrama which has become tedious to participants and spectators alike. For a painstaking chronicler like Gibbon, history seemed to be nothing but a record of crimes, follies and misfortunes. Somewhat more perceptive, though shackled by a rationalist framework of truncated idealism, Hegel at least identified the central issue in his laconic observation that if men learn anything from history, it is that they learn nothing at all. Clearly, there is something about human beings that is mulish and proud, that mutilates inner aspirations and divine hopes. When the innate power of learning is obscured, human beings fall prey to an unrelenting succession of misshapen thoughts, distorted emotions and self-negating actions. This intimate if inverse connection between the spiritual anatomy of man and the outward play of events was sensed by Gandhi in his conclusion that history, as ordinarily conceived, is merely a grandiose record of the interruptions of soul-force.

From a diagnostic standpoint, it is as if a heavy stone lodged in the spine were to block the inflow of Divine Light from the top of the head. The baby's fontanelle, connected with the *Brahmarandhra chakra*, is soft in the first months of life, but, owing to the karma of past misuse of powers, astral calcification of that vital aperture reaches to an unprecedented degree in modern man. Thus the "shades of the prison-house begin to close upon the growing boy", and the essential *nadis* become listless in the absence of the divine efflux. This morbid condition cannot be corrected from below or from without; it is only a radical realignment of one's inner mental and devotional posture that will restore the free flow of the currents in the spiritual spinal cord. One has to learn before teaching. One must be still and listen before speaking. One must meditate before attempting to conceive and create or engage in outward action.

If human beings are to be more than animals, if they are to reclaim their descent from the Divine, there can be no fakery and foolery, no pretence or deception. They must take their stand as fallible learners, growing and acknowledging errors through candour and self-correction, clearly and cleanly admitting their ignorance but firmly and fearlessly strengthening their own willingness to learn. Regardless of all exoteric and external tokens of class and caste, of culture and social station, each individual must become a humble, though self-accredited, ambassador of goodwill in a global society of learning. If in future lives such honest seekers are to approach the true Mystery temples, they must begin now by laying aside any false sense of superiority and inferiority, all unctuousness and hypocrisy, and learn to greet each other as souls with pride in the beauty and bounty of all lands and in the nobility of common folk and the ancestors of the earth, thereby acknowledging their mutual membership in mankind. Along with its ancient gurus and preceptors, the human race — most of whose mature graduates are not incarnated at any given time — is waiting to see how many true learners may emerge in our epoch. How many are willing to acknowledge in daily practice what they really know about playing a musical instrument? It is only through years of discipline that one may learn any true art, whether it be meditation or the practice of political diplomacy, the therapeutics of self-transcendence or authentic friendship for one's comrades in humane endeavours.

As Cicero taught, divine nature has no interest in perpetually underwriting human folly. Twentieth century America with its celluloid media is neither the first, nor will it be the last, society to be disabused of its self-perpetuated delusions. Even Americans can wisely use their magnificent resources in libraries, the finest available on earth, and really begin to learn. The moment one truly begins to learn, one starts to speak from knowledge, with the accents of genuine confidence that naturally combine with a sense of proportion, without adolescent exaggerations and extravagances. Mature men and women honour their sacred obligations to their children and their moral debts to their fathers and mothers; authentic learners are proud of their illiterate grandparents and rustic ancestors who helped in their own way to make possible the opportunities of the present. The emergence of a widely diffused sense of individual integrity in the common cause of human learning is a mighty undertaking, rooted in a spiritual reformation of the human psyche. It requires saying adieu to the homogenization and humbug of modern mass education, and courageously choosing the elevating ideal of lifelong learning based upon spiritual self-education through ethical self-renewal in the altruistic service of others.

Many more people in the world are ready for this today than in any previous epoch. Yet some who desperately want to learn do not know how because they imagine that they cannot start until everyone else does. This is the peasant mentality at its most timid, but it is not the true state of mind of pastoral exemplars of the *grihastha ashrama*, who have nurtured and sustained humanity over a myriad centuries. Whilst every village and town has its share of those who substitute pretension and crudity for learning and life, there are always a scattered few who are willing to be Promethean. These are the humble pioneers who husband the new seeds and who plan ahead for the coming year's crop. In villages results count, but they are essentially those supported by nature's rhythms. Without the ingenuity and inventiveness of farmers in responding to Nature, the subsidies of kings and courts are of no avail, and if in contemporary capitals people have become insensitive to the rhythms of nature and thereby cut off from their sense of the need to learn, so much the worse for them. To the extent that any group of people imagines itself divorced from the natural necessity of learning, its culture is a sham and its society a fabric of deceit built on ignorance. Puzzled and frightened by the raucousness and violence caused by its own unacknowledged delusions, it moves through a succession of misunderstood non-crises to utilitarian non-solutions, unable to learn because unwilling to listen either to its own inner voice or to the wisdom of others.

As H.P. Blavatsky noted in the last century, wherever spiritual truth is dishonoured and elementary discrimination is lacking, the mysteries of nature cannot be divulged. One must begin by honouring the humblest truths by honest application and through some philosophical comprehension before one may raise one's hand to the latch which guards the gate of the Greater Mysteries. Initially, one must be willing to honour the Delphic injunction "Know thyself" on the planes of relative learning, and thereby restore the power of inner perception before one may apprehend any absolute truth.

> Absolute truth is *the symbol of Eternity,* and no *finite* mind can ever grasp the eternal, hence, no truth in its fulness can ever dawn upon it. To reach the state during which man sees and senses it, we have to paralyze the senses of the external man of clay. This is a difficult task, we may be told, and most people will, at this rate, prefer to remain satisfied with relative truths, no doubt. But to approach even terrestrial truths requires, first of all, *love of truth for its own sake,* for otherwise no recognition of it will follow.
>
> H.P. BLAVATSKY

The Victorian age, with all its cant and hypocrisy as well as its latent sense of human dignity and integrity preserved through the recollection of the Enlightenment, is gone. It is now obvious to many that there was neither irony nor polemic, but only compassion, in the stern warnings that H.P. Blavatsky delivered on behalf of the Mahatmas to Theosophists and non-Theosophists alike. The collapse of the acquisitive and parochial civilizations of the past two millennia is approaching completion, and on behalf of the Aquarian dawn of the global civilization of the future, it was essential since 1963 to encourage rebels and victims alike to come out of the old and decaying order. This anarchic rebellion entailed the risk that the weak would become like Trishanku in the Indian myth, who was suspended between heaven and earth, neither able to land on his feet in the world nor capable of scaling celestial heights. This was a great but well-calculated risk, because large numbers of pilgrim-souls have awakened to a sense of their common humanity, both in the old world and the new.

Whilst the wisest statesmen and most perceptive peoples of the globe did not think that the Second World War had drained all the sources of discord on the earth, they were nonetheless willing to move towards the establishment of a juridical basis of enduring peace. What they did not foresee was that their endeavours on behalf of a new era of security and welfare for the whole of humanity would be flouted by the flagrant jingoists of the so-called American century, backed by sectarian bigotry and pervasive racism. Like Lisa in Dostoevsky's *Notes From The Underground,* they may not have comprehended the details of what America claimed to know, but they soon understood that their smug benefactor was so self-deluded as to be incapable of offering timely help. Perhaps now a growing core of Americans has realized that the decent peoples of the world dislike self-righteous bullies. They do not like the bombing of defenseless people, nor do they wish to see what happened to Dresden recur *ad nauseam* after the war. Rather, they expect true courage and ethical sensitivity from the proud champions of freedom and human solidarity. No one capable of resonating to the authentic meaning behind the American experiment could be but saddened to see it turning into a vulgar display of chauvinistic rhetoric and moral cowardice, an unholy alliance of Mammon, Moloch and Beelzebub.

It was the strange karma of the modern Theosophical

Movement to attract many souls who were able neither to stand up in the world nor to renounce it for the sake of the spiritual welfare of humanity, and so in the nineteenth century it largely failed in America. Although it quickly travelled to England and Europe and also found receptive soil abroad, from India to Japan, in North America it engendered a crop of delusions, despite the sacrifices of a few pioneers. People actually thought that simply because they were middle-class salvationists they could pretend to be the chosen race of forerunners of future humanity. These pathetic delusions do not belong to the past, but have persisted like poison amongst pseudo-spiritual coteries and the crowded ranks of those who have not yet learnt that they cannot get something for nothing, or purchase wisdom for a price. Whilst America welcomed the wretched of the earth with a noble promise of liberty and justice for all, it also pampered the shallow autodidacts and plausible hypocrites who treated America as a land where anything goes and all is permitted. Many of these and their descendants eventually congregated in California and in the environs of the city of the angels (which its original Indian inhabitants had prophetically associated with demons). Blind greed, the perverse refusal to learn and the profanation of the sacred are so widespread today that the anger of humanity is sufficiently aroused to call for a halt to the further spread of the diseases of the psyche. The time for fascination with the pathology of the soul is past.

America must now take a firm stand and foster human beings who can marry, bring up children, and can love without merely demanding to be loved. They must learn to show true and direct personal charity to the deserving, and not just presume on some evangelical committee to plan out other lives. They must learn to esteem the ethical dignity of their neighbours every day of the year, regardless of race, creed, sect or ideology. What is required is nothing superhuman, but merely the reduction of subhuman activity through the exemplification of true values, and by a cool recognition of the enormous difference between delusive posturing and the real world in which diverse human beings are born, grow old and die, burdened by the sorrows caused by their own ignorance. Though they suffer, they may learn by acknowledging their errors, and paralysing their pride rather than their spiritual faculties. Relinquishing both conceit and guilt, they can learn to say that they are sorry when they hurt others, and they may begin to learn the manners of the common man and the authentic accents of the voice of mankind. Then they may take their place once again in the community of man by refusing to live like tawdry traducers, cheats and fakes. Each and all must learn to live lives built upon intrinsic value and reality, not upon appearances and noisy self-assertion. The heavenly maiden of Truth can descend only in a context congenial to her, the soil of an impartial, unprejudiced mind, receptive to pure spiritual consciousness.

Whilst it is true that the mad rush of material civilization leaves one little time for reflection, thus increasing the irksomeness of a life of empty custom and barren conventionality, this alienation from humanity and Nature is the inescapable karma of past lives. The real danger in the present is that the simulation and deceit of conventional existence will be mistaken for the true substance of fellow-feeling and concern for others. Whatever its varied masks, selfishness remains the same, and its inflammation through 'double ignorance' is the primary disease of the soul.

> SELFISHNESS, the first-born of Ignorance, and the fruit of the teaching which asserts that for every newly-born infant a new soul, *separate and distinct* from the Universal Soul, is 'created' — this Selfishness is the impassable wall between the *personal* Self and Truth. It is the prolific mother of all human vices, *Lie* being born out of the necessity for dissembling, and *Hypocrisy* out of the desire to mask *Lie*. It is the fungus growing and strengthening with age in every human heart in which it has devoured all better feelings. Selfishness kills every noble impulse in our natures, and is the one deity, fearing no faithlessness or desertion from its votaries. Hence, we see it reign supreme in the world and in

so-called fashionable society. As a result, we live, and
move, and have our being in this god of darkness under
his trinitarian aspect of Sham, Humbug and Falsehood,
called RESPECTABILITY.

H.P. BLAVATSKY

There is nothing more cleansing than the truth, for, as Jesus
taught, it is by learning and knowing the truth that one becomes
free. Wherever the truth is obscured, whether by individuals or
governments, responsibility is weakened, and with it the
connection between the higher Triad and the lower principles.
Hence, it is a form of needless self-destruction to be continually
speaking of the so-called predicament of the age, and never facing
one's own failings. The critical question is not what is wrong with
the world, but what is one's own individual responsibility for
particular choices and acts. There is need for less talk of nihilism
and Nietzsche and more attention to one's individual
responsibility to parents, to spouse and children, and to those
nobler human souls with whom one has the privilege of
associating in the pilgrimage of life. Vast numbers of people in
America and all over the globe are pleased with the prospect of
the termination of a tired old cycle of cowardly irresponsibility,
and the burgeoning promise of a saner and more cooperative way
of life. Many young people are aware that what Lenin called the
bourgeoisification of the proletariat is doomed. The time has come
for perceptive Americans of all ages to cherish their common
ancestry with the rest of mankind, neither from gorilla nor
Jehovah, but from the solar Fathers of the human race, the
Agnishwatha Pitris, the Lords of Light, who long ago breathed
life into those who were human in form but devoid of
self-consciousness. Through the controlled power of mystic
ideation, they lit up the divine spark in the soul which makes
possible both learning and choice, and thereby all spiritual, moral
and mental growth.

The authentic learner will seek to rekindle and strengthen
that light, the Akashic lustre in the saddened eyes of every human

being. Witnessing the world with eyes of maturity, of honesty and truth, one must learn to be on the side of germinal goodness, not debasement, of inner beauty, not crudity, of light itself, not shadow, and above all, the needs of the many rather than the cravings of a few. One must make a decisive break with the endless chain of personal self-pity, and affirm pure 'I am I' consciousness in order to prepare to take one's true place, stand confidently in the Light of the Spiritual Sun, and ardently follow the Way of Wisdom-Compassion. That way is as high as the stars. It is also as near as the next step, for it is the way of humanity. It is the way of humility and true affirmation, and the way of the inmost camaraderie of spirit which is more profound and potent than outward speech can convey.

When people are lost in silent thought, like Rodin's statue, asking not who they are or what is their tribe and pedigree, but thinking of the nature of man and the future of all mankind, that is the sign of growth. When people learn to forget themselves and their petty concerns, and to think instead of the stars and of all the souls on earth and of the resources of the globe and of world peace and government, then they will discern the great challenge of our time. They will see that they must come out of the multitude and out of the forests of delusion and exemplify through their endeavours the true meaning of human existence. They will live richly yet humbly and without guarantees or scapegoats, but purely for the joy of breathing benevolently and working quietly. Guided by a calm and secure intuition of the possibilities of the academies, ashrams and monasteries of the future, the initiation chambers, mystic rites, and sacred sanctuaries to be spread all over the globe, those who courageously seek the privilege of inclusion without any glory other than in the joy of participation may stand up and be counted. Though they make their mistakes and are put through many trials, they will still govern themselves and crucify the pride of self rather than the *imago* of Christos, spurning the Kamsa within the mind rather than the life-giving gift of Krishna.

Present in every human heart, and hidden by the veil of the mystery of the *Atman*, the life-giving power and spirit of eternal

Truth finds its voice in the languages of love, of truth, and of purity of intention, purpose and will that is awakened when one gains the priceless privilege of being in the orbit of the self-luminous Mahatmas and their Avatar on earth. Like the central sun and the sacred planets, they are ever present in their invisible forms. Having nothing to prove to human beings of any age or clime, they are simply *yogins* who love mankind. Masters of themselves, they are the illustrious servants of the human race and the inimitable embodiments of the unmanifest universe of divine obeisance and sacred learning. In the mystical language of the *Anugita*:

> Glory, brilliance and greatness, enlightenment, victory, perfection and power — these seven rays follow after this same Sun (Kshetragna, the Higher Self). . . . Those whose wishes are reduced (unselfish) . . . whose sins (passions) are burnt up by restraint, merging the Self in the Self, devote themselves to Brahman.
>
> *The Secret Doctrine*, ii 639

If the highest *jnanis* are also the purest *bhaktas*, responding in magical sympathy to the cosmic will of Krishna, entering the stream of incarnation or abiding in the regions of invisible space only for the sake of service, can souls on earth who aspire to learn take any other standard? In the present period of human transformation, the opportunities for growth are great although the law of retrogression claims its toll amongst the weak. It may help to recall Longfellow's reminder that "Dust thou art, to dust returnest, was not spoken of the soul." One need not be like a dumb driven creature; but through unassuming heroism one may live a real life of earnest striving after the good. In a time of profanation one must refine the potent energy of thought through the living idea of the sacred, and though one might have humour and humanity, this need never be at the expense of another human being. One should recognize that *ahimsa* sweetens the breath, that non-violence dignifies the human being and straightens the spine, and that prostration adds inches to one's stature and health to one's frame. Integrity resides in the ability to recognize the difference between what one knows and what one does not know, coupled with a commitment to make good use of the divine gift of the power of learning right until the moment of death, so that one may arrive at the farther shore of earthly life with a sense of having contributed to that which was vaster and more profound than anything that could be contained in the compass of one lifetime.

To recover one's own inheritance as a Manasic being, and to resonate to the Avataric vibration which reverberates throughout the invisible world, one must raise one's horizons of thought. One must renounce the confined chronologies and parsimonious ontologies of Western thought. Almost by definition, a Westerner is an individual who believes in only one life. Yet there are many both in America and throughout the world who take rebirth for granted, integrating it into their way of life. Whilst there is a risk that one may speak in terms of many lives but act in terms of one life (which is cheating), once the mind and heart are firmly fixed upon the idea of karma, there is a spontaneous recovery of the capacity to learn and to show reverence and kinship to other human souls. Like the majority of mankind and the ancient inhabitants of the New World, the early Americans, including the Founding Fathers, believed in reincarnation. What, then, is the point of cowardice? Reincarnation is not merely a fashionable topic of conversation for actors and prostitutes sharing autobiographies, nor is it only designed for behind-the-scenes discussions. It should be brought out into the open, as the great sages have always done. If one has doubts, one must ask oneself if there is any reason to affirm another alternative. If so, then freely adopt the philosophy of the behaviourists and nihilists who openly expect to end their existence at death. As Jesus taught, either blow hot or blow cold, for the lukewarm are spewed forth.

If you choose the language of karma and the logic of reincarnation, universal unity and causation, and human solidarity, then you must also accept that theory is only as good as its practice. On this clarified and purified basis it becomes possible to make some small difference by one's life to the lives of others through showing true reverence and humility and an authentic agnosticism because of the ineffability of the One, the universality of the Law of Karma, the intricacy and exactitude of philosophical astrology, and the mysterious mathematics of sum-totals pertaining to the series of reincarnations. Thus one may learn to take an accurate account of the heavy toll exacted by the blockage of the Divine Light in the interior principles. A strenuous effort is required to learn the ABC's of occultism, and it would be folly to expect to discover the origins of consciousness through the self-restricted evidence of only one of its states. The ontological depths of *Prajna* can only be approached after there is a thorough mastery of the psychological and moral planes of human existence. Through firm detachment and unwavering attention, one must make oneself invulnerable to the siren calls of the past and cloying fantasies about the future, for the *narjol* is not safe until after having crossed beyond the regions of illusion, in which, as the *Anugita* teaches:

> ... fancies are the gadflies and mosquitoes, in which grief and joy are cold and heat, in which delusion is the blinding darkness, avarice, the beasts of prey and reptiles, and desire and anger are the obstructors.
>
> *The Secret Doctrine*, ii 637

Above all, if one would seek freedom from the forests of delusion, from the enslavement of *Manas* to the senses, one must turn to the one and only source which can give protection and refuge, the *Kshetragna* within the sun. This is not to be understood in terms of any of the foolish salvation myths built up by failed disciples, but rather because of the logic and the law of the reflection of supernal light. Try to see the world not from below above but from above below. Try to see the world through the eyes of all those *yogins*, Mahatmas, who live both in the Himalayan crests of consciousness and in the lowliest heart of every sincere and aspiring human being. They can pass through any metal or substance named by man, and be simultaneously in many places. Established in the transcendental freedom of *Mahat*, they travel at will throughout the planes of the globe, though this has nothing to do with pseudo-occult notions of astral travel. They are Masters; their life-atoms are so pure that they can never hurt a single being. Supremely benevolent, men of truth who never know what it is to foster a lie, they are perfected in the practice of *Karma Yoga*, using many guises, playing jokes, veiling themselves constantly and thereby always guarding and protecting each and every human being without exception. They are what they are before they ever take illusory birth in the races of man, and they do not become anything different. Taking on illusory bodies of form from time to time for the instruction of mankind, Avatars create before mortal eyes a re-enactment of the path towards supreme enlightenment, but it is only a foolish fancy that supposes, for example, that Christ was not Christ, that Buddha was not Buddha, aeons before taking birth in a mortal frame. It was only for the sake of instruction that Jesus the Chrestos became Christos seemingly in three years, or that Gautama the Prince became the Enlightened Buddha through his travail in the forest on behalf of mankind.

Buddha taught that the entire world is like a lake of lotuses, each representing beings in different stages of *maya*. He explained that his life was not for the sake of those few who had already approached the Light of the Spiritual Sun, nor for those so deeply plunged in the mud of *maya* and *moha* that they could make no significant progress in their present incarnation, but rather for those in the middle, struggling to come out, those who need the assurance and the confidence that they too can move further up through the swirling currents of earth life and reach the surface of the waters and open to the sun. All such births of spiritual Teachers of Mankind are conscious incarnations of beings who knew millions of years ago who they were, and who, in enacting their self-knowledge that spells out as self-conquest, assume a compassionate veil.

In the *Bhagavad Gita*, Lord Krishna explains that there are seven classes of human beings. There are those who are wicked, those who are deluded, and those who are totally drunk with passion. These three classes neither know nor recognize Krishna.

Then there are the four classes of true and good beings who have some degree of recognition: the sufferers and afflicted, who, in their pain, desperately want to find peace and give their lives meaning; those who seek truth and spiritual knowledge which could be used for self-transformation, knowledge that by use they could convert into wisdom which, through suffering, becomes compassion; and then there are those who are wise and yet seek further wisdom, understanding that the basis of all wisdom is the knowledge of Krishna. Finally, there are those who already know Krishna because they are already a part of Krishna. These beings are the dearest unto Krishna; eternally united to him, they are never apart from him. They are the Mahatmas difficult to find. They became Mahatmas in the only way that any human being ever can, out of many lives of struggle and search, of honest striving and pure devotion. They are the custodians of the Seventh Mystery, that most secret Wisdom, which ever lives in the heart of every being and from which ultimately none is excluded.

Krishna explains that when he comes into the world, any beings who recognize him at any level and truly place their hearts on him — in their thoughts and dreams, their hopes and aspirations — and who truly think of him in times of trouble will be helped. Those who truly love him for his own sake and not for their own will certainly find the grace that comes with such honest love. Those whose minds are still enthralled within the forest of illusions, and who seek therein their good, will under karma find there the sad fruits of their misguided search. But as Bhagavan revealed in the *Anugita*, for those who have learnt to subdue their senses and for whom the light of *Buddhi-Manas* has begun to dawn,

> another forest shines forth, in which *intelligence is the tree*, and emancipation the fruit, and which possesses shade (*in the form of*) tranquillity, which depends on Knowledge, which has contentment for its water, and the KSHETRAGNA (the '*Supreme* SELF,' says Krishna, in the Bhagavad Gita) within for the Sun. . . . Those people who understand the forest of Knowledge (Brahman, or

SELF) praise tranquillity. And aspiring to that forest, they
are (re-) born so as not to lose courage. Such indeed, is
this holy forest . . . and understanding it, they (the Sages)
act accordingly, being directed by the KSHETRAGNA.
The Secret Doctrine, ii 638-640

Those who seek for nothing in the world but only wish to
serve humanity and Krishna in the heart of every being are
'fortune's favoured soldiers'. They alone come to Krishna, realizing
that they are already in him though he is not contained in them,
for he is everywhere and cannot be only in a few. This is the
supreme mystery of the *Adhyatman,* the comprehension of which
dispels all darkness. It is the mystery of immortality veiled by the
appearances of the life and death of beings. It is the supreme glory
and light of the Divine made visible by the Divine, and it is beyond
all light and darkness, beyond all the wondrous and myriad forms
and shapes of the celestial and terrestrial worlds which are only
the veil upon itself. It is the very Self of Wisdom and Compassion,
and the secure refuge of truth sought by all beings in the vast vale
of soul-making called the world. It is the deathless core of
fearlessness in all the prisoners in all the dungeons of the world,
in the hearts of all the children who hope against hope that there
will be a tomorrow, hope that despite the errors of generals, the
follies of politicians, the ignorance of pseudo-spiritual leaders,
there will be peace and goodwill amongst men, and there will be
some rare breeze over the Himalayas which comes to bless all
beings.

THE VIGIL NIGHT
OF HUMANITY

If the Higher Mind-Entity — the permanent and the immortal — is of the divine homogeneous essence of 'Alaya-Akasa,' or Mahat, — its reflection, the Personal Mind, is, as a temporary 'Principle,' of the Substance of the Astral Light. As a pure ray of the 'Son of the Universal Mind,' it could perform no functions in the body, and would remain powerless over the turbulent organs of Matter. Thus, while its inner constitution is Manasic, its 'body,' or rather functioning essence, is heterogeneous, and leavened with the Astral Light, the lowest element of Ether. It is a part of the mission of the Manasic Ray, to get gradually rid of the blind, deceptive element which, though it makes of it an active spiritual entity on this plane, still brings it into so close contact with matter as to entirely becloud its divine nature and stultify its intuitions.

H.P. BLAVATSKY

The poet Tennyson proclaimed: "Ring out the old, ring in the new." There is, at this point in the history of human evolution, a tremendous and unprecedented golden opportunity. Its origin is not in outward forms and institutions, but in consciousness itself; its promise is rooted in a radical restructuring of the ratios in human consciousness between the unmanifest and manifest. Since this revolution arises within the very principle of Manasic self-consciousness, it can be neither understood nor entered through tellurian conceptions of human history or egoity below the fourth plane. Yet, everywhere, men and women of moral courage can glimpse this subtle transformation through the intimations of awakened intuition, and can authentically respond to the noumenal initiatives of our time. Each may uncover within himself the spiritual resources to contribute to the humanity of the future and the strength of mind to take those decisions at the moment of death which will assure participation in that future.

Before the dawning of the new order of the ages, in which the relations of nations will be changed significantly, humanity will witness the dismantling of the old structures. The clarion call has been sounded and it will be maintained continuously until all the obsolete megaliths that wallow in the debris of the past and the humbug of history, and until all the appalling vicissitudes of the Karma of Israel over two thousand years, will come to an end, and end not with a bang but a whimper. It is the solemn duty of those who have had the sacred privilege of entering the orbit of the 1975 Cycle to draw apart, in the words of St. Paul, from the multitudes of fatalists and to insert themselves into the whole human family. This is not easy, for everyone is a victim of his own karma over millions of years. All this karma may be strangely brought together in a concentrated form in a single lifetime, through a process which defies analysis and baffles imitation, and which can only be glimpsed intermittently, in hints and whispers, until the moment of death, when the immortal soul lays down its garment and gains, at last, some inkling of the hidden meaning of human life.

One of the long-standing problems with the western world, especially over the past two hundred and fifty years, has been its baseless assumption that the entire world owes it an explanation. The many owe no explanation to the few, and above all, there is no explanation owed to the ignorant and uninitiated by the Society of Sages. Krishna owes no one any explanation. If this is understood, it will become clear that human beings have assumed needless burdens of false knowledge. Through a mistaken conception of knowledge they assume that what they repeat below the fourth plane they truly know, because they have failed to grasp the crucial distinction between 'knowing how' and 'knowing that'. Reading a textbook on carpentry does not ensure that one can become a carpenter. A cookbook does not make a chef. If this is true of carpentry and cooking, of music and mathematics, it is even more true of spiritual wisdom. The mere fact of repeating words below the fourth plane does not admit the soul of man to the stream of search. No one becomes a mountain climber by dreaming about it, or by exchanging images and fantasies with others. The truth can only be known by testing and training one's psyche, and this cannot be done without first asking *who* is really testing and training the psyche. If a human being were merely one of the six specialized principles of human nature, it would be impossible to engage in self-redemption.

All the principles of man are derivatives and reflections, on different planes of substance, of One Life, One Light and One Energy. When a human being ascends above the fourth plane and becomes immortal, living in the instrument but in the name of the music, inhabiting the vessel but in the name of the Light, remaining in the mask but in the name of the Nameless, he has become attuned to humanity at large. Anyone at any time can become more attentive to the vast milling crowds of human souls, who, though they may wander in the dark and sometimes tumble in the dust, come together in the dusk. As souls, all withdraw into deep sleep and come closer to the Divine within, finding in "nature's second course" the nourishment and strength which enables them to arise the next day and continue with courage their pilgrimage. To become attentive to the cry of the human race, to become responsive to the immemorial march of all human souls on this vast and uncharted pilgrimage, is also to come closer to Krishna within, and to comprehend the affirmation: "I am seated in the hearts of all beings and from me comes knowledge and memory and loss of both."

There is that facet of the Logos which is karma, the complex interaction of all life-atoms below the fourth plane in the great wheel of life, as Buddha called it. All of these participate at different rates and with different degrees of semi-unconsciousness — partial, imperfect self-consciousness —in the long pilgrimage. Therefore, human beings generally do not know who they are, where they are or what goal they seek. This threefold ignorance is an integral part of the human enterprise. In the modern world, those who failed spiritually, being unable to maintain even minimal standards of what it is to be human, developed theories based upon the corruption of consciousness to apply to most human beings, who, however imperfect, are not warped in the essential intuitions of the heart. It is the tragedy of man and of human history that the monstrous necromancy and extreme sickness of so few should have imposed so great and so intolerable a burden upon large masses of human beings. This is the fault of modern miseducation, rooted in false ideas of human life, which asserts the quaint dogma — for which there is no evidence and never will be — that the human being is the body, that there is only one life, that this is a universe without moral law, that everything is chaos and without meaning, and that by counting the heads of the mindless, by collating the opinions of cerebrating machines, there is an accredited basis for either Truth or Equality or Freedom. There is none, and therefore the ritual of democracy has failed. All the deceptive tokenism that resulted from the eighteenth century revolution has evaporated.

Each human being is a Monad or individual, a ray of the Divine, immortal in essence, yet only potentially so as an incarnated ray working in vestures that are evidently mortal. These vestures, ever changing and evanescent, compel every human being to interact with all the seven kingdoms of nature. There is not an animal, not a plant or mineral, not a star or galaxy or planet, which does not feel every subterranean influence in nature. Therefore, all human beings are brought together in a vast solidarity of being in which breathe millions upon millions of centres of light in all the variegated kingdoms of nature. In finding itself, humanity must rediscover its ontological basis in the entire cosmic scheme. Five million years ago in Atlantis, human beings sought the mystery fires but then, alas, degraded them. They sought thaumaturgic powers at the expense of the majority of mankind. They exploited the theurgic traditions of their wiser ancestors. They generated the intoxicating idea of individual perfection, for which exclusiveness there is no cosmic provision in the grand scheme of evolution. There is not a human being on earth who could truly ascend above the planes without coming into a compassionate relationship with all life. The true Teaching, which has always existed in the world, guarded in sanctuaries around the globe, reminds us that no one can ever make any real spiritual progress except on behalf of all humanity.

No one can separate himself from the meanest and most wretched of the earth. As soon as human beings utter the sacred sound of the AUM, yet harbour selfish thoughts and intentions, consolidating them and presuming to judge harshly a single being (let alone those who have played such sacrificial roles throughout eighteen million years), they are warped and self-condemned. They cannot hope to benefit at the moment of death from the regenerative compassion of the Bodhisattvas. It is in blind ignorance that human beings perform these extraordinary antics, becoming mere mediumistic entities, collections of diseased and distorted life-atoms, brought together by a pathetic preoccupation with personal failure. The very idea is false. It is false at the very root. There can be no solace for the individual except in the context of universal enlightenment, universal progress and universal welfare. Any human being not threatened by the fact that other human souls exist, not disturbed by the fact that humanity is on the march, can receive help, but only in proportion under law and provided that he does not ask for any more than he deserves and not at the expense of any other being.

Thus, when the Avataric affirmation of Krishna is made and humanity is given its warning, this is done with a calm indifference to the opinions of individuals but with an unqualified insistence upon the simple proposition that the whole is greater than the part, that the tree is greater than the branch, that the mighty forest is greater than any individual tree. That eternal principle is the enduring basis of the custodianship of the sacred Mysteries amongst the Brotherhood of Bodhisattvas, who serve Krishna faithfully in ceaseless and effortless devotion, without let or hindrance, "without variableness or shadow of turning". This principle has been assiduously upheld without exception in every ancient nation and civilization of the earth, and it will not be forgotten in the future. The doors of the Mystery Temples must remain forever sealed, except to those whose Buddhic intuition resonates to the larger vision, the deeper purpose of all humanity.

> All ancient nations knew this. But though all had their Mysteries and their Hierophants, not all could be equally taught the great metaphysical doctrine; and while a few elect received such truths at their initiation, the masses were allowed to approach them with the greatest caution and only within the farthest limits of fact. 'From the DIVINE ALL proceeded Amun, the Divine Wisdom . . . give it not to the unworthy,' says a Book of Hermes. Paul, the 'wise *Master-Builder,*' but echoes Thoth-Hermes when telling the Corinthians 'We speak Wisdom among them that are perfect (the initiated) . . . *divine* Wisdom in a MYSTERY, even the *hidden* Wisdom.'
>
> H.P. Blavatsky

The golden tones of the humanity of the future have already begun to ring out around the globe, and have been greeted with gladness in the hearts of myriads of unknown human beings in every land. For those who have not yet felt it fully, or only intermittently within themselves, the problem is tunnel vision, an inability to see beyond and outside the narrow horizon of one's own myopic perception. This tunnel vision is a great obstacle to each and every one who wishes to come out of the multitude, especially in this extremely visual culture, descended from the peasants of the earth. In narrowness and instantaneity there is no basis for growth and enlightenment. The eyes and ears are proverbial liars. Rather, one must learn to use the eye of mind, to awaken the eye of the soul. Above all, in mystic meditation one must draw within one's own sanctuary in one's inmost heart, because only there can one come closer to the Logos in the Cosmos, closer to the living god in every man, woman and child on this earth. Many people are ready for this, now more than ever. But there are also, alas, some who are part of the sickness of the past.

Each human being, as a self-determining agent, is responsible for the opportunities and obstacles of his own making. Therefore, each must learn that to wish all human beings well means to hope that everyone may become a friend of the best in himself, may draw apart from the snake of separateness and the slime of selfishness, and emerge from the pit of ignorance, learning instead to use the senses and organs, and especially the sacred organ of the Logos called the tongue, on behalf of universal good. Yet, one cannot learn to affirm the authentic accents of human brotherhood all at once. Those who have made resolves to do so should not expect that they are abruptly going to become new people. At the same time, new beginnings are indeed possible.

All human beings know that they have had many opportunities to make some small difference to the quality of their life and consciousness. It is possible to make a much greater difference in the presence of the Guru and the Divine Wisdom, especially if one makes use of every opportunity, in the dawn and at twilight, at midday and perhaps even at midnight. Everyone can find some few moments during the day to devote himself to the sacred purpose of self-regeneration. That is the critical message of metapsychology. And that is why the opportunity is given to various individuals, though they may be ignorant of the *ABCs* of the *Sanatana Dharma*, to do that which over a hundred years very few could do effectively, to study Gupta Vidya, the Secret Doctrine, in a way that provides the basis for meditation. When the teachings are meditated upon daily, in conjunction with the use of *bija sutras* (mantrams given for the sake of creating a current that may be carried throughout the day), together with self-correction, hope is awakened. Regardless of the gravity effect from the past, individuals may make a new beginning; the more that beginning is made on behalf of all that lives, the more that beginning will become a holy resolve. It will be blessed by all the gods and guardians of the globe, and by the Avatar of the age.

This has nothing to do with nineteenth century rituals and Victorian habits, with slavish adherence to calendars and clocks. No one need labour under false burdens of expectation and regret bolstered by pseudo-psychological theories of human nature. These are but the rationalizations and residues of the failure of individuals to sort out their own lives, to see and acknowledge the nature of their obligations, needs and wants. Today, all over the globe, more courageous men and women than ever before are preparing themselves to become true learners and have already sensed and saluted in their hearts a new current of global awakening. Seeing beyond roles and discerning the principles of metapsychology within their own experience, by honest and voluntary work they are making their own modest but genuine contributions to the whole, thus inserting themselves into the humanity of the future and quietly unravelling the spiritual promise glimpsed in the vigil night of meditation.

The quintessential meaning of the contemporary revolution in human self-awareness is contained in the metapsychological teachings that are the basis of *Buddhi Yoga*. The moral diversity human beings exhibit, ranging from pure compassion to abject selfishness, is to be understood in terms of the distinction between human individuality and its transitory mask, the personality. The tendency of the outward character is determined by the inward polarity of *Manas*. As H.P. Blavatsky explains:

> The mind is dual in its potentiality: it is physical and metaphysical. The higher part of the mind is connected with the spiritual soul or Buddhi, the lower with the animal soul, the Kama principle. There are persons who never think with the higher faculties of their mind at all; those who do so are the minority and are thus, in a way, *beyond,* if not above, the average of human kind. These will think even upon ordinary matters on that *higher* plane.
>
> H.P. BLAVATSKY

The faculty of the mind that predominates in any given lifetime is a function of all the past thoughts and feelings of the Monad in its varied incarnations over millions of years. The selection of the life-atoms that constitute the mortal vestures proceeds under strict law, rooted in the metaphysical unity beyond the cosmos and apportioning the elements to the vestures according to the individual's acknowledgement, or denial, of that unity. When, over a course of lives, an individual has neglected the development of the higher faculties of *Manas*, the noumenal potential of spiritual consciousness becomes obscured by the thick encrustation of life-atoms impressed with selfishness.

> This is why it is so very difficult for a materialist — the metaphysical portion of whose brain is almost atrophied — to raise himself, or for one who is naturally spiritually minded, to descend to the level of the matter-of-fact vulgar thought. Optimism and pessimism depend on it also in a large measure.
>
> H.P. BLAVATSKY

If one's thinking is noetic, based upon that which is larger and more universal, and if, in this light, one considers calmly the lower and that which is lesser, one will be an optimistic person, glad that there are billions of human beings in the world, happy that children are being born, and above all, eager to greet the future. If, on the other hand, one is amongst those unfortunate people who have made pernicious alliances with the dark side of the moon, coming under its shadow through preoccupation with one's own shadow, one is *in extremis*. For such, no matter how many years of physical life may remain, it is, in fact, too late. At the moment of death, they will find that they have wasted their lives. Through meditation upon the shadow, through fascination with excreta, they have become afraid of the light. No one else has done this to them. They have excluded themselves from the school of human evolution and are unable to move onward with the awesome pilgrimage of humanity.

There are many such people in the world today, and, owing to their own selfishness, they are experiencing an extreme form of psychological terror. They, along with their inordinate selfishness, must and will disappear. Like *rakshasa* ghouls of the graveyard, they will make a great deal of noise before they are finished, but disappear they will because it is too late in Manasic evolution for abnormal selfishness. All human beings are, of course, concerned with survival and self-preservation to some degree, but there is a world of difference between this furtive selfishness and frenetic ego sickness. Ego sickness is abnormal selfishness; it has already created by the power of thought the very avenging demons which will destroy it. These incubi and succubi pursue the abnormally selfish in sleep and in waking life, all the time, until these dark monsters — created out of greed, out of fear of being wrong and making a fresh start, out of fear of the facts of spiritual life, out of exploitation of the patience and kindness, the generosity and magnanimity of others —surround their creator and close in for the kill.

This is no mere figure of speech, though it was graphically illustrated by Aldous Huxley in *The Devils of Loudun*. It is not merely a possibility, but a grave fact in the metaphysical realms of human existence beyond the veil of physical life. It is rooted in the capacity of manasic thought-energy to disturb and impress the atoms of the astral light. Drawing from the science of optics, accessible in a crude form to her readers in the nineteenth century, H.P. Blavatsky explains:

> ...the rays of thought have the same potentiality for producing forms in the astral atmosphere as the sunrays have with regard to a lens. Every thought so evolved with energy from the brain, creates *nolens volens* a shape.
>
> H.P. BLAVATSKY

One may have the illusion of free will, but this production of astral forms through the power of thought proceeds involuntarily. In the case of an ordinary human being, both this form and the process of its formation are entirely unconscious. One simply does not know what one has done. By contrast, however, in the case of an Adept, who chooses each thought with a beneficent and well-directed motive, the mental emanation can be sent forth with enough of his will and intelligence to accomplish his purpose. The Adept needs no visible media, no complex computer or elaborate postal service. He can instantly transmit a thought over millions of miles. Thus, all Adepts are in immediate and effortless communication with each other, and Adepts in the Army of the Voice are able to take orders from their Chief, who transmits the will of the Logos instantly to agents all over the globe, who thereby know what exactly they have to do.

Whilst this instant alertness to the Light of the Logos and the Voice of Vach will not be earned by humanity as a whole until future Rounds, the moment has come for men and women everywhere to choose between love of the Light and morbid slavery to shadows. The logic of Manasic evolution implies a division between forms fostered by astral attachment and vestures evolved through altruistic meditation. Each alternation of day and night, each cycle of birth, death and reincarnation, each pulse-beat and each breath taken is a living moment of choice, a link in the endless chain of potential spiritual growth. With every mental exhalation, one emanates into the common atmosphere either fresh blessings for all or the foul snares of one's future bondage. As the Monad's karma accumulates over the aeons, it does so amidst the vastly larger totals affecting the entire race, which are continuously adjusted by the Lipikas under the impersonal guidance of the laws of invisible Nature. It is the unwavering will of the Logos that every sentient atom of life shall realize its ultimate unity with the One Life, and become thereby an active centre of beneficent light energy, consecrated to the law of sacrifice — the law of its own being.

Manasic humanity today is at a moment like the dawn of Venus, filled with the promise of a future wherein societies and civilizations founded upon the sacrificial love of wisdom will flourish. Every dawn dispels the shadows of the night; they are wise in their time who learn to love the light they cannot yet see in its fullness, whose harbinger they can recognize in the bright messenger of the dawn. In a few brief hours on the clock of human evolution, the Sun of Truth will arise for all who are courageous enough to turn towards the East, and mankind will rediscover itself. Having chosen the noetic light of *Buddhi* within, it will find itself in the company and service of the Servants of the Logos, and engaged in the compassionate travail of the true City of Man.

THE PILGRIMAGE OF HUMANITY

Paranirvana is that supreme state of unconditioned consciousness which connotes freedom from the entire process of becoming, the 'chain of dependent origination' and involuntary incarnations. The soul's pilgrimage over eighteen million years of self-conscious existence, and for a much longer period in the future, is truly an awesome and arduous journey through the great Circle of Necessity. Each immortal soul has been repeatedly embodied in the seven kingdoms of Nature, and participated in every possible form through a collective monadic host. Each individual monad has at some remote time experienced the myriad modes of mineral, vegetable and animal life, as well as the variegated centres of consciousness of the three elemental kingdoms. In more recent manvantaric time every human being has traversed the tremendous gamut of contrasting states of mind that are induced by the polarities of self-conscious existence. All this is possible and necessary, according to arcane metaphysics, because "every atom in the Universe has the potentiality of self-consciousness in it, and is, like the Monads of Leibnitz, a Universe in itself, and *for* itself. *It is an atom and an angel.*" The Paranirvanic consummation of the soul's pilgrimage presupposes the existential realization that the individual self-consciousness of human beings is the dim reflection of the universal self-consciousness of the Dhyanis. These are the Buddhas of Contemplation, such as Amitabha overbrooding Gautama Sakyamuni, "manifesting through him whenever this great Soul incarnates on earth as He did in Tzon-kha-pa".

Since the enormous potential for divine regeneration is present in every atom, the conventional distinction between animate and inanimate matter is extremely misleading. Everything is alive through awareness; all is consciousness. A few people know intuitively, and many sense psychically, what the ancient schools of wisdom openly taught — that spiritual growth involves the interaction of incipiently self-conscious invisible centres of energy with already perfected human monads. The Hindu teachings about the thirty-three crores of *devas* and *devatas*, echoed in mythic allusions to sylphs, salamanders, undines and gnomes, are all references to elementals. In every single elemental life and in every point of invisible space there is potential self-consciousness and some degree of active intelligence. Owing to this ubiquitous presence throughout the course of evolution, the deeper the self-consciousness of human beings, the more effectively they can quicken the intellectual unfoldment of what is potentially present in the whole of life. In Gupta Vidya there are strict rules about magnetic specialization, an essential prerequisite to the creation through meditation of beneficent channels for consciousness. Nourished by meditation and protected by magnetic purity, consciousness becomes so charged with universal light that it can exercise complete control over the entire sphere of perception and activity.

There is a sum-total of potentials in consciousness, perception and energy that pertains to each self-conscious human monad over eighteen million years. This sum-total has a necessary connection with the spectrum of possibilities in any given lifetime for any human being. Owing to the immersion of consciousness in illusory time, the real person does not consist solely of what is seen at any particular moment, but is constituted by the sum of all the varied and changing conditions from the initial appearance in material form to eventual disappearance from the earth. From birth till death each human incarnation is a series of transformations that is seemingly endless, but which may be partly understood by considering the permutations and combinations of the seven sacred planets and twelve zodiacal signs acting through a variety of aspects and angles. Yet the myriads of transformations a human being undergoes on earth from birth to death are all encompassed by the small circle of time within which a single life is lived. Therefore there is a sum-total, which in turn is included within a much vaster sum-total, unknown to human beings in general, but which exists from eternity in the future and passes by degrees through matter to exist for eternity in the past. To intuit this existence is to awaken to the immense potential of self-consciousness as the guiding force of evolution; to sense its presence in each event is to embark on the path of *Paranirvana*. To witness its universal dimensions, so that the past and future lie before one like an open book, is to become a Mahatma for whom the grand sum-total is archetypally reflected in the earthly existence of every human soul.

It is possible in principle for the immortal soul to draw into the realm of self-conscious awareness any portion of the experience and knowledge that is already summed up in its immemorial pilgrimage. This would have been very difficult to conceive in the nineteenth century, but is more comprehensible in the age of DNA and the microprocessor. One needs little familiarity with electronics to recognize that millions of items of information can be registered in minute devices, and little awareness of contemporary biology to apprehend that every possible transformation of a human body over a lifetime is potentially present in the embryonic germ cell. Ancient wisdom teaches that by the end of the seventh month of development much more than can be grasped by modern biology is already inscribed in the foetal vesture as a set of possibilities. Crucial among these is the noetic capacity to make a decisive difference in the extent to which one draws upon and experiences the sum-total of possible configurations. By deep thought and study, by the daily use of true knowledge, by meditation and calm contemplation, by creative interaction with Nature and with other minds, human beings can affect the degree to which they self-consciously experience what is actually going on in all the vestures from the moment of birth to the moment of death.

Maya or illusion is inextricably involved in the idea of separate existence as a monad. From the philosophical perspective of universal self-consciousness, the immense pilgrimage of the human soul is somewhat unreal. Even from the standpoint of the monad enduring over eighteen million years, a hundred lives in succession is mayavic, rather like glancing through a few slides. A single life on earth is barely an instant, if entire solar systems which emerge and disappear over millions upon millions of years are mere winks in the Eye of Self-existence. What then is the meaning and value of a single human life? While there is an extraordinary range in potential human awareness, most beings are "living and partly living", in the phrase of T.S. Eliot. They are hardly aware of the dynamic processes behind incarnate existence, and from the perspective of the immortal soul they are not awake and scarcely alive. One has to come out of the psychic sleep of a lifetime for there to be a moment of true spiritual awakening to universal causation, human solidarity and the reality of a law-governed universe working ceaselessly through thought, will and feeling, on a cosmic plane but also in and through every single human being on earth. Spiritual awakening is not merely a shift in one's plane of consciousness, but a fundamental alteration of perspective regarding consciousness itself beyond all its planes of embodiment and manifestation.

> Maya or illusion is an element which enters into all finite things, for everything that exists has only a relative, not an absolute, reality, since the appearance which the hidden noumenon assumes for any observer depends upon his power of cognition. To the untrained eye of the savage, a painting is at first an unmeaning confusion of streaks and daubs of colour, while an educated eye sees instantly a face or a landscape. Nothing is permanent except the one hidden absolute existence which contains in itself the noumena of all realities. The existences belonging to every plane of being, up to the highest Dhyan-Chohans, are, in degree, of the nature of shadows cast by a magic lantern on a colourless screen; but all things are relatively real, for the cogniser is also a reflection, and the things cognised are therefore as real to him as himself.
>
> *The Secret Doctrine,* i 39

The Dhyan Chohans, including even the supernally numinous Ah-Hi, exist only during the *manvantara,* and at the end of it are reabsorbed into the Divine Darkness. How then can there be enlightened human beings much greater than Dhyan Chohans, capable of remaining awake in *Paranirvana* during the long night of non-manifestation? Only the highest Initiate can know the full meaning of the 'Ring Pass-Not' and hence the ultimate terminus of manvantaric growth, as well as the Infinity beyond. But by considering the principle that every human being is an admixture of all the elements of existence gradually perfected over myriads of lives, it is evident that every moment affects what will happen to a human being a million years from now, just as at every moment each individual is affected by what happened a million years ago. In a law-governed cosmos there can be no other way to make sense of the vastitude of human experience, the commonality of human potential, and the immeasurable range of states of mind and degrees of human freedom. As a compound of the essences of all the celestial hierarchies, and as That *(Tat)* which is beyond every essence, state and condition, the self-conscious being may succeed in rising beyond any hierarchy, class or combination of them.

Man can neither propitiate nor command the *devas.* There are no special favours in cosmic evolution. The Religion of Responsibility requires that each self-conscious human soul must strip away the suffocating mask of the personal ego to arrive at the full knowledge of the non-separateness of the Higher Self, the divine Triad overbrooding the incarnated human being. Typically, the Triad is far above the head and cannot come closer without something like a bursting of the skull, but the Triad itself is in total unison with the one absolute Self, the cosmic Triad. Through experiential knowledge of this transcendental unity, any soul can, even during terrestrial life, become 'as One of Us'. By eating of the fruit of Divine Wisdom which dispels soul-ignorance, human beings can become like the Elohim or Dhyanis, but they can also do much more than that. Yet even on that exalted plane, the spirit of solidarity and perfect harmony which reigns in each hierarchy in nature must extend over and protect them in every particular.

In the *Book of Job* it is suggested that no man's burden is greater than he can bear. There is that divine spark in all human beings which is capable of enduring every kind of trial, and at the moment of death it affords them a fleeting glimpse of the real world to which they belonged even while partly asleep during a lifetime of living and partly living. This psychic drowsiness is due to the desire to exist as a separate being in a form, and this thirst *(trishna)* is what all mystical training seeks to overcome. Unless one begins by subduing and transcending the intense will to exist as a separate being, one is not ready to enter the Path of spiritual enlightenment. One must relinquish existence as a physical or astral form, as a wandering mind and wavering heart, letting go of false, fickle and fleeting concerns induced by the shifting scenery and elusive imagery of sense-objects. One must renounce the belief that one belongs to a restricted circle of friends and foes, while fulfilling one's obligations to each and every human being one encounters the best one knows how. To enter into the community of mankind, to rebecome the ray that is truly oneself, is to begin what Krishna calls 'the divine discipline'. As one acquires a more universal perspective in relation to the masks of time — memory and desire, regret and anticipation, and the irrational fears that consolidate the shadow — they fall away and one's eyes are opened to the noumenal light of the invisible world. Then, ascending through a series of progressive awakenings, one can dissipate every kind of crippling self-concern until one's only reason for living is a profound sense of sacred obligation in the sphere of self-chosen duties. Through daily practice one experiences a deeper kinship with all that lives and breathes, a greater love of other human beings, a truer realization of the cosmic Self, a profounder conviction of universal brotherhood. One may thus come out of the world of the 'living dead' and approach the sanctuaries of sages who are awake even during *pralaya,* the night of non-manifestation.

The long and difficult journey, too vast to be fitted into any temporal scheme, may be seen in terms of realizing Universal Mind as absolute abstract Thought and hence as the permanent possibility of mental action, of which manifested mind is the concrete expression. Manifest cosmic mind includes the Ah-hi, the Dhyan Chohans and the collective hosts of spiritual beings which are the transmitters of Divine Thought and universal will. These are the intelligent Forces that affect every blade of grass, every pebble and everything that moves in this cosmos in which nothing is at rest. They inscribe and enact in Nature its laws, while they themselves act according to laws impressed upon them by still higher powers. Universal Mind comes into manifestation through cosmic hierarchies that are somewhat comparable to an army made up of divisions, brigades and regiments, each of which has its distinct individuality. The analogy is imperfect because cosmically there is freedom of action and mathematically defined responsibility for each and every grouping. Each is contained in a larger individuality from which it derives inspiration, and each contains lesser individualities to which it owes sacrificial service.

The Army of the Voice is an archetypal expression of what the *Bhagavad Gita* calls *Adhiyajna*, the primordial power of ceaseless sacrifice that makes life in any form possible. The *Adhiyajna* is present whenever a human being is breathed into or breathed out of a cosmic body or vesture. Each is a blessed beneficiary of the ceaseless cosmic sacrifice, from dawn to dusk, from birth to death, and at the *sandhyas* initiating *manvantara* and *pralaya*. It is through gratitude and devotion to the Logos as *Adhiyajna*, maintained over many lifetimes and ascending through ordered levels of manifestation, that human beings are most truly human. This gradual ascent is the work of the whole of evolution, and in the end it takes the host of immortal souls to the great day of 'Be-With-Us', which is not a fixed locus or final epoch but a sublime state of spiritual consciousness.

'It must not be supposed that the Logos is but a single centre of energy manifested from Parabrahmam; there are innumerable other centres . . . and their number is almost infinite in the bosom of Parabrahmam.' Hence the expressions, 'The Day of Come to us' and 'The Day of Be with us,' etc. Just as the square is the Symbol of the Four sacred Forces or Powers — Tetraktis — so the Circle shows the boundary within the Infinity that no man can cross, even in spirit, nor Deva nor Dhyan Chohan. The Spirits of those who 'descend and ascend' during the course of cyclic evolution shall cross the 'iron-bound world' only on the day of their approach to the threshold of Paranirvana.

The Secret Doctrine, i 134

If one wholly merges with the very highest radiations of the most unconditioned consciousness, one cannot possibly manifest or have any relationship to anything in time and space. Therefore the desire for liberation of human beings is merely a delusive anticipation of that highest consummation which comes under the law of cycles only at the end of a *manvantara.* Yet every pilgrim soul is eternally impelled from within by an immortal longing for reunion with its essential nature, its transcendent source.

If they reach it — they will rest in the bosom of Parabrahmam, or the 'Unknown Darkness,' which shall then become for all of them Light — during the whole period of Mahapralaya, the 'Great NIGHT,' namely, 311,040,000,000,000 years of absorption in Brahm. The day of 'Be-With-Us' is this period of rest or Paranirvana.

The 'Monad,' born of the nature and the very Essence of the 'Seven' (its highest principle becoming immediately enshrined in the Seventh Cosmic Element), has to perform its septenary gyration throughout the Cycle of Being and forms, from the highest to the lowest; and then again from man to God. At the threshold of Paranirvana it reassumes its primeval Essence and becomes the Absolute once more.

The Secret Doctrine, i 134 - 135

If this is the sublime promise and prospect for the whole of humanity at the end of an immense period of evolution, the meaning of individual enlightenment is the uninterrupted ascent towards universal self-consciousness. It presupposes the capacity to reach by intense meditation to the very threshold of that state and to choose an appropriate focus of noumenal, though relative, existence from which to overbrood one's manifesting self. One would ascend as high as one could, wholly centered upon the Spiritual Sun, with a supreme resolve to be of ceaseless benefit to the whole of life. At the summit one would stay at a critical distance from the threshold of enlightenment so as to be of effective help to beings lost in ignorance and confusion and wandering at their peril. For the *yogin* who has mastered many modes of training, this involves the ability to achieve at will within all his vestures full mastery of the true *kundalini*, the pristine power of *Buddhi*. A humble aspirant intently using the sacred teaching about the Spiritual Sun may have little knowledge of the psycho-spiritual centres and the higher states of consciousness, but may nevertheless experience and renew each day a deep sense of the oneness and transcendence of all life, which in reality is beyond form and colour, as the limitless light of electric intelligence. By preserving this sense intact within the heart as an unspoken but ever-present awareness, the chela is opening the door to a series of timely initiations by the Guru.

Those who have fulfilled such training encounter again at the final stage the fundamental choice between liberation and renunciation. Before this point is reached some may find at the moment of death, because of the sum-total of their desire for absorption, that the energy is moving upwards and they may be enabled to enter into a kind of lesser *nirvana* which to them may look like *Paranirvana*. But those *yogins* who have renounced the slightest desire for individual bliss or absorption, and have long since vowed to serve the whole of the human race, do not seek anything less than universal enlightenment. Fully cognizant of higher states of consciousness, they are able to remain fixed in the *turiya* state of spiritual wakefulness even amidst the delusive conditions of the world. Bearing witness to the Spirit in Silence while moving in and through the planes of maya, they are able to act as unseen helpers to that latent spark of aspiration present in all souls and atoms. In the light of authentic understanding of the true meaning of *Moksha*, H.P. Blavatsky cites the *Visishtadwaita Catechism*, suggesting that even its teachings are at one with Gnostic tenets regarding the deliverance of Sophia Achamoth, lost and labouring in the waters of ignorance on her way towards Supreme Light, by Krishna-Christos:

> After reaching Moksha (a state of bliss meaning 'release from Bandha' or bondage), bliss is enjoyed by it in a place called PARAMAPADHA, which place is not material, but made of Suddasatwa (the essence, of which the body of Iswara — 'the Lord' — is formed). There, Muktas or Jivatmas (Monads) who have attained Moksha, are never again subject to the qualities of either matter or Karma. 'But if they choose, *for the sake of doing good to the world*, they may incarnate on Earth.' The way to Paramapadha, or the immaterial worlds, from this world, is called Devayana. When a person has attained Moksha and the body dies: —
>
> 'The Jiva (Soul) goes with Sukshma Sarira from the heart of the body, to the Brahmarandra in the crown of the head, traversing Sushumna, a nerve connecting the heart with the Brahmarandra. The Jiva breaks through the Brahmarandra and goes to the region of the Sun (Suryamandala) through the solar Rays. Then it goes, through a dark spot in the Sun, to Paramapadha. The Jiva is directed on its way by the Supreme Wisdom acquired by Yoga. The Jiva thus proceeds to Paramapadha by the aid of Athivahikas (bearers in transit), known by the names of Archi-Ahas...Aditya, Prajapati, etc. The Archis here mentioned are certain pure Souls, etc., etc.'
>
> *The Secret Doctrine*, i 132

Anyone who daily thinks of the Spiritual Sun as the transcendent source of all light, life-energy and intelligence in the whole of Nature and humanity, and invokes it on behalf of universal good, cannot but be utterly suffused with the profoundest reverence, gratitude and obeisance to the enlightened beings that have attained *Paramapadha*. One cannot regularly contemplate the highest invisible forces within the Spiritual Sun without deriving from that source the beneficence of the creative, sustaining and regenerative energy that nourishes the divine hierarchies. When one senses the noumenal radiation of the metacosmic source of the hierarchies, one sees them all as sharing in a single light-essence which is hidden in every atom and also abides within the Cave of the Heart. Individuals who experience this, either in an ecstatic vision or in a series of profound meditations, come into a sacred orbit where great silence, deep calm and immense humility are needed to protect the integrity, the stability and the continuity of the experience. If one does not train in advance and at all times in this way, becoming increasingly tranquil, steadfast and humble, one will never really be able to breathe at the rarefied altitudes of spiritual awareness. One will simply not be able to partake of those supernal states of being that bring one closer to the *Atma-Buddhi-Manas* of the sun, and therefore to the Mahatmas, the Buddhas and the Dhyanis. Those who come into this orbit but cannot sustain it will be rapidly propelled downwards and the whole process will reverse itself. Because divine force can destroy as readily as it creates, this most sacred teaching was always preserved in silence in the oldest cultures of the human race. It is only hinted at in *The Secret Doctrine* in the hope that intuitive individuals who have a deep love of the human family, reverential gratitude to the Mahatmas, and a heroic and invulnerable determination to serve the Army of the Voice and to walk the Path, will resolve to use the teaching for the benefit of all souls.

Self-conscious human monads traversing the Circle of Necessity are eternal witnesses to the boundless compassion and unconditional benevolence of the *Adhiyajna*. Whenever individuals forget themselves and work for a larger group — whether for their family, community or society, or for the whole of humanity, or the entirety of nature — they become aware of a larger life and a vaster realm of being wherein there is an effortless surrender of the mayavic self. Millions upon millions of human beings seek forms of meritorious self-transcendence, but this does not mean that they will necessarily attain to pure self-consciousness, which requires intense meditation and preparation for initiation. Daily meditation is the essential starting-point, and if one enjoys calm contemplation and the silence of meditation one will in a short time, perhaps seven to fourteen years, become able to do whatever has to be done in the world while rooted in the immovable mind. This divine discipline, which each person has to accomplish in order to exist self-consciously as Spirit, gives meaning, beauty and purpose to all human life and evolution. Alas, while every human being is a vital part of the universal pilgrimage, in nearly every case virtually nothing of this journey is known to the incarnated soul. This means that its real life is hidden on another plane and it cannot ever connect with life on this plane without self-discipline. The earlier one makes a conscious effort to connect in any lifetime, the better it is for the soul. But when one moves in meditation beyond the earthly scene, one senses the strength and majesty of the *Guruparampara* chain and the Brotherhood of Bodhisattvas, the golden fellowship of Initiates from whom descend all the Avatars and Divine Incarnations in recorded and unrecorded time. Beyond the manifested hierarchies is the Self-existent Concealed Lord, parentless and one with the universal *Parabrahm*. This sacred mystery must be pondered within one's inmost sanctuary through deep meditation, so that one may come closer in one's secret, spiritual heart to the Source of all life, light and energy throughout this resplendent cosmos in which resonates the still, sad music of humanity.

TOWARDS
ENLIGHTENMENT

DEGREES OF ENLIGHTENMENT

The names of the deities of a certain mystic class change with every Manvantara. Thus the twelve great gods, Jayas, created by Brahmā to assist him in the work of creation in the very beginning of the Kalpa, and who, lost in Samadhi, neglected to create — whereupon they were cursed to be repeatedly born in each Manvantara till the seventh — are respectively called Ajitas, Tushitas, Satyas, Haris, Vaikunthas, Sadhyas *and* Adityas: *they are* Tushitas (*in the second Kalpa) and* Adityas *in this* Vaivasvata *period, besides other names for each age. But they are identical with the* Manasa *or* Rajasas, *and these with our incarnating Dhyan Chohans. They are all classes of the* Gnana-devas. . . . *There are real* Devagnanams, *and to these classes of* Devas *belong the* Adityas, *the* Vairajas, *the* Kumaras, *the* Asuras, *and all those high celestial beings whom Occult teaching calls* Manaswin, *the* Wise, *foremost of all.*

The Secret Doctrine, ii 90

According to the ancient Puranas, the first gods were the Virajas, the Agnishvatta Pitris, the gods and fathers of the gods. Beheld by Brahmā with the all-seeing eye of yoga, the Agnishvattas inhabit the eternal sphere called Virajaloka. From these incorporeal Pitris, unshadowed by any astral phantom, come all the Hosts of the *Manasa*, the spiritual ancestors who endowed nascent humanity with the potency of self-conscious thought over eighteen million years ago. The recognition and realization of this divine heredity is essential to the seminal work of the Theosophical Movement, which was, is and ever shall be the progressive elevation of the *Buddhi* and *Manas* of the human race. All human beings are pristine rays of *Mahat*, universal mind, and therefore all human beings are inherently capable of universal self-consciousness, transcending every object and every subject. The buddhi-manasic potential of humanity is not, in principle, limited by any field that requires the focussing of consciousness upon any specific class of particulars. Divine self-consciousness has not only the effortless capacity for intense interior concentration upon any class of objects, but also the assured capacity for freeing itself from confinement through any class of particulars. Human consciousness is intrinsically capable of conceiving all possible as well as all actual beings, all possible and actual subjects and objects. Through the joyous awareness of their essentially divine nature, human beings are capable not only of seeing humanity and the entirety of manifested Nature in terms of all that may be known about the present and the past, but also of visualizing the vast range of possibilities constituting the future of Nature and Humanity.

It was the divine intent of the solar ancestors of the human race that humanity should awaken and master this latent capacity for *kriyashakti*. This would naturally encompass the ability to visualize the future development of flora and fauna and of the elemental kingdoms, as well as the mineral, vegetable and animal kingdoms. In particular, far-sighted individuals may fearlessly extend the horizon of human powers and possibilities, and imagine what fully self-conscious human beings might be like in the far distant future. This sovereign capacity of human beings to go far beyond any particular set of facts is not a matter of mere idle speculation or sporadic invention. If this sacred activity of calmly visualizing the future is sustained with deep concentration that transcends the realm of memory and sensation, it will penetrate with depth and intensity into a much subtler plane of existence, wherein all matter is undifferentiated, primordial and fiery. This is the plane of the supersensuous aether, the *Akasha*, which is exceedingly subtle, plastic and pliable to persistent ideation.

Through such intense concentration, human beings may actually help fashion the noumenal prototypes of the future. This is a sacred theurgic activity, and to be able to sustain it one would not only have to become practised and proficient in deep meditation, but also to become dispassionate and detached towards the existing world of objects and subjects. Certainly, one would have to free oneself from the crude memory of cursory events that impinge, mostly through sensation, pleasure and pain, upon the agitated personality. In fact, one would have to disengage oneself from all the chaotic affinities that one has formed in the astral body with ephemeral events, meretricious attractions and concretizing tendencies. To engage in this profound self-purification, one must learn to stay in a meditative state of voidness, experiencing what St. John of the Cross called the dark night of the soul. After purging all the lower affinities and supplanting them with finer tendencies originating in the higher Self, one may gradually become directly conscious of the higher affinities of the immortal soul. It is at this point that the awakened soul may become immediately aware of the different classes of hierarchies and creators involved in the spiritual lineage of humanity. Among the myriad classes of creators, human beings have a special affinity with highly evolved divine intelligences allied with the *sukshma sharira*, what might be called the subliminal aspect of the astral form. Every human being has recognizable affinities with the myriad gods, and with all the divine intelligences that endlessly circulate within the supersensuous ether of Space. Potentially, human consciousness may inhabit not merely spaces on and around the earth, but also interplanetary spaces, intrasolar spaces and spaces extending even to those that circle round the nucleus of the central Spiritual Sun.

The profound nature and enormous range of human potential is hardly comprehensible to most ordinary human beings. Even a partial incarnation of true buddhi-manasic genius will produce a highly sensitive individual capable of remarkable flashes of genius, extraordinary vision and divine intuition. Mozart was one such genius, a shining example of a free spirit who inhabited a world that has no relationship to the world as we know it. These rare souls may be expansively buoyant in their relationships to human beings and also be daringly outspoken and maddeningly unorganized in a worldly sense. For such a kaleidoscopic mind, replete with musical vibrations — the endless permutations, patterns and resonances of Akashic sound — it is very difficult to make a practical accommodation to ordinary human consciousness. Instead, such boisterous beings are in continual communication with the *devas*, with divine beings and divine intelligences, and are effortlessly capable of experiencing the music of the spheres as well as the divine dance *(lila)* of the noumenal plane.

Even such souls, however, can scarcely give a sufficient indication of the immense range of creative ideation. It flourishes freely in a realm impossible to map, impossible to delimit or even to define. Whether one talks in the language of comparison and contrast, or in terms of individuation and universalization, no category can convey enough about the inexhaustible range of possible conceptions that belong to the vast realm of seminal ideation. Yet if one begins to discern something of the nature of these wondrous possibilities, it becomes clear that there can be conscious alterations, by controlled ideation, in human beings, which not only transcend *kama manas* — the brain-mind caught up in the volatile and ever-changing realm of sensory particulars — but may even gain a skilful mastery at some level over hosts of elementals, and then delegate many of the functions that belong to the lower quaternary to a trained set of elementals.

Everyone has some experience, at a preliminary level, of such training. An extremely experienced cook, even an experienced driver, may have some sense of being involved with intelligences or elementals that seem to function without constant guidance. These entities have been programmed, one might say, to respond flexibly and to become extremely sensitive to all the actual and possible features of a situation. Whilst one may gain some elementary sense of this from such ordinary examples, it is inadequate to convey a full sense of the complete mastery over elementals that one finds, for example, in Shakespeare's *The Tempest*. Prospero the Magus has in Ariel a highly skilled controller over the elemental field who is at the same time a perfect instrument of Prospero. This entirely realistic example reveals the ever-present possibility in human ideation of delegating whole classes of functions through trained elementals. In practice, this requires a transformed relationship between the Lunar Pitris — who have given humanity all the elements of its lower quaternary — and the Solar Pitris — who have lit up in humanity the flame of self-consciousness. Only by forming self-conscious affinities with the Agnishvatta Pitris, who are responsible for all the *Manasa*, may one gain such mastery.

To establish that relationship one must move to a realm of meta-ethics and of noetic magic, far removed from all ordinary conceptions. What in other people are involuntary and compulsive tendencies can, in fact, be brought together in ways in which there is a precision in the orchestration of elemental intelligences in the performance of a wide variety of activities. All these activities would be commanded by the astral shadow of the Lunar Pitris, which itself has become highly responsible and wholly responsive to the Solar Dhyani who has become more fully incarnated. Here it is helpful to draw an analogy with the macro-processes of evolution, which may be put in terms of the following stages:

> Three stages in the elemental side; the mineral kingdom; three stages in the objective physical side — these are the seven links of the evolutionary chain. A descent of spirit into matter, equivalent to an ascent in physical evolution; a re-ascent from the deepest depths of materiality (the mineral) towards its *status quo ante*, with a corresponding dissipation of concrete organisms up to Nirvana — the vanishing point of differentiated matter.
>
> *Five Years of Theosophy*

The progressive descent of spirit into matter involves an increasing obscuration of spirit. To be able to elaborate, extend and experience the matrix of matter, there must be a temporary loss of conscious access to innate, timeless and unbounded spirituality. On the other side of the evolutionary arc, to be able to free the spiritual will is to reduce and refine, to concentrate and reshape matter, so that one becomes less involved with gross life-atoms and more capable of dealing with the most sensitive, refined and supersensuous life-atoms. These in turn are capable of responding as naturally and as reliably to the spiritual will as a fine musical instrument to the hands of a master. Such a maestro is not focussed upon either instrument or script, but having mastered them both, creates and re-creates sound through his own metaphysical imagination.

Long before this can happen to human beings in general, long before the beginning of the Sixth Race, there must be a conscious development, within the Fifth Sub-Race of the Fifth Race, of an impartial, impersonal and universal sense of justice in the moral realm. This can only come from a freedom from all possible roles and a capacity to enact them freely, while at the same time being able to see beyond them. The vanguard of the Fifth Root Race in the Fifth Sub-Race arose essentially in Europe and Scandinavia, going back to ancient Nordic conceptions of law, self-respect, honour and freedom. Later, the whole range of Germanic peoples, coming down to the Mediterranean world, and above all the rich heritage of England and France, contributed to this remarkable development. The greatest creative geniuses over thousands of years in that part of the world have created complex languages and also a scintillating spectrum of conceptual possibilities that is still to be fully assimilated by many human beings. Unfortunately, most human beings, especially in the last hundred years, have become mentally slavish and morally parasitic, subsisting only because of mass education and mass culture. Strutting and posturing, they cling to copies upon copies of the shadows of shadows of the original insights of the greatest minds. Even the better products of contemporary culture scarcely have even an indirect awareness of secondary and third-order reflections of the seminal ideation of the vanguard of the Fifth Sub-Race. To break this destructive cycle of degradation, it is necessary to go beyond the outward ephemera of contemporary culture by developing the power of meditation with a degree of continuity and skill that is paralleled by the development of a responsible detachment, rooted in the fact that one has discharged all one's duties. Only when one fulfils all one's familiar obligations in many spheres can one become truly detached — free to contemplate and free to go beyond the claims of the world — and also free to give full support to an arduous programme of systematic and continuous spiritual meditation.

This theurgic activity, which is now so crucial to the Fifth Sub-Race, was laid down in its essentials in the First Sub-Race of the Fifth Root Race in India. Here in the 1975 Cycle one may be helped through a variety of sacred texts, especially through the *Yoga Vasishtha*. Even though it might have been written down relatively recently (namely, in the last two thousand years), it actually records the teachings given a million years ago in the time of Rama by the sage Vasishtha. The *Yoga Vasishtha* sets forth the holy discourses given by the Sage in the court of Rama, the great King-Initiate and incarnated Avatar who was no other than the being who later became Krishna. Rama invited the Rishi, who was beyond time, outside history and representative of the realm of the transcendent, to transmit the quintessence of the highest wisdom in regard to the Self, in regard to mind, error, happiness, virtue, and also in regard to the highest exemplification of living liberation, the *Jivanmuktas*. The Sage offered disquisition upon disquisition, repeatedly and in diverse modes, using rich and telling metaphors, but always reverting to certain central questions based upon the relation between the real and the unreal. Here the terms 'real' and 'unreal' are not applied merely to the world of fugitive sense-perceptions, but to immense periods of time, to entire worlds and *manvantaras*. From that elevated standpoint, one is asked to generate an active sense of reality which is more fundamental, more durable and much more meaningful, and which therefore can be carried over millions upon millions of years. That is the exalted philosophical level at which Vasishtha speaks. At the core of his Teachings are profound questions about the relation of the unmanifest to the manifest.

In the *Yoga Vasishtha* the supreme basis of a consecrated life of conscious immortality and ceaseless contemplation was provided at the beginning, as also in the later climactic development, of the Fifth Root Race. To rise in consciousness to this level, much less go beyond it, is to develop a radically new attitude towards the whole concept of conquest and control, a heightened sense of the invisible world of elementals and an entirely new conception of noetic magic involving the exercise of *kriyashakti*, creative visualization. This requires the sovereign capacity to alchemize and transform all one's lower vestures. And it is the testimony of the Sage that this is possible only if one can activate potentials in the subtlest vestures. It is essential to awaken certain higher subdivisions of *Manas* in relation to specific subdivisions of *Buddhi* and to bring them together.

This daring programme, which goes directly to the heart of the Theosophical Movement, is really a concerted effort to stimulate the metaphysical imagination of thinking beings who have the courage and freedom to see beyond the limits of their environment, beyond the parameters of their parochial, familial and cultural affinities. Those who can go beyond these customary limitations, and who can truly adopt a universal perspective of the human heritage, will be able to see behind all the great myths of all humanity certain inspiring central conceptions which throw light not only upon the forgotten language of dreams and visions, but also upon the world as it is. A true awakening of spiritual imagination inevitably and wholly changes one's view of what it is to be alive and who one is. It also generates a rich inner life, joyous and serene, but rooted in a relaxed mastery over all the obligations of one's outer life. Whilst accomplishing all of these with ease, completing them with only a portion of oneself, one will keep free the rest of oneself to continue to gestate the highest conceptions.

The effortless performance of every obligation, whilst established in transcendence of the outer world, involves a rethinking of the fundamental nature of attention to good and evil, to right and wrong. This would also be connected with a reconceptualization of what are seen as limitation and imperfection, suffering and misfortune, in the so-called real world. Through a meditative metaphysical awareness of the *Agathon* outside space and time, one must develop a compassionate and therapeutic understanding of the moral opposites in manifestation.

> Good and Evil are twins, the progeny of Space and Time, under the sway of Maya. Separate them, by cutting off one from the other, and they will both die. Neither exists *per se*, since each has to be generated and created out of the other, in order to come into being; both must be known and appreciated before becoming objects of perception, hence, in mortal mind, they must be divided.
>
> *The Secret Doctrine,* ii 96

Good and evil as an inseparable pair of opposites may be thought of in terms of the relationship of manifested and differentiated light and shadow. Here one is speaking not of noumenal light, not of that which originates from the centre of the hexagon, the light of *Daiviprakriti,* nor even of Fohat, which is the synthesis of all phenomenal light-energies. Rather, one is addressing a level that is much below the level of primordial manifestation and is concerned with the world of chaos and contrast, the realm of highly concretized perceptions. Generally, human beings have a narrowly limited view of light and, therefore, also of shadow. As the human instruments are imperfect, they give a dull and distorted conception of light and shadow. This is the inevitable outcome of the limited spatio-temporal horizon which engages consciousness in the sensorium. It operates especially strongly in memory and sensation, through the notion of the past and through expectations focussed upon a concretized and foreshortened future. All these perceptions and conceptions are under the sway of *maya.* There is, therefore, an element of unreality and exaggeration, an element of deception, in all moral concepts derived from such consciousness.

This may be seen at work in many ways. One might belong

to a particular family, a certain class or to some specific community. Within such a context, it might appear that there is an extraordinary difference between human beings, such that they are clearly divided between 'the good guys' and 'the bad guys'. Some insight into the deceptive nature of contrast may be found in the work of the novelist Claude Houghton, who specialized most of his life in studying criminals and defending them. Moving in the underworld of London, he won the respect of a large number of criminals. He discovered in that underworld many senior police officers whose whole task was to befriend the most important of the crooks. He thus discovered a very complicated kind of understanding between both sets of individuals. Behind the façade of social life and its facile generalizations, he saw there were innumerable unexpected and complicated shades and blendings of goodness and evil, of strength and weakness, of courage and timidity, that mocked any exaggerated contrast of good and evil. Some of the authentic complexity of human beings can also be seen in Shakespearean plays, where every character has an element of absurdity and a possibility of transcendence; everyone is changing all the time, and by the end may, in unexpected ways, be elevated.

Seen from the objective standpoint of a great dramatist, the entire gamut of human character is so great that one must begin to accept that any sort of harsh contrast between good and evil is subjective and deceptive. Such contrasts are based upon external signs and are limited owing to the habitually limited contexts in consciousness in which people ordinarily move. Yet it is precisely these limitations which impose upon individuals tremendous burdens of fear and expectation, as well as induce them to indulge in judgementalism. From the exalted standpoint of an enlightened being, as Buddha once said, all differences between all human beings are as nothing compared to the tremendous difference between the enlightened and the unenlightened. Once one registers the huge abyss separating the great benefactors and divine ancestors of the human race from ordinary human beings, one can clearly see the relativity of one's perceptions regarding good and evil, right and wrong. Even more is required if one is going to be not merely an objective observer or a sympathetic judge, but a mature being responsible for others. Again, one may be helped by examples — a wise mother with a large family made up of difficult and easy children, or a wise schoolteacher, who truly wants to release the potential and do the best for a large class of different people. One might also think of a wise healer, a shaman, who must not only diagnose but also cure a great variety of suffering individuals. But whilst such examples can help clarify the nature of compassion, they serve only as dim approximations of the boundless compassion and beatific grace of the enlightened.

The only way to move towards that distant goal is through practical altruism now. If one truly desires to awaken *Buddhi*, one must begin to learn how to act non-judgementally and responsibly on behalf of others. Human beings who are not merely concerned with judging, let alone absolutizing, the differences between human beings, but who want to help human beings to change their condition, have to engage, either semi-consciously or with full self-consciousness, in a kind of spiritual alchemy. They must first help to change the vocabulary of people. They must minimize the use of the words 'cannot' and 'impossible'. They must discourage the phrase "I won't". They must stress what can be done here and now. Instead of saying that nothing can be done, people must be encouraged to discover the first step that can be taken right now. This requires an alchemical alteration in one's view of what is bad. That which is bad is that which is still alterable. Inflexibility resides purely on the plane of effects. Considered on the plane of causes, it is based upon a false idea which, though persistent and therefore strong, can nevertheless be modified and qualified. In time, indeed, it can be replaced by the true idea of which it is a distorted reflection or even a polar opposite.

To be able to assist others in altering their perception of what is limited or limiting, to be able to help others to see opportunities where they would otherwise feel blanked out, is an alchemical art. It involves being able to see the dynamic relationship between limited goods and limited evils. Potentials of the greater good often lie within limited evils, just as the dangers of shadows often lie in prospects that seem to offer the greater good. This alchemical art is difficult to describe because it can only be learnt through daily practice. Put simply, no one can really know anything about human nature if he or she becomes an expert in human weakness. At best, one can only become a candidate for maleficent magic, or sorcery. To have any authentic knowledge of human nature and to help human beings grow, one has to become an ingenious expert on the inherent good in human beings. One must be able to put the case for any and every human being on earth.

If one truly wishes to help humanity, one must, like a good physician, be willing to recognize illnesses for what they are and call things by their proper names. One cannot soft-pedal or deny the existence of extreme and unnatural selfishness.

> Spirituality is on its ascending arc, and the animal or physical impedes it from steadily progressing on the path of its evolution only when the selfishness of the *personality* has so strongly infected the real *inner* man with its lethal *virus*, that the upward attraction has lost all its power on the thinking reasonable man. In sober truth, vice and wickedness are an *abnormal, unnatural* manifestation, at this period of our human evolution — at least they ought to be so. The fact that mankind was never more selfish and vicious than it is now, civilized nations having succeeded in making of the first an ethical characteristic, of the second an art, is an additional proof of the exceptional nature of the phenomenon.
>
> *Ibid.,* ii 110

There is nothing more horrifying than the kamarupic portrait of an extremely selfish personality. There is nothing more ugly than *tanha,* the desperate clinging to the physical body. These common evils are, in fact, much more difficult to dispel than the so-called dramatic examples of evil that so fascinate popular culture.

The wise individual who truly wants to gain a greater knowledge of human nature must grow deaf to the chaotic sounds that emerge from the hollow sounding-box of the insecure personality. He must see every person from the profound standpoint of the indwelling ray of the immortal soul, the trapped ray of universal mind. Those who are in right earnest in wanting to work actively for the humanity of the future must experience a good deal of what one of the Mahatmas characterized as "swimming *in adversus flumen.*" To be able to gain a dynamic and therapeutic view of human nature, they must go far beyond any absolutizing or relativistic conceptions of good and evil. They must, on behalf of the future, restore a consciousness of the ineffable presence within themselves, and all humanity, of that which was in the beginning, the divine light of *Mahat,* the sacred lineage of the Agnishvatta Pitris.

The seeds of Wisdom cannot sprout and grow in airless space. To live and reap experience, the mind needs breadth and depth and points to draw it towards the Diamond Soul. Seek not those points in Maya's realm; but soar beyond illusions, search the eternal and the changeless SAT, *mistrusting fancy's false suggestions.*

The Voice of the Silence

THE PATH OF RENUNCIATION

Renounce and then enjoy this world.
Isopanishad

Starting upon the long journey immaculate; descending more and more into sinful matter, and having connected himself with every atom in manifested Space — *the* Pilgrim, *having struggled through and suffered in every form of life and being, is only at the bottom of the valley of matter, and half through his cycle, when he has identified himself with collective Humanity. This,* he has made in his own image. *In order to progress upwards and homewards, the 'God' has now to ascend the weary uphill path of the Golgotha of Life. It is the martyrdom of self-conscious existence. Like Visvakarman he has to sacrifice* himself to himself *in order to redeem all creatures, to resurrect from the many into the* One Life. *Then he ascends into heaven indeed; where, plunged into the incomprehensible absolute Being and Bliss of Paranirvana, he reigns unconditionally, and whence he will re-descend again . . .*
The Secret Doctrine, i 268

The immortal individuality of every human being is overbrooded by a luminous Dhyani, and it persists as a distinct Monad during its entire Manvantaric pilgrimage of myriad incarnations in mortal vestures. As *Atman*, the Monad is one in fiery essence with *Paramatman*; as the Buddhic vehicle it is the Dhyan Chohanic light-energy; and as self-conscious *Manas*, the individual Monad is an integral portion of the Great Sacrifice, the mysterious *Adhiyajna*, the ensouling Mind and Heart of all humanity. Immovably fixed at the highest pole of the spectrum of consciousness, the Divine Prototype is both the noumenal cause and silent watcher of its successive projections into the shadowy region of phenomenal change. The partial incarnation of the immortal Monad in every personality is a sacrificial participation in the shadowy side of existence. It carries into every descent a luminous spark of the supernal light of compassionate awareness, thus endowing each of its lunar vestures with the personal prerogative of reflective consciousness, choice and discrimination, moral conscience and responsibility.

All self-consciousness is inherently ethical in essence, and is made possible through the voluntary sacrifice of the Immortal Triad. And yet, much of what is sensed and mirrored by the human Ego in its incarnation into a mortal vesture cannot serve the moral purposes of its immemorial pilgrimage, owing to the recurrent subversion of Manasic ideation through the sway of unregulated *kama* and attendant rationalizations of weakness and servility. For the human being the grossest plane and enslaving principle are not the physical, with its molecular matter constructed out of countless elemental 'lives', but the chaotic astral plane of frustrated cravings, fears and foolish imaginings. These form clouds of vapour which obscure mental perception and obstruct the noetic capacity to focus the Buddhic light of the *Atman* with alertness and awareness, deliberation and detachment, calmness and creativity.

To render the priceless privilege of noetic insight relevant in daily life requires strength of concentration, serenity of feeling and skill in action. This creative state of being necessitates the withdrawal of the wandering mind from the hypnotic spell of nebulous sensations, compulsive reactions and repressed emotions. The analytical mind must be yoked to a still centre through the persistent negation of the false identity gleaned from the succession of humdrum events and the melodramatic moods of the shadowy self. The self-sacrifice of noetic consciousness enables the reflected rays within the lunar realm of heterogeneous matter and cloudy confusion to draw back to the parent sun and profit from its cosmic splendour. Everything turns upon true self-consciousness, which is the Manvantaric gift of the God in man as well as the grace of the Guru given to the selfless devotee in any auspicious cycle of growth.

The profound challenge to human beings moving in the realm of the mortal and the conditioned is to awaken a therapeutic awareness of the potential and the unmanifest. Each and every human being is invariably helped in deep dreamless sleep when the Immortal Self is in its original state of timeless consciousness, analogous at its own level to Paranirvanic unconditionality. Thus it is possible for everyday life to go on even amidst the psychic confusion, the complicated enmeshing of events, and the karmic burden of all the misused and contaminated life-atoms that make matter seem sinful. The daily replenishment from the inner reserves of noetic consciousness is made possible through the magic of *sushupti*. To sustain this vibration in waking life and utilize the resources of deep meditation in the sphere of mundane duties, one needs continually to let go of all mental habits of narrow self-reference. One must break up the inert assemblage of ingrained tendencies which consolidate into a shallow conception of isolated identity. Even when through moralistic discipline this conditioned self becomes increasingly righteous, bound up with ostentatious virtues, with self-protective habits, with worthy resolves and pious aspirations, it still acts as a fragile crystallization of fickle identity and an arbitrary limitation upon the attributeless Self.

The Path of true spiritual self-consciousness commences at that crucial point where one is ready to live in and through diverse beings. This is neither the natural stance of humanity in general nor the mental posture of many human beings who have a fleeting attraction to the Path of self-redemption. Nevertheless, every soul has some implicit sense of human growth, some elementary empathy towards others, which enables language itself to be meaningful. The unspoken reciprocities that make everyday interaction and humane understanding possible even at the simplest level presuppose a pervasive intersubjectivity in self-consciousness. This is the unmanifest Mahabuddhic potential behind collective evolution at every level, but to be able to get beyond its instinctual and outward modes, individuals must consciously and confidently identify with the Mind and Heart of all Humanity.

The silent martyrdom of self-conscious existence becomes real enough with the cool recognition that everyone's limitation is also one's own. The harrowing pain at the inability of higher consciousness to avail itself fully of vestures provided under karma must be experienced by the awakened individual as a mere instance of universal pain. The intense realization of human suffering is not a once-and-for-all attainment, but a continuous Buddhimanasic expansion of awareness and a quickening of sensitivity together with an intense longing, on behalf of the entire human race, for Divine Wisdom. One must learn to keep awake and to sleep, to eat and bathe and work cheerfully on behalf of all living beings. One must enjoy traversing the daily round of familiar duties and sacrificial obligations, consecrating all these to *Lokasangraha*, the welfare of the world. Above all, one must discover the disarming simplicity of joyous devotion through selfless acts, sacred studies and deep meditations offered, like a leaf, a flower or a fruit, to Krishna, the Great Giver. This unconditional love and ceaseless sacrifice must be attempted by all those who would wish to come out and be separate, in the words of Paul, who would like to relinquish their illusory existence and begin to live anew, immersed in the potent current of spiritual evolution.

The true martyrdom of self-conscious existence necessarily entails the total renunciation of any possible concept of personal identity and also of individual progress. Monadic individuation has validity and meaning solely in the sacred act of, and entirely for the sake of, intelligently focussing the universal light of the *Atman*. It has no other function. To be able to renounce this individuality completely, relinquishing at the core even the seed-idea of any conception of personal virtue, individual excellence or spiritual progress separate from the whole of humanity, is to blend the mind with the soul, and even more the light of the soul with the luminous Paramatmic essence of the *Adhiyajna*, the Great

Sacrifice. *Agniyoga* burns out the root illusion of individuality in the fires of self-purgation.

When many first encounter the vast perspective and true proportions of the Secret Path of Renunciation, they become bewildered because they hastily assume they are inherently incapable of following it. The origin of this instinctual response is actually the delusive notion, deeply embedded in the unrefined psyche, that man is a fortuitous concurrence of atoms fatigued by external stimuli, involuntary emotions, incoherent thoughts and the appalling waste of energy through pseudo-knowledge. The personality is reinforced by a defensive posture of false omniscience at the mundane level which is nothing but mulish obstinacy and a pathological refusal to see the light. This arises from the fear-ridden reluctance to learn from others, to risk the pain of growth in awareness, to give moral shocks to the lunar vesture so that it can be shaken out of its automatic and habitual responses, all of which are based upon intertwined illusions in relation to time, space, motion, causality, karma, and above all, selfhood. To let go of such mental trappings and emotional reactions, learning to recognize the subtler and specious forms in which they reappear and relinquishing them yet again, must produce a triple revolution in awareness — in the subject of one's creative contemplation, in the object of one's constant devotion, and in one's intrinsic capacity to consecrate the simplest acts of life.

This fundamental revolution in thought and feeling, word and deed, will alchemically transmute the ways in which one looks at the world and employs the sense-organs of hearing, taste, smell and touch. The more one can calmly sit down and, in the light of the potent ideal of universal compassion, concede the absurdity of much that many people call living in the world, the more one can give a radical shake-up to the entire system. One can quietly begin in the silence after the storm, to induce a necessary state of separation of all the elements which have coagulated into ossified structures, breaking up the clusters and refining life-atoms through meditation upon voidness and fullness. By blanking out and refusing to give energy or indulgence to these many false identities or masks of the soul, one can reawaken noetic insight within a stream of consciousness of the sacredness of life and the One Source of Light-Energy.

Simpler peoples living in uncluttered cultures have often employed effective and graphic images to represent the corruption of consciousness through a false sense of personal identity. An angry person is sometimes portrayed as possessed by a malevolent red devil dancing upon his head. Children taught to think in terms of such powerful if intuitive images soon become aware that to fall into a state of temper is to give oneself over to some perverse manikin, to some demonic imp which may itself be a simulacrum or shadow of one's own unacknowledged fears. To think imaginatively of elementals in this way is to begin to see that a great portion of what one calls oneself and one's own is a costly delusion, for which the karmic negation is breakdown, despair and death.

One's personal identity has no continuity whatsoever except through repetition of signs and sounds, and no intrinsic validity except through passive acquiescence or emotional reinforcement from the outside. Inevitably, Nature responds in the language of suffering, giving repeated shocks to the psyche and in this way some progress is made in inward freedom from the inertia of delusion. If there were no suffering, which is the merciful teacher and stern awakener of consciousness, there would be no way for the cowardly individual to let go of obsessions. Thanks to therapeutic suffering there is at least some stimulus and hope for renunciation of outworn preoccupations. But as people relinquish illusions, they become so infatuated with a new sense of liberated selfhood that they resent any reminder of their past errors and persisting misconceptions of themselves and others. Thus they erect fresh barriers between their self-image and the rest of humanity, falling prey repeatedly to possession or obsession by elemental forces coloured by entrenched kamamanasic rationalizations.

How many people in the presence of children with temper

tantrums think back to their own temper tantrums? How many people recognize in the illusions of those ten or fifteen years younger the reminders of similar snares in their youth? How many, when they see people ten or twenty years older who are trapped in a pathetic refusal to learn afresh from life, can see analogies with their own resistance to learn and their own crippling fear of coming to terms with their costly errors? Anyone so blessed by karma as to have heard the inspiring teaching concerning the Path of Renunciation should show the courage to overcome smug self-centeredness and enslavement to pride and prejudice. In a strictly unmetaphorical sense, the disciple's sojourn on earth should be a compassionate mode of wise participation in the lives of other human beings through the empathetic recognition of every possible illusion and its alchemical transmutation. Many people prefer not to recollect what they were five or ten years ago in negative terms, but would rather live in the undisturbed oblivion of their current self-image and thoughtless drift. This is a sad waste of their present incarnation, unpardonable in a would-be disciple, without any real benefit to the immortal soul. The higher principles cannot effectively incarnate and the Divine Triad cannot be invoked as a guardian and guide unless the individual purges his consciousness of whatsoever obscures the thread of moral purpose.

The true seeker finds a firm basis for spiritual resolve by focussing concentrated attention upon a universal perspective, while gaining skill in action in the arena of daily duties. The sacred task of purifying and perfecting manasic self-consciousness, through effortless renunciation and sacrificial self-transcendence, takes many lives. Humanity, in general, will become fully Manasic only in the distant future, in the Fifth Race of the Fifth Round. The further development of *Manas* that should take place in the present Fifth and in the coming Sixth Sub-race of the Fifth Root Race in the Fourth Round is proportionately small for myriads of human beings who are half asleep most of the time. This is readily confirmed by considering how much of the potency of thought is untapped, because so little thinking is truly universal, and how much the volatile energy of volitional desire is wasted, because extremely little is expended on behalf of the immortal individuality.

Most of what people call feeling is mere emotion, which causes wear and tear in the astral vesture. This wastage has as its ideational basis an arbitrary one-life assumption, which is only rendered hypocritical by those who pay lip-service to a salvationist belief in reincarnation but are actually captive to bodily cycles and a physical conception of age and vitality. Yet, while many human beings are not able to be highly Manasic, if any have drawn under the karma of former lives into the proximity of *Brahma Vach* or Divine Wisdom, the spiritual ideation of the deathless race of Seers and Sages, then great indeed is their privilege and its attendant responsibility.

Manas, which descends from and corresponds to *Akasha,* the fifth universal cosmic principle, can be existentially recognized in terms of the strong sense of individual responsibility: the more fully *Manas* is developed, the deeper is one's responsibility and the stronger one's capacity for choice. The full potential of *Manas* can only be intimated through an exacting conception of individual responsibility wherein one is accountable for every thought and feeling, and for every life-atom that at any given time is an integral part of one's vestures or merely passes in and through one's radius of influence. So immense is the Akashic potential of the fully awakened *Manas* that the perfected Masters are literally responsible for the welfare of worlds.

Such a Promethean conception is far removed from the feeble notions of most thinking men and women of the present Round. It is downright alien to that noisy minority which is terrified of taking responsibility for the simplest things, for elementary errors, for past mistakes and present failures, for endemic and *tamasic* tendencies which act as mental blocks or emotional obstructions in the lunar and physical vestures. The refusal to accept responsibility, which is a cowardly refusal to become Manasic, is a vain attempt to be mindless, to become a retarded soul unable to keep pace with the high purposes of evolution. All of this has got to be paid for, not only through the tragic condition of the ray that gradually weakens its connection with the Divine Triad, but also through the immeasurable agony of those lofty souls who suffer for the sake of the whole, who do not have any sense of 'mine' and 'thine' in relation to the collective illusions of egotistic pride and ignorant selfishness of the human race. Those who truly aspire to the Path of Renunciation, also called the Path of Woe — mental woe for all souls trapped in the abject wretchedness of living death or indefinitely mired in ignorance and irresponsibility — should ponder deeply the sacred image of the cosmic sacrifice of Visvakarman in the steep Golgotha of life. Then, at the revelatory moment of death, they may come to have a flash of understanding strong enough to evoke a mighty resolve to return as early as possible in the next life into the spiritual service of suffering humanity. Hence the need for spiritual knowledge, self-study and daily meditation.

In a universe of justice the voluntary discipline of sacrifice presupposes the power of choice of every single human being. *Manas* spells moral responsibility, and it connotes freedom of choice as well as the fearless acceptance of the full consequences of past choices. A Manasic being welcomes everything that comes under merciful karma as a necessary consequence of choices in other lives, self-determination at the moment of birth, and the continuous stream of self-definition originating at the causal level of ideation. The truly Manasic being would never condescend to assign any portion of his character or circumstance entirely to an outside agency or source — whether heredity, environment, the collective Karma of society or humanity. All such alibis, excuses and evasions would be morally unworthy of a Manasic being. One might coolly consider these mitigating factors when one wishes to understand the unknown karma of other beings, especially as one cannot arrogate to oneself the vicarious burden of responsibility which other persons must assume voluntarily. It is with selfless humility and spontaneous reverence before the mystery of every Ego that the Bodhisattva seeks broader explanations for the sake of a compassionate understanding, a non-moralistic or constructive appraisal of the spiritual predicament of human souls. If one thinks seriously about the metaphysical basis of sacrifice, the ethics of responsibility would logically follow, including the moral codes of discipleship. Also, one would see with the clarity of compassion that what is customarily called living is largely a series of pathetic contortions based upon a sad legacy of fears inherited from past lives of irresponsibility and evasion.

Persisting in such a course of self-destruction can only lead at some point to a total rupture of the connection with the Divine, unless there is a courageous if traumatic confrontation with these downward tendencies. For humanity as a whole, there eventually must come such a crucial moment of choice in the Fifth Round, but for individuals who have entered the Path, it can come much earlier than for the majority of mankind. When the twin gifts of *Manas* — moral responsibility and noetic choice — are strengthened through use by a burgeoning Buddhic awareness of cosmic sacrifice, then, as the *Stanzas* teach:

> The thread between the *silent watcher* and his *shadow* (man) becomes stronger — with every re-incarnation.

This is what should happen in every human life, and if it does not, there is something seriously wrong. In every incarnation the *sutratman* should become stronger between the Silent Watcher — the overbrooding Dhyani or Divine Prototype at the upper rung of the ladder of being — and the lunar shadow at the lower rung. Gupta Vidya teaches that the two highest classes of Dhyanis — the Watchers connected with the seventh principle and the Architects connected with the sixth principle — furnished the various races of humanity with divine Kings and Instructors:

> It is the latter who taught humanity their arts and sciences, and the former who revealed to the incarnated Monads that had just shaken off their vehicles of the

lower Kingdoms — and who had, therefore, lost every
recollection of their divine origin — the great spiritual
truths of the transcendental worlds.

The Secret Doctrine, i 267

If, despite this sacred lineage and divine descent which lends to
man the sacrificial light of self-consciousness, he nonetheless
desecrates the gift of creative imagination through moral
turpitude, then there is a tragic loosening or sundering of the vital
connection with the immortal Monad. Turpitude means taking
pride in what is vile and base and pleasure in what is shameful; it
is bravado in the service of Satan. Such terrible misuse of the will
and the potency of thought imperils the life-giving connection
between the higher Triad and the lower quaternary, and gravely
increases the risk of running loose and "astray into the lunar path."
     There is enormous moral danger in any pseudo-scientific
categories of thought or pseudo-religious forms of worship that
encourage disguised irresponsibility in the name of pseudo-
freedom or pseudo-determinism or pseudo-salvation. Once one
goes astray into the lunar path, all manner of unholy alliances
are made between the astral form and nefarious swarms of
tortured elementals, soulless elementaries and evil sorcerers, as also
massive legions of malignant, gangrenous and leprous thought-
forms going back to Atlantean times. One becomes the helpless
prey of whole classes of images intimately associated with the
appalling abuse of spiritual knowledge, creative potency and
mental energies. This inevitably attracts a host of soul-ailments
and diseases, and those who succumb to them face formidable
obstructions to finding a human form or congenial conditions
in which one can foster spiritual intuitions. Even if, at one level,
one wants to aspire heavenward, the entire system seems to
conspire against the promise of progress owing to spinal
blockages, mental deposits and astral deformities.
     To purge oneself of spiritual pollution and to heal the moral
scars it leaves in the lunar vesture, one must meditate deeply and
continuously, with an intensely devout wish to restore and

strengthen the fragile connection with the immortal spirit of
Atma-Buddhi. One must immerse oneself in the Buddhic current
of the healing waters of wisdom, the elixir of *Hermes*, the
indestructible spark of divine conscience, which is consubstantial
with the fiery essence of the Dhyanis (the Angirasa descended
from Agni). This is like bathing in the luminous stream of Divine
Wisdom, the only Jordan whose waters can baptize in the name
of the Father in Heaven, the *Mahaguru* on earth, the God in man.
The therapeutic restoration of the right relationship between the
reflected ray and its divine parent cannot come by ritual chanting
and monotonous mutterings, by what is mistaken for prayer,
worship or meditation.

Rectification must proceed from intense thought, conscious
strengthening of the strongest altruistic feelings in oneself, and
by an unconditional vow and irreversible determination. This
would be enormously helped by invoking and activating the
higher faculties which have their analogues with lower *manas* and
with *prana*. The manifest energy of *prana* must reflect something
of the continuity and self-luminous, self-created spiritual energy
of the invisible *Atman*. The polarity of *kama* must be purified
through devotion and directed by that inward tropism and vertical
movement towards the Divine Triad which could confer the
benediction of gratitude and reverence towards the *Ishtaguru* and
the Brotherhood of Bodhisattvas. Lower *manas* must be brought
into firm alignment with higher *Manas*, especially through the
use of silence and conscious control of speech. If there are daily
duties to perform, one should take a universal ideal, a potent
mantram, dwell upon these and then look upon obligations as
sacred, with a joyous recognition of responsibility and choice.

It is unwise to spend too much time on only one thing and
to evade other duties. It is wiser to keep moving with cheerfulness
while blending the elements of refined thinking, feeling and
breathing into a single stream of sacrificial ideation. One must
even be delighted to discover obstacles, understanding that so-
called bad karma is what one unconsciously or unknowingly
desired for one's discipline. Karma is not only what one deserves,

but also what one really wants, because it offers a golden opportunity for transmuting past errors and persisting obstacles. Even tainted life-atoms must be welcomed and cleansed, or they will take their revenge if their demand for attention is spurned. They must indeed be discouraged from performing their ludicrous devil dances, and can be gently coaxed into the presence of potent thoughts and feelings of pure benevolence.

Wise devotees who make this regenerative programme the basis of spiritual alchemy will combine continuity of daily practice in modest and moderate doses with the Himalayan strength of unconditional and irrevocable, irreversible commitment. The secret doctrine of *Buddhi Yoga* teaches that though it take a long time to perfect this practice, it needs only moral courage, not the mere passage of time, to give it a firm basis. The spiritual will is released through meditation upon *Vach*, nourished through devotion to Krishna, and intensified through the yoga of *tapas*, consecrated to Shiva. Thus, throughout human evolution, wise individuals in all the ancient centres of Initiation took irrevocable vows and made irreversible commitments. In each life they reaffirmed the irreversibility of their striving on the Path because this alone releases the spiritual will that invites the *Atman* to descend into the vestures and assume divine kingship.

Mental and moral courage, constancy of zeal and concentration of purpose are the three talismans of self-regeneration. Herein lies the clue to the strength of unconditional affirmations. A part of the shadowy self always attempts to be conditional and crafty; one has to renounce allegiance to this pretentious enemy through the sovereign act of unconditional affirmation. There is no other way. When a seeker recognizes this psychological truth through life upon life, the length of the process matters little if the philosophical basis is sound and the spiritual resolve is firm and unconditional. It is a high tragedy that many people for whom access to the sacred teachings was made easy never truly chose the Path because they never really initiated the heroic and sacrificial resolve of *Manas*.

Every seeker must freely choose the Path sometime, choose

it wholly, unequivocally and completely. Each must choose it whole-heartedly and single-mindedly without introducing those seemingly small qualifications which are tiny apertures through which the vermin rush in from the region of spiritual vampires and intellectual vultures. And when the vermin come, they breed fast and make short work of the contaminated structure. To seal off every mental reservation, egotistic escape-route and moral evasion, one must make a supreme, unconditional and absolute affirmation on the Bodhisattva Path, renouncing all possible concessions to conditionality and cowardice. Herein lies the dignity of the sacred and the divinity of a Vow or *Vrata*, sanctified by *Rta* or cosmic rightness and its ceaseless rhythm in the *anahata*, the immortal centre of incarnated *Manas*. A person who invokes *Vach* takes a mighty step towards Enlightenment because his or her spiritual energy-field is enormously intensified by the immaculate light of *Atma-Buddhi*. The Lanoo must be calm and patient, moving step by step along the Path, day by day, week by week, month by month. After a point it becomes wholly natural to stay firmly within the noetic current of life-giving wisdom and compassion which streams forth from Krishna and the Lodge of Mahatmas.

KNOWLEDGE AND NEGLIGENCE

Fix thy Soul's gaze upon the star whose ray thou art,
the flaming star that shines within the lightless depths of
ever-being, the boundless fields of the Unknown.
                              The Voice of the Silence

Every human being is endowed with a mind which is a focussing mirror for concentrated thought and cognition. Every being in the seven kingdoms of Nature is sentient at some level of intrinsic and potential intelligence and apperception. Human beings, as self-conscious monads, are capable of deliberate reflection, of making every item in the external world an object of intense thought, and also pondering upon themselves in relation to other selves. If all beings participate in an expanding universe of mind, in degrees of awareness which are heightened by the plastic power of self-consciousness, what is the basis of the ubiquitous distinction between knower and known, subject and object? If there is to be an intelligible universe of multiple manifestation arising from a single source but only partly related to it, there must also be an array of minds capable of focussing the light of universal awareness in varying degrees in relation to fields of cognition that are partly governed by the porosity of material vestures — the physical body, the astral form, the subtler veils that belong to every being and which are more distinctly differentiated at the human level. Consciousness in a world of heterogeneous objects differentiated through a variety of vestures must necessarily involve the ever-changing contrast between the knower and the known. It takes a long series of meditations to discern the unmodified unity behind the multiplicity of objects. To understand this ethically is even more difficult. It means using the persistent distinction between subject and object as the foothold for recovering a sense of unity in the realm of relativities and contrasts.

Ethically, the thinking individual encounters the need to put oneself into the position of another person, who is both an active knower and a moral agent. Given the initial difficulty of apprehending the contrast of subject and object, how can one comprehend the mystical teaching of Shankaracharya which seems to suggest that the knower is an illusion? If the knower is an illusion, what sense is to be made of knowing? If a person sees the illusion of separateness, what meaning may be assigned to percepts, concepts and the very act of cognition? Such questions merely start the protracted process of enquiry into the knower, the known and knowing. A person who has passed through a preliminary period of earnest questioning may reach a point where he or she may meditate upon the ancient teaching concerning the *Atman* and the *Atmajnani*. The *Atman*, the one source of all light, life and energy, is itself the pristine reflection of the attributeless reality of the Divine Ground, *Brahman*. The *Atman* is the light in every atom and the Logos overbrooding every human being. It is the fully incarnated deity in the *Atmajnani*, the self-governed Sage, the initiator into *Atmavidya*, the wisdom of the *Atman*.

How can the ordinary human being make use of a recondite teaching about what seems far beyond everyday experience and ordinary modes of thinking? The kernel of Shankaracharya's teaching is that in reality there is no above and beyond, there is no near and far. *Atmavidya* is itself dimensionless like the *Atman*. The *Atman* is without axes in either physical or conceptual space. The *Atman* is omnipresent, homogeneous and impenetrable. If the light of the *Atman* is hidden in the heart of every human being, its radiance is reflected in all human longings. One must love the *Atman* if one hopes to focus upon the light of the *Atman* and if one aspires to unite completely with the *Atman*. True meditation is self-sustaining to some degree. For the Sage it is utterly uninterrupted at all times because he is ever established in that exalted state of meditation. He merely assumes a mayavic form for the sake of serving a self-chosen mission of mercy in the sphere of cyclic time. If every human being daily comes closer to the *Atman* in deep sleep, everyone is essentially capable of that Atmic awareness which transcends the polarity of known and unknown, knower and knowing. Human beings live ostensibly in a world of fugitive time, fragmented space and differentiated objects. Time is differentiated in terms of seconds and minutes, days and months, for the sake of availing oneself of cyclic rhythms and linear succession. Space is differentiated by place and relationship, and this helps one to locate oneself and one's role in a world of shifting boundaries and continuous reconstruction.

How can one make use of a metaphysical teaching that is typically realized only in a few moments of dreamless sleep every night? The only way this can become continually relevant is by a conscious exercise of contemplation. We need to enter repeatedly into that state of consciousness which transcends the polarities and pairs of opposites, the fluctuating contrasts of light and shade. Since this is far from easy, the opportunity must be taken to do something in this direction on a regular basis, to concentrate the mind on a central truth, to see it from the standpoint of one's own immediate needs but also to grasp it philosophically and impersonally. To look at an idea independently of one's personal standpoint requires effort; to see it from the standpoint of many other people is even more difficult. Nonetheless, it is vital to sustain the effort, to increase continuity by recognizing and overcoming discontinuities. So as long as there is discontinuity in consciousness, the mind will be captive to the sharp distinction between the knower and the known and knowing, will reinforce rather than transcend the sense of separateness. Self-correction is the basis of science and philosophy, but such correction is usually confined to the level of perception or awareness at which the error is identified and the subsequent correction is applied.

Through daily meditation one has a firm basis for self-study, for scrutinizing one's sets of thoughts, behaviour patterns and modes of cognition in terms of discontinuity and continuity. If one is truly trying to maintain continuity, then one is most concerned to examine why one loses it. By persisting in self-study on a regular basis, one may come to see clearly the causes of recurring patterns of deviation, forgetfulness and irresponsibility. At some point of intensive enquiry, one isolates the root causes of sporadic effort, shallow resolve and diffused desire. Shankaracharya teaches that the chief cause of bondage is captivity to a false identity which has no basis in reality but is merely like a photograph one mistakes for oneself. The true Self cannot be known until one can consciously live in and through other beings. Every person does this to a limited extent. Otherwise, there would be no possibility of communication, no extension of empathy, no growth in understanding. Yet human beings are not sufficiently motivated to strengthen the innate capacity for transcendence of the false self. Scattering of consciousness arises through mistaken identification with the persona, with name and form, likes and dislikes, borrowed opinions and ill-digested insights, with everything that is like excess luggage which cannot be carried by the immortal soul at the moment of death when the lower vestures are discarded. For the immortal soul — the *Atman* in its pristine ray — there is no illusion of separateness, no tension through duality, no captivity to the conceptualization of particulars.

> The *Atman* dwells within, free from attachment and beyond all action. A man must separate this *Atman* from every object of experience, as a stalk of grass is separated from its enveloping sheath. Then he must dissolve into the *Atman* all those appearances which make up the world of name and form. He is indeed a free soul who can remain thus absorbed in the *Atman* alone.

The persistent asking of the question "Who am I?" raises a person beyond the boundaries of the personality. The lower mind is typically trapped in the realm of external differentiation, of comparison and contrast. It is fragmented through the fleeting succession of states of consciousness which produces the illusion of time. It is delusively dependent through its polarization between past and future, regrets and anticipations, fears and fantasies. Through deep meditation it is indeed possible to silence the lower mind and initiate a state of true calm. It is essential to release the serene awareness of the higher mind, which is inherently capable of abstraction, universalization and thinking through particulars *(dianoia)*. By repeated and regular efforts in meditation and self-scrutiny, one could correct the more glaring discontinuities. One might make it a daily practice to prepare before sleep by reflecting upon the *Anahata*, the deathless vibration in the secret heart, the ceaseless pulsation of the AUM. This could be fused with a true feeling of compassion for all beings, as evoked by *The Voice of the Silence* in its poignant lament:

> Alas, alas, that all men should possess Alaya, be one with the Great Soul, and that possessing it, Alaya should so little avail them! Behold how like the moon, reflected in the tranquil waves, Alaya is reflected by the small and by the great, is mirrored in the tiniest atoms, yet fails to reach the heart of all. Alas, that so few men should profit by the gift, the priceless boon of learning truth, the right perception of existing things, the knowledge of the non-existent!

All rays of light emanate from a single source. Once one has abstracted from habitual identification with a name and a form and assumed the mental posture of an individual ray of light, one may experience the effulgence of the *Atman*. Self-knowledge will spontaneously arise through active contemplation, which will be food for the soul. If one found that despite proper preparation at night, one still woke up with no lucid recollection in the mind, intense self-questioning is needed. Who is the 'I' that entered *sushupti* and what is the 'I' that cannot remember? One has to make daily experiments with truth. All of this is valuable and valid as a process of knowing, though it is only the partial awareness of a partly self-conscious being of dim reflections of a deeper realm. Nothing learnt is ever lost by the immortal soul. It is important to see the painful process of progressive knowing as constructive and continuous. It is helpful to lose the thraldom and tension of effort by devotedly meditating upon the invisible form of the Guru, the *Atmajnani* in whom the knower, knowing and the known are all one. This is uplifting because it elevates one's level of consciousness to meditate on the Self as incarnated in a fully self-conscious Sage, who is outside time and yet in contact with the temporal, who is beyond visible space yet omnipresent, and always accessible on subtler planes of manifestation.

One is only partly awake when asking questions about the true Self; one is more awake when one actively meditates and even more awake when one ardently seeks the Knower of the *Atman*. The *Atmajnani* is in a steady state of *turiya,* continuous spiritual wakefulness. Total wakefulness is only possible on the plane of the *Atman,* wherein no distinctions made by the mind have any meaning. It is a pure, primordial state of consciousness which is incommunicable. It can neither be described nor characterized but it is approached to some extent when emptying out, when negating and questioning. It is the miniature light in the eyes of every human being. To kindle the small spark of light into the blazing fire of divine wisdom is the task of many lifetimes. The *yogin* is fully consumed, says Shankaracharya, in the fire of true knowledge. The important thing for each and every person is to make an honest effort to keep moving towards an ideal state of inward freedom. One must grasp all available opportunities for greater knowing, for deeper self-knowledge, profounder knowledge of the Self and pure selflessness.

The feeling of responsibility is the first step towards selflessness. All spiritual Teachers promulgate what everyone already knows at some level — that everything adds up, that nothing is lost, that no one can evade anything. The homilies and proverbs of all traditions only point to the accumulated wisdom of humanity. The half-asleep individual has lost the key and does not know how to use the heritage of universal truth. Great

Teachers descend amidst humanity so that a second birth is possible for the disciples who are ready. This profound awakening of spiritual consciousness takes place among many at critical thresholds in human evolution. The karma of the whole of humanity for the duration of an epoch is nobly assumed by one of the Brotherhood of Sages, who comes into the world and becomes responsible for the progress of humanity during a cycle of awakening. The Bodhisattva elevates the idea of responsibility to its greatest height. What does it mean to be responsible for an age and to be responsible for the whole of humanity? This is an awesome and staggering conception. How can it be even sensed by those who refuse to recognize their errors and the future consequences to be faced?

In general, an awareness of individual responsibility is the mark of a *Manasa,* a thinking being and moral agent. Though one cannot put everything right in this life and all the people one has affected are no longer around or alive, still some things can be rectified right now. It is possible to clean up one's copybook significantly without any clues to the complex mathematics of the cosmos. It is a waste of energy to fret and fume over the past, which is already part of our present make-up. Every cell of one's being carries the imprint of every thought, feeling, emotion, word and deed that one emanated in this life. At least, one can be responsible in relation to what one can see. At the present point of history the sense of responsibility has been enormously heightened for the whole of humanity. Never before have there been so many millions of human beings in search of divine wisdom, the science of self-regeneration. *The Voice of the Silence* instructs the disciple: "Look not behind or thou art lost." It is an exercise in futility to look behind because what has receded will recur. Instead of idle regret, it is possible to use the gospel of gratitude to transmute every precipitation of Karma into an avenue for fundamental growth through courageous self-correction.

Gratitude is no longer a threatening term, even in the United States. Many people everywhere respond to the beauty of reverence as it is truly innate to the human soul. Miseducation may foster mental presumption but it cannot extinguish the immortal spark of devotion. In all human beings there are natural feelings and intuitions which can be awakened and quickened. It would indeed be wrong to think that purely by penitence one could wipe out the consequences of past irresponsibility. This is a costly failure to understand the law of ethical causation. If one already has wronged others wilfully or thoughtlessly, feelings of remorse or empathy cannot erase past debts. This untenable doctrine of moral evasion did much harm over two thousand years. It was a travesty of true religion, an arbitrary breach of natural harmony. The irresponsible dogma of vicarious atonement traduced the exalted ethical teaching of Jesus. He taught that the Divine is not mocked: as ye sow, so shall ye reap. This is a central tenet in the teachings of all Initiates, and the erosion of the idea of responsibility is everywhere the consequence of priestcraft and ceremonialism. There are myriad ways in which people run away from the mature acceptance of full responsibility for past misdeeds. The Aquarian sees that true responsibility begins in the realm of thought and must include every thought. Surely one can appreciate the profound integrity of the teaching that every thought connects each human being with every other. The intuitive recognition of universal interdependence and of human solidarity is the basis of an ever-expanding conception of moral responsibility, renewed and refined through successive lives of earthly probation by a galaxy of immortal souls in a vast pilgrimage of self-discovery reaching towards universal self-consciousness.

It is helpful to make a start by recognizing that to become more selfless, one must become more responsible. This is a critical clue for daily self-study. When embarked upon self-therapy, the moment one even begins to blame anyone else, one should see that one is going wrong. The moment one looks for excuses one is off course. The moment one is compulsively peering around or seems too tired to face the truth, one is vainly running away from the Self, from the Wheel of Dharma, from the *Atman* and the *Atmajnanis*. One may crouch and kneel and beg for forgiveness but the Law can exempt nothing and no one. *Atmajnanis* work in harmony with the *Atman,* and the *Atman* is Karma. Sages dare not still the movement of Karma. The disciple under trial should fundamentally rethink all relationships — to Teachers, to companions, to dependents and to oneself. One will need far more than a few crumbs of self-knowledge garnered carelessly, while holding onto a convenient self-image. One needs a stronger current through a deeper meditation upon the *Atman* and the *Agathon,* the central source of universal good. This will arouse increased wakefulness so that one can recognize seemingly remote connections between causes and consequences. One can come alive as a human being, a moral agent, an immortal soul, as a person who is truly trying to do the best without settling for a smug and shadowy sense of responsibility. One is willing and ready to assume the fullness of responsibility that constitutes the dignity and divinity of being human in a universe ruled by rigid justice. Thus one can strengthen one's clear perception, in others and in oneself, of those graces which are universal among human beings, which are conveyed through authentic gestures of gratitude, reverence and renunciation. Some people have dim memories of other times when they sought to cut corners in ways that might apparently make sense if there is only one life, but which make no sense whatsoever if there are successive incarnations and if every event has a hidden lesson which must be mastered.

To grasp the rudiments of the Philosophy of Perfectibility and to learn the axioms of the Science of Spirituality, one must deepen the sense of the sacred through some daily exemplification of the Religion of Responsibility. Shankara taught that negligence, the inversion of responsibility, is death. Negligence in breathing results in physical death; negligence of the mind leads to atrophy of the power to think. Negligence of the conscience culminates in moral blindness and negligence of the soul obscures intuition and inhibits the creative will. The immortal soul cannot make sufficient use of its instruments to fulfil its purposes on earth. Since negligence works at all levels and is ruinous to oneself, what is the deeper negligence of which Shankaracharya speaks? In terms of the mathematics of the soul, a feeble or a distorted use of opportunities for growth blocks future possibilities over lives. This is the worst kind of negligence. If one has the priceless gift of access to the waters of life-giving wisdom and neglects one's opportunity, one will be propelled backwards in ways that become irreversible. If one comes into the presence of a life-giving source of wisdom, one is hardly expected to be perfect, and one is certainly not immune from mistakes and misconceptions, let alone trials and tribulations. Teachers may even recommend strong medicine at certain times to enable the weak to observe minimums. Any human being who comes any closer to a life-giving source of wisdom must either go up or go down. As Gandhi saw, human nature is such that it must always either soar or sink. What determines this is negligence in relation to what one knows in some measure. This spiritual teaching of Shankara necessarily means that one must make a much better use of the future time available on earth, which will determine, at the moment of death, the outcome of succeeding lives. Each one is already carrying the burden of former lives, especially the last three, and to some extent can explain one's present patterns in terms of entrenched tendencies. If these are so tenacious, it is because they were not begun recently but were fostered through recurring rationalizations, excuses and reinforcement.

One has therefore to cut to the very core of one's psyche, and this will need courage and care. That does not mean one should brood over one's shadow, or exaggerate one's personal self. The more one broods, the worse it will get, and the more one talks about it, the more it will lengthen. This is such a potent teaching that anybody who continued in this way even after knowing better would be much worse off. One must always exercise the privilege of speech with care, and never be negligent in the use of sound. Invoking the words of divine wisdom on behalf of the shadowy persona can lead to corruption of consciousness and astral pollution. Past negligence and misuse can be carefully corrected by present observation of compulsive patterns and neglected needs of the soul. There is hope because the immortal soul can always take control of its sluggish vestures, but this cannot be done overnight if there has been a solidification in the vestures through long-standing neglect of meditation and self-study. Be more deliberate, thoughtful and detached; then one will be more relaxed. Let go. Do not try to do everything all at once, but daily do something constructive. Find a balance that is appropriate, and it is wise to aim higher than one's weaknesses would suggest, while also making due allowance for the resistance offered by deeply lodged tendencies. Find out what works as a stimulus to growth and how one's golden moments may be renewed and fused into an active force for good.

Making a sincere start can release the spiritual will, the calm assurance that one is honest, one's perception is clear and one's mind is unclouded. The mists of illusion are dispelled precisely because one has seen through a glass darkly. There is no need to claim that when one sees clearly, one sees everything. Having found that one can see as clearly as possible what it is essential to do, then relax the tension of striving. The *Atman* is without any strain and is felt by the power of calmness. The *Atman* is pure joy, pellucid truth and self-sustaining strength. The pristine quality of pure love is the pathway to self-knowledge. These cannot be aroused at once but they are all latent in oneself. Though the mind has been blunted by negligence in meditation, it still has considerable elasticity and unrecognized resilience. One may discern in the heart the resonance of the *Atman*, even though the heart might have been obscured and wounded by perverted emotions and distorted feelings. Like a wounded soldier, one can still summon the unseen resources of the spirit.

There is a hidden current of continuity that preserves humanity. This is much deeper and more mysterious than the mere instinct of physical survival. The profounder the continuity, the greater the universality. One may learn as much as one can in relation to as much as one knows, in relation to as much as one can use with as much courage and strength as one can summon. With the *Atman* there is nothing to run away from, nothing to run away to. The *Atman* is everywhere. Though its light is ever available, it can only be reached by raising one's consciousness to the universality of the empyrean. When one is seemingly on one's own, one is mostly if unconsciously in contact with the lower forces in Nature. When one ardently seeks divine wisdom and meditates upon the *Atmajnani,* one comes into the radius of an invisible fellowship of disciples on the Path of disinterested service to Humanity.

All growth really depends upon the extent of repeated self-correction in all one's patterns of use, misuse, non-use and abuse. The fundamental negligence of which Shankaracharya speaks consists in forgetting the Self in the realm of the non-Self. This is consistently mistaking the non-Self for the Self. The spiritual Teacher is not addressing the lower mind, but is reaching to the silent inner Self. One must see beyond the visible, and what is thought to be invisible is only so in relation to the visible. If selfhood is seen as a series of veils, the more earnestly one unties the mental knots that result in recurring negligence and repeated forgetfulness, the more easily one will unravel the finer threads of subtler causes. As spiritual wakefulness increases, there will be a distinct replenishment through calmness, contentment and cheerfulness. The *Atman* knows no differentiation or death. Like a vast waveless expanse of water, it is eternally free and indivisible. It is pure consciousness and the Witness of all experiences. Its intrinsic nature is joy, it is beyond form and action, it is the changeless Knower of all that is changeable. It is infinite, impartite and inexhaustible.

> Let there be no negligence in your devotion. Negligence in the practice of recollection is death — this has been declared by the seer Sanat Kumara.
>
> For a spiritual seeker, there is no greater evil than negligence in recollection. From it arises delusion. From delusion arises egoism. From egoism comes bondage and from bondage misery.
>
> Through negligence in recollection, a man is

distracted from awareness of his divine nature. He who is thus distracted falls — and the fallen always come to ruin. It is very hard for them to rise again. . . .

Control speech by mental effort; control the mind by the faculty of discrimination; control this faculty by the individual will, merge individuality in the infinite absolute *Atman* and reach supreme peace.

SHANKARACHARYA

SPIRITUAL ATTENTION

Sit evenly, erect, at ease, with palms folded on the lap, with eyes fixed on the nose; cleanse your lungs by taking a deep breath, holding it in and then discharging it, raise in your heart the OM *sounding like the tolling of a bell, and in the lotus of your heart, contemplate My form as encircled by light.*

The path of knowledge is for those who are weary of life; those who still have desires should pursue the path of sublimation through works; and to those who are not completely indifferent nor too much attached the devotional path bears fruit.

Perform your actions for Me and with thoughts fixed on Me; untainted like the sky, see yourself within your self; consider all beings as Myself and adore them; bow to everybody, high or low, great or small, kind or cruel; by seeing Me constantly in all, rid yourself of jealousy, intolerance, violence and egoism. Casting aside your pride, prestige, and sense of shame, fall prostrate in humility before all, down to the dog and ass. This is the knowledge of the learned, the wisdom of the wise — that man attains the Real with the unreal and the Immortal with the mortal.

KRISHNA to UDDHAVA

The universe is mostly unmanifest, and every human being is a microcosmic reflection of the entire egg-like cosmos. Each individual is a vast but largely hidden force-field, but all are manifesting with varying degrees of knowledge, deliberation and discrimination. These diversities are the product of a long history of use, overuse and misuse of the sheaths and vestures in which immortal monads have been embodied in myriad environments over eighteen million years. Given this far-reaching perspective, how can any person use this potent teaching in order to become a better human being? How can an individual become more attentive and discriminating in using the sacred gift of creative imagination, training the mind as an instrument for concentrated thought, directed with a benevolent feeling towards goals compatible with the purposes of all living beings, towards universal good? Strange as it may seem, everyone can discover indispensable clues for answering this question in the simple fact that he or she is a certain kind of human being. The whole story is recorded from head to toe: the way a person walks and talks; the way a person holds himself or herself; the way a person thinks, feels and acts; the way a person relates to other beings; but, above all, the way a person lives through waking and sleeping from day to day, passing through the three halls of consciousness — *jagrat, swapna* and *sushupti* — connecting moments in childhood through the seasons of human life, growing, maturing and mellowing with intermittent glimpses of wisdom.

Every person can test motives and methods in the daily attempts to translate thought and intention into outer modes of expression. If someone gets a chance to work upon certain details of some part of a larger work in which the levels of motivation markedly vary, that person can learn through what karma brings to him or her. If, by mistake, one became involved in more than one can manage, this would be known within a short time because one would get burnt. To be unready is to have a shrunken sense of self and therefore a force-field that is very congested with blurred, contradictory and weak currents liable to short circuits and shocks. As long as there is the opportunity to learn and to correct, it is always possible to make a difference because all human beings are capable in their finest moments of the highest possible motivation. There is hardly a person who has not had moments of pure love of the human race. There are few who have gone through the whole of life without even once having looked at the stars and sky and wondered at the magnitude of the universe. Nature cannot support a human being who cannot ever negate the suffocation of confinement within shallow perspectives of mind and heart. As long as there is the beneficence of sleep, every human being has abundant opportunities to renew the larger Self, the greater motive, the fuller perspective. The problem then is not that a human being is without spiritual resources, but rather how to make those resources tapped during deep dreamless sleep relevant when one is out in the field of duty, *Kurukshetra*. Wakeful deployment of resources will require sufficient noetic detachment to avert captivity to compulsive activity, and thereby avoid being cut off from the greater Self. When the only correction available is sleep, it is too inefficient to rely upon automatically because the daily passage through confused dream states vitiates the healing effects of deeper dreamless states.

Meditation is the source of noetic understanding, but this depends upon an initial humbling of the false self that otherwise undermines every effort. Learning without unlearning is not only useless, but, like eating without elimination, it can be fatal. Bad habits must be unlearnt while learning new ways of doing things that come from new ways of thinking, and in this continuous process one has to be courageous in assessing one's spiritual strivings. By seeing where one is going wrong and why, it is possible to make significant connections between causes and consequences and then see where a real difference can be made. It is always possible to make a difference, but only on the basis of self-examination that leaves one more determined and relaxed — more relaxed because of seeing oneself in relation to the whole of humanity. Without running away from the facts, it is possible to take an honest inventory, and if this is done, one will soon begin to discover that it is not that one's motive is entirely bad or that one is altogether no good. It is rather that one is not very good at learning because of having created blockages in the self through pride, blockages in the mind through prejudice, blockages in the heart through partiality, blockages in the will through perversity. These blockages precipitate very quickly in the presence of great resolves, and if they are not faced, it is difficult to avoid walking backwards. But if this realization brings a sense of defeat, that means one never really understood the teaching of Karma. The Self that has to make the effort of understanding is that ray of the immortal soul which is put in charge of the kingdom in which the different parts of one's being must be dynamically balanced. When there is a greater harmony within, it is possible to contribute more to harmony without. This is what each is meant to do. The general accounting can be left to Karma. By altering radically one's attitude to work, to motive and method, and one's way of balancing them, there is the opportunity for growth on the basis of a larger and a firmer recognition of the invisible forces, realities and laws constantly at work in Nature and in oneself.

One must use with care those living messengers called words, and this reference to messengers has to do with different classes of elementals, all the myriad invisible centres of energy that permeate the diverse departments of Nature. To be full of the fire of devotion and to do the best work one can, one must have the right basis in thinking. The immortal soul is capable of immortal love, of immortal longings that may summon the life-essence that permeates this globe, the omnipresent spirit that is dateless and deathless. Everyone is inherently capable of an unending, unconditional love and courage and endurance, ready "to suffer woes hope thinks infinite". The depth of devotion depends upon the level of being. Those who are unafraid of death, who see themselves neither in terms of the body nor in terms of the mind, but as immortal monads, can generate and sustain devotion to the greater hearts and minds of the Bodhisattvas. This constant devotion is in the context of universal mind or *Mahat*, and the hebdomadal heart of the cosmos. They come under the protection of supreme compassion, the universal umbrella of Dharma. When devotion thus becomes a sovereign talisman, it is continually enriched by *yajna* and *tapas*, sacrificial meditation. The wise are those who, starting from small drops of genuine devotion, humility and wisdom, make them grow. They are wise because they grow the way Nature grows. They will, of course, make mistakes, but as long as they maintain their original recognition of the utter simplicity, the transparency and truth of devotion, they can strengthen the current of resolve and regeneration. Magic is possible where there is authenticity, continuity and a sense of proportion, where there is sacrifice, care and a willingness to learn, as well as a capacity to merge the little self in the greater Self.

The path of spiritual attention is not easy, although anyone can make a beginning by trying to understand. Those who still have desires should pursue the path of sublimation through sacrificial works. To those who are neither completely indifferent nor too much attached, the devotional path bears fruit. One is not expected to be perfectly indifferent to everything nor suddenly to show effortless mastery in the practice of devotion. Devotees have their many limitations, but they are expected to moderate their attachment to the fruits of results. Then the path of devotion will bear fruit at the moment of death or in other lives. The mathematics of the universe is exact; one merely does the best one can and leaves the rest to the Law. It is necessary to elevate what is mortal and unreal with the help of a mental posture which involves true obeisance. To remember properly the original moment is to gain glimpses into the future. The divisions of time into night and day, clock time and calendars, engender an illusory sense of past and present and future. It may be that in a certain year upon a certain day one had a spiritual awakening because one came into the presence of spiritual wisdom. If so, to be true to that means to keep going back again and again to the original moment, because the more one can do that, the more one will come closer to the Teachers of Wisdom. If on any issue one understood the original moment, then one would see that the whole story is compressed in that original moment. In that is already determined and defined the future outcome of everything that is connected with that original moment.

One cannot awaken the powers of spiritual attention if one is preoccupied with externals. One cannot be spiritually awake and attentive if one has forgotten that one is an immortal soul. Even if at some level one knew it and then forgot it, that is going to have an effect upon the power of attention. Understanding means making connections. When one truly enjoys thinking about what one is trying to recall, then one can summon other ideas connected with the same line of thinking. Correlations begin to emerge and connections can be made. With calm and detachment and true love of something larger than oneself, there can be access to a vaster perspective. The reason why people forget and why they fantasize is that they do not really know in the present. The reason they do not know in the present is that they are not fully attentive as immortal souls. They are misled by the sensorium, by the shadowy screen of prejudice, by the film of false anticipation and by the burden of failure, shame and regret. Therefore, they have neither lightness nor freedom nor joy, neither do they have any fullness of receptivity and devotion. The path of spiritual reminiscence has to be summoned, and the future is obscure to those who desperately want clues or cues from the outside.

Human beings define themselves during the day by how they relate to deep sleep, and during their lifetime by how they relate to their golden moments. They could know their karma if only they would have the courage to look at their vows, at their highest moments and the extent of their fidelity to them. If they can say that they have at some level made an effort to be true but failed, then they should go on and say that they are willing for Karma to work. They must be honest with themselves if they would gain the strength they need through rekindling a golden moment. This could again become real for them in the present. Then they do not have to see their future only in terms of failures, betrayals, forgetfulness and loss of vision. They could see it in terms of a renewal of vision and a rekindling of strength.

To work with Karma is to learn why one is what one is at any given time on any plane, to look at one's strengths and with the help of this awareness to recognize the seeds of former resolve. One always has the opportunity to be grateful to those who made it possible, to have the courage to look at one's weaknesses and understand calmly how they arose, and be determined to counteract them. Then one has a sense of actually shaping the future on the basis of true knowledge, not on the basis of mere chance or the whim of a capricious god. This is true spiritual knowledge based upon a courageous correction of one's own relationship to the divine spirit within, the indwelling Ishwara.

Great teachers work under a law where every genuine striving is noticed, but all human beings throughout the world come under the same law. Those who can see the past, the present and the future simultaneously will only let their gaze fall where it is merited, because where it falls there is a tremendous quickening of opportunities for growth, but also an enormous increase of the hazards of neglect. In a dynamic universe of thought and of consciousness, a great difference can be made in one's understanding of causality and of energy through one's concept of time which is determined by one's concept of selfhood and being. This is truly a function of how one thinks at this moment today, how one sleeps tonight and how one wakes up tomorrow, in a cycle of progressive awakenings through meditation and ethical practice, not for the sake of oneself but for the sake of all living beings in the visible and invisible cosmos.

SPIRITUAL WILL

The vital interrelationship of Nature and of humanity, as well as the complex process of evolution and of history, is essentially the manifestation of unity in diversity. Every human being is a compact kingdom with manifold centres of energy that are microcosmic foci connected with macrocosmic influences. There is a fundamental logic to the vast unfolding from One Source through rays of light in myriad directions into numerous centres that are all held together by a single Fohatic force, an ordering principle of energy. The logic of emanation is the same for the cosmos and for the individual. The arcane teaching of the divine Hierarchies, of Dhyani Buddhas, of the three sets of Builders and of the mysterious Lipika conveys intimations of invisible, ever-present, noumenal patterns that underlie this immense cosmos of which every human being is an integral part. The ordered movement of the vast whole is also mirrored in the small, in all the atoms, and is paradigmatically present in the symmetries and asymmetries of the human form with its differentiated and specialized organs of perception and of action.

Modern man, burdened by irrelevant and chaotic cerebration, often fails to ask the critical, central questions: What does it mean to have a human form? Why does the face have seven orifices? What does it mean to have a hand with five fingers? Why is one finger called the index finger and what is the purpose of pointing in human life? What is the significance of the thumb and what is its connection with will and determination, which must be both strong and flexible? Can flexibility and fluidity be combined in human life in ways analogous to what is exemplified in the physical world by all the lunar hierarchies impressed with the intelligence that comes from higher planes? What is the function of the little finger, which is associated with Mercury? What is the connection between speech and this seemingly unimportant digit which is important for those who have skill in the use of hands, whether in instrumental music or in craftsmanship? When one is ready to ask questions of this kind, taking nothing for granted, then one can look at statues of the Buddha and of various gods in many traditions, where the placement of the hand is extraordinarily significant: whether it is pointing above, pointing below, whether it is extended outwards, whether it is in the form of an oblation or receiving an offering, or in the familiar *mudra* of the hand that blesses. What is the meaning of joining the thumb and the central finger, which is given great importance in mystical texts like the *Hymn to Dakshinamurti?*

The moment one begins to raise such innocent questions about the most evident aspects of human existence, it immediately becomes clear that pseudo-sophisticated people are prisoners of the false idea that they already know. And yet self-reliance and spontaneous trust are so scarce in the world of the half-educated. Many people are so lacking in elementary self-knowledge that when a person meets another, instead of a natural response of receptivity and trust, there is an entrenched bias engendered by fear and suspicion. This has been consolidated through the establishment of a Nietzschean conceptual framework in which all human relationships are viewed simply in terms of domination and being dominated. This obsessive standpoint drains human relationships of deeper content, of spiritual meaning and moral consciousness. All moral categories and considerations become irrelevant when one entirely focuses upon an ethically neutral and colourless conception of the will. To assume and act as if everything turns upon the master-slave relation is a major block to the development of self-consciousness, as Hegel recognized. Humanity has left behind its feverish preoccupation with false dominance in formal structures. The seventeenth and eighteenth centuries witnessed the emergence of a higher plateau of individual and collective self-consciousness. All men and women are the inheritors of the Enlightenment, with its unequivocal affirmation of the inalienable dignity of the individual, who can creatively relate to other human beings in meaningful dialogue and constructive cooperation.

Rooted in a simplistic but assertive mentality, dissolving all moral issues, the language of confrontation and of submission is irrelevant to the universal human condition and to the hierarchical complexity of Nature. Any person with a modicum of thought who begins to ask questions about the marvellous intricacy and dynamic interrelationships of Nature — questions about the sun and the stars, the trees and forests, the rivers and oceans, and above all about human growth — will readily recognize that no real understanding of the organic processes of Nature can be properly expressed in terms of such jejune categories as dominance and submission. Nor can any meaningful truths about the archetypal relations between teachers and disciples, parents and children, friends and companions, be apprehended through the truncated notion of an amoral will. Human life is poetic, musical and poignant. It has an open texture, with recurrent rhythms, and it continuously participates in concurrent cycles. To know this is to recognize, when viewing the frail fabric of modern societies, that human evolution has not abrogated the primordial principles of mutuality and interdependence, but indeed abnormal human beings and societies have become alienated from their inner resources of true strength and warmth, trust and reciprocity. The Golden Rule remains universal in scope and significance. There is not a culture or portion of the human race, not an epoch in history, in which the Golden Rule was not understood. Without this awareness there would be no social survival, let alone its translation into the language of roles and obligations and into the logic of markets. Reciprocity is intrinsic to the human condition.

By rethinking fundamentally what it means to confer the potency of ideation upon primal facts such as the conscious use of the human hand, one can discard much muddled thinking which is the prolific parent of a vast progeny of distrustful, fearful, weak and wayward thoughts that are constantly tending in a downward direction. Spiritual will can be strengthened when a person meditates upon the cosmic activity which is partly conveyed through creation myths, and may be grasped metaphysically in terms of the abstract becoming more and more, yet only incompletely, concrete. There must be a firm recognition of the necessary gap — inherently unbridgeable — between the unconditioned and the conditioned, between noumenal light and its phenomenal reflections. For those who begin to sense this in the ever-changing world, it can help to initiate a revolution in their everyday relationships. The true occultist starts at the simple level of constant thoughtfulness and moves to a mode of awareness whereby he can effortlessly put himself into the position of another human being.

It is the hallmark of spiritual maturity that one has no sense of psychological distance from another, that one cannot only salute but also share the unspoken subjectivity of another human being. When a thoughtful person begins to look at others in this way, the need for involuntary karma and mere extensions to superficial human contact will be replaced by the inward capacity, through every opportunity that comes naturally, to discover the universal meaning of human evolution, the potential richness and actual limitations of human nature, and the shared pathos of the spiritual pilgrimage of humanity. As depth of awareness is gained, it is possible to educate one's perceptions and one's responses to the world, cleansing the mind and the heart, and releasing the spiritual will. One can cultivate a real taste for the rarefied altitudes of Himalayan heights whereupon sublime truths are experienced as noumenal realities.

The awakening of intuitive insight is an essential prerequisite to authentic participation in human life. Noetic awakening presupposes that one learns to take nothing for granted, and repeatedly re-creates a sense of wonder and openness. It is necessary to increase silence in relation to speech, contemplation in relation to action, and deliberation in relation to impetuous response. Living from within, each day becomes charged with rich significance and is a vital link in a continuous thread of creative ideation. So immense are the potentials of human consciousness that for a true *yogin* a single day is like an entire incarnation. When individuals truly kindle the spark of *Buddhi-Manas,* they can rapidly move away from the nether region of dark distrust and abject dependence, and actively think in terms of the high prerogatives and vast possibilities of human life. Through calm contemplation they can come closer to the highest energies in the cosmos. Through proper alignment with what is above and within, they readily perceive the world as a shadowy reflection of reality, and also see beyond fleeting images to the hidden core of what gives vitality and continuity to the stream of consciousness. The restoration of Buddhic perception gives a preliminary understanding of what it is like to become constitutionally incapable of distrust, delusion, cowardice and craving. The mental portrait of the self-governed Sage, who ever remains in effortless attunement to the parentless Source, becomes a transforming reality in daily life. One no longer inhabits the terrestrial region of time and space in which linger many deluded souls for whom one feels true compassion, but one ascends to the empyrean of divine ideation.

Noble resolves and self-binding commitments are accessible to the spiritual will that is allied with the active aspect of *Buddhi*, which is *Kundalini*. In the manifest world Fohat is cosmic electricity, which vitalizes everything and is the intelligent guiding force behind all combinations, permutations and separations which occur throughout all the kingdoms of Nature. But in the unmanifest realm Fohat is pure consciousness, the energy of potential ideation. This plane of spiritual unity and volition cannot be approached except by intensely developing the power of abstraction. Suppose that a person starts simply with the difficult but necessary meditation upon the corpse. Every human being knows that one day the body will be stiff like a log of wood, and whether it is burnt or buried it will have already begun to disintegrate from what is arbitrarily called the moment of death, about which there is much uncertainty. When is that moment of death? Is it when the heart ceases to beat and the breathing stops, or is it when electrical activity in the brain subsides? Theosophically, there are further critical questions about the progressive withdrawal of the immortal monad from its different vestures. The astral that is bound up with the physical body must go with the disintegrating body because even for disintegration there must be an invisible basis of intelligence, provided by the gross astral. But there are other aspects of the astral that are connected with the departing principles. Profound meditation upon one's corpse and the moment of death can result in a critical distance and increasing freedom from personal anticipations about the coming weeks, months and years. If a person finds anything morbid in this meditation, it is because consciousness has become escapist, delusive and pleasure-oriented. But if one is ardently concerned with meaning and significance, with ethical considerations of right and wrong, with obligation and responsibility, then one may calmly and detachedly see the moment of death as the completion of a cycle of fulfilment of earthly duties and spiritual exercises.

It is necessary to move in thought far beyond this initial meditation upon death. One must think of oneself as having lived through and relinquished a wide range of mortal bodies, as having been through innumerable sets of experiences in many different contexts, enacting myriad roles. For the immortal soul the only significant question is whether one learnt anything deeply meaningful about the world and from any opportunities for the elevation of consciousness that it offered. How many times was one able to come into contact with spiritual teachers, and in how many lives was one able to intuit something of the meaning of initiation? As one persists in such questions, one begins to live in and through other people, experiencing an intense interest in the human condition as a whole. Seeing the world through many eyes, one identifies with the standpoint of myriad souls. One begins to discover the secret of the *yogin* and the Adept: that the more one withdraws within, the more one can universalize one's own concern for the human race. By giving up the false idea that what is visible is necessarily more real than what is invisible, that one has more pressing obligations to those one sees than to those one does not see, one realizes that human evolution could not have continued, that people would not have planted trees for their descendants, without some awareness of the hidden basis of human solidarity. When one has attained some appreciation of this vital fact, it would be of great benefit to meditate upon the sacred Catechism in *The Secret Doctrine*:

> The Master is made to ask the pupil:
> '*Lift thy head, oh Lanoo; dost thou see one, or countless lights above thee, burning in the dark midnight sky?*'
> '*I sense one Flame, oh Gurudeva, I see countless undetached sparks shining in it.*'
> '*Thou sayest well. And now look around and into thyself. That light which burns inside thee, dost thou feel it different in anywise from the light that shines in thy Brother-men?*'
> '*It is in no way different, though the prisoner is held in bondage by Karma, and though its outer garments delude the ignorant into saying, "Thy Soul and My Soul."*'
> The Secret Doctrine, i 120

Any person who begins such meditations and persists in them will experience a tremendous cleansing preparatory to the re-education of the powers of perception and action. Eventually, one no more sees the world as the world sees itself, in terms of separation and contrast, dominance and distrust, dependence and change. Instead one learns to see the world in terms of the continuity behind the change, in terms of that which is deathless within that which is ever dying. One begins to sense the noumenal reality of divine ideation behind the flux of fleeting phenomena. When a person starts to think, feel and respond in the light of this transformed way of looking at the world, deliberately choosing ideas, lines of thought, self-reliant acts of service, feelings of compassion, benevolence and trust, then one's whole conception of reality is altered. Even the sense of being bound down by the persona begins to loosen up gradually. Through this regenerative experience one comes to recognize that the motion that is visible is only a surface phenomenon and that the highest energy resides only where all external forces are gathered and withdrawn to a still centre.

By the mystic power of ideation one has supersensuous insight and a much sharper sense of the universe as unitary. Until there is Buddhic awareness of the omnipresence and radical unity of unmanifest Fohat, there can be no truly free will and self-reliance, but only compulsive restlessness and passive reaction. Free will in the spiritual sense only begins when one enters into a realm of pure freedom from form, flux and change, and from the temporal succession of states of consciousness. This can be readily tested. If one feels that the first moment that one contacted the Divine Wisdom is *now*, then one is free, but if it seems years ago, then one is enslaved by the past. If one feels that one's moment of death is *now*, one is free, but if it seems to lurk in the future, one is mesmerized by change. When one can burst the artificial boundaries of past and future within the present moment, then one begins to experience the spiritual will that is free, powerful and beneficent, and which, because it is unbounded, can lend enormous courage and confidence to the deliberate choice of thoughts and the continuous direction of attention. Where the attention or the eye of the Adept falls there is a tremendous intensification of noetic life-currents. There is an intimate relation between the Fohatic energies of ideation and attention focussed in the Eye of Shiva and the Kriyashaktic power of quickening spiritual and material life.

In their self-training all disciples must progressively learn to master the power of attention preparatory to any real initiation. First, one has to learn to withhold attention, and one has to do it many times over until it becomes a totally natural process. Lowering one's eyes when going out into the world, holding one's tongue when in company, restraining one's hands from grasping at objects, the disciple learns by withdrawing and withholding attention how it is possible to choose a great idea out of the voidness and how to choose by acceptance what comes under karma in the world. There is nothing personal in this because through heightened awareness one sees that what is chosen at any given time is but one out of myriad possibilities. In this way one is not caught in the delusions resulting from a sensationalist fuss about events. Events do not have any such exaggerated meaning because one always sees that about which Gurudeva speaks — the one undivided Flame. One hears all the time that which is inaudible, like that which is in the fathomless depths of the ocean and in the farthest reaches of space — "the VOICE unbroken, that resounds throughout eternities, exempt from change, from sin exempt, the Seven Sounds in one, THE VOICE OF THE SILENCE."

Once one becomes a witness to the incredible ordering of life-atoms and a Buddhic perceiver of the immense possibilities they represent, they truly become one's pupils, friends and servants in the great work of universal evolution. Ultimately, one can even overcome the contrast between subjectivity and objectivity, between spirit and matter. Because people do not do this voluntarily, Fohat at one level makes incarnation possible, binding *Atma-Buddhi* to *Manas*. When *Manas* manifests as a man of mighty meditation, it becomes one with *Atman,* and *Buddhi* generates that subtle breath of silent Fohatic energy whereby one withdraws from all reflections of light into the empyrean of Divine Truth. The less one is caught up in the agitations of manifested Fohat, the more one feels the intensity of strength of the field of inaudible, unexpressed feeling-energy of *Atma-Buddhi* radiating from the eternal realm of *Sat.*

> This 'World of Truth' can be described only in the words of the Commentary as 'A bright star dropped from the heart of Eternity; the beacon of hope on whose Seven Rays hang the Seven Worlds of Being.' Truly so; since those are the Seven Lights whose reflections are the human immortal Monads — the Atma, or the irradiating Spirit of every creature of the human family.
>
> *Ibid.*, i 120

SPIRITUAL PERCEPTION

The possession of a physical third eye ... was enjoyed by the men of the Third Root-Race down to nearly the middle period of the Third SUB-race of the Fourth Root-Race, when the consolidation and perfection of the human frame made it disappear from the outward anatomy of man. Psychically and spiritually, however, its mental and visual perceptions lasted till nearly the end of the Fourth Race, when its functions, owing to the materiality and depraved condition of mankind, died out altogether before the submersion of the bulk of the Atlantean continent.

The Secret Doctrine, ii 306

The ancient atrophy of the Third Eye, together with the possibility of its reawakening, is integral to the teachings of Gupta Vidya. The elusive nature of that eye lies veiled in many myths and legends about the idyllic childhood of humanity and its paradisaic innocence. This lost and largely forgotten Elysium was not some sheltered sanctuary, but rather a pervasive state of consciousness. Within a triple scheme of human evolution, comprising spiritual, intellectual and physiological modes of development, the whole of humanity, at the dawn of evolution, enjoyed a foretaste of the glorious fullness of human potential, to be unfolded towards the close of the Seventh Round. During the enormous cycles of human evolution upon earth, there has been an alternation of longer and shorter periods of relative obscuration of the spiritual faculties of humanity. Some of these phases were intensified by human errors and avoidable tragedies. These became overlapping factors in succeeding cycles of obscuration and clarity in the human vestures, resulting from the centrifugal and centripetal forces behind evolution. The actual condition and constitution of human vestures in any epoch is the product of complex causes.

Mature wisdom calls for a strong sense of moral responsibility for the collective consequences of past conduct as well as active cooperation with the inexorable cycles of Nature. These include the familiar cycle of birth and death, the slow succession of the Golden, Silver, Bronze and Iron Ages, the emergence and disappearance of continents and also the myriad vicissitudes in the alteration and refinement of human vestures. The original awakening, subsequent atrophy and future recovery of the Third Eye is a moral saga illustrating the interweaving of cyclic necessity and moral responsibility. Even conscientious students of Gupta Vidya find it very difficult to preserve a proper balance in relation to the poignant theme of the atrophy of the Third Eye. It is upsetting to think of the vast majority of human beings as spiritually marred by the appalling consequences of the flagrant misuse of the higher faculties during earlier races. The inherent inability of most people even to consider the hidden Third Eye as the active organ of spiritual vision is the karmic heirloom of all humanity. And yet, the need to arouse the latent power of spiritual vision poses a profound and inescapable challenge to all aspirants on the path of spiritual enlightenment. We need to ask what was natural and what was unnatural about the early evolution and eventual petrification of the Third Eye.

Myths, legends and folklore indicate that, in archaic periods of prehistory, human beings were gigantic in stature and possessed a 'Cyclopean' eye located in the forehead. Gupta Vidya assigns these distant epochs to the Third and early Fourth Root Races. According to arcane wisdom, the placement of this eye in the forehead is a poetic licence: the true locus was at the back of the head. What we now call the Third Eye was then the dominant organ of vision. To understand this, one must appreciate the primacy of the astral and inner vestures in relation to the organs of action and sensory faculties of the physical body.

The *First* Race is shown in Occult sciences as spiritual within and ethereal without; the *second,* psycho-spiritual mentally, and ethero-physical bodily;

the *third*, still bereft of intellect in its beginning, is astro-physical in its body, and lives an inner life, in which the psycho-spiritual element is in no way interfered with as yet by the hardly nascent physiological senses. Its two front eyes look before them without seeing either past or future. But the 'third eye' *'embraces* ETERNITY'.

Ibid., 298-299

As an organ, the 'Cyclopean' eye belongs to the subtler vestures which antedate the emergence of the physical form with its familiar organs. The physical body, together with its complex and delicate physiological structure, constitutes a "coat of skin" which evolved from within outward, covering the astral vesture. This development took place at that point in cyclic evolution when there was a maximum involvement of Spirit in matter, correlative with the maximum differentiation of objective substance. The complete involvement of human souls in physical matter took place simultaneously with the infusion of the self-conscious Manasic ray into a set of developing human vestures. Once *Manas* was awakened, the Third Eye — which in reality is the *first eye* — served as the organ of spiritual sight, untrammelled in its activity by the nascent physiological vesture. Its mirror in the physical body is the pineal gland, intuitively identified by Descartes as the seat of the soul. In the animal kingdom, whose vestures were formed from the residues of human evolution, a similar physiological structure served as the organ of vision.

Therefore, while the 'Cyclopean' eye was, and still *is*, in man the organ of *spiritual* sight, in the animal it was that of objective vision. And this eye, having performed its function, was replaced, in the course of physical evolution from the simple to the complex, by two eyes, and thus was stored and laid aside by nature for further use in Aeons to come. This explains why the pineal gland reached its highest development

proportionately with the lowest physical development.
It is the vertebrata in which it is the most prominent
and objective and in man it is most carefully hidden
and inaccessible, except to the anatomist.

Ibid., 299-300

These developments, encompassing millions of years and vast cycles of racial evolution, are all part of what may be called the programme of Nature. They marked the momentous intersection of the activity of the *Barhishad* or Lunar Pitris and the *Agnishwatha* or Solar Pitris. These two groups of ancestors endowed humanity with, respectively, its differentiated material vestures on several planes and its inward spiritual principles, especially *Manas* or self-conscious moral intelligence. The natural exercise of spiritual vision guided by self-conscious intelligence constituted the foundation of the Golden Age at the dawn of humanity. As the inevitable tide of physiological evolution gradually caused the 'Cyclopean' eye to recede, human beings experienced a painful sense of loss. With much greater dependence upon the two front eyes during the early Fourth Root Race or Atlantean civilization, there were desperate physiological attempts to recover what had been lost. Many Atlanteans could not comprehend that their loss had to do with consciousness and with form. They became enormously preoccupied with forms and externals, and thereby brought about a diminution in the power and scope of consciousness itself at its most autonomous level. None of the repeated efforts to tinker with the physiological organs or to create substitutes by whatever means could quicken or reawaken the spiritual function of the Third Eye. Atlanteans became increasingly involved in something fundamentally unnatural which could only produce a consolidated concretization of consciousness. Eventually, quite apart from the loss of the Third Eye in the physical organism, there was an obscuration of spiritual perception associated with the Third Eye. This became a tremendous handicap to human evolution.

It was not necessary then, nor is it now, that all human beings remain spiritually blind, regardless of physiological evolution or the widespread atrophy of the pineal gland. The deliberate awakening of spiritual vision is integral to the exacting discipline of initiation into the Mysteries. Such preparatory training is based upon a truly philosophic understanding of human nature and incarnation, and upon a systematic ethical and psychological development which excludes short-cuts and adventitious aids. Mahatmas and Initiates who have guided and guarded the spiritual progress of humanity for over eighteen million years have continually made accessible the time-honoured path that leads to inward enlightenment. The *Commentaries* on the *Stanzas of Dzyan* convey the need for magnetic purity and proper guidance:

> *There were four-armed human creatures in those early days of the male-females* (hermaphrodites); *with one head, yet three eyes. They could see before them and behind them. A KALPA later* (after the separation of the sexes) *men having fallen into matter, their spiritual vision became dim; and coordinately the third eye commenced to lose its power. . . . When the Fourth* (Race) *arrived at its middle age, the inner vision had to be awakened, and* acquired by artificial stimuli . . . . *The third eye, likewise, getting gradually* PETRIFIED, *soon disappeared. The double-faced became the one-faced, and the eye was drawn deep into the head and is now buried under the hair. During the activity of the inner man* (during trances and spiritual visions) *the eye swells and expands. The Arhat sees and feels it, and regulates his action accordingly . . . . The undefiled* Lanoo (disciple, chela) *need fear no danger; he who keeps himself not in purity* (who is not chaste) *will receive no help from the 'deva eye.'*
>
> *Ibid.*, 294 - 295

During the descent of Spirit into matter, the spiritual and physiological processes are strictly coordinate. For example, if there is a loss in the inward power of seeing, the organ of sight is also commensurately weakened. This is equally true of all human faculties and their physical centres. Various atrophied organs survive in the human constitution, and these are hardly understood by contemporary physiology or medicine. They are virtually irrelevant to the vast majority of human beings. Sages of old knew that the disciplines which can truly help to reawaken inner vision are radically different from the artificial stimuli avidly sought during the latter Atlantean age. Yet, the appeal of these poor substitutes points to the pervasiveness and inevitability of the eclipse of the inner senses by overdeveloped outer senses. Most human beings shared in this psycho-physical heredity that was caused by the gross abuse of faculties and powers during the Atlantean period.

If there is an excessive development of the physiological eyes at the expense of the Third Eye during a particular phase of evolution, and if all human beings are involuntary participants in this process, then as later phases of evolution are reached human beings could awaken flashes of that original interior perception. As the balance of evolution shifts from the phase of involution of Spirit into matter to the evolution of Spirit out of matter, there is a corresponding lightening of the vestures and a quickening of the veiled organs of inner vision. Human beings could have flashes of perception, even though they might not be able to recover that perception fully, let alone quickly. In meditation they might experience a certain swelling and expansion, an agitation or heating up, connected with the intensity of activity in the pineal gland. No known physiological function may be assigned to the pineal gland, and however much medical practitioners study the human corpse, they will never discover its real importance during life. Some do recognize that the pineal gland indirectly regulates hormone-producing glands, and it is now known that in animals it is sensitive to light. In fact, human beings can during deep contemplation or during some states of ecstatic trance have flashes of the expansion and contraction that affect the pineal gland and pituitary body. These in turn affect their perception of images and sounds. Even though there was an inescapable element in the loss of its original function, the

Third Eye itself was not wholly lost. It is still dormant and remains intact in the subtle vestures. The problem for present humanity is the proper coordination between the functioning of the Third Eye in the subtle vestures and the physical body with its two eyes and the atrophied pineal organ.

If the natural veiling of spiritual sight through the inordinate development of the physiological vesture was the whole story, then humanity would not have melancholy recollections of the Golden Age, nor such a strong propensity towards gloom and doom, externalization and salvationism. In fact, the persisting dominance of entire theologies based upon guilt and sin at this particular point in human evolution is itself indicative of the perfidious moral history connected with the loss of the Third Eye. No matter how much contrasting theories of guilt and sin claim to account for the present human predicament, they can only gain credence through vulnerabilities in the human psyche. These revolve around a morbid sense of failure, pretence and pride, which are the unnatural result of past misuse of spiritual powers. Human beings may identify evil with violence and separativeness, with everything that is inimical and arises out of blindness and greed, stupidity and self-deception. Nonetheless, all these represent secondary effects. At the causal level, evil pertains to the perverse misuse of the very highest spiritual gifts. Such misuse induced religions to fall victim to priestcraft and lose touch with the Mysteries. Spiritual evil made human beings, who innately have extraordinary powers such as *Kriyashakti* and *Itchashakti,* lose all of them. Spiritual evil and deliberate misuse were a violation of the evolutionary programme of Nature.

> When spirituality and all the divine powers and attributes of the deva-man of the Third had been made the hand-maidens of the newly-awakened physiological and psychic passions of the physical man, instead of the reverse, the eye lost its powers. But such was the law of Evolution, and it was, in strict accuracy, no FALL. The sin was not in using those newly-developed powers, but

in *misusing* them; in making of the tabernacle, designed
to contain a god, the fane of every *spiritual* iniquity.

Ibid., 302

The deleterious consequences of this profanation cannot be
blamed upon the logic of descent of Spirit into matter. They are
the terrible karma of those who, far from merely becoming
enslaved by selfish desire and sensory indulgence, in fact became
proficient in treachery, blasphemy, profanation and betrayal of the
sacred, especially in sacrificing the welfare of others for the sake
of self. This has nothing to do with any passing weakness owing
to a natural obscuration of faculties. Whatever the 'ills' that
mortal flesh may be heir to, the physical body is not the source
of spiritual iniquity. As H.P. Blavatsky indicated,

> the reader who would feel perplexed at the use of the
> term 'spiritual' instead of 'physical' iniquity, is reminded
> of the fact that there can be no physical iniquity. The
> body is simply the irresponsible organ, the tool of the
> *psychic*, if not of the 'Spiritual man'. While in the case
> of the Atlanteans, it was precisely the Spiritual being
> which sinned, the Spirit element being still the 'Master'
> principle in man in those days. Thus it is in those days
> that the heaviest Karma of the Fifth Race was generated
> by our Monads.
>
> *Ibid.*, 302

One must calmly contemplate how this spiritual sin arose
and how it engendered enormous ruthlessness and extreme
selfishness as well as an overpowering obsession with external
dominance and a deeply entrenched resistance to admitting any
fault, acknowledging any responsibility or making any amends.
Through the perverse misuse of the highest powers with which
they were entrusted, vast numbers of sick souls were trapped in a
tragic condition wherein they were unable and unwilling to come
to terms with their own karma and virtually incapable of finding
or even seeking their proper place in the moral order of the

cosmos and of society. Owing to this diseased perversion and compulsive inversion, an appalling corruption of consciousness resulted, which cannot be suddenly remedied at some future point in evolution, even when the interconnection between the subtle centres and physiological organs is radically altered. It is indeed imperative for the spiritually corrupt to begin now to reverse the karma of past misuse if they would at all reawaken spiritual vision and continue to participate in self-conscious human evolution in future races.

Certainly, it would be of great help to seek, and show true humility, amidst the company of stronger souls whose karma is untainted by ingratitude and perfidy in former lives. It is always salutary for everyone to admire and emulate freedom from a sense of separativeness wherever one sees it in others. This is ever preferable to the contagion of abject selfishness, stark ingratitude, rancour and envy. Anyone can attempt to make real for oneself the latent spiritual goodness, purity and innocence that one can re-cognize in any others around. Authentic admiration and emulation can be powerful purifiers for any human being, let alone for those who come into the magnetic orbit of a spiritual Teacher. It can bring one in closer touch with one's own spiritual heritage from the Third Root Race, which is even now recapitulated in childhood and infancy. Nonetheless, the root causes of spiritual and moral blindness must be faced. Until they are confronted, the proper awakening of spiritual vision is impossible. This brings up the ultimate question of authentically accommodating the idea of universal compassion and enlightenment.

Can one develop sufficient self-transcendence and such a profound concern for the spiritual welfare of all human souls that one's entire conception of desire is revolutionized? When this becomes possible, one can be so creative and so saturated with universal compassion that one simply does not have any craving, let alone a compulsive need, to consider any other human being as a mere object for one's own sensuous gratification. There is a radical change in one's level of consciousness, and this has a decisive effect on the tropism and texture of elements and life-atoms in the subtle vestures and in the physical body. The flow of energy within the spinal cord is transformed, affecting the interaction between the pineal gland and the pituitary body, together with the medulla oblongata and the multiple centres of the brain.

It is only if one apprehends the necessity of these fundamental transformations in human nature that one can recognize that the essential logic of human evolution did not envisage such damage to spiritual vision. To grasp this is to be ready to engage in an examination of one's motives, one's potentials, one's capacities and the hindrances that obstruct one's consciousness. Through *tapas* and daily meditation one may appreciate the feasibility of increasing continuity of consciousness between waking and sleeping, between life and death, bridging all the pairs of opposites and transcending the succession of time. One may then come to comprehend that the Third Eye has retreated from without inwardly because an earlier phase of the logic of evolution extruded it from within without. The withdrawal inward of the organ of the Third Eye corresponds to a greater withdrawal of consciousness from concretization, which is indeed crucial in the current phase of human growth and maturation. Concretization of consciousness does not refer only to the amount of stimuli on the physical or sensory plane; it also takes place through limiting concepts and mental ossification, through craving for certainty, through harsh judgementalism and an addiction to self-pity and even nihilism. The inability to restore the fluidity of ideation on metaphysical abstractions, spiritual ideas and moral ideals is the sad consequence of concretization and externalization.

Whatever corruption of consciousness originally occurred has been compounded many times over through repeated failures to come to terms with the propensity to prolong spiritual iniquity and accelerate self-destruction. This cannot be put right instantly, and to imagine otherwise is only a symptom of the basic problem. One must resolve to try, to try and try again. In order to strengthen this resolve, the Teachers of Gupta Vidya have sought to share relevant portions of arcane knowledge about the history of the Third and Fourth Root Races. Some understanding of past evolution is essential if one seeks to grasp the logic and significance of systematic self-training and self-testing. In order to rejoin the forward movement of humanity, one must realize that all human beings are fallen gods, disinherited from their divine estate through the loss of the eye of wisdom. As a result, they have become almost exclusively dependent upon sensory perception. And yet, the actual range of the physical sense-organs has become narrower and narrower over time. Since the energy of spiritual life is independent of physical form and matter, the more preoccupied one is with the physical form and with sense-perceptions, the more one is alienated from the true source of strength, volition and self-direction.

When individuals initially confront this problem, they run the risk of entangling themselves in what might be called a meta-problem. Contacting the Teachings of Gupta Vidya and reading about the earlier races of humanity, the karma of Atlantis and the loss of the Third Eye release latent forces within one's nature. The processes which originally held one back can repeat themselves in one's apprehension and use of arcane wisdom. If one's basic loyalty is to the world and to one's self-image on the personal plane, then whatever vows and resolves one adopts can only operate and have force on that plane. One may maintain a sanctimonious charade reminiscent of hypocritical religion and monkish façades. One may even manage to conceal the persistent play-acting from oneself for a long time. Inevitably, the time comes when one recoils from the sham with self-loathing and a mixture of indignation and despair. This is a tragic and pitiable condition for any human soul. The danger of becoming trapped in this meta-problem must be coolly confronted, since the restoration of spiritual vision cannot occur without unleashing the very tendencies that originally led to spiritual blindness.

Typically, this problem shows itself in a grasping attitude towards the Teachings of Gupta Vidya. Instead of putting oneself in the position of a postulant who is wide awake, who absorbs through osmosis and calmly assimilates the Teachings, seeking to apply them to daily duties and encounters, one becomes addicted to over-analysis and judgementalism. Through one's continuing contact with the Teachings, there is a powerful quickening of the energies available to the restless lower mind and the attendant risk that these energies will be appropriated by the *ahankaric* and acquisitive self. When the individual receives more spiritual food than he or she is able to assimilate on a higher plane, then *kama manas* becomes hyperactive, destructive and harsh. Fascinated with its own weaknesses and faults, it ceaselessly looks for vulnerabilities in others and even becomes adroit in self-serving rationalizations and endless excuses. As a result there arises a powerful blockage to the release of intuitive insight.

It is through the power of Buddhic intuition that individuals are initially drawn to the Teachings of Gupta Vidya. In learning a language, one must try to speak, making mistakes, correcting them, and thereby gradually gaining facility. If this is true of ordinary language, it is much more so with the language of the soul. Spiritual intuition is like fire. It is only through the use of real fire that fuel can be kindled, and wherever real fire is used, there is the risk that it will be misused. This is paradigmatically true with regard to the Promethean fire of mind given to humanity over eighteen million years ago. Every neophyte who would approach the Mystery-fires must be prepared to assume full responsibility for the right use of the fire of knowledge. The more one has the proper qualifications to become a *chela*, the more one is able to assimilate and reflect deeply and patiently upon the Teachings, endowing them with vivid relevance to daily life. The fire of *Buddhi* can become quickened through the study, contemplation and practice of Gupta Vidya. As Krishna affirmed in the *Bhagavad Gita*, in the course of time spiritual knowledge will spring up spontaneously within oneself.

In order to release soul-memory and activate one's higher faculties, one must be fortunate enough to have come consciously and voluntarily to the spiritual life, not out of any compensatory motives but out of love and reverence for Divine Wisdom and with a deep longing to benefit humanity. Only those who live and breathe benevolently can avoid the awful consequences of misappropriating the higher energies in the service of the lower, thereby forfeiting the great opportunity gained under karma of coming closer to the immemorial Teachings and to authentic spiritual Teachers. For such seekers who are suffused with a profound humility and a deep desire for learning for the sake of others, there will be a natural protection. True *shravakas* or learners will be able to use the archetypal method from the first, proceeding from above below and from within without and emphasizing at each stage the steady assimilation of mental and spiritual food through moral practice. There need be no partiality and imbalance, no one-sidedness or bias, in the apprehension and application of Gupta Vidya. As Mahatma M. pointed out,

> In our doctrine you will find necessary the synthetic method; you will have to embrace the whole — that is to say to blend the *macrocosm* and microcosm together — before you are enabled to study the parts separately or analyze them with profit to your understanding. Cosmology is the physiology of the universe spiritualized, for there is but one Law.

In order to embrace the whole, one must grasp the fundamental continuity of cosmic and human evolution, establishing one's consciousness in a current of Buddhic compassion and unconditional love for all that lives. One must learn to move back and forth continuously between the macrocosmic and the microcosmic. One must strive to see the relevance of universal ideation to specific contexts. One must ever seek to bridge the universal and the particular in waking consciousness, maximizing the good even in highly imperfect situations. Tremendous aid can come through the Buddhic stream of Hermetic wisdom pouring forth from the Brotherhood of Bodhisattvas. With a mind moistened by wisdom and compassion, one may return again and again in meditation and self-study to seek appropriate connections and correspondences between the macrocosm and the microcosm. Drawing upon the rich resources of Gupta Vidya, one must grasp its universal synthesis before attempting to study the parts separately or analytically. This means that one must engage in daily *tapas* or mental asceticism. In the Aquarian Age we need to relinquish the entrenched modes of the inductive and analytic mind, replacing them by cultivated skill in deep concentration, creative imagination and calm receptivity towards universal ideation. In this way one will come to comprehend the connections between the most primordial and abstract and the most dense and differentiated levels of manifestation of consciousness and matter. The continuity of consciousness which one seeks is, in fact, a mode of mirroring the metaphysical integrity of cosmic unity.

If one can learn to let go of the rationalizing pseudo-intelligence of the personality, then one can begin to draw upon the natural strength of *Manas*. One must learn to take the simplest ideas and apply them universally. Action based upon spiritual insight has a moral simplicity that neither can be understood nor imitated by the lower mind. For a long time in the life of any disciple, it is wise to consider the spiritual vision of the Third Eye as equivalent to moral discrimination. This is eloquently illustrated in the life of Mohandas Gandhi, who was skilful in finding potent analogies between the circulation of blood and global economics or psychological health. Anyone who arouses *Buddhi* can take seriously the integrity of the cosmos and deduce practical wisdom. One can learn to perceive vital connections between the mental and spiritual health of individuals and society as a whole, and apply these perceptions to oneself.

If one gains some proficiency in this daily use of Buddhic intuition, one will soon find that it becomes meaningful to use the myths and symbols of Gupta Vidya as a basis for meditation upon the structure and function of the human form. One must learn to contemplate the cosmic dimension of human existence and become capable of deriving from such contemplation a vital sense of sanctity, plasticity and potentiality in relation to the physical body. Great philosophers and mystics have done this, seeing in the human form the paradigmatic metaphor for all growth. They have used the analogy of sight when speaking of soul-knowledge and spiritual wisdom, referring to the eye of the soul and the mind's eye. But even to appreciate this analogy, one must to some degree awaken *Buddhi*. Just as one can hardly convey the operation of sight and vision to a person born blind, one cannot readily communicate the nature of spiritual vision to those in whom it is totally blocked. Similarly, one could hardly convey the thrills and challenges of mental perception to persons with undeveloped mental sight.

As the ability to apprehend analogies is itself an essential element in soul-vision and also conducive to the awakening of the inward capacity for noetic insight, it is always wise to recognize and acknowledge the limits and levels of human experience. Without actually developing spiritual and mental insight and tasting the ineffable bliss of authentic mystical vision, one cannot comprehend or even appreciate the scope and range of possible peak experiences. Owing to the pervasive principle of continuity in the cosmic order and in human nature, there is the ever-present possibility of transcending the limits of known and shared experience. By using analogies and correspondences to move from the familiar and the bounded to the unfamiliar and the unbounded, one may gain sufficient skill in the dialectical art to subdue the mind and absorb it into the pulsating consciousness of the spiritual heart. In a mystical sense, one can make the mind whole, and enlist it into the service of the heart, while at the same time making the heart intelligent and strong.

In order to attain a state of heightened spiritual awareness and effortless vigilance, compassion and receptivity, it is essential to recognize and remove persisting discontinuities in consciousness. The familiar gaps between sleeping and waking, between dreaming and deep sleep, between ephemeral fantasies and enduring commitments, are connected with lesions in the subtle vestures which induce a fragmentation and distortion of spiritual insights. One must patiently identify these deficiencies, seek out their root causes, and initiate an appropriate course of corrective exercises. In the meantime, it is meaningful to establish and strengthen a continuous current of deep ideation upon the highest conceivable ideals, principles and goals relevant to the future of humanity. The mind and heart may be fused through an ardent devotion to Bodhisattvic exemplars of continuity of consciousness in the ceaseless service of all humanity. Through this very attempt, even the sick may slowly heal themselves and seek *satsang*, the company of the wise, who can help to nurture the seed of *bodhichitta*, the potent resolve to awaken the Wisdom Eye for the sake of universal welfare.

POLARITY AND DISCRIMINATION

As a lamp in a windless spot does not flicker, so is the man of subdued thought who practises union in the Self.
SHRI KRISHNA

It is intrinsic to the complex nature of man that though he necessarily participates in the ever-present polarity of the three qualities *(gunas),* he is always capable of mirroring spaceless wisdom in the theatre of time. According to the ancient teachings of the sages, man is essentially aloof from all the modifications of his mind. Man is more than the medley of bodily movements, more than the sum-total of his desires, and stronger than the torrent of thoughts that rush forth in a frenzied procession before his inward eye. Man is vaster than his variegated states of consciousness. Every person is beyond all possible modes of manifestation, for at the root there is an inmost core of consciousness wherein one is free from the familiar pairs of opposites. There is hardly a human being who does not savour golden moments of release and reconciliation, a deep feeling of joyous freedom, a firm sense of the falling away of fetters. There is not a person who does not experience, while tossed between the polarities of inertia and impetuosity, intervals of rhythmic, harmonious movement. Every person, in principle, is conscious of boundless space, ceaseless motion and eternal duration. These transcend the clumsy categories into which human life is conventionally divided. Man has the potential power of going beyond yesterday, today and tomorrow, here, there and everywhere. It is this central truth, as Krishna suggests in the *Bhagavad Gita,* that makes man capable of union with the Universal Self. Each can become a true man of meditation, with an inalienable freedom from captivity to the *gunas* as well as a creative participation in the three qualities — in illumination, in the desires and passions of the world, and in the enveloping fog of obscuration, darkness and ignorance. At all times, the immortal soul is uninvolved.

In Buddhist literature the elephant symbolized the magnanimous potentials of human nature. The impersonal majesty, gentle friendliness and steady reliability of elephants are familiar to all, and there is scarcely anyone who cannot appreciate the story of the six blind men and the elephant. One of them clasped the tail and concluded that the elephant was a rope; another held the trunk and decided that the elephant was a huge serpent; the blind man who grasped a leg thought the elephant was like a tree; stroking the ear, another surmised the elephant to be a fan; touching the elephant's side, the fifth man took the elephant to be a wall; and finally, seizing a tusk, the sixth man feared the elephant was a spear. So they all came to conflicting views. A seventh person, standing apart and clearly seeing that there are six paradigmatic standpoints corresponding to north, south, east, west, above and below, could cherish a synthesizing insight. All six perspectives are partially true, but none of them expresses the whole truth. Buddha often spoke of the elephant as signifying the Bodhisattva, with his wisdom and compassion. The Bodhisattva, like the elephant, is incapable of forgetting anything which is relevant to what he needs to know. At the same time, he is suffused by supreme detachment. The Bodhisattva's eyes, like those of the elephant, are gentle and full of tenderness, gladdening all around. The Bodhisattva teaches what it is to be truly human, to be abundantly affectionate, to love generously. Just as little children can approach elephants with no fear of being hurt, so too may all men and women approach the Bodhisattvas.

The elephant displays a marvellous blending of the three qualities. The elephant is tamasic; no one who sees a quiet pachyderm weighing four tons is likely to regard the animal as restless. There is a tremendous stability to the elephant. At the same time, though it is tamasic, it relishes harmless pleasures, as every child knows who has had the satisfaction of offering bananas to an elephant. Yet the elephant is proverbially patient and long-suffering, with a majestic indifference to the curiosity of passers-by. In this way the elephant indicates the enormous potential strength of soul, mind and character in every human being. Furthermore, the elephant shows the most harmonious movements, swishing its tail or swaying its trunk. When it raises its trunk, it salutes the boundless sky, its tusks ever pointing upwards. To take an elephant's-eye view of the world is to appreciate the immensity of what is above by saluting the vastness of the sky while at the same time standing very firmly on the ground. When in motion the elephant is an enchanting sight. Bartok, commenting on a delightful passage in one of Beethoven's symphonies, said that it was like the stately yet playful movement of elephants dancing. Such music employs the bass notes of heavy instruments and at the same time conveys to intuitive listeners a quality reminiscent of those haunting times in history when great events converged. Elephants are symbolic reminders of the momentous changes that are gestating today on the globe, seminal movements which are the unacknowledged reflections of the sacrificial ideation of Bodhisattvas.

Remaining rooted in immovable contemplation upon the spaceless, the soundless, the boundless, the Bodhisattvas are motionless in mind and in will, yet rhythmic and deliberate in thought and creation. They participate in the vicissitudes of historical cycles sufficiently to understand human beings who are still captive to the bonds of matter, but at the same time they remain in a seeming state of non-activity because they have no incentive or motivation to act for the sake of results. They simply do not live for the fruits of action, and are beyond praise and blame, while effortlessly exemplifying the religion of responsibility.

The *Bhagavad Gita* intimates that perfectibility is a meaningful ideal because it is rooted in the very ground of one's being. In effect, Krishna's teaching is echoed in the injunction of Christ: "Be ye therefore perfect, even as your Father which is in Heaven is perfect." If every human being can summon an active faith in the possibility of perfection, then each can vitally participate in the vicissitudes of space and time, the perplexing imperfections of this world. If one can avoid consolidating through guilt-ridden tamasic obsession or precipitating through the intensely rajasic and disordered buzzing of the brain, or seeking self-satisfaction through a static, sattvic equilibrium, then one may become an apprentice in the art of alchemical self-transmutation.

One could repeatedly rise above the three qualities and thereby recognize in this great teaching an assured basis for the principle of indefinite growth in the context of cool detachment and joyous renunciation. So long as the three qualities are not merely properties of matter and mind but also grounded in the very nature of differentiated reality, human beings can self-consciously seek the One in the many and then discern the many in the One. Eventually a point is reached when it is possible simultaneously to see the One in the many and the many in the One. The *Bhagavad Gita* blends three types of knowledge with the three gunas. In the fourteenth and seventeenth chapters the three qualities are differentiated at many levels, including faith, charity, action, knowledge, the discriminative faculty of *Buddhi*, the power of steadfastness and the potency of meditation.

In regard to discrimination of duty Krishna offers a dialectical teaching that can accommodate a variety of situations owing to its central logic. Quintessentially, it is a philosophy in which there is no intrinsic separation of the knower from the known. Anyone with a strictly conventional view of his obligations is apt to be attached to results. He becomes so conditioned and conditional that he can attempt something solely in the hope of reward. This is magnified unmistakably in an effete commercial culture where one never initiates anything unless it can be weighed and measured, bought and sold. Today many people are waking up to the absurdity of the logic of the cash register when applied to human encounters. Those who perform duties in a rajasic sense have no real discrimination. They are ever agitated by the desire for results, and, therefore, can only discharge their duties by setting false values upon them. They have somehow to set apart certain acts and duties from all others. Not only are they inflexible, but they are also preoccupied with the language of comparison and contrast. They soon start comparing and contrasting, whether in self-awareness or meditation, in drug-taking or erotic activity, in stocks and shares or success measured in terms of dollars and cents. As they are constantly involved in making comparisons which are misleading, they cling to a derivative and parasitic conception of duty. They cannot generate the supreme, serene sense of obligation of the truly free man who voluntarily binds himself by a fundamental commitment and chooses to honour it through every trial.

Alternatively, consider the person who decides to remain true to a sacred teaching and to a fundamental negation of false values. Here one may sense the strength of clear-sightedness brought over from previous lives in order to carry out a line of inward resolve. Such souls show the power of calm discrimination between essentials and non-essentials. The more tough-minded a person remains in preserving a pattern of self-chosen obligations — or as Krishna says, in doing *only* what is necessary — the more he is always, in every situation, ready to negate the superfluous while concentrating on what is needed. This produces a level of discriminative wisdom which is rather like the use and enjoyment of light. Some mystical poets compare this to the light that radiates from a red-hot piece of glowing coal. *Tamas* would be the same coal when it is inert. When a fire is put out, there is a death of rajasic radiance and there results a stone-like state concealing an inner process of disintegration. Discriminative wisdom exists at many levels. Herein lies the great strength and generous hope of the teaching of the *Bhagavad Gita*. Every rivulet of discrimination enhances the active power of *Buddhi*. Even if one merely has a few drops of the waters of devotion and humbly consecrates them at the inmost altar of Krishna, it is possible to negate in advance any attachment to consequences. Engaging in action in a sacrificial spirit, with pure joy and the willing acceptance of pain, the true devotee will certainly be delivered from a network of errors and miseries. In the progress of time he will surely experience tranquillity of thought.

'Dharma' in Sanskrit has a very different connotation from any strenuous conceptions of duty, Calvinistic or Teutonic. There is instead a firm yet relaxed sense of obligation which is self-sustaining and also spontaneous. In the *Bhagavad Gita* dharma is ascribed to fire, the sky, all objects in space, all phenomena in time, and the categories of selfhood. Dharma is that which *holds*: anything which holds up a human being, anything which sustains him, anything which helps him to keep going — is rooted in his duty. If dharma upholds every person, anyone can regulate and refine dharma through Buddhic discrimination. This is the sovereign talisman of every human being. All persons inherently possess godlike faculties of imagination, creativity, freedom and serenity. All are capable of exalted conceptions of calm, and can expand their perspectives and horizons while at the same time bringing a godlike faculty of intense concentration to every task.

The great Teachers of mankind have always reminded all of the privilege of incarnation into a human form. Many people, however, are liable to be so rajasic at the moment of death that they will soon be propelled back into incarnation in circumstances they do not like. There are also those who are so receptive in life to the summerland of ghosts, demons and disintegrating entities, *pisachas* and *rakshasas*, that at the moment of death they are drawn into the underworld of psychic corpses. Human beings are innately divine, but there are myriad degrees of differentiation in the manifestation of divine light. The light shines in all, but in all it does not shine equally. By using whatever in consciousness is an authentic mirroring of supernal light in the concrete contexts of daily obligations, one's own light will grow. The rays of truth can fall upon those who ardently desire to rescue the mind from the darkness of ignorance. It is critical for human beings to keep relighting themselves, to wipe out the ignorance that consolidates out of inertia and delusion in that pseudo-entity absolutized as the personal self. In the eyes of the sages there are only rays of light accompanied by long shadows masquerading as personalities.

Krishna speaks in the sixteenth chapter of those who are born with demonic qualities, and provides a perfect portrait of the contemporary dying culture in Kali Yuga. He also offers a compelling picture of the graces and excellences of those who evoke memories of the Golden Age. The demonic qualities, resulting in spiritual inertia, are the product of misuse in previous lives. Everyone who abused any power must face the consequences in the future. For three or four lives he may find his will blunted, his faculties castrated, his potencies circumcised, until he can thoroughly learn the proper use of his powers. There is a compelling passage in *The Dream of Ravan* wherein we are given a graphic analogy between states of mind and diseases. Theosophically, all ailments are caused in the realm of the mind; all ailments are rooted in the subtler vestures. *Sattva* corresponds to the *karana sarira,* the causal body, comprising the most fundamental ideas of selfhood in relation to which one generates a sense of reality. There is a correspondence between *rajas,* the principle of chaotic desire, and the *sukshma sarira,* the astral form. When this is irradiated by the Light of the Logos, it can show a reflected radiance. In all human beings there are glimmerings of noble aspiration, the yearning to do good. This is the source of fellow-feeling, the kindness of a mother for her children, the solicitude of a doctor for a pregnant woman whose baby he is delivering. These are mere intimations of that sattvic quality which can make a human being magnanimous, noble and free.

The astral body is lunar and is affected by the phases of the moon. It is vulnerable to pollution, especially through self-hatred, perverse ambition and self-dramatization. This is accompanied by the ever-thickening anxiety which deep down in the soul represents the fear that one may not return in a human form. With the disconnection between what the soul knows in sleep and what the mind fears in waking life, there is an acute sense of being unworthy of the rich resources of life. This enormous sense of inadequacy is coupled with the terror of loneliness, aggravated by the inability to share the joys and sorrows of others. It is pathetic to be preoccupied with success and failure. There is nothing more tedious than continuously adding up the figures in one's own account. When such a person gives himself a rest, he mistakes chaotic images in the brain for thinking, or the mechanical borrowing of sounds and gestures for sacred mantrams. Mantrams must be intoned with tremendous deliberation.

When persons find that they are like leaky jars and at the same time suffer a painful inner congestion, they must recognize that there is no release except through fundamental measures. There is no protection for the lazy and the weak, nor for those who indulge in self-pity but who are perversely strong-willed. These spiritual and moral cowards, drawing on frustration and hatred from previous lives, would either like to rearrange everything instantly, or steal their way, with drugs or incantations, into the magic casements of mystical states of consciousness. Many, through memories from previous lives, would like to think that simply by holding a book they will be saved. Any possibility of redemption, however, depends upon the degree and continuity of their genuine concern for other human beings.

There is an enigmatic story in *The Bhagavatam* about a man who became wicked. He had several children, named after gods and goddesses, and at the moment of death he happened to cry out the name of his son Narayana. Because he uttered this divine name in a mood of resignation when the god of Death came, he suddenly began to see the light. The god of Death took counsel with the attendants of Vishnu, who asked, "Can you take him away when he has uttered this sacred sound?" Then they told this man that he could have another lease on life, but they warned him that henceforth no accidental sounding of the divine name would protect him. From now onwards he must deliberately and daily intone it. The gods knew that in his sounding of the name there was a residual sincerity reaching out to Lord Narayana, and that if he got another chance, he would deeply repent and generate constancy of devotion. There are few experiences that are so chastening as a narrow escape from death. Unfortunately, many people have not used their time to think through their fundamental view of life, but it is always possible to reflect that there are other human beings on earth, that the world is a wonderful place, that one's life is not one's own to throw away.

One is indebted to one's parents and teachers for myriad opportunities to learn, and just because one fails to reflect calmly upon the good in oneself does not mean that one cannot grasp such opportunities or that one must continually brood on limitations. To do so is demonic. There are large numbers of people with abundant energies and considerable powers, but unable to use them effectively because of past misuse, owing to excessive meditation upon themselves and of extreme callousness in regard to means and ends. They have played the ancient game of gaining confidence at the expense of others, but for such there is no cosmic protection. He who seeks to gain at the expense of another is lost in life after life. But he who seeks to grow in the service and the loving acceptance of all others, can always reflect upon the good in all human beings, and thereby release the good in himself.

Demonic inertia arises through a whole way of thinking that is false. If one thinks that this world exists for enjoyment only, that human beings are merely the ephemeral accidental product of the pleasure of a man and a woman, that everyone is in competition for wealth and fame and status, and if one ceaselessly caters to all such absurdities and stupidities, one develops an asuric nature. Anyone who really wants to rise above this condition could do no better than to ponder upon the seventeenth chapter of the *Bhagavad Gita*, the philosophical nature of the three qualities, and the sixteenth chapter, which gives the portraits of the demonic personality as well as the godlike being. A sensible person who wishes to travel on the road to true discipleship, will find that simply by studying these chapters calmly he could see clearly the convergence of attitudes and qualities that strengthens the demonic or godlike nature in man. Instead of indulging in self-pity and self-contempt, the sincere seeker of wisdom will allow his whole nature to become absorbed in contemplation on the godlike qualities.

The whole of the *Bhagavad Gita* is replete with magnificent portraits of sages. The magic of meditation is such that by merely focussing upon them, they can release a light-energy which streams downward, freeing a person from the bondage of self-created illusions and self-destructive acts. Rid of the specious notion that he is somebody special, he can freely accept his cosmic potential as a point in space and joyously deliver himself with the dignity of man *qua* man. It is only when he is ready that Krishna confers upon Arjuna the exalted title of Nara (man), an individual ray of Divine Light. When a person can truly witness the divine in every human being, he can also see that every time anyone torments himself, he tortures Krishna. No one has such a right. One's parents did not give a body simply for the sake of crucifying the Christos-Krishna within. One has to free oneself from all obsessive identification with the shadow and salute the empyrean with the cool assurance of one who does not fear the light or is not threatened by the fact that other human beings exist, and whose stance is firmly rooted in the Divine Ground that transcends the *gunas* and the playful polarities of *Purusha* and *Prakriti*.

INTEGRATION AND RECURRENCE

If, on the one hand, a great portion of the educated public is running into atheism and scepticism, on the other hand, we find an evident current of mysticism forcing its way into science. It is the sign of an irrepressible need in humanity to assure itself that there is a Power Paramount over matter; an occult and mysterious law which governs the world, and which we should rather study and closely watch, trying to adapt ourselves to it, than blindly deny, and break our heads against the rock of destiny. More than one thoughtful mind, while studying the fortunes and reverses of nations and great empires, has been deeply struck by one identical feature in their history, namely, the inevitable recurrence of similar historical events reaching in turn every one of them, and after the same lapse of time. This analogy is found between the events to be substantially the same on the whole, though there may be more or less difference as to the outward form of details.

The Theosophist, July 1880   H.P. BLAVATSKY

Cyclic causation or the eternal law of periodicity stands midway between the affirmation of the Absolute and the postulate of progressive enlightenment in the set of fundamental axioms of Gupta Vidya. Pointing to the inexorable alternation of day and night, of birth and death, of *manvantara* and *pralaya*, cyclic law ensures that all events along with their participants, great or small, are comprehended within the archetypal logic of the Logos in the cosmos. Gupta Vidya indicates the mayavic nature of all manifestation in relation to the Absolute, whilst at the same time stressing that karmic responsibility is the pivot of all spiritual growth. The essential significance of the complex doctrine of cycles sometimes seems difficult to grasp in theory or to apply in practice. If the mind misconceives the metaphysical distinction between TAT and *maya*, then the dignity of spiritual striving through cycles under karma will be minimized. Self-examination and self-correction may be neglected owing to a false and merely intellectualist theory of transcendence. Conversely, the mind which embraces a too literalized conception of the immanence of the Absolute will find itself mired in experience with no accessible power of transcendence. It will tend to acquiesce in a sanguine or despairing doctrine of mechanical destiny which is psychological fatalism resulting from a mistaken conflation of causality with the ephemeral forms of outward events.

The true teaching of cyclic causation implies neither a trivialization nor a mechanization of life in a vesture in terrestrial time. Instead, it intimates the mysterious power of harmony, the irresistible force of necessity, which resides in the eternal balance of the manifest and the unmanifest in every living form and phase of the One Life. The ceaseless vibratory motion of the unmanifest Logos is the stimulus of the complex sets and subsets of hierarchies of being constituting the universe; and of the intricate and interlocking cycles and subcycles of events that measure out its existence. The intimate relationship between temporal identity and cyclic existence is symbolized in the identification of the lifetime of Brahmā with the existence of the universe, a teaching which also conveys the true meaning of immortality in *Hiranyagarbha.*

From the standpoint of universal unity and causation, the universe is a virtual image of the eternal motion or vibration of the unmanifest Word, scintillating around a set of points of nodal resonance within that Word itself. From the standpoint of individual beings involved in action, the universe is an aggregation of interlocking periodic processes susceptible to reasoned explanation in terms of laws. Understanding the nature of cycles and what initiates them, together with apprehending the mystery of cyclic causation itself, requires a progressive fusion of these two standpoints. The exalted paradigm of the union of Eternity and

Time is *Adhiyajna,* seated near the circle of infinite eternal light and radiating compassionate guidance to all beings who toil in the coils of Time. Established in Boundless Duration, all times past, present and future lie before his eye like an open book. He is Shiva, the Mahayogin, the leader of the hosts of Kumaras, and also Kronos-Saturn, the lord of sidereal time and the ruler of Aquarius. If humanity is the child of cyclic destiny, Shiva is the spur to the spiritual regeneration of humanity. And, if the Mahatmas and Bodhisattvas, the supreme devotees of Shiva, live to regenerate the world, then it is the sacred privilege and responsibility of those who receive their Teachings to learn to live and breathe for the sake of service to all beings.

It is in this spirit that H.P. Blavatsky, in her essay entitled "The Theory of Cycles", suggested several keys to the interpretation of cyclical phenomena. We can readily discern the vast variety of periodic phenomena which has already been noticed in history, in geology, in meteorology and in virtually every other arena of human experience. We can also recognize the statistical recurrence of certain elements in reference to economics, to wars and peace, to the rise and fall of empires, to epidemics and revolutions, and also to natural cataclysms, periods of extraordinary cold and heat. H.P. Blavatsky's intent was not merely to persuade the reader of the pervasiveness of periodic phenomena through the multiplication of examples, but rather to convey the immanent influence of the power of number and of mathematics within all cyclic phenomena. She reviewed the original analysis of certain historical cycles made by Dr. E. Zasse and published in the *Prussian Journal of Statistics.* Dr. Zasse presented an account of a series of historical waves, each consisting of five segments of two hundred and fifty years, which have swept over the Eurasian land mass from east to west.

According to Dr. Zasse's chronology, which began at approximately 2000 B.C., the year 2000 of the present era should mark the conclusion of the fourth such wave, and the inception of yet another wave from the east. Commenting briefly upon the importance of one-hundred-year cycles within the longer cycles indicated by Dr. Zasse, H.P. Blavatsky cited his analysis of ten-year and fifty-year cycles of war and revolution affecting European nations. In order to draw attention away from external events and to direct it towards deeper psychological causes, she pointed out:

> The periods of the strengthening and weakening of the warlike excitement of the European nations represent a wave strikingly regular in its periodicity, flowing incessantly, as if propelled onward by some invisible fixed law. This same mysterious law seems at the same time to make these events coincide with astronomical wave or cycle, which, at every new revolution, is accompanied by the very marked appearance of spots in the sun.

Elsewhere, both in *Isis Unveiled* and *The Secret Doctrine*, she made reference to the eleven-year sunspot cycle, suggesting something of its occult significance in the respiration and heartbeat of the solar system.

During the nineteenth century a number of scientists speculated about the relationship of sidereal and terrestrial events. Dr. Stanley Jevons, one of the founders of econometrics, saw a correlation between sunspot cycles and the rises and falls of economic output and productivity. Jevons went so far as to speculate that "the commercial world might be a body so mentally constituted . . . as to be capable of vibrating in a period of ten years". In *The Secret Doctrine*, H.P. Blavatsky observed:

> Drs. Jevons and Babbage believe that every thought, displacing the particles of the brain and setting them in motion, scatters them throughout the Universe, and they think that 'each particle of the existing matter must be a register of all that has happened'.
>
> *The Secret Doctrine*, i 104

Correlating this idea to the occult conception of the enduring impress of thought upon the subtle matter of the invisible human vestures, H.P. Blavatsky intimated the vital relationship between the impress of sidereal influences upon the psyche and the cyclic destiny of human souls.

> The Hindu *Chitra-Gupta* who reads out the account of every Soul's life from his register, called Agra-Sandhani; the 'Assessors' who read theirs from the heart of the defunct, which becomes an open book before (whether) Yama, Minos, Osiris, or Karma — are all so many copies of, and variants from the Lipika, and their Astral Records. Nevertheless, the Lipika are not deities connected with Death, but with Life Eternal.
>
> Connected as the Lipika are with the destiny of every man and the birth of every child, whose life is already traced in the Astral Light — not fatalistically, but only because the future, like the PAST, is ever alive in the PRESENT — they may also be said to exercise an influence on the Science of Horoscopy.
>
> *The Secret Doctrine*, i 105

From such considerations a complex picture emerges of a myriad overlapping cycles and subcycles on several planes of existence. Whilst the enormous breadth and depth of cyclic phenomena would render elusive and exacting analysis of cycles for the neophyte in Gupta Vidya, one should attempt to nurture a cool apprehension of the regular periodicity in the excitement of mental and physical forces affecting both collective and distributive karma. It may help to begin with a relatively simple example. Consider the case of a single family living within a larger household and a local community. Each member of the family is born at a different moment. Each, therefore, has a different constellation in the ascendant at the moment of birth, and each has different cycles determined by the positions of the moon, the planets and the stars in the heavens at the moment of birth. For each, the angular relationships between these sidereal bodies —

and their placement relative to the zenith and horizon in the place of the individual's birth — will vary. Already, even at the simplest level, one can see an inherent complexity to the cyclic destiny of every individual.

Within the lifetime of the individual a variety of cycles and subcycles will operate, some marked off by septenates of years and having to do with the incarnation of the higher principles, and others governed by a cycle slightly more than eighteen years having to do with the revolution of the nodes of the moon. Each of these cycles will have its own subcycles, and these in turn will be comprised of still smaller cycles, down to those which may last only a few weeks, a few days, even a few hours. Although this kind of mathematics can be most readily handled with the help of a minicomputer, it is not beyond the capacity of the human brain. Nor should it be forgotten that several people live together in families, and that there is a close interaction between what is happening in the orbit of the father, the mother, the children and all the ancestors of each. Owing to the complex overlapping and intersecting of the mathematics applying to each individual and to a specific group of individuals, one might think of constellations of energy-fields wherein many people produce an immense clustering of elements, all of which obey the laws of cycles. If one passes from the limits of a single family to the scope of a mini-commune or even a small community, it is evident that the degree of complexity involved in comprehending the cycles at work will become very great.

In order to understand the activity and overlapping of cycles on any broad scale, one must adopt a set of categories that has nothing to do with the perceptions and propensities of the personal nature. To the integrative and synthetic vision of the Adept, the interplay and interaction of human beings on the terrestrial plane are resolved into the occult correspondences of sounds, colours and numbers. Individual human beings are seen as having manvantaric stars, or rays of individuality, which pertain to them throughout the vast cycle of their incarnations. Within each incarnation that individuality takes up a personal existence connected with a personal star or ray. Whilst the tone, coloration and number associated even with the latter is generally unknown to most human beings in incarnation, and only crudely guessed at by contemporary theories of personality, the still more fundamental elements of individual identity as a Monad are scarcely even conceived. Yet, for the Adept the world of human interaction consists of a series of mathematically governed octaves of colour and sound beyond the comprehension of even the most speculative forms of modern painting and music. Nonetheless, if an individual is privileged to have received spiritual instruction regarding the nature of colour, sound and number, then he may begin to make experiments. By taking one of the simple colour charts available, he could discover how, out of the primary colours, complex shades and hues may be derived. Also he could gain some insight into what the developed artist means by a pure colour — an extremely pure blue or a luminous gold.

All such experiments are clearly relative to perception and to circumstance, because the pigments used will inevitably introduce a tincture which is part of the physical chemistry of what is called colour. And, whilst discrimination of colours on the physical plane can be heightened to an extraordinary degree — as exemplified by silk dyers, for instance — this skill represents only the most mundane aspect of the conscious refinement of colour vision. There is a tremendous difference between what is ordinarily perceived as colour and what is potentially perceptible on the subtler planes. Many are aware of the possibilities of subtle hearing or melodious colouring in music, whether it be through Indian music, with its refined system of quarter tones and complex rhythms, or through classical European music, with its intricate system of voices and use of silences. By playing a raga or a symphony, one can transform the entire elemental field of one's room. When one listens to such music, cycles overlap and the psyche fluctuates, in ways intensified by the collective nature of these forces. By noetically imposing upon the field some elevating spiritual note, one can gain the benefit of the fluidic nature of the field without being drawn into or absorbed by the psychical atmosphere.

If colour, sound and number can work such soothing charms, they can also work destructively. Great deliberation and intelligent sifting are, therefore, paramount in the use of alchemical knowledge. There are secrets locked within the spectrum, within the octave and within the series of numbers from 1 through 7, which can kill as well as heal. Without discrimination based upon purity of motive, any attempt to manipulate these Fohatic factors of cyclic destiny is likely to result in either unconscious grey or even black magic. In the realm of unconscious motivation, this will emerge through impulsiveness, particularly in speech, and a tragically misplaced sense of timing. Despite these dangers, inherent to a universe in which Manasic beings have free choice, persistently shines the ever-present possibility open to each human being to help Nature and harmonize with her through cycles, striving for the elevation of the human condition. Neither the ideas of Pythagoras on the mysterious influence of colours, numbers and sound, nor the theories of the ancient world-religions and philosophies, are so bizarre or so irrelevant as sectarian dogmatists and secular empiricists would pretend.

H.P. Blavatsky's aim in hinting at the occult foundations of the law of cycles was to restore the rights of ancient wisdom, and she recognized that nine out of ten human beings are somewhat open to the Teachings of Gupta Vidya. There is, alas, always the tenth person who has a problem — whether it be materialism, soul-blindness or suggestibility — and therefore goes around proclaiming some sort of superstitious humbug or general nihilism out of nervousness and a lack of courage, traceable to previous lives. And as long as some people talk shallow nonsense about sacred matters without real knowledge, this will tend to reinforce the skeptic. Hence, there exists a kind of see-saw action between people who talk about the sacred but do not really know it, and those who hear about it but refuse to consider it because their survival depends upon their illusions. All this waste provides a negative example of the cyclic reinforcement of social attitudes. As the Upanishadic and Socratic traditions demonstrate, the dialectics of speech and silence can convey as well as obscure the highest knowledge.

H.P. Blavatsky knew that the time was fast approaching when more and more people would emerge who have the courage both to examine ancient wisdom and to correlate it with the discoveries of science. It was for those who would ask questions, and make their own investigations by looking at the heavens and looking within themselves through meditation, that she partially unveiled the teachings of Gupta Vidya. Those who use these teachings — and daily consult *The Voice of the Silence* — in order to understand the profounder visions and longings of their hearts will progressively gain confidence in charting the seas of the psychic unconscious. With steadiness and persistence, they will become more skilled in handling the take-off and landing, the vertical ascent and descent in consciousness, so critical to the Aquarian Age. The ability to sustain oneself in any state of consciousness or meditation and the related ability to move deliberately from one plane or state of consciousness to another with relaxed control depend upon one's access to a fixed point of reference or vibration within consciousness. If the sevenfold human constitution were likened to a miniature solar system, the centre of consciousness would reside on one of the planets of that system.

Despite all the variations and fluctuations of cyclic existence affecting states of consciousness, all points of view within the system revolve in complex orbits around the central sun of the *Atman*. The motions of attention from one point to another are regulated by that central sun in accordance with its breath and heartbeat. As in the macrocosm of the universe, so too in the microcosm of human nature — all the oscillating motions and emanations of the MONAD and the Monad are comprised in an original fundamental vibration.

> All are contained within the *Maha-Yug*, the 'Great Age' or Cycle of the Manu calculation, which itself revolves between two eternities — the 'Pralayas' or *Nights of Brahma*. As, in the objective world of matter, or the system of effects, the minor constellations and planets gravitate each and all around the sun, so in the

world of the subjective, or the system of causes, these
innumerable cycles all gravitate between that which the
finite intellect of the ordinary mortal regards as eternity,
and the still finite, but more profound, intuition of the
sage and philosopher views as but an eternity within
THE ETERNITY. 'As above, so it is below', runs the
old Hermetic maxim.

Ibid.

In so far as individuals can assimilate this radical perspective
within themselves, they will not be so dependent upon transient
fashion and fickle opinion, nor will they be so susceptible to
volatile psychic influences. In a society where many have scarcely
any conception of self-magnetization and magnetic purity, they
perpetually throw off negative emanations through speech and
the eyes and thought. Through the natural rhythms of daily life —
the cycle of waking and sleeping, of going to work and returning
home, of interacting with family and friends — strong focal points
are established for the aggregation of psychic impressions. If one
has not prepared oneself through proper meditation to use these
focal points for the strengthening of positive vibrations, then they
will by default turn into rats' nests of negativity. Through
identification with the personal nature, one may tend to take every
one of these disturbances literally and personally, and thereby
make it the hooking-point for further infestation of the psyche.
If, instead, one strengthens a meditative awareness of the
manvantaric vibration of the Avatar, then these inevitable
collecting-points in terrestrial consciousness can become powerful
regenerative agents enabling one to meet one's own karmic
responsibility and to lighten the burden of others.

Meditation upon the cosmos as a complex hierarchy of
interacting cycles radiating from a common source may be aided
by simple, yet suggestive, diagrams. One *yantra* represents a spiral
seashell with a lotus at the centre, the outside of which is like the
head of a coiling serpent. The diagram is in ceaseless motion. At
the same time, because of the harmonizing of different strata —
which resemble the skins of the earthy layers of language and

concept, and even the different hierarchies of reality — the *yin-yang* alternation within the different strata harmonizes with the lotus-like sun in the centre. Thus, lines of emanation radiate out from the centre and return to it. Through meditation upon such a *yantra* one can break the fixity of the static geometry and the limited algebra governing one's responses to the world, and move on to a more dynamic and topological post-Newtonian conception of space, a more fluidic and flexible post-Euclidian geometry, and a more interactive conception of a post-Cartesian algebra founded upon matrices and groups. As one gains a sense of Aquarian meta-mathematics and meta-geometry, founded upon the triadic meta-logic of Gupta Vidya, one will prepare oneself to participate self-consciously in the dialectical calculus of the cosmos. Daily meditation can provide the basis for dynamic integration of distilled perceptions.

Cycles are not mechanical recurrences of events, but living curves of dynamic causation. Every individual has a karmic curve, and at each point has potential access to the sum total of karmic energies generating that curve. Through noetic conceptions of maxima and minima, of curvature and inflexion, one can self-consciously generate a line of life's meditation. Through the Buddhic powers of correlation and discrimination, of integration and differentiation, one can penetrate the deceptive surface of events and reach towards the underlying planes of causation. Most individuals, alas, fail to maximize their opportunities because their notions of cause and effect are mistaken. This may be discerned by comparing the concepts of explanation and definition. If told that the term 'lion' is defined as 'a large carnivorous feline mammal found most often in Africa and Asia, with a tawny body, a tufted tail and a shaggy mane', one will not think that the phrase defining 'lion' is actually a lion in any way. One will understand that the term being defined and the phrase doing the defining both have the same meaning. Similarly, if one is told that a certain event is to be explained by the occurrence of certain other events, one should not think that the events constituting the explanation are the cause of the given event, but rather that both the explained event and the explaining events are manifestations of the same cause.

To the eye of Shiva the entire universe and all its cyclic phenomena comprise a single harmonious consequence of one Causeless Cause, the Karmic Sum Total symbolized by the lifetime of Brahmā. Most human beings are unable to maximize their opportunities even under the lesser, though still vast, sum totals and karmic curves of individual Monadic existence, prefigured by the manvantaric star. They die hardly having used one percent of their potential brain-power, and hardly having tapped one-tenth of one percent of their far more powerful heart-energy. If the spiritual and mystical heart is not exercised, it begins to atrophy. If, however, it is strengthened through the exercise of dispassion and devotion, it gains strength, firing the synapses of the nervous system and stimulating the cells in the centres of the brain. Through heart-energy, through an abundant love of one's fellow men, of their children and their families, one begins to break down the false boundary of the *persona* and its limited view of family and friendship. As this barrier is dissolved, other human beings, and the world at large seem less alien and less hostile. Life becomes more meaningful and challenging through the perception that all other human beings are immortal souls, like oneself, capable of reciprocity in spiritual aspiration. One can tap more and more of one's heart-energy, and thus quicken the Buddhic mind and even release the spiritual will.

Then, passing beyond the narrow horizon of personal existence, one may naturally insert oneself into the broader evolutionary development of humanity. One will learn to discard that which is perverse, whilst turning that in oneself which is unique and individual to the good of others, all the while strengthening an inward sense of that which is common to all and confined by none. As Mahatma K.H. taught in the last century:

Whenever any question of evolution or development in any Kingdom presents itself to you bear constantly in mind that everything comes under the Septenary rule of series in their correspondences and mutual relation through nature.

In the evolution of man there is a topmost point, a bottom point, a descending arc, and an ascending arc. As it is 'Spirit' which transforms itself into 'matter' and (not 'matter' which ascends — but) matter which *resolves once more into spirit,* of course the first race evolution and the last on a planet (as in each round) must be more etherial, more spiritual, the fourth or lowermost one most physical (progressively of course in each round) and at the same time — *as physical intelligence is the masked manifestation of spiritual intelligence* — each evolved race in the downward arc must be more physically intelligent than its predecessor, and each in the upward arc have a more refined form of mentality commingled with spiritual intuitiveness.

One must not forget for even a moment that there are seven colours, seven sounds, seven days of the week, seven principles in the cosmos and in man, that the physical body has seven layers of skin and that every seven years one experiences important and irreversible changes in the mortal vestures. It will thus become possible to draw those kinds of Buddhic analogies and correspondences which are essential to the comprehension of cycles and the alchemical task of noetic integration. Disabused of any false dichotomy between spirit and matter, one will come to understand that if spirit transforms itself into matter and matter resolves itself once more into spirit, then matter is nothing but a passive lower expression of spirit, whilst spirit is, through ideation, an intensification of the energy-field in matter with a transforming power. How much one can bring this power to bear will depend upon one's degree of constancy in remembering the septenary rule. Without comprehending the entire series, it is not possible to enjoy the entire spectrum or to employ the seven notes with accuracy and timing.

To do the right thing at the right time depends upon a lively awareness of the subtle phases and stable conditions of prevailing cycles. In the Aquarian Age it is helpful to acknowledge that human beings, having begun in the First Root Race as extremely ethereal and spiritual beings, have now completed their arc of descent into matter and are engaged in a progressive process of etherealization and spiritualization. In the Fifth Root Race, going from the Fifth Sub-Race to the Sixth Sub-Race, this process is giving birth to a profound spiritual sensitization of intelligence through the elevation of life-atoms. This is connected with the cosmic electricity of *Daiviprakriti*, the Light of the Logos. All the modes of physical and astral intelligence throughout the various kingdoms of Nature are nothing but masked manifestations of the synthesizing spiritual intelligence of *Mahat*. Along the upward involutionary arc of growth and spirituality, each human being, each individuated ray of *Mahat* in *Manas*, must self-consciously cultivate what Mahatma K.H. calls a "refined form of mentality commingled with spiritual intuitiveness". Refined mentality is *Manas-Taijasi*, and spiritual intuitiveness *Buddhi*. Thus, *Buddhi-Manas-Taijasi* is the colouring, the tonality and the number of the Avataric impulse in the present cycle. It is the spiritual essence of secular monasticism which, from its present *bija* or seed state, will flourish as a new mode of self-regenerating civilization in the maturing phases of the Aquarian Age. Like seeds that lie beneath the protection of mountain snows, every element of spiritual intuition, of mental refinement, and of the heart radiance that comes through compassion out of the mystic marriage (*hieros gamos*) of truth and love is being helped and nourished at this sacred moment and hour in the evolutionary history of mankind. Such seeds, sown in trust by courageous pioneers in the chill midnight of outward darkness, will bring forth a rich harvest for mankind in the warmer dawns of the foreseeable future.

INSIGHT AND ENERGY

The Universe really is motion and nothing else.

PLATO

Energy is generated by cosmic ideation within the ever-potential field of cosmic electricity. On the subtlest levels of abstraction there is an incredible rapidity of rhythmic motion in a diaphanous, undifferentiated, homogeneous material medium. At that level of cosmic unity there can be no sharp distinction between ideation or thought and motion or electricity involving atomic particles. *Alayavijnana*, cosmic consciousness, is the storehouse and the penultimate source of all the energy moving on all planes of awareness and matter through descending degrees of differentiation and varying rates of motion, elaborating different curves of cyclic origination, alteration, decay and destruction. When contrasted with this cosmic perspective, the early modern distinction between kinetic and potential in the natural sciences, stemming from crucial moves made in the eighteenth and early nineteenth centuries — especially in the contributions of Young who connected energy with work — is inadequate.

Even at a physical level, problems remain in regard to what is potential and what is actual. Potentially, there is energy in a suspended object to the extent to which it has not fallen. If it were to fall, it would release energy, but if it is fixed in place, it is not going to fall. If it has potential energy in terms of the notion of a falling object though it is an object that is secured, what kind of energy is in fact involved though it is not visible as active energy in motion? It might be said that gravity exerts a measurable pull upon it, but what is that? A person may thus try, in a Socratic way, to ask the sorts of questions which the pioneers of the modern natural sciences raised, but now in reference to the conceptual framework of contemporary mechanics, biology or chemistry.

Galileo once puzzled in church about the uniformity in the time intervals of the oscillations of a pendulum despite the diminishing of the arc of oscillation. Beginning to ask basic questions with the help of examples will show that the distinction between potential and actual is relative to those who are at a certain point in a realm of actualization. For someone at a point of stasis or standstill, all motion is relative to that position, and as objects move at the same rate along parallel lines, each appears motionless to the other.

In a Leibnizian sense, all possible worlds exist in the divine mind, but there seems to be only one particular world of which we are a part. This world must be a complex manifestation, through myriad monads, of one primordial monadic essence within the divine light. If, for example, one took a blank sheet of paper and set down three variables in relation to some problem, a number of models or different combinations of possible alternatives could emerge. If the problem is simple enough and one is sufficiently logical at that level of simplicity, it is possible to exhaust the alternatives. This soon becomes tedious for a thinking person who wishes to see what further permutations and combinations could be made. Meditation is a constant cancelling in thought of crystallization inherent in particularization. Non-attachment is a logical pre-condition for self-consciously handling matter at a rate of extremely rapid motion, like the speed of light, and shaping out of homogeneous substance a suitable vehicle for the concentrated noetic energy that streams forth from an ever-present awareness of the unconditioned and the unmanifest. Noetic insight is much richer than merely handling alternatives in a dry-as-dust, arid manner wherein an attenuated scheme of logic results in circumscribed logical possibilities.

Self-conscious thinkers are aware that through every thought they produce a progeny, that through every image they emanate a whole procession of elementals. This is not very difficult to imagine when one knows that merely by dropping fifty cents on the floor a million ergs are released. The erg is a minute unit of measurement and yet a wealth of energy and motion is involved.

More generally, the earth's entire energy resources, the focus of many self-elected prophets of doomsday, are minuscule in comparison to the energy released by the sun. In about fifteen minutes the sun radiates upon our planet more energy than the whole world consumes in a year. Here one directly confronts the poverty of conventional categories of thought in relation to demonstrable evidence for the tremendous plenitude in regard to solar heat, light and electromagnetic energy. Contemporary science is still crude, awkward and assertive due to its state of adolescence.

In a metaphysically impoverished climate, merely to say that people ought to think of logical possibilities will not help them to tap noetic energy. We might enlist a concept like vision from religion and myth. The advantage of the term 'vision' is that everyone can understand the use of the eyes, and knows at some level what is involved in seeing even though most have not really thought much about it. Even without being an artist, a person knows that one critical element in seeing is perspective. A more crucial element is the capacity to be able to handle different perspectives over a period of time. Still better, though more difficult, is the ability to handle various perspectives simultaneously. Even on the physical plane there are rich imaginative possibilities which are forfeited through fixation or through having a wandering eye. Most people are simply not able to exercise the full potential of the godlike faculty of sight on the physical plane. When people think that by the aid of a drug, a technique, a text, they could suddenly have a vision, see sights, forms and sounds, and even have some sensation of light, the word 'vision' becomes so plebeianized, even in its mystic sense, that many hazards are connected with its use. There is no cognitive content to that kind of concept. People who have had what they sincerely believe are valid and beautiful visionary experiences may very quickly trivialize them by depicting them in the language of emotion. Does this give one real knowledge? Does it permanently transform one's view of the world? At one level, it does give the recognition that the world of superficial appearances is a lie and that much so-called knowledge is empty and pretentious. This recognition has a certain value but it is not very constructive.

Although it is a useful exercise to insert a philosophical notion like logical possibility or vision into the common conception of potential and kinetic motion, this moves us no closer to a grasp of higher states of consciousness. Such states cannot be unlocked by any stolen key because they presuppose a distinct moral requirement — disinterested, altruistic, detached receptivity. It has to be disinterested to release a high level of energy. It has to be altruistic, for unless one can release pure energy one would be burnt up at the higher levels. This is a merciful protection because few could truly handle the power of a cosmic vision. With Nietzsche, many might say, "Let the veil remain." The larger the vision, the greater the corresponding compassion required. The more penetrating the insight, the greater the necessary detachment and the single-minded concentration needed. One must be sufficiently strong and unafraid, not wanting anything for oneself that is not legitimate and which cannot be effortlessly secured like the breathing of air or the drinking of water. The moral require-ment for tapping high energies is not an arbitrary imposition upon self-conscious beings by some capricious authority. It is actually a psychological pre-condition for being able to maintain a poise which is needed to sustain subtler vestures in realms of consciousness wherein the crucial distinction is not between actual and potential, but rather the ontological distinction between potentiality and potency.

Metaphysical imagination, continuous reflection and deep meditation are required for real understanding. One could learn by looking at Nature, the inimitable teacher. Nature is a servant of Adepts, but a teacher to everyone else. Even on the physical plane, potential energy has something to do with height. Consider what happens to the immense electrical energy potentially available in the downward trickle of mountain streams. Where does it come from? It represents nature's work as an alchemist in taking the moisture in the ocean and evaporating it through heat.

Through the evaporation and raising of moisture to a sufficient height, nature is able to convert alchemically that water so that it is not energically the same as it is when at sea level. There are only a few drops where a stream begins, but there is a vast potential energy present. Yet that potential energy is in fact an actual energy in relation to the potential energy which went into the whole process of alchemization begun by heat and which will also be present when the process is complete.

There is something in higher states of consciousness analogous to the experience of a condition which is neither hot nor cold, but where there is a vivifying participation in the cool blue flames of a soft light which can release a steady stream of energy and which could be used at will in any direction on any plane beginning with ideation and working downward. One soon reaches a point where one has to relinquish conventional distinctions and also recognize the poverty of all mundane concepts. There is some similarity between the image-making power of a newborn babe, innocently floating on the ocean of life, and the disciplined imagination, gently guided by a benevolent will, of the detached and all-seeing Adept. There is more similarity between these than between the disciplined imagination of the Adept and the impressionistic visions of excitable prophets. These latter are chaotic, and have only a limited validity in relation to the illusions of men in the realm of so-called reality made up of divisive and tortuous, impotent and aborted, actualizations. Confused visions are not merely crude and delusive, but actually generate a perverse and demonic energy.

Patanjali's *Yoga Sutras* refers to two kinds of energy. One kind of energy, which might be called a sort of higher *prana*, gives one level of understanding. The other kind of energy cannot remotely be tapped, except through a serene continuity of consciousness called *sama* or similitude. In such a state, a person can consciously make luminous the sphere surrounding his *rupa* and effortlessly sustain self-luminosity. This is only possible at a high level of ceaseless meditation upon the one secondless, universal source of divine light. It involves the theurgy wherein a person sees all beings as spheres of light within a vast universe which is a limitless, boundless sphere of light. From this perspective, one would be able self-consciously to transmute every atom of one's grosser vestures and radiate out, from above below and from within without, that supreme self-luminous noetic energy which can light up the atoms and arouse the potentials that slumber in human beings. No society, group or civilization can self-consciously harness this energy — even for the sake of the collective good — without fulfilling the moral and psychological prerequisites that are needed. There is no possibility of access to Akashic energy without fulfilling the ethical preconditions that prevent its misuse. People might, however, in a misguided search for the Alkahest, foster a multitude of delusions. Strictly speaking, all the psychic states are shadowy and insignificant in relation to the wisdom of noetic insight.

One could, with unwavering detachment, profound disinterestedness, and unconditional benevolence towards all, sustain a higher indifference in relation to every aspect of this world of manifestation, and yet see all relativities from the standpoint of unconditioned consciousness in which the self-luminosity of the divine is ceaselessly present. It is necessary to discriminate between the turbulent atmosphere of divisive, separative thought coalescing with psychic forces and the pellucid strength generated by the noetic energies of sustained altruistic thought. Proximity on the physical plane has nothing to do with co-adunition and consubstantiality on higher planes of consciousness. Human beings carry their own problems around them, creating and living in their own world. Maya or deception accompanies the notion that because people are close together on the physical planes they therefore share a common access to the same current of ideation. The situation is quite different if persons are consciously aware of the thoughts and energies they release. At the highest level, there is no real distinction between thoughts and feelings and noetic energies. They are intermeshed. They are emanations which involve noetic thought, Buddhic feeling and spiritual energy. These emanations will always bless, but especially those who are willing to expel from their own vestures chaotic and befouled energies.

All aspirants must do something on their own. It cannot be done for them. They must aid in the conscious and continual purgation of these muddled matrices, the fuel of their *kama manas*, so that the void can be filled by streams of noetic energy. But this would be very misleading if a person expected it to happen suddenly: hence Plato's metaphor of the leaky jar in *Gorgias*. If a person made it a habit of allowing himself to befilled up with foul matrices only to eliminate them, merely out of soul-disgust, and then was able out of unconscious receptivity to receive a great outpouring of higher energy — it could not be retained. One cannot retain noetic energies if one has cut astral grooves that can only channel lower emanations. One would be like a leaky jar that has been so befouled that every time it is emptied, and pure fresh water is put into it, the fresh water gets contaminated. In the process of dynamic interchange of life-atoms, the fresh water would be expelled by evaporation.

A person has to do those basic things which will help produce more fundamental, stable, reliable and long-term changes in his vestures. One must establish points of contact and connections between the highest thoughts, feelings and states which one can maintain in daily life. One can experience the vibrant ocean of life-energy when at sunrise or at sunset one is able to experience the majesty and joy of the burgeoning light hidden behind the vast vista of Nature's wealth of manifestation. Old cultures practised self-conscious modes of purification. What is the equivalent on the mental plane to bathing, to becoming ready to receive the manna that one hopes will fall from heaven? What is the equivalent of wanting to share it on the plane of thought and feeling with those who need help, or with those whom through the natural course of events one could help? One's own integrity and honesty, as well as toughness, are involved. Fearlessness is the defining characteristic of spiritual strength, and is the only basis upon which one could release truly noetic energy. No man could suddenly jump from being a concatenation of fears to supreme fearlessness. The very fact that one wants to jump means one is somewhere afraid of failure, hoping for spiritual favours or that partiality will work on one's behalf. What is that self that one is so anxious to protect, and on behalf of which one has to be so afraid and to seek favours?

In the *Bhagavad Gita* one could see unlimited applications of the central teachings, not merely to life conceived in terms of events, external decisions and particular duties, but in terms of a noble and noetic consciousness that must be vigilantly maintained with increasing detachment and without fear or wish for favour. Then, in a state of inward receptivity, one could enter the world of divine light, the light of the Logos within every man and behind and beyond the universe, a world in which every thought and feeling is instantaneously translated into altruistic action for the sake of all.

SELF-EMANCIPATION

BUDDHI YOGA

*Every form on earth, and every speck (atom) in Space
strives in its efforts towards self-formulation to follow the
model placed for it in the* 'HEAVENLY MAN.'
The Secret Doctrine, i 183

Monadic evolution aims initially at establishing individuated centres of human self-consciousness. Once millions upon millions of these have emerged under natural law, the distinctive purpose of human evolution thereafter is to arouse and activate universal self-consciousness through a series of progressive awakenings. The monad "in its absolute totality and awakened condition" as "the culmination of the divine incarnations on earth" represents a critical state which will be fully perfected at the end of the Seventh Round by the whole of humanity, under the common cosmic laws of growth and retardation. In this long process there are many casualties and tragedies, but there are also shining examples of truly heroic, Promethean self-emancipation by moral geniuses. Having sunk into the depths of matter, such exemplars have pulled themselves up by self-effort and emerged through creative suffering into exalted states of enlightened consciousness, through which they could keep pace with the Avataric Saviours and Teachers of the entire human race. At all times the spiritual vanguard at the forefront of human evolution points towards the noetic possibilities of human life and architectonic perfection in spiritual consciousness. Every creative advance in monadic evolution depends upon the critical range and potent fullness of self-consciousness. Through its depth of perception in reference to the world, it impels a natural movement towards the Heavenly Man, the Divine Prototype, the Daimon of the immortal Self in every human being. By withdrawal from the selfish clutches of the grosser vestures and the demoniac tendencies, the human Monad reascends through *Buddhi Yoga* to the state of transcendental union with its parent Self, the universal Ishwara, the Logos in the cosmos and the God in man.

The degrees of differentiation in the Monadic Host below the human kingdom, as well as the distinctive marks of the human Monad, are conveyed by H.P. Blavatsky in a critical series of propositions which commences with a reference to the earliest period in the ethereal formation of the earth chain:

> The Monadic Host may be roughly divided into three great classes: —
> 1. The most developed Monads (the Lunar Gods or 'Spirits,' called, in India, the Pitris), whose function it is to pass in the first Round through the whole triple cycle of the mineral, vegetable, and animal kingdoms in their most ethereal, filmy, and rudimentary forms, in order to clothe themselves in, and assimilate, the nature of the newly formed chain.
> *The Secret Doctrine,* i 174

These Monads come over progressively from the previous lunar chain in a series of stages in order to animate all the nascent forms in the coalescing matrix of the earth chain. These lunar forms, extremely subtle and refined in the First Round, incipiently belong from the first to the seven different kingdoms. Then come "those monads that are the first to reach the human stage during the three and a half Rounds." This great descent of the Monadic Host does not take place all at once, but over immense cycles of man-vantaric time, and according to the innate characteristics of these Monads, reflecting an inherent sevenfold division. Owing to the degrees of development that have already taken place, all human Monads roughly fall into seven classes connected with the seven cosmic hierarchies, the seven planets and other sets of seven in Nature. They come therefore in a certain order, and those Monads that are the first to reach the human stage during the three and a half Rounds become Men, or attain to self-consciousness, by the middle of the Fourth Round. These constitute most of Humanity.

The key to the internal continuity of this entire process, linking together these various stages and phases on diverse planes and globes, is given in the ideational power of the Monad, manifesting as self-conscious intelligence:

> The MONAD emerges from its state of spiritual and intellectual unconsciousness; and, skipping the first two planes — too near the ABSOLUTE to permit of any correlation with anything on a lower plane — it gets direct into the plane of Mentality. But there is no plane in the whole universe with a wider margin, or a wider field of action in its almost endless gradations of perceptive and apperceptive qualities, than this plane.
>
> *The Secret Doctrine*, i 175

The term 'mentality' is used here to indicate *Manas* or self-consciousness, and has little or nothing to do with what is normally called mind or brain-power. Manasic beings function on a plane of consciousness saturated with inexhaustible possibilities for mental creation acting through ideal projections, pictures and images. Through this power, or rather through its truncated specialization on the plane of incarnation, all human beings, most of the time unconsciously and ignorantly, are constantly creating affinities with different classes of living centres of energy. Since there is no intrinsic difference between Spirit and Matter, but only an extrinsic difference of degree, the two are inseparable, and one can neither find ideation without substance nor energy without form. This continual coalescence or interaction of energy and form, of ideation and substance, is a pervasive principle in this dynamic universe of ceaseless change and has an intimate bearing upon the whole course of human evolution. Not only do human beings experience alterations of state in the brain-mind and modifications of the vestures at every moment, but correlative changes are also experienced at the level of cohesion in the mineral kingdom, and at the level of instinct in the animal kingdom. In the human kingdom these interrelated changes encompass emotion and feeling in the realm of 'affect', the sense of comparison and contrast, identification and differentiation, in the realm of intellectual awareness, as well as the power of noetic discrimination in recognizing subtle nuances of meaning and in the continual interplay of light and darkness.

These evolutionary processes on the plane of mentality produce the human sense-organs, which are perfected through imaginative precision. Indeed, they must be contemplated calmly and carefully, as without proper mental attention they will remain under-utilized. Most persons are barely able to tap all that is possible even within the entire range of the seven sense-powers. Most people barely hear, barely see, barely touch, barely taste and barely smell, much less activate higher sense-powers. As an obvious example, anyone who develops a refined ability to differentiate the most subtle fragrances will regard the ordinary sense of smell as extremely crude. This would be true not only in regard to herbs or perfumes, but especially in regard to the familiar experience of cooking. It is quite possible to develop and refine the capacity to recognize the invisible essences underlying what seems to be physical food, and to be directly aware of the myriad effects of different combinations of spiritual essences upon the sevenfold human constitution, with its latent forty-nine fires. Such sensory refinement has to do with wise magnetic attunement, and vitally affects the vestures in both their constitution and composition. The alchemical process of distilling the combinations and correlations of essences in each of the invisible vestures proceeds through *etherealization* which must necessarily work through the spiritual will.

The spiritual will alone is constantly able to alchemize, renovate and refine the life-atoms of the vestures, increasing their lightness and porosity to Divine Light. When the vestures are suffused by that Light, it becomes possible to think, feel, act, breathe, smell, taste, touch, see and hear benevolently. One is enabled to employ Divine Wisdom as a science governing every relationship to the atoms that one touches and blesses. The process of refinement involves the full and vast range of Monads that have passed collectively through the various kingdoms at different levels, coming down from the most ethereal in the early Rounds to the existing fourth stage with its kaleidoscopic variety of alternative opportunities for apperceptive and perceptive consciousness. Passing this mid-point, the cycle of monadic evolution moves upwards again to that plane which was in the beginning a state of spiritual and intellectual unconsciousness for the Monads, but which must become the plane of universal self-consciousness for perfected Monads by the end of the Seventh Round.

Behind and beyond all these changes of state and form there remains, unchanging and intact, one and the same Monad. It is an inward centre of light which does not participate in all the many alterations that affect the vestures. To put it differently, there must be beyond all the material vestures the perpetual motion of the *Atman*, which is the indwelling noumenal and invisible core of every Monad. Those who regularly meditate derive much benefit from the instruction of the *Catechism* of Gupta Vidya, which teaches one to draw inwards in consciousness to an inmost noumenal centre or point, which then immediately becomes a point in a line, a point in a cross, and finally the central point in relation to all possible forms. By entering into the Divine Darkness of pure abstraction, by becoming a Point without extension and receding behind all the planes of differentiation, one removes all awareness of forms and all evidence that there are many Monads. In the absence of manifest light, one experiences a deeper sense of the unity of all Monads and fundamentally destroys the all-pervasive illusion that there are many different beings separate from each other, sitting or moving in their separate bodies. Krishna teaches that the Eye of Wisdom has the intrinsic capacity to distinguish Spirit itself from a world of diverse objects and ultimately destroys the persisting illusion of manifold objects. When noetic consciousness has majestically risen above separations of objects and forms, it now experiences the world differently, omnidimensionally and in depth, entering the noumenal realm of what is unmanifest on the illusory plane of contrasts, beyond which there is the homogeneous plane of radiant matter, which lends luminosity to the subtlest vestures of the immortal Soul. This elevation of consciousness to a *laya* point is an experiment through which one can visualize at a preliminary level the plenitude of the field of noetic ideation, but it may be taken even further and simultaneously applied to all classes of human beings throughout the earth. This requires the progressive deepening of one's perception through intense meditation, so that over a period of time one may gain a greater sense of the noumenal depths of life-energy, and the magical properties of the Alkahest, the universal solvent.

The Monad, which is essentially ever the same, participates through the various vestures in succeeding cycles of partial or total obscuration of Spirit or of Matter. Everything occurring in daily life could be seen entirely in terms of the continuous ascent or descent from the One, or in terms of obscuration and illumination, but these could pertain either to Matter or to Spirit. Once one has grasped this philosophical and metaphysical basis for comprehending the complex scheme of monadic life and transformation, one can reckon with the fact that there are seven kingdoms of Monads:

> The first group comprises three degrees of elementals, or nascent centres of forces — from the first stage of differentiation of (from) Mulaprakriti (or rather Pradhana, primordial homogeneous matter) to its third degree — *i.e.*, from full unconsciousness to semi-perception; the second or higher group embraces the kingdoms from vegetable to man; the mineral kingdom thus forming the central or turning point in the degrees of the 'Monadic Essence', considered as an evoluting energy. Three stages (sub-physical) on the elemental side; the mineral kingdom; three stages on the objective physical side — these are the (first or preliminary) seven links of the evolutionary chain.
>
> *The Secret Doctrine*, i 176

Between the three elemental kingdoms on the subjective side and the vegetable, animal and human kingdoms on the objective side, lies the mineral kingdom. Poised in the fourth, or balance position, the Mineral Monad becomes crucially important. Indeed, one cannot understand either Evolution or Magic without apprehending the process of immetalization through which the abstract *Monas* reaches a maximum of condensation in the mineral kingdom. After this stage there comes a rapid dispersion, a continuous loosening up, which then produces the three kingdoms on the ascending arc. Viewed in one way, there is "a descent of spirit into matter equivalent to an ascent in physical evolution."

The more Spirit descends into Matter, the more there is conscious evolution on the physical plane. This is part of the cosmic sacrifice, because the bringing down of Spirit into Matter enables the latter at a greater level of density to evolve further and thus be quickened by noetic intelligence. If, for example, one handles with natural reverence and spiritual wakefulness any so-called object, which may seem to be a book, a piece of jade or a wristwatch, but which is actually an aggregate of elementals and life-atoms, then one can wisely instruct and initiate. Those who are truly awake spiritually can take anything, and with selfless love they can quicken latent intelligence, vivifying active awareness and higher self-consciousness. It is not as if there is not much to do in this visible universe. At any given moment one can touch and elevate every sentient point of energy. Looked at in this way, all life becomes extraordinarily meaningful, holding innumerable opportunities to aid monadic life in "a re-ascent from the deepest depths of materiality (the mineral) towards its *status quo ante*."

Since reascent implies a corresponding dissipation of the concrete organism, it is frightening to most people as it means the renunciation of identification with the sense of being in a body. Hence it is a disadvantage for them to have clocks and calendars. By thinking in terms of the distance or closeness in years to birth or death, and the waste of time since the birth of the body, little indeed is done for the care or tendance of the immortal soul. Seeing this makes many people nervous, but this is to lose the proper perspective. One must see all life in the context of the invisible whole. One cannot reascend consciously without a progressive series of dissipations and a continual breaking up of *skandhas* accumulated throughout a lifetime. For instance, an emotional person needs to reduce the liabilities of the lower vestures to certain basic patterns of consolidation and break up these unhelpful clusters at their very core. Whence the need to belong? What is this concern to appropriate? Whence the desire for material or psychological security? One must burst the consolidating sources of emotion in order to keep pace with forward Manasic evolution. Humanity is in the Fifth Race of the Fourth Round, the long epoch of *Manas*, and to be emotional is only to go racially backwards. To catch up with the forward impulse of humanity in the Fifth Race means becoming a self-sufficient being of creative thought and deep meditation, freed from the evanescent impulses of mere emotional reaction.

In order progressively to dissipate and dissolve the elements by which, through the desire for consolidation, people limit and bind themselves, the persisting root of illusion must be sought in the mind. The mental image of oneself as separate from other human beings, feverishly moving places but periodically depressed if not ascending all the time, is entirely false. Each human being is merely one of myriads of centres of sensation and observation, but while such centres in the lower kingdoms have a certain precision, humans are all too often lazily and inefficiently trying to observe and record on the basis of mayavic conceptions amidst a kind of day-dreamy existence. It is an important and difficult task to cut through this veil of illusion, and this can only be done by coming down from the cosmic to the mundane. First, one must rise upwards to a cosmic perspective and perceive the whole universe from a unitary standpoint. Then one can come down to oneself and one's daily orbit of duties and obligations. Human beings are assuming an impossible task when they attempt the opposite, starting with the lower self and then trying to dispel their root illusions. Only by ascending to the universal and then descending to the particular can one find greater meaning in every atom and every aspect of oneself, as well as every event upon life's journey and the soul's pilgrimage.

Hermetic wisdom holds that everything in the universe follows analogy, that as it is above, so it is below, and that man is a microcosm of the universe. H.P. Blavatsky expresses this axiom in exact terms which clearly show the critical relevance of the evolution of human mentality to corresponding transformations in the subhuman kingdoms: "That which takes place on the spiritual plane repeats itself on the Cosmic plane. Concretion follows the lines of abstraction; corresponding to the highest must be the lowest; the material to the spiritual." Pointing to the dangers of the anti-intuitive, or below-above approach to the task of liberating consciousness from the bonds of form, she warns: "It would be very misleading to imagine a Monad as a separate Entity trailing its slow way in a distinct path through the lower Kingdoms, and after an incalculable series of transformations flowering into a human being." To think in such a limiting and linear way is to repeat the error of nineteenth century Darwinian speculation, effectually cutting oneself off both from the prospects of emancipation and the possibilities of service to the entire life-stream of evolution — monadic, mental and astral. To think of oneself and a tiny pebble, and to suppose that the pebble or stone is a separate entity which will eventually become an equally separate human being, is essentially false.

The Monadic Host is a collective force below the human level, working conjointly, by descent of Spirit into Matter, to raise all that which has become differentiated to a higher power of porosity or luminous reflection of intelligence. Until the human stage the indestructible monadic spark of the One Central Fire is only collectively involved in evolution as part of the great Monadic Host. At the human stage it becomes creatively capable by the potent power of self-reflection, *Svasamvedana,* of being able to consider itself as an object of its own thought and imagination. This is an extraordinary power, denied to the animal, which the human being has, the sacred gift of visualization. Thought is an essentially divine power belonging to human beings, and when exercised properly it can become an irresistibly potent agent of transformation in human nature and Nature in general. The collective Monadic Host in its descent is only a vast collection of creative centres because the atom "is not a particle of something, animated by a psychic something, destined after aeons to blossom as a man. But it is a concrete manifestation of the Universal Energy which itself has not yet become individualized." The human Monad is that same universal energy, not separate in any way, but individuated.

Many of the problems that arise in trying to understand this process are due to thinking in terms of terrene rather than aquatic analogies. When one thinks of the ocean, it is clear that there is no less differentiation there than on the earth. But the untutored and ungoverned senses are practised liars. Hence there is a profound need for true science. Occultism begins in the recognition that raw sense-perceptions not only tell nothing, but are actually poor reporters of inaccurate information. They falsely convey an impression that there are myriad separate things 'out there'. This is why people who close their eyes and begin to meditate work hard from early on to destroy this delusion. It is sometimes held that this misconception is strong in human life because of the deception of language and the actual activities of naming and particularization, but these themselves arise merely from a priori consolidation in consciousness of one's image as a separate being. These psychological differentiations exist only as incomplete reflections.

In essence, there is no differentiation. All drops in the ocean are within one great collective being, and the moment one speaks of 'drops', this is only in relation to some water taken out of the ocean and put in a jar. These are ephemeral 'drops'. What applies to the ocean also applies to the earth and everything else, contrary to what the casual eye reports. To understand this truly at its root requires the return, through the power of abstract meditation, to the noumenal source of consciousness, and then smoothly descending in concentrated thought. One thus takes hold of a single torch in the darkness, lighting it up, and through it one may light up other receptive beings. In a sense this is mayavic because all Monads are exactly the same, whether manifest or not, whether illuminated or in darkness. Yet, to recover a sense of true being independently of what has happened in the external fields of sensory contrast, material disaggregation, seeming cohesion and dispersion, and mayavic manifestation, is to recover a noetic sense of the entire ocean and its invisible, unfathomable depths. Then, as *Manasa,* one may readily appreciate the depth of responsibility implied by the statement that "The ocean (of matter) does not divide into its potential and constituent drops until the sweep of the life-impulse reaches the evolutionary stage of man-birth."

The seemingly unbridgeable gap between the human and the other Monads is no more than the deceptive difference between the drop within the ocean and the drop outside the ocean. The teleological significance of the drop having been taken out of the ocean is that the cosmic power of that Monad, consciously to mirror the whole, is greater when it is locked into a certain vesture, the boundaries of which it must burst by the power of meditation. There is a deep meaning to the Orphic saying, quoted by Plato and Socrates, that the human body is like a tomb. The body is a temple, potentially, but in practice it is a tomb in which there is a confinement of the human Monad. Like a bird that is only freed from its cage at night, the Monad is ordinarily free only during deep sleep. Waking life is a kind of pralayic death to the immortal soul, and deep sleep, which is a temporary state of death or amnesia for the brain-mind, is truly regeneration and the elixir of life for the immortal soul. The soul is locked up and cannot come into its own except in deep sleep because its jailer, the brain-mind or personal ray, has assumed a parasitic false identity. Like a monkey or an automaton, it obscures the light which can only be gestated in silence. The personal ray is addicted to manifestation: the greater its desire to manifest, the longer and intenser the imprisonment of the immortal soul. From this, all the ascetic rules logically follow. The deeper the desire for meditation and calmness, for drawing within, and for self-forgetfulness in a state of active wakefulness to the noumenal realm of universal unity and life, the richer the possibilities for release of the spark of *Buddhi-Manas* from the *Atman* (the divine flame), and of establishing the still centre of one's inmost being, thus regaining the sovereign throne which has been usurped by *kama manas*.

If *kama manas* were an entity on its own, it could not ever displace itself. But *kama manas* is like an unruly child, an uproarious upstart in relation to *Manas*, a pathetic cheat that has stolen the light of self-consciousness and appropriated it on behalf of name and form. It did not mean to do all of this, but it caught the habit in the company of other people doing the same thing. During what is called 'growing up', it became inextricably involved in the extraordinary exaggeration that there are different and competing actors out there. Then, through compulsive consolidation of the personal consciousness, this became a dangerous habit. The child is bewildered when it first goes to school because it is expected increasingly to identify itself with something external. It may have already been given much aid in separativeness at home, especially where there were other children from which to differentiate itself. This banal phenomenon is somewhat unavoidable, but it is a spiritual hindrance to the incarnation of the immortal soul. Hence the importance of being able repeatedly to recollect, in a Platonic sense, one's true awareness of who one is as an 'I am I', an invisible centre of divine light-energy, essentially independent of all external impressions, conceptions, perceptions and forms. The mystical ability to release the potency and will of the indwelling Monad in waking life is the defining mark of spiritual wakefulness. When one sees rays of light, not forms, and when one sees oneself only as a ray of light and never as a form, then the human Monad begins to become progressively self-conscious in waking life. A truly self-conscious being in the midst of people who are not self-conscious can, while maintaining total silence, have an alchemical effect upon other people. At a minimum, they will be more apologetic rather than boastful about being bound up with the sensorium. If one maintains inward continuity of spiritual wakefulness, one can be a potent force for lighting up latent self-consciousness and giving spiritual life to all other beings.

This sacred privilege, exemplified by all the Avatars, is the fruition of the life-giving power of the perfected Monad. "As the Monads are uncompounded things . . . it is the spiritual essence which vivifies them in their degree of differentiation." There is that golden germ in the immortal Monad which vivifies even while it differentiates. The power to give life is always derived from the higher principles, which is why science will never be able to fabricate a living being through genetic manipulation. The divine power to give life derives entirely from the spiritual essence of the highest principles in the cosmos and in Man,

> which properly constitutes the Monad — not the atomic aggregation, which is only the vehicle and the substance through which thrill the lower and the higher degrees of intelligence.
>
> Leibnitz conceived of the Monads as elementary and indestructible units endowed with the power *of giving and receiving* with respect to other units, and thus of determining all spiritual and physical phenomena.
>
> It may be wrong on strictly metaphysical lines to call Atma-Buddhi a MONAD, since in the materialistic view it is dual and therefore compound.
>
> *The Secret Doctrine*, i 179

One should not imagine rigid Aristotelian rifts between *Buddhi* and *Manas*, between *Atman* and *Buddhi*, or between *Atman* and *Buddhi-Manas*. These are really the three hypostases or aspects of one abstract reality. All the human principles should be seen as specializations of a supreme principle, different kinds of lenses through which one central light can be focussed at varying degrees of differentiation. This fundamental fact is itself the enduring basis of analogy and correspondence in nature, and hence of the myriad opportunities people have, with the help of simple analogies, to recognize how the same light is focussed in different ways in all beings. But all seekers must apply these sacred analogies to themselves through the practice of *Buddhi Yoga*. "As Matter is

Spirit, and *vice versa;* and since the Universe and the Deity which informs it are unthinkable apart from each other; so in the case of *Atma-Buddhi.*" One cannot think of light in the human constitution apart from the Light of the Logos in the cosmos and the Divine Darkness beyond. And if one thinks of the Light of the Logos, the noumenal light within *Mulaprakriti,* the Ishwara and the *Paramatman,* then one will readily salute the inward light in *Buddhi-Manas,* in every human being. Everything at any given degree of differentiation is simply a specialization of a higher principle manifesting through the matrix of a different lens or focussing medium. To realize this fully is irreversibly to alter one's way of looking at the world and oneself.

Darkness from the standpoint of the sense-organs is metaphysically closer to Light, and primordial Light is permanently hidden within the Divine Darkness. Upon entering a condition of visual darkness, by analogy and correspondence one may experience resonances of a deeper state of spiritual darkness wherein meditation upon Non-Being results in an ineffable experience of primordial Light. Since all nature can be understood in terms of analogy and correspondence, everything on the physical plane is not only isomorphic, but also isodynamic with something on a higher plane. On the physical plane artificial light generates an illusory kaleidoscopic world, in contrast with which the darkness of abstraction is closer to the noumenal; so with the noetic mind that meditates. But mere exposure to the evocative power of physical darkness will not alter the ephemeral mental conceptions of human beings. This is why most people, though they go daily into deep sleep and come closer to the ideographic language of the immortal Soul, find that it avails them naught the next day. They have little basis for believing during the day that only the previous night they entered into their ancestral kingdom of Divine Light. There are blockages in bringing back the noumenal light of true knowledge gained in deep sleep through the chaos of *swapna,* the chaos of fascination with form, mostly arising through ignorant fear and wishful thinking.

So long as there is in human beings a compressed, congested

view of the separative self conceived in terms of innate deficiency, such blockages will persist. They derive from millennia of mutilation of the nimbus of human beings and have to do with causal factors connected with the misuse of magic, with creedal religion and exploitative social structures, but also with the persistent if pathetic refusal of many persons to accept fully their own responsibility and consequent karma. There is a stark alienation between human beings and their myriad opportunities for good in each life because as they learnt language, like Caliban in *The Tempest*, they learnt faster to curse than to bless. The recent story of humanity is a complicated and sometimes sordid tale of base ingratitude arising from fear and guilt, owing to many golden opportunities being misused through the failure to share them with others. Humanity thereby engendered certain ingrained patterns, so that the fresh opportunities given frequently in deep sleep or at certain waking moments will not make a lasting difference unless there is a calm and careful recognition of the diverse modes of karmic bondage.

Put simply, two distinct requirements must be fulfilled: *first,* one has to get beyond oneself, going in consciousness to the core of what is common, cosmic and transcendent until one can come down and be wide awake in the world of particularities and contrasts, the arena of illusion, ignorance and delusion; *secondly,* one must also acknowledge in detail, at least unto oneself, one's persisting delusions, because if one looks for commonality at the expense of fruitful diversity, one evades one's ethical responsibility. If one is unduly caught up in the world, one is running away from the One Light, but if one vainly tries to grab instantly the light of spiritual will, one is running away from past karma. Therefore one has to recognize frankly that every moment is a precious opportunity to learn, that everything which comes in life is really one's guru in disguise. At every moment of each day, the stream of life is rushing in to teach the soul if it is willing to learn. If one takes proper advantage of these golden opportunities, one can clean and polish the lenses of the vestures. By working upon one's different vestures in deep meditation several times a day, and also by going beyond them during deep sleep, a point will come at which one is refining them deftly from both ends rather like a person who is both visualizing a plan for a new arrangement in a room and also cleaning out objects as they are. The one activity need not preclude the other. One can have some time each day to think out a new way of arranging everything, and new ways of thinking. Meanwhile, one can also dust each object as it is, keeping things as neatly as possible within the existing arrangement.

Applying the analogy to the vestures, one can simultaneously increase slowly the porosity of the grosser vestures to the light while also working through the subtlest vestures to invite the beatific descent of the Divine Light. As the grosser vestures are continually renovated and cleaned, and as the subtlest vestures experience through meditation the infusion of noumenal light, a point comes at which the two processes can be brought together, realigning all the vestures from a fresh standpoint. This process must be renewed and repeated again and again. The search for the spiritual is really hard work, and while it is good that so many people have rebelled against a social structure which was using labour as a means of confinement to a narrow bourgeois conception of the world, the deeper purpose of this widespread and anomic rebellion was not to encourage indolence and indiscipline. Work and discipline can be done in an Aquarian mode, as a form of silent worship and spontaneous sacrifice, flowing forth from a selfless motive to be of true service to humanity and to elevate human and global consciousness, thus furthering the noble impulse of monadic evolution.

Light on the Path teaches "Kill out ambition. . . . Work as those work who are ambitious." Taken up in isolation, this is indeed difficult, but where it is done on behalf of the whole, without concern for any rewards to one's precarious self-image, it is much easier. This does not mean that there is no longer any ambition whatsoever. The diseases of the soul are still there to be healed, but where individuals work collectively, there is a quantum jump to a point at which they are less concerned with living a banal life of petty personal ambition. Yet, to work as those work who are ambitious is truly difficult for many weak-willed individuals. To work mainly for a loftier purpose, to generate a tremendous energy but out of a cheerful sense of obligation and as a modest contribution to the whole, even though there is no payoff to the personal ray, is hard for the persona. One must replace lunar emanations by solar energies. The sun does not wax and wane, but ceaselessly emanates light, life and energy so that in and around every human being there is a magnetic field of self-sustaining motions of the Spiritual Will, the Spiritual Heart and the Spiritual Mind. All that waxes and wanes, participating feebly in the vicissitudes of change, is secondary and instrumental. It is ephemeral and relatively unreal when seen from the noetic standpoint of the Spiritual Sun, mirrored in *Atma-Buddhi-Manas*.

Atma-Buddhi is the invisible sun in man, the *Atman* being like the invisible disc itself, and *Buddhi* is its centrifugal light. *Manas* is the centripetal organ for focussing that light, the seat of pure thought and spiritual will. What is below is like the moon which receives reflected light from the sun. *Manas* would be rather like Venus, the fixed star in highest heaven, Lucifer-Hesperus. This has nothing to do with the personal mind, which is extremely fickle and volatile, ever-changing and in a constant state of self-obscuration. The ordinary mind has developed into a perverse instrument because it is fiercely gripped within the cruel claws and greedy tentacles of the demon of selfish desire. *Kama manas* is like a motor-power driving the personal man to a pseudo-life sustained by futile fears of death and the obscure past. Inwardly, these fears stem from the loss of the birth vision. People become vulnerable to plausible but absurd eschatologies because in every human soul there is the sad loss of an earlier vision which can only be recaptured by conscious effort. Until it is sufficiently recovered, one is necessarily subject to a creeping fear of the divine judgement which comes at the moment of death. Yet, there is much truth to what Shakespeare says, that life is but a poor shadow that struts upon the stage for a brief hour, full of sound and fury, signifying nothing. For the immortal soul there is little benefit, typically, in most of what is called earthly life.

Therefore, the immortal soul must indeed make the most of a few moments of time in daily meditation and deep sleep, so that it may become capable of sustaining its own pure visions of the Good. This does not mean that at other times there is no creative activity, on the subtler planes of non-manifestation, but all this has little to do with the reflected ray. Until its periodic pain becomes the basis of a life of search for meaning, and until it is blended through *Buddhi Yoga* with the vaster suffering of all humanity, one cannot hope to awaken to the real life of the immortal Monad. When one enters what *The Voice of the Silence* calls the Path of Woe, then one will eventually come to discover the ineffable *ananda* of the Divine Light streaming forth from the Divine Darkness, the changeless *alpha* and *omega* of monadic life beyond all form, stretching until the farthest shore of formless existence.

The Dewdrop slips into the shining sea.

OM MANI PADME HUM

SELF-MAGNETIZATION

Thus proceed the cycles of the septenary evolution, in Septennial nature; the Spiritual or divine; the psychic or semi-divine; the intellectual, the passional, the instinctual, or cognitional; the semicorporeal and the purely material or physical natures. All these evolve and progress cyclically, passing from one into another, in a double, centrifugal and centripetal way, one in the ultimate essence, seven in their aspects. . . . Thus far, for individual, human, sentient, animal and vegetable life, each the microcosm of its higher macrocosm. The same for the Universe, which manifests periodically, for purposes of the collective progress of the countless lives, the outbreathings of the One Life; in order that through the Ever-Becoming, every cosmic atom in this infinite Universe, passing from the formless and the intangible, through the material natures of the semi-terrestrial, down to matter in full generation, and then back again, reascending at each new period higher and nearer the final goal; that each atom, we say, may reach through individual merits and efforts that plane where it re-becomes the one unconditioned ALL.

The Secret Doctrine, i 267-268

Throughout manifested Nature and in all beings — human, animal, vegetable, mineral and elemental — there is a universally diffused magnetic field in which one common vital principle circulates that may be controlled by the perfected human will. Beyond the illusion of time produced by the succession of finite states of consciousness, every present moment of manifest life is both a summation of a series of moments that goes back into the night of time and the dawn of cosmic manifestation, and also an emanation from a single stream of consciousness, an immortal ray of light that travels through a long journey over eighteen million years and stretches into future time.

The emergence from past time and the entry into the future are illusory in so far as these alterations in awareness or modifications of mind only affect the elemental vestures. Made up of changing combinations of sentient lives, these enveloping vestures are involved in an ever-revolving motion under a universal law, which balances every outgoing and ingoing — the Great Breath. In every human soul there is an innate tropism, a natural propensity towards the Good at some level of self-persistence. Not a living being on earth lacks a germ of good, a spark of truth and a ray of supernal light. Nothing could survive in the realm of form apart from this essential element of universal light-energy which makes cohesion possible. But this same law of balance also decrees the dispersion of life-atoms, providing for decay and death as well as for birth and growth, and hence permits not only rebirth but also regeneration or retrogression.

The path leading to conscious immortality, to freedom from the grip of all-devouring Time, must necessarily involve a spiritual process of progressive self-regeneration; it is founded upon detachment from form, veneration of the universal sacrifice of life, and serene meditation upon the One Light beyond all manifestation. The Buddhas of Contemplation are constantly established in the pristine unmodified state of cosmic meditation. Krishna, the Logos incarnate, instructs Arjuna: "Out of a single portion of myself I create this entire universe and remain apart." This is the highest standpoint conceivable in cosmic evolution. It is a supreme state of freedom which is accessible only at the summit of enlightenment, attained by those Bodhisattvas who have become illumined beings in the fullest sense, capable of mastering all the vestures of incarnation and remaining in effortless attunement to the Great Breath, the Soundless Sound. Acting in time but abiding outside time, moving in space yet resting beyond all visible space, they remain in an Atmic state of eternal motion which is motionless in comparison with all modes of motion recognizable on the external planes of matter.

This is the ultimate object of mystic meditation and continuous contemplation by the developing disciple who sits ready for *Dubjed* (Initiation). After a long period of preparatory discipline, the neophyte reaches repose wherein it is meaningful to ask whether, and in what sense, there is any essential difference between such fundamental conceptions as space, causality, time and motion. Are they merely conceptually interdependent facets of a single reality, or are they ontologically separate? To the ordinary mind they would seem to be separate because the familiar framework of cognition identifies a spatio-temporal context or sphere in which one is firmly focussed upon a single point of concentration. The mind would persistently seek to focus upon a seed-idea as the germ or cause of a new train of self-reproductive thought which might take root in the Tree of Life, and in successive lives of spiritual discipline the seed may sprout into the Tree of Immortality.

The disciplined mind could also become intensely aware of the rates and phases of breathing and soon discover that it is impossible to go from the in-breath to the out-breath, or from the out-breath to the in-breath, without a minimal pause or interval, some sort of *laya* point. Many a monk seeks to prolong the interval of stillness between inbreathing and outbreathing, or between outbreathing and inbreathing. At this stage the discursive mind notices that there are distinct differences of time intervals in varying contexts. With steadfast persistence in such a simple exercise, these differences become less important, especially when there is a decisive shift of attention from physical to mental breathing. A heightened concentration of awareness is possible when one can smoothly dissolve the seemingly discrete intervals between breathing in and breathing out. This can arouse the power of noetic discernment, giving a finer sense of the particularity of each moment, and sharpening the intensity of awareness. This will help in time to attain an assured sense of what is essential in every momentary experience, of the hidden core meaning in a humdrum day of familiar events and responses. There is that which is truly valuable in every context of human interaction, but the discerning soul can only learn from each day by rendering gentle service to all that lives. Within a limited sphere of duty — on a single day for a particular period of time while meeting other beings — one must pierce the veil of unconscious collective processes, which otherwise leave one a victim, more acted upon than acting, mentally passive rather than spiritually awake.

Buddhic insights are best understood in terms of the attempt to transcend all divisions, to go beyond every sense of separateness. It may be initially difficult to avoid the feeling that one is oneself, that one has a neighbour, that one is passing other human beings, that one meets A and B and C while at work. This is an illusion which is needed at a certain stage of differentiation but which must be transcended on the Path. The goal is first to see only rays of light in those who masquerade under different names and diverse forms, and then to go further: not only to see no differences but also to see oneself in each and every other person one encounters. This means projecting not one's lower self, (that merely inverts the process), but one's truest Self. The aim is to see the best one knows in each and every human being, and also to recognize the best in each and every human being as present in oneself. This psychological process takes years of sustained self-training and self-correction, with concrete tests applied to the reflected ray which is involved in the many pairs of opposites — heat and cold, loss and gain, growth and decay, fame and ignominy, creation and destruction, and so on. These are all part of the ethical burden of incarnation, while one is alive and awake, and while one is moving in and through a world of many minds and hearts, lives and souls, each of whom is on a solitary pilgrimage.

It is the longest journey for each and every human being, dateless and deathless: no landmarks are on the visible plane, but all are eternally enshrined within the tablets of the astral light and upon the records of *Akasha*, the fiery mist out of which the Golden Egg encircling the universe is constituted. Consubstantial with the universal *Hiranyagarbha*, there is that which is like a minute portion of it, and provides protection for each and every human being. It is largely potential, but may be activated during deep meditation, when one has abstracted from the physical body with its senses and organs, and from the reflected ray of the lower mind with its likes and dislikes, fears and hopes, hates and suspicions, its pride, conceit, delusion and illusion. All of these, endemic to the assemblage of lower lives, can be let go and the mind may be withdrawn to that still, motionless centre unmodified by colour, by limitation, by form, by change, by seeming movements of succession in time or coadunition in space. All of these could be transcended because one could bring consciousness to a still centre in the place between the eyes where the eternal motion of *Alaya-Akasha* becomes the alchemical elixir of life.

> *Whatsoever quits the Laya State, becomes active life; it is drawn into the vortex of* MOTION *(the alchemical solvent of Life); Spirit and Matter are the two States of the* ONE, *which is neither Spirit nor Matter, both being the absolute life, latent. . . . Spirit is the first differentiation of (and in)* SPACE; *and Matter the first differentiation of Spirit. That, which is neither Spirit nor matter — that is* IT — *the Causeless* CAUSE *of Spirit and Matter, which are the Cause of Kosmos. And* THAT *we call the* ONE LIFE *or the Intra-Cosmic Breath.*
>
> The Secret Doctrine, i 258

What is true of the phases and pauses of breathing is also true of the cycles and seasons of Nature, as well as the divisions of lifetimes. At every level of organisation of the countless lives mirroring the One Life, unseen creators and destroyers are constantly engaged in a sort of combat. At the molecular level this may be seen in reference to the microbes and life-atoms which make up the vestures, and in their aggregate action give rise to the four phases of human life, comparable, according to Pythagoras, with the four seasons. Attentive observation of Nature reveals a function in her economy for each and every thing. There is a function for the sere and yellow leaf of autumn which must die when the chlorophyll has so saturated the leaf that the green has become a yellow-brown. It is a breaking-up — a function of Shiva — which allows its restoration to the mud of the earth so that all of those lives are released. They go into the non-manifest only to re-enter in new arrangements the realm of the manifest. The ceaseless activity in Nature is at all times constructive, requiring the disintegration and rebuilding of structures, expressing a distinct beauty in every one of the seasons. If one can experience through meditation the continuous process of construction, destruction and regeneration that persists throughout human life, one becomes much more willing to accept these different phases and their distinct characteristics in terms of the total economy of human life. Through the incarnation of the projected ray there is an impingement of the subtler vestures upon the astral and the physical. By the power of thought one can enable what is in the higher vestures to act magnetically upon the lower vestures. By mere reaction and emotion, one may intensify the obscuring reaction of the lower vestures upon the higher vestures.

This is the choice life continually affords to a human being. Either one chooses to become more deliberate and ideative by the magnetizing power of thought, functioning in terms of manifold cycles rather than the overall cycle of the gross astral, and so, by the power of higher thought, discovering and giving significance, beauty and meaning to life-atoms at each stage. Or one can merely be emotional, using language and thought to rationalize emotion, building up an ego and defending it, corroding the channels of connection between the higher and the lesser vestures till there is an atrophy of creative centres. After a point, the more one does this, the harder it is to gain the power of attention, to hold an idea, to become completely absorbed in a therapeutic teaching. Instead, through self-examination and meditation, one ought to learn to take advantage of the properties and powers of the higher which do not belong to the same cycles that work upon the lower vestures. So, to achieve a total renovation of the lower vestures from the standpoint of the immortal individuality will take many years. One must be willing to look back at seven, fourteen, twenty-one years of life and courageously acknowledge the chaotic patterns of so-called thinking and feeling which mauled, weakened and atrophied the constructive, creative and consecrating powers of the correlative faculty of *Manas* reflected in all these vestures. Without either being irresponsibly fatalistic, or delusively emotional, one must acknowledge that a thorough renewal requires many years of courageous effort. Damage done over a long time can have no instant solution. To succumb to the flattery that suggests otherwise is to deny oneself the opportunity to learn properly the alchemical art of self-regeneration.

Rather, one must resolve to spend a number of years establishing and strengthening countervailing tendencies, recognizing old tendencies when they come, and counteracting them with deft precision. Robert Crosbie suggested that as soon as one discerns a mood or tendency which is deleterious, one should immediately think of the opposite. Ineffectually thinking of the opposite, and being unable to do anything when the challenge has already come to full flower, is like refusing to treat a disease when its initial symptoms appear. It is precisely when a tendency from the past first registers in awareness that one must act calmly. Like wise soldiers in times of great crisis, one must become especially cool and exceptionally slow. One must find the correct countervailing mood; and until one ties the ailment and remedy together, it is hard to break up a mood. But if one makes the effort with total trust in the law of cycles, and does this sufficiently often, it will begin to happen naturally. Then it will wear away the old tendencies until they fall away, and a refreshed class of life-atoms will become a permanent component of one's vestures.

The metaphysical basis of this theurgic work of self-regeneration lies in the ultimate identity of all life, both in the physical realms studied by chemistry and physiology, and in the invisible realm of life-atoms:

The Occult doctrine is far more explicit. It says: —
Not only the chemical compounds are the same, but the same infinitesmal *invisible lives* compose the atoms of the bodies of the mountain and the daisy, of man and the ant, of the elephant, and of the tree which shelters him from the sun. Each particle — whether you call it organic or inorganic — *is a life*. Every atom and molecule in the Universe is both *life-giving* and *death-giving* to that form, inasmuch as it builds by aggregation universes and the ephemeral vehicles ready to receive the transmigrating soul, and as eternally destroys and changes the *forms* and expels those souls from their temporary abodes. It creates and kills; it is self-generating and self-destroying; it brings into being, and annihilates, that mystery of mysteries — the *living body* of man, animal, or plant, every second in time and space; and it generates equally life and death, beauty and ugliness, good and bad, and even the agreeable and disagreeable, the beneficent and maleficent sensations. It is that mysterious LIFE, represented collectively by countless myriads of lives, that follows in its own sporadic way, the hitherto incomprehensible law of Atavism.

The Secret Doctrine, i 261

There is an atavistic return to psychic tendencies of the past, as well as elements of physical heredity, and they go back over many lives, connecting with patterns over many generations. All of these are in the astral light, permeating the lower vestures so that any attempt to assign a single extraneous cause, or to blame them on other individuals in this life, would be unphilosophical. There are so many life-atoms involved in the vestures that every day through thought, breath and speech, one charges enough life-atoms to affect many lives. It is absurd to try, on the basis of some narrow span of illusory time, to blame all one's ills upon a single lifetime. One must, at some point, penetrate to the causal level, and mentally cleanse one's sense-perceptions. To understand how Manasic concentration of *Buddhi-Akasha* can purge and purify the lower vestures, one must grasp the correlative action of thought upon the fiery lives of the lower vestures as they alternate in their function of building and destroying:

> The 'fiery lives' are the seventh and highest sub-division of the plane of matter, and correspond in the individual with the One Life of the Universe, though only on that plane. The microbes of science are the first and lowest subdivision on the second plane — that of material *prana* (or life). The physical body of man undergoes a complete change of structure every seven years, and its destruction and preservation are due to the alternate function of the fiery lives as 'destroyers' and 'builders.' They are 'builders' by sacrificing themselves in the form of vitality to restrain the destructive influence of the microbes, and, by supplying the microbes with what is necessary, they compel them under that restraint to build up the material body and its cells. They are 'destroyers' also when that restraint is removed and the microbes, unsupplied with vital constructive energy, are left to run riot as destructive *agents*. Thus, during the first half of a man's life (the first *five* periods of seven years each) the 'fiery lives' are indirectly engaged in the process of building up man's material body; life is on the ascending scale, and the force is used in construction and increase.
>
> *The Secret Doctrine*, i 262-263

Any individual who is magnetized through great ideas and benevolent currents of thought and feeling during that period should be so grateful that he cannot awaken on any single day without feeling this gratitude intensely. The ideal *chela* who is going to gain the elixir of life, wakes up daily with a virtually inexpressible awareness of the privilege to be able to breathe, when he has already contacted the Teachers of *Brahma Vach*. A person who experienced this gratitude in any significant degree in those early years is extremely fortunate; through constant gratitude one gives enormous strength to the subtler vesture of ideation. One is therefore ready in the subsequent period to put to proper use all that has been evolved. "After this period is passed the age of retrogression commences, and, the work of the 'fiery lives' exhausting their strength, the work of destruction and decrease also commences." On the physical plane, this is a reflection of what occurs on all planes and involves the subtlest energies. The subtler the energies, the more they are affected by whether the will, motive and impulse of thought and feeling are benevolent or malevolent, selfless or selfish. That is ultimately the only issue. Because people in general cannot handle this, metaphysically and mathematically, through meditation and ideation, they require a system of external ethics that puts a brake upon their selfish misuse of life-atoms. Because the body was given a certain name, because others acknowledged that there was a separate being, they were misled into thinking that one owns everything. In truth, one owns nothing.

It is an abnormal notion in human evolution that one owns anything at all. Not only is everything held in trust, but one is a Manasically individuated being chiefly for the sake of expressing gratitude. There is no higher reason. The sole purpose of human sound and speech is to be able to resonate with gratitude to the cosmic sound, *Nada Brahman.* By using the measure of gratitude, which is appropriate to the symmetrical ways of life of the civilization of the future, one can see the abnormality of a great deal of contemporary existence. One can also see how difficult it is to reverse these tendencies because people constantly contaminate the few grains of rice they receive from the Wisdom Religion with the muck and the mire of the shallow culture that surrounds them and suffocates their innate intuitions. Nonetheless, if they develop a genuine capacity to use the Teaching on a day-to-day basis, and if they are also willing to be patient and to work in terms of seven-year cycles, they can decisively amend their own patterns, structures and cycles, replacing former tendencies by new powers and new levels of creativity, continuity and choice. They can begin to benefit from painful construction (which takes place through lower destruction), endured with a selfless attitude of sacrifice, renunciation and detachment.

When the 'Devourers' (in whom the men of science are invited to see, with some show of reason, atoms of the Fire-Mist, if they will, as the Occultist will offer no objection to this); when the 'Devourers,' we say, have differentiated 'the fire-atoms' by a peculiar process of segmentation, the latter become life-germs, which aggregate according to the laws of cohesion and affinity. Then the life-germs produce lives of another kind, which work on the structure of our globes.

The Secret Doctrine, i 259

At the foundation of all the seven subdivisions, and corresponding to *Manas*, is *Akasha*, the fifth cosmic principle which is fiery, but not like fire on the physical plane. It is also watery, airy, but it is none of these as they are known in terms of ordinary conceptions of fire, water and air. *Akasha* is the very essence of higher *Manas*, hence of ideation and thought. Ideation is a sacred word, not to be confused with what people call thinking, which is really the mind chattering away. To ideate is to blend the energy of ideation and a universal truth. It is to moisten, to vivify, a universal truth by calmly and repeatedly dwelling upon that idea so that it becomes an abstract image or a matrix that can act upon the will through *Akasha*. Through abstract meditation the perfected will can guide the material correlates of *Akasha*, following a series which corresponds to the successive differentiations of the proto-elements underlying the various globes of the earth chain. Beginning with Fire and the fire-atoms in the First Round, these proceed through Air, Water and Earth in the succeeding Rounds. Since each of these elements is the source of the diverse properties of the subtler vestures behind the physical, all the globes and all the Rounds have their connections with different aspects of the human being. According to the ancient Commentaries on the *Stanzas of Dzyan*: "*It is through and from the radiations of the seven bodies of the seven orders of Dhyanis, that the seven discrete quantities (Elements), whose motion and harmonious Union produce the manifested Universe of Matter, are born.*" H.P. Blavatsky points to the necessary nexus between these substantial elements and spiritual consciousness:

> *Our physical light is the manifestation on our plane*
> and the reflected radiance of the *Divine* Light
> emanating from the collective body of those who are
> called the 'LIGHTS' and the 'FLAMES.'
>
> *The Secret Doctrine*, i 259

A person who truly begins to understand the possibility of the process of alchemical transmutation inherent in incarnated life will set apart both time and space every day, as well as appropriate symbols and magnetic centres of association, with a continuous stream of creative ideation. This is difficult in the course of a crowded day in the presence of others; but one can sit alone at night and propel these divine ideas to act as living forces. If one adopts the proper mental posture — one of great reverence, gratitude and obeisance to all Divine Hierarchies — these forces will act infallibly. But the process is hard, unless one is genuinely grown up. Unless one has been taught gratitude as a child, seeing it practised by others, one will not understand the sacred idea of intelligent obedience. Knowing nothing about truly free will, and therefore living compulsively in terms of wants, a shadowy life becomes established which makes it difficult to summon pure mental images. One must assail the root of false identity, expose it as a lie, and let it all go. One must break it apart. It is especially important not to cooperate with those types of language that contaminate, corrupt and misuse spiritual truths, including mindless appeals to experience "for its own sake" and vain assertions of illusory free will that are merely popular forms of lunar game-playing. At some point, these will take their inevitable toll, and will weaken the capacity of the mind to focus Buddhic Light, blocking opportunities for self-regeneration.

Instead of consigning oneself to the captivity of psychological delusions and temporal illusions through moribund attachment to fleeting forms, one must renounce separative and self-limiting life. Then one can enjoy the pulse of universal life. When each day becomes a constant "thank you" to the entire human race, one takes one's true place in the human family. One recognizes that the human family, in some mysterious, unthanked, but also unobtrusive manner, has made it possible to breathe and to eat, to live and to sleep, to walk on this good earth. Meditation is a kind of thankfulness; and when it is thankful it is cool, like the "cold brightness" of the fire-atoms of the First Round, for it is freed altogether from the lie and lust of self. It is freed from any care for the shadow, and from any attachment to the mask. By voiding altogether the personal self, by making it a zero, one enjoys living, in and through all beings. Meditation becomes a "thank you", which lightens one's load, increases the light in the eyes, deepens the power of silence and changes the tone of one's voice. One acquires a cool appreciation of the human condition, of its poignancy and its pain, but also of its silent grandeur, its inward dignity, and its unscrutinized meaning. Then one begins to recognize that manifested life is merely a participation in formation, preservation and destruction, the three aspects of the OM, the three hypostases of the manifesting spirit of the Supreme Spirit by which title Prithivi, the earth, greets Vishnu, the Logos.

The earth as a whole engages in a daily greeting of Narayana, and this celebration of life is expressed in the endless re-enactment of the triune activity: firstly of formation, germination, creation, the giving of birth; secondly of preservation, support, stability and survival; and thirdly of destruction, dissolution, rearrangement, regeneration. Thus, at the hidden core of life is that which does not perish with manifested forms, *Achyuta*, the abstract Triad. When meditation has reached a certain point within the ever-expanding sphere of higher awareness, there is a recognition and reverence of the cosmic Triad which is incarnated in those who are enlightened. Then, there is an irreversible increase in the light of awareness of the invisible guardians of the human race. Humanity is an orphan; but there are those who guide and guard its destiny. As one becomes profoundly moved by the Great Sacrifice, one is able to make each day count more as a contribution in a life-count well lived. At the moment of death one will recognize that one has brought a golden thread of gratitude from the first moment of birth to a state that resembles death, but merely is a prelude to rebirth, a preface to the resumption of one's true vesture wherein, self-consciously, one can return to the world to serve on behalf of all that breathes.

THE VERBUM

When our Soul (mind) evokes a thought, the representative sign of that thought is self-engraved upon the astral fluid, which is the receptacle and, so to say, the mirror of all the manifestations of being.

The sign expresses the thing: the thing is the (hidden or occult) virtue of the sign.

To pronounce a word is to evoke a thought, and make it present: the magnetic potency of the human speech is the commencement of every manifestation in the Occult World. To utter a Name is not only to define a Being (an Entity), but to place it under and condemn it through the emission of the Word (Verbum), to the influence of one or more Occult potencies. Things are, for every one of us, that which it (the Word) makes them while naming them. The Word (Verbum) or the speech of every man is, quite unconsciously to himself, a BLESSING or a CURSE; this is why our present ignorance about the properties or attributes of the IDEA as well as about the attributes and properties of MATTER, is often fatal to us.

Yes, names (and words) are either BENEFICENT or MALEFICENT; they are, in a certain sense, either venomous or health-giving, according to the hidden influences attached by Supreme Wisdom to their elements, that is to say, to the LETTERS which compose them, and the NUMBERS correlative to these letters.

The Secret Doctrine, i 93-94

Those who have had the resplendent karma of receiving the sacred teaching about the Verbum should move rapidly from the state of irresponsibility into the realm of responsibility in the gestation of sound associated with thought. This is a practical teaching that can be used even if one has yet to acquire a detailed knowledge of the hidden properties of matter on subtle planes of existence. Anyone may make a true beginning by trying to conserve speech-energy, by becoming more deliberate and careful in the choice of thoughts and words. Calmly sitting down in the privacy of one's own solitude to read aloud *The Voice of the Silence*, or excerpts from *The Secret Doctrine*, one can make a radical change in one's magnetic field. Infusing this endeavour with a profound sense of the sacred, a vital depth is touched in one's daily awareness of the invisible centres of consciousness and in one's capacity to direct benevolently different groupings of life-atoms, to purify and render them worthy of the divine temple, the human form wherein burns the flame of self-consciousness kindled by the Sons of Fire.

The priceless gift of noetic self-awareness can be brought to bear upon each of the different centres of consciousness. Even though in its spiritual essence *Manas* is entirely disconnected from the discordant sensorium, it effectively can, through the pristine radiation of its own potent light, magnetize, consecrate and intensify as well as make precise and benevolent the organs of perception. Those who value this immense privilege seriously enough to carry out a series of initial experiments with truth within themselves will gain a greater awareness through deliberation of the dignity and the divinity of being human. They will discover what it means to reverse the current of negative thought, centered upon the sense of futility of the personal self, and they will lighten the load of dead-weight elementals impressed with past pretences, desperation and despair.

The orbit of the sacred is revolutionary; it is subversive to the *status quo* of one's previous somnambulic existence. Lest one cultivate the fatal craft of becoming schizoid, one must assiduously practise the arcane teaching about the Verbum by consciously choosing and assuming full responsibility for one's thought-currents. Instead of excusing one's passive tendencies, one must learn to direct one's attention to what one deliberately intends, to sublime themes that elevate the mind, to daily exercises in spiritual alchemy. Individuals must think to the core the quintessential prerogative of being human. Rather than irresponsibly pretending that the whole of life is episodic, they must acknowledge that days make up weeks, weeks make up months, months make up years, years make up decades in a lifetime, and each incarnation is an integral part of a long series of lives. In a universe where sowing and reaping are inextricably interwoven, human beings have to do what agriculturists know and gardeners practise, preparing the soil, pulling out weeds, planting at the right time and patiently cooperating with the seasons and cycles of Nature. If some are afraid to do this, it is because they mistakenly believe that they are infallible experts on the subject of themselves. This is a fundamental error. When a person gains glimpses of self-knowledge, a sure sign of growth is the increased willingness to breathe the refreshing air of agnosticism. One is ready to recognize that there is a profound mystery to every human being, that the last person one knows is oneself. Not until the bonds of personality are loosened can that self be truly known. The soul abides in the Silence, and when the restless mind ceases from thoughts and words, it may be merged into the inmost shrine of the heart, so that when one opens the eyes and utters a sound, one feels it is a sacred privilege to breathe as the votary of the Logos, of Brahma Vach.

If a person ventured to make daily experiments with truth, it would be helpful to formulate some working rules which make due allowance for the plastic potency of one's own vestures. After all, different people have different propensities. Some are very vocal on worldly matters but they are utterly unable to speak about the spiritual. Others speak endlessly about the spiritual until words lose all meaning. Still others speak as if they already know what they have only remotely glimpsed. Others mix vibrations, speaking of the sacred and then lapsing into the profane. Sacred language cannot be properly enunciated if one inserts into it a sense of the separative 'I' because the kamamanasic 'I' has to vacate its false authority within the human being so that the immortal individuality may affirm spiritual truths through an invulnerable personality. The metaphysical basis of this process lies in the fact that the more indivisible the mental energy involved in universal, abstract, impersonal ideas, the more rarefied and homogeneous is the matter within which these ideas clothe themselves. As divine ideation draws the mind to a still centre, through deep meditation upon boundless duration, abstract space and pure being, one approaches a plane of consciousness where matter is radically different from what is normally understood. Matter becomes light-energy. It is cool Akashic fire which has a distinctive texture, a peculiar tensility and volatility, ethereal properties for which there are no adequate analogues on the physical plane.

A person sitting for long hours by a log fire may start to see behind and around the flames a noumenal light and may begin to have an inkling of the invisible fire behind the veil of the visible. It is possible for any person to arouse the subtler senses by reaching towards universal ideas, and through intense ideation one may become conscious of noumenal matter. This arcane teaching rests upon the presupposition that what is called knowing or interacting is an imperfect experience of consubstantiality. One only knows what is on the grosser planes through the grossness in oneself. Any suggestion that it is outside is misleading, for if it were not in oneself it could not be seen. A highly evolved being may be able to take the most mundane of subjects and see it from the standpoint of the subtlest abstraction, thus elevating the entire field. On the other hand, most human beings only too often do the opposite. They may even take a sublime conception and drag it down to the densest plane of sensory awareness.

Control of thought and speech is an essential ingredient of soul etiquette and spiritual discrimination. It represents good taste at the highest level, where one may enrich a spontaneous longing for Brahma Vach, the *Agathon*, the Ineffable Good. Out of repeated meditation one must gain such a strong, lively and self-perpetuating sense of the Ineffable Good at the core of the Divine Darkness behind the shimmering veils of the universe, that one is securely anchored in that state of spiritual awareness. And therefore, as Plato suggested in the Allegory of the Cave, when seemingly descending into the world of heterogeneity, one is able to use wisely one's eyes and ears and above all, one's tongue, so that one is acutely conscious of every available opportunity to give a forward impulse to human evolution. Where one encounters anything meretricious on the lower planes, it will roll off like water off a duck's back. It simply will not inhere because of the intense activation and vigilant preservation of one's noetic awareness. The importance of this mental discipline will soon become evident to those who are courageous enough to become steadfast in its practice, not for their protection, but for the sake of universal enlightenment. Not only can they begin to discharge their debt to the sacred Teaching by converting it into what they could use, but they could actively contribute to the creation of the magnetic field in which spiritual instruction could be integrated into new modes of secular monasticism.

It is the responsibility of those who have received the Teaching to test themselves by experiments and exercises, by resolutions and by vows, for the sake of other human beings who have not been so privileged, and therefore cannot understand how they are constantly harming themselves by the sounds emitted through their tongues and vocal chords. They have created recurrent karma even through a single violent outburst. Given the mathematics of the process, it takes a long time to create a strong field of refined vibrations. Destruction takes very little time, and through violence masses of life-atoms have stamped on them some memory of revenge. As W.Q. Judge explains in "The Persian Student's Doctrine", at some point they will return and take their toll for the abuse given to them. Many people are self-alienated because they have misused too many life-atoms for too long and therefore fear that something like nemesis is coming to them. This supposedly malign fate is nothing other than what they themselves have summoned, but unless they grasp the logic of karma and reincarnation, there is little they can do to mitigate their own misery.

If one has been so fortunate as to encounter these teachings, then instead of vainly brooding over what one might have done ten lives ago, one should right now release the strongest vibration of which one is capable. One will be doing so in a magnetic field in which there are unknown but tougher beings than oneself who are also doing it in their own consciousness. One will have the benefit of that collective current as well as the inestimable benediction of Initiates. If one attempts this earnestly, one will begin to feel worthy of inhabiting the human form, with its far-ranging faculties of perception and action, which myriads of ancestors and their spiritual instructors have produced and perfected over aeons. The golden opportunity is open to all to correct the persisting mistakes of the past and to insert the strongest current into the immediate future, and that means one has to get to the root-cause which is the immovable mind. Just as one can sense the depths of the ocean or the idea of bare space, one can make the mind immovable and inconceivably strong. One may associate it with an inward posture and meditate upon its potential fixity, analogous to the snowy pillars of Amarnath. As Robert Crosbie suggests, one should meditate upon the idea of steadiness itself. One might think of familiar examples of what is fixed, from the pole-star to the unthanked lamp that lights a city street for stragglers in the night. Above all, if one would learn steadfastness in maintaining the highest spiritual vibration, one must meditate upon the Bodhisattvas and Mahatmas, and Shiva, the patron and paradigm of true ascetics.

The initiation of any sacred sound-vibration, when based upon exact spiritual knowledge, can set the keynote of an entire epoch. In that Avataric tradition, when Krishna struck a keynote, as with Buddha, Shankara and Pythagoras, the highest karma of a cycle was determined. This has a bearing upon the classes of souls drawn into incarnation as well as the pressures that vacate souls unable to keep pace with the current, and also upon all the invisible forces and energies that have been rearranged and affected. At all times there are people who may be contemporaneous with the sounding of such a keynote, but apart from a vague sense that something is going on, they may not be able to participate in it because, as Buddha said in the *Dhammapada,* the ladle of a soup bowl, even though it serves the most delicious soup over the lifetime of that bowl, will never become the taste of the soup. Mere physical proximity makes no difference to consciousness. Spiritual teachers think and speak in terms of millennia and of millions of beings, and in many a Buddhist text it is said that the Buddha taught all three worlds. In these worlds there are those who, by self-conscious awareness of what is seminal, can receive the reverberation of the keynote and become capable of benefiting by its translation into uses that may be exemplary and helpful to other beings. There would be no survival for the human race over eighteen million years but for the continuous compassion of the Brotherhood of Bodhisattvas.

The karma of the earth is much better than the karma of most of the beings who inhabit it, and it is the sacred reservoir of the sacrificial ideation of holy beings that sustains humanity. These are the invisible potencies and guardians that protect the human race and provide the forward impulse behind human evolution. Even though whole groups of entities, by receiving the accumulated karma of their own perverse acts, may vacate the scene of history, Humanity moves onward. This is because the power of spiritual continuity is much stronger in the universe than the discordant discontinuities of fragmented consciousness. All discontinuities must very quickly produce disconnections, and when there are disconnections between the centres, this is rather like a wireless set that does not work anymore or a car that has broken down. But in regard to the astral, breakdown is not a matter which can be mechanically adjusted. It is a function of tropism, whole classes of life-atoms and elementals which develop destructive tendencies that become cumulative and cataclysmic.

The practical implication lies in the inexorable fact that whatever karma any human being generates between the age of twenty-one and thirty-five must be properly adjusted between the age of thirty-five and forty-nine. These twenty-eight critical years out of a human being's average of seventy are more intense than the period before twenty-one, despite the extenuating theories of those who want to blame heredity or environment or childhood.

The middle period is crucial because the power of thought is activated in a manner that has a vital bearing upon the twenty-one years that complete the average span. There is a cyclical rhythm in every human life which is related to the mystery of numbers and the mathematics of collective cycles. To be able to work with these laws and cycles is what has always been valued as wisdom throughout the history of the human race. Wisdom always works with the processes of life and its continuities through generations that are understood by all peoples. Anything that is not based upon this organic pattern is unnatural and a sign of ignorance, of cutting oneself off from what it is to be human, from the whole of life, from the laws of Nature and from the historical currents that move towards righteousness, enlightenment and growth.

These forward currents have their ultimate origin in the manifesting power of the Verbum, which through its cyclic descent establishes the manvantaric world — "the one 'Whirlwind' (or motion) finally giving the impulse to the form, and the initial motion, regulated and sustained by the never-resting Breaths — the Dhyan Chohans." These are, in turn, the ancestors and archetypes of the Buddhas of Ceaseless Contemplation, who exemplify to mankind *dhyana par excellence*. They seem distant to human beings, and seem to represent an impossible ideal of fixity and continuity only because human beings have mistakenly identified themselves with those elements in themselves that are discontinuous. On this basis, immortality itself becomes impossible to understand because that composite mind which is discontinuous is meant to disintegrate. It is ceaselessly involved in the flux, it is essentially unreal, it is rather like the interplay of light and shadow upon a screen wherein is reflected at a great distance an image projected from a magic lantern. The immortal individuality of every human being inhabits a luminous sphere or noumenal field which is saturated with the highest creative reverberations. Through *sushupti* and meditation each person may come closer to the great galaxy of perfected minds and hearts which are engaged in ceaseless contemplation, and also to the

Dhyanis presiding over the whole of manifestation.

The Dhyanis are at the apex of complex hierarchies which are difficult to understand because the entire Teaching about spiritual hierarchies is numerological, mystical and shrouded in a secret cipher. These exalted intelligences are intimately involved, as daimons, with every single human being. This is closely related to what happens at the moment of death, when every person comes into contact with a being of light. That is the true Father-spirit, the Dhyani overbrooding each human being. Even if a person, for lack of contemplation and meditation or due to misidentification with the body and the persona (namarupa), never really thought of the overbrooding Dhyani, at the moment of death the presence of the Dhyani is essential to enable a smooth separation of the higher Triad from the lower quaternary. The spiritually wise have taught in all times and cultures that the individual who consciously chooses during waking life to think of that which happens involuntarily to the mind in sleep, and of that which comes as a gift at the moment of death, is able to maintain a ceaseless current of benevolent ideation. Only such a person is truly able to live, which is why The Voice of the Silence enjoins: "Give up thy life, if thou would'st live." Without dying unto the world, without dying as a separative self, without relinquishing the petty personal concerns which are mostly muddled and confused through a fundamental ignorance of causality, conscious immortality is impossible. The blustering tyrant, kama manas, must cast off all pretensions and invoke the immortal sovereign spirit to descend and enter the temple, don the vestures and assume its sovereignty over its kingdom so that the soul's true mission may be fulfilled. This is what is meant by inviting Krishna to become the charioteer, transforming Kurukshetra into Dharmakshetra, the field of triumphant righteousness.

Shankara transmitted the wisdom of Initiates and taught that "Fire is beyond time — that is the highest guru." There is a Father-fire in the Spiritual Sun which is formless and invisible and which is triune, but which on the reflected plane is a sevenfold fire that participates in the manifested world. If the typical human being is sevenfold as a differentiated being, though strictly unitary, that person can become an integrated being, intact within and living from within without. By meditating in the lower vestures upon the higher Triad, one can get closer and closer to the cosmic Triad until there is a permanent reversal of polarity. Then there is a continual awareness of the ubiquitous reality of the primordial Triad of Agni, Vayu and Surya, of Fire, Breath and the Spiritual Sun. When these are seen as one, and when this becomes the subject as well as object of meditation, it is possible to make a revolutionary difference in the internal relations between life-atoms in one's subtlest vestures. Then one is able to control at will the lower principles while seemingly participating in the world of differentiated forms which is mayavic and unreal. The secret life of the soul is constant, continuous and replete with the pure joy of effortless attunement to the whole, to the music of the spheres, to the rhythms of invisible Nature. This is the blessed privilege accessible to every human being, to become capable of entering into the pristine current of the Dhyani, to become self-consciously aware upon every plane of the inaudible hum in the heart, the ceaseless vibration that comes from the Soundless Sound.

The sacred teachings concerning the Spiritual Sun, the Verbum and the Dhyanis cannot be understood unless they are used daily, and this is inconceivable unless one is inherently capable of apprehending and experiencing them. There is a self-validating nature to Divine Wisdom. When one finds a seminal idea, a mantramic phrase which truly sparks off some light in the head and in the heart, and one feels impelled to use it, then by reflecting upon it and by remaining in that current and using it one can transform the magnetic field of awareness, which in turn can draw the mind further onward. Those who engage in regular meditation upon OM TAT SAT will find that their attention is again and again taken back to *Hiranyagarbha,* the golden egg, and to that which is beyond it and is represented by the Spiritual Sun. If one is always reaching out to the Source, then one can take the teachings concerning entire classes of seminal energies and gain some sense of how these work, usually when one is very still, in a state of deep silence, and when one has brought to a point one's whole consciousness and then expanded it while staying within that current. If one really touched the core and experienced joy, one would naturally want to return to it again and again. It is really important to touch that realm which is so overwhelmingly joyous and profoundly illuminating that one's whole being wants to go in that direction as often as possible. This can produce a line of life's meditation. When that truly happens, the *sadhaka* or seeker begins to live in the current of Divine Wisdom and then many discoveries are possible, so that when one hears about the Kumaras, our spiritual progenitors, one can resonate in the different centres of one's being.

A simple but crucial exercise is not to go to bed and not to wake up without deliberately giving oneself a chance to dissociate, saying, "I am not the body, I am not the astral form, I am not my likes and dislikes, I am not this name." As one comes closer to the recognition that one is THAT which is beginningless and endless, not just in words but in thought, one will begin to centre oneself in the spiritual heart of one's being. Most of what is called living is off-centre, and therefore one is alienated from the inmost depths of one's being. If one practised a regular exercise before going into sleep and on waking, and then tried to link these two points through a third point during the day, one would establish a triad through which the mind is firmly brought back to the same central theme of true selfhood. By making connections between points in consciousness, one begins to initiate a current in which one can stay continuously. Then it becomes natural to familiarize oneself with the different classes of obstructions and obstacles that deflect one from the current. One naturally welcomes every opportunity through reading and thinking and through listening, where one can be brought back to the main current which then becomes the living power of Divine Wisdom. In the course of time there is a progressive incarnation of the higher principles and therefore a natural evacuation of those classes of tendencies which cannot really occupy the same space in which the diviner energies are operating. To realize the beneficent and purifying power of the Verbum on a sustained and regular basis is the great purpose of all invocations of Brahma Vach, so that as many as possible may enter the current of divine ideation which is the guiding force of cosmic and human evolution.

KRIYASHAKTI

Kama . . . is in the Rig Veda (x, 129) *the personification of that feeling which leads and propels to creation. He was the* first movement *that stirred the* ONE, *after its manifestation from the purely abstract principle, to create,* 'Desire first arose in It, which was the primal germ of mind; *and which sages, searching with their intellect, have discovered to be the bond which connects Entity with Non-Entity.' A hymn in the Atharva Veda exalts Kama into a supreme God and Creator, and says: 'Kama was born the first. Him, neither gods nor fathers (Pitara) nor men have equalled.'. . . The* Atharva Veda *identifies him with* Agni, *but makes him superior to that god. The* Taittariya Brahmana *makes him allegorically the son of Dharma (moral religious duty, piety and justice) and of Sraddha (faith). Elsewhere Kama is born from the heart of Brahmā; therefore he is* Atma-Bhu 'Self-Existent', *and* Aja, *the 'unborn.'*

The Secret Doctrine, ii 176

There is a vital connection between *Kriyashakti*, the creative potency of self-conscious thought, and Kamadeva, the Rig Vedic deity of compassion. At the highest metaphysical level, *Kriyashakti* is equivalent to the most primal currents of cosmic creativity and impulsion. This supreme potency of self-conscious thought is capable of bodying forth from the most sublime states of transcendental awareness an unbroken stream of emanations that may serve as sources of strength for all aspirants on lower planes of consciousness. Like all the mighty *shakti* powers hidden in the human constitution, *Kriyashakti* can be fully aroused and made active only out of the most compassionate and universal motives. The divine imagination can be awakened only in the service of universal good. This capacity to enact in manifestation an ideal vision of the *Agathon* is a self-conscious embodiment of the creative compassion of the cosmos symbolized in Kamadeva. Ordinarily, the current of *kama* is a force that makes for human bondage. This impact of *kama*, however, is but a shadowy reflection of the cosmic principle of divine creativity and universal compassion.

The Rig Vedic Hymn to Creation highlights the intimate relationship between pre-cosmic desire at the most primordial level and pre-cosmic ideation. Pre-cosmic ideation connotes a great deal more than mere passive contemplation of abstract ideas. Indeed, the very concept of ideation implies active volition. At the most primeval level of the cosmos, on the plane of *Mahat*, this volitional agency is represented as the primal seed or germ of mind. It is the pristine ground and unmanifest matrix of universal self-existence. As the causeless Germ in the Root, it is *Atma-Bhu* and *Aja* — Self-Existent and Unborn. It is the unmanifest Logoic Heart of the cosmos-to-be, the ineffable self-conscious source which radiates through every dimension of space, and the transcendental reflection of the unknowable Absolute. Between the ineffable zero of Be-ness and the infinitude of existing beings, it swells and vibrates with the pure desire to create, the volition of the One to become the many. It is within this mysterious Root of the cosmos that the highest Rishis have found and realized "the bond which connects entity with non-entity." Such a Rishi has plumbed to its depth the problem of identity and mastered the meaning of universal self-existence in Deity. The fully perfected human being has become one with Deity, one with God. He is therefore able to understand from within his own universal self-consciousness the deific principle of cosmic creation. He has become one of the rays streaming forth from the heart of the Spiritual Sun. He has become attuned in consciousness and being to the kernel of the mystery of the One and the many.

Apart from this most mysterious and sacred realization, it is logically and psychologically impossible to resolve the impasse between the unconditional and the conditioned. In the arcane metaphysics of Gupta Vidya, the One without a second, by its very nature, can have no relationship to the world of differentiated time and space, the realm of manifested subjects and objects. How, then, is it possible to account for the world of differentiation? To the uninitiated mind it would seem that either there must be a god who creates the world out of nothing or that the world and all its life are a godless accident sprung from material chaos. Yet this apparent dilemma — anthropomorphism or atheism — is but a false dichotomy. Through travelling the inward path of meditation (*dhyana*) it is possible to apprehend the bond between that One, which is eternally absolute, and the world of time and of manifestation. To understand is to become and to participate in the mystery. One must merge in consciousness with the Logos, become refulgent like the sun with the unconditioned potentiality of Divine Thought and diffuse the rays of unconstrained creativity throughout universal space.

The universal indifference of the Logos to all possible modes and forms of manifestation is equivalent to its universal compassion and benevolence. As the mystical mirror of the *Agathon*, it is neither subject to itself nor possessed of any object. It is neither added to nor subtracted from by the appearance or disappearance of the manifested cosmos. To begin to conceive of it, one might think of a realm of the unmanifest causally prior to the region of the manifest. Even this, however, may only confuse minds addicted to thinking in terms of subjects and objects. It is extremely difficult to sunder Deity from its emanations, to distinguish between the subliminal force of abstract terms like TAT, *Daiviprakriti* and *Mulaprakriti* and the Unmanifest Logos. Ultimately, even these words are themselves emanations from that plane of transcendental self-existence. They are themselves reflections and radiations, focussed out of compassion and for the sake of understanding, of the consciousness of enlightened beings. They are meant to serve as the basis for deep meditation and an inward ascent in noetic consciousness.

Through intensity of devotion in meditation upon such potent ideas, even the neophyte can come to sense some glimmering of the mystery of the relation between Entity and Non-Entity. When one ideates in the realm of pure thought, without reference to objects or temporality, one will in the end experience within oneself the intrinsic continuity extending from one pole of that meditation — which is voidness — to the other pole —which is fullness and plenitude. Through this mystical experience of emptiness and plenitude within the same state of universal consciousness, one experiences something of the mystery of Fohat, something of the mystery of the bond connecting Entity with Non-Entity.

Hidden within the folds of this mystery is the ultimate metaphysical basis of all *Kriyashakti*, all creative imagination. At this highest level one must understand the whole universe as the product of the highest *Kriyashakti*. One must therefore recognize the consubstantiality of the essential nature of each human being with the Divine Ground that is prior and unrelated to all manifestation. This recognition can come about only through entering into that realm of pure being which is the Divine Darkness prior to all worlds and to all forms. The highest basis of creativity is, naturally enough, very far removed from worldly notions and tokens of creativity. It has nothing to do with concretized desires for results impelled by an acute sense of deficiency and want. It is completely free from any illusions foisted by an incomplete self-consciousness upon that which is necessarily mutable and mortal. In spanning the poles of pure voidness and pure plenitude, this highest Kriyashaktic creativity transcends all limited modes of affirmation and negation, whether in relation to space or time or motion. It is neither tinged with the angularity of self-interest nor trammelled by the distortions of exaggeration and denial.

Something of the supreme self-confidence of self-existence is conveyed in the hymn of the *Atharva Veda* which portrays Kamadeva as the offspring of Dharma and Shraddha. *Dharma* in this sense refers to supreme necessity, flowing forth from precosmic harmony or *Rta* as its architectonic embodiment in abstract space. On the one side, it is the stern decree of necessity, imposing harmony upon the relations of all manifested beings; on the other side, it is the compassionate fitness of all things and the vital sense of everlasting right. In the primal exercise of pure cosmic *Kriyashakti*, there is an element of seeming involuntariness, of that which is both binding and holy. In this dharma there is a solemnity and sacredness which far transcends all derivative notions of destiny and faith, all earthly promises and prospects. Standing prior to all of these, and serving as the root of all legitimate aspiration, dharma is the unwavering and authentic imperative of the truth of Self-Existence. It is the abstract principle of integrity and the fount of all obligation and its fulfilment.

At the same time, there is in that pure cosmic *Kriyashakti* an element of *shraddha* or faith. This faith is an unshakeable conviction of the inherent value of the action of *Kriyashakti*, independent of entropy and of the reflection of creativity in the complex processes of change. It is the unbroken assurance of the Divine, which is unborn and undying; it is the full freedom of selflessness, the formless joy and boundless beneficence that gives freely of itself without a shadow or hint of calculation. Thus, the allegorical offspring of Dharma and Shraddha is the mystical power of divine creation at the heart of the invisible cosmos. It is *Kriyashakti* personified as Kamadeva, the infinite potency of Divine Thought and the Law of laws, Compassion Absolute. It is *Eros* in its most profound philosophical sense, the awesome creative and therapeutic force extolled in *The Banquet* of Plato. Whether one speaks of it as pure love or cosmic creativity, it cannot be understood without reference to a world that is unmanifest and a state of being which is prior to manifestation. Before the dawn of manvantaric manifestation, pure thought and pure creative desire become fused within the primal germ of mind. This spirit of unconditioned self-existence was called by H.P. Blavatsky "Love without an object." As the mystical confluence of *shraddha* and *dharma*, it is both the source and the fulfilment of all devotion and discipline, all love and service. It is the one flame burning without wick, fuel or stand amidst the boundless field of the Divine Darkness.

This highest Logoic centre of the cosmos is the primordial source from which all differentiated beings come into existence and to which they return. It is all in all, and the binding force of all. In it the many live, move and have their being. It is the law of growth and the entelechy of all existence. All the manifested processes of cosmic life, with their complex interplay of creation, continuity and change, are crystalline aspects of the metabiological Logoic life within and beyond the cosmos. As that universal current of life is itself unborn and self-existent, there is that in its reflected modes which cannot be construed in terms of any finite sequence of antecedents or formal set of preconditions. The mystery of life outside the cosmos, yet also at its root, is mirrored in the myriad living beings that people the cosmos on its different planes. Each is a spark of that original creativity, and each is an embodiment of its law. Thus, whilst there is comprehensible transmission and continuity among living forms, there are also sudden changes and creative transmutations of living form that cannot be reduced to finite causes. These changes do not, however, represent randomness or disorder within the cosmos. Rather, instead of being traceable to the action of the parts, they represent the living presence of the whole in each, the presence of the One amidst and within the many.

On the physical plane this is the problem of heredity and variation which has intrigued intrepid thinkers throughout the centuries. Since Pythagoras inserted the idea of evolution into early European thought, many philosophers have ardently sought to account for biological continuity and change. The rich resources of ancient thought have been largely eclipsed since the nineteenth century by empirical science's narrow and obsessive interpretation of Darwin's thought. When one considers Darwinian notions in the light of a broader stream of thought in world culture, their exclusive respectability can hardly be defended. For though there is evidently something plausible in Darwinian explanations of speciation and variation, there is also something grossly inadequate. What it accomplishes by way of concrete explanation, it achieves at the cost of mechanistic assumptions. By insisting upon the mechanical efficacy of transmission of characteristics at the level of individual instances, it renders collective evolution utterly random and chaotic. Whilst freeing biological thought from the arbitrary anthropomorphism and hazy teleologies of the Middle Ages, it leaves life to languish as a statistical accident, a blind offspring of a philosophy that is itself blind to the potency of ideation.

The price of this shallow materialism and narrow empiricism is a persistent inability to conceive of the nature of the creative potential inherent within human beings. Without taking into account the logic of the Logos on the plane of *Akasha*, it is impossible to form any adequate conception of the nature of the modes of transmission of life on the physiological plane. Genetic transmission can only account for some of the variations within patterns that themselves cannot be explained by physical heredity. In order to understand the conception, gestation and birth of even a single human form, one must allow for the invisible progenitors such as the Lunar Pitris. Certainly, to gain some grasp of the elusive logic of human procreation, as it applies to the entire race, one must see the present mode of procreation in relation to a series of different modes in the past and the future. One must consider the complex history of anthropogenesis, recognizing the diverse roles played by differing hosts of creators and Pitris in the formation and ensoulment of human vestures on the earth. At the very least, one must attempt to abstract one's *idea* of human procreation from its present *means* of accomplishment. Hence, one is helped by mythic accounts of the mysterious modes of birth that characterized the earlier human races — the *chhaya* birth, the sweat-born, the egg-born and the androgynous. Citing a telling example from zoology, H.P. Blavatsky pleaded for a more open-minded approach to the nature of human reproduction.

> The very interesting polyp *Stauridium* passes alternately from gemmation into the sex method of reproduction. Curiously enough, though it grows merely as a polyp on a stalk, it produces gemmules, which ultimately develop into a sea-nettle or *Medusa*. The Medusa is utterly dissimilar to its parent-organism,

the *Stauridium*. It also reproduces itself differently, by sexual method, and from the resulting eggs, *Stauridia* once more put in an appearance. This striking fact may assist many to understand that a form may be evolved — as in the *sexual* Lemurians from *Hermaphrodite* parentage — quite unlike its immediate progenitors. It is, moreover, unquestionable that in the case of *human* incarnations the law of Karma, racial or individual, overrides the subordinate tendencies of 'Heredity', its servant.

Ibid., 177-8

The cosmic law of Karma, which works through all race evolution, is involved in the descent of the Kumaras, the solar ancestors who endowed nascent humanity with the power of *Manas* over eighteen million years ago during the Third Root Race. That same law of inherited Karma is also involved in the procrastination of some of that host, as in their eventual retribution whereby they were projected into senseless forms. Similarly, the law of Karma comprehends the vast scope of the hosts of the Lunar Pitris working up the materials of the living lower kingdoms throughout the preceding Rounds. This complex karma of all humanity over millions upon millions of years is involved in the changes and continuities affecting the human race. That karma involves the activity of beings of surpassing wisdom and power as well as myriads upon myriads of elementals, the living atoms of Nature's sounding-board. It should not be surprising, therefore, that it is impossible to explain or anticipate everything that is transmitted through human beings merely through some theory of physical heredity, however complicated in terms of modern biochemistry and microbiology. Whilst it is possible to gain helpful lessons through a microscopic study of its physical manifestations, there are far more important insights to be gained by rising in consciousness to a more global awareness of human life. It is in the multi-dimensional life of humanity as a whole that the deepest mysteries are to be discerned regarding the Logoic processes of creation, continuity and change.

Similarly, abstracting from the present human condition and attempting to recover in consciousness some awareness of the earlier androgynous condition of humanity can help in coming to understand Kriyashaktic creativity. Before the separation of the sexes took place over eighteen million years ago, human beings in the Third Root Race were hermaphroditic or androgynous. Subsequently, the familiar form of division into male and female has prevailed. In so far as human beings generate in consciousness an exaggerated sense of specialization or polarization through being male or female, they will experience either a false sense of insufficiency or a false sense of self-sufficiency on the lunar plane, which acts as an obstacle to creativity. Once polarization has taken place, there is an intrinsic incompleteness in the male principle and a corresponding if deceptive wholeness or self-sufficiency in the female principle. Each of these could inhibit that potent force of fearlessness and detachment in the realm of imagination which is required to release the higher creative will. Until one overcomes the lower psychic sense of completeness or incompleteness that accompanies the astral form, one cannot tap that authentic fearlessness which enables one to enter the Divine Darkness prior to all worlds and all forms. One must readily transcend the polarity of the astral form that refers to being male or female if one seeks to recover an inner sense of the stern necessity and divine compassion of mental and spiritual creation, and if one is to root oneself in the supreme faith and abiding self-existence of the immortal Triad.

The wings of ideation are typically weighted down through identification with the astral and physical form. One's capacities for meditation and creativity are clipped through attachment to that which is merely a mutable projection. The force of this attachment is increased by the activity of *kamamanas*, particularly through speech and cerebration. All of these cause the astral to bloat until it becomes quite heavy. It is significant that in hinting about the after-death states of consciousness, Plato in the *Phaedo* uses as the primary pair of opposites the heavy and the light. Those whose souls were weighted down in life are weighted down even in death. In contrast, those who lightened themselves in life experience, effortlessly, a degree of lightness after death. They are able to ascend to the higher planes of consciousness. To experience the ultimate in lightness and effortlessness combined with fearlessness, detachment and faith in creativity, one must transcend altogether the astral plane. One must develop an inward sense of being that can function freely through the *karana sharira*, the permanent vesture which is the basis of the permanent astral body.

A developed disciple of *Brahma Vach* can gestate such an astral body in any life, and continue to do so over succeeding lives. Thus he, like an Adept, will eventually be able to exercise some volitional control over incarnation and to conceive and contemplate a voluntary incarnation. This process, continuing through many lifetimes, involves the hatching out of astral matter of a particular kind of permanent astral vesture, which itself is emanated out of the *karana sharira* out of the purest vesture which might be called 'the meditation body'. It is what is sometimes called in Buddhist literature the Buddha-nature or Buddha-body. Only through profound meditation can one gain a sense of the potential reality of that subtle vesture of meditation. And only then can one transcend without effort the seeming insufficiency and false sufficiency that belongs to the astral plane through the separation of the sexes.

Long before an individual attains to this advanced and deliberate state of self-evolution, he can gain a provisional and theoretical understanding of *Kriyashakti* arising out of meditation as the paradigm of creativity. Citing the mysterious role played by *Kriyashakti* in the evolution of humanity and the presence of this power as latent in every human being, H.P. Blavatsky characterized *Kriyashakti* as

> the mysterious *power of thought* which enables it to produce external, perceptible, phenomenal results by its own inherent energy. The ancients held that any idea will manifest itself *externally* if one's attention (and Will)

is deeply concentrated upon it; similarly, an intense volition will be followed by the desired result. A Yogi generally performs his wonders by means of Itchasakti (Will-power) and Kriyasakti.

Ibid., 173

Human beings in every walk of life have had intimations of the reality of such powers, and even realized that what the Inner Self truly wishes is what ultimately is handed down through justice. This is *Kriyashakti* at the simplest level. This relationship of intense volition to tangible result cannot be understood inductively or in terms of likes and dislikes. One cannot even begin to ponder the idea of what one's inner Self — the *Ishwara* within — chooses without attaining a high degree of detachment. According to Patanjali, *vairagya,* or detachment, is indifference to everything but the Supreme Soul, rooted in a sense of supreme fitness and inner moral necessity. To act for and as the Supreme Self is to embody both *dharma* and *shraddha,* moral necessity and spiritual conviction. Paradoxically, when the mind and heart are concentrated deeply upon that which is totally right, one no longer desires anything for oneself. Then one will reach one's goal. This process of mental and spiritual creativity through and on behalf of universal good is experienced through mystic meditation. In the perfected human being, permanently rooted in consciousness on the plane of *Akasha, Kriyashakti* unfolds as the ceaseless capacity of compassionate ideation extended in protective benevolence over all beings.

This divine capacity of the perfected human being is derived from the creative heart of the Logos. Its exercise by Buddhas and Mahatmas is inseparable from the creative compassion in the primal germ of mind at the origin of the cosmos. All phenomenal matter is only a kind of appearance which, at the root, is in essence inseparable from Root Matter or *Mulaprakriti.* In that primordial matter, which is the invisible essence behind all phenomenal matter, there is *Daiviprakriti,* the primordial Divine Light which is also Life in the highest sense. That eternal Life is also Light and Electricity at the earliest precosmic level. All of these are reflected at the dawn of manifestation in cosmic electricity or in the Light of the Logos in manifestation. They are reflected in the life that then becomes the Fohatic energy, which maintains an entire set of worlds in manifestation. At the primordial level, Light and Life can be summoned out of the *Mulaprakriti* which is hidden in phenomenal matter. Kamadeva is this highest energy of the purest ideation awakened in the primal germ of mind through *Kriyashakti* on the plane of the Logos. It is through *Kriyashakti* that the Lords of Wisdom, the Kumaras, the eldest sons of Brahmā born of the body of night, created progeny in the Third Root Race of humanity. That progeny was and is both a single wondrous Being and a radiant Host of beings,

> the so-called SONS OF WILL AND YOGA, or the 'ancestors' (the *spiritual* forefathers) of all the subsequent and present Arhats, or Mahatmas, [created] in a truly *immaculate* way. They were indeed *created*, not *begotten*, as were their brethren of the Fourth Race, who were generated sexually after the separation of sexes, the *Fall of man.* For creation is but the result of will acting on phenomenal matter, the calling forth out of it the primordial divine *Light* and eternal *Life*. They were the 'holy seed-grain' of the future Saviours of Humanity.
>
> *Ibid.*

The gestation and emanation of a new nucleus of Mahatmas and Adepts set apart for the coming races of humanity arose out of the original meditation of the highest divine beings in the Third Root Race. This is *Kriyashakti* in its most exalted sense. It is intimately connected with the mysteries of initiation, whereby a Bodhisattva can, out of the light of the Dhyani Buddha which is within himself, project a Manushi Buddha and a Nirmanakaya. It is also possible, through *Kriyashakti,* to project a certain type of human being which becomes a model and a redemptive saviour for races to come. This, associated with Padmapani Bodhisattva, is the highest and most sacred form of creativity. Every human being has within himself the principle of Christos, Chenresi, Avalokiteshvara or Padmapani Buddha. Every human being has within the spiritual essence of the universal light of the universal Logos which is eternal Life, and which encompasses each and every form of divine creativity.

Attempt, I entreat you, to mark what I say with as keen an observation as you can. He who has been disciplined to this point in Love, by contemplating beautiful objects gradually, and in their order, now arriving at the end of all that concerns Love, on a sudden beholds a beauty wonderful in its nature. This is it, O Socrates, for the sake of which all the former labours were endured. It is eternal, unproduced, indestructible; neither subject to increase nor decay; not, like other things, partly beautiful and partly deformed; not at one time beautiful and at another time not; not beautiful in relation to one thing and deformed in relation to another; not here beautiful and there deformed; not beautiful in the estimation of one person and deformed in that of another; nor can this supreme beauty be figured to the imagination like a beautiful face, or beautiful hands, or any portion of the body, nor like any discourse, nor any science. Nor does it subsist in any other that lives or is, either in earth, or in heaven, or in any other place; but it is eternally uniform and consistent, and monoeidic with itself. All other things are beautiful through a participation of it, with this condition, that although they are subject to production and decay, it never becomes more or less, or endures any change. When anyone, ascending from a correct system of Love, begins to contemplate this supreme beauty, he already touches the consummation of his labour.

The Banquet   PLATO

THE EYE OF SHIVA

When the Fourth (Race) *arrived at its middle age, the inner vision had to be awakened, and* acquired by artificial stimuli, *the process of which was known to the old sages. . . . The third eye, likewise, getting gradually* PETRIFIED, *soon disappeared. The double-faced became the one-faced, and the eye was drawn deep into the head and is now buried under the hair. During the activity of the inner man* (during trances and spiritual visions) *the eye swells and expands. The Arhat sees and feels it, and regulates his action accordingly. . . . The undefiled Lanoo* (disciple, chela) *need fear no danger; he who keeps himself not in purity* (who is not chaste) *will receive no help from the 'deva eye.'*

The Secret Doctrine, ii 294-295

The priceless gift of spiritual vision veiled in the arcane symbolism of the Eye of Shiva is the sacred heritage of future humanity, but it will remain hidden, like the Biblical treasure in the field, until all lesser lights are renounced. From the time of the sacrificial descent of the Agnishwatha Pitris into the Monadic Host of incipient humanity over eighteen million years ago, the fiery spark of noetic insight has been enshrined in the inmost heart of each and every immortal soul. In the earliest epochs of evolving humanity, the light of soul-vision irradiated and suffused the mortal vestures, giving meaning and direction to daily conduct, a fullness of fellow-feeling in society, and grateful reverence to the lustrous presence of spiritual elders and teachers. The spontaneous devotion of the Third Root Race sprang from its lucid awareness of the supernal light within the human breast, and its natural intention to cherish and consecrate that living trust. Effortless purity and exquisite delicacy of soul-etiquette, qualities so scarce in the present age, were the widely prevalent marks of undefiled self-consciousness in the earliest races. The light has not wholly dimmed nor has the vision vanished beyond recall.

The indestructible Light of the Logos antedates all worlds and endures as the permanent possibility of vision. The sacred organ of spiritual perception in man has become obscured and even atrophied through misuse of its potency. By misappropriating the universal energies of the Higher Triad for the sake of the separative concerns of the mortal self, the vital connection between the permanent and impermanent vestures was damaged, dulling the psycho-physical senses, rendering them fickle and deceptive at best. As the final consequence of follies and misdeeds, the crucial brain-centres associated with the channels of spiritual awareness were petrified. The diminished estate of contemporary humanity is the direct and inevitable consequence of its individual and collective immorality in the past. Most of the world's present ills and sufferings, along with its apparent indifference to its future welfare can be traced to deliberate if forgotten choices in distant eras.

Like Milton's Samson, shorn of power and blinded through folly, mankind is helplessly chained to the cyclic round through no fault but its own. Similarly, if it is to recover the lost light of its spiritual immortality, this can only come about through sacrificial deeds of self-regeneration and self-correction, thus emulating the mighty *Yogin*, Shiva. Gupta Vidya teaches the mysterious tenet that the Third Eye is indissolubly connected with Karma, a teaching which is as telling in relation to the future as it is pertinent to the past. Both past and future are merely facets of the eternal present viewed from the standpoint of differentiated consciousness. So too, cause and effect in discontinuous action are but aspects of universal harmony in manifestation through centrifugal and centripetal modes of motion. In the *Bhagavad Gita* neither the Divine Eye of Krishna nor the Cosmic Vision that it confers is fanciful or fortuitous. The Avataric descent of the Logos and the lending of the Divine Eye to Arjuna are objective representations in the temporal realm of archetypal realities in the timeless realm of spirit. It was Arjuna who, through self-righteous identification with his own mask, placed limits upon Lord Krishna and thereby felt himself cut off from immortality.

Having truncated the sense of self, he alienated himself from the Logos, and fell into dark despair when faced with his self-chosen dharma.

If ignorant identification with the mask is the primary cause of human bondage, it is inseparable from a correlative caricature of Deity and Law. There is an intimate connection between anthropomorphic religion and the exteriorized personification of universal law as a cruel and avenging power. In regard to the Greek conception of Nemesis, H.P. Blavatsky pointed out that originally Nemesis was not a goddess, but rather a moral feeling which stood as the barrier to evil and immorality. Through anthropomorphizing fancy, this feeling was progressively externalized and personified into an ever-fatal and punitive goddess. Such an unphilosophical conception, itself a symptom and result of the corruption of consciousness, must be rejected in order to restore a sterling sense of responsibility under Natural Law.

> Karma has never sought to destroy intellectual and individual liberty, like the God invented by the Monotheists. It has not involved its decrees in darkness purposely to perplex man; nor shall it punish him who dares to scrutinise its mysteries. On the contrary, he who unveils through study and meditation its intricate paths, and throws light on those dark ways, in the windings of which so many men perish owing to their ignorance of the labyrinth of life, is working for the good of his fellow-men.
>
> *The Secret Doctrine,* ii 305

Philosophically, the impersonality of the unknown and unknowable divine Principle is inseparable from the impartiality of universal and immutable justice. To be confused about the former is to be confounded by the latter. It is a curious, though undeniable, fact that just two hundred years ago the founders of the American Republic saw fit to place a graphic representation of the Divine Eye of Wisdom on the Great Seal. And, though that eye has been prodigally printed on every dollar bill for nearly fifty years, hardly one out of a hundred Americans has really noticed it, and scarcely one out of a hundred thousand has seriously thought about it. Perhaps one in a million has sought to put it to use, and one in ten million might have been able to sustain true meditation upon the Eye for a period of months or years. Virtually all have gone on spending the dollar without any reverence for the Third Eye, a prolific waste of the world's resources for which Karma is now exacting its toll. Such is the karma of a nation condemned by its founders to an acceptance of the logic of universal brotherhood.

There is nothing more threatening to the shadowy persona than universal brotherhood. As human beings walk away from the sun, the shadow lengthens. As they walk towards the sun, the shadow declines. It is significant, from the standpoint of karma, that the Founding Fathers identified the radiant eye over the pyramid as the eye of providence, and not the Eye of Wisdom. This confusion, though well-intentioned, degrades the divine Principle by making it the whimsical despot invoked as providence. If this suggests that Americans, like all peoples, have still much to learn, the Founding Fathers were ready to recognize this and were well aware that the republic they established would need a continuous process of ethical education aimed at a time centuries hence when men and women everywhere could grasp the true meaning of universal brotherhood and its ontological foundations.

Moral learning and the recovery of metaphysical insight are not the result of formal education or the exclusive privilege of any social class. In fact, many ordinary people of the world, unburdened by the dichotomies of modern thought, the tedium of high school and the conformist sophistry of college, are more likely to appreciate the real nature of learning. Travelling many paths and byways to and from their daily labours, they often enjoy the privilege of looking at the stars. Though they may not comprehend the configurations of the planets or the constellations of the zodiac, at least they are humbly aware that there is a vast sky above their heads. They may be unfamiliar with arcane knowledge about the hierarchies of Dhyanis, Rishis and *devas* associated with the heavenly hosts, but as they journey into the dawn, gazing upward and greeting the stars, they travel a sure, if slow and painful, path to self-enlightenment. None but the wise can surmise what thoughts men and women hold in their minds at death. Even in life neither parents nor children, neither relatives nor friends, really know anything about the deepest thoughts and feelings that move other human beings as they travel up and down the roads of the ancient lands of the earth.

There are many mysteries surrounding human beings, above all the mystery of the Ego, and the more deeply this is felt, the more silent one is about them. Amongst those who most keenly sense the mystery of the soul, one will not find facile references to the Third Eye. Such persons will not be tempted to speak out of turn about sacred matters because they will be too busy learning the proper use of their two eyes, and gaining self-respect through the cultivation of skill in action. Every traveller knows that it is necessary to keep both eyes on the road and to remain flexible. One must learn to discern when it is appropriate to go faster and when it is apposite to go slower. There is an essential discipline in coordinating the right and left eyes which must be mastered at some preliminary level before one can travel safely upon the roads of life. If watchful and vigilant travellers should grow weary along the way and pause to rest for a few moments under the empyrean — where there are no boundaries — they can collect themselves and draw within, experiencing an exhilarating sense of release from the clamour and cacophony of the age. When they are withdrawn from the noises of the world and repose in inward silence, they may experience moments of serene self-forgetfulness and even communion with the *daimon*. Through the immense strength of vision of the immortal soul, every human being receives some benediction during deep, dreamless sleep, what Shakespeare called "the balm of hurt minds."

If this is the common source of impersonal inspiration in every human being, one might ask why it seemingly avails so many so little. If all share in a universal opportunity for self-education and spiritual growth, yet societies and nations find themselves mired in self-perpetuating ignorance and delusion, one could ask what went wrong with the human species in general. If men and women of the earliest civilizations of the earth enjoyed the illumination of the inner eye in waking life, one must seek for the causes of the loss of vision in actions carried out despite its guidance. As H.P. Blavatsky explains:

> The 'eye of Siva' did not become entirely atrophied before the close of the Fourth Race. When spirituality and all the divine powers and attributes of the deva-man of the Third had been made the hand-maidens of the newly-awakened physiological and psychic passions of the physical man, instead of the reverse, the eye lost its powers. . . . The sin was not in using those newly-developed powers, but in *misusing* them; in making of the tabernacle, designed to contain a god, the fane of every *spiritual* iniquity. And if we say 'sin' it is merely that everyone should understand our meaning; as the term *Karma* would be the right one to use in this case; while the reader who would feel perplexed at the use of the term 'spiritual' instead of 'physical' iniquity, is reminded of the fact that there can be no physical iniquity. The body is simply the irresponsible organ, the tool of the *psychic*, if not of the 'Spiritual man.'
>
> *The Secret Doctrine*, ii 302

The duration and extent of this appalling abuse and tragic inversion of the gift of self-consciousness were neither brief nor trivial, but rather involved vast numbers of human beings over millions of years. Whilst the last remnants of the Atlantean continent subsided some twelve thousand years ago, and the Fifth Root Race began a million years before that, one must take into account the preceding four million years of the Fourth Root Race to understand the scale of the period of decline. One must also take into account the millions of years between the emergence of the godlike beings of the Third Race, over eighteen million years ago, and the commencement of the Atlantean Fourth Race about five million years ago. It should be evident that the magnitude and sway of the karmic forces set in motion by the earlier races of humanity are too enormous to be encompassed within the stunted theories of modern social scientists. Indeed, virtually all the presuppositions and working assumptions of modern writers are the pathetic consequences of that ancient blindness. As such, they can scarcely offer contemporary humanity a reasonable explanation or solution for its current predicament. If the narrow and reductionist theories of secular history are useless in this regard, the anthropomorphic religions of the past few millennia are even worse.

The fateful events depicted in the *Stanzas of Dzyan* are not to be understood as a mere chronology of past evolution. These far-reaching events are sadly re-enacted in the life of every human being, as may be seen by considering what happens to a newborn child. Until approximately the age of three, every infant possesses an active spiritual awareness, but then, unfortunately, it is given a shadowy sense of 'I' bound up with wants and deficiencies. Too many foolish mothers are continually asking "Does Baby want this? Does Baby want that?" whereas, of course, the baby wants nothing. Although its physical organism may be either too warm or too cold, too dry or too wet, or may need feeding or washing, as a conscious being it is complete and lacks nothing. Yet, through misplaced solicitude the infant is psychically crippled, giving it a shadowy and deprivatory sense of self. Thus, the child grows up with a strong sense of self-deficiency. But this is at least partly corrected at around the age of seven under the compassion of the cosmic Law, when there is a descent of the ray of higher *Manas*.

There is no human being who is without help because, on the average, there is always present some sense of being a thinking individual, capable of choice and self-determination. Whatever one's fate or future, and whatever one's range of alternatives, it is always possible to become more responsible, having lit up the spark of innate responsibility after the age of seven. If this is securely done before the age of fourteen, then a child is fortunate because he or she is able to pass through the tumultuous, stormy and exaggerated time of puberty with a sense of proportion and balance. If there is proper preparation by those whom the child trusts, there is a distinct beauty to that period because the creative imagination is ready for great mythic inspiration. If a child is given myths, images, pictures, stories and symbols of all that is noble and elevating, then these become living presences to the child, who is thus able to emancipate the psyche from the clutches of adolescence. Whilst performing its duties at school, learning myriad lessons, respecting its diverse teachers and keeping aloof from delinquent children who are either misled or perversely ignorant, the sensible child can enjoy a healthy growth in the freely chosen company of those who do the difficult things in life, like doing physical exercise, venturing to play a musical instrument, mastering arithmetic and learning to read and write with enjoyment. By befriending those who enjoy learning, it is feasible to fuse work and play. Then, at the stage where a child naturally looks for ideals and longs to see them mirrored in others, it is possible to develop true respect and affection, and indeed there could be a burgeoning of immortal longings behind the mortal masquerade of emotions.

Whilst the period of maturation can be beautiful if it is well handled, typically and unfortunately, owing to the collective karma of society and of ancestors, instead of being helped, the child is overwhelmed by the newly awakened physiological powers and psychic passions. If, as Plato hinted, the Third Eye may ideally begin to function around the age of thirty-five, this cannot happen unless the process was initiated at the age of seven. If, under Karma, this was not possible, then one should at least begin around the age of twenty-one or even twenty-eight. Yet, if none of these things can be done, then one may still hope that after thirty-five one will be able to recapitulate some of the lost opportunities of the first thirty-five years by truly loving and admiring children, and being on the side of other people who are younger than oneself. Though this may be against the grain of a parasitic culture, which seeks to devour each succeeding generation through the delusions of its predecessor, it is nonetheless an essential requirement of the 1975 Cycle.

It is possible to find joy in the growth of other people, and those who truly have their minds open to the future will be on the side of children and their grandchildren, the unknown and unborn generations that will come after. In order to be on the side of people who are not before one's eyes, one must actively exercise one's imagination, not fabricating any false roles for oneself, nor assuming false burdens. The children of future generations cannot be saved by indoctrination. They do not need to be saved, because they are immortal souls. They need no vicarious atonement, but they may be aided under Karma. One can prevent them from being self-destroyed, but that can only be done by the magic of eloquent example. If, despite mistakes, one could show that it is possible to breathe benevolence and incarnate the spirit of universal brotherhood, then children, who are observant by nature, will quietly notice the effortless example set by elders. Children are quick to discern one's willingness to learn from them and from others, and through this they will also recognize that despite the hollow pretensions of contemporary culture, true learning is an integral part of the constitutional birthright of Americans and of every contributor to the City of Man.

Through an enlarged conception of the spiritual birthright of reincarnating egos, it can be shown that the plentiful exercise of the sovereign powers of thought, learning and meditation are secured for every human being by the moral order of the cosmos. Whilst they may be ignorantly denied or discouraged in corrupt societies, they are fully encouraged and actively fostered by the Brotherhood of Bodhisattvas. There is nothing in the constitution of human nature to prevent a person from meditating at any time, nor need one travel to or live in any cloistered shelter to exercise freely these prerogatives. Whether one's journey through life carries one over crowded city streets or quiet forest paths, there is no external circumstance of life which negates the possibility of meditation. Neither does the mere passage of years set aside or subvert one's capacity and need to think and learn. There are many old people who, despite advanced age and the force of habit, set an example to the young by calmly demonstrating that they are still willing to learn and still willing to look to the promise of the future. If courageous individuals are willing to learn at the age of seventy, then why cannot younger people learn at the age of forty or thirty or twenty? If old people can begin to learn what it means to get their mental luggage ready for the next incarnation, then it is certainly possible for others to do so at the age of forty. At a time when social pioneers and spiritual pathfinders show a spontaneous readiness to greet each other as citizens of the world, beholden to no party or partial electorate but rather to the whole of humanity, can any individual consider himself or herself as anything less than a denizen of the cosmopolis, the City of Man?

In the infancy of humanity, when all alike were secure in their joyous awareness of immortality, birth and death were viewed as no more strange than the putting on or taking off of a garment. In general, the human race has passed on from childlike wonder to adolescent bewilderment and into the self-questioning of youth amidst a burgeoning of the fires of creativity around the time of its puberty. Now, despite half-hidden and half-denied memories of old errors, it is possible for humanity to get ready for the next stage, which is the maturation of adulthood. Humanity is coming of age, becoming adult. More precisely, in terms of the total scheme of human evolution and the complex cosmogonic tables of Gupta Vidya, humanity is somewhere around the age of thirty-five, even a bit past it. Humanity is at that critical point when it must experience a radical metamorphosis. A significant and pioneering portion of humanity is ready to graduate to full maturity. They have used their two eyes carefully and learnt something about spiritual responsibility, meditating upon collective Karma and the vital connections between moral causes and social consequences. They have become more mindful and therefore more patient, more deliberate and therefore more discriminating. Through detachment from personal existence they have gained greater continuity of consciousness and a more profound compassion for their fellow beings. Other human beings, however, who are as yet unable to do this will have to try harder. They will have to exert themselves more intensively so that they can atone for lost time and make amends for past misdeeds.

It is for this reason that H.P. Blavatsky took such pains to explain the distinction between the natural psycho-physical changes affecting the relationship of the early races to the Third Eye and the unnatural degradation of the spiritual principles in man in the later portions of the Fourth Race. The former is a natural and inevitable part of the process of evolution, but the latter was not. Not every human being has committed every spiritual iniquity, of course. Most human beings are extremely weak-willed, and it is highly unlikely that they actively launched on a career represented by Sodom and Gomorrah. It is much more likely that their selfishness was nothing more than banal. Abnormal selfishness involves bringing a high degree of concentration to one's selfishness, such as is required to become a ruthless captain of industry or a crafty manipulator of the media. Most human beings do not have sufficiently intense experience in grey or black magic to achieve such ends. To understand the heavy Karma of the latter portion of the Fourth Root Race, one must set aside the spell of fascination with the venal forms of iniquity and seek a philosophic understanding of the sprouting of spiritual evil. Suppose that one has received potent spiritual Teachings, and that one uses them to show off to one's neighbour. This is a dangerous step even if it seems innocuous; it can rapidly lead to using the Teachings on behalf of one's separative self, when in fact one received the teachings only for the sake of service to others.

Although one may not self-consciously intend to show off to others, nevertheless, in a society pervaded by bottomless insecurity and lack of spiritual decorum, it is quite plausible that many will turn to the Teachings chiefly in order to gain personal confidence. This, however, is a serious error and will inevitably result, at the moment of death, in all one's intellectual learning being stripped away. In order to avoid this pathos at death, one should long before that time master the personality, which is merely a tool or instrument and in itself of no consequence other than as a transient vesture of the Immortal Soul. Once the root idea of the Immortal Soul as the Being-in-charge pervades one's consciousness, *kama manas* must wholly relinquish its false posture of dominance. The Immortal Soul cannot take possession of its temple until the ratiocinative mind has abdicated from its ascendancy and the heart has been cleansed. The spiritual path leading to the awakening of the Third Eye begins with an assured recognition of the Divine Light within, and is consummated in the fullness and purity of that Light. Hence it is said that the path begins and ends outside the lower self.

Since the true danger is that the Spiritual Light will be deflected and dragged down into the realm of the psychic and the personal the practical issue is how the lunar mind can be pacified during the period of its attenuation. Whether it be through music, gardening, swimming or walking, there is a wide variety of ways in which one can pacify and silence the lunar mind, stilling its thoughts and preventing them from polluting one's intuitions. In doing this, it is foolish and even absurd to declaim against the body, the irresponsible organ and tool of the psychic nature, called "brother ass" by Francis of Assisi. If the body is restless, this puts a strain upon the astral because it is engaged in involuntary movement. Therefore, one needs to replace involuntary movements by deliberate movements without becoming inflexible. This points to the art of deep relaxation, the *yoga* of mental resilience.

It is possible to learn to move at will the different limbs of the body while at the same time not being rigid, remaining calm, natural and relaxed. Physically, this will relieve heat and pressure in the blood, and give a cool rhythm to the rate and beat of the heart. Psychologically, one can learn to let go in the mind the false burdens and images, which only serve to obscure the path of duty through a delusive sense of personal melodrama. It is much easier to let go when one has given up the intoxicating notion of personal progress and its attendant fantasies about the paramount priority of one's own odyssey. The world depends upon the entirety of humanity, and as one of billions of Monads engaged in spiritual evolution on this globe, one can make a modest yet effective contribution to the future of humanity. The critical question is whether one is making any contribution at all or going in the opposite direction — behaving irresponsibly as if one had more real knowledge than one does.

The fundamental problem with the Atlanteans was that they pretended to know when they did not. They mistook the nascent vision within themselves for the fullness of enlightenment, and disowning with base ingratitude their spiritual benefactors, they employed their powers for self-aggrandizement and self-righteously rationalized the consequences. When under Karma their presumption failed, they lapsed into the impotence and blindness brought upon themselves by their own misuse of opportunities. The karma of this misuse takes the form of a serious damage to the astral spine and to the flow of the magical elixir from the top of the head down to what is below the solar plexus. This organic and astral damage cannot be blamed upon parents, grandparents or ancestors, who were merely the karmic instruments for bringing into the present that which each human soul has earned for itself in another life. This can be tested by examining one's own motivation and conduct over the past seven, fourteen or twenty-one years, and discerning therein the seeds of ingratitude, selfishness, pride, presumption, misuse and abuse of opportunities. Yet, lest one become caught in self-pity, one must not be afraid to look at oneself both as a baby and as an aged person approaching the moment of death. One should break down the identification with the body-image and see oneself in relation to many and diverse human beings. Whenever one encounters another, one should think "There I am," without enhancing the sense of 'I'. By strengthening empathy for others, one will find that the sense of self is attenuated until it becomes a potent instrument for the purpose of using effectively the Teaching, a cipher in myriad cosmogonic equations.

What looks impossibly difficult is actually not so arduous if one begins correctly with a few small and simple examples. Many people have lost opportunities because of pseudo-dramatics which never helped anyone. Growing up means doing that which would help others. It is like trying to fix an old toy for the sake of a child. To do this, one must improvise and be constructive. No one would think very much of an appliance repairman who came and spent a week at their expense mourning the fact that the machine had broken down. Rather, one is grateful to the repairman who fixes it and moves on. This means not that one should be functional and utilitarian, but rather that one must seek to be constructive in facing difficulties. The point has now been reached when humanity is sufficiently grown-up not to be impressed by Atlantean gestures and well-worn excuses. A vanguard of human beings is fast emerging who are able to shoulder responsibility naturally and with ease. They find self-forgetfulness enjoyable and self-actualization as natural as breathing. At such a time, a great deal that is tortuous and redundant begins to fade away. Meanwhile, however, everything pathological concentrates in all the life-atoms that have been tortured by what is unnatural and ravenously seize the opportunity to manifest wherever possible. Those who are passive and irresponsible day-dreamers tend to become saturated with such lunar life-atoms, and as they walk in and out of the corridors of this world, they falter and fall prey to dark moods and despair.

The present time of metamorphosis offers a propitious opportunity for deep meditation upon the boundless ocean of space and upon Karma as a compassionate law that applies to all of Nature and humanity. When one has truly begun to gain an inkling of the law of Karma as the law of one's own being, inseparably binding each to all for the sake of the common good, then one can begin to meditate upon the Third Eye of the highest beings and see the Eye of Shiva over the Pyramid of Initiation which protects the whole of humanity. Feeling a thrill even to be a part of the human race under that omnipotent protection, one will renounce all personal fantasies regarding the Third Eye and begin to invoke its beneficence for all souls. The right use of the two eyes is the vital starting-point upon the path which leads through meditation and withdrawal from the sense organs to the point between the eyes, of which Krishna speaks. It is easier now to comprehend the compassion of the strong, the wisdom of stillness and the effortless celibacy of the twice-born.

One could say that the entire Teaching of Gupta Vidya is a metaphysical prelude to profound meditation, but this is to say a great deal. *Sanatana Dharma* provides conceptual maps and gives a firm basis for the cleansing and purifying of the emotional nature and the lunar mind. It aids human beings in disabusing themselves of the false burdens and feeble memories of the lunar form. It prepares individuals to enter the sacred orbit of the Mahatmas and thereby, especially in a strong cycle, into the aura of the Avatar. It is possible to do much in a short time if one can stay simple and honest, be regular and not neglect the small things of life, the daily obligations of pilgrim-souls. One must honour the small and renounce grandiose ideas about oneself. When one does this cheerfully, there will be a legitimate soul-satisfaction that one can carry a sublime thought through the day, into sleep, and further into the next day, with a singleness of purpose, of heart, mind and will.

Through continuity of consciousness there is a radical healing that takes place within one's whole nature, and an authentic gain in self-respect. Like a person who late in life learns a new language and is thrilled that he can learn the alphabet and write his first sentence, so too any human being at any age can so strengthen the antaskaranic connection with the Higher Self that life takes on a new depth of meaning and expression. It is a difficult discipline initially, but if one faithfully keeps at it in a non-strenuous way, doing it only out of love for one's fellow men and out of gratitude to one's Teachers, there will be infallible help from the Eye of Shiva and the Flute of Krishna. If the motive is to make a potent contribution to the grandchildren of one's grandchildren, and if one lets go of the mayavic tension of the personal self, then the sense of the sacred deepens until one is able to make holy resolves and charge them with a silent power for good. That power is the light in the Divine Eye of the Logos in the Cosmos and the god in man, and it is eternally available to every humble but mature pilgrim-soul seeking the privilege of entry into the emerging family of mankind.

Rudra Siva, the great *Yogi*, the forefather of all the Adepts — in Esotericism one of the greatest Kings of the Divine Dynasties. Called 'the Earliest' and the 'Last', he is the patron of the Third, Fourth, and the Fifth Root-Races. For, in his earliest character, he is the ascetic *Dig-ambara*, 'clothed with the Elements', *Trilochana*, 'the *three*-eyed'; *Pancha-anana*, 'the five-faced', an allusion to the past four and the present fifth race. . . . He is the 'God of Time', Saturn-Kronos, as his *damaru* (drum), in the shape of an hour-glass, shows.

The Secret Doctrine, ii 502

SPIRITUAL WAKEFULNESS

Paranishpanna, remember, is the summum bonum, *the Absolute, hence the same as Paranirvana. Besides being the final state it is that condition of subjectivity which has no relation to anything but the one absolute truth (Para-marthasatya) on its plane. It is that state which leads one to appreciate correctly the full meaning of Non-Being, which, as explained, is absolute Being. Sooner or later, all that now seemingly* exists, will be in reality and actually *in the state of Paranishpanna. But there is a great difference between* conscious *and* unconscious *'being.' The condition of Paranishpanna, without Paramartha, the Self-analysing consciousness (Svasamvedana), is no bliss, but simply extinction (for Seven Eternities).*

The Secret Doctrine, i 53-54

Wakeful consciousness, *Turiya*, in eternal duration is the vital core of authentic participation in *Brahma Vach*. The practical embodiment of potent ideals depends upon the fusion of individual consciousness with boundless duration. The alchemical transformation of life into eternal Life is equivalent to the mystical passage from death to immortality. All self-conscious spiritual growth is a function of continuity and discontinuity of consciousness, associated with the phenomena of birth, death and rebirth. The more sedulously individuals sift through the world's particulars, the more meaningful and enduring are their perceptions, the keener are their differentiations between various levels of reality. Thus, they can also recognize the relative unreality of all things. The capacity to affirm and negate at the same time rests upon the rootedness of souls in a timeless realm of reality above the phenomenal processes of change, above the shifting dichotomies of subject and object or past and future. With abstracted attention and attained alertness, they may consider life in terms of one great forward push at the cosmic and at the human level. This evolutionary thrust is progressing neither chaotically nor arbitrarily but under the laws of cause, effect and further cause.

Life may be viewed as an arrow, directed from the past to the future. It may also be seen from the standpoint of Deity, a circle with its centre everywhere and its circumference nowhere. To combine both perspectives is the prerogative of man, who can both expand and contract, diffuse and deepen the range and reach of self-consciousness. Paradoxically, the more one's consciousness is located beyond the particulars of time, the more attentive one may be to them. Timelessness is neither inertia nor indifference. It is not a blurring of impressions of mortality, but an intense sharpening and heightening of perceptions relevant to learning and living and delivering one's dharma. All elemental lives, moving in and through myriad shifting shadowy forms, participate at some level in incipient or higher degrees of abstract subjectivity, the basis for the distinction between the different kingdoms. Each represents the different degrees of power of the matter-moving *Nous*, the animating soul of the universe immanent in every atom, manifested in man, and inseparable from the ONE LIFE, or *Jivatma*, the transcendental and wholly immaterial ground of all design in living nature. This soul of the world, or *Alaya*, has a dual aspect correlative with the alternations of *Maha-Manvantara* and *Maha-Pralaya*.

> Alaya, though eternal and changeless in its inner essence on the planes which are unreachable by either men or Cosmic Gods (Dhyani Buddhas), alters during the active life-period with respect to the lower planes, ours included. During that time not only the Dhyani-Buddhas are one with Alaya in Soul and Essence, but even the man strong in the Yoga (mystic meditation) 'is able to merge his soul with it.'
>
> *Ibid.*, 48

Furthermore:

> In the Yogacharya system of the contemplative Mahayana school, Alaya is both the Universal Soul

(Anima Mundi) and the Self of a progressed adept.
'He who is strong in the Yoga can introduce at will his
Alaya by means of meditation into the true Nature of
Existence.'

Ibid., 49

In its absolute and eternal aspect, *Alaya* precedes the
sevenfold differentiation of *Prakriti*, is the unevolved cause of
comprehension of all the diverse manifestations of life in the seven
kingdoms. During the period of manifestation it is the vital basis
of intelligence distributed by degrees throughout the kingdoms
of evolved life. The human capacity to merge through meditation
the self-conscious soul — *Alaya* in one aspect — with *Alaya* in its
eternal aspect is the basis of conscious immortality and boundless
compassion. The more deeply and irreversibly one can do this,
the more one can retain wakefulness outside the realm of temporal
change and remain consciously rooted in what is called pure
Being, which is also pure Non-Being. This ultimate spiritual
wakefulness can only be attained by abstraction, by blanking out
all impressions and by meditating upon both the ceaseless and
cyclical disintegration of worlds. In *Maha-Pralaya* all possible
concepts and worlds are reabsorbed into the one primordial
material substratum, which, having reabsorbed into itself all the
elements, falls into a state of total latency wherein ideation is
potentially present but without any urge to manifest. It is then
that the *Alaya* of the universe is in *Paramartha*, entirely
transcendent comprehension and absolute true Being.

The capacity to void the mind through meditation and to
become aware of what seems like non-being whilst one's body is
asleep is essential to the realization of true Being and presupposes
a fundamental alteration of one's conceptions of life and vitality.
To a great extent, mechanistic views of life arise because of a
narrowness of perception, together with an action-centered view
of vitality. A healthy antidote to societies caught up in the frenetic
rush of consumption is to spend leisure time by the ocean
listening to its ancient rhythms, or in the mountains silently

attentive to nature's sounds. In these ways one can approach a deeper and more undifferentiated field of consciousness that is motion at a subtle level of vibration. To do this self-consciously, to establish within oneself a permanent core of silence, is the task of meditation.

Initially, one must set aside some time daily and blank out everything: one's total sense of identity, one's memories and expectations, all images and all impressions. Doing so, one gradually enters with adoration into the most abstract homogeneous realm accessible. As one gains a progressive kinship with the realm of Divine Darkness, free of the interplay of light and shadow that characterizes the world of relativities, one begins to sense within oneself living depths upon depths in consciousness. Philosophically, this negation of all limited states of consciousness, of all illusory distinctions between spirit, soul and matter, is equivalent to the affirmation of universal life and absolute freedom. Real vitality has its basis in the realm of non-being that is beyond the calculus of sequential causation.

As the Upanishads teach, the spiritual path is like the razor's edge. The effort to realize true immortal life in non-being requires the utmost discrimination with regard to motive. At every point, one must keep in mind the archetypal distinction between liberation and renunciation. Everything in the Teachings of Gupta Vidya may be viewed in the context of a search for heightened awareness, or merely as a quest for escape. The desire for extinction is extremely strong throughout nature, whether conceived in terms of *Maha-Pralaya* at the end of an age of Brahmā, or in terms of *Nitya Pralaya*, ceaseless dissolution. Everything in manifest Nature is reabsorbed into the whole. In human beings this force of dissolution may be converted into a desire for extinction because many do not wish to engage spiritually in a world pervaded by shallow values, frozen expressions and limited conceptions. Through the principle of negation, Nature balances the over-assertion of the manifested ray with disengagement in sleep or in death. Whilst the human desire for extinction can reflect the final reabsorption of everything into the whole, this desire itself reflects attachment to manifested existence. It betrays a wish for escape, an irresponsible quest for liberation. This is entirely different from the search for self-conscious attunement to universal self-consciousness, the state of those who are awake during the Night of non-manifestation.

Without the self-conscious realization of *Alaya*, without *Paramartha*, the *Paranirvana* of the universe is mere extinction. Unless and until the divine essence in oneself, which is one with the essence in the heart of every atom, is made the self-conscious basis of boundless compassion towards all beings, the soul cannot realize the permanent potential of universal and eternal life.

> Thus, an iron ball placed under the scorching rays of the sun will get heated through, but will not feel or appreciate the warmth, while a man will. It is only 'with a mind clear and undarkened by personality, and an assimilation of the merit of manifold existences devoted to being in its collectivity (the whole living and sentient Universe)', that one gets rid of personal existence, merging into, becoming one with, the Absolute, and continuing in full possession of Paramartha.
>
> *Ibid.*, 54

The fundamental distinction between liberation and renunciation implies that true love is proportional to spiritual wakefulness. The capacity to love all life-atoms depends upon one's understanding of their various orders and functions within the World Soul. Through appropriate arrangement and discipline, they must be given a chance to become apprenticed in discipleship, even at the level of unself-consciousness and incipient consciousness. No mere facility with intellectual constructions or recourse to ritual techniques is going to sustain the tremendous power of attention needed for this learning. This capacity of the soul for wakefulness is dependent upon previous lives of meditation, renunciation and service. Thus, in the meta-psychological perspective of Gupta Vidya, there is no basis for understanding soul powers and the development of magical possibilities, whether in their beneficent or maleficent uses, apart from an understanding of karma and reincarnation.

Every human being has brought into the world some distinctive experience of the immortal soul and its theurgic powers, some indelible marks of past proficiency and past deficiency. Spiritual growth cannot, therefore, be explained by the principle of desire operating in the present. Filtered through the distorting prism of *kama manas,* the ideal principle of aspiration becomes a concretized impression of temporal and temporary desires. Such illusory impressions are merely projections out of *tanha,* the root desire to exist and subsist in a form or body in a world that is limited in space and time. There can be no true wakefulness, no release of the spiritual will, and no moral and mental growth based upon such an obscured and distorted sense of self-existence.

> The real person or thing does not consist solely of what is seen at any particular moment, but is composed of the sum of all its various and changing conditions from its appearance in the material form to its disappearance from the earth. It is these 'sum-totals' that exist from eternity in the 'future', and pass by degrees through matter, to exist for eternity in the 'past'.
>
> *Ibid.,* 37

The deeper conception of time which is needed to understand these karmic sum-totals can only arise from an extraordinary detachment. Burdened by individual and collective karma on the one hand, confronted by the necessity of supreme detachment on the other, many find it difficult to retain a vital enthusiasm for the world. They must realize that even the most magnanimous souls cannot give themselves fully to every living being without voiding every element of meretricious attraction to the shadowy self. Detachment from the personal self is necessary for those who wish to view the world without bondage to attachments and illusions. The inner ray of *Alaya* cannot be freed for the exhilaration of universal compassion until it is disengaged in consciousness from its own reflection localized in time and space upon the waves of differentiated matter. This disengagement, equivalent to awakening true continuity of consciousness, proceeds through an undivided process of unfoldment that may be represented by an orderly series of law-governed phases. If these stages are not clearly understood, the nature of detachment may be distorted and its motives debased. Each stage accompanies a growing transcendence of the illusion of time and comprehension of Karma. At the same time, each stage represents a growing awakening to essential degrees of *Alaya* or noetic intelligence. Souls progress from the restraint of the lower self or personality by the divine Self or individuality to the restraint of the Self divine by the Eternal, in which even the latent consciousness of desire and *tanha* is torn out. Thus the soul is merged in self-consciousness with the eternal essence of *Alaya*.

The first problem of withdrawal of consciousness from form may be understood best through the relationship between karmic attachment and memory. So long as karmic attachment operates through personal memories, individuals will experience pleasant and unpleasant reactions. As Shri Shankaracharya taught, "So long as we experience pleasure and pain, karma is still working through us." The more violent these emotional reactions, the stronger is the dead weight of karma. In extreme cases, a terrible and intensely traumatic experience in previous lives, coupled perhaps with a short or non-existent *devachan*, may bring about a tremendous burden on consciousness in the present incarnation. Attracted, under karma, to parents and companions bound by likes and dislikes, one may likewise experience emotional extremism. But, whatever its cause, volatility is invariably symptomatic of a high degree of karmic bondage. Its victims must learn painfully over a lifetime to void a false sense of reality or romance, of security or expectation. The seeming burdens of karma are in direct proportion to the delusions that must be voided.

An Initiate, seeing the aura of a human being mired in

delusion, knows that at the moment of that being's death one question remains: Has his understanding of the *ABCs* of life improved since his birth? If so, the individual can begin to discharge the debt of karma. Thus, if he is fortunate, the individual will gravitate to environments where there is little attention to likes and dislikes and where the options for the personality are fewer. Through successive incarnations, Karma compassionately reduces opportunities for protracted delusion until the individual is compelled to learn essential lessons. In terms of the self-conscious pursuit of moral and metaphysical ideals, Karma operates with the same dispassion, progressively narrowing the margins for error. Individuals vary in their degrees of wakefulness in proportion to their kamic attachment. They burden consciousness with fragmented memories, which must be distinguished from soul reminiscence, a reflection of universal memory beyond parochial and ephemeral likes and dislikes. As an individual learns to overcome the blurring of attention induced by personal memory, he will receive greater aid through moral allegiance to chosen ideals. Plato and Gandhi wisely recognized that most people in the Age of Zeus, Kali Yuga, are burdened by hostile memories and desperately in need of hospitable ideals.

Transmitting ideals to children and pupils through example and through precept is both beneficent and constructive. Their capacity for credible ideals increases with practice, and, as attention is focussed upon the possibilities of the future, it continues to develop. Naturally, ideals recede as they are approached, but they are nonetheless essential; they provide directions, if not destinations, and propel the individual ever forwards. As long as there are ideals, pointing to the imaginative possibilities of the foreseeable future, one can appreciate the salutary lessons of karma without becoming overburdened by collective memories of failure. Ultimately, all potent and transcendental ideals have their origins in Divine Thought, and their realization cannot be restricted to the solitary pilgrimage of any individual soul. As presented in the portraits of perfect enlightenment in various scriptures, they represent the source and apex of universal spiritual unfoldment. The true mystery of ideals is bound up with that of Avatars and Manus, the exalted incarnations and prototypes guiding and overbrooding manifestation, but rooted in the unmanifest Divine Thought and the Host of Anupadaka.

At the simplest level, the development of a mature consciousness of magnanimous ideals is central to the ethical growth of human beings, individually and collectively. The more potent ideals any living culture can express, the greater the hope it preserves. As a society grows weary, its scintillating ideals evaporate. From the era of Arthurian legends to Victorian dreams, England was characterized by its rich, understated yet resonant ideals. Now, all those souls engaged in this exuberant period of flowering have vanished or incarnated in Africa, Asia and elsewhere. Contemporary Englishmen and women find themselves unable to vitalize the ideals they inherited and succumb to nostalgia. Likewise, the Scandinavians passed through this transformation of ideals into memories long ago and then purged themselves of the corrosive tendency of self-flattery. Such purgation is particularly difficult in America, because to this day, America is the dumping ground of the world's malcontents. Whenever America begins to grow up, it receives a burden of memories dumped by new immigrants from declining or dissipated cultures. Thus, through kamic attachment or karmic precipitation, societies become weighted down by memories, and soon they find themselves caught in a downward cycle. Yet, if an individual or a society can become electrically charged by ethical ideals, can rekindle a sense of wonder towards creative possibilities, can look to the future with cool confidence, a life-giving and forward-looking current is released.

The capacity for intense involvement with the beauty of ideals is central to the problems of pessimism and optimism, apathy and initiative, for individuals as for societies. Viewed more metaphysically, the problem of attachment and memory is founded in the illusion of time itself. If one understands the present moment as merely a mathematical line separating those logical constructs called the past and the future, the present amounts to a virtually invisible and illusory division constantly in movement. Thus, everything is constantly absorbed from the past into the future. According to Buddhist metaphysics, however, "The Past time is the Present time, as also the Future, which, though it has not come into existence, still is." From this perspective, both the future and the past exist even now, because everything that has happened to humanity over eighteen million years is summed up here and now within the subtle vestures, whilst everything that will happen in myriad lifetimes to come is already implicit in the programming of our invisible vestures. Coping with this in a meaningful philosophical way, and without costly escapism, requires a meticulous attention to timing.

One must gain sufficient detachment from the past, the present and the future in the ordinary sense, from memories and ideals, to be able to see the abstract open texture of universal possibilities that the present, that imperceptible mathematical line, represents. Albertus Magnus is said to have made a homunculus, which could only come alive if the correct operation were performed at a certain moment. As that moment approached, the homunculus said, "Time will be, Time is, Time was." Because the key was not promptly applied as it said "Time is," it rapidly went on to "Time was." Such is the condition of human beings caught up in the past and the future, oblivious to what is pregnant in the present moment. Here one encounters the paradox of time and wakefulness. The more timeless one's consciousness in the true philosophical sense of expanding self-consciousness, the better one can appreciate the present moment and the sharper one's sense of timing.

The so-called realists, constantly marshalling convenient or frightening facts from the past, are only compensating for their lack of lively awareness in the enigmatic present. Whilst prating of proven realism, they entirely miss the present moment. Through the karmic process of acceleration of contagious delusion, operating on the social plane, those individuals with the most constrained sense of duration and most misplaced sense of realism tend to become the strident spokesmen of declining cultures in a dark age. Under the guise of accredited authority, misusing the channels of the media, they feverishly seek to impress their own confined consciousness upon others, parading the language of fear, pragmatism and survival. As, alas, many souls are susceptible to the pulls of pleasure and pain, this pseudo-realism becomes a dominant thought-form for a generation, and is passed on from parents to children as an insidious cowardice concerning the future. True realists, however, are those who are imaginatively practical with regard to ideals. They evidence no such impotence. Knowing that the negation of form is essential to the realization of ideals, they see the present moment rather as the wise view the moment of death, the great destroyer of illusions. Only when one releases the fragments can one see the picture as a whole, distil the quintessential from every experience, and free oneself from obscuring projections and distortions.

All negations of false continuity of consciousness are vital opportunities to awaken to a deeper continuity in consciousness. It is in this light that one should view the immemorial teachings of Gupta Vidya: nothing on this earth has real duration, nothing remains for a moment without change. So too Krishna asserts in the *Bhagavad Gita* that he, as the manifested Logos, never remains for a moment inactive. The blurring sense of duration that accompanies sensory awareness, like the blurred impression on the retina caused by an electric spark, is due to identification with transitory form. It is impossible to gain a right perception of reality, of the relationship of the immortal soul to its evolving vestures, without withdrawing attention from such nebulous images of personal consciousness.

No one could say that a bar of metal dropped into the sea came into existence as it left the air, and ceased to exist as it entered the water, and that the bar itself consisted only of that cross-section thereof which at any given moment coincided with the mathematical plane that separates, and, at the same time, joins, the atmosphere and the ocean. Even so of persons and things, which, dropping out of the to-be into the has-been, out of the future into the past — present momentarily to our senses a cross-section, as it were, of their total selves, as they pass through time and space (as matter) on their way from one eternity to another: and these two constitute that 'duration' in which alone anything has true existence, were our senses but able to cognize it there.

Ibid., 37

Fundamentally, the illusion of time must be traced to the experience and expression of ideation through a limiting vesture. Mind, at every level of manifestation, is equivalent to a summation of states of consciousness grouped under thought, will and feeling. During manifestation these mutable aggregates are the basis of capricious memory; during non-manifestation they fall into complete abeyance. Thus, when divine thought or universal ideation is unmanifest, the mental basis of temporal existence has ceased to be.

A noumenon can become a phenomenon on any plane of existence only by manifesting on that plane through an appropriate basis or vehicle; and during the long night of rest called Pralaya, when all the existences are dissolved, the 'UNIVERSAL MIND' remains as a permanent possibility of mental action, or as that abstract absolute thought, of which mind is the concrete relative manifestation.

Ibid., 38

It is from within this plenum of divine thought, eternal duration and absolute harmony that the deathless Watchers in the Night maintain their calm and compassionate vigil over the entire spectrum of manifested life. Viewing *Mahat* and *Manas* from above below, they calculate the sum-totals of collective human karma and, through benevolent ideation, ameliorate the agonizing condition of trapped human souls. This is the predicament of the parrot mind, of the partisan heart, of the deluded soul enslaved by externals. The temporal confinement of the projected personal ray has obscured the Buddhi-Manasic Ego and impeded its active realization of its authentic inheritance as a ray of Universal Mind. It is essential to strengthen the self-redemptive conception of the *antaskarana* bridge between the immortal and the mortal egos. Through meditation upon the higher pole of egoity, it is possible to withdraw the mind from limitations. This is the basis of true self-abnegation, self-discipline and clear-sightedness.

As this clarity of vision matures into spiritual wakefulness, one can reverse the polarity of the different centres in the lunar vesture, thereby affecting the desire-nature, sensory states and the deepest feelings. So great is the potential of the pure crystalline ray of *Alaya* that even such a profound change can take place at any time. But the transformation must be thorough and fundamental, with no quarter given to mental laziness or moral cowardice. All dullness of attention is caused by a fear of non-being acting through *tanhaic* attachment to some limited view of life. Human beings are like shadowy creatures, clutching to the trappings of existence because they are terrified of real life, like mountaineers paralyzed by fear, grasping on to precipitous ledges. They must let go their frozen grip on the niches of illusory security, if they wish to regain the freedom to move and to aid each other. They must ever be willing to be thrown back totally upon themselves, relying upon no outward circumstances or props, but only upon invisible and unbreakable cords of compassion linking one with all. Thus, they may approach the *mysterium tremendum*, the noumenal realm of Non-Being, wherein true Being lies, in the bosom of the Eternally Self-Existent. By entering the *Nivritti Marga*, the path of inwardness, one may commence the mystic return to Maha-Shiva.

Thou hast to saturate thyself with pure Alaya, become as one with Nature's Soul-Thought. At one with it thou art invincible; in separation, thou becomest the playground of

Samvritti, origin of all the world's delusions.

All is impermanent in man except the pure bright essence of Alaya. Man is its crystal ray; a beam of light immaculate within, a form of clay material upon the lower surface. That beam is thy life-guide and thy true Self, the Watcher and the silent Thinker, the victim of thy lower Self.

The Voice of the Silence

THE MESSAGE OF BUDDHA

It is necessary to state the main message of Gautama Buddha in a manner which makes apparent the basis of its universal appeal. The teachings of Buddha can be studied under various heads. One can explore the foundations of Buddhist metaphysics, or interest oneself in the formulation and implications of Buddhist ethics. One may also enquire into the complex structure and contemporary relevance of Buddhist psychology, or concern oneself, as only a few have done, with deriving from the discourses of Buddha a complete, coherent social and political philosophy. All these form part of one central message, and have the compelling characteristic of an organic unity between the different aspects of Buddhist thought. In a sense, they are all derived from the various facets of a myriad-minded genius whose long life had remarkable phases in a single-hearted quest for the meaning of the spiritual pilgrimage of suffering humanity. He was an effortless master of many skills and diverse modes of teaching, a sage who denied that he was divinely chosen or uniquely endowed and simply claimed that, unlike most people, he was fully awake. He moved among the unlettered as well as the learned, among kings and scavengers, among the poor, the lowly and the wretched, attracting men and women of all ages and all trades, welcoming especially the most afflicted into the universal fellowship of the Sangha. If he struck the ordinary observer as markedly different from all others, he was consistent in stressing that human beings differ in degree, not in kind, though the gap between the enlightened and the unenlightened is always greater than all other comparisons and contrasts.

It is, therefore, essential to consider the vital elements in the message of Gautama Buddha in the light of certain universal keys that can be applied by all seekers of wisdom. It is easy but wrong to imagine that Buddha was a very special sort of spiritual teacher who came to provide a unique kind of moral message to humanity for a purpose different from that which was behind the efforts of spiritual teachers before and after him. This would only obscure his repeated reference to the noble lineage of Tathagatas — those who have tread and shown the path to enlightenment in ways that are now unknown and unrecorded. To see Buddha as he saw himself is to see him in the light of the universal pilgrimage and the latent wisdom of all humanity. It is in the light of the *Philosophia Perennis* or the *Sanatana Dharma*, itself only a mirroring of the innate wisdom of Amitabha, the one Divine Spirit or overbrooding Logos, that the message of Gautama Buddha can best be comprehended. Before we can properly receive this message, we must ask ourselves: What manner of man was Lord Buddha? From whom did he come, and for whom did he renounce his royal estate and transmit the results of his intense struggles? What was his chief aim and the deeper significance of his extraordinary impact upon so many who were estranged from traditional sources of solace?

Gautama Buddha was a master man and not a god, a sage who achieved self-mastery through arduous strivings, carried on through many lives on earth and brought to fruition in his last recorded life — the life we imperfectly know from several chronicles that have come down over two and half millenia. He attained to Bodhi Dharma, the supreme state of wisdom, because he fully developed in himself the faculty possessed by all of us, the noetic faculty of Buddhi. It was through the complete unfoldment of Buddhi — unerring intuitive insight, spiritual and moral discernment, universal and omnidirectional perception — that Buddha himself became possible, vindicating the promise and potential of enlightenment as a feasible goal for one and all who persist against all odds in the quest for universal meaning and enduring peace of mind. The self-chosen title of 'Buddha' assumed by the great-souled Gautama after his complete renunciation of earthly happiness and his eventual disavowal of prolonged austerities is validated only after the climactic vision that followed a tempestuous period of intrepid questioning and self-study. His profound enlightenment is inseparable from his persistent and probing inquiries and introversion, and his teaching stressed the integral connection between wisdom-compassion and the method of investigation as well as the testing of the insights and errors accruing from ascetic contemplation. If the Jataka tales and other chronicles make allusions to the previous incarnations of Gautama Buddha, it is also true that some Mahayana texts stress the importance of seeing his life as a conscious enactment of the universal quest of humanity rather than the terminus of a series of struggles over successive lives on earth.

Spiritual life, like all earthly endeavour, is a process of progressive repetition, sifting the golden grains of insight from the dross of compulsive experience. It takes the form of a steady spiral-like ascent, going round and round through similar phases, yet all the time going higher and deeper in one's awareness of quintessential truth and meaning. 'Great Sifter' is the name of the Heart Doctrine as well as of the cosmic wheel of karma and dharma. Lord Buddha, the Great Master, by his extraordinary and exemplary sacrifice on behalf of all who are afflicted, demonstrated to ordinary human beings the possibility of effective self-emancipation from the fetters of existence through the removal of inward hindrances to the release of salvific wisdom.

Whence did he come? Ultimately, from nowhere else than the same source from which all beings have come, the One Great Spirit from which, far back in the dawn of human self-consciousness, we all derived our noetic intelligence, and since when we have gone through various stages of embodiment in the vestures provided by elemental Nature, rendered appropriate by the inexorable law of ethical causation. In a deeper sense Gautama Buddha came from a spiritual lineage of little known sages and illuminated seers, who sensed early in life that he had already gained the gnosis of the initiated in his previous incarnations, but he needed to probe the subtle errors and specious rationalizations that hinder the release of innate wisdom among so many seekers and anchorites. If such wisdom is latent in all souls and can be spontaneously released at the moment of ripeness, determined by the karma of the age as well as of one's previous lives, it is imperative to contemplate the impersonal truth of universal suffering and universal self-redemption. The subtle balance between conscious striving and letting go of the very self that strives is beautifully and abundantly suggested in the *Gandavyuha Sutra* and cognate texts in the *Prajnaparamita* canon, as well as in the ancient *Puranas* of India and the parables of a host of later teachers, from China to Burma, who truly followed in the footsteps of Gautama Buddha and his *Buddhavachana*, the vast outpourings of his authentic teaching.

At the same time, it is important to notice that Buddha came immediately to the people of Northern India, Hindus of all castes, Jains, protagonists of antiquated schools of thought and attenuated techniques of yoga, polemicists and disillusioned ritualists, armchair monists and ardent dualists, atheists and agnostics, emaciated ascetics and fatalistic followers of outworn theistic formulas, confirmed cynics and bewildered nihilists, and many victims of decadent social structures. He was determined to destroy irrational idolatry and the exclusive patronage of oppressive priestcraft, and, above all, to counter all blind belief with the challenge of concrete instantiation. He knew from his own early experiences that the true spirit of ancient Hindu thought and practice had receded owing to the excessive importance given to the letter of canonical law and to mere mechanical ritual. Gautama Buddha was in every way a revolutionary thinker whose teaching was subversive to existing social practices that engendered what the *Bhagavad Gita* calls the false piety of bewildered souls. At the same time, he cannot be understood if he is confined to a particular historical context and to a distinctively religious mission.

His eye for essentials led him to seek for fundamental answers to fundamental questions that concern human beings in all possible social conditions. He came not only to confront and challenge the exclusivism of traditional elites, but also to teach those rare souls who were ready for that training in advanced meditation which he alone could give, and who were waiting on the threshold of final spiritual realization. Some of these remarkable disciples had been taught by him in previous lives and there was a flash of mutual recognition when they met him. While his advanced teaching took place in the middle phase of his post-enlightenment sojourns, his last phase was devoted to conveying the essential truths in a manner that met the needs of many lay disciples. Occasionally he encountered some kings and queens from neighbouring kingdoms, and thereby his plea for spiritual tolerance and non-violent resolution of conflicts laid the basis for fresh approaches to political and social ethics. This eventually culminated, in the reign of King Ashoka, in the emergence of a large-scale Buddhist social system.

Gautama Buddha's chief aim was to re-discover and re-state the timeless wisdom of the Tathagatas, the *Sanatana Dharma* or Eternal Religion, by showing the corruptions into which its latest forms in India had fallen. His extraordinary impact upon the India of his time and subsequently upon the entire Eastern world was based upon his remarkable life of renunciation, enlightenment, compassion and sacrifice. His teachings have come down in a large collection of texts embodying his numerous discourses in diverse contexts. These were faithfully rendered into several languages over centuries and carefully preserved in monasteries in India, Ladakh, Nepal, Sri Lanka, Tibet, Burma, Thailand, Cambodia, Korea, Japan, Mongolia, China and the U.S.S.R.

Lord Buddha urged his disciples to refrain from idle metaphysical disputation and vain speculation upon abstruse matters 'not tending to edification.' He taught not that there was nothing divine or deific in Nature and Humanity, but rather that there was no anthropomorphic creator upon whom the burden of human sins could be thrown, or to whose arbitrary act the creation of the cosmos could be ascribed. The whole universe is the manifold and variegated expression of a single, unitary Life Principle. This works through various ever-changing forms on different planes under an omnipresent Law of complex causation. Subjects and objects, acts and events, mental processes and physical phenomena, are related to each other in cause-effect-cause sequences, every effect carrying within itself the potency of further causation, just as it in itself is the product of prior causation.

Buddha not only proclaimed the existence of One Life Principle but also pointed to the interconnectedness of everything, the root causes of embodied existence, and the Chain of Dependent Origination. Any particular position or condition in space and time must be viewed as a part in relation to the whole, and not in terms of the illusory ego or the separative self. The latter is a projection in a particular situation, from which complete knowledge cannot be gained, and from which all such relative perceptions contain within themselves the elements of error and delusion, *samvritisatya*. Error and evil are inherently relative, removable only by attaining to the standpoint of universal consciousness, *paramarthasatya*. This can only be gained by going within oneself, cutting through the mental fetters of false egoity, and experiencing in the deeper voidness the unitary nature of all subjects and objects, all beings in their common, indivisible and essential nature.

The spiritual individuality of every person, though enduring and causally significant compared to the ephemeral epiphenomena of the present, is itself relative and illusory in comparison to the Universal Adibuddha. The Life Principle of the cosmos is not exhausted in any one set of embodiments, nor can it be described by any definition, for it is essentially attributeless. Therefore, whenever Buddha was asked about the Absolute, Deity, or the Supreme Self, his only answer was utter silence. His silence should not be taken for atheism, the denial of a divine Principle in Nature and Man; rather he intimated that the state or universal self-consciousness is itself the highest possible form of gnosis. In order to attain even a measure of spiritual wisdom, one must cast off the shackles of habitual identification with the individual self and its salvation, let alone the mutable and composite mask of the personality. Probing conceptual and linguistic analysis, such as in the *Milindapanha* and elsewhere, can show the systematically elusive nature of the 'I' as well as of the entire assemblage of sense-data.

These are some of the salient elements in the metaphysics of the Abhidhamma, and they are sufficient to enable us to see the distinctive import of Buddhist ethics, as derived from Buddhist metaphysics. The diverse laws which regulate the interrelationship between the innumerable phenomena of the world around us, and of which we are an integral part, are all varied expressions of One Law, which is only the One Life in its ceaseless centripetal and centrifugal action. Buddha chose to stress the law-governed nature of the cosmos rather than its deific essence for the sake of human understanding and the assumption by all persons of their inalienable moral responsibilites. There is only one Law — the Law of Karma, of ethical causation and cosmic harmony. All aspects of this universal Law give rise to differing conditions of consciousness and embodied existence. All the problems which face men and women, especially the omnipresence of suffering and the inescapable nature of evil and culpable ignorance, may be met successfully. They are merely aspects of the ceaseless operation of the One Law of universal unity and human solidarity, and ordinary human beings may proceed from some knowledge of these aspects to a greater understanding of the whole, and then to a calm contemplation of the cosmic life-process and the One Life Principle. They may then begin to meditate upon cosmic consciousness, the mighty host of Tathagatas, and the Great Unknowable.

Buddhist ethics in its most familiar form is widely disseminated as comprising the critical eight steps of the Noble (Arya) Path. The teaching concerning the Eightfold Path is known as the Fourth Truth, the first three Truths being really statements of metaphysics based upon empirical evidence, introspection and meditation. First of all, suffering exists. Suffering is ubiquitous and inevitable. Secondly, the cause of suffering is craving — ignorant, selfish and possessive desire. Thirdly, the cure of suffering is the removal of the false sense of egotistic attachment and personal possession, so that each individual is no longer caught in the meshes of his or her own making, but goes beyond it, looking inwards and heavenwards. Fourthly, the very existence of the Path of enlightenment is the Fourth Truth. The existence of the Path is itself a metaphysical truth, fully realized by Buddhas and

Bodhisattvas who bear witness for the sake of all who suffer that deliverance is possible, that the means to deliverance is at hand and in accordance with the Law, that *dhamma* is fully in harmony with the Law of Karma, which is thus seen by the enlightened as the Law which ever moves to Righteousness. The Path ever exists. It is not something invented or first propounded by Gautama Buddha. He made it more readily evident and accessible to the multitudes by walking the Path himself and by vindicating the promise and prospect of enlightenment for one and all. To take the triple refuge — in the Buddha, the Dhamma and the Sangha — is to recognize the daily relevance of the Noble Eightfold Path.

The First Step on the Eightfold Path is *Right Knowledge*. Gautama Buddha wished to show all earnest seekers for enlightenment the possibility and importance of attaining a rational understanding of the cosmic process, of the law of karma and reincarnation, and of the complexities of human nature. Both wisdom and method, *prajna* and *upaya*, require the calm adoption of a scrupulously rational approach to the subject-matter of traditional religions. Buddha came to curb blind belief and to show that the intelligibility of the cosmos must be matched by an individual's reliance on reason, as well as experience and insight or illumination. Self-knowledge must be gained, not for the sake of the edification of the illusory personal self, but rather to gain a clear understanding of the cosmic process and to assist all in the universal quest for enlightenment. Thus the Second Step on the Path is *Right Motive*. With *Right Motive* one sustains the search for *Right Knowledge*, and *Right Knowledge* in turn strengthens the *Right Motive*. Both require of the seeker a deep scrutiny of the workings of the mind, the assemblage of acquired mental habits and grooves, the interplay of compulsive emotions and contradictory volitions, the repressed desires and hidden longings of the heart.

As the seeker becomes increasingly concerned with self-testing, he becomes more deliberate and restrained in the expression of *Right Knowledge* and *Right Motive* through speech and act. Self-knowledge is not gained from outside, but rather released from within. *Right Speech* arises naturally as one seeks to gain and manifest growing self-knowledge for the highest possible motive, and with the concern for pure and proper speech one gains a greater insight into *Right Action*. In going from within outwards, one is less concerned with prohibitions and permissions, rites and ceremonials, but more honest and perceptive in seeing the hindrances to inward continuity of consciousness in ill-considered speech and action. As one becomes more secure in *Right Knowledge* and *Right Motive,* one is better able to discriminate between what is truly necessary and what is superfluous, what is truly relevant and what is redundant, what is truly helpful to others and what is harmful. Thus *Right Speech* and *Right Action* heighten the seeker's sense of moral responsibility as well as sensitivity to the needs of others. This naturally strengthens the concern with *Right Livelihood* and alters one's entire standpoint towards wants and needs, outward skills and inward satisfaction.

The sixth crucial step is *Right Effort.* The seeker soon realizes that it is paramount, in the sphere of daily duties, to keep to the main spiritual pursuit uninterrupted. Perseverance in the main task amidst the cares and distractions of ordinary life demands a stringent standard of sustained mindfulness and concomitant self-restraint. This requires *Right Concentration* and *Right Meditation,* the seventh and eighth steps on the Path. The seeker has to grasp fully the tenacious proclivities of the mind in the grip of conscious and unconscious desires as well as the latent crystalline clarity of the pure mind, freed from craving and purged by illuminative insight. Hence various spiritual exercises in mind control, self-examination, the preservation of deep calmness, proportionality and purity of heart become indispensable. Meditation upon voidness and fullness can increase the seeker's insight into the dialectic of transcendental wisdom in the *prajnaparamita* texts as well as reveal the indissoluble connection between wisdom *(prajna)* and unconditional compassion *(mahakaruna).* Heightened self-awareness and its progressive universalization become the basis of serene self-transcendence, effortless altruism and joyous detachment. To move closer to enlightenment is to become invulnerable in personality, impermeable to the titanic forces of the *mahamaya*, the Great Delusion, and irreversible in one's dedication to the enlightenment and redemption of all beings.

The Eightfold Path demonstrates that Buddhist ethics, Buddhist psychology and Buddhist metaphysics are closely interlinked at all stages of the progressive awakenings of seekers of enlightenment. Even if a person is not ready to grasp the great goal and the deeper significance of the Eightfold Path, it is possible to begin to gain a greater measure of control in one's life. Anyone can benefit from the rudiments of Buddhist psychology as taught in Vipassana training, which focusses upon gaining greater awareness of one's breathing, one's likes and dislikes, one's unacknowledged desires, weaknesses and strengths. Philosophically, the essential basis of Buddhist psychology is powerfully simple and can be understood by all. No one can deny the existence of the One Life Principle. Any exaggerated emphasis or misuse of its particular manifestations is, in fact, a denial and desecration of the One Life Principle. Every single vice or weakness arises from the inflated and false valuations ascribed to the various forms, powers and manifestations of the One Life. It is possible to extract from every experience the essence and to enjoy the simple activity of daily sifting of the essential from the redundant, thereby increasing one's self-awareness and one's sensitivity to the needs of others and oneself. One will soon come to see that without a modicum of self-discipline and self-control, there is a considerable wastage of energy and effort and much avoidable pain and misery. It is always pertinent to seek a steady, self-sustaining state of mental peace, balance and fulfilment.

Buddhist social and political philosophy is centred chiefly upon the principle of conformity to and emulation of the cosmic Wheel of Law. The moral Law is the ordered expression of the ceaseless re-establishment of cosmic harmony and human solidarity. Every human being must be seen as a probationary learner gaining experience in the School of Life, suffering for a purpose that cannot be discovered without inserting oneself into the universal pilgrimage of all beings, and seeking for spiritual freedom based upon a knowledge of causes and consequences. The Buddhist State must necessarily be a full-fledged Welfare State which provides all citizens with an ethical environment in which the true needs of human life may be met by self-reliant and altruistic action. Its chief emphasis must be upon universal life-long education and spiritual enlightenment. It must consciously mirror the Great Law of moral interdependence and ethical causation and inculcate in all persons the accept-ance of full responsibility for individual and social welfare. An individual's right relationship with the cosmos and with Nature is fundamental if he is to establish a right relationship with society. Whilst many lack the knowledge needed to grasp cosmic and social interdependence at a causal level, they could begin by stressing right relations with their kinsfolk and neighbours.

Thus the entire message of Gautama Buddha constitutes a wonderful unity, universal in scope, applicable to all human beings, and powerfully re-stated by different Teachers in different ways. Buddha gave to one and all the prospect of validating and pursuing a single-minded spiritual quest for meaning, enlightenment and redemption. He taught, not escape into some celestial retreat, but the gaining of *nirvana* in *samsara*, progressive enlightenment in the company of one's fellows and voluntary reincarnation for the sake of sharing the hard-won fruits of self-knowledge and inner peace with suffering humanity. His own exemplary life was the beautiful and lustrous realization of three paramount principles — the principle of regeneration, the principle of renunciation and the principal of reverence. We must regenerate ourselves as he did, we must gain more and more wisdom and compassion and then renounce the fruits of our spiritual strivings; thus, by a series of steps, each greater than the last, we come to the final step, the supreme renunciation of individual bliss which he superbly demonstrated in his own life. Above all, we must take refuge in the Tathagata light of Buddha and in the Order of Disciples he came to re-establish upon the earth. We must show reverence to the Buddhas and to all beings, for without reverence nothing worthwhile is possible in human life.

Caxton Hall, London
March 25, 1952

COGNITION AND FREEDOM

If anyone says that the Tathagata comes or goes, sits or reclines, he fails to understand my teaching. Why? The Tathagata has neither whence nor whither, and therefore he is called the Tathagata.

The Diamond Sutra

All growth in self-conscious beings is based upon self-determination checked by karma, the consequences of past causation. The immortal soul, as a self-subsisting being, is engaged in an awesome pilgrimage within a vast Circle of Necessity extending over an immense period of time. Within this manvantaric matrix, each must give meaning to the assumption of responsibility in the light of the central teaching of the *Diamond Sutra*. Over millennia myriads of human beings are involved in elaborating modes of perception and awareness which generate diverse emphases in thought-forms, in language, and in ways and means of interacting with those abstractions called institutions, roles and rules. Archetypally, these divergences may be seen in relation to the invisible centre of an invisible circle, which is also the topological centre of an equilateral triangle. There is no priority to any of the angles made by any two lines of the triad. At the same time, there must be a fourth point, in relation to which the triad may be seen as a whole. The geometry of the universe involves an appearance of stability which masks the living arithmetic of ceaseless development.

To begin to ponder upon the wisdom of the *Diamond Sutra*, the climactic message of Buddha, we should reflect upon the fundamental identity of all monads. Every human being knows that in the context of the collective interdependence of beings under law, all discriminations between persons become illusory and irrelevant. Death does not discriminate between persons; an epidemic does not favour some and punish others. Men who sail on long voyages are silent witnesses to the majesty, impersonality and profound impartiality of the ocean, which is often compared to the whole of life. 'Law' is merely a word given to the totality of interdependent relations that constitute a world or a system. One of the core statements of the *Diamond Sutra* is that the system is no-system. Consider any example — a school, a nation, an economy — and look at manuals, rules, and diagrams of edifices. Anyone can be induced to see a spatial field over a period of time in terms of determinate points and discrete relationships. Nevertheless, there is a freedom and an unstructured quality in human relationships. There is an indefinable improvisation in the relationship between a mother and her child, between a husband and his wife. These designations merely indicate persons in distinct roles, relative to particular contexts.

In the *Diamond Sutra* the problem of specification is raised by the wisest of the Buddha's disciples who have mastered the divine dialectic of Buddhist ontology, which negates the substantiality of visible forms and the rigidity of discriminations relative to objects of sense-perception. Most people entertain an unphilosophical notion of some kind of timetable or guide book for travel in terms of a predetermined starting-point and a fixed terminus. Yet anyone who wanders in the mountains or roams about like a nomad, neither threatened by nor dependent upon maps, knows that all of these are arbitrary localized representations in what appears as a boundless field from a high altitude. Anyone from a great city who merely happens to fly over its towering structures experiences a sort of release from overdrawn lines and discovers something of the lightness of a bird on the wing. Every human being is capable of a certain freedom and largeness, a magnanimity which is beyond the possibility of specification and analysis, and transcends all formal limitations. At the very moment someone says he is this or that, the object of the statement is becoming something else. We are always living some sort of parasitic and derivative existence because of restrictively conceptualizing consciousness, which itself is essentially as unbounded as the sky, as free space, as the vast and unfathomable ocean. Even the concepts of law and evolution merely refer to a process of ceaseless breathing in and out, a cyclical manifestation in time, which itself cannot be caught within the circle. We can never see a circle from outside if we are identified with any point in the circle.

Immense implications would emerge for the daily lives of human beings if they could seriously ask whether the *onus probandi* is in the wrong place all the time. They could look at babies and try to work back in consciousness to a time when they were less confined. Look at a person before he is obsessed with grades and degrees; watch a person over a weekend when he forsakes the distinctions that men make during the week. Every human being senses that he or she is more than all the conventionalized distinctions, which are devices for the solidification of matter and thereby a conceptual prison for consciousness. Human beings must give themselves the opportunity, deliberately and self-consciously, to focus their attention upon the forgotten truth that the mind cannot ever encompass reality. The very thought of space reaching out in every direction has a purifying and liberating effect upon the mind. This is because of fixed presuppositions and assumptions in relation to matter and spirit, which are merely two aspects of one and the same homogeneous substance-principle. Although called by many names, in the *Diamond Sutra*, it is depicted as the fusion of the void with the white heat of thought bursting its own boundaries. The separation of inner from outer, man from the world, the infinite space within from the dimensionally defined though limitless space without, has a corrective and therapeutic function in relation to recovery of self-awareness within the context of shared awareness. If we think of many centres of light blended together, counting and differentiating become irrelevant. One experiences the joy and the thrill of a flood of light, but even this is only from the standpoint of the sense-organs. What looks like a flood of light may in fact be only a mirage, a film or veil upon that incredible voidness of absolute darkness which is necessarily true light.

In delivering the *Diamond Sutra* the Buddha was stretching the serene minds and spatial perspectives of those few disciples gathered around him who already sensed that plane of consciousness where the Buddha abides even while in manifestation. They were able to accommodate the magnitude of vision of the Bodhisattvic state. The Bodhisattva is a being who has mastered the wisdom of compassion. Wisdom manifests as an unmodified state of calm consciousness. Everything else in relation to it is like an evanescent bubble. Thinking about this untrammelled perspective can help us to understand our own time. What individuals have failed to do on their own is happening collectively: there is a shared experience of voiding old forms and the past criteria of frozen meanings, all of which can no longer be maintained because the very will to impose them has weakened, and the defensive will to react against them is on the decline. The moment individuals try to capture this awareness of voiding the old in terms of isms or nihilisms, they experience the painful gap between soul-awareness and the cool capacity of spiritual wakefulness to master and radiate through every mode of expression with the precision one would find in music or mathematics. The Buddha was, in effect, extolling the music of the Soundless Sound, the mathematics of the zero. He was an artist speaking and singing, but also gently chiding. He effortlessly embodied, in an inimitable manner, the inexhaustible plenty of the boundless ocean of wisdom *(Prajna)* and compassion *(Karuna)*.

If a person really begins to see simultaneously from alternative standpoints and can make this a living reality in consciousness, while recognizing that this is still based upon a relative but always mistaken assumption of separate selfhood, then he is doing what is suggested in one puzzling place in the *Diamond Sutra*. The question is asked, why is the Absolute in persons? This is philosophically strange when so much has been said to void all attributes of Absoluteness. Any person can, as much as any other, embody and maintain self-consciously the serene awareness of the whole. This suggests that though our language and thought are riddled with pairs of opposites, the activity in itself, *tathata*, the thing in itself which is truly a process, is so overwhelmingly profound that it creates a Buddha-field. How is this possible? When people get together they collectively create a shared but nonetheless dependent sense of reality, but the moment a sufficient number of persons lose interest in that form of sharing, the entire field becomes absurd. This is a fact about human consciousness which requires and presupposes differentiation. The differentiation is constantly cancelled by the interaction which cannot be sustained except in terms of the false supports provided by the seeming continuity and substantiality of what is unreal unless beings attach and assume a reality to it. This is only a way of saying that a human being can never stay still. No man can ever experience total immobility. If he did, he would cease to be alive. Equally, the mere fact of always changing does not by itself mean anything in relation to the motive of unfolding the five eyes of which the *Diamond Sutra* speaks. Motive itself is the vast motor-force of Fohat, an ocean of energy in ceaseless motion.

If the entire universe is a golden egg in which there is a fructifying principle of expansion, a breathing outwards, then all particular acts and motives are as unreal relative to the pulsation in the cosmic egg as an appendage which imagines it exists on its own, that it is not in fact wholly dependent. Every organ and cell of the human body depend upon that incredibly intricate network of nerve centres and invisible capillary streams of electromagnetic threads in subtle matter that binds together 10^{70} light-atoms. The thought is overwhelming because human beings normally settle for less. Whether they talk a moral language, a seemingly philosophical idiom, or a scientific-mechanistic jargon, they are engaged in some sort of collective self-mutilation. One might think, as Tolstoy wrote in *War and Peace,* that there is no set of reasons sufficient to convey the rationale behind the bizarre course of history. Is there really free will? Tolstoy asked of the Napoleonic war whether it was all caused by one particular man with his obvious limitations, or whether perhaps there was a vaster force operating. When we seem to sense that greater force at work, it matters little who fills the role for the consummation of the collective Karma of the aggregates of human beings that masquerade as nations and races. We come to see what Schopenhauer stressed in the nineteenth century. The notion of personal will is possibly a tragic illusion. To this extent the behaviourists are right, but only from the standpoint of differentiated separateness which dilutes and destroys the mind. What behaviourists are doing in one direction is similar to what drug addicts are doing in another. There is a common, desperate need to wipe out some essential features of consciousness and experience.

Supposing a man, when he looked at his life, saw that he could not particularize, did not plan, or deliberately intend most of what he did. When he begins to make experiments with the vast storehouse of energy that is the universe, with every centre of which he is linked through one of the various elements and substances in his being, he attempts to do what Nature does and becomes an alchemist. Every such apprentice alchemist will soon discover the extraordinary powers of concentrated thought and of controlled creative imagination. Few persons today think that the problems of some years ago, which at the time seemed so impossibly cosmic, were more than turbulences in teacups. Given the logic of identification, this is part of the ineluctable process of the prismatic scattering of undifferentiated consciousness into seven rays, which soon become obscured in a kaleidoscopic shadow-play. There is, in Platonic language, a series of reduced reflections, rather like an array of poor reproductions from a negative. There is a deep sense in which all human beings are dreamily involved in a secondary kind of existence. When men begin to wake up to the vastness and potency of cosmic will — rather than fear a grotesque God whimsically manipulating the world — they will see that there is nothing greater on earth than the sovereign dignity and majesty of self-consciousness. There is an amazing plasticity, power, flexibility and range to human consciousness, but also myriad possibilities of polarization through a perverse disinclination to focus steadily on a worthy goal. We drift into false assumptions about 'I' as 'Mr. So-and-So', deciding now to do this, and to do that tomorrow. There is a recurrent constriction of consciousness. There is ever the danger of losing our awareness of the internality which must be unbounded in relation to the unending variety of fields of cognition. It was recognized even by someone as inverted in spiritual perception yet insightful as Hobbes, who said that cognition is rather like conceiving or giving birth. Imagining, on the other hand, is not like conceiving. The imagination is so fertile, capable of such an immense progeny, that one cannot limit its richness in terms of certain strenuous acts of cognition.

Our very language comes in the way of becoming self-consciously aware of what we already know. If we did not already know it, no communication would ever convey to us the consubstantiality of consciousness, behind and beyond possible focussing points of perception, and the intelligent, boundless universe as a vast though arbitrary aggregation of innumerable possible fields. This is the most difficult and crucial of all subjects for reflection. One can initially understand it by application to specific matters and then by learning to be free-wheeling in thought. This makes real the connection between unconditioned and conditioned. If a person has thought this through — being engaged in *dianoia* — he finds that the whole notion of motive is transformed. While the universe cannot protect one's private intentions, through thought one can insert anything one chooses into the total good. Even though one does not fully know what that is, one can recognize it. One can equally visualize going in the opposite direction, unless one has blinded oneself to the point of enjoying a psycho-physical death-wish. We find we cannot explain easily the gesture of Jesus to Dostoevski's Grand Inquisitor. We cannot fathom the smile of a Mona Lisa or the inscrutable expression on the face of the Egyptian Sphinx. If a person suddenly did something without quite knowing why, in an atmosphere of acceptance and hope, with a great deal of give and take and a freedom from the burden of judgement, he or she would be astonished at how much human beings can improvise. And yet, they do it all the time when they care for each other. But when the demon of judgementalism, mired in a self-destructive shadowy self, and therefore a desperate insecurity, slithers like a snake into the picture, then nothing looks quite right. Everything is open to suspicion, so human beings torture themselves and nourish illogical attitudes.

The tradition that goes back to Gautama Buddha and before, and which came down through teachers like Pythagoras and Shankaracharya, venerates the universal mind, the jewelled storehouse of all thought. At one with it any human being is invincible, but separated from it a person is a playground of illusions, inversions and deceptions. When anyone really thinks through the message of the *Diamond Sutra*, he soon finds that the meaning of life is totally different because he was overlooking that which was obvious from the first. There is an omnidirectional reflection of light in even the rough-cut diamond. Each is reminiscent, in its own way, of the Kohinoor — the renowned 108 carat 'Fullness of Light'. Many have wondered about its enigmatic history traced through many kingdoms. Its story is shrouded in the secret annals of Initiates. There exist beings capable in consciousness of maintaining a boundless field of awareness in a manner that can be hooked to any point in space-time. The human mind when perfected in its powers is capable of impressing matter at a noumenal level merely by the magnetic touch of a finger or through a deft rearrangement of life-atoms. Nature is itself the carrier of myriad impresses across millennia, converting coal eventually into a diamond.

In Gupta Vidya there are no such firm distinctions as we tend to make between metaphysical, mythic and metaphorical. Reality is one. The sages speak in terms of a total knowledge of all correspondences, and at the same time they can make endless substitutes and conversions because they effortlessly handle all the polarities — north, south, east, west, above, below — and yet they know that all of these are relativities. The *Diamond Sutra* is addressed to the Diamond Soul in every man, the hidden centre of the limitless light of awareness. We may be misled by physical analogies, but this noumenal light of mental awareness can create, sustain and dissolve entire fields of cognition. We know from common experience that few things can survive when totally ignored by all, and also that when human beings seize upon something, they lend it verisimilitude. The truly wise man both negates and affirms as he walks through life. Having found meaning and reality in abiding as a motionless being clothed in refined matter, he is like a person who has gone back into the egg. This is a puzzling phenomenon because we do not have physical representations which adequately depict the magic and beauty of self-transformation. When we reflect upon the diamond and the sun, we can conceive of subtle interactions over immense distances in time and of space. Yet a meteorite suddenly penetrating the atmosphere of the earth can instantly convert into diamonds whatever comes in its way. The laser beam of Buddhic perception can reach to the core *(tattva)* of anything and everything because it bypasses the region of dependent and secondary causation. It penetrates to the very root.

The *Diamond Sutra* teaches that any person can, in principle, see to the core of conditioned reality. He can do this through a clear-sighted recognition of the dimensionless cause of unconditioned reality within himself and everyone else. The jewel is within one's reach; one has to use it. When a person is ready to replace angular views with a rounded vision, he can activate the magnetic sphere of influence around him. At all times human beings, on all planes, either speed up or slow down. They exhibit either restlessness or inertia and cannot move equally in all directions at the same time. As one moves away from homogeneity into the realm of the differentiated, what one man cannot use, another man will appropriate. This applies not only to human beings but to all whirling centres of energy. Nature abhors a vacuum. There is nothing that is wholly unused except on the visible plane, and even this is mayavic. One's whole conception of the world of which one is a part can be profoundly altered. To the unfolding Buddhic perception of a person who is truly awake, the logic of relations in diverse realms of matter and consciousness has nothing to do with those eyes and ears which Heraclitus designated as false witnesses to the soul. If human beings had always trusted to the unreliable reports of their physical sense-organs, there would have been no real knowledge of any kind. It is thanks to the light of intelligence and self-reflection that there is knowledge. Souls that are fully awake radiate the inimitable lustre of the diamond through the magical fusion of wisdom and compassion. Buddha exemplified the sovereign human capacity of voiding the seeming full whilst also showing an unspoken, ever-present sympathy for everything that lives and breathes.

Whenever a person realizes the self-subsisting nature of truth, he enjoys the ineffable freedom which commands the power to see through the eyes of others, with and for them. He finds exhilaration in the expansion of consciousness that encompasses myriad perspectives. A point comes when one can do this not intermittently and by degrees, but ceaselessly by going to the very core, like the sage on a mountain who forgets there is a mountain, who sees no distinctions amidst the plains and between souls, but is replete with cosmic affirmation from what looks like bare negation in a limitless, azure expanse. These are imperfect representations of noumenal realities in the realm of consciousness. Every person has within him or her the possibility of coming closer to the Diamond Soul, the true Self of all. It is transcendent and need not be transfixed one-dimensionally or in as many dimensions as one may count, because it has a solidity and depth inseparable from the void. It is that which constantly rediscovers the voidness of the seeming full — the striking keynote of Buddha — and thereby prepares a person to do that which Krishna taught — to see the fullness of the seeming void. To bring these two archetypal modes together is the noble prospect and the divine destiny of the forerunners of the Aquarian Age. This is a time which spares no illusions or shadows, but which is spacious and fertile in opportunities for such expansion of awareness as may attract credible and sharable representations from the realm of *Akasha* into the free spaces among human beings.

ENLIGHTENMENT

The 'last vibration of the Seventh Eternity' was 'fore-ordained' — by no God in particular, but occurred in virtue of the eternal and changeless LAW *which causes the great periods of Activity and Rest, called so graphically, and at the same time so poetically, the 'Days and Nights of Brahmā.' The expansion 'from within without' of the Mother, called elsewhere the 'Waters of Space,' 'Universal Matrix,' etc., does not allude to an expansion from a small centre or focus, but, without reference to size or limitation or area, means the development of limitless subjectivity into as limitless objectivity. 'The ever (to us) invisible and immaterial Substance present in eternity, threw its periodical shadow from its own plane into the lap of Maya.'*

The Secret Doctrine, i 62-63

The transcendence of *maya*, the awakening of wisdom and the realization of immortality are three in one. Though they may be distinguished for the sake of understanding and therapeutic meditation, they are in truth but aspects of unified perfection. Like the triple hypostases of the *Atman*, they form a purely noumenal matrix hinting at the inconceivable ideal of full enlightenment. That enlightenment has no specific ground, is not a state and is no event. Tautologically, it is the realization of the Real. Philosophically, it is the consummation of *philos* in *sophia*, the two becoming one, the extinction of divisions between subject and object. Inaccessible through mere affirmation or even negation, it is the One Truth (SAT) beyond all illusion, ignorance and death. It may be approached only by following the small, old path, the path that begins and ends outside of self. One must first become the path to enter it, and then one must realize that one travels on that path "without moving."

Ultimately, there can be no true comprehension of enlightenment or of the path outside of enlightenment itself.

Mortality cannot judge of immortality; *avidya* cannot conceive of *vidya*. The insubstantial self of mayavic matter cannot encompass the boundlessness of the Real. The shadow cannot comprehend the light that casts it. Whether understood in terms of the attraction and repulsion of *tanha* that constricts motivation and the will, or in terms of the delusion of the mind through dichotomies, the lesser and partial cannot comprehend the supreme and complete. Nonetheless, there is latent in every human being the precious seed of enlightenment, *bodhichitta*. Consubstantial with the highest planes of cosmic substance, it is the core of that consciousness perfected by Buddhas and Bodhisattvas. It is the immutable ground of immortality, inseparable from the One Life or the Rootless Root of all manifestation. To begin to understand the permanent possibility of enlightenment pervading manifested life, one must ponder the ontological status of that unmanifest wisdom, the possibility of which is envisaged by esoteric philosophy.

In the *Bhagavad Gita*, Lord Krishna tells Arjuna that there is no non-existence for that which is, and no existence for that which is not. If supreme and boundless unmanifest wisdom constitutes reality, there can be no non-existence of wisdom bound up with what are called illusion, ignorance and death. Similarly, if these three themselves are not reality, then they are nothing which can pass into non-existence with the awakening of wisdom. If unmanifest wisdom is without antecedent, it is also without residue. Typically, however, human beings conceive of enlightenment as some sort of real change — a contradiction in terms. Put crudely, they suppose either that eternal wisdom has somehow become real, or that the unreal realm of *maya* has somehow become non-existent. Too objective a mind will produce the first misconception, too subjective a turn of mind will produce the second. In either case, the theoretical and, what is the same thing, the practical possibility of enlightenment is obscured. This root imbalance or eccentricity in the soul's vestures and in human understanding is multiplied a myriad times, affecting every arena of mundane thought and action.

In order to ameliorate this condition, H.P. Blavatsky devoted considerable attention, in *The Secret Doctrine*, to the emerging phases of manifestation from the long night of *Pralaya*. Whilst these considerations are so abstract as to be of immediate interest only to the highest Adepts, they nevertheless have a direct relevance to all who seek to enter the path. If absolute abstract Space, unconditioned Consciousness and boundless Duration are the fundamental terms in the equation of manifestation, then they must also be the ultimate factors in any adequate conception of self-reference, self-regeneration and self-realization. Through meditation upon *Mulaprakriti* and *Prakriti*, *Parabrahm* and *Mahat*, boundless Duration and conditioned Time, the mind can be balanced and brought into proper orientation to the problem of Self and non-self. As this inner posture is steadied by devotion, entry onto the path will come through intuition and a strengthening of the heart.

Non-self has its roots in a process which H.P. Blavatsky characterized as "the development of limitless subjectivity into as limitless objectivity." Put more symbolically, in terms of *Mulaprakriti*,

> the ever (to us) invisible and immaterial Substance present in eternity, threw its periodical shadow from its own plane into the lap of Maya.
>
> *Ibid.,* 62-63

Mulaprakriti is pre-cosmic Root Substance, the noumenal origin of all differentiations and types of matter — the latter term referring to the aggregate of objects of possible perception. *Mulaprakriti* is wholly noumenal and so subjective that it cannot remotely be imagined by the human mind through extrapolation from a world of phenomenal objects. Even the subtlest abstractions employed in the sciences involving intra-atomic particles and fields, will not yield a conception of the abstractness of *Mulaprakriti*.

To be able to visualize *Mulaprakriti*, one must imagine the disappearance of all worlds, all planets and all galaxies, a dissolution so complete that no thing remains. When this negation is pushed to the fullest cosmic level, one must visualize in what may be called absolute abstract Space a primordial substratum or field. At that level of abstraction, space and substance mutually imply each other. This inconceivable degree of abstract homogeneity and limitless subjectivity is prior to all worlds and continues to be at the hidden root whilst all worlds manifest and are dissolved. Therefore, it is eternal. Having no reference to change, it is unchangeable and thus ever exists in eternity. *Mulaprakriti*, unmodified homogeneous *prima materia*, must not be confused with the objectivized conception of prime matter entertained by nineteenth century scientists, for it represents the most noumenal and primal conception of substance, beyond all objectivized universals. That it cannot be imagined is attested even by contemporary cosmology with its limited notion of beginnings and endings, or of one specific Big Bang. Other more audacious astronomers will not surrender to a belief in temporal finitude.

Once one can begin to conceive of *Mulaprakriti* as an invisible and immaterial substance present in eternity, and by definition unrelated to time, one must consider its relationship to matter in any possible system of worlds. In an objective world, even the most subtle abstract manifesting or manifested matter at the sub-atomic level is only a shadow. It is, in the words of the *Commentaries*, a shadow thrown from that homogeneous eternal realm into the lap of maya. One analogous approach is to think first of darkness and light, then of a series of reflections. But even such analogies are inadequate because they are based upon a conditioned view of space as characterized by extension, and of time as characterized by succession. Such assumptions, rooted in the illusion of a separative personal existence, cannot comprehend pure primal pre-cosmic *Mulaprakriti*. Such limiting conceptions obscure recondite questions in contemporary science about the reversibility of events. But they also obscure the Divine Darkness, which is only a metaphorical expression for this invisible and immaterial substance, that is mystically said to cast a periodical shadow. The casting of this shadow already assumes the emergence of a world of seeming objectivity divided into planes and rays. Even at the most primordial level of this assumed division into what are called the primary seven Dhyan Chohans, comparable to the Ah-Hi, there is the assumption of a kind of shadowy partial existence. And that shadowing continues, replicating itself a myriad times, so that on the densest possible plane of objective matter the one primal substance is shadowed by a dazzlingly complex panorama of forms, changing and interacting, scintillating in ceaseless transformation.

To gain an accurate conception of the ontological status of this boundless plane of seeming objectivity arisen from limitless subjectivity, absolute abstract Space, one must take account of the potency of ideation and intelligence in the unfolding of cosmic process. If one overlooks noetic intelligence and pursues only matter and substance, the immense realm of *prakriti,* one will derive the impression that all these forms of matter are ultimately shadowy by reference to *Mulaprakriti,* which is timeless, without immanence and involvement even in the vastest periods of time. It is beyond them; thus it has been called a veil upon the Absolute, a veil upon *Parabrahm,* almost indistinguishable from the Absolute. Just as the Absolute, if it is to be truly the Absolute, cannot enter any possible relationship with anything relative, so too *Mulaprakriti* cannot possibly be converted into anything else. It cannot possibly be related to any form of *prakriti.* This puzzling and challenging fact must be counterbalanced by similar considerations with regard to intelligence.

At the level of immaterial Root Substance, there must also be a pre-cosmic Ideation which is pure subjectivity, unconditioned, unmodified consciousness. This pure potential subjectivity is prior to any modified consciousness restricted by any object, by any relations between objects, or by any limited modes of self-reference. In gestating pure subjectivity, one comprehends that a totally negative field is ontologically prior to the act of negation. Again, one should ask what conceivable relationship there could be between this pure limitless subjectivity and the limitless realm of objective existence. In the abstruse metaphysics of the ancient Hindu schools, it is taught that the Absolute, *Parabrahm*, could be viewed as *nirguna* — attributeless. As soon as one predicates attributes of the Absolute, one has obscured the attributeless Absolute, *Nirguna Brahman*. To remain true to the pure thread of philosophic thought, one must withhold all qualifications and predications of the Absolute. One cannot even say that It was, It is or It will be.

What *Mulaprakriti* is to *prakriti* — primal Root Substance to noumenal matter — *Nirguna Brahman*, the attributeless Absolute, is to *Mahat* or cosmic mind. To gain any intuition of the profound meaning of this paradigmatic truth, one must meditate upon the early passages from the *Stanzas of Dzyan*, which characterize the long night of non-manifestation — *Maha Pralaya*.

> THE ETERNAL PARENT (Space), WRAPPED IN HER EVER INVISIBLE ROBES, HAD SLUMBERED ONCE AGAIN FOR SEVEN ETERNITIES.
> TIME WAS NOT, FOR IT LAY ASLEEP IN THE INFINITE BOSOM OF DURATION.
> UNIVERSAL MIND WAS NOT, FOR THERE WERE NO AH-HI TO CONTAIN IT.

These *Stanzas* attempt the virtually impossible task of characterizing an immense period of total non-manifestation, wherein matter, mind and time were not. Whilst these *Stanzas* have a vital significance for those at certain high levels of abstract meditation, striving after universal self-consciousness, they also have a great theoretical importance for human beings merely trying to emancipate themselves from fragmented consciousness in a world of objects.

The apprentice at meditation must begin by considering non-manifestation metaphysically. One must first conceive of the possibility, and then proceed to ponder further questions, which may be resolved through the instruction of the *Stanzas*. From total non-manifestation, where the Absolute *is* as much as during a period of manifestation, there is an anticipation of manifestation as a whole. Something analogous to this may be experienced in the early morning hours, in the passage from extreme darkness to a noumenal participation in the progressive dawn. Because embodied human beings are already subjects and objects, minds in forms, they can conceive of this process in two ways: by visualizing *Nirguna Brahman*, the attributeless Absolute, generating the possibility of universal mind, which in turn becomes *Mahat*, the cosmic mind of a particular system; or by visualizing *Mulaprakriti*, primordial pre-cosmic Substance, becoming the noumenon of matter in relation to a sphere of potential existence. We may move either from unlimited pre-cosmic Ideation or from unlimited pre-cosmic Substance through the most abstract sense of limit — limit in the most extreme degree applying to millions upon millions of years and to myriads of worlds within worlds.

The purpose of this profound meditation is to shatter the association of space with extension and of time with succession. These conceptions must be destroyed at the root, so that one may return to the deepest possible ground of pure potential universal awareness. At every point, there is, predictably, the risk that the deepening of consciousness may be arrested through identification with material forms, even the most subtle. But there is another and equally profound risk, the fundamental nature of which can be readily grasped by those who have spent some time with the Indian schools of philosophy, especially Vedanta. H.P. Blavatsky noted that:

> With some schools, Mahat is 'the first-born' of Pradhana (undifferentiated substance, or the periodical aspect of Mulaprakriti, the root of Nature), which (Pradhana) is called Maya, the Illusion.
>
> *Ibid.*, 62

Unlike the various Vedantin doctrines, the esoteric teachings do not hold that *Mahat* is derived from the illusory or periodic aspect of *Mulaprakriti*. As H.P. Blavatsky explained, the Wisdom-Religion holds that

> while Mulaprakriti, the noumenon, is self-existing and without any origin — is, in short, parentless, Anupadaka (as one with Brahman) — Prakriti, its phenomenon, is periodical and no better than a phantasm of the former, so Mahat, with the Occultists, the first-born of Gnana (or *gnosis)* knowledge, wisdom or the Logos — is a phantasm reflected from the Absolute NIRGUNA (Parabrahm, the one reality, 'devoid of attributes and qualities'; see Upanishads); while with some Vedantins Mahat is a manifestation of Prakriti, or Matter.
>
> *Ibid.,* 62

Because these idealistic schools of thought strongly stress the need for union between the individual *Jivatman* and the *Paramatman*, one with *Parabrahm*, they also seem to suggest that the whole world is an illusion, from that philosophical standpoint which sees even the cosmic mind — *Mahat* — as only an outgrowth or outcome of *prakriti,* or matter. Yet if it is *only* an outgrowth of matter, it becomes totally unreal. Earlier in *The Secret Doctrine,* H.P. Blavatsky discussed a similar divergence between the views of the Yogachara and Madhyamika schools of Mahayana Buddhism, concerning their understanding of the terms *Paramartha* and *Alaya.* Calling the Yogacharas the great spiritualists and the Madhyamikas the great nihilists, she again drew a distinction between too vehement idealism and the Teachings of Theosophia or *Brahma Vak.*

If *Mahat* is prior to *prakriti,* one might be tempted to ask whether *Mahat* is prior to *Mulaprakriti.* But *Mahat* is to *Nirguna Brahman* as *prakriti* is to *Mulaprakriti,* which is *Anupadaka.* The precedence of *Mahat* to *prakriti* is the key; ideation and consciousness are prior to everything else, save the veil over *Parabrahm.* If an individual human being ardently longs to attain to universal self-consciousness, he or she must be able to reduce everything to its homogeneous essence, to see through the relative reality and unreality of the world, yet acknowledge that in the world of unreal time there is that which is consubstantial with the Absolute. In the language of *Ishopanishad,* it is erroneous to reject either the Transcendent or the Immanent. The Absolute is neither. One must come to sense the Transcendent in the Immanent, and, as a first step in meditation, the Immanent in the Transcendent. *Parabrahm* is neither Being nor Non-Being; IT IS BE-NESS.

To gain universal self-consciousness one has to experience the continuity of consciousness from the highest to the lowest, from the most boundless to the most limited. This is perhaps the hidden intent of Vedanta, all too often obscured by schools of idealism, which emphasize the subjective approach to metaphysics. Subjective idealists like Berkeley, phenomenalists, even German phenomenologists — all, like Vedanta, are fundamentally concerned with the distinction between Being and Becoming. All require a doctrine of maya which involves either saying that maya is a superimposition or that it is an unreal shadow. But whatever it is, it leaves intact the fundamental ground, and therefore one has to cancel everything out and go back to that fundamental ground to gain enlightenment. Unfortunately, this view could become a justification for those who want to become absorbed in the whole, negating everything, without gaining universal self-consciousness and coming back into the world with that self-consciousness intact. Yet, it is just this process which enshrines clues to the sacred mystery of incarnation, especially of the Avatar.

To convey something of the development of limitless objectivity out of limitless subjectivity, it is helpful to employ concepts like expansion and contraction. When talking at the most macrocosmic level of the unmanifest and the manifest, non-being and being, it would be better to avoid such terms. To understand the *Stanzas* when they speak of an expansion "from within without", it is necessary to purge the notion of expansion of any spatial reference. The entire range of mundane experience equally constrains the capacity to devise diagrams and models. For the expansion of the *Stanzas* is purely metaphysical and has no relation to objective space. It is best intimated by the lotus, which is phanerogamous, *i.e.,* contains in its seed form the complete flower in miniature, just as an embryo develops into a human being. Because it is completely present in prototype, the unfoldment of the lotus is merely an elaboration of what is already present. This is the closest analogy to the unfoldment from the prototypic universal ideas in the cosmic mind into the world of many types and forms. But becoming accustomed to so lofty a conception is like acclimatizing oneself to the rarefied altitude of high mountains. Just as one must learn to breathe the thin air, while maintaining activity, so one must in meditation learn to give a sense of reality on the mental plane where there are no forms and beings but only Darkness. This cannot be done without purging all those notions that have been acquired through manifested existence in a world circumscribed by limited space and time.

Just as the cosmic lotus flowers in a space without extension, so too it flowers in a time without succession. Thus, the esoteric philosophy

> divides boundless duration into unconditionally eternal and universal Time and a conditioned one *(Khandakala)*. One is the abstraction or noumenon of infinite time *(Kala)*; the other its phenomenon appearing periodically, as the effect of *Mahat* (the Universal Intelligence limited by Manvantaric duration).
>
> *Ibid.,* 62

These two different dimensions of time — *Kala* and *Khanda-kala* — stand to each other as *Parabrahm* and *Mulaprakriti* to *Mahat* and *prakriti*. It is possible to recognize that there is an unconditional, eternal and universal time that has nothing to do with clocks and chronometers. It is a time that has to do with consciousness, but not with embodied, differentiated and externalizing consciousness. When through meditation consciousness is deliberately turned inward, when it can do what Nature does when *Pralaya* comes, then it is possible to approach unconditional, eternal, universal time. But one must recognize that conditioned time is merely an effect of *Mahat* and a characteristic of *prakriti*. Boundless Duration is prior to *Mahat*, and therefore closer to *Mulaprakriti* and *Parabrahm*.

To understand this and to make it the basis of meditation, it is helpful to ponder upon the process of universal dissolution. The powerful mythic and poetic descriptions of the onset of the night of *Pralaya* in a variety of Indian texts can be made the basis of a purifying and meditative discipline. One can learn to experience within oneself the progress of universal dissolution, experiencing the destruction and absorption of the element of earth into water, the absorption of water into fire, of fire into air, and of air into ether — the rudimentary property of which is sound. Even that is dissolved into what may be called a seed of consciousness on the plane of *Mahat*, the primary property of which is *Buddhi* at the universal level. Even that must ultimately be transcended. All the elements are progressively gathered back into one element, and that is converted from a single universal field of sound through a root or germ of consciousness back into a field of pure ideation — and beyond. Hence the potency of A-U-M, merging back into the soundless OM. If one sees all manifestation as one vast golden egg of Brahmā, in that luminous egg (*Hiranyagarbha*) the same process is ever taking place.

The Dawn of manifestation and the Twilight of the onset of *Pralaya* are not to be thought of as two points of sequential time separated by vast intervals. They are metaphysically fused in boundless duration as ceaseless creation — *Nitya Swarga* — and ceaseless dissolution — *Nitya Pralaya*. The individual who, through meditation upon these ideas, arouses intuition can reverse all that has happened since entering the mother's womb. Having experienced the shock of being thrown into the womb, and having progressively become involved through a series of identifications and limitations, human beings may be seen as fallen gods. Therefore, to overcome the bonds of illusion, ignorance and death, it is necessary to reverse this process, but not at the crude concretized level of those who talk of the primal scream and going back to the womb. It must be reversed cosmically, because nothing can ever be done fundamentally at the individual level unless it is understood cosmically.

This is the indispensable foundation of the Wisdom-Religion, of *Brahma Vidya*. As above, so below. As below, so above. In the below one must reach for the above; one must concern oneself with all humanity, on a metaphysical level, before any fundamental and irreversible change can be made in oneself. To understand this intuitively is to see that when one withdraws in meditation, at a steady and high level of abstraction, one is striving to experience the night of non-manifestation, where there are no worlds. To be able to do this is to empty and reabsorb all elements, dissolving everything elementally and at the level of ideation. To transcend the veils of conditioned existence whilst retaining full awareness is to realize the one primal Root Substance in boundless Duration. That is pure self-consciousness — *Atma Vidya*, one with the supreme attributeless unmanifest wisdom in *Parabrahm*.

> *Say not that It is One, as there can be no second, nothing other than That. There is neither uniqueness nor commonality, neither entity nor non-entity; this secondless One is neither void nor plenum. How can I convey this supreme wisdom?*
>
> SHRI SHANKARACHARYA

THE YOGA SUTRAS

THEORY, PRACTICE
AND DARSHANAS

*To contemplate these things is the privilege of the gods,
and to do so is also the aspiration of the immortal soul of
man generally — though only in a few cases is such
aspiration realized.*

PLATO

I *THEORIA* AND *PRAXIS*

Throughout its long and largely unrecorded history, Indian thought preserved its central concern with ontology and epistemology, with noetic psychology as the indispensable bridge between metaphysics and ethics, employing introspection and self-testing as well as logical tools, continually confronting the instruments of cognition with the fruits of contemplation. Through its immemorial oral teachings and a vast variety of written texts, the fusion of *theoria* and *praxis,* theory and practice, was never sacrificed to the demands of academic specialization or the compartmentalization of human endeavour. Diverse schools of thought shared the conviction that true understanding must flow from the repeated application of received truths. Coming to know is a dynamic, dialectical process in which thought stimulates contemplation and regulates conduct, and in turn is refined by them. Although an individual who would be healthy and whole thinks, feels and acts, gnosis necessarily involves the fusion of thought, will and feeling, resulting in *metanoia,* a radically altered state of being. The Pythagorean conception of a philosopher as a lover of wisdom is close to the standpoint of an earnest seeker of truth in the Indian tradition.

Indian thought did not suffer the traumatic cognitive disruption caused by the emergence of ecclesiastical Christianity in the Mediterranean world, where an excessive concern with specification of right belief, sanctioned and safeguarded by an institutional conception of religious authority and censorship, sundered thought and action to such an extent that it became common to think one way and act in another with seeming impunity. The chasms which opened up between thought, will and feeling provided fertile soil for every kind of psychopathology, in part because such a fragmentation of the human being engenders inversions, obsessions and even perversities, and also in part because for a thousand years it has been virtually impossible to hold up a credible paradigm of the whole and healthy human being. The philosophical quest became obscured in the modern West by the linear succession of schools, each resulting from a violent reaction to its predecessors, each claiming to possess the Truth more or less exclusively, and often insisting upon the sole validity of its method of proceeding. The slavish concern with academic respectability and the fear of anathematization resulted in the increasing alienation of thought from being, of cognition from conduct, and philosophical disputation from the problems of daily life.

Indian thought did not spurn the accumulated wisdom of its ancients in favour of current fashions and did not experience a violent disruption of its traditional hospitality to multiple standpoints. The so-called *astika* or orthodox schools found no difficulty in combining their veneration of the Vedic hymns with a wide and diverse range of views, and even the *nastika* or heterodox schools, which repudiated the canonical 'authority' of the Vedas, retained much of Vedic and Upanishadic metaphysics and almost the whole of their psychology and ethics. Indian philosophical schools could not see themselves as exclusive bearers of the total Truth. They emerged together from a long-standing and continuous effort to enhance our common understanding of God, Man and Nature, and they came to be considered as *darshanas* or paradigmatic standpoints, shedding light from different angles on noumenal and phenomenal realities. They refrained from claiming that any illumination which can be rendered in words — or even in thoughts — can be either final or complete.

II THE SIX SCHOOLS

It may be pointed out here that a system of philosophy however lofty and true it may be should not be expected to give us an absolutely correct picture of the transcendent truths as they really exist. Because philosophy works through the medium of the intellect and the intellect has its inherent limitations, it cannot understand or formulate truths which are beyond its scope. . . . We have to accept these limitations when we use the intellect as an instrument for understanding and discovering these truths in the initial stages. It is no use throwing away this instrument, poor and imperfect though it is, because it gives us at least some help in organizing our effort to know the truth in the only way it can be known — by Self-realization.

I.K. TAIMNI

The ageless and dateless Vedas, especially the exalted hymns of the *Rig Veda,* have long been esteemed as the direct expression of what gods and divine seers, *rishis* or immortal sages, saw when they peered into the imperishable centre of Being which is also the origin of the entire cosmos. The *Upanishads* (from *upa, ni* and *sad,* meaning 'to sit down near' a sage or *guru),* included in the Vedas, constitute the highest transmission of the fruits of illumination attained by these *rishis.* Often cast in the form of memorable dialogues between spiritual teachers and disciples, they represent rich glimpses of truth, not pieced together from disparate intellectual insights, but as they are at once revealed to the divine eye, *divya chakshu,* which looks into the core of Reality, freely intimated in idioms, metaphors and mantras suited to the awakening consciousness and spiritual potentials of diverse disciples. However divergent their modes of expression, they are all addressed to those who are ready to learn, willing to meditate deeply, and seek greater self-knowledge through intensive self-questioning. The Upanishads do not purport to provide discursive knowledge, conceptual clarification or speculative dogmas, but rather focus on the fundamental themes which concern the soul as a calm spectator of the temporal succession of states of mind from birth to death, seeking for what is essential amidst the ephemeral, the enduring within the transient, the abiding universals behind the flux of fleeting appearances.

From this standpoint, they are truly therapeutic in that they heal the sickness of the soul caused by passivity, ignorance and delusion. This ignorance is not that of the malformed or malfunctioning personality, maimed by childhood traumas or habitual vices. It is the more fundamental ignorance (*avidya*) of the adroit and well-adapted person who has learnt to cope with the demands of living and fulfil his duties in the world at a certain level without, however, coming to terms with the causes of his longings and limitations, his dreams and discontinuities, his entrenched expectations and his hidden potentials. The sages spoke to those who had a measure of integrity and honesty and were willing to examine their presuppositions, but lacked the fuller vision and deeper wisdom that require a sustained search and systematic meditation. For such an undertaking, mental clarity, moral sensitivity, relaxed self-control and spiritual courage are needed, as well as a willingness to withdraw for a period from worldly concerns. The therapeutics of self-transcendence is rooted in a recondite psychology which accommodates the vast spectrum of self-consciousness, different levels of cognition and degrees of development, reaching up to the highest conceivable self-enlightenment.

Upanishadic thought presupposed the concrete and not merely conceptual continuity of God, Nature and Humanity. Furthermore, Man is the self-conscious microcosm of the macrocosm, where the part is not only inseparably one with the whole but also reflects and resonates with it. Man could neither be contemplated properly nor fully comprehended in any context less than the entirety of visible and invisible Nature, and so too, ethics, logic and psychology could not be sundered from metaphysics. 'Is', the way things are, is vitally linked to 'must', the ways things must be, as well as to 'ought', the way human beings should think and act, through 'can', the active exploration of human potentialities and possibilities, which are not different, save in scope and degree, from cosmic potencies. A truly noetic psychology bridges metaphysics and ethics through a conscious mirroring of *ṛta*, ordered cosmic harmony, in *dharma*, righteous human conduct that freely acknowledges what is due to each and every aspect of Nature, including all humanity, past, present and future.

The ancient sages resolved the One-many problem at the mystical, psychological, ethical and social levels by affirming the radical metaphysical and spiritual unity of all life, whilst fully recognizing (and refusing to diminish through any form of reductionism) the immense diversity of human types and the progressive awakenings of human consciousness at different stages of material evolution and spiritual involution. The immemorial pilgrimage of humanity can be both universally celebrated and act as a constant stimulus to individual growth. Truth, like the sun shining over the summits of a Himalayan range, is one, and the pathways to it are as many and varied as there are people to tread them.

As if emulating the sculptor's six perspectives to render accurately any specific form in space, ancient Indian thinkers stressed six *darshanas*, which are sometimes called the six schools of philosophy. These are *astika* or orthodox in that they all find inspiration in different ways in the Vedas. And like the sculptor's triple set of perspectives — front-back, left side-right side, top-bottom — the six *darshanas* have been seen as three complementarities, polarized directions that together mark the trajectory of laser light through the unfathomable reaches of ineffable wisdom. Each standpoint has its integrity and coherence in that it demands nothing less than the deliberate and radical reconstitution of consciousness from its unregenerate and unthinking modes of passive acceptance of the world. Yet none can claim absoluteness, finality or infallibility, for such asseverations would imply that limited conceptions and discursive thought can capture ultimate Reality. Rather, each *darshana* points with unerring accuracy towards that cognition which can be gained only by complete assimilation, practical self-transformation and absorption into it. At the least, every *darshana* corresponds with a familiar state of mind of the seeker, a legitimate and verifiable mode of cognition which makes sense of the world and the self at some level.

All genuine seekers are free to adopt any one or more of the *darshanas* at any time and even to defend their chosen standpoint against the others, but they must concede the possibility of synthesizing and transcending the six standpoints in a seventh mode which culminates in *taraka*, transcendental, self-luminous gnosis, the goal of complete enlightenment often associated with the secret, incommunicable way of *buddhiyoga* intimated in the fourth, seventh and eighteenth chapters of the *Bhagavad Gita*.

Although scholars have speculated on the sequential emergence of the *darshanas*, and though patterns of interplay can be discerned in their full flowering, their roots lie in the ancient texts and they arise together as distinctive standpoints. It has also been held that the six schools grew out of sixty-two systems of thought lost in the mists of antiquity. At any rate, it is generally agreed that each of the later six schools was inspired by a sage and teacher who struck the keynote which has reverberated throughout its growth, refinement and elaboration. As the six schools are complementary to each other, they are traditionally viewed as the six branches of a single tree. All six provide a theoretical explanation of ultimate Reality and a practical means of emancipation. The oldest are Yoga and Sankhya, the next being Vaishesika and Nyaya, and the last pair are Purva Mimansa and Vedanta (sometimes called Uttara Mimansa). The founders of these schools are considered to be Patanjali of Yoga, Kapila of Sankhya, Kanada of Vaishesika, Gautama of Nyaya, Jaimini of Purva Mimansa and Vyasa of Vedanta, though the last is also assigned to Badarayana. All of them propounded the tenets of their philosophical systems or schools in the form of short *sutras*, whose elucidation required and stimulated elaborate commentaries. Since about 200 C.E., a vast crop of secondary works has emerged which has generated some significant discussions as well as a welter of scholastic disputation and didactic controversies, moving far away from *praxis* into the forests of *theoria*, or reducing *praxis* to rigid codes and *theoria* to sterile formulas. At the same time, there has remained a remarkable vitality to most of these schools, owing to their transmission by long lineages which have included many extraordinary teachers and exemplars. This cannot be recovered merely through the study of texts, however systematic and rigorous, in a philosophical tradition which is essentially oral, even though exceptional powers of accurate recall have been displayed in regard to the texts.

Nyaya and Vaishesika are schools primarily concerned with analytic approaches to the objects of knowledge, using carefully tested principles of logic. The word *nyaya* suggests that by which the mind reaches a conclusion, and since the word also means 'right' or 'just', Nyaya is the science of correct thinking. The founder of this school, Gautama, lived about 150 B.C.E., and its source-book is the *Nyaya Sutra*. Whilst knowledge requires an object, a knowing subject and a state of knowing, the validity of cognition depends upon *pramana*, the means of cognition. There are four acceptable *pramanas*, of which *pratyaksha* — direct perception or intuition — is most important. Perception requires the mind, *manas*, to mediate between the self and the senses, and perception may be determinate or indeterminate. Determinate perception reveals the class to which an object of knowledge belongs, its specific qualities and the union of the two. Indeterminate perception is simple apprehension without regard to genus or qualities. In the Nyaya school, indeterminate perception is not knowledge but rather its prerequisite and starting-point.

Anumana or inference is the second *pramana* or means of cognition. It involves a fivefold syllogism which includes a universal statement, an illustrative example and an application to the instance at hand. *Upamana* is the apt use of analogy, in which the similarities which make the analogy come alive are essential and not superficial. *Shabda*, sound or verbal expression, is the credible testimony of authority, which requires not uncritical acceptance but the thoughtful consideration of words, meanings and the modes of reference. As the analytic structure of Nyaya logic suggests, its basic approach to reality is atomistic, and so the test of claims of truth is often effectiveness in application, especially in the realm of action. Typically, logical discussion of a proposition takes the form of a syllogism with five parts: the proposition *(pratijna)*, the cause *(hetu)*, the exemplification *(drishtanta)*, the recapitulation *(upanaya)* and the conclusion *(nigamana)*.

However divergent their views on metaphysics and ethics, all schools accept and use Nyaya canons of sound reasoning. A thorough training in logic is required not only in all philosophical reasoning, exposition and disputation, but it is also needed by those who seek to stress mastery of *praxis* over a lifetime and thereby become spiritual exemplars. This at once conveys the enormous strength of an immemorial tradition as well as the pitiable deficiencies of most professors and pundits, let alone the self-styled so-called exoteric *gurus* of the contemporary East. Neither thaumaturgic wonders nor mass hypnosis can compensate for mental muddles and shallow thinking; indeed, they become insuperable obstacles to even a good measure of gnosis and noetic theurgy, let alone authentic enlightenment and self-mastery.

The Vaishesika school complements Nyaya in its distinct pluralism. Its founder, Kanada, also known as Kanabhaksha, lived around 200 C.E., and his chief work is the *Vaishesika Sutra*. Its emphasis on particulars is reflected in its name, since *vishesha* means 'particularity', and it is concerned with properly delineating the categories of objects of experience. These objects of experience, *padarthas*, are six: substance *(dravya)*, quality *(guna)*, and karma or movement and activity (forming the triplicity of objective existence), and generality *(samanya)*, particularity *(vishesha)* and *samavayi* or inherence (forming a triad of modes of intellectual discernment which require valid logical inference). A seventh object of experience, non-existence *(shunya)*, was eventually added to the six as a strictly logical necessity. The Vaishesika point of view recognizes nine irreducible substances: earth, water, air, fire, aether *(akasha)*, time, space, self and mind, all of which are distinct from the qualities which inhere in them. The self is necessarily a substance — a substrate of qualities — because consciousness cannot be a property of the physical body, the sense-organs or the brain-mind. Although the self as a substance must be everywhere pervasive, its everyday capacity for feeling, willing and knowing is focussed in the bodily organism.

Since the self experiences the consequences of its own deeds, there is, according to Vaishesika, a plurality of souls, each of which has its *vishesha,* individuality or particularity. What we experience is made up of parts, and is non-eternal, but the ultimate components — atoms — are eternal. Individuality is formed by imperceptible souls and certain atoms, which engender the organ of thought. At certain times, during immense cosmogonic cycles, nothing is visible, as both souls and atoms are asleep, but when a new cycle of creation begins, these souls reunite with certain atoms. Gautama asserted that even during incarnated existence, emancipation may be attained through ascetic detachment and the highest stages of contemplative absorption or *samadhi.* Though the Vaishesika school wedded an atomistic standpoint to a strict atheism, over time thinkers accepted a rationalistic concept of Deity as a prime mover in the universe, a philosophical requisite acceptable to Nyaya. The two schools or systems were combined by Kusumanjali of Udayana about 900 C.E. in his proof of the existence of God. Since then, both schools have been theistic. The Jains claim early parentage for the Vaishesika system, and this merely illustrates what is very common in the Indian tradition, that innovators like Gautama and Kanada were reformulating an already ancient school rather than starting *de novo.*

The Purva Mimansa of Jaimini took as its point of departure neither knowledge nor the objects of experience, but *dharma,* duty, as enjoined in the Vedas and Upanishads. As the accredited sources of dharma, these sacred texts are not the promulgations of some deity who condescended to step into time and set down principles of correct conduct. Rather, the wisdom in such texts is eternal and uncreate, and true rishis have always been able to see them and to translate that clear vision into mantramic sounds and memorable utterances. Hence Mimansa consecrates the mind to penetrating the words which constitute this sacred transmission. Central to the Mimansa school is the theory of self-evidence — *svata pramana*: truth is its own guarantee and the consecrated practice of faith provides its own validation. Repeated testings will yield correct results by exposing discrepancies and validating real cognitions. There is a recognizable consensus amidst the independent visions of great seers, and each individual must recognize or rediscover this consensus by proper use and concentrated enactment of mantras and hymns. Every sound in the fifty-two letters of Sanskrit has a cosmogonic significance and a theurgic effect. Inspired mantras are exact mathematical combinations of sounds which emanate potent vibrations that can transform the magnetic sphere around the individual as well as the magnetosphere of the earth. Self-testing without self-deception can become a sacred activity, which is *sui generis*.

From the Mimansa perspective, every act is necessarily connected to perceptible results. One might say that the effects are inherent in the act, just as the fruit of the tree is in the seed which grew and blossomed. There is no ontological difference between act and result, for the apparent gap between them is merely the consequence of the operation of time. Since the fruit of a deed may not follow immediately upon the act, or even manifest in the same lifetime, the necessary connection between act and result takes the form of *apurva*, an unseen force which is the unbreakable link between them. This testable postulate gives significance to the concept of *dharma* in all its meanings — 'duty', 'path', 'teaching', 'religion', 'natural law', 'righteousness', 'accordance with cosmic harmony' — but it cannot by itself secure complete liberation from conditioned existence. Social duties are important, but spiritual duties are even more crucial, and the saying "To thine own self be true" has an array of meanings reaching up to the highest demands of soul-tendance. In the continual effort to work off past karma and generate good karma, there is unavoidable tension between different duties, social and spiritual. The best actions, paradigmatically illustrated in Vedic invocations and rituals, lead to exalted conditions, even to some heavenly condition or blissful state. Nonetheless, as the various *darshanas* interacted and exchanged insights, Mimansa came to consider the highest action as resulting in a cessation of advances and retreats on the field of merit, whereby *dharma* and *adharma* were swallowed up in a sublime and transcendental state of unbroken awareness of the divine.

In striving to penetrate the deepest arcane meaning of the sacred texts, Mimansa thinkers accepted the four *pramanas* or modes of knowledge set forth in Nyaya, and added two others: *arthapatti* or postulation, and *abhava* or negation and non-existence. They did this in part because, given their view of the unqualified eternality of the Vedas, they held that all cognition is valid at some level and to some degree. There can be no false knowledge; whatever is known is necessarily true. As a consequence, they saw no reason to prove the truth of any cognition. Rather, they sought to demonstrate its falsity, for if disproof were successful, it would show that there had been no cognition at all. The promise of gnosis rests upon the sovereign method of falsifiability rather than a vain attempt to seek total verification in a public sense. Shifting the onus of proof in this way can accommodate the uncreate Vedas, which are indubitably true and which constitute the gold standard against which all other claims to truth are measured. Mimansa rests upon the presupposition of the supremacy of Divine Wisdom, the sovereignty of the Revealed Word and the possibility of its repeated realization. Even among those who cannot accept the liturgical or revelatory validity and adequacy of the Vedas, the logic of disproof can find powerful and even rigorous application. As a method, it became important to the philosophers of Vedanta.

Vedanta, meaning 'the end or goal of the Vedas', sometimes also called Uttara Mimansa, addresses the spiritual and philosophical themes of the Upanishads, which are considered to complete and form the essence of the Vedas. Badarayana's magisterial *Brahma Sutras* ordered the Upanishadic Teachings in a logically coherent sequence which considers the nature of the supreme *Brahman*, the ultimate Reality, and the question of the embodiment of the unconditioned Self. Each of the five hundred and fifty-five *sutras* (literally, 'threads') are extremely short and aphoristic, requiring a copious commentary to be understood. In explaining their meaning, various commentators presented Vedantic doctrines in different ways. Shankaracharya, the chief of the commentators and perhaps the greatest philosopher in the Indian tradition, espoused the *advaita*, non-dual, form of Vedanta, the purest form of monism, which has never been excelled. He asked whether in human experience there is anything which is impervious to doubt. Noting that every object of cognition — whether dependent on the senses, the memory or pure conceptualization — can be doubted, he recognized in the doubter that which is beyond doubt of any kind. Even if one reduces all claims to mere avowals — bare assertions about what one seems to experience — there nonetheless remains that which avows. It is proof of itself, because nothing can disprove it. In this, it is also different from everything else, and this difference is indicated by the distinction between subject and object. The experiencing Self is subject; what it experiences is an object. Unlike objects, nothing can affect it: it is immutable and immortal.

For Shankara, this Self *(Atman)* is *Sat-Chit-Ananda,* being or existence, consciousness or cognition, and unqualified bliss. If there were no world, there would be no objects of experience, and so although the world as it is experienced is not ultimately real, it is neither *abhava,* non-existent, nor *shunya,* void. Ignorance is the result of confusing *Atman,* the unconditioned subject, with *anatman,* the external world. From the standpoint of the cosmos, the world is subject to space, time and causality, but since these categories arise from nascent experience, they are inherently inadequate save to point beyond themselves to the absolute, immutable, self-identical *Brahman,* which is absolute Being *(Sat).* *Atman* is *Brahman,* for the immutable singularity of the absolute subject, the Self, is not merely isomorphic, but radically identical with the transcendent singularity of the ultimate Reality. Individuals who have yet to realize this fundamental truth, which is in fact the whole Truth, impose out of ignorance various attitudes and conceptions on the world, like the man who mistakes an old piece of rope discarded on the trail for a poisonous serpent. He reacts to the serpent, but his responses are inappropriate and cause him to suffer unnecessarily, because there is no serpent on the trail to threaten him. Nonetheless, the rope *is* there. For Shankara, the noumenal world is real, and when a person realizes its true nature, gaining wisdom thereby, his responses will be appropriate and cease to cause suffering. He will realize that he *is* the *Atman* and that the *Atman* is *Brahman*.

Although *Brahman* is ultimately *nirguna*, without qualities, the aspirant to supreme knowledge begins by recognizing that the highest expression of *Brahman* to the finite mind is Ishvara, which is *Saguna Brahman*, Supreme Reality conceived through the modes of pure logic. Taking Ishvara, which points beyond itself to That (TAT), as his goal and paradigm, the individual assimilates himself to Ishvara through the triple path of ethics, knowledge and devotion — the *karma*, *jnana* and *bhakti yogas* of the *Bhagavad Gita* — until *moksha*, emancipation and self-realization, is attained. For Shankara, *moksha* is not the disappearance of the world but the dissolution of *avidya*, ignorance.

Ramanuja, who lived much later than Shankara, adopted a qualified non-dualism, Vishishtadvaita Vedanta, by holding that the supreme *Brahman* manifests as selves and matter. For him, both are dependent on *Brahman*, and so selves, not being identical with the Ultimate, always retain their separate identity. As a consequence, they are dependent on *Brahman*, and that dependency expresses itself self-consciously as *bhakti* or devotion. In this context, however, the dependence which is manifest as *bhakti* is absurd unless *Brahman* is thought to be personal in some degree, and so *Brahman* cannot be undifferentiated. Emancipation or freedom is not union with the divine, but rather the irreversible and unwavering intuition of Deity. The Self is not identical with *Brahman*, but its true nature is this intuition, which is freedom.

Faith that *Brahman* exists is sufficient, and individual souls are parts of *Brahman*, who is the creator of universes. Yet *Brahman* does not create anything new; what so appears is merely a modification of the subtle and the invisible to the gross which we can see and sense. Because we can commune with this God by prayer, devotion and faith, there is the possibility of human redemption from ignorance and delusion. The individual is not effaced when he is redeemed; he maintains his self-identity and enjoys the fruits of his faith.

About a century and a half after Ramanuja, Madhava promulgated a dualistic *(dvaita)* Vedanta, in which he taught that *Brahman*, selves and the world are separate and eternal, even though the latter two depend forever upon the first. From this standpoint, *Brahman* directs the world, since all else is dependent, and is therefore both transcendent and immanent. As that which can free the self, *Brahman* is identified with Vishnu. Whereas the ultimate Reality or *Brahman* is neither independent *(svatantra)* nor dependent *(paratantra)*, God or Vishnu is independent, whereas souls and matter are dependent. God did not cause the cosmos but is part of it, and by his presence keeps it in motion. Individual souls are dependent on *Brahman* but are also active agents with responsibilities which require the recognition of the omnipresence and omnipotence of God. For the individual self, there exists either the bondage which results from ignorance and the karma produced through acting ignorantly, or release effected through the adoration, worship and service of Deity. The self is free when its devotion is pure and perpetual. Although the later forms of Vedanta lower the sights of human potentiality from the lofty goal of universal self-consciousness and conscious immortality taught by Shankaracharya, they all recognize the essential difference between bondage and freedom. The one is productive of suffering and the other offers emancipation from it. But whereas for Shankara the means of emancipation is wisdom *(jnana)* as the basis of devotion *(bhakti)* and *nishkama karma* or disinterested action, the separation between *Atman* and *Brahman* is crucial for Ramanuja and necessitates total *bhakti*, whilst for Madhava there are five distinctions within his dualism — between God and soul, God and matter, soul and matter, one form of matter and another, and especially between one soul and another — thus requiring from all souls total obeisance to the omnipresent and omnipotent God.

Suffering is the starting point of the Sankhya *darshana* which provides the general conceptual framework of Yoga philosophy. Patanjali set out the Taraka Raja Yoga system, linking transcendental and self-luminous wisdom *(taraka)* with the alchemy of mental transformation, and like the exponents of other schools, he borrowed those concepts and insights which could best delineate his perspective. Since he found Sankhya metaphysics useful to understanding, like a sturdy boat used to cross a stream and then left behind when the opposite bank has been reached, many thinkers have traditionally presented Sankhya as the theory for which Yoga is the practice. This approach can aid understanding, providing one recognizes from the first and at all times that yoga is the path to metaconsciousness, for which no system of concepts and discursive reasoning, however erudite, rigorous and philosophical, is adequate. More than any other school or system, Yoga is essentially experiential, in the broadest, fullest and deepest meaning of that term.

SANKHYA YOGA

The term 'Sankhya' is ultimately derived from the Sanskrit root *khya*, meaning 'to know', and the prefix *san*, 'exact'. Exact knowing is most adequately represented by Sankhya, 'number', and since the precision of numbers requires meticulous discernment, Sankhya is that *darshana* which involves a thorough discernment of reality and is expressed through the enumeration of diverse categories of existence. Philosophically, Sankhya is dualistic in its discernment of the Self *(purusha)* from the non-self *(prakriti)*. In distinguishing sharply between *purusha*, Self or Spirit, on the one hand, and *prakriti*, non-self or matter, on the other, the Sankhya standpoint requires a rigorous redefinition of numerous terms used by various schools. Even though later Sankhya freely drew from the Vedic-Upanishadic storehouse of wisdom which intimates a rich variety of philosophical views, its earliest concern does not appear to have been philosophical in the sense of delineating a comprehensive conceptual scheme which describes and explains reality. Early Sankhya asked, "What is real?" and only later on added the question, "How does it all fit together?"

Enumerations of the categories of reality varied with individual thinkers and historical periods, but the standard classification of twenty-five *tattvas* or fundamental principles of reality is useful for a general understanding of the *darshana*. Simply stated, Sankhya holds that two radically distinct realities exist: *purusha*, which can be translated 'Spirit', 'Self' or 'pure consciousness', and *mulaprakriti*, or 'pre-cosmic matter', 'non-self' or 'materiality'. Nothing can be predicated of *purusha* except as a corrective negation; no positive attribute, process or intention can be affirmed of it, though it is behind all the activity of the world. It might be called the Perceiver or the Witness, but, strictly speaking, no intentionality can be implied by these words, and so *purusha* cannot be conceived primarily as a knower. *Mulaprakriti*, however, can be understood as pure potential because it undergoes ceaseless transformation at several levels. Thus, of the twenty-five traditional *tattvas*, only these two are distinct. The remaining twenty-three are transformations or modifications of *mulaprakriti*. *Purusha* and *mulaprakriti* stand outside conceptual cognition, which arises within the flux of the other *tattvas*. They abide outside space and time, are simple, independent and inherently unchanging, and they have no relation to one another apart from their universal, simultaneous and mutual presence.

Mulaprakriti is characterized by three qualities or *gunas: sattva* or intelligent and noetic activity, *rajas* or passionate and compulsive activity, and *tamas* or ignorant and impotent lethargy, represented in the Upanishads by the colours white, red and black. If *mulaprakriti* were the only ultimate reality, its qualities would have forever remained in a homogeneous balance, without undergoing change, evolution or transformation. Since *purusha* is co-present with *mulaprakriti*, the symmetrical homogeneity of *mulaprakriti* was disturbed, and this broken symmetry resulted in a progressive differentiation which became the world of ordinary experience. True knowledge or pure cognition demands a return to that primordial stillness which marks the utter disentanglement of Self from non-self. The process which moved the *gunas* out of their perfect mutual balance cannot be described or even alluded to through analogies, in part because the process occurred outside space and time (and gave rise to them), and in part because no description of what initiated this universal transformation can be given in the language of logically subsequent and therefore necessarily less universal change. In other words, all transformation known to the intellect occurs in some context — minimally that of the intellect itself — whilst the primordial process of transformation occurred out of all context, save for the mere co-presence of *purusha* and *mulaprakriti*.

This imbalance gave rise, first of all, logically speaking, to *mahat* or *buddhi*. These terms refer to universal consciousness, primordial consciousness or intellect in the classical and neo-Platonic sense of the word. *Mahat* in turn gave rise to *ahankara,* the sense of 'I' or egoity. (*Ahankara* literally means 'I-making'.) Egoity as a principle or *tattva* generated a host of offspring or evolutes, the first of which was *Manas* or mind, which is both the capacity for sensation and the mental ability to act, or intellectual volition. It also produced the five *buddhindriyas* or capacities for sensation: *shrota* (hearing), *tvac* (touching), *chaksus* (seeing), *rasana* (tasting) and *ghrana* (smelling). In addition to sensation, *ahankara* gave rise to their dynamic and material correlates, the five *karmendriyas* or capacities for action, and the five *tanmatras* or subtle elements. The five *karmendriyas* are *vach* (speaking), *pani* (grasping), *pada* (moving), *payu* (eliminating) and *upastha* (procreating), whilst the five *tanmatras* include *shabda* (sound), *sparsha* (touch), *rupa* (form), *rasa* (taste) and *gandha* (smell). The *tanmatras* are called 'subtle' because they produce the *mahabhutas* or gross elements which can be perceived by ordinary human beings. They are *akasha* (aether or empirical space), *vayu* (air), *tejas* (fire, and by extension, light), *ap* (water) and *prithivi* (earth).

This seemingly elaborate system of the elements of existence (*tattvas*) is a rigorous attempt to reduce the kaleidoscope of reality to its simplest comprehensible components, without either engaging in a reductionism which explains away or denies what does not fit its classification, or falling prey to a facile monism which avoids a serious examination of visible and invisible Nature. Throughout the long history of Sankhya thought, enumerations have varied, but this general classification has held firm. Whilst some philosophers have suggested alternative orders of evolution, for instance, making the subtle elements give rise to the capacities for sensation and action, Ishvarakrishna expressed the classical consensus in offering this classification of twenty-five *tattvas.*

Once the fundamental enumeration was understood, Sankhya thinkers arranged the *tattvas* by sets to grasp more clearly their relationships to one another. At the most general level, *purusha* is neither generated nor generating, whilst *mulaprakriti* is ungenerated but generating. *Buddhi, ahankara* and the *tanmatras* are both generated and generating, and *manas,* the *buddhindriyas, karmendriyas* and *mahabhutas* are generated and do not generate anything in turn. In terms of their mutual relationships, one can speak of kinds of *tattvas* and indicate an order of dependence from the standpoint of the material world.

No matter how subtle and elaborate the analysis, however, one has at best described ways in which consciousness functions in *prakriti*, the material world. If one affirms that *purusha* and *prakriti* are radically and fundamentally separate, one cannot avoid the challenge which vexed Descartes: how can *res cogitans*, thinking substance, be in any way connected with *res extensa*, extended (material) substance? Sankhya avoided the most fundamental problem of Cartesian dualism by willingly admitting that there can be no connection, linkage or interaction between *purusha* and *prakriti*. Since consciousness is a fact, this exceptional claim involved a redefinition of consciousness itself. Consciousness is necessarily transcendent, unconnected with *prakriti*, and therefore it can have neither cognitive nor intuitive awareness, since those are activities which involve some centre or egoity and surrounding field from which it separates itself or with which it identifies. Egoity or perspective requires some mode of action, and all action involves the *gunas*, which belong exclusively to *prakriti*. Consciousness, *purusha*, is mere presence, *sakshitva*, without action, dynamics or content. Awareness, *chittavritti*, is therefore a function of *prakriti*, even though it would not have come into being — any more than anything would have evolved or the *gunas* would have become unstable — without the universal presence of *purusha*. Thus it is said that *purusha* is unique in that it is neither generated nor generating, whereas all other *tattvas* are either generating, generated or both.

In this view, mind is material. Given its capacity for awareness, it can intuit the presence of *purusha*, but it is not that *purusha*. All mental functions are part of the complex activity of *prakriti*. Consciousness is bare subjectivity without a shadow of objective content, and it cannot be said to have goals, desires or intentions. *Purusha* can be said to exist *(sat)* — indeed, it necessarily exists — and its essential and sole specifiable nature is *chit*, consciousness.

Unlike the Vedantin *Atman,* however, it cannot also be said to be *ananda,* bliss, for *purusha* is the pure witness, *sakshi,* with no causal connection to or participation in *prakriti.* Yet it is necessary, for the *gunas* could not be said to be active save in the presence of some principle of sentience. Without *purusha* there could be no *prakriti.* This is not the simple idealistic and phenomenological standpoint summarized in Berkeley's famous dictum, *esse est percipi,* "to be is to be perceived". Rather, it is closer to the recognition grounded in Newtonian mechanics that, should the universe achieve a condition of total entropy, it could not be said to exist, for there would be no possibility of differentiation in it. Nor could its existence be denied. The presence of *purusha,* according to Sankhya, is as necessary as is its utter lack of content.

Given the distinction between unqualified, unmodified subjectivity as true or pure consciousness, and awareness, which is the qualified appearance of consciousness in the world, consciousness appears as what it cannot be. It appears to cause and initiate, but cannot do so, since *purusha* cannot be said to be active in any sense; it appears to entertain ideas and chains of thought, but it can in reality do neither. Rather, the action of the *gunas* appears as the activity of consciousness until the actual nature of consciousness is realized. The extreme break with previous understanding resulting from this realization — that consciousness has no content and that content is not conscious — is emancipation, the freeing of *purusha* from false bondage to *prakriti.* It is akin to the Vedantin realization of *Atman* free of any taint of *maya,* and the Buddhist realization of *shunyata.* Philosophical conceptualization is incapable of describing this realization, for pure consciousness can only appear, even to the subtlest cognitive understanding, as nothing. For Sankhya, *purusha* is not nothing, but it is nothing that partakes of *prakriti* (which all awareness does).

Sankhya's unusual distinction between consciousness and what are ordinarily considered its functions and contents implies an operational view of *purusha.* Even though no properties can be predicated of *purusha*, the mind or intellect intuits the necessity of consciousness behind it, as it were. That is, the mind becomes aware that it is not itself pure consciousness. Since this awareness arises in individual minds, *purusha* is recognized by one or another egoity. Without being able to attribute qualities to *purusha*, it must therefore be treated philosophically as a plurality. Hence it is said that there are literally innumerable *purushas*, none of which have any distinguishing characteristics. The Leibnizian law of the identity of indiscernibles cannot be applied to *purusha*, despite the philosophical temptation to do so, precisely because philosophy necessarily stops at the limit of *prakriti*. *Purusha* is outside space and time, and so is also beyond space-time identities. Since the minimum requirements of differentiation involve at least an indirect reference to either space or time, their negation in the concept of indiscernibility also involves such a reference, and cannot be applied to *purusha*. Even though Sankhya affirms a plurality of *purushas*, this stance is less the result of metaphysical certitude than of the limitations imposed by consistency of method. The plurality of *purushas* is the consequence of the limits of understanding.

Within the enormous and diverse history of Indian thought, the six *darshanas* viewed themselves and one another in two ways. Internally, each standpoint sought clarity, completeness and consistency without reference to other *darshanas*. Since, however, the *darshanas* were committed to the proposition that they were six separate and viable perspectives on the same reality, they readily drew upon one another's insights and terminology and forged mutually dependent relationships. They were less concerned with declaring one another true or false than with understanding the value and limitations of each in respect to a complete realization of the ultimate and divine nature of things. Whilst some Western philosophers have pointed to the unprovable Indian presupposition that the heart of existence is divine, the *darshanas* reverse this standpoint by affirming that the core of reality is, almost definitionally, the only basis for thinking of the divine. In other words, reality is the criterion of the divine, and no other standard can make philosophical sense of the sacred, much less give it a practical place in human psychology and ethics. In their later developments, the *darshanas* strengthened their internal conceptual structures and ethical architectonics by taking one another's positions as foils for self-clarification. Earlier developments were absorbed into later understanding and exposition. Historically, Sankhya assimilated and redefined much of what had originally belonged to Nyaya and Vaishesika, and even Mimansa, only to find much of its terminology and psychology incorporated into Vedanta, the most trenchantly philosophical of the *darshanas*. At the same time, later Sankhya borrowed freely from Vedantin philosophical concepts to rethink its own philosophical difficulties.

Despite Sankhya's unique distinction between consciousness and awareness, which allowed it to preserve its fundamental dualism in the face of monistic arguments — and thereby avoid the metaphysical problems attending monistic views — it could not avoid one fundamental philosophical question: What is it to say that *prakriti* is dynamic because of the presence of *purusha*? To say that *prakriti* reflects the presence of *purusha*, or that *purusha* is reflected in *prakriti*, preserves a rigid distinction between the two, for neither an object reflected in a mirror nor the mirror is affected by the other. But Sankhya characterizes the ordinary human condition as one of suffering, which is the manifest expression of the condition of *avidya*, ignorance. This condition arises because *purusha* falsely identifies with *prakriti* and its evolutes. Liberation, *mukti*, is the result of *viveka*, discrimination, which is the highest knowledge. Even though *viveka* might be equated with pure perception as the *sakshi* or Witness, the process of attaining it suggests either an intention on the part of *purusha* or a response on the part of *prakriti*, if not both. How then can *purusha* be said to have no relation, including no passive relation, to *prakriti*? Even Ishvarakrishna's enchanting metaphor of the dancer before the host of spectators does not answer the question, for there is a significant relationship between performer and audience.

Such questions are worthy of notice but are misplaced from the Sankhya standpoint. If philosophical understanding is inherently limited to the functions of the mind (which is an evolute of *prakriti*), it can encompass neither total awareness (*purusha*) nor the fact that both *purusha* and *prakriti* exist. This is the supreme and unanswerable mystery of Sankhya philosophy, the point at which Sankhya declares that questions must have an end. It is not, however, an unaskable or meaningless question. If its answer cannot be found in philosophy, that is because it is dissolved in *mukti*, freedom from ignorance, through perfect *viveka*, discrimination. In Sankhya as in Vedanta, philosophy ends where realization begins. Philosophy does not resolve the ultimate questions, even though it brings great clarity to cognition. Philosophy prepares, refines and orients the mind towards a significantly different activity, broadly called 'meditation', the rigorous cultivation of clarity of discrimination and concentrated, pellucid insight. The possibility of this is provided for by Sankhya metaphysics through its stress on the asymmetry between *purusha* and *prakriti*, despite their co-presence. *Prakriti* depends on *purusha*, but *purusha* is independent of everything; *purusha* is pure consciousness, whilst *prakriti* is unself-conscious. *Prakriti* continues to evolve because individual selves in it do not realize that they are really *purusha* and, therefore, can separate themselves from *prakriti*, whilst there can never be complete annihilation of everything or of primordial matter.

Whereas Yoga accepted the postulates of Sankhya and also utilized its categories and classifications, all these being in accord with the experiences of developed *yogins*, there are significant divergences between Yoga and Sankhya. The oldest Yoga could have been agnostic in the sense implicit in the *Rig Veda* Hymn to Creation, but Patanjali's Yoga is distinctly theistic, diverging in this way from atheistic Sankhya. Whilst Sankhya is a speculative system, or at least a conceptual framework, Yoga is explicitly experiential and therefore linked to an established as well as evolving consensus among advanced *yogins*. This is both illustrated and reinforced by the fact that whereas Sankhya maps out the

inner world of disciplined ideation in terms of thirteen evolutes —
buddhi, ahankara, manas and the ten *indriyas* — Patanjali's Yoga
subsumes all these under *chitta* or consciousness, which is resilient,
elastic and dynamic, including the known, the conceivable, the
cosmic as well as the unknown. Whereas Sankhya is one of the
most self-sufficient or closed systems, Yoga retains, as a term and
in its philosophy, a conspicuously open texture which characterizes
all Indian thought at its best. From the Vedic hymns to even
contemporary discourse, it is always open-ended in reference to
cosmic and human evolution, degrees of adeptship and levels of
initiatory illumination. It is ever seeing, reaching and aspiring,
beyond the boundaries of the highest thought, volition and
feeling; beyond worlds and rationalist systems and doctrinaire
theologies; beyond the limits of inspired utterance as well as all
languages and all possible modes of creative expression.
Philosophy and mathematics, poetry and myth, idea and icon, are
all invaluable aids to the image-making faculty, but they all must
point beyond themselves, whilst they coalesce and collapse in the
unfathomable depths of the Ineffable, before which the best
minds and hearts must whisper *neti neti*, "not this, not that".
There is only the Soundless Sound, the ceaseless AUM in
Boundless Space and Eternal Duration.

PATANJALI'S
TARAKA RAJA YOGA

A lmost nothing is known about the sage who wrote the *Yoga Sutras*. The dating of his life has varied widely between the fourth century B.C.E. and the sixth century C.E., but the fourth century B.C.E. is the period noted for the appearance of aphoristic literature. Traditional Indian literature, especially the *Padma Purana,* includes brief references to Patanjali, indicating that he was born in Illavrita Varsha. Bharata Varsha is the ancient designation of Greater India as an integral part of Jambudvipa, the world as conceived in classical topography, but Illavrita Varsha is not one of its subdivisions. It is an exalted realm inhabited by the gods and enlightened beings who have transcended even the rarefied celestial regions encompassed by the sevenfold Jambudvipa. Patanjali is said to be the son of Angira and Sati, to have married Lolupa, whom he discovered in the hollow of a tree on the northern slope of Mount Sumeru, and to have reduced the degenerate denizens of Bhotabhandra to ashes with fire from his mouth. Such legendary details conceal more than they reveal and suggest that Patanjali was a great Rishi who descended to earth in order to share the fruits of his wisdom with those who were ready to receive it.

Some commentators identify the author of the *Yoga Sutras* with the Patanjali who wrote the *Mahabhashya* or *Great Commentary* on Panini's famous treatise on Sanskrit grammar sometime between the third and first centuries B.C.E. Although several scholars have contended that internal evidence contradicts such an identification, others have not found this reasoning conclusive. King Bhoja, who wrote a well-known commentary in the tenth century, was inclined to ascribe both works to a single author, perhaps partly as a reaction to others who placed Patanjali several centuries C.E. owing to his alleged implicit criticisms of late Buddhist doctrines. A more venerable tradition, however, rejects this identification altogether and holds that the author of the *Yoga Sutras* lived long before the commentator on Panini. In this view, oblique references to Buddhist doctrines are actually allusions to modes of thought found in some Upanishads.

In addition to our lack of definite knowledge about Patanjali's life, confusion arises from contrasting appraisals of the *Yoga Sutras* itself. There is a strong consensus that the *Yoga Sutras* represents a masterly compendium of various Yoga practices which can be traced back through the Upanishads to the Vedas. Many forms of Yoga existed by the time this treatise was written, and Patanjali came at the end of a long and ancient line of *yogins*. In accord with the free-thinking tradition of *shramanas*, forest recluses and wandering mendicants, the ultimate vindication of the Yoga system is to be found in the lifelong experiences of its ardent votaries and exemplars. The *Yoga Sutras* constitutes a practitioner's manual, and has long been cherished as the pristine expression of Raja Yoga. The basic texts of Raja Yoga are Patanjali's *Yoga Sutras*, the *Yogabhashya* of Vyasa and the *Tattvavaisharadi* of Vachaspati Mishra. Hatha Yoga was formulated by Gorakshanatha, who lived around 1200 C.E. The main texts of this school are the *Goraksha Sutaka*, the *Hathayoga Pradipika* of Yogindra of the fifteenth century, and the later *Shivasamhita*. Whereas Hatha Yoga stresses breath regulation and bodily discipline, Raja Yoga is essentially concerned with mind control, meditation and self-study.

The *Yoga Sutras* of Patanjali is universal in the manner of the *Bhagavad Gita*, including a diversity of standpoints whilst fusing Sankhya metaphysics with *bhakti* or self-surrender. There is room for differences of emphasis, but every diligent user of Patanjali's aphorisms is enabled to refine aspirations, clarify thoughts, strengthen efforts, and sharpen focus on essentials in spiritual self-discipline. Accommodating a variety of exercises — mind control, visualization, breath, posture, moral training — Patanjali brings together the best in differing approaches, providing an integrated discipline marked by moderation, flexibility and balance, as well as degrees of depth in meditative absorption. The text eludes any simple classification within the vast resources of Indian sacred literature and *a fortiori* among the manifold scriptures of the world. Although it does not resist philosophical analysis in the way many mystical treatises do, it is primarily a practical aid to the quest for spiritual freedom, which transcends the concerns of theoretical clarification. Yet like any arcane science which necessarily pushes beyond the shifting boundaries of sensory experience, beyond conventional concepts of inductive reasoning and mundane reality, it reaffirms at every point its vital connection with the universal search for meaning and deliverance from bondage to shared illusions. It is a summons to systematic self-mastery which can aspire to the summits of gnosis.

The actual text as it has come down to the present may not be exactly what Patanjali penned. Perhaps he reformulated in terse aphoristic language crucial insights found in time-honoured but long-forgotten texts. Perhaps he borrowed terms and phrases from diverse schools of thought and training. References to breath control, *pranayama.* can be found in the oldest Upanishads, and the lineaments of systems of Yoga may be discerned in the *Maitrayana, Shvetashvatara* and *Katha Upanishads,* and veiled instructions are given in the 'Yoga' Upanishads — *Yogatattva, Dhyanabindu, Hamsa, Amritanada, Shandilya, Varaha, Mandala Brahmana, Nadabindu* and *Yogakundali* — though a leaning towards Sankhya metaphysics occurs only in the *Maitrayana.* The *Mahabharata* mentions the Sankhya and the Yoga as ancient systems of thought. Hiranyagarbha is traditionally regarded as the propounder of Yoga, just as Kapila is known as the original expounder of Sankhya. The *Ahirbudhnya* states that Hiranyagarbha disclosed the entire science of Yoga in two texts — the *Nirodha Samhita* and the *Karma Samhita.* The former treatise has been called the *Yoganushasanam,* and Patanjali also begins his work with the same term. He also stresses *nirodha* in the first section of his work.

In general, the affinities of the *Yoga Sutras* with the texts of Hiranyagarbha suggest that Patanjali was an adherent of the Hiranyagarbha school of Yoga, and yet his own manner of treatment of the subject is distinctive. His reliance upon the fundamental principles of Sankhya entitle him to be considered as also belonging to the Sankhya Yoga school. On the other hand, the significant variations of the later Sankhya of Ishvarakrishna from older traditions of proto-Sankhya point to the advantage of not subsuming the *Yoga Sutras* under broader systems. The author of *Yuktidipika* stresses that for Patanjali there are twelve capacities, unlike Ishvarakrishna's thirteen, that egoity is not a separate principle for Patanjali but is bound up with intellect and volition. Furthermore, Patanjali held that the subtle body is created anew with each embodiment and lasts only as long as a particular embodiment, and also that the capacities can only function from within. Altogether, Patanjali's work provides a unique synthesis of standpoints and is backed by the testimony of the accumulated wisdom derived from the experiences of many practitioners and earlier lineages of teachers.

Some scholars and commentators have speculated that Patanjali wrote only the first three *padas* of the *Yoga Sutras,* whilst the exceptionally short fourth *pada* was added later. Indeed, as early as the writings of King Bhoja, one verse in the fourth *pada* (IV. 16) was recognized as a line interpolated from Vyasa's seventh commentary in which he dissented from Vijnanavadin Buddhists. Other interpolations may have occurred even in the first three *padas,* such as III.22, which some classical commentators questioned. The fact that the third *pada* ends with the word *iti* ('thus', 'so', usually indicating the end of a text), as it does at the end of the fourth *pada,* might suggest that the original contained only three books. However, the philosophical significance of the fourth *pada* is such that the coherence of the entire text need not be questioned on the basis of inconclusive speculations.

Al-Biruni translated into Arabic a book he called *Kitab Patanjal (The Book of Patanjali),* which he said was famous throughout India. Although his text has an aim similar to the *Yoga Sutras* and uses many of the same concepts, it is more theistic in its content and even has a slightly Sufi tone. It is not the text now known as the *Yoga Sutras,* but it may be a kind of paraphrase popular at the time, rather like the *Dnyaneshwari,* which stands both as an independent work and a helpful restatement of the *Bhagavad Gita*. The *Kitab* translated by al-Biruni illustrates the pervasive influence of Patanjali's work throughout the Indian subcontinent.

For the practical aspirant to inner tranquillity and spiritual realization, the recurring speculations of scholars and commentators, stimulated by the lack of exact historical information about the author and the text, are of secondary value. Whatever the precise details regarding the composition of the treatise as it has come down through the centuries, it is clearly an integrated whole, every verse of which is helpful not only for theoretical understanding but also for sustained practice. The *Yoga Sutras* constitutes a complete text on meditation and is invaluable in that every *sutra* demands deep reflection and repeated application. Patanjali advocated less a doctrinaire method than a generous framework with which one can make experiments with truth, grow in comprehension and initiate progressive awakenings to the supernal reality of the Logos in the cosmos.

The word *yoga* is derived from the Sanskrit verbal root *yuj*, 'to yoke' or 'to join', related to the Latin *jungere*, 'to join', 'to unite'. In its broadest usages it can mean addition in arithmetic; in astronomy it refers to the conjunction of stars and planets; in grammar it is the joining of letters and words. In Mimamsa philosophy it indicates the force of a sentence made up of united words, whilst in Nyaya logic it signifies the power of the parts taken together. In medicine it denotes the compounding of herbs and other substances. In general, *yoga* and *viyoga* pertain to the processes of synthesis and analysis in both theoretical and applied sciences. Panini distinguishes between the root *yuj* in the sense of concentration *(samadhi)* and *yujir* in the sense of joining or connecting. Buddhists have used the term *yoga* to designate the withdrawal of the mind from all mental and sensory objects. Vaishesika philosophy means by *yoga* the concentrated attention to a single subject through mental abstraction from all contexts. Whereas the followers of Ramanuja use the term to depict the fervent aspiration to join one's *ishtadeva* or chosen deity, Vedanta chiefly uses the term to characterize the complete union of the human soul with the divine spirit, a connotation compatible with its use in Yoga philosophy. In addition, Patanjali uses the term *yoga* to refer to the deliberate cessation of all mental modifications.

Every method of self-mastery, the systematic removal of ignorance and the progressive realization of Truth, can be called *yoga*, but in its deepest sense it signifies the union of one's apparent and fugitive self with one's essential nature and true being, or the conscious union of the embodied self with the Supreme Spirit. The *Maitrayana Upanishad* states:

> Carried along by the waves of the qualities darkened in his imagination, unstable, fickle, crippled, full of desires, vacillating, he enters into belief, believing I am he, this is mine, and he binds his self by his self as a bird with a net. Therefore a man, being possessed of will, imagination and belief, is a slave, but he who is the opposite is free. For this reason let a man stand free from will, imagination and belief. This is the sign of liberty, this is the path that leads to *brahman*, this is the opening of the door, and through it he will go to the other shore of darkness.

Thus, *yoga* refers to the removal of bondage and the consequent attainment of true spiritual freedom. Whenever yoga goes beyond this and actually implies the fusion of an individual with his ideal, whether viewed as his real nature, his true self or the universal spirit, it is gnostic self-realization and universal self-consciousness, a self-sustaining state of serene enlightenment. Patanjali's metaphysical and epistemological debt to Sankhya is crucial to a proper comprehension of the *Yoga Sutras*, but his distinct stress on *praxis* rather than *theoria* shows a deep insight of his own into the phases and problems that are encountered by earnest practitioners of Yoga. His chief concern was to show how and by what means the spirit, trammelled in the world of matter, can withdraw completely from it and attain total emancipation by transforming matter into its original state and thus realize its own pristine nature. This applies at all levels of self-awakening, from the initial cessation of mental modifications, through degrees of meditative absorption, to the climactic experience of spiritual freedom.

Patanjali organized the *Yoga Sutras* into four *padas* or books which suggest his architectonic intent. Samadhi Pada, the first book, deals with concentration of mind *(samadhi)*, without which no serious practice of Yoga is possible. Since *samadhi* is necessarily experiential, this *pada* explores the hindrances to and the practical steps needed to achieve alert quietude. Both restraint of the senses and of the discursive intellect are essential for *samadhi*. Having set forth what must be done to attain and maintain meditative absorption, the second book, Sadhana Pada, provides the method or means required to establish full concentration. Any effort to subdue the tendency of the mind to become diffuse, fragmented or agitated demands a resolute, consistent and continuous practice of self-imposed, steadfast restraint, *tapas*, which cannot become stable without a commensurate disinterest in all phenomena. This relaxed disinterestedness, *vairagya*, has nothing to do with passive indifference, positive disgust, inert apathy or feeble-minded *ennui* as often experienced in the midst of desperation and tension in daily affairs. Those are really the self-protective responses of one who is captive to the pleasure-pain principle and is deeply vulnerable to the flux of events and the vicissitudes of fortune. *Vairagya* implies a conscious transcendence of the pleasure-pain principle through a radical reappraisal of expectations, memories and habits. The pleasure-pain principle, dependent upon passivity, ignorance and servility for its operation, is replaced by a reality principle rooted in an active, noetic apprehension of psycho-spiritual causation. Only when this impersonal perspective is gained can the *yogin* safely begin to alter significantly his psycho-physical nature through breath control, *pranayama*, and other exercises.

The third book, Vibhuti Pada, considers complete meditative absorption, *sanyama*, its characteristics and consequences. Once calm, continuous attention is mastered, one can discover an even more transcendent mode of meditation which has no object of cognition whatsoever. Since levels of consciousness correspond to planes of being, to step behind the uttermost veil of consciousness is also to rise above all manifestations of matter. From that wholly transcendent standpoint beyond the ever-changing contrast between spirit and matter, one may choose any conceivable state of consciousness and, by implication, any possible material condition. Now the *yogin* becomes capable of tapping all the *siddhis* or theurgic powers. These prodigious mental and moral feats are indeed magical, although there is nothing miraculous or even supernatural about them. They represent the refined capacities and exalted abilities of the perfected human being. Just as any person who has achieved proficiency in some specialized skill or knowledge should be careful to use it wisely and precisely, so too the *yogin* whose spiritual and mental powers may seem practically unlimited must not waste his energy or misuse his hard-won gifts. If he were to do so, he would risk getting entangled in worldly concerns in the myriad ways from which he had sought to free himself. Instead, the mind must be merged into the inmost spirit, the result of which is *kaivalya*, steadfast isolation or eventual emancipation from the bonds of illusion and the meretricious glamour of terrestrial existence.

In Kaivalya Pada, the fourth book which crowns the *Yoga Sutras*, Patanjali conveys the true nature of isolation or supreme spiritual freedom insofar as it is possible to do so in words. Since *kaivalya* is the term used for the sublime state of consciousness in which the enlightened soul has gone beyond the differentiating sense of 'I am', it cannot be characterized in the conceptual languages that are dependent on the subject-object distinction. Isolation is not nothingness, nor is it a static condition. Patanjali throws light on this state of gnosis by providing a metaphysical and metapsychological explanation of cosmic and human intellection, the operation of karma and the deep-seated persistence of the tendency of self-limitation. By showing how the suppression of modifications of consciousness can enable it to realize its true nature as pure potential and master the lessons of manifested Nature, he intimates the immense potency of the highest meditations and the inscrutable purpose of cosmic selfhood.

The metapsychology of the *Yoga Sutras* bridges complex metaphysics and compelling ethics, creative transcendence and critical immanence, in an original, inspiring and penetrating style, whilst its aphoristic method leaves much unsaid, throwing aspirants back upon themselves with a powerful stimulus to self-testing and self- discovery. Despite his sophisticated use of Sankhya concepts and presuppositions, Patanjali's text has a universal appeal for all ardent aspirants to Raja Yoga. He conveys the vast spectrum of consciousness, diagnoses the common predicament of human bondage to mental ailments, and offers practical guidance on the arduous pathway of lifelong contemplation that could lead to the summit of self-mastery and spiritual freedom.

SAMADHI PADA

Through study let one practise yoga,
Through yoga *let one concentrate on study.*
By perfection in study and in yoga
The Supreme Soul shines forth clearly.

VYASA

The classic text of Patanjali opens with the simplest statement: *"atha yoganushasanam*," "Now begins instruction in yoga." The typical reader today might well expect this terse announcement to be followed by a full explanation of the term *yoga* and its diverse meanings, perhaps a polemical digression on different schools of thought and some methodological guidance concerning the best way to use the text. None of this occurs. Rather, Patanjali set down his most famous words: *"yogash chitta-vritti-nirodhah*," "*Yoga* is the restraint of the modifications of the mind." He stated the essential meaning of yoga without any argument or illustration, as if he were providing a basic axiom. He thus showed at the very start that he was concerned with practical instruction rather than theoretical exposition. He thereby took for granted that the user of the text already had some understanding of the task of yoga and was ready to undergo a demanding daily discipline.

Yoga psychology differs radically from more recent, and especially post-Freudian, schools of thought in its stress on self-emancipation rather than on self-acceptance in relation to social norms or psychic tensions. Most modern varieties of psychology, including even the recent humanistic preoccupation with self-actualization as propounded by Abraham Maslow and elaborated in different directions by Carl Rogers and Rollo May, essentially aim at an integration and harmonizing of otherwise disparate and conflicting elements in a person in contemporary society. For Patanjali, all these identifiable elements — thoughts, feelings, intentions, motives and desires (conscious and unconscious) — are *chittavrittis*, mental modifications which must be seen as hindrances to contemplative calm. Even if they are deftly balanced and fully integrated, the individual would at best be a mature person marked by thoughtful and creative responses in a world of suffering and ignorance. Conquering, not coping, transcending, not reconciling, were Patanjali's chief concerns. For him, the latter were by-products of the former, and never the reverse. The psychology of self-emancipation means the deliberate and self-conscious restraint of everything that is productive of mental confusion, weakness and pain.

Patanjali's stipulative definition of yoga might seem dogmatic, but this reaction springs from ignorance of his central purpose and unstated presuppositions. Patanjali wrote not from the standpoint of revealed scripture, academic scholarship or of theoretical clarification, but from the standpoint of concrete experience through controlled experiment. If truth is ontologically bound up and intimately fused with self-transcendence, then what from the standpoint of self-emancipation is a stark description is, from the standpoint of the unenlightened, an arbitrary prescription. What would be the naturalistic fallacy on a single plane of manifested Nature becomes a necessary line of thought when multiple planes of unmanifested Nature are taken into account. The ability to alter states of consciousness presupposes the capacity to emulate the architectonics of a higher and less differentiated plane on a lower and more fragmented plane of percepts and concepts. In other words, yoga is that science in which the descriptions of reality necessarily function as prescriptions for those who have not experienced it. The analogy would be closer to music or mathematics than to the visual arts or the empirical sciences as normally understood.

Skilful methods are those which provide apt descriptions, giving the instructional guidance needed. Hence, in the hands of a spiritual master, the actual method to be pursued varies with each aspirant, for it is the vital and original link between the adept's transcendent *(taraka)* wisdom and the disciple's mental temperament and devotion (*bhakti*). There is a reciprocal interaction between the readiness to receive and the mode of giving — of disciple and master. For Patanjali, the true nature of *chitta*, the mind, can be known only when it is not modified by external influences and their internal impresses. For as long as modifications persist without being deliberately chosen for a purpose, the mind unwittingly identifies with them, falling into passivity, habitude, and the pain which results from a state of fragmentation and self-alienation.

Since mental modifications ramify in myriad directions, their root causes need to be grasped clearly if they are to be firmly removed. The essential principle to be understood is central to the second and third of Gautama Buddha's Four Noble Truths. Those persistent misconceptions which, directly or indirectly, produce discontent and suffering have a distinctive set of causes which, if eliminated, inevitably ensure the cessation of their concomitant effects. Patanjali pointed to five *chittavrittis* which are distinct and yet share the common tendency to be pleasurable or painful. Whilst yoga psychology fully acknowledges the strength of the pleasure principle — the propensity to be drawn towards pleasurable sensations as if by a magnet and to be repelled by painful ones — it denies its relevance to real individuation as a moral agent, a Manushya whose name comes from *manas*, 'mind', the root of which is *man*, 'to think'. Self-emancipation, the culmination in yoga of self-transcendence, requires the complete subordination of the pleasure-pain principle to the reality principle. Reality, in this view, has nothing to do with involuntary change, the inherent propensity of *prakriti*, matter, and not *purusha*, spirit, whilst pleasure and pain are necessarily bound up with conditioning and change. This is why the most attractive states of mind seem so readily and recurrently to alter into the most repugnant states. In general, mental modifications obscure and obstruct the intrinsically blissful nature of pure consciousness, the serene state of mind of the "spectator without a spectacle".

The five types of mental modifications are: *correct cognition*, based on direct perception, valid inference and verbal testimony;

misconception, based upon something other than itself, namely the five *kleshas* or sources of sorrow — ignorance, egoism, attachment, hate and the fear of death, according to the *Yogabhashya*; *fantasy,* engendered by words and concepts, when and to the degree that they do not refer to reality; *sleep,* which occurs when other modifications cease and the mind is emptied of mental contents; and *memory,* which is the result of clinging to, or at least not letting go of, objects or images of subjective experiences. The *chittavrittis* can be diagrammatically depicted as follows:

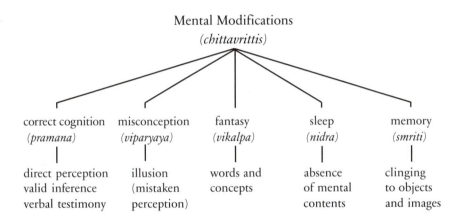

Mental Modifications (*chittavrittis*)				
correct cognition (*pramana*)	misconception (*viparyaya*)	fantasy (*vikalpa*)	sleep (*nidra*)	memory (*smriti*)
direct perception valid inference verbal testimony	illusion (mistaken perception)	words and concepts	absence of mental contents	clinging to objects and images

Although this array of mental modifications is easy to outline, its implications are extensive and radical. When Patanjali included correct cognition amongst the mental modifications, he was adhering to strict theoretical and practical consistency. He was concerned to deny that mundane insight, discursive thought and even scriptural authority can free the mind from bondage to delusion and suffering. Yet without a preliminary apprehension of yoga philosophy, how could one adopt its methods and hope to achieve its aims?

In part the answer lies in a proper grasp of the pervasiveness of *maya* or illusion. If everything that conceals the changeless Real is *maya,* then the human being who seeks to know the Real by conventional methods is trapped in some sort of metaphysical split or even schizophrenia. Philosophers from the pre-Socratics and Platonists to Descartes and Spinoza recognized that a substance cannot become what it is not. To say that human beings are intrinsically capable of attaining *kaivalya*, self-emancipation or transcendence of *maya*, is to affirm that they are quintessentially what they seek. Their inmost nature is one with the Real. On the other hand, to say that they have to strive in earnest to realize fully what they essentially are implies that they have allowed themselves to become captive to *maya* through persistent self-limitation.

Given this delusive condition, the mere temporary cessation of modifications, such as occurs in sleep, will not help to liberate man's immortal spirit. As *maya* is pervasive illusion, humanity as it knows itself is a part of it. Ignorant or involuntary withdrawal from its action only makes it unconscious, and this is why sleep is classed as one of the *chittavrittis*. Rather, one has to master the rules of *maya* and learn how to extricate oneself gradually from it. Otherwise, one only makes random moves, embedding oneself in deeper ignorance and greater suffering. Patanjali taught that deliverance can only come through *abhyasa*, assiduous practice, and *vairagya*, dispassionate detachment. *Abhyasa* is the active opposite of passive sleep, and *vairagya* frees one from all attachments, including the *kleshas*, which induce misconceptions. Together, these two mirror in the world of change that which is changeless beyond it. In the language of the *Isha Upanishad*, one has to find the transcendent in the immanent, and for Patanjali, *abhyasa* and *vairagya* constitute exactly that mode of awareness.

For Patanjali, however, *abhyasa* is not just striving to *do* something; it is rather the effort to *be* something. "*Abhyasa* is the continuous effort to abide in a steady state." According to the *Yogabhashya*, *abhyasa* is the attempt to preserve *prashantavahita*, continuity of mind or consciousness which is both fully awake and without fluctuations. Like all such spiritual exercises, *abhyasa* becomes richer, more refined and more relaxed with persistence that comes from repeated effort, moral earnestness and joyous devotion. *Abhyasa* is the constant criterion for all effort, and the indispensable tool, whenever and however taken up.

Vairagya cannot be merely passive disinterest in the content of experience any more than sleep can substitute for wakeful serenity. It is true detachment whilst being fully aware of the relative significance of objects, and this element of self-conscious maintenance of calm detachment is exactly what makes it real *vairagya*. Through *vairagya*, one comes to know the world for what it is because one recognizes that every object of sense, whether seen or unseen, is an assemblage of evanescent attributes or qualities *(gunas)* of *prakriti*, whereas the enduring reality, from the standpoint of the seeker for emancipation, is *purusha*, the Self of all. Shankaracharya stated: "The seer of *purusha* becomes one who is freed from rejecting or accepting anything. . . . Detachment is extreme clarity of cognition."

Abhyasa and *vairagya* are fused in the intense yet serene mental absorption known as *samadhi*. Patanjali characterized *samadhi* (which means 'concentration', 'contemplation' and 'meditation', depending on the context) in relation to a succession of stages, for if *samadhi* signifies a specific state, the contemplative seeker would either abide in it or fail to do so. But Patanjali knew that no one can suddenly bridge the gap between fragmented, distracted consciousness and wholly unified meditation. Rather, concentration *(samadhi)* proceeds by degrees for one who persists in the effort, because one progressively overcomes everything that hinders it. In the arduous ascent from greater degrees of relative *maya* towards greater degrees of reality, the transformation of consciousness requires a calm apprehension of those higher states. The conscious descent from exalted planes of being requires the capacity to bring down a clearer awareness of reality into the grosser regions of *maya*. Continuous self-transformation on the ascent must be converted into confident self-transmutation on the descent.

Patanjali saw in the evolving process of meditation several broad but distinct levels of *samadhi*. The first is *sanprajnata samadhi*, cognitive contemplation, in which the meditator is aware of a distinction between himself and the thought he entertains. This form of meditation is also called *sabija samadhi,* or meditation with a seed *(bija)* wherein some object or specific theme serves as a focal point on which to settle the mind in a steady state. Since such a point is extrinsic to pure consciousness, the basic distinction between thinker and thought persists. In its least abstracted form, *sanprajnata samadhi* involves *vitarka* (reasoning), *vichara* (deliberation), *ananda* (bliss) and *asmita* (the sense of 'I'). Meditation is some sort of *bhavana,* or becoming that upon which one ponders, for consciousness identifies with, takes on and virtually becomes what it contemplates. Meditation on a seed passes through stages in which these types of conditioning recede and vanish as the focal point of consciousness passes beyond every kind of deliberation and even bliss itself, until only *asmita* or the pure sense of 'I' remains. Even this, however, is a limiting focus which can be transcended.

Asanprajnata samadhi arises out of meditation on a seed though it is itself seedless. Here supreme detachment frees one from even the subtlest cognition and one enters *nirbija samadhi,* meditation without a seed, which is self-sustaining because free of any supporting focalization on an object. From the standpoint of the succession of objects of thought — the type of consciousness all human beings experience in a chaotic or fragmentary way and a few encounter even in meditation on a seed — *nirbija samadhi* is non-existence or emptiness, for it is absolutely quiescent consciousness. Nonetheless, it is not the highest consciousness attainable, for it is the retreat of mind to a neutral *(laya)* centre from which it can begin to operate on a wholly different plane of being. This elevated form of pure consciousness is similar to a state experienced in a disembodied condition between death and rebirth, when consciousness is free of the involvement with vestures needed for manifestation in differentiated matter. Just as an individual becomes unconscious when falling into deep dreamless sleep, because consciousness fails to remain alert except in conditions of differentiation, so too consciousness in a body becomes unconscious and forgetful of its intrinsic nature on higher planes. *Samadhi* aims to restore that essential awareness self-consciously, making the alert meditator capable of altering planes of consciousness without any loss of awareness.

For earnest practitioners, Patanjali taught, *samadhi* is attained in several distinct but interrelated ways — through *shraddha* (faith), *virya* (energy), *smriti* (retentiveness) and *prajna* (intellectual insight) — which are vital prerequisites for the meta-psychological yoga of *samadhi*. *Shraddha* is the calm and confident conviction that yoga is efficacious, coupled with the wholehearted orientation of one's psychic, moral and mental nature towards experiential confirmation. Undistracted *shraddha* of this sort leads naturally to *virya*, energy which releases the resolve to reach the goal and the resourceful courage needed to persist in seeking it. In *The Voice of the Silence*, an ancient text of spiritual discipline, *virya* is viewed as the fifth of seven keys required to unlock seven portals on the path to wisdom. In this text, *virya* follows upon *dana, shila, kshanti* and *viraga* (*vairagya*) — charity, harmony in conduct, patience, and detachment in regard to the fruits of action — all suggesting the hidden depths of *shraddha* which can release dauntless energy in the pursuit of Truth.

Smriti implies the refinement of memory which helps to extract the essential lesson of each experience without the needless elaboration of irrelevancies. It requires the perception of significant connections and the summoning of full recollection, the soul-memory stressed by Plato wherein one awakens powers and potentialities transcending the experiences of a lifetime. *Prajna*, released by such inner awakenings, enables consciousness to turn within and cognize the deeper layers of oneself. Seen and strengthened in this manner, one's innate soul-wisdom becomes the basis of one's progressive understanding of the integral connection between freedom and necessity. In time, the 'is' of external facticity becomes a vital pointer to the 'ought' of the spiritual Path and the 'can' of one's true selfhood.

Supreme meditation, the most complete *samadhi*, is possible for those who can bring clarity, control and imaginative intensity to daily practice. Yet Patanjali's instructions, like those of an athletic coach who guides the gifted but also aids those who show lesser promise, apply to every seeker who sincerely strives to make a modest beginning in the direction of the highest *samadhi* as well as to those able to make its attainment the constant target of their contemplations. He spoke explicitly of those whose progress is rapid but also of those whose efforts are mild or moderate. An individual's strivings are stimulated to the degree they recognize that they are ever reaching beyond themselves as they have come to think of themselves through habit, convention, weakness and every form of ignorance. Rather than naïvely thinking that one is suddenly going to surmount every obstacle and obscuration in one's own nature, one can sedulously foster *bhakti*, total devotion and willing surrender to Ishvara, the Supreme Spirit immanent in all souls, even if one has hardly begun to grasp one's true self-hood. Such sustained devotion is *ishvarapranidhana*, the potent invocation of the Supreme Self through persistent surrender to It, isomorphic on the plane of consciousness with abnegation of the fruits of all acts to Krishna on the plane of conduct, as taught in the *Bhagavad Gita*.

Ishvara is *saguna brahman*, the supreme repository of all resplendent qualities, in contrast to *nirguna brahman*, the attributeless Absolute. Ishvara is *purusha*, "untouched by troubles, actions and their results" (I.24), immanent in all *prakriti*. Cherishing the one source of all is the means by which one moves through degrees of *samadhi*, culminating in the complete union of the individual and the cosmic, the state of *kaivalya* or isolation. Like Kether, the crown in the Kabbalah, Ishvara is at once the single motivating force behind the cosmic activity of *prakriti* and the utterly transcendent *(nirguna) purusha* or pure spirit. What exists in each human soul as the latent bud of omniscience is awakened and it expands into the realm of infinitude in Ishvara itself. Untouched by time and therefore untrammelled by ordinary consciousness which is time-bound, Ishvara is the supreme Initiator of all, from the ancient Rishis to the humble disciple sitting in meditation. Ishvara is OM, the primal sound, the basic keynote of all being, the source of the music of the spheres, mirrored in the myriad manifestations of *prakriti*. Surrender to Ishvara is aided by the silent repetition of the sacred OM and by deep meditation upon its mystery and meaning. When *bhakti* flows freely in this rapturous rhythm, consciousness readily turns inward and removes all hindrances to progress in *samadhi*.

Surrender to the luminous core of one's consciousness, which is more powerful than one's strongest proclivities, initiates a mighty countervailing force against the cumulative momentum generated by the *chittavrittis*. As the mind has grown accustomed to indulge, identify with and even cherish ceaseless modifications, any attempt to check those modifications runs against the self-reproducing tenacity of long-established habits, impressions and tendencies. The *chittavrittis* are virtually infinite in their discrete manifestations and yet are amenable to broad classification on the basis of essential traits. The hindrances which aggravate mental distraction, fragmented consciousness and continual modification are disease, dullness, doubt, heedlessness, indolence, addiction to objects of sense, distorted perception, and failure to stabilize the mind in any particular state. Though distinct from each other, these distractions are all accompanied by sorrow *(duhkha)*, depression, bodily agitation and irregular breathing. They can, however, be most effectively eliminated through *abhyasa*, or constant practice of a single truth or principle. Whilst any profound truth which deeply moves one can be chosen, to the degree that it is true — and so to the degree that it is efficacious over time — it is *ekatattva*, the one principle, which in Sankhya philosophy is *purusha* or pure spirit.

Overcoming mental obstructions through *abhyasa* in respect to one principle requires the progressive purification of the mind, freeing it from the froth and dross of old patterns fostered by feeble and fickle attention. Most seekers typically find easiest and most effective a concerted effort to expand the feeling of friendliness towards all beings, compassion for every creature, inward gladness and a cool detachment in regard to pleasure and pain, virtue and vice. On the physical plane of human nature, one can learn to make one's breathing calm and even, steady and rhythmical. Through intense concentration, one can begin to awaken subtler perceptions which are not subject to hindrances in the way the ordinary sense-organs are, to an almost grotesque extent. One may even activate a spark of *buddhi,* pure insight and deep penetration, sensing the vast ocean of supernal cosmic light which interpenetrates and encloses everything. Some seekers will find it more feasible to contemplate the lustrous splendour of a mythic, historical or living being who is a paragon of supreme self-mastery. Others may benefit by brooding on flashes of reminiscence that recur in dreams or come from deep dreamless sleep. Patanjali also pointed out that one could gain mental stability by meditating intently upon what one most ardently desired. In the words of Charles Johnston, "Love is a form of knowledge", when it is profound and sacrificial, constant and unconditional.

All such efforts to surmount the hindrances which distract the mind are aids to deep meditation, and when they have fully worked their benevolent magic, the becalmed mind becomes the effortless master of everything which comes into the horizon of consciousness, from the atomic to the infinite. When all the hindrances disappear, mental modifications cease and the mind "becomes like a transparent crystal, attaining the power of transformation, taking on the colour of what it rests on, whether it be the cognizer, the cognized or the act of cognition." (I.41) When the mind is distracted through discursive trains of thought, it tends to oscillate between passive disorientation and aggressive attempts to conceal its ignorance through contentious and partisan fixations. But when the memory is purged of external traces and encrusted conditionality, and the mind is withdrawn from all limiting conceptions — including even its abstract self-image, thus focussed solely on *ekatattva*, truth alone — it is free from obscuration, unclouded *(nirvitarka)*, and sees each truth as a whole. It notices the subtle elements behind shifting appearances, including the noumenal, primordial and undifferentiated sources and causes of all mental modifications.

This serene self-emancipation of consciousness is called *sabija samadhi*, meditation with a seed, the fulcrum for gaining all knowledge. In this sublime condition, the mind has become as pellucid as crystal and mirrors the spiritual light of *purusha*, whence dawns direct insight *(prajna)* into the ultimate Truth.

Unlike other methods of cognizing truth — which concern this or that and hence are involved with *samvritti satya*, relative truths, though truths nonetheless — *prajna* has but one single object for its focus, the Supreme Truth itself *(paramartha satya)*. Its power displaces and transcends all lesser forms of truth, exiling them permanently from consciousness. Beyond this lies only that indescribable state called *nirbija samadhi*, meditation without a seed, wherein the mind lets go of even Truth itself *as an object*. When the mind ceases to function, the *Yogabhashya* teaches, *purusha* becomes isolated, pure and liberated. Mind has become the pure instrument that guides the soul ever closer to that threshold where, when reached, spirit steps from false finitude into inconceivable infinitude, leaving the mind behind, passing into *kaivalya*, total isolation or supreme freedom. The last psychic veil is drawn aside and the spiritual man stands with unveiled vision. As M.N. Dvivedi commented, "The mind thus having nothing to rest upon exhausts itself . . . and *purusha* alone shines in perfect bliss and peace." "The Light," I.K. Taimni remarked, "which was up to this stage illuminating other objects now illuminates Itself, for it has withdrawn beyond the realm of these objects. The Seer is now established in his own Self."

Having depicted the entire path leading from ignorance and bewilderment to beatific illumination, Patanjali saw only two tasks remaining: (1) to explain in detail the diverse means for attaining concentration and meditation, and (2) to elucidate the idea of *kaivalya* or isolation, in so far as it is possible to convey it through words.

SADHANA PADA

*A person without self-discipline cannot attain
perfection in* yoga. . . . *An undisturbed course of self-
purificatory conduct should be practised.*

Yogabhashya

Patanjali initiated his teaching concerning *praxis* by calling
attention to the three chief elements in the discipline
of yoga: *tapas,* austerity, self-restraint and eventually
self-mastery; *svadhyaya,* self-study, self-examination, including
calm contemplation of *purusha,* the Supreme Self; and *ishvarapranidhana,* self-surrender to the Lord, the omnipresent divine
spirit within the secret heart. The threefold practice or *sadhana*
can remove the *kleshas* or afflictions which imprison *purusha* and
thus facilitate *samadhi* or meditative absorption. This arduous
alchemical effort was summed up succinctly by Shankaracharya:
"Right vision *(samyagdarshana)* is the means to transcendental
aloneness *(kaivalya).* . . . Yoga practice, being the means to right
vision, comes before it. . . . Ignorance is destroyed when directly
confronted by right vision." The *kleshas,* though varied in their
myriad manifestations, are essentially five: *avidya,* ignorance;
asmita, egoism; *raga,* attachment; *dvesha,* aversion; and *abhinivesha,*
tenacious clinging to mundane existence. Ignorance, however, is
the broad field in which all the other *kleshas* arise, because they
are no more than distinct specializations of ignorance.

Ignorance is a fundamental inverted confusion which
mistakes *prakriti* for *purusha,* the false for the true, the impure for
the pure, and the painful for the pleasurable — a persisting
malaise which might have been difficult to comprehend in the
past but which is now a familiar condition in contemporary
psychology. Springing from fundamental ignorance, egoism
(asmita) confuses the potency of the Seer *(purusha)* with the power
of sight *(buddhi).* Attachment *(raga)* is the pursuit of what is

mistaken to be pleasurable, whilst aversion *(dvesha)* flees from what is believed to be painful. These two constitute the primary pair of opposites on the psychological level in the field of ignorance, and all other pairs of opposites are derived from them. Clinging to phenomenal existence *(abhinivesha)* is the logical outcome of the operation of ignorance, and once aroused is self-sustaining through the inertia of habit, so that countervailing measures are needed to eradicate it, together with the other *kleshas*.

Through ignorance *(avidya)* there is an obscuration of the cosmic Self *(purusha)*, a fundamental misidentification of what is real, a persistent misconception which carries its own distinct logic within the complex dialectic of *maya*:

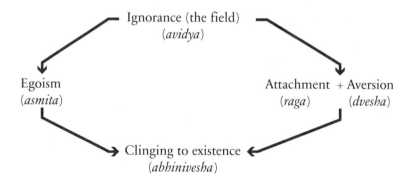

Since the *kleshas* are engendered by a persistent error, at root mistaking *prakriti* for *purusha*, or attributing the essential characteristics of *purusha* to one or another aspect of *prakriti*, they can be eliminated only by a radical reversal of the downward tendency of alienation and retreat from truth. This fundamental correction, as far-reaching as the entrenched habit of inversion which necessitates it, is *dhyana*, meditation, together with the mental and moral exercises which strengthen it. To say, as Hindu and Buddhist thinkers alike assert, that karma is rooted in *avidya* is to imply that the ramifying results of karma now experienced, or yet to be experienced in a future incarnation, are all rooted in the *kleshas*.

In the graphic language of spiritual physiology, the *kleshas* constitute a psychic colouring or peculiar obsession which forms a persisting matrix of karma, the results of which must eventually be experienced, and also creates mental deposits which channel mental energies into repeatedly reinforcing the *kleshas*. *Dhyana* alone can effectively eradicate these mental deposits while providing the clear detachment *(vairagya)* and cool patience *(kshanti)* to exhaust and dissolve the karmic matrix over time. As long as the *kleshas* remain, involuntary incarnation into bodies captive to the pleasure-pain principle is inescapable. Elation and depression are the inevitable effects of such embodiment. Since these are the product of egoism and the polarity of attraction and aversion, rooted in ignorance and resulting in the tenacious clinging to mundane existence, the discerning *yogin* comes to see that the truth of spiritual freedom and the rapture of limitless love transcend the *kleshas* entirely. All karma brings discord and distress, including the insistent pains of loss and gain, growth and decay.

Karma means *parinama*, change, and this invariably induces the longing to recover what is receding, to enhance what is emerging, or to sustain a static balance where no thing can endure. To be drawn to some objects and conditions and to be disinclined towards others is indeed to foster *tapa*, anxious brooding over what might be lost or what one might be forced to encounter. All experiences leave residual impressions, *samskaras*, which agitate the mind and stimulate desires to have or to avoid possible future experiences. In general, the *gunas* or root qualities of *prakriti* — *sattva*, *rajas* and *tamas*: luminosity, action and inertia; purity, restlessness and languor; or harmony, volatility and fixity — persist in ceaselessly shifting permutations which continually modify the uncontrolled mind. For these reasons, Patanjali taught, all life without spiritual freedom is fraught with sorrow. Through yoga, it is not possible to avoid consequences already set in motion, but it is feasible to destroy the *kleshas* and thereby remove the causal chain of suffering.

Metaphysically, *buddhi*, intuitive intellect, is closer to *purusha* than any other aspect of *prakriti*. Nonetheless, *buddhi* is still what is seen by *purusha*, the Perceiver, and it is through confounding the Perceiver with what is perceived at the supersensuous level that suffering arises. *Prakriti*, consisting of the *gunas*, is the entire field, enclosing the objective world and the organs of sensation. It exists solely for the sake of the soul's education and emancipation. The *Yogabhashya* teaches that identification of the Perceiver with the seen constitutes experience, "whilst realizing the true nature of *purusha* is emancipation." In the realm of *prakriti*, wherein the Perceiver is captive to the ever-changing panorama of Nature, the *gunas*, which may be construed as the properties of perceptible objects but which are really propensities from the standpoint of psycho-mental faculties, act at every level of conscious awareness.

At the level of differentiated consciousness, *vitarka*, wherein the mind scrutinizes specific objects and features, the *gunas* are particularized *(vishesha)*. When consciousness apprehends archetypes, laws and abstract concepts *(vichara)*, the *gunas* are archetypal *(avishesha)*. When the *gunas* are discerned as signs and signatures *(linga)*, objects are resolved into symbols of differentiation in a universal field of complete objectivity, and consciousness experiences ecstasy *(ananda)*. Though discrete, objects are no longer distinguished in contrast to one another or through divergent characteristics; they are distinct but seen as parts of a single whole. They are apprehended through *buddhi* or intuitive insight.

The *gunas* are *alinga* — signless, irresolvable, undifferentiated — and lose their distinction from consciousness itself when objects dissolve in the recognition that consciousness and its modifications alone constitute the noumenal and phenomenal world. Hence, pure consciousness *(lingamatra)*, which is the simple, unqualified sense of 'I', subsists in a pristine noumenal condition *(alinga)* wherein it does not witness the ceaseless operation of the *gunas*. This divine consciousness is the highest state of meditative absorption, beyond which lies complete emancipation, *purusha* without any tincture of *prakriti*.

The Perceiver is pure vision, apprehending ideas seemingly through the mind. Once final emancipation, which is the ultimate aim and purpose of all experience, is attained, *purusha* no longer encounters the confusion of spirit and matter through mental modifications. As experience, correctly understood, culminates in eventual self-emancipation, *kaivalya*, Patanjali held that 'the very essence of the visible is that it exists for the sake of the Seer, the Self alone' (II.21).

The world does not vanish for all others when a man of meditation attains *kaivalya*; they remain in confusion until they also attain the same utterly transcendent state of awareness. Here Yoga philosophy exhausts its conceptual and descriptive vocabulary. Whether one asserts that there is an indefinite number of *purushas*, each capable of attaining *kaivalya*, or one states that *purusha* attains *kaivalya* in this instance but not that, is a matter of indifference, for one perforce invokes enumeration, time and space — terms properly applying to *prakriti* alone — to characterize a wholly transcendent reality. The pervasive existential fact is that *prakriti* persists so long as there are beings trapped through ignorance, and the vital psychological truth is that no being who attains the transcendent *(taraka)* reality of unqualified, pure *purusha* can do so vicariously for another. Through their hard-won wisdom and compassion, emancipated seers and sages can point the way with unerring accuracy. They know how to make their magnanimous guidance most effective for every human being, but each seeker must make the ascent unaided.

If the cosmos as considered in contemporary physics resolved itself into a condition of undisturbed entropy, or if, in the language of Sankhya, the *gunas* achieved total and enduring equilibrium, Nature *(prakriti)* would cease to exist, since there would be nothing to be perceived. Ignorance and its inseparable concomitant, suffering, arise from a broken symmetry in Nature. In contemporary thought there is no adequate explanation for the origin of that 'cosmic disaster', for the emergence of sentience is said to occur *within* the broken symmetry. If the scientific community were trained to use the language of Sankhya and Yoga philosophy, it would have to speak of the origin of *purusha*, consciousness, within the evolutionary permutations and convolutions of *prakriti*. Sankhya and Yoga teach, however, that *purusha*, sempiternal and independent, perceives *prakriti* and indirectly gives rise to the broken symmetry itself, the anti-entropic condition which is the activity of the *gunas*. For Patanjali, *prakriti* must necessarily exist, for it is through experience — conjunction with *prakriti* — that *purusha* knows itself as it is. But when *purusha* wrongly apprehends *prakriti*, as it must until it knows itself truly as it is, ignorance and all the entangling *kleshas* arise. When *purusha* attains *kaivalya*, emancipation, it sees without error, and this is gained through experience in self-correction and self-mastery. From the highest standpoint, this means that *purusha* preserves its freedom and intrinsic purity by avoiding mistaken assumptions and false conclusions. From the standpoint of any individual involved in *prakriti*, unbroken discriminative cognition (*vivekakhyati*) is the sole means to emancipation, for it releases the abiding sense of reality (*purusha*) in him. The dual process of removing the *kleshas* and reflecting on the Self (*purusha*) assures the progressive and climactic attainment of emancipation (*kaivalya*) such that ignorance does not arise again.

Having delineated the path to *kaivalya*, Patanjali discoursed in some detail on the seven successive stages of yoga which lead to *samadhi*, full meditative absorption, but he insisted that, even though each stage must be passed in succession, truth and wisdom dawn progressively upon the aspirant to stimulate his endeavour. Yoga is successive, gradual and recursive, the path of ascent which alone leads from darkness to light, from ignorance to transcendental wisdom, from death and recurring rebirth to conscious immortality and universal self-consciousness. Although the stages through which consciousness must ascend are sequential in one sense, the practice of Taraka Raja Yoga involves eight limbs or aspects which are logically successive but ethically and psychologically simultaneous. In fact, one can hardly pursue one part of Patanjali's eight-limbed yoga (*ashtangayoga*) without also attending to its other divisions. Just as a human being, despite his ignorance, is an integrated whole, so too *ashtangayoga*, despite its logical sequence, is an integral unity. Patanjali enumerated the eight *(ashta)* limbs *(anga)* of this Taraka Raja Yoga as five which concern karma and lay the foundation for meditation, and three which constitute meditation itself: restraint *(yama)*, binding observance *(niyama)*, posture *(asana)*, regulation of breath *(pranayama)*, abstraction and withdrawal from the senses *(pratyahara)*; concentration *(dharana)*, contemplation *(dhyana)* and complete meditative absorption *(samadhi)*.

The *yamas* or restraints are five, constituting a firm ethical foundation for spiritual growth, starting with *ahimsa* (non-violence) and including *satya* (truth), *asteya* (non-stealing), *brahmacharya* (continence) and *aparigraha* (non-possession). Shankaracharya held that *ahimsa* — non-violence, harmlessness, defencelessness in Shelley's phrase — is the most important of the *yamas* and *niyamas*, and is the root of restraint. Like all constraints and observances, *ahimsa* must not be interpreted narrowly but should be seen in its widest sense. For Shankaracharya, this meant that *ahimsa* should be practised in body, speech and mind so that one avoids harming others in any way, even through an unkind thought. *Ahimsa* can be taken to include the classical Greek sense of *sophrosyne*, a sense of proportion which voids all excess, the state of mind which can avoid even unintentional harm to a single being in the cosmos. In employing *ahimsa* as a talismanic tool of political and social reform, Gandhi exemplified the central importance and far-reaching scope of *ahimsa*. For Patanjali, however, *ahimsa* and the other *yamas* and *niyamas* constitute the daily moral discipline needed to pursue Taraka Raja Yoga. Taraka Raja Yoga is not a narrowly technical or specialized practice to be added to other instrumental activities in the world; it is rather the indispensable means for radically transforming one's essential perception of, and therefore one's entire relation to, the world. From the standpoint of Self-knowledge, which is ultimate gnosis, there are no greater disciplines. Hence the *yamas* are not altered by condition and circumstance, social class or nationality, nor by time nor the actual level of spiritual attainment. Together they constitute the awesome *mahavrata* or Great Vow, the first crucial step to true spiritual freedom.

The *niyamas* or binding observances are also five, constituting the positive dimension of ethical probity. They are *shaucha* (purity), *santosha* (contentment), *tapas* (austerity, self-discipline), *svadhyaya* (self-study) and *ishvarapranidhana* (surrender to the Lord). Like the *yamas*, the *niyamas* cannot be fully grasped as specific and bounded concepts. First of all, they should be seen as evolving conceptions — for example, purity of thought is deepened through purity of conduct — and then they will rapidly unfold subtler levels of meaning as the aspirant attains more intensive depths of meditation. Purity of volition is thus ever enriched and refined. The greatest obstacles to the restraints and binding observances are those thoughts which run in the opposite direction — thinking of impure things or acts, wishing to do harm for a perceived injustice, self-indulgence, self-deception and self-assertion. Such illicit and destructive thoughts are perverse precisely because they belie and defeat the initial commitment to the *yamas* and *niyamas*. Instead of suppressing such scattered thoughts or wallowing in hideous self-pity, one must firmly and deliberately insert into the mind their potent opposites — love for hate, tenderness for temerity, sweetness for spite, virile confidence for the devilry of self-doubt, authentic self-conquest for compulsive self-indulgence. Thus what begins as a shrewd defence against deleterious thoughts becomes a deft substitution of one kind of thought for another and results in sublimation, the skilful transformation of the tonality and texture of consciousness. Strict and consistent measures are needed to deal with subversive thoughts, not in order to repress them or to hide guilt for having them, but only because they induce depression and self-loathing, with predictable and pathetic consequences. Facing unworthy thoughts firmly, and thereby exorcising them, is to free oneself from their nefarious spell.

When any object is forcibly confined, it exerts crude pressure against its external constraints. In the ethical realm, effortless self-restraint produces a powerful glow of well-being which others can appreciate and even emulate. When, for example, one is established in *ahimsa*, others do become aware of an encompassing and inclusive love, and latent or overt hostility dissolves around one's radius of benevolence. *Satya*, truth, is the path of least resistance amongst the shifting ratios of the *gunas*, and when one is clearly established in truth, the predictable consequences of thought, word and deed are constructive and consistent. Similarly, strengthening oneself through *asteya* (non-stealing), one desists from every form of misappropriation, even on the plane of thought and feeling, and discovers what is apposite on all sides. Nature protects and even provides for those who do not appropriate its abundant resources. *Brahmacharya*, selfless continence in thought and conduct, fosters vitality and vigour. *Aparigraha*, non-possessiveness, promotes noetic insight into the deeper meaning and purpose of one's probationary sojourn on earth.

Expansiveness too has its compelling effects. *Shaucha*, inward and outer purity, protects the mind and body from moral and magnetic pollution, and prevents one from tarnishing or misusing others. One acquires a dependable degree of serenity, control of the senses and one-pointedness in concentration, thus preparing oneself for the direct apprehension of *purusha*, the Self. *Santosha*, deep contentment, assures satisfaction not through the gratification of wants (which can at most provide a temporary escape from frustration), but rather through the progressive cessation of craving and its prolific yearnings and regrets. *Tapas*, austerity, penance or self-discipline, removes pollution inherited from one's own past and releases the full potentials of mind, senses and body, including those psychic faculties mistakenly called supernormal only because seldom developed. *Svadhyaya*, self-study, calls for careful study and calm reflection, including the diligent recitation and deep contemplation of texts, thus giving voice to potent mantras and sacred utterances. It achieves its apotheosis through direct communion with the *ishtadevata*, the chosen deity upon whom one has concentrated one's complete attention, will and imagination. This exalted state readily leads to *ishvarapranidhana*, one-pointed and single-hearted devotion to the

Lord. Such devotion soon deepens until one enters the succeeding stages of meditative absorption *(samadhi)*.

With the firm foundation of *yamas* and *niyamas,* one can begin to benefit from the noetic discipline of intense meditation and become modestly proficient in it over a lifetime of service to humanity. Since the untrained mind is easily distracted by external and internal disturbance, real meditation is aided by an alert and relaxed bodily vesture. To this end, a steady posture *(asana)* is chosen, not to indulge the acrobatic antics of the shallow Hatha Yogin, but rather to subdue and command the body, whilst retaining its alertness and resilience. The correct posture will be firm and flexible without violating the mind's vigorous concentration and precise focus. Once the appropriate *asana* is assumed by each neophyte, the mind is becalmed and turned towards the Infinite, becoming wholly impervious to bodily movement and change, immersed in the boundless space of the akashic empyrean. Thus the impact of the oscillating pairs of opposites upon the volatile brain mind, captivated by sharp contrasts and idle speculations, and the agitation of the body through recurring sensations are at least temporarily muted. In this state of serene peace, the effortless regulation of rhythmic breath *(pranayama)* becomes as natural as floating on the waters of space. Just as the mind and body are intimately interlinked at every point, such that even holding a firm physical posture aids the calming of the mind, so too *pranayama* points to silent mental breathing as well as smooth respiration.

Prana, which includes the solar life-breath, is the efflux of the constant flow of cosmic energy, regulated by the ideation of *purusha* and radiating from the luminous substance of pure *prakriti.* From the *nadabrahman* — the Divine Resonance and perpetual motion of absolute Spirit — and the global respiration of the earth reverberating at its hidden core, its slowly rolling mantle and its shifting crust, to the inspiration and expiration of every creature in the cosmos, the ocean of *prana* permeates and purifies all planes of being. In the human constitution, irregular, spasmodic or strained, uneven breathing can disturb the homeostatic equilibrium of the body and cause fragmented, uncoordinated modes of awareness. Proper breathing oxygenates the physical system optimally, and also aids the mind in maintaining a steady rhythm of unbroken ideation, fusing thought, will and energy. *Pranayama* begins with deliberate exhalation, so that the lungs are generously emptied and the unusable matter expelled into them is made to exit the bodily temple. Thereupon, slow inbreathing invites oxygen to permeate the entire lung system and penetrate the blood, arteries, nerves and cells. Holding the breath in a benevolent pause permits the respiratory system to adjust gently to the next phase of oxygenation and detoxification. When these rhythmic movements are marked by due measure and proportion, mantramically fused into the inaudible OM, there is a distinct improvement in psycho-physical health and a remarkable increase of vigilance and vigour.

The fourth step in *pranayama* transcends the physiological dimensions of respiration for which they are a preparation. The highest *pranayama* becomes possible when one has gained sufficient sensitivity through the earlier stages of *pranayama* to sense and direct the divine flow of *prana* throughout one's entropic psychophysical system. Then one may, through mental volition alone, fuse mental serenity and single-mindedness with psycho-physical equilibrium, and also convey subtle pranic currents, charged with selfless ideation, to various *padmas* or vital centres *(chakras)* in the body. Since each of the seven *padmas* is precisely correlated with the corresponding state of concentrated consciousness, the fearless equipoise needed to activate these magnetic centres and the benevolent *siddhis* or theurgic powers thereby released requires the commensurate and controlled alteration in the tonality and texture of consciousness. When the highest *padma* is effortlessly and gently touched by mind-directed *prana,* non-violent consciousness simultaneously attains full *samadhi.* "Thus is worn away," said Patanjali, "the veil which obscures the light" (II.52), thereby pointing to the subduing of the *kleshas* and the neutralization of karma through the progressive awakening of discriminative insight and intuitive wisdom.

The process of purification is not an end in itself, but the necessary condition to prepare the mind for *dharana,* complete concentration. *Pranayama,* delusive and dangerous when misappropriated for selfish purposes pursued through subtle enslavement by the *kleshas,* is hereby integrated into Patanjali's eightfold yoga as a preliminary step towards subduing the restless mind, freeing it to become the servant of the immortal soul, seeking greater wisdom, self-mastery and universal self-consciousness. *Pratyahara,* abstraction and disassociation of sensory perception from sense-objects, is now accessible. Withdrawal of the senses from their objects of attraction does not destroy them. Rather, the subtler senses take on the plastic and fluidic nature of the serene mind itself. Without the myriad distractions of familiar and strange sense-objects, the senses become subtilized and pliant, no longer pulling consciousness towards internal images, external objects or captivating sense-data. Instead, the noetic mind firmly expels images and subdues impulses, gaining sovereign mastery over them. Patanjali ended the second *pada* here, having shown the pathway to proper preparation for profound meditation. The significance of the last three interconnected *angas* or stages of yoga is indicated by the fact that Patanjali set them apart in the third *pada* for his authoritative exposition.

The preparatory discipline or *sadhana* of the second *pada* has been thus strikingly extolled by Rishi Vasishtha:

> He engaged in the practice of Raja Yoga, remaining silent and graceful in countenance. He abstracted his senses from their objects as the oil is separated from the sesamum seed, withdrawing their organs within himself as the turtle contracts his limbs under his hard shell.
>
> With his steady mind he cast all external sensations far off from himself, as a rich and brilliant gem, shedding a coating of dust, then scattered its rays to a distance. Without coming in contact with them, he

compressed his sensations within himself, as a tree in the cold season compresses its sap within its bark. . . .

He confined his subdued mind in the cave of his heart, as a great elephant is imprisoned in a cavern of the Vindhya Mountain when it has been brought by stratagem under subjection. When his soul had gained its clarity, resembling the serenity of the autumnal sky, it forsook all unsteadiness, like the calm ocean unagitated by any winds.

Yoga Vasishtha Maharamayana

VIBHUTI PADA

Attention is the first and indispensable step in all knowledge. Attention to spiritual things is the first step to spiritual knowledge.
CHARLES JOHNSTON

Patanjali commenced the third *pada* of the *Yoga Sutras* with a compelling distinction between three phases of meditation. *Dharana* is full concentration, the focussing of consciousness on a particular point, which may be any object in the world or a subject chosen by the mind. The ability to fix attention is strengthened by the practice of the first five *angas* of Patanjali's *ashtangayoga,* for without some cultivation of them the mind tends to meander and drift in every direction. *Dhyana* is meditation in the technical sense of the term, meaning the calm sustaining of focussed attention. In *dhyana,* consciousness still encounters some modifications, but they all flow in one direction and are not disturbed by other fluctuations of any sort. Rather like iron — consisting of molecules clustered together in various ways, their axes oriented in different directions — undergoes a shift of alignment of all molecules in a single direction when magnetized, so too consciousness can become unidirectional through experiencing a current of continuity in time.

    Samadhi, broadly characterized as 'meditative absorption' or 'full meditation', signifies the deepening of *dhyana* until the chosen object of meditation stands alone and consciousness is no longer aware of itself as contemplating an object. In *samadhi,* consciousness loses the sense of separateness from what is contemplated and, in effect, becomes one with it. Like a person wholly lost in their work, "the object stands by itself," in the words of the *Yogabhashya,* as if there were only the object itself. Although these three phases can be viewed as separate and successive, when they occur together in one simultaneous act they constitute *sanyama,* serene constraint or luminous concentration. The novice who nonetheless is capable of entering *samadhi* may take a long time to move from *dharana* to deep *samadhi,* because he experiences the entire movement as a radical change in consciousness. But the adept in *sanyama* can include all three in a virtually instantaneous act, thus arousing the ability to move from one object of contemplation to another almost effortlessly.

Prajna, cognitive insight, the resplendent light of wisdom, or intuitive apprehension, comes as a result of mastering *sanyama.* Although *prajna* is the highest level of knowledge to which philosophy can aspire, it is not the supreme state, for it halts at the threshold of *vivekakhyati,* pristine awareness of Reality, which can be neither articulated nor elucidated. *Sanyama,* Patanjali taught, is not completely mastered all at once. Rather, once *sanyama* is attained, it is strengthened in stages by deft application to different objects and levels of being. Each such application reveals the divine light as it manifests in that context, until the adept practitioner of exalted *sanyama* can focus entirely on *purusha* itself. In *sanyama* the patient aspirant glimpses the divine radiance, the resplendent reflection of *purusha,* wherever he focusses attention, but in time he will behold only *purusha.* In the *Bhagavad Gita,* Krishna asked Arjuna to see Himself in all things, but in the climactic cosmic vision, Arjuna witnessed the cosmic form (*vishvarupa*) of the Lord. *Sanyama* is wholly internal, whilst the first five yoga practices are external. Though all the *angas* are crucial to yoga, the last three, harmoniously synthesized in *sanyama,* constitute yoga proper. Since this is the central aim of everything stated so far in the *Yoga Sutras, sanyama* received considerable emphasis from Patanjali.

Nirodha, restraint, cessation or interception, is essential to *sanyama* because it is concerned neither with different states nor objects of consciousness, but chiefly with the process of transformation or replacement of the contents of consciousness. In *sanyama* the definite shift from one object of attention to another — and these can be wholly abstract and mental objects — involves a change of mental impression. As an object fades from mental view, another appears on the mental horizon to take its place. But like the pregnant moment just before dawn, when night is fleeing and the first light of day is sensed but has not yet shown itself, there is a suspended moment when what is fading has receded and the new object of focus is yet to appear. This is *nirodhaparinama*, the moment, however fleeting, between successive modifications when, according to the *Yogabhashya*, "the mind has nothing but subliminal impressions". (III.9) Should the mind lose its alertness at just that point, it would fall into a somnolent state, for in *sanyama*, consciousness is wholly absorbed in the object of consciousness, whilst in *nirodhaparinama* that object has vanished. But if it remains fully awake, it gains a powerful glimpse of the tranquil state of non-modification, and may thus pass through the *laya* or still point of equilibrium to enter into a higher plane. With sufficient practice, the *yogin* learns to extend *nirodha* and abide in it long enough to initiate this transition. The less accomplished, if they do not get caught in the torpor of the penultimate void, may notice the passage of *nirodha* as a missed opportunity. With persistent effort, the *yogin* learns to remain in *nirodha*, relishing the peaceful, smooth flow of cosmic consciousness and reaching the highest *samadhi*.

Samadhiparinama, meditative transformation, occurs when *nirodha* is experienced not simply as a negation of objects of consciousness but rather as a positive meditation on nothingness. One-pointedness of consciousness has been so mastered through the progressive displacement of all distractions that *ekagrata*, one-pointedness, alone subsists, and this becomes *ekagrataparinama*, total one-pointedness. It is as if the seed of meditation, first sought and recovered every single time the mind wandered and was sharply brought back to a focus, then firmly fixed in focus, had been split asunder until nothing remained but the empty core upon which the mind settles peacefully. Here the besetting tendency to fluctuate has become feeble, whilst the propensity to apply restraint is strong. Since all states of consciousness are necessarily correlated with states of matter, both being products of the *gunas* stimulated to action by the presence of *purusha*, the depiction of consciousness also pertains to matter. The powerful transformation of consciousness is precisely matched in the continual transformations of matter, though the ordinary eye fails to apprehend the critical states in the transformation of matter, just as it remains largely unaware of *nirodha*. Nonetheless, there is a single substratum, *dharmin*, which underlies all change, whether in consciousness or in matter, and this is *prakriti*, the primeval root of all phenomena. For Patanjali, this means that all transformations are phenomenal in respect to *prakriti*, the *prima materia* in its essential nature, and, like *purusha*, ever unmodified. The ceaseless fluctuations of mind and world are merely countless variations of succession owing to alterations of cause. Realizing this, the *yogin* who has mastered *sanyama*, and thereby controls the mind at will, can equally control all processes of gestation and growth.

Having elucidated the nature of concentration as the sole means for discovering and transforming consciousness at all levels, Patanjali turned to the remarkable phenomenal effects possible through *sanyama*. Any fundamental change in consciousness initiates a corresponding change in and around one's vestures. A decisive shift in the operation and balance of the *gunas*, in thought, focus and awareness, reverberates throughout the oscillating ratios between the *gunas* everywhere. Since any significant refocussing of the mind produces dazzling insights and diverse phenomena, Patanjali conveyed their range and scope. For yoga they are not important in themselves because the goal is *kaivalya*, liberation, but they are vitally important as aids or obstacles on the way to achieving the goal. Patanjali could not dismiss or overlook them, since they are real enough and inescapable, and so he delineated them clearly, knowing fully that all such arcane information can be abused. One who willingly uses such knowledge to stray off the arduous path to emancipation brings misery upon himself. One who would use this knowledge wisely needs to understand the many ways one can be misled into wasting the abundant resources accessible to the *yogin*. Profound alterations in states of consciousness through *sanyama* can bring about awakened powers called *siddhis,* attainments, many of which may seem to be supernatural and supernormal to the average person. They are, however, neither miraculous nor super-natural, since they suspend, circumvent or violate no laws. Rather, they merely indicate the immense powers of controlled consciousness within the perspective of great Nature, powers that are largely latent, untapped and dormant in most human beings. They are suggestive parameters of the operation of the vast scope and potency of consciousness in diverse arenas of *prakriti.*

Sanyama, the electric fusion of *dharana, dhyana* and *samadhi,* can release preternatural knowledge of past and future; the *yogin* gains profound insight into the metaphysical mystery of time. The future is ever conditioned by the past, and the past is accurately reflected in every aspect of the future. The present is strictly not a period of time; it is that ceaselessly moving point which marks the continual transition from future to past. Comprehending causality, seeing the effect in the cause, like the tree in the seed, the *yogin* perceives past and future alike by concentrating on the three phases of transformation experienced in the present and which, at the critical points of transformation, indicate the eternal, changeless substratum hidden behind them. Once conscious awareness is fixed beyond the temporal succession of states of consciousness, causality ceases to be experienced as a series of interrelated events — since the succession is itself the operation of past karma — and is perceived as an integrated whole in the timeless present. Thus past and future are seen from the same transcendent perspective as the timeless present. Freeing oneself from captivity to the mechanical succession of moments in clock time, one can rise beyond temporality and grasp causality noetically rather than phenomenally.

Although language is often viewed as an arbitrary and conventional system of communication, interpersonal understanding and mental telepathy as well as rapport between receptive and congenial minds are based on more than mere convention. Just as time is experienced as internal to the subject when the mind is mechanical, whilst causality is not necessarily time-bound, the evolution of language cannot dispense with intersubjectivity, shared clusters of concepts, rites and rituals, habits and customs, races and cultures. The deepest meaning of sounds is subtle and elusive, dissolving meanings and expectations. The linkage connected to the possibility of speech as well as to the potency of the primordial OM, the secret name of Ishvara, is *sphota*, the ineffable and inscrutable meaning intimated by sounds and speech. Through *sanyama*, the *yogin* can so deftly discern sound, meaning and idea that he instantly grasps the meaning, whatever the utterance of any person. Not only does he readily understand what is said by anyone, however awkward, disingenuous or deceptive the utterance, but he also apprehends the meaning of any sound uttered by any sentient being, whether birds and beasts, insects, trees or aquatic creatures.

The focussing power of *sanyama* enables the *yogin* to explore the subtlest impressions retained on the mental screen, and in so doing he can summon them into the light of consciousness. In this way, he can examine his entire mental inheritance and even discern previous lives. Knowing the exact correlations between states of consciousness and external conditions, he can recognize the linkage between latent memories and the traumas they induce, as well as the integral connection between past impressions and their inevitable karmic effects, thereby recollecting the patterns of previous incarnations. Similarly, by directing his yogic focus on the *pratyaya* or content of any mind functioning through a set of vestures, he can cognize that mental condition. Since all such mental contents are mirrored in the features and gestures of another, he can read the thoughts of another by looking at the person, and he can make the same determination by examining any portion of the expressed thought of another. Rather like a hologram, each and every aspect of an individual reflects the evolving structure of the whole being. Through *sanyama*, any facet of the person can reveal his psychic and mental make-up. Such attention will not, however, unveil the underlying structure of another's deepest consciousness, since that is hidden even to the person scrutinized. To discover the inward depths of the person, the *yogin* has to take the subject as the sole object of his sustained concentration and not merely that subject's mental contents. The ultimate question "Who are you?" can be resolved only in the way the question "Who am I?" is taken as a theme of intense meditation.

For Patanjali, as for different schools of Indian thought and for Plato *(Republic,* Book VI), seeing is a positive act and not merely a passive reception of light refracted from an object in the line of sight. Seeing involves the confluence of light (an aspect of *sattvaguna)* from the object of sight and the light from the eye of the seer, an active power (another aspect of *sattva).* The *yogin* can direct *sanyama* to the form and colour of his own body and draw in the light radiating from it, centring it wholly within his mind, *manas,* so that the *sattva* from the eye of another cannot fuse with it. Thus the body of the *yogin* cannot be seen, for he has made himself invisible. Similarly, by meditation upon the ultimate basis of any sensory power, the element essential to that sense, and its corresponding sense-organ, the *yogin* can become soundless, intangible and beyond the limited range of all the bodily senses. With the proper inversion of the process, he can dampen or delete any sense-image, like glaring lights or background noise, either converting them into mild sensations or blanketing them entirely.

If the *yogin* should choose to practise *sanyama* on his past karma, he can obtain unerring insight into every causal chain he once initiated. Recognizing which tendencies are being expended and at what rates, as well as those lines of force which cannot bear fruit in this life, he may discern the time of his death — that point wherein the fruition of karma ensures the complete cessation of vital bodily functions. At the same time, such knowledge readily gives warnings of future events, all of which are the inevitable fruition of karma, and thus the *yogin* readily sees in each moment signs and portents of the future. He does not perceive, in such instances, something that is present only to his penetrating gaze. Rather, he is only reading correctly the futurity which ever lurks in present events, just as gold ore inheres in the dull rock even though only the trained eye of the prospector can see it and know it for what it is. Whilst such practical wisdom allows the *yogin* to foresee mental and physical conditions, he can also discern more fundamental changes which are due to the inexorable working of overlapping cycles, and, even more, he can focus on those critical points which trace the curve of potentiality for permanent spiritual change, or *metanoia*.

By focussing on *maitri*, kindliness, or any similar grace of character, the *yogin* can fortify that virtue in himself, thereby increasing his mental and moral strength and becoming the shining exemplar and serene repository of a host of spiritual graces. The *yogin* can activate and master any power manifest in Nature and mirrored in the human microcosm, refining its operation through his vestures, honing his inward poise and inimitable timeliness in its benevolent use. Thus, by contemplating the *sattva* or light within, discarding the reflected lights imperfectly and intermittently transmitted through the sensory apparatus, the *yogin* can investigate and come to cognize every subtle thing, whether small, hidden, veiled or very distant. He can discern the atom *(anu)* by deploying the light within, for all light is ultimately one. Should he choose to practise *sanyama* in respect to the sun, he can come to know the harmonies of the solar system from the standpoint of its hidden structure as a matrix of solar energies. Further, he can know all solar systems by analogy with ours, and so his comprehension of cosmic forces expressed in, through and around the sun is more than mere familiarity with the structure of a physical system. He also grasps the architectonics — psychic, mental and spiritual — of all such systems. Similarly, his concentration on the moon yields insights into the intricate arrangements of the stars, since, like the moon, they are all in motion around multiple centres. By concentrating on the pole-star — whose arcane significance is far more than what is commonly assumed on the basis of its visible locus in the sidereal vault — he discerns the motions of the stars in relation to one another, not just on the physical plane but also as the shimmering veil of Ishvara, the manifested Logos of the cosmos.

Directing the power of *sanyama* upon the soul's vestures, the *yogin* can calmly concentrate on the solar plexus, connected with the pivotal *chakra* or psycho-spiritual centre in the human constitution, and thus thoroughly grasp the structure and dynamics of the physical body. By concentrating on the pit of the throat, connected with the trachea, he can control hunger and thirst. Since hunger and thirst are physical expressions at one level of being which have corresponding correlates and functions at every level, his concentration can also affect mental and psychic cravings, since he has mastered the *prana* or vital energy flowing from this particular *chakra*. More specifically, by concentrating on the *nadi*, or nerve-centre called the 'tortoise', below the trachea, the *yogin* gains mental, psychic and physical steadiness, facilitating enormous feats of strength.

If *sanyama* is directed to the divine light in the head, the *yogin* can come to see *siddhas*, perfected beings. This supple light is hidden in the central *sushumna* nerve in the spinal column, and emanates that pristine vibration *(suddhasattva)* which is magnetically linked to the sun and is transmitted through the moon. Concentrating on that supernal light, the *yogin* can perceive those perfected beings whose luminous and translucent vestures are irradiated by the light of the Logos *(daiviprakriti)*. Similarly, concentration on the laser light of spiritual intuition, *kundalini* released by *buddhi*, results in flashes of inward illumination. This light emanates from *pratibha*, the pure intellect which is self-luminous and omnidirectional, constant and complete, unconnected with earthly aims and objects. Focussing on its radiance releases *taraka jnana*, the transcendental gnosis which has been aptly termed 'the knowledge that saves'. This primeval wisdom is wholly unconditioned by any temporal concern for self or the external world, is self-validating and self-shining, the ultimate goal of Taraka Raja Yoga. It puts one in close communion with Ishvara whilst preserving a vital link, like a silver thread, with the world of woe, illusion and ignorance. *Pratibha* is that crystalline intellection exemplified by Bodhisattvas who have transcended all conditionality, yet seek to serve ceaselessly all souls trapped in the chains of bondage. By concentration on the secret, spiritual heart — the *anahata chakra* — the *yogin* becomes attuned to cosmic intellection, for the *anahata* is man's sacred connection with cosmic consciousness, reverberating until near death with the inaudible yet ever pulsating OM.

Should the *yogin* master all these marvellous *siddhis*, he would still remain ensnared in the world which is pervaded by pain and nescience, until he is prepared to take the next, absolutely vital step in the mastery of *taraka jnana*. Any individual involuntarily participates in the stream of sensory experience by blindly assenting to the pleasure-pain principle. This will last as long as he cannot discriminate between *purusha*, the cosmic Self, and the individuating principle of spiritual insight, *sattva*. Even the subtlest light shining in the incomprehensible darkness of pure Spirit, *purusha*, must be transcended. The *Yogabhashya* states the central issue: "It has therefore been asked in the *Upanishad*: By what means can the Knower be known?" *Sanyama* must be entirely directed to *purusha* so that it is perfectly mirrored in the serene light of noetic understanding *(sattva)*. *Buddhi*, that intuitive faculty of divine discernment through which the highest *sattva* expresses itself, becomes a pellucid mirror for *purusha*. Just as *purusha*, cosmically and individually, penetrates and comprehends *prakriti*, so too the highest *prakriti* now becomes the indispensable means for apprehending *purusha*. This is the basis for *svasamvedana*, ultimate self-knowledge, the paradigm for all possible self-study at any and every level of consciousness and being. Once this fundamental revolution has occurred, self-consciousness can turn back to the world of objects — which once plunged it into a state of delusion and later gave rise to a series of obstacles to be surmounted — and adopt a steadfast, universal standpoint flowing from all-potent, pure awareness. What once needed various mental and psycho-physical mechanisms can now be accomplished without adventitious aids, thereby dispensing altogether with all conditionality and systemic error.

In practice, the *yogin* can now freely and directly exercise the powers commonly connected with the lower sense-organs, without dependence on sensory data. Hence his sight, hearing, smell, taste and especially touch are extra-sensory, far greater in range and reach than ever before, precisely because there is no longer reliance on imperfect sensory mechanisms conditioned by physical space and psychological time. What were once obstructions to the deepest meditation (*samadhi*) can now serve as talismanic aids in benefitting both Nature and Humanity. The *yogin* can, for example, choose at will to enter another's body with full consent, because his mind is no longer entangled with a physical or astral vesture and because he knows the precise conduits through which minds are tethered to bodies. Having risen above any and all temptation to gratify the thirst for sensation or the craving for experience, he can employ his extraordinary powers and extra-sensory faculties solely for the sake of universal enlightenment and the welfare of the weak.

Having gained complete self-mastery, the *yogin* can now exercise benevolent control over invisible and visible Nature (*prakriti*) for the *Agathon*, the greatest good of all. Since even his own vestures are now viewed as external to him, his relation to them has become wholly isomorphic with his conscious connection to the vital centres in the Great Macrocosm. By mastering *udana*, one of the five currents of *prana*, chiefly connected with vertical motion, the *yogin* makes his body essentially impervious to external influences, including the presence of gravity and the inevitability of death. By mastering *samana*, the current of *prana* which governs metabolic and systemic processes, he can render his body self-luminous and radiant, as Jesus did during his climactic transfiguration and as Moses is said to have done during his salvific descent from Mount Sinai. Knowing the integral connection between the inner ear and *akasha*, the supple light and etheric empyrean in invisible space, the trained *yogin* can hear anything that ever impressed itself, however distantly, upon that universal, homogeneous and supersensuous medium. Similarly, knowing the vital connection between the astral body and *akasha*, he can make his body light and even weightless, and also as pliable and versatile as a superb musical instrument.

From the standpoint of self-consciousness, the *yogin* who has mastered *taraka jnana* can practise *mahavideha,* the power of making the mind wholly incorporeal, so that it abides in pure and perfect awareness beyond even *buddhi.* Such a state of cosmic consciousness is indescribable, though it can be identified as that exalted condition in which no light anywhere is absent from his mental horizon. From the standpoint of Nature, the perfected *yogin* has total control of matter and can fully comprehend it in its subtlest and most minute forms. He can manifest through his vestures the entire spectrum of possibilities of universal self-consciousness and effortless control over matter — merging into the atom, magnifying himself into the galactic sphere, making the human temple worthy of every perfection, including grace, beauty, strength, porosity, malleability and rock-like hardness. Controlling the seven sense-organs, the masterly *yogin* knows precisely how they function on the spiritual, mental, moral and physical planes, and he can instantaneously cognize anything he chooses. Comprehending and controlling *pradhana,* the common principle and substratum of invisible Nature, he can direct every change and mutation in material *prakriti.* He is no longer subject to the instruments he employs, for the entire cosmos has become his Aeolian harp and sounding-board.

The *yogin's* total grasp of the elusive and ever-shifting distinction between *purusha* and *prakriti,* especially between the universal Self and the individuating principle of understanding *(sattva),* between subject and object at all levels, becomes the basis for his unostentatious sovereignty over every possible state of existence. His complete comprehension of the Soundless Sound (OM), of the Sound in the Light and the Light in the Sound, results in what is tantamount to serene omnipotence and silent omniscience. Yet although the perfected *yogin* is a Magus, a Master of gnosis, wholly lifted out of the sphere of *prakriti* and supremely free, self-existent and self-conquered, he does not allow even the shadow of attachment to transcendental joy to stain his sphere of benevolence to all. Complete and invulnerable non-attachment, *vairagya,* can destroy the lurking seeds of self-concern and susceptibility to delusion, and he may thus approach the threshold of *kaivalya,* supreme self-emancipation. If, however, he is enthralled by the glorious deities and celestial wonders he encounters in the spiritual empyrean, he could rekindle the dormant yearning for terrestrial life, with its fast-proliferating chain of earthly entanglements. But if he steadfastly practises *sanyama* on the *kalachakra,* the Wheel of Time, and even more, penetrates the last veil of *kala,* the mystery of Being, Becoming and Be-ness, the infinitude of the Eternal Now hidden within the infinitesimal core of the passing moment, he can dissolve without trace the divine *yogamaya* of conditioned space-time. Such unfathomable depths of consciousness transcend the very boundaries of gnosis and cannot be conveyed in any language, conceptual or ontological.

The purest and most perfect awareness is indistinguishable from the direct apprehension of ultimate Reality wherein, in the words of Shankaracharya, the very distinctions between seer, seeing and sight, or knower, knowing and known, wholly vanish. Here, for example, the Leibnizian principle of the identity of indiscernibles collapses in thought and language. Knowing eternity-in-time in its irreducible moments, even indistinguishable events or objects can be instantaneously separated in an ecstatic, simultaneous apprehension of the One without a second, of the One mirrored in the many, of the many co-present in the One, of the tree of knowledge within the tree of life. And yet nothing is known by species, genus or class: each thing is known by its instantaneous co-presence. *Taraka jnana* is thus not only omniscient in its range but simultaneous in its scope. The *yogin* knows at once all that can possibly be known, in a world of commonalities, comparisons and contrasts, and infinitesimal parts within infinite wholes.

Supreme emancipation, *kaivalya,* dawns only when *purusha* shines unhindered and *sattva* receives the full measure of light. *Purusha* is no longer veiled, obscured or mirrored by the faculties and functions of *prakriti,* and *buddhi* becomes unconditional, untainted by any teleological or temporal trace. There is no more any consciousness of seeking the light, which the aspirant legitimately entertains, or of radiating the light, which the recently omniscient *yogin* experiences. There is now solely the supernal and omnipresent, ever-existing light of *purusha,* abiding in its intrinsic splendour of supreme freedom, and this is *kaivalya,* the supreme state of being "aloof and unattached, like *akasha*" (*Srimad Bhagavatam* VI). Since this is the ultimate goal of Taraka Raja Yoga, in terms of which each spiritual potency, skill and striving must be calibrated, Patanjali devoted the concluding fourth *pada* to this exalted theme.

In the memorable words of the Sage Kapila to Devahuti, the daughter of Manu:

> The moment his mind ceases to discriminate, by reason of the activities of the senses, between objects which are not intrinsically different, looking upon some as pleasant, on others as not, that moment he sees with his own mind his own SELF, equable and self-luminous, free from likes and dislikes, and completely aloof, serenely established in the intuition of transcendental rapture. Pure Consciousness is spoken of variously as *parabrahm, paramatman, Ishvara* or *purusha.* The Lord, the One without a second, masquerades as the multiplicity of seer, seen and so on. The one goal of all yoga, practised perfectly with all its ancillary disciplines, is the attainment by the *yogin* of total detachment from the world. . . .
>
> At the same time he should learn to see the SELF in all creatures, and all creatures in the SELF, making no difference between them, even as in all creatures he recognizes the presence of the gross elements. Just as fire looks different in the diverse logs that it burns, owing to the difference between the logs, so too does the SELF seem different in the varied bodies it indwells. The *yogin,* vanquishing thus the inscrutable *maya* of the Lord, which deludes the *jiva* and is the cause of the phenomenal world, rests secure in his own true state.
>
> *Srimad Bhagavatam* III

KAIVALYA PADA

With the fulfilment of their twofold purpose, the experience and the emancipation of the SELF, *and with the cessation of mutations, the* gunas *cannot manifest even for a moment.*

Yogabhashya

Patanjali provided a vast perspective on consciousness and its varied levels, as well as the necessary and sufficient conditions for sustained meditation. He set forth the essential prerequisites to meditation, the persisting obstacles to be overcome by the conscientious seeker, and the awesome powers and exhilarating experiences resulting from the progressive attainment of *samadhi*. In the fourth *pada*, the heart of which is *kaivalya*, the ultimate aim and transcendental culmination of the discipline of Taraka Raja Yoga, Patanjali epitomized the entire process from the standpoint of the adept *yogin* in meditation. He was thus able to offer a rounded exposition which might otherwise remain obscure. The *Yoga Sutras* is for daily use, and not dilettantish perusal. Its compelling logic is intrinsically self-validating as well as capable of continuous self-testing. Its reasonableness and efficacy are endorsed by a long succession of accredited seers and seekers.

The *siddhis*, or arcane, supernormal and spiritual powers, may be inborn in any incarnation. Although they may appear spontaneous or superfluous to the superficial eye, they are strictly the products of profound meditations in previous lives, as they depend for their development on mastery of the mind and its myriad correlations amongst the manifold elements in the cosmos. Since individual consciousness may have undergone such strenuous discipline in prior incarnations but not in the present life, the imprint of these practices in the immortal soul can be retained without conscious remembrance of the fact. If, however, it is not supported and strengthened by conscious discipline (*abhyasa*) in this life, the manifestation of unusual mental capacities and uncommon *siddhis* may be sporadic, relatively uncontrolled and precariously inconstant. Furthermore, because all knowledge is recollection, in a Platonic sense, and the residues of the past linger in the present, *siddhis* can sometimes be stimulated by hallucinogenic drugs and herbs like verbena, or by sacred chants and time-honoured incantations, although the effects of external aids are notoriously uneven and ever unpredictable. Systematic austerities (*tapas*) may also release something of the attainments of previous incarnations, but true *samadhi* alone provides the rigorous, progressive and reliable pathway to self-mastery and sovereignty over the subtle forces of Nature. With such complete command of the *gunas* or modes of *prakriti* as it manifests in the mind and in the external world, the adept *yogin* can alter his nature from one class of being (the human) to another (a *deva* or god, in a broad sense of the term), if the karmic conditions in life are congenial and conducive to rapid development. Even then, the wise practitioner would not pursue this discipline except from the highest of motives, for anything less would hinder *prakrityapurat,* the 'flow of *prakriti*' needed for its safe and smooth accomplishment.

No significant change of human nature would be possible if it merely depended upon instrumental causes, for these can only rearrange components or unveil hidden but pre-existent features. Hence, doing good deeds cannot transform one's composite nature, nor need they bear that burden, for one's inmost nature is *purusha,* Self alone, and this is reflected by pure consciousness, *buddhi.* Right conduct on the moral and mental planes can remove various obstructions to the rapid unfoldment of the vast potential of consciousness and that complete realization of *purusha* known as self-emancipation (*kaivalya*). To the *yogin,* his mind serves as the director of any number of mental matrices or emanated minds which can carry out semi-independent functions under its supervision. Just as the presence of *purusha* quickens and facilitates the fertile expansion of consciousness, so too the controlled mind of the *yogin* stimulates intellection everywhere. The *yogin* can work through the receptive minds of mature disciples, aiding all humanity by strengthening its spiritual aspirations. Whether mental aspects of the *yogin* or the sympathetic minds of others, no matrix of consciousness is free of *samskaras* or mental deposits, save the *yogin*'s mind born of meditation. Only the consciousness integrated by pure *dhyana* is devoid of all impediment.

The *yogin* is above good and evil acts, not because he has become indifferent to the consequences of action, but rather because he is naturally disposed to remove all obstructions and mental deposits. Good conduct as well as bad bears fruit for the doer, but the *yogin* acts in such complete accord with Nature that what he does responds to necessity, being neither pure *(sattva)* nor polluted *(tamas)* nor mixed, like that of most human beings. His conduct follows a fourth course, that of *nishkama* or desirelessness, so that he cannot be said to do what he wishes, but rather he only does what needs to be done. *Nishkama* karma, the fruition of pure desireless action, neither returns nor clings to the *yogin*. Being one with Nature, he ceases to be a separative centre of focus or agency, and his actions, strictly speaking, are no longer 'his', being the spontaneous play of *prakriti* before *purusha*. Hence, he leaves no impressions or residues in his consciousness even whilst doing his duty with single-minded precision, since he acts as the willing instrument of *purusha* immanent in *prakriti*. He has only former mental deposits, resulting from past karma, which he meticulously removes to attain total freedom.

The *yogin*'s assiduously nurtured capacities disallow the emergence of fresh karma, the results of which could adhere to him because he is no longer subject to *vasana*, the force of craving and the unchecked impulse for life in form, with its attendant consequences. But he cannot instantly dissolve karma generated long ago, for whatever was the result of *vasana* in the past must inevitably linger, although the *yogin* is aware of its antecedents and does not become distracted or discouraged by it. In addition to the results that are already manifest, the force of craving and the *vasanas* (identifiable traces of unfulfilled longings and the cumulative karma they rapidly engender) deposit unconscious residues in the mind. These are more difficult to discern, for they are not recurring modifications of consciousness such as those induced by specific objects of desire, but are subtle tinctures or discolorations in the lens of cognition, hard to detect, recognize and remove. Being unconscious, and unknown to the thinker, they will appear only when conditions are ripe, and the yogin must patiently wait for their emergence in order to eliminate them. Even though immense periods of time and many incarnations may intervene between the initial insertion of the *vasanas* into consciousness and their eventual emergence, they are neither dissolved nor transformed, for they are retained in a stream of soul reminiscence which is not brain-dependent, and which indeed provides a basis of continuity. This stream of latent reminiscence is revealed in the sometimes sudden appearance of surprising tendencies that seem out of character, but are nonetheless inescapable in the strict operation of karma.

Although any specific *vasana* could, in principle, be traced to a particular point in time — some previous incarnation — when the stream of consciousness encountered a similar cluster of thoughts, feelings or acts, *vasana* or desire in general is atemporal. It is coeval with mind *(chitta)* and with the cosmos. Whilst any distinct *vasana* could first appear only when a congenial psycho-physical structure arose to make its manifestation possible, *vasana* as a force is an inextricable element in the matrices of differentiated matter. Just because the propensity to enjoyment or self-indulgence is an integral aspect of the cosmic process — the captivating dance of *prakriti* before *purusha* — the overcoming of all such propensities demands a deliberate choice maintained over time through Taraka Raja Yoga, the discipline of transcendental detachment. *Vasana* finds its support in the mutable mind, which is the action of *prakriti* owing to the proximity of *purusha*. Only when the mind is fully awake, wholly focussed and serenely steadfast will *vasana* vanish. This is equivalent to the potential ability of *prakriti* to behold *purusha* qua *purusha* without wavering, and this is only possible as a deliberate act — *buddhi* reflecting *purusha* without distortion or fluctuation.

Considered from the temporal standpoint, the protracted continuity of *vasana* as a strong force and the specific *vasanas* as persisting matrices of memory suggest the arbitrariness of the divisions of time into past, present and future. Each *vasana* is but a seed which inevitably grows into a plant and bears appropriate fruit: knowing the seed, one can cognize all future states of development. In the present lie latent the past and the future, just as the present was contained in the future and will remain until it slides speedily into the past. The underlying reality cannot be understood without seeing the present as no more than a moving phase through the limitless continuum of time, all of which is latent save for the swiftly passing moment. When all the *vasanas* have been consigned to the past, and when even the very basis of desire ceases to bother consciousness, *kaivalya* alone abides. All continuous change and the ramifying consequences of change are the tumultuous activity of the *gunas,* and when that relentless activity belongs to the past, no longer swaying the mind of the *yogin,* the *gunas* have ceased their incessant interplay in the stream of consciousness. Becoming latent, they have ceased to manifest and have become dormant or homogeneous, leaving intact the luminous vision of serene self- emancipation *(kaivalya).*

An object is what it is not because of some unique substratum, for the ultimate substratum of everything is the same. An object is distinct only because of the complex configuration of the *gunas,* the ceaseless interplay of which constitutes its nature. The fluid geometry of Nature, with the shifting ratios of *gunas,* permits some objects to persist longer than others, but the principle remains the same and endurance is merely relative. Even though an object survives for a time, the mutual activity of the *gunas* which constitutes each mind is different and alters at varying rates. Hence each person cognizes the object distinctively. The object is independent of each and every mind, though all apprehension of the object is entirely mind-dependent. Whether an object is known or not is the result of whether or not a particular mind is attracted to it. *Purusha,* however, cannot be a mental object. Rather, it is seen directly when the mind remains focussed upon it and does not move. Significantly, direct awareness of *purusha* occurs when the mind ceases to act, which in Sankhya philosophy is equivalent to saying that the mind ceases to be what it is. *Purusha* witnesses all mental modifications and is the true Knower precisely because it does not alter or waver.

The mind is not self-luminous and cannot know itself by its own effort. Subject to change, it can be seen as an object by another, and ceaselessly changing, it cannot know itself, for change cannot discern change, just as relativities cannot calibrate relativities. *Purusha,* the ever changeless, is alone the Knower, whose reflection is cast upon consciousness, which then knows derivatively. Since the mind moves from moment to moment, it cannot both function as that which cognizes and that which is cognized. Hence, that which cognizes the mind whilst it cognizes objects (and so undergoes modification) is above the mind. Since consciousness operates on many levels, the level of awareness which apprehends consciousness necessarily transcends the level of the apprehended consciousness. Ultimately, *purusha* comprehends all consciousness. One cannot speak of one mind knowing another within itself, as if the human being were constituted by many minds — an erroneous view encouraged by the limitations of descriptive and conceptual languages; one would have to posit an infinite regress of such minds, each knowing the one 'below' or 'in front of' itself, since none could know itself. The absurdity of an infinite series of minds within the consciousness of each individual is shown clearly by the problem of memory. Which mind would then remember? All of them? An infinitude of interacting memories would result in utter confusion of consciousness.

Self-cognition is possible when the relativating nature of the mind — its constant fluctuation which is the activity of the *gunas* — ceases. Pure consciousness desists from deploying the mind and so can know it, and when it does so, it ceases to be involved in any sort of movement from moment to moment. "The self-knowledge spoken of here," W.Q. Judge wrote, "is that interior illumination desired by all mystics, and is not merely a knowledge of self in the ordinary sense." Likening consciousness to light and the mind to a globe, I.K. Taimni suggested a striking metaphor: "If a light is enclosed within a translucent globe, it reveals the globe. If the globe is removed, the light reveals itself." This revelation is not knowledge in any ordinary sense, because within it there is no subject-object distinction, no separation of perceiver, perceived and perception; there is only the eternal Reality of the Self-illuminated *purusha*. Although the mind, acted upon by the *gunas* and so consisting wholly of *prakriti*, is not consciousness, it is tinctured by *purusha* and receives its luminous hue from it, even whilst suffused with the gaudier colours of the world of objects. It seems to be both conscious and non-conscious, and so those who do not know *purusha* but experience its effects in *prakriti* mistake the mind, an instrument, for consciousness itself, when in fact the true cognizer of objects impressed upon the mind is *purusha*. This root error — mistaking the organ of perception for the power of perception — is the origin of all ignorance, illusion and sorrow.

"The mind, which is essentially an assemblage," the *Yogabhashya* teaches, "cannot act on its own to serve its own interests." (IV.24) Modified by a chaotic series of new impressions and weighed down by myriad deposits from past impressions, the mind cannot act for itself even though it thinks it does. From a teleological standpoint, the mind exists solely for *purusha*, and despite an individual's deep-seated, ignorant confusion — the inexorable cause of sorrow — all mental activity arises in association with the Self, which it unknowingly seeks. Impressions engender a *maya* of independent activity which is dispelled in *samadhi*, wherein the nature of the mind is discerned. When the Perceiver, *purusha*, sees beyond the confusion of ordinary cerebrations, there is no identification of the power of sight with the instrument of seeing, and it is entirely unaffected by the attributes, tendencies and images of the mind. The fully awakened, alert and tranquil mind, settled in the supreme stillness of *samadhi*, speedily learns correct cognition and moves steadily in the direction of *kaivalya*, self-emancipation. In fact, it is *purusha* hidden behind the gossamer veils of intellection whose light illumines the way, but, in the apt analogy of I.K. Taimni, like the magnet attracting iron filings, the mind seems to move towards the magnetic *purusha*, when in truth the invisible power of *purusha* draws the mind to itself. At this exalted stage, the individual seeks nothing except the total freedom of self-emancipation. Even when the mind, like a guided missile locked on to its target, moves without the slightest wavering or change of course towards the luminous *purusha*, old impressions will cyclically reassert themselves, owing to their unspent momentum. They can be eliminated by the same methods developed for dissolving the *kleshas* or afflictions, except that here the *yogin* knows them already for what they are and can instantaneously destroy them, or return them to complete dormancy, through undisturbed discernment (*vivekakhyati*) of the True Self (*purusha*).

When the *yogin* abides in this peaceful state wherein *purusha* alone stands at the focal point of his entire consciousness, he verges on *prasankhyana*, omniscience or complete illumination. Since any lurking attachment can be a hindrance to self-realization, he must renounce even the desire for the highest illumination, save insofar as it may elevate all existence. From the inception of his spiritual quest in lives long past, *viveka* (discrimination) and *vairagya* (detachment) have been crucial to his endeavours. As *viveka* culminates in *vivekakhyati* (discernment of the Real), so too *vairagya* culminates in *paravairagya*, supreme detachment towards the highest conceivable fruit of effort, *prasankhyana*. When this occurs, *samadhi* becomes *dharmamegha*, the rain cloud of righteousness, which is perpetual discernment of *purusha* or unending enlightenment. The circle is closed, the line returns upon itself, and the *yogin* passes from linear time into the omnidirectional realization of *purusha*, the Self, rising above time to the Eternal Now which transcends every moment though implicit in temporal succession. All the residues of the afflictions (*kleshas*) simply drop away as water runs off an impervious surface, and the *yogin* finds self-emancipation even in embodied life. *Dharmamegha samadhi* destroys the residuum of karma and the *kleshas* at the root, so that they can never arise again. The *yogin* has attained that supreme felicity from which there is no falling away.

The *yogin's* cognition becomes infinite and without any limit whatsoever, for of the three *gunas, rajas* and *tamas* have ceased to be active. But even this cognition is transcended, for the stilling of *rajas* and *tamas* deprives *sattva* of a contrasting field for expression, and so all three *gunas* become quiescent. This can be conceived as their merger into homogeneous latency or as their cessation, for they no longer sustain the process of ceaseless transformation. Without such transformation, there is no existence as evident in Nature (*prakriti*), and yet since they remain latent they still exist for all those who live in ignorance. As all knowledge depends upon transformations of consciousness which occur through the succession of moments (*kshanas*), knowledge is limited by the discontinuity of moments. For the *yogin* who has reached the threshold of *kaivalya*, the succession of moments is seen as a discrete continuum and is wholly transcended. His knowledge is no longer bound by temporal succession because he beholds the process as a whole. Rather than being subject to the transformations of the world, he sees them as an endless succession of discrete states, whilst his transcendental (*taraka*) knowledge is continuous and complete. He is now the Perceiver (*purusha*), utterly unaffected by the passing show of phenomenal Nature (*prakriti*).

The *gunas,* no longer stirred to activity by the presence of *purusha,* are reabsorbed into absolute latency, and *purusha* abides in its own essential nature, without any trace of ignorance, misconception, confusion and sorrow. For the *yogin,* experience comes to an end, for he has become one with his true nature, which is *purusha,* the energy of pure consciousness — devoid of moments — which is cosmic ideation, upon which all noumena and phenomena depend. This is complete emancipation,

kaivalya, and supreme peace, *nirvana. Kaivalya* is the ineffable
state of stillness — though such terms are wholly inadequate,
metaphysically and metapsychologically — which is the self-
existence of *purusha* in and as itself. The *yogin* is no longer captive
to the central duality postulated in Sankhya philosophy, for he
beholds *purusha*, which is himself, in the entire cosmos, and the
entire cosmos, which is also himself, in *purusha*. For him, as in
Mahayana mysticism, *nirvana* is *samsara* and vice versa. Since there
is no separation between the two, there is no room for even the
subtlest error, and so sin and sorrow vanish forever. *Sat-Chit-
Ananda*, Being, Consciousness and Bliss, constitute for him the
fullness of *purusha*, which nonetheless abides beyond them as the
attributeless Self.

What, one might ask, does the *yogin* do now? Does he abide
forever in unalloyed bliss? Such questions cannot be raised, for
the *yogin* is no longer a creature of time and space. Rather than
being now or doing then, he always was, is and will be, for he
lives in the Eternal Now. Even though consciousness, bound by
time, change and error, makes of such an inconceivable condition
a frozen ecstasy, no picture of it can be anything but a fantasy
rooted in ignorance. The *yogin* is entirely free and moves through
sublime states of awareness which the unenlightened mind can
neither imagine nor articulate, and therefore Patanjali, a true Sage,
remained silent. When the *yogin* ceases to be a part of the temporal
process and becomes indistinguishable from it — on the principle
of the identity of indiscernibles — he becomes its creator. He was
there in the beginning and he is its *eschaton*, the end and goal
beyond which there is only Silence.

In the memorable words of *Shrimad Bhagavatam*, Book XI:

> The yogin, having discarded the notions of 'good'
> and 'bad', though experiencing the objects of the senses
> in all their diversity, is no more addicted to them than
> the wind to the places where it happens to blow. The
> yogin who has realized the SELF, though he seems to
> identify with the properties of the material vesture he

inhabits, is no more attached to them than the breeze is attached to the fragrant scent it carries. Even whilst remaining in the body, the Sage should think of his soul as unattached to the body and the like, and unlimited just as the sky is, not only because it is present in all Nature, animate and inanimate, as the invariable concomitant, but being identical with the Supreme, it is also all pervading. . . .

Pure and kind-hearted by nature, the Sage is like water, in that he is a sanctifying influence in the lives of those who purify themselves by seeing, touching or speaking of him. Radiating power, enhanced by austerities, possessing nothing, yet imperturbable, the *yogin* who has steadied his mind remains unsoiled like the fire, regardless of what he may consume. . . . While the creation and destruction of the bodies that the SELF assumes proceeds every moment at the hands of Time, which rushes like a swift stream, the SELF remains unnoticed, like the emergence and subsidence of tongues of flame in a burning fire.

BETWEEN HEAVEN AND EARTH

BETWEEN HEAVEN
AND EARTH

The great antique heart, how like a child's in its simplicity, like a man's in its earnest solemnity and depth! heaven lies over him whersoever he goes or stands on the earth; making all the earth a mystic temple to him, the earth's business all a kind of worship. Glimpses of bright creatures flash in the common sunlight; angels yet hover, doing God's messages among men. . . . A great law of duty, high as these two infinitudes (heaven and hell), dwarfing all else, annihilating all else — it was a reality, and it is one: the garment only of it is dead; the essence of it lives through all times and all eternity!

The essence of our being, the mystery in us that calls itself 'I,' — what words have we for such things? — it is a breath of Heaven, the highest Being reveals himself in man. This body, these faculties, this life of ours, is it not all as a vesture for the UNNAMED?

THOMAS CARLYLE

Rounds and Races are integral to cosmic and human evolution. This septenary teaching is of crucial significance to the conceptual framework of Gupta Vidya. Metaphysics and ethics are fused in one unbroken series of instinctual and intuitive states of unfolding monadic consciousness in slowly evolving material vestures. Of the seven planes of Kosmic consciousness, the lower four *rupa* planes provide the seemingly objective matrix for the seven globes of the Earth Chain. The upper three *arupa* planes are almost incomprehensible by the uninitiated and are closely connected with the ineffable mystery of Mahatic self-consciousness, at once the source and support of universal progress upon the seven globes of human evolution.

> These seven *planes* correspond to the seven *states*
> of consciousness in man. It remains with him to attune
> the three higher states in himself to the three higher
> planes in Kosmos. But before he can attempt to attune,
> he must awaken the three 'seats' to life and activity.
>   *The Secret Doctrine*, i 199

Any human being who is truly serious about activating these dormant spiritual centres and selflessly attuning them to the three higher planes of Kosmic consciousness must think away entirely from the enveloping vestures and move upon the "waters of Space", the empyrean of 'airy nothings', the Akashic void within the Hebdomadic Heart, the Kingdom of Heaven on Earth. In the alchemical process of progressive self-attenuation the enlightened person makes fruitful discoveries about the limits and possibilities, the tendencies and tropisms, of all the varying classes of elementals in the illusory vestures. If any seeker of truth is Buddhic regarding the broad scheme of evolution, which is triple in function and sevenfold in the great circlings of globes by the Monadic Host, then the voluntary assumption of incarnation by Divine Self-consciousness at a certain critical stage of global evolution yields a richer view of the true stature of being human, God *in actu*.

If any sensitive person fully thought out what it means to be a self-conscious being, making meaningful connections in reference to all aspects of life and death, then one would verily become capable of cooperating with the evolutionary scheme by staying in line with those gods and sages who are the unthanked Teachers of Humanity. No such fundamental revolution in consciousness is possible without becoming intensely aware of both motive and method. Motive has to do with morality in the metaphysical sense, the rate of vibration of one's spiritual volition. Is the individual soul consciously seeking to help, heal and elevate every single life-atom? Or, owing to fear, ignorance, suspicion and doubt, is the fugitive soul trapped in a mechanical repetition of moribund hostilities inimical to those whom it irrationally and unintentionally injures? Through unremitting attention to such internal obstructions, one could rise above the lower or lunar planes of consciousness, seeing compulsive tendencies for what they are, and thus introduce by renewed acts of noetic will a strong current of spiritual benevolence. This would be the basis of Bodhisattvic ethics, a joyous mode of relaxed breathing. In pursuing this Aquarian life-style, one is certain to encounter various difficulties in the realm of the mind in regard to one's permeability to astral forces, one's personal vulnerability to reversals, perversion and pride, and also a strange susceptibility to distortions and awkwardnesses that come between what is spontaneously felt at the core of one's being and its deliberate enactment in the chaotic context of social intercourse.

One would have to become mathematically objective about the fluctuating patterns of mental deposits and tendencies that have cut deep grooves in the volatile vestures of personal existence. One would have to see all this in relation to human evolution as a whole, asking relevant questions about the uncouth Fourth Race as well as concerning what one really learnt in the first sub-race of the Fifth Race of original thinkers and theophilanthropists who were effortlessly capable of creative ideation and concentrated endeavour. In asking such questions one has to lift ethical sensitivity beyond the level of the individual monad, through active concern with all humanity, to cosmic planes of cognition. In so doing one could gradually come to make fundamental readjustments in the elusive relationship between one's lower and higher centres of perception, volition and empathy.

Although such a prospect of self-sovereignty may seem to be an enormous evolutionary advance, in retrospect, once it is attained, it will be seen as no more than a self-conscious restoration of the primeval modes of moral awareness of the Third Root Race. Soon after their descent, the gods — the pristine Sons of Wisdom who incarnated into the Third Race — engendered through *Kriyashakti* the sacred progeny of the truly twice-born, the fabled Sons of Ad, the mythic 'Sons of the Fire-Mist', the immaculate Sons of Will and Yoga. What they emanated in unison was a wondrous collective being (Bodhisattvic Golden Egg), a mysterious Bodhi-Tree and deathless fountainhead, the Tree of Noetic Wisdom, from which arose all the initiated Adepts and god-men, gurus and sages of the human race in subsequent epochs of evolution. The arcane teachings affirm that Dakshinamurti, the Initiator of Initiates, was the original Jagadguru (Amitabha), Rishi Narayan or Shri Krishna, the Ancient of Days who stood as Shiva (Avalokiteshwara) behind Buddha, Shankara, Pythagoras and Plato, Confucius and Lao Tzu, Christ and Paul, Count St. Germain and Claude St. Martin, Cagliostro and Mesmer, H.P. Blavatsky and W.Q. Judge. There have always existed on earth the secret mystery-temples in which the whole life of the neophyte through a series of preparatory initiations must eventually lead to grateful prostration before the Great Sacrifice *(Adhiyajna)* and a Host of Hierophants, the Buddhas of Contemplation, silently sustaining the whole world, the Wheel of Samsara, the Great Chain of Being. It was H.P. Blavatsky's accredited privilege to transmit this ancient and sacred teaching in a memorable hymnody in *The Secret Doctrine,* from which every Lanoo may derive inspiration and strength in reawakening the mighty power of sacrifice, the invocation of *Adhiyajna* through *Agniyoga* by the grace of *Adi Sanat,* the *Mahat-Atman.*

> The 'BEING' just referred to, which has to remain nameless, is the *Tree* from which, in subsequent ages, all the great *historically* known Sages and Hierophants, such as the Rishi Kapila, Hermes, Enoch, Orpheus, etc., etc., have branched off. As objective *man,* he is the mysterious (to the profane — the ever invisible) yet ever present Personage about whom legends are rife in the East, especially among the Occultists and the students of the Sacred Science. It is he who changes form, yet remains ever the same. And it is he again who holds spiritual sway over the *initiated* Adepts throughout the whole world. He is, as said, the 'Nameless One' who has so many names, and yet whose names and whose very nature are unknown. He is *the* 'Initiator,' called the 'GREAT SACRIFICE.' For, sitting at the threshold of

LIGHT, he looks into it from within the circle of Darkness, which he will not cross; nor will he quit his post till the last day of this life-cycle. Why does the solitary Watcher remain at his self-chosen post? Why does he sit by the fountain of primeval Wisdom, of which he drinks no longer, as he has naught to learn which he does not know — aye, neither on this Earth, nor in its heaven? Because the lonely, sore-footed pilgrims on their way back to their *home* are never sure to the last moment of not losing their way in this limitless desert of illusion and matter called Earth-Life. Because he would fain show the way to that region of freedom and light, from which he is a voluntary exile himself, to every prisoner who has succeeded in liberating himself from the bonds of flesh and illusion. Because, in short, he has sacrificed himself for the sake of mankind, though but a few Elect may profit by the GREAT SACRIFICE.

It is under the direct, silent guidance of this MAHA — (great) — GURU that all the other less divine Teachers and instructors of mankind became, from the first awakening of human consciousness, the guides of early Humanity. It is through these 'Sons of God' that infant humanity got its first notions of all the arts and sciences, as well as of spiritual knowledge; and it is they who have laid the first foundation-stone of those ancient civilizations that puzzle so sorely our modern generation of students and scholars.

Ibid., i 207-208

This sublime portrait must speak to the imperishable spiritual intuition in the inmost heart of every human being who seeks to cross the threshold. It is truly a theme for reflection, and if used as the basis of deep and daily meditation, it should act upon the sovereign spiritual will. It should lend hidden strength to the capacity to marshal and concentrate in one's divine sphere all sacrificial thoughts, feelings, energies, words and acts. It should also give the indestructible strength to remain like the solitary

Watcher totally bound to his self-chosen post. The very idea of any shadow of turning or variation from one's sacred commitment would be deeply repugnant to one's nature. The esoteric teaching given above was always whispered but only enacted within the *sanctum sanctorum* of the Mystery Schools. It is a theurgic teaching meant to fire a human being through *Agniyoga* and arouse soul-memories (anamnesis) from pre-manvantaric aeons in cosmic evolution. To be able to incarnate such a therapeutic teaching is to light up the rising flame of resolve such as will never be extinguished in the mighty task of universal enlightenment.

Many seekers have genuinely attempted such an authentic and generous discipline but have still been unable to extricate themselves from their own inane servitude to their shadow, their envy and suspicion, their compulsive expansion of that shadow of inherent inferiority through fear and doubt, through obsessional thinking and delusional feeling, and the over-whelming chaos of undeliberate, undiscriminating responses to the worlds of form. This is not only fatal but also like a terminal case of cancer in a human being who has used the priceless boon of truth for blocking the door to the humanity of the future. Regardless, however, of the mistakes and failures of most neophytes, there must come a decisive moment of choice when one is prepared to combine solemnity and simplicity in a joyous acceptance of one's own spiritual mission as a pilgrim-soul, as a true disciple upon the Path, as a vigilant listener to the utterance of Divine Wisdom, as a Happy Warrior in the Army of the Voice, and as a creative restorer of the natural order of spontaneous fellow-feeling towards the whole of humanity.

One must cherish constantly the light of daring, the moral courage to take the Kwan Yin pledge — an irrevocable decision that confers true dignity, spiritual wakefulness and the resonance of responsibility. For such a sacred resolve to be an exemplar of spiritual strength, all of one's being must be involved, without withholding any asset or evading any obligation. Nature is by no means ungenerous in affording seasonal opportunities for honest rededication to self-renewal and service. The fortnight commencing with the winter solstice and culminating on the fourth of January, consecrated to Hermes-Buddha, marks the potent seed-time for the coming year. Soren Kierkegaard observed that "Life can only be understood backwards, but it must be lived forwards." It is important that a sensitive person should prepare for the future by taking a firm, all-inclusive, unconditional position gestated out of deep reflection. One should set apart abundant time for that noble purpose to be truly able to generate the permanent basis of alchemical resolution and spiritual will. Then as one comes down from that exalted state of *samadhi*, enriched by constant meditation and manvantaric sleep, one could renew and resume this profound preparation in the dawn and the dusk, using all the precious time available to "get ready for Dubjed." If this is done between the ages of fourteen and thirty-five, then the time between the solstice and fourth of January could be used annually to light the fires in all souls of the irrevocable and effortlessly selfless commitment to the whole of life and to all the solar and lunar ancestors. If anyone truly performed this *yajna* in the sacred name of the Guru of Gurus, the Hierophant of Hierophants, the Initiator of Initiates, one would receive untold benefits from the service of Krishna, the Purna Avatar, the Logos in the Cosmos and the God in man.

Those who wish to enjoy this sanctification might well look back calmly at the lost years and wasted lives, not in self-serving images in elaborate detail but philosophically in terms of ingrained tendencies and fear-ridden preoccupations. Even through looking back over one year, one could make many discoveries about human vulnerabilities, excuses and rationalizations. One may also see in one's pseudo-Promethean struggles the neglected hooking-points that support one's better self in surviving the *pralaya* of a disintegrating bimillennial epoch and in widely sharing all one's truest perceptions and finest perspectives. While venturing upon this meditative retrospection, one must recognize that one is only seeking the sacred tribe of those who have effortlessly renewed their Bodhisattvic pledges in recurring cycles of descent and incarnations of ascent for the sake of all. One is imbibing strength from those to whom this is as natural as breathing, as effortless as meditating upon the mantrams of Lanoos and Arhats. Having assimilated the sacred teaching of *Jnana Yajna*, one must deeply desire *(Itchasakti)* to insert one's own labours of love and acts of devotion into the Great Sacrifice (Maha Yajna). People are both cursed and blessed by being told these things, because if they listen to Krishna's secret teaching and do nothing about it, then their karma is needlessly burdensome. There is always a risk assumed in intoning Brahma Vach. In general, Gandhi's axiom is fundamental: human nature is such that it must either soar or sink, and whether one goes forward or backward is determined by the benevolent use of modern knowledge and ancient Wisdom.

When spiritual knowledge is made the enduring basis of deep reflection, where it is moistened by the liquid fire of devotion to Universal Good and by the concentrated current of aspiration, then it becomes a breakthrough into inner space. With noetic insight, one can burn out at the core all those defeatist devices of thinking, feeling, speaking and acting which continually toss the initiative back to the illusory self, thereby making spiritual life seem a wearisome, defensive and cheerless struggle, with tension and tightness, and little sweetness or light. In fact, the taking of a Vow during a rising cycle of immense promise for mankind means the restoration of the reins of kingship to the Sovereign Self, and the firm refusal to allow the initiative to be smothered in the ashes of vain hopes and burnt-out ideals. This requires a period of intense *tapas,* a time of mental and physical fasting, self-renewal through silence, abstention and calmness: otherwise, one remains compulsively caught up in muddy streams of sterile emanations and the accompanying flotsam of fuzzy elementals that crowd in and clog the nerve-currents of noetic will. At the root of this dismal predicament is the false idea of who one is and a delusive image of oneself as the egocentric pivot of a world upon which one may make myriad claims. The sacrificial, humane, adult, mellow and mature outlook is the exact opposite. Dag Hammarskjöld once wrote that human life involves a bringing together of oil and air, and then there is a spark. The moment one thinks of rights, there is no spark; the oil and air will never come together. Sadly, human beings repeatedly abort, murder or damage their own chances as souls because they cannot get rid of this fundamentally false idea of a separate self, and even more sadly, in the light of divine teaching, they sometimes cling to it with melodramatic versatility. This is such piteous karma that it is all too poignant to contemplate — on behalf of a single human soul. Therefore one should, for the sake of all, awake, arise and seek the Great Sacrifice, and seek a pellucid reflection in the waters of wisdom. Thus the soil of the brain-mind is stirred, washed and prepared to receive the hidden seed of moral resolution, releasing the spiritual will in silence and secrecy, strengthened by inner humility and true courage during the seed-time of the golden harvest that will feed the hungry.

Those who are dedicated to serve Krishna should meditate upon the hymnody to the Great Sacrifice, or the rhapsody of the Self-Governed Sage in the second chapter of the *Bhagavad Gita*, or on any one of the magnificent portraits of Avatars (Magus-Teachers) in any sacred text, each of which is a great gift which Rishis (Sages) are ceaselessly beatified to hear and chant. If this is the endearing characteristic of all Mahatmas and Bodhisattvas, surely the least any human being can do who has the golden opportunity to use such a text is to become somewhat worthy of the sacred privilege. It is now time to awake from preparatory slumber and truly meditate upon those mantramic texts (in Sanskritic English or German and Russian) and taking even a few sentences, think deeply about their meaning and use. All sacred texts will suggest to their ardent devotees the different stages in reference to mind control, the method of collecting the mind, and the infallible means for removing the delusion and commotion of worldly concern. Having learnt how to settle the mind in a state of calm so that it is like the still lagoon or swan lake, one can let it expand like the blue vault of the sky when enshrined in that serene state. In time, one will come to see the golden sphere of cosmic light within the hollow of the heart in the expanding universe of the *Hiranyagarbha*, the Egg of Brahmā. This will reverse the polarities in the *laya* centres for those who persist in the discipline of selflessness. This secret teaching is jewelled in the hidden heart of every authentic tradition, is always given for the sake of all humanity to those who silently serve the City of Man. Since samsara is merely a mirage of the mind, the disciple must examine and expunge all thoughts that pollute the holy avenues of expression. To do this, one has to meditate upon mighty spiritual conceptions, readily forgetting oneself and thrilling with a feeling of universal gratitude and individual responsibility, reverence and renunciation. From within the spiritual heart, one must evoke the cool courage to look at one's faults with the unerring eye of Buddhic discernment.

It is always crucial to growth that the positive meditations shall be far greater than the negative sacrifices, and that one should really savour the sheer joy of mental procreation and self-cancellation. One should lose one's morbid taste for self-righteous condemnation and image-crippling which is rooted in the paralysing fear of failure and sprouts into the cankerous weeds of an asuric and demonic way of life. Thinking in terms of votive offerings rather than death sentences could vitalize that vacuum in the brain and the heart where lies hidden the elixir of decisiveness and definiteness, a crispness and magnanimity which authenticate the true signature of selfhood. Too many human beings have repeatedly subverted their lives owing to their obsession with their own repulsiveness instead of learning the lesson that they must confront the lie in the soul which conceals the virginal beauty within the antediluvian monster. They have hugely enjoyed meditating upon themselves as total failures, thereby insulting the integrity of the Mahatmas and also doing immeasurable harm because they would have been able to do much good with even a little of this mental prostration to Krishna. One has to recover an exquisite sense of the sacred, the numinous and the unmanifest. One has to reach out repeatedly to that light of the Logos which is above the cerebrum, that which is without any limits or reservations, that divine lustre which can never be mirrored except through *Buddhi* in *Manas*. This is the pristine ray of *Mahat-Atman*, the Universal Self of the Maha Yogin serenely seated upon Mount Kailaś while dancing amidst the ghouls of the graveyard, releasing them from self-torture and their unending cruelty to gnomes and undines, sylphs and salamanders. *Buddhi* is latent in every atom, and yet as *Buddhi* mirrors *Atman*, there is an infallible result, a humbling decisiveness and sovereign assurance which comes from nowhere else than the transcendental Buddhas of Compassion. *Nishchaya* in Sanskrit means 'without any shadow'. When a true *yogin*, from the depths of his or her meditation upon human suffering and the need for Divine Wisdom, vitalizes that immaculate light of the *Atman* in the inmost brain, perfectly mirrored in the cells of the occipital lobe, there arises an ancient assurance and selfless certainty which is concealed and can never be erased. It can never be shown to the blasphemous even though it remains as a hidden lamp behind the borrowed mask. The light of true conviction engenders an irreversible current through *Sachakriya*, a sacred affirmation of the truth of a lifetime. Even though a fallen disciple has languished for long with wasted words, harsh sounds, violent speech, empty offerings, even though enormous karma has been generated by the Atlantean *rakshasa* (monster), all of which will have to be rendered in full account in future lives, nevertheless if he invokes the grace of Krishna-Christos through penitential meditations upon the Soundless Sound, he can place the demonic dwarf beneath the feet of the Divine Dancer and rescue from the debris of shipwreck the white dove of peace, the olive branch of humility, and the self-cancelled pledge of true service.

   All who take advantage of this matchless means of true self-renewal can inaugurate a fundamental change in the polluted *Manas* through *Agniyoga*, the sacred science of baptism through the fires of self-purgation. *Kama manas*, the inverted reflection of *Manas*, becomes constricted through the cohesion of the delusive image of personal identity bound up with intellectual auto-eroticism, physical sensations, sights and sounds, deceptive externalities, and the knots of perversion tightening the myriad cords of foreshortened conceptions of space-time. *Kama manas* is the externalizing and rationalizing mind that needlessly negates others as well as oneself. It is the mediocre mis-educated insecure mind that cuts up everything and dismisses the divine with faint praise and the sneer of guilty derision! *Kama manas* is discontinuous and it creates a monotonous movement from one extreme to the opposite so that it cannot come to rest, but is constantly enslaved by restless caution and is constitutionally incapable of transcending its own meanness and spiritual sterility. All of this is the unnatural legacy of the Fourth Race of graceless giants. Whilst, in the economy of Nature, even such tendencies to grossness represent the tortured descent of the light of consciousness to the lesser hierarchies and lower emanations, the excess of humbug with which this self-assassination is perpetrated through cowardly speech is indeed abnormal. This is the origin of obsessive guilt and compulsive fear, arising from the degradation of the Holy of Holies, the desecration of the sacred tabernacle, the massacre of innocents, the endlessly evasive abdication of responsibility through pride in hypocrisy, self-torment, and the dressing up of moral blindness in the cloak of false modesty. On the other hand, all human beings of every race and tribe, every creed and nihilistic sect, innately enjoy a residual sense of decency, a feeling for tenderness, forgiveness and magnanimity towards the unloved. This is innate in all human beings because it was the great gift of the gods to the Third Race of Innocents. Without a spark of empathy there would be no *conatus*, no basis for a rational self-preservation except in the case of those soulless beings who behave like machines and robots. Knowing all this at some level, one can invoke the blessing of the Avatars to fan the faint spark of *Buddhi* buried within the burnt-out charcoal of a self-throttled *Manas*. Krishna hinted in the *Uttara Gita* that even the elongated shadow of self-betrayal could be slowly shrunk by self-attenuation through sacred speech and abstention from harm to the helpless life-atoms.

Each and all must restore what is natural to the whole of humanity and was exemplified *par excellence* by the authentically initiated Brahmins of antiquity who had little to do with the India of recent millennia, but were true transmitters of the oral traditions of theurgic utterance until the time of betrayal of the Buddha except in cloistered sanctuaries of *yogins* and *sannyasins*.

> When, moved by the law of Evolution, the Lords of Wisdom infused into him the spark of consciousness, the first feeling it awoke to life and activity was a sense of solidarity, of one-ness with his spiritual creators. As the child's first feeling is for its mother and nurse, so the first aspirations of the awakening consciousness in primitive man were for those whose element he felt within himself, and who yet were outside, and independent of him. DEVOTION arose out of that feeling, and became the first and foremost motor in his nature; for it is the only one which is natural in our heart, which is innate in us. . . .
>
> It lives undeniably, and has settled in all its ineradicable strength and power in the Asiatic Aryan heart from the Third Race direct through its first 'mind-born' sons, — the fruits of *Kriyasakti*. As time rolled on the holy caste of Initiates produced but rarely, and from age to age, such perfect creatures: beings apart, inwardly, though the same as those who produced them, outwardly.
>
> *Ibid.*, 210-211

The Initiates of the deathless Race scattered the seeds of primordial wisdom among all the races of men and the Mystery Schools in cloistered gardens, caves and sanctuaries around the globe. The innate feeling of devotion throbbed in the sacred chamber of every human heart, but to be able to exemplify it naturally and instantly has become the lost art of magnanimity in the age of Varna Shankar or the Tower of Babel. The gift of graciousness cannot be bequeathed by external structures or physical heredity in Kali Yuga, the Age of Iron. The class of souls which delayed incarnation — owing to pride in purity, cowardly caution, fear of involvement in the mire of human fallibility, and a stubbornly selfish refusal to move into more differentiated realms — paradoxically became those very beings who, once they had incarnated, were captive to carnality, weakness of will, and fear-ridden worship of the printed word. The iron of self-contempt and false toughness, image-crippling and spiritual circumcision, entered into their souls, their blood and brain-cells. In the legends and myths of antiquity, the original fear of incarnation, owing to deficiency in active meditation upon the entire scale of ascent and descent, resulted in the perverse or compulsive pollution of the powers of thought, imagination and reverence for life. The resulting corruption of consciousness and simian imitativeness became the karmic burden of the Pratyeka Buddhas of spiritual selfishness. The atoms of matter were tainted by the double sin of the mindless and miscegenation. As a result, many gluttonous men and women are constantly caught up in those material particles, or become mediumistic through foul thoughts and fear of invasion. Among the sorcerers, traducers and traitors the power of the *Aum* was lost. The Third Eye closed, with a consequent suffocation of spiritual intuitions in the moral dwarfs of humanity.

The therapeutic restoration of the porosity of the brain-mind to the light of *Atma-Buddhi* is possible. It depends upon the progressive exemplification of five criteria of what is natural to human self-consciousness. *First* is the irrepressible feeling of reverence for the unbroken line of descent of the Great Sacrifice of the Hierophantic Host under the eternal Initiator of Initiates, the evergreen Trees of Knowledge, Enlightenment and Immortality. Honouring others is innate to the human heart: it would show as a true reverence for Nature, for the Spiritual Sun and its myriad rays among all humanity, for all the constellations and the seven kingdoms and the Illustrious Predecessors, Light-Bringers and Pathfinders, reverence that is natural. Anything less is unnatural and abnormal, a moral monstrosity. *Secondly,* there is a longing for the ideal forms and archetypes, a great joy in withdrawing from the pressure of concern with the concrete to the empyrean of invisible potentials, a pure love of Truth, Beauty and Goodness in all forms, selfless ideation on metaphysical paradigms, parapolitical ideals and Universal Good — the Agathon. *Thirdly,* and this is certainly a very decisive test, an innate, instructive and ineradicable conviction (regardless of culture) that the sexual act is sacred, that the Lesser Mysteries of Eros must mirror the pristine Light of the Logos invoked through Sound and Silence in the Greater Mysteries. Anything else runs the risk of ever-increasing desecration of the dignity of human beings, the sanctity of the Holy of Holies, as well as the fecundity of human potentials. *Fourthly,* there is devotion, the only feeling natural to the hearts of men and women of all races, common to the human babe and the young of animals. Devotion, understood rightly, shows in the Rishis and Sages as well as in a child's simplicity which co-exists with authentic solemnity and inner depth. Inherent in the human heart is the ever-present sense of the sacred and the feeling that everything in human worship of the Divine is worthy of minimal respect. This is magically shown in that which corresponds to *Manas* among all the senses, the synthesizing sense of touch. The *fifth* criterion of culture is a recognition of the human body as a temple, not a tomb, of the pilgrim-soul in every person.

> There is but one temple in the universe, and that is the body of man. Nothing is holier than that high form. . . . We touch heaven when we lay our hand on a human body! . . . If well meditated it will turn out to be a scientific fact; the expression . . . of the actual truth of the thing. We are the miracle of miracles, — the great inscrutable Mystery.
>
> *Ibid.,* 212

The pervasive sense of the sacred and universal respect for freedom of thought and choice have become obscured in many victims of modernity owing to a hypnotic fascination with corruption and evil, forgetfulness of the divine mission of the immortal Soul, alienation from others and oneself, especially through fear of failure, estrangement through loneliness, distrust of oneself, and possible misuse in former lives due to cowardice and false ideas connected with evasion of the laws of Nature. Corruption of consciousness must be healed, and what is natural must be restored through the Golden Rule of reciprocity. Already, since 1963, many souls have taken birth in diverse cultures who have a recognition of the need to restore the ethical foundation of human society. This transcends the claims of all cultures to pre-eminence. Such souls will increase in number until a time comes when there will be so many for whom this is so natural that any encouragement given them will help the regeneration of the human race. This will be a distinctly different class of souls from those who came mauled and tormented by the degradation of two world wars, which helped to make popular the works of the corrupt. The attempt to make normal what was abnormal has failed, so far. It was tried in every way, but once the alternatives are known, then what is abnormal had to become more and more desperate and self-destructive because it could not any more pretend to be normal.

The twilight hour of sadists and masochists has now struck, and myriads of pilgrim-souls seek the Midnight Sun and the sacred constellation of the Aquarian Age, which began soon after the *fin de siècle*. The invisible dawn of the cosmopolis is summoned by the flute of the divine cowherd, beckoning home the matured innocents that dared to dream of a Golden Age. Meanwhile, Nataraja of Kailas and Kala-Hamsa enacts the Tandava Dance over the heads of epicurean giants, stoical dwarfs and cynical eunuchs. The age of sectarian religions, technocratic politics and cultural envy is dead. *Kama manas* has been dethroned by *Buddhi-Taijasi,* the Light of the Logos. The age of humanistic science, authentic spirituality and mini-communes has just begun, foreshadowing the end of the twentieth century and the emergence of the City of Man. The inevitable return of initiative to the scattered supporters of what is innate, universal and spiritual, merely suggests that no special pleading is needed for true gratitude and an authentic sense of the sacred. Despite the failures of so many, the philosophy of perfectibility, the religion of responsibility and the science of spirituality will spread far and wide, like the myriad branches of the Ashwatha tree, with its roots in heaven.

The collective self-consciousness that has been perverted must be released through love and wit. If one sees clearly the sacredness of the indestructible teaching of antiquity, one can recognize the Kama Manasic self-interest of Arjuna as a necessary tool in the service of Krishna in the Great War between psyche and nous, the Tower of Babel and the New Jerusalem, the head and the heart of every human being on earth. The true spark of universal brotherhood, reverence for teachers, gratitude to the good earth, and reticent sanctity may, even from a spark, be fanned into the fires of creativity in the service of the civilization of the future. This is the great hope which hides the golden promise. If even a few theophilanthropists would now serve the Bodhi-Tree and the City of Man, the Isle of the Blessed would be grateful beyond measure. Every such sincere effort is assuredly of help in relieving the pain of the human heart, which is widespread today, and also in laying down the universal cornerstones of the academies and ashrams of the future. All cultures need to rediscover what it means to be truly humane. Builders of bridges between Heaven and Earth are few and far between, and always have been; they may be readily recognized by their unswerving fidelity to pledges on behalf of mankind. Citizens of the cosmopolis will unite when they have nothing to lose but their masks of misanthropy — or their fugitive souls, on earth as in heaven.

SPECTATOR AND PARTICIPANT

... those who 'ascend and descend' are the 'Hosts' of what we loosely call 'celestial Beings'. But they are, in fact, nothing of the kind. They are Entities of the higher worlds in the hierarchy of Being, so immeasurably high that, to us, they must appear as Gods, and collectively — GOD. ... there may be a certain limited communication between some of those worlds and our own. To the highest, we are taught, belong the seven orders of the purely divine Spirits; to the six lower ones belong hierarchies that can occasionally he seen and heard by men, and who do communicate with their progeny of the Earth; which progeny is indissolubly linked with them, each principle in man having its direct source in the nature of those great Beings, who furnish us with the respective invisible elements in us.

The Secret Doctrine, i 132-133

In the mystical language of *The Voice of the Silence*, every human being is both agent and witness, both radiator and radiation. As an immortal *Atma-Buddhic* Monad, each human being is a spectator in eternal Duration. As a ray of the ever Unmanifest, each Monad can see what all other Monads can see, through the eyes of the highest *Anupadaka*, the Mahatmas and silent watchers during the night of *pralaya*. Each human being can witness the deaths of civilizations, of beings, even of his own body, just as Mahatmas observe the deaths of worlds, galaxies and all that is at *Maha Pralaya*. Every human being is also a participant, a *Manasa*, a pristine ray capable of pure self-conscious awareness and creative thought, authentic individuation as an 'I am I' consciousness. This active individuality, the *sutratman* that threads the soul's incarnations like jewelled beads upon a string, affords endless opportunities for learning and service. At the same time, each human being is also a spectator and participant in a more immediate spatial and temporal sense.

As a projected ray of *Manas* caught up in *kama* and involved with the astral plane, each human being is also a cerebrating animal ensnared in expectations and excuses, rationalizations and regrets, fantasies and frustrations. On the planes of the lower quaternary, every human being is immersed in vast fields of elementals and *devas*, all the hosts of secondary forces that are under the control of the four Maharajas spoken of in Hindu mythology. These Regents of the four cardinal points of the compass are the channels through which karma is transmitted magnetically, forming and affecting the organs of perception and action of the incarnated human being.

Given the archetypal logic of the involution of spirit into form, it is truly vital that the boundless potential of the Monad must be awakened through the trials of incarnation on the lower planes. The depth and complexity of the lessons to be learnt ensure that each human being will pass many lives of apprenticeship before realizing the ideals of universality in consciousness and freedom from karma. The inherent integrity of the Monad and its consubstantiality with cosmic truth guarantee that it will not rest content until it has wrought this task through to the end, however long it takes. Owing to the integrity of the innumerable intelligences constituting the planes of the lower quaternary, which are themselves ultimately derived from the same Monadic plane of existence as humanity, and which constitute the incipient human kingdoms of future evolution, every self-conscious abuse or misuse of human capacities is exactly mirrored in the lower human vestures. If incarnated human beings find themselves passive and drowsy participants, dim-sighted and dull-witted observers, caught in a seemingly chaotic and confusing world, that is the result of their own past self-neglect. The forces of *tamas* and *rajas* predominate in the *linga sharira* and its vital energy, rendering the temple of the physical form mostly unused and even useless.

The emphasis in incarnated consciousness is almost entirely upon the lower centres. Because the spleen, the liver and the stomach are over-active, most people are caught up to the point of emotional exhaustion. This condition reacts upon the solar plexus, creating a congestion that interferes with both physical and mental digestion, assimilation and elimination. In effect, human beings have handed over their instruments to myriads of entities that execute a kind of a devil dance through a human body. Very few human beings are noetically involved in the processes that ordinarily pass for eating, sleeping, bathing, speaking or making love. A pathetically large proportion of what passes for human life is simply a shadow-play of elementals resulting from human resignation of responsibility. Yet, people are deceived into supposing that they are engaged in meaningful human activity because they have manufactured particular elementals drawn around the *namarupa*, the name and form, which mimic authentic action.

If, through suffering and solicitude for others, one begins to gain a sense of the magnitude of this dismal delusion, it is natural to want to restore dignity to one's own life through a search for knowledge and for the means of making a genuine contribution to the lives of others. Having thus raised one's sights, one may be prepared to read the *Stanzas of Dzyan* and resonate to the ancient accent and self-validating summons of Gupta Vidya.

> LEARN WHAT WE, WHO DESCEND FROM THE
> PRIMORDIAL SEVEN, WE, WHO ARE BORN FROM THE
> PRIMORDIAL FLAME, HAVE LEARNED FROM OUR
> FATHERS.
>
> *Ibid.,* 88

Here speaks the voice of the primordial Mysteries, the voice of all the self-shining Initiates who speak by thinking and think by ideating. Arrayed around a common ineffable centre, like the Buddhas and Bodhisattvas in Tibetan *tankas,* they are ceaselessly engaged in fathomless meditation. Through their adoration and compassion they continually point to Amitabha, to Avalokiteshwara, the one Source and the primordial Flame. This is the divine Tetraktys, the sacred four, the eternal self-existent One called the concealed Lord and also known as the androgyne Father-Mother, the direct emanation from the primordial Flame. From this emanate the primordial seven, the highest *Ah-Hi*, the divine breaths; from those emanate the Manasaputras as well as the builders of form. The primordial seven, the highest beings on the scale of existence, latent during *pralaya* and active during *manvantara*, constitute the ray of the Tetraktys, which is eternal in essence and periodic in manifestation.

The same Teaching is given in terms of the seven Kumaras, the eldest mind-born sons of Brahmā sprung from the fourfold mystery. Brahmā is *Hiranyagarbha*, the resplendent Spiritual Sun, the effulgent golden egg which is like the aura of the entire cosmos.

> In the Rig Veda it is said: — 'THAT, the one Lord of all beings . . . the one animating principle of gods and man,' arose, in the beginning, in the Golden Womb, Hiranyagarbha — which is the Mundane Egg or sphere of our Universe.
>
> *Ibid.*, 89

From that One and the egg, the inseparable and androgyne *Hiranyagarbha-Prajapati*, emanate the Three-in-One, the Tetraktys or sacred Four. The original triune rays in the Tetraktys are the primeval Vedic Trimurti of Agni, Vayu and Surya — spiritual fire, spiritual air and spiritual sun. From these emanate the other seven. Together they constitute either the seven or the ten, depending upon how one counts the original Three-in-One. However reckoned, one must not emphasize any separation between Agni, Vayu and Surya or between these three and the primordial seven, the *Ah-Hi*.

It is best to think of them as one while meditating at dawn, at sunset, at midday and midnight. Whether one employs a sacred mantram or invocation to draw one's entire attention to the great Mystery, or whether one has the idea of it so impacted in the consciousness that it may be linked to anything before the mind's eye, this is the path of those who are serious about living a life of constant gratitude. Once a taste for it is developed, it is pure bliss. It is better to spend time in gratitude than in brooding over the shadow. At the highest level of maintaining a current of ideation, where one becomes a true man of meditation in silence, the One, the egg, the Three-in-One, the seven and the ten are all comprehended within the supreme *Paramatman,* called *guhya* or secret. Even in thinking of it one must exercise reticence, never thinking about it carelessly or mechanically. It must be assimilated and allowed to cohere in secret.

This indivisible unity of *Sarvatman,* the Supreme Soul, has been portrayed in many mystic images — such as that of Vishnu seated upon Adishesha amidst the great ocean of space with Brahmā springing forth from his navel. The symbol of the Spiritual Sun riding a chariot drawn by seven steeds has the same meaning. Hence it is said: *"The seven Lords of Being lie concealed in* Sarvatman *like thoughts in one brain."* This is the basis of the highest meditation and the highest magic, giving strength to the continuous maintenance of one's consciousness as a monadic spectator. Constant adoration of the *Ah-Hi,* the Seven-in-One, the Trimurti of Agni, Vayu and Surya, is the inherent and essential activity of the Monad. Owing to its constant adoration of the primordial One, the primordial Three, the primordial Seven, the Monad is able to maintain ceaseless awareness in eternal Duration. Hence, it can understand Krishna speaking in his highest aspect when he states: *"I established this whole universe with a single portion of myself and remain separate."* This is Krishna as Narayana, the first Logos. He is also Ishwara, the second Logos and the Avatar. He is all these simultaneously, and, as he reveals to Arjuna, he is the Supreme Self — *Sarvatman* — dwelling in secret within every human heart.

The fundamental question facing human beings as obligatory participants in incarnated life is how to sustain this mystical awareness. Owing to the very nature of the vestures of incarnation, one will have to cope with multiples, with matter and with sense-experience. Differentiated, fragmented patterns of thought will arise in the lower mind as the sense-organs prompt comparisons and contrasts. To reaffirm the One in the many and to benefit, as a participant, from the standpoint of the spectator, one may, therefore, meditate upon the Soundless Sound of *Nada Brahman* in its unmanifest essence and in its multiple differentiations as the Army of the Voice. One may meditate upon the OM as the ceaseless eternal sound and also as the great affirmation of the Army of the Voice symbolized by *Oeaohoo*.

> The 'Army of the Voice', is the prototype of the 'Host of the Logos', or the 'WORD' of the Sepher Jezirah, called in the Secret Doctrine 'the One Number issued from No-Number' — the One Eternal Principle.
>
> *Ibid.*, 94

Here, in the arcane code language of Gupta Vidya, fully accessible only to hierophants but amenable to contemplation by any earnest seeker at any level, is a clue to the relationship of sound and number. From zero comes one; that one, when taken together with the zero, makes ten. These are the one from the egg, which are followed by the six and the five, yielding 1065, the value of the first-born who answers to the numbers 7, 14 and 21. This particular sequence of numbers, connected with *Hiranyagarbha*, Brahmā and Vak, intimates the archetypal logic of the pre-cosmic and the logic of the cosmic.

> The esoteric theogony begins with the One, manifested, therefore not eternal in its presence and being, if eternal in its essence; the number of the numbers and numbered — the latter proceeding from the Voice, the feminine Vach, Satarupa 'of the hundred forms', or Nature. It is from this number 10, or creative nature, the Mother (the occult cypher, or 'nought', ever procreating and multiplying in union with the Unit '1', one, or the spirit of Life), that the whole Universe proceeded.
>
> *Ibid.*, 94

Guided by Vak, Sarasvati, Isis, the Army of the Voice is ceaselessly at work as the conscious intelligent host in invisible mystic Nature. Acting with mathematical precision through the fiery force of the Fohatic whirlwind, Vak establishes the Army of the Voice in abstract space reflecting divine Thought. First, the germs of wheels are established in the six directions of space, which represent the junction of pure spirit and matter, the *arupa* and the *rupa*, symbolized by the interlaced triangles or Vishnu's *chakra*. At each angle stands an army of the Sons of Light, whilst the Lipika, the recorders of karma, stand in the middle. The Dhyanic hosts at the angles are mystic watchers, appointed to watch over each respective region from the beginning to the end of the *manvantara*. This is the Divine World, called the 'first' because the manifestation which precedes it, the world of SAT, is the realm of noumena in their primary manifestation. Coeval and coexistent with the One Life, and with that through which the direct energy radiating from the One Reality reaches all beings,

> this 'World of Truth' can be described only in the words of the Commentary as 'A bright star dropped from the heart of Eternity; the beacon of hope on whose Seven Rays hang the Seven Worlds of Being.' Truly so; since those are the Seven Lights whose reflections are the human immortal Monads — the Atma, or the irradiating Spirit of every creature of the human family.
>
> *Ibid.*, 120

From this septenary light proceeds the Divine World, the countless candles lit at the primeval source, the Buddhas or formless divine Souls of the last *arupa* world, the world of the Lipikas and their mystic watchers. Fohat as divine love seeks to unite the pure Spirit, the ray inseparable from the one Absolute, with the divine Soul, the two constituting in man the Monad, and in Nature the first link between the ever-unconditioned and the manifested. Next in the series of developments concerning the cosmic and human principles comes the building of a set of four winged wheels at the corners of a great square. At each of the four cardinal points stands a Regent, one of the four Maharajas, and his host. These guardians of the world are the *Lokapalas*, including Indra in the east, Yama in the south, Varuna in the west, and Kubera in the north. By analogy and correspondence, what applies to the entire cosmos may also be applied to this tiny globe that we call the earth. Even though it is but a speck of dust in the vast sidereal cosmos, there is that on earth which corresponds to the four Regents and their hosts at the four cardinal points of the compass.

Each of the four Regents who rule over the cosmical forces of the four directions and the four primitive elements leads a host of spiritual beings, acting as the protectors of mankind throughout its evolution. Whenever human beings make pilgrimages to the icy northern lands of the midnight sun, whenever they greet the sun rising in the east, or turn with reverence to any direction of the compass, they may salute the spiritual heritage of humanity, and invoke the protection of its guardians, guides and mystic watchers. Anyone who even remotely begins to apprehend this will readily appreciate that the universe, the earth and humanity are fully protected. Human anxiety, individually or collectively, does not reflect any chaotic uncertainty in the cosmos, but only a fear of not being able to acquire a suitable vesture and environment in the future.

If one recognizes that the universe is fully protected through the Army of the Voice, then the question becomes simple: Is one on the side of the universe, or is one, owing to an inability to control breathing and thought, a slavish fascination with foolish opinions, against life? It is better to train in silence to become a silent servant, attentive to the inner voice. One may not hear the voice until the moment of death, the time of which is uncertain, but not distant in any event. If one earnestly listens to the voice in waking, in meditation and in sleep, one will certainly receive intimations. One will learn how to become a silent server of the human race. As each human being has set in motion certain causes through the potency of thought, magnetically awakening and attracting the reaction of the corresponding powers in the sidereal world, the destiny of each human being is connected with one or other of the constellations and their presiding planetary spirits, the *Lokapalas* of the four cardinal and four intermediate points of the compass. These beings rule the forces that direct the physical and material agents required to carry out the decrees of karma. Through them and through the Lipika, the recorders of karma, the destiny of every human being is intimately interwoven with the hosts of the Army of the Voice.

To see oneself as a part of mankind acting under the benevolent protection and karmic discipline of the Army of the Voice is to bid goodbye to identification with one's compulsive, competitive, raucous animal nature. It means becoming a true human being, with a deep inner strength and an enormous willingness to learn, to heighten retention and wakefulness, and to develop a continual reverence for the human race and its invisible guardians. In practice, this means withdrawing attention from external relations, and focussing upon that which is on top of the head of every human being. By seeing oneself and others only as the light that is above the head, one may learn how to move from morn to night, acting towards other human beings with dignity and silence.

Through a growing awareness of one's assured place amidst the Army of the Voice, one may gain a stronger, sharper and more refined sense of dharma. At the same time, one will bring a sweeter gentleness and subtle fragrance to the performance of duty, nurtured in meditation and harvested through sacrificial action. One's tone of voice will improve, attaining a clarity and a kindness that does not hurt or exclude others. But this venture requires a constant, patient redefinition of oneself. Each day and every week one should refine one's tone of voice, one's attitude towards duty, and one's actions towards one's fellow men. If one has been the source of pollution through fascination with shadows, then one should restore a higher awareness, physically and mentally. One should ask how, through self-correction, one can improve the sphere of duty in the coming days and weeks. This should not be done neurotically out of self-concern, but noetically out of concern for others, through meditation and through invocations that draw one closer to the Voice.

As one grows in this discipline, it will begin to have an irresistible effect upon one's faculties of perception and action. Through one's purified thought one will begin to resonate to the currents of magnetic force on the invisible planes presided over by the four Regents. Were it not for the ceaseless activity of these cosmic agencies, it would not be possible to lend intelligence to sight. The human eye is extremely mysterious. It contains a minute pin-point of eternal light-substance — *suddhasattva* — the substance of the Dhyani Buddhas and of Ishwara. This pin-point of light in the centre of the eye is the gift of the divine Fathers of the human race, the Light-Bringers who illuminated the minds of human beings over eighteen million years ago. One must treat the eyes as sacred, taking care over their spiritual cleansing. One must look intelligently and benevolently, as an immortal soul gazing upon other immortal souls. One does not want the wandering eye, the fixated eye or the day-dreamy eye. Instead, while using both eyes, one should try to think of the Third Eye, the invisible eye of compassion, negation and transcendence. Great souls sometimes choose to take incarnation as blind persons so that they can avoid the distractions of sight. The physical eyes must be used with scrupulous care. Likewise, one must use the ears to become a good listener, catching not only what is on the physical plane but also the inaudible sounds of nature. Through the sounds of the ocean, the forests and even noisy cities, one may train the ear, tuning in to the resonances of the Soundless Sound.

> It is through the four high Rulers over the four points and Elements that our five senses may become cognisant of the hidden truths of Nature.
>
> *Ibid.*, 125

Through the refinement of the senses, one may come to see to the root of the four elements. As one does so, one will become aware of magnetic currents that pass out of oneself and come into oneself whenever one uses the senses. As a constant transmitter of magnetism, one will be concerned with beneficent motives and with sending out strong, healthy vibrations. One will also want to guard against perceiving that which one cannot handle. This is the message of the statue of the three monkeys: see no evil, hear no evil, speak no evil. They are a reminder not to see, to hear or to speak unnecessarily. By taking up this discipline and without having to enter a monastery, one will begin to move in line with Nature's harmony and rhythms. One will participate cooperatively with the twenty-eight-day lunar cycle, the seven-day cycle of the week, the thirty-odd days of the solar month, the seasons of the year, and so on. As a participant in Nature, through mastery of the vestures, one will learn to retain and extend one's awareness of the invisible and universal ground of Nature and man, benefiting and being benefited by the ordered numerical sets of the hosts of the Army of the Voice.

Through expanding and deepening one's awareness and participation in the invisible universe, one will gradually reduce fascination with the shadow. The enemy is not fascinating, but only a pathetic knot of muddled thinking. On the physical plane, neglect of exercise may cause a congestion in the spine, a kind of stiffening of the nerves, which results in backaches and a loss of physical mobility. This is part of ageing and may be met with proper measures. But those suffering from mental arthritis or cerebral congestion experience psychological pain and a lack of mobility that prevents them from doing their duty. They need to heed the advice of *The Voice of the Silence*: "*Mind is like a mirror; it gathers dust while it reflects. It needs the gentle breezes of soul-wisdom to brush away the dust of our illusions.*"

If the mind is tied up in self-made knots, it is because of terrible illusions as a child, perhaps becoming a chela of Hollywood, addicted to day-dreaming. The best thing is to see these for what they are, while showing compassion for those enslaved by them. Perhaps one was averse to homework or mathematics or afraid of having to look after oneself without one's parents. In addition to developing such barriers to true self-dependence, one may have deemed oneself a 'sensitive' person, when in truth one was weak-willed and afraid. Human beings learn to play these games over a number of lives. In themselves they are uninteresting, but they indicate an unwillingness to be quiet and to take one's place in the human family. They represent diseases of the soul and the mind, as well as of the astral form. There is some one thing about oneself that must be faced; until that is faced, the knot will not unravel. This itself must not, however, be turned into a protracted drama out of pride. The knot will never be loosened by brooding on the shadow.

The oldest and wisest course is to begin to practise altruism. Try to live for others. Try to see beyond the self, by forgetting the self. Everyone is entitled to look earnestly at the sky under which all human beings live and to look lovingly at the earth upon which all human beings walk. Everyone is entitled to think with gratitude of the elements, which offer help from all directions and all departments of Nature. But one must first practise self-forgetfulness, dutifulness and detachment. Through taking an intense interest in humanity and in the possibilities of the human condition, one may develop a deep love for the spiritual family into which one has entered. Seeing this as one's own true family, linked up to the mighty Brotherhood of Bodhisattvas, one may let go of the tension of self-concern. Then at the right time, through help in dreamless sleep and in daily meditation, the truly devoted and totally faithful will come to see the knot for what it is and it will loosen up. There is no point in worrying about these things, because that is how the knot was formed in the first place. Anxiety contracts, benevolence expands. Following the *ABCs*, one should move from anxiety to benevolence, and then to contentment. Then one may return to *A*, recognizing that it does not stand for anxiety but rather for the *Atman*, the Absolute and the *Ah-Hi*; that *B* stands for the Brotherhood, for the Builders and for the Great Breath. When one learns to see life with childlike simplicity, one can begin to get ready to receive the ancient Catechism:

"Lift thy head, oh Lanoo; dost thou see one, or countless lights above thee, burning in the dark midnight sky?"

"I sense one Flame, oh Gurudeva, I see countless undetached sparks shining in it."

"Thou sayest well. And now look around and into thyself. That light which burns inside thee, dost thou feel it different in anywise from the light that shines in thy Brother-men?"

"It is in no way different, though the prisoner is held in bondage by Karma, and though its outer garments delude the ignorant into saying, 'Thy Soul and My Soul.'"

Ibid., 120

RELATIONSHIP AND SOLITUDE

True Love in this differs from gold and clay,
That to divide is not to take away.
Love is like understanding that grows bright
Gazing on many truths; 't is like thy light,
Imagination! which, from earth and sky,
And from the depths of human fantasy,
As from a thousand prisms and mirrors, fills
The Universe with glorious beams, and kills
Error, the worm, with many a sun-like arrow
Of its reverberated lightning.

PERCY BYSSHE SHELLEY

The principle that all human beings should be treated as ends in themselves and not as means constitutes the core of Kantian morality. It rests upon an older conception of the world as a coherent structure intelligible to the pure reason of man. This world is a moral order precisely because human beings are an integral part of it. The human mind, by an act of pure, universal, impersonal reason, is able to discern the ethical order within the natural order. Each human being is a self-determining agent within a universe which itself may be seen as a kingdom of ends. Every human being as a responsible agent can become a monarch within his or her own modest kingdom by living in terms of ends that are self-chosen. We rule ourselves by making those ends meaningful in our lives.

For the practical realization of this possibility, we must assume that every human being is inherently capable of acting spontaneously without interfering with other human beings. We know that this noble mode of action is not achieved because reason is clouded by irrational passion. Pure universal affirmation is distorted, dissolved and even destroyed in the midst of the blinding partialities of confused human beings captive to conflicting impulses, aims, motives and desires. Suppose, however, that these self-chosen ends were intrinsically compatible, and that each person, in willing an end, asked the question, "If everyone wills this end, is it compatible for all human beings individually to pursue it without mutual interference?" At one level, a general answer would only yield a formal criterion of action. Is there a practical way, however, in which we could readily recognize in ourselves any fall from the autonomous state of a self-determining, rational being? We must identify any desire to interfere with others as springing from a part of ourselves which cannot be underwritten by the moral order and which the universe cannot protect.

Although theoretical formulations have a certain value, nonetheless, in the familiar but treacherous territory of tortuous rationalization and sinuous self-deception, as well as the psychological pessimism of our time, they only communicate negatively. And yet, while we may not fully know what it means to pursue our own ends without interfering with other individuals, we can surely recognize instances where one human being is crudely using another. We recognize this in its extreme form in politics, but the idea that any government could have total control over the human mind is self-contradictory if human beings are intrinsically self-determining agents. This also applies to any theory of continuous interference through conditioning, any supposedly benevolent, massive manipulation such as 'Skinnerism.'

The crucial challenge is whether we can, long before we are confronted by extreme cases, apply to all contexts a truly philosophical framework of indefinite growth in human relationships. Can we recognize not only the obvious ways in which we use other people, but also the pure ideal wherein we determine a chosen end without ever treating anyone else as a means? Can we understand the complexities of lower *Manas* solely through the desire for universal affirmation? We need a more complex view of human nature and especially a subtler understanding of the mind. It is not enough to see human beings merely in terms of use and misuse, least of all in the Benthamite language of self-interest, because people generally do not really know what is to their advantage over a long period of time in every context. All utilitarian formulations eventually tend to break down. It may even be better to think away altogether, in human relationships, from the ends-means dichotomy because it has been tainted by narrow and short-sighted perspectives.

Is there a nobler way by which we can come to understand what it is for two human beings to help each other, to share with each other, and not to use each other? Even though the sacred idea of love is degraded every day, there is no human being who does not understand what love means at some level. The counterfeit of love is false romantic idealization which soon becomes empty and irrelevant. True love involves the many complexities of human beings, the manifest weaknesses and also the hidden poignancy in the archetypal relationships between father and child, husband and wife, teacher and pupil, and between two friends. If two people can sense something beyond themselves, can they also see how the direction of their relationship could be meaningful? Even though in their weakest moments there is a tendency for either to take advantage of the other unconsciously or in the name of the good, is there still a feasible possibility of self-correction? Must relationships tend to become prisons or can they evolve in the direction of liberation? In the everyday contexts of human relationships, the critical question is whether we are becoming more tyrannical in relation to others or are allowing our closest encounters to enhance the joys of individuation.

These fundamental inquiries hurt because any pertinent discovery of the subtle forms by which the tyrannical will masquerades as love destroys our delusive relationships. Mere intellectual awareness does not help, and this is the point we have reached in contemporary culture. People know so much about all abuses of trust that they are terrified of any irrevocable commitment. They are afraid to spend time with their relatives; afraid to assume burdens of responsibility in relation to children;

afraid of intimacy with others and most of all afraid of deep introspection and meditative solitude. Relationships have broken down because many have become painfully aware of all the ambiguities, perversions and tyrannical elements in the human psyche. The atmosphere is so polluted that we almost dare not breathe. Therefore, the most simple, natural analogies, let alone idyllic models of archetypal relationships, do not speak to the disillusioned. They need a fundamental solution and not only an acute awareness of human failings. There is no total solution in the empirical realm that is compatible with the sum-total of goodness in the universe, but a fundamental solution can emerge when individuals are willing to rethink their conceptions of themselves.

The therapeutic counsel of the great healers of souls is as relevant now as it was in the days of Buddha and Christ. There are those whom the immemorial teaching does not transform, even though they spend a lifetime with it. There are those who are afraid it is going to alter them and therefore never enter the stream. There are those who progressively find it affecting them, and are able by an unspoken trust to use it and be benefitted by it. And then there are those very few who are deeply grateful for the supreme privilege of witnessing the presence of this timeless teaching. They are constantly focussed upon the eternal example nobly re-enacted by Avatars who portray the magnificent capacity to maintain, with beautiful balance and ceaseless rhythm, the awesome heights of cosmic detachment and boundless love. These mighty men of meditation are also illustrious exemplars of the art of living and masterly archers in the arena of action. They cannot be understood in terms of external marks or signs. It is only through their inner light that individuals can come into closer contact with the inner lives of beings so much wiser and nobler than themselves. Those who cherish this truth may find the inner light within their own silent sanctuary through deep meditation, in their incommunicable experience of poignant emotions, in response to soul-stirring music, or in their ethical endeavours through honesty and self-examination.

Human beings willing to take their lives into their own hands can acknowledge when they have used a person as a means to their own end, and see this as unworthy. Highly evolved souls who fall into such abuses will go into a period of penance. They will engage in a chosen discipline of thought and action so as to atone for their past misuse. Penance is not to be understood in terms of externals. True *tapas* touches the core of one's inward integrity. It fosters a calm reliance upon the great law of universal unity and ethical causation. It is rooted in the wisdom that protects right relationships. The tragedy of the human condition is that when we make moral discoveries we cannot readily go back to those we have wronged and rectify matters. Either it would be too painful or the individuals involved are not accessible. But we can correct our relationships at a higher level of integrity. We could prepare ourselves, in a practical way, to come out of the old and smaller circles of loyalty. We could authentically enter into the family of man and become members of that brotherhood of human beings who do their utmost, in the depths of solitude and self-examination as well as in the gamut of their relationships in daily life, to re-enact in simple situations what at an exalted level is effortlessly exemplified by the Brotherhood of Bodhisattvas.

Those who make this heroic effort become pioneers who point to the civilization of the future. They gestate new modes in the realm of pure ideation and bring them down into the region of the visible, laying foundations for a more joyous age in which there will be less defensiveness, fear and strain in the fit between theory and practice. Some want to get there straightaway, but they have never really asked themselves whether they have paid off their debts, or even faced up to the consequences of what they did before. This is a common error, but nonetheless it is insupportable in a cosmos that is a moral order. We cannot erase what went before, though we can make every new beginning count and insert it into a broader context. The great opportunity that the Aquarian Age offers is to gain a sense of proportion in relation to oneself, entering into an invisible brotherhood of comrades who are making similar attempts. Their mutual bonds come alive through their inmost reverence for their teachers, who exemplify in an ideal mode what their disciples strive to make real in their lives through sincere emulation to the best of their knowledge.

We need to function freely in the invisible realm of growth where all formulations can only be initial points of departure, and all interactions may serve as tentative embodiments of ideals. We know today, even in terms of the inverted insights of the lunar psychology now so widely disseminated, that our responses to others are in part truths about ourselves. We are aware that weak people are going to see weakness everywhere, or are going to be threatened by stronger people who remind them only more acutely of their own weakness. In the worst cases, the weak either try to pull down the stronger through image-crippling or try to live off them vampirically. On the opposite side, there are divine equivalents to these demoniac extremes, because evil is merely a privation of the good. Evil is only a shadow cast by a good which is not static: the more we seek it, the more it moves through degrees of relative manifestation extending into the unmanifest realm and beyond into that which cannot be called 'good' or 'true' or 'beautiful' or anything, because it is beyond all appellations and attributes.

There is then a process that is the opposite of vampirization. Instead of subtracting from someone else for our own benefit every time we see something that is strong or admirable, we could try to be silent learners. This is not easy. Very great souls, wherever they are born, reveal themselves as archetypal learners. By learning all the time they readily assimilate the best from those they encounter, and thus rapidly learn in every direction. *Light on the Path* gives the most comprehensive and precise instruction: "No man is your enemy: no man is your friend. All alike are your teachers." This mode of learning is a way of drawing from others which enriches all. The archetypal mode is so basic that it cannot remotely resemble institutionalized, routinized, inherited conceptions of learning. One can enact a whole *manvantara* within a single night if one is serious about learning, simply by sitting quietly in a restaurant and watching people coming and going, working and conversing. Learning is ceaselessly going on everywhere but it can become truly self-conscious only if one is sufficiently humble.

It is absurd to insist that there is no alternative to manipulation in human relationships. What makes vampirization possible is a kind of perverted strength, a determined persistence in weakness. An Initiate will see in such sad cases not a weakling, but an old sorcerer playing sick games behind a weak exterior, using the guise of weakness for the sake of sordid traffic in human vulnerability. There is present a reflected ray of the divine, but its strength shows itself demoniacally, inverted through a perverse determination which can only push the person along the inclined slope that culminates in the irreversible utter loneliness, annihilation, and extinction of the vital connection with the *Atman*. We need to meditate deeply on the opposite to see to the very core of what is happening. We can only do this if we can witness what we see with a commensurate compassion. The self-destructive sorcery of vampirization and manipulation must be met by a tremendous love, such as that of Krishna, Buddha, or Christ, for the faint spark of moral perception in that unfortunate human being desperately needs to be fanned before it is wholly extinguished.

Meditation upon the nature of good and evil also points to a process that is the opposite of the demoniac tendency, through extreme insecurity, of breaking down the images of stronger people. True learners, in contrast to fickle sycophants, are skilled in the enjoyment of excellence. They are willing to worship the imprint of impersonal truths about human nature in the acts and utterances of noble souls, wherever they may be discerned. Diverse individuals may find kinship with exemplars of human excellence in ancient myths, in recorded history, and in the secret fraternity of living sages. If we sit down and calmly reflect upon the best persons we have ever known, upon those we most respect, we may come to see the finer qualities hidden in the creative depths of these beings. Continuous effort generates strength. If we love enough we will readily recognize that we are initially not worthy enough to appreciate all the excellences of higher beings. We need knowledge, self-study, and the companionship of those who are our comrades in the quest for wisdom. Then we become intuitively capable of drawing to that orbit wherein we sense without profanation a sacred dissemination and steady diffusion of ideals that may be incarnated by degrees. This is the only possible strength compatible with a spiritual cosmogony and an emanationist conception of human evolution.

Strength is truly that which is compatible with further growth. This is no static notion of strength and there can be no external measure of it. Human beings are the greatest cowards when they will not admit a mistake and when they will not face themselves. The greatest heroes are the ones who show the courage needed for constant self-correction. True strength has nothing to do with indices of power in the visible realm. It shows itself in the inner life of man, in psychological struggles, and in the moral sphere. As we begin to gain a little of this inward strength, we prepare ourselves for more. Then it becomes natural and spontaneous to rejoice in the existence of those stronger than ourselves.

It is possible even now to recover something of that faded memory of the joys which were once experienced in families where one could insert one's whole conception of oneself into a larger fellowship. We can no longer do this mechanically in Kali Yuga, least of all in a competitive society, and in relation to the family as defined merely in terms of blood ties and physical heredity. We have to re-discover and re-create the small family before we can join the greater family of man. We need to think about humanity as a whole, the human situation, human needs, human sufferings, and the glaring gap between the human predicament and all the expertise in the corridors of power. But we should not presume that we know enough about such matters. It would be better to seek to become effective servants of Mahatmas who alone have the wisdom needed to enlighten and elevate the whole of the human race, but who cannot do so without the help of companions. Drawn out of different cultures, they are the global forerunners who are willing to serve as "Fortune's favoured soldiers" in the Army of the Voice.

These companions realize that true solitude is not loneliness, but the experience of a more intense fellowship that goes beyond the human kingdom. It is a fellowship not merely with nature seen in terms of its four kingdoms — mineral, vegetable, animal and human — but a fellowship that includes three invisible elemental kingdoms. Even more, it is a fellowship with living forces that are neither remote abstractions nor anthropo-morphized entities. Through this fellowship we may experience the thrill of the discovery that within the human body there is a universe intimately bound up with a vast universe which includes many more worlds than what either visually or conceptually we call the cosmos. Deep, steady and regular meditation, supported by the integrity of self-study, becomes after a point as natural as breathing. It becomes continuous with the whole of one's life, and then a person can never be lonely in the ordinary sense, because one will be unafraid. If there is no limiting conception of oneself which makes one vulnerable, there is nothing to fear.

To explain this in detail would be futile because an explanation would say nothing to someone who does not have some experience of it. The best way to understand it is to focus one's consciousness, within the solitude of one's own life, upon those passages in the great devotional texts which give the capacity — within the alembic of one's purified imagination, the matrix of one's serene ideation, and the warmth of one's expanding heart — to tap through meditation the ideation, benevolence and compassion of beings who have gained enlightenment. An infallible test of whether one has truly entered the stream is that one recognizes one's predecessors, the Tathagatas. People who only attempt meditation for a while, and keep pretending that they have the last word or the final answer, are pitiable failures. The individual who has an authentic inner life feels a profound veneration for a vast brotherhood of beings who have walked that way before. Many people experience a comparable feeling on trips to the mountains, especially when they are alone for a long time.

They experience an exhilaration at seeing another human being. There is a comradeship which we can experience but are not ready to verbalize.

We can find in such fruitful encounters preparatory anticipations of the solidarity experienced through the discipline of discipleship, meditating as steadily as a spinning top, while also engaged in creative action. Enjoying comradeship with the Brotherhood of Bodhisattvas, the disciple is strengthened by his constant awareness of Their boundless compassion. Simply to think of their infinite sacrificial wisdom fortifies him. This is a profound experience, and anyone can earn it by making the necessary effort. But in the sacred realm no false coins will serve, and there can be no cheating or manipulation. As in René Daumal's *Mount Analogue,* the only thing that entitles one to go further is being able to extract a particular kind of pearl-like substance that one can only get by risking great danger, coming close to precipitous waterfalls and crashing cascades. Progress is made solely by daring, the willingness to go through repeated trials, and by magnanimity.

Though depicted in different ways by many teachers throughout vast ages, the trials of a disciple are very real. No strength is gained by any who are unwilling to be tested and tried, or who are afraid of trying. This will always be the case, as long as the universe has the integrity necessary to accommodate the continuities between great beings and every person alive. In a universe of law, the only way in which it is possible to go through the journey is step by step. As suggested in the story of Job, one's burden will never be greater than one can bear. But at any given time, the trial one is undergoing will seem as if it is too much. Jesus exemplified this at his supreme trial when he faced the thought that he might have been forsaken. Even though such thoughts may occur, the disciple can persist. Faith will triumph over doubt, and *kama manas* will finally be sloughed off like the skin of a snake. The new self emerges at that very point where one is willing to let go of the whole assemblage of past limitations. But this cannot be done once and for all. It has to be done repeatedly.

There will be many trials, and, for those who are simply not able to understand what is involved, the warning is given at the outset that this is the Path of Woe. The Rosicrucian motto enjoins: "Know, dare, will," and, above all, "remain silent." If candidates are willing to fulfil such precise qualifications, they will be able to travel the whole Path. It is that kind of journey where, if one gains a self-sustaining measure of growth on the Path, a point is reached, earlier than one might think, where there is no more anxiety or concern about one's own good. When that point is passed, one is truly fortunate, because then it is possible to keep going while seeing beyond the calculus of consequences. A faith can be fostered which is founded in understanding and reinforced from within by a high resolve embodied in the realm of sacrificial action, depicted forcefully in the *Bhagavad Gita*. Inevitably, one may appear to lose ground at times, but a person who is ambivalent and dithering cannot augment his faith. All despondency has to be cast off. While this cannot be done at the beginning, it will be required as one grows. It can be done provided one always keeps looking ahead to that which is beyond oneself, and which encompasses all other human beings.

One must show a warm gratitude to those pilgrims on the path who, having gone further up, are beckoning to the persons below. This is little understood in the world of inversions or in the language of lower *Manas* which has tarnished all images of the truths of the spiritual life. We can become ready for more and more, however, by using every increment of authentic experience. It is the constant effort to bring many individuals to this hunger for genuine learning and to give them some meaningful hope, that constitutes the great sacrifice of the Mahatmas. Their ceaseless and magnanimous work is vaster at all times than any individual can comprehend, but at the same time it has precision in relation to the law of cycles. They work with vast cyclic forces and know what can be done in any year in any place at any level in relation to the greatest good of all. One will make marvellous discoveries as one climbs more, finding that the precision, detachment and selflessness needed are truly awe-inspiring. But a person will be proud to have become worthy even to know this much, and if he looks back at what he was a long time ago or sees those still struggling below, he will recognize a profound kinship and want to help in every way.

There is another telling insight in *Mount Analogue*. Pilgrims find they reach a stage where they cannot take the next step forward, where they have to sit and wait until those who are still struggling below have come up to their level. Those who would not do for others what has been done for them will never make further progress in the spiritual life. The door will be shut. Such persons may build up a pattern where, in their concern to keep going, they forget what they have already been through. They fail to empathize fully with those who are still struggling. A balance must be struck on the Path which can only be genuine and dynamic when produced by a rhythmic alternation between withdrawals and involvements, *nivritti* and *pravritti*, meditation and skill in the art of action, solitude and relationship. Disciples can integrate solitude into every week, into every day, and eventually integrate it into themselves so that they are within their spheres all the time and can see in all particular relationships mirrorings of vaster relationships with all living beings. They begin every week by deliberation in regard to what they can do for someone else and by self-study with regard to how they may apply what they have learned from others and how they may correct various sins of omission and commission. A person who regularly undertakes this can carry it out everywhere, even in the simplest relationships.

The most unspoken, intimate relationships reflect the very highest relations, which at the pinnacle of the spiritual life is that of disciple and teacher, but which at the cloud-obscured peak of enlightenment is like that between a child and a mother. The *chela* directly experiences these sacred relationships, which are inconceivable to human beings as they are. Yet, we can see them mirrored even in the awkward stumblings of ordinary men. Hence, as suggested in the great images given by Plato, those who recognize that the ladder of love extends into the elusive realms of the ineffable, can also see the reflections of that divine magic in its simplest manifestations among ordinary people. When a person can do this, there is no more dichotomy between authentic relationship and inner solitude.

An evolving human being and a developing disciple experience that which seems mysterious — what it is to be of the world and one with it and yet out of it and not in it at all. When we experience this in sufficient measure, we may more readily understand what it means to be a being who can remain awake during *pralaya* and yet also be uninvolved whilst fully engaged during manifestation in the work of the world. We come to see that for an ascending consciousness there are levels upon levels of negation and affirmation. This pair ultimately become like two poles that are symmetrically related to a higher pole which is beyond because it can never manifest and is unconditioned. This is most meaningful when seen, not as an image or a metaphor, but as a living reality within, pointing to the One beyond and above the Waters of Space, which "breathes breathless." It is possible to remain in that ground of Being which is Non-Being. It is feasible to understand the vast meshing of karmic causation and at the same time, while standing outside it, to feel no sense of separateness from the most ignorant beings, toiling and hurting themselves and somehow through their stumblings, growing towards a greater freedom than they can recognize while still hiding in the shadows. Those who approach these transcendental recognitions will truly feel it a sacred privilege to "profit by the gift, the priceless boon of learning truth, the right perception of existing things, the knowledge of the non-existent."

DRAWING THE LARGER CIRCLE

'Great Sifter' is the name of the 'Heart Doctrine',
O Disciple. The wheel of the Good Law moves swiftly on. It
grinds by night and day. The worthless husks it drives from
out the golden grain, the refuse from the flour. The hand of
Karma guides the wheel; the revolutions mark the beatings
of the karmic heart.

The Voice of the Silence

The 1975 cycle will continue to precipitate momentous choices for individuals and societies. What are the vital elements in this decisive choosing, and what will be the chief consequences? There is in the life of every human being a series of minor choices which add up to a crucial choice, but often it is made with incomplete knowledge of its critical nature. To grow and to age is to recognize with increasing clarity that all events in the past have had their irreversible consequences. Therefore, within any shallow philosophy centred essentially on the physical body and premised upon a single incarnation, a personal sense of futility and fatalism looms large as one comes closer to the moment of death. As with individuals, so with civilizations. Civilizations are apt to conduct the deepest reflection upon their storied past in times of depression, either out of self-indulgent nostalgia or sheer bewilderment at their bygone glory. This has shadowed every great civilization in its hour of decline, and today we are witnessing this in Western Europe and in the nostalgic mood which is intermittent in the United States. Civilizations seek to cling to something of the past, and perceptive chroniclers like Toynbee in England or Jaspers in Switzerland sense that something went wrong as early as before 1914, that the seeds of today's malaise lay far back in the past. When we look back to that past we surmise that a lot could have been avoided, that there were viable alternatives and missed opportunities. This is the sad state of societies as well as individuals who, because of narrowness of perspective and myopia in relation to the future, impose upon their lives a delusive dependence upon their own edited versions of a truncated past. But whenever human beings are willing to rethink their basic assumptions about themselves, about their shrouded past and about their cloudy future, then they do not need to edit. They do not have to limit unduly the horizon of their gaze.

This is difficult to understand initially. One might think in terms of the extreme example of a person with Promethean foresight who can discern in the cycles of this century long-term factors that go back a thousand years into the past and will go forward a thousand years into the future. In the Victorian Age, T.H. Huxley observed that in the myriad worlds around us there is no reason why there cannot be beings with an intelligence as far beyond our present level as ours is beyond that of the black beetle, and with a control over nature as far beyond our own as ours is beyond that of the snail. He also suggested that even ordinary human beings can look back and forward over a millennium and make broad projections. It is, in principle, possible for there to be beings in the universe who can see all pasts and all futures. The power of choice is partly a function of the scope of perspective. With wider perspectives our choices become more intelligent, but as they become more informed, we readily recognize that there are many factors that are constant. One cannot wish away causes generated over a long cycle. The more clearly a person sees what he cannot alter right now in this incarnation, the more effectively he can use his energies to alter what he can. All this requires a measure of balance, but most human beings are unable to choose wisely by clearly facing the alternatives before them. All too often they vainly hope that by proceeding in one direction, everything else will automatically come to them. Energy cannot move in all directions at once, and though there are many planes of matter, it is always the case that everything adds up in a mathematical universe. One's capacity to choose is a function of one's knowledge, not merely of particular causal chains but also of what is at the very core of the phenomenal process of becoming: breathing in and breathing out. Ideally, if one could comprehend the meaning of a single day, one would by analogy be able to understand what is enacted over a lifetime.

It has been taught that for the truly wise, each day is like a new incarnation. In a small space they see the subtle motions of unbounded space. In a single moment they can grasp quintessentially the infinite possibilities that are spread out in eternal duration. They can retain in consciousness the freedom that belongs to those who are not rushing to manifest, while displaying a shrewd awareness of what it is possible to manifest with a due respect for the feelings of others, for collective strengths and weaknesses, for the limits and possibilities of the current cycle. The teachings of Gupta Vidya offer the vast perspective of over eighteen million years of human history and also of the sixth sub-race which will emerge far in the future but which must clearly have some relationship to the fifth sub-race — now visibly on the decline — that flowered forth in Europe and partly in America. At this point of time there is, by analogy and correspondence, a critical moment of choice bearing upon the alternatives that confront our intelligence.

The ratiocinative mind has become adept, because of modern upbringing and so-called education, because of so much dichotomous thinking since Aristotle, at rationalizing its wants, desires and limitations. Now we find at a global level the logical limit of this rationalizing mind, which insists there is not enough room or food on earth for all human beings on our globe. This no-exit barrier in thinking arises because of assumptions that were too limited from the start. It hinges upon a view of the universe which is incompatible with the vast resources of the creative imagination, with the inventiveness displayed in the last three centuries in building up the structures of applied science and sophisticated civilization. Even this is merely a recent example of the immense resourcefulness of the human race over many millennia. The type of thinking which is inductive, inferential and dichotomous, functioning within the perspective of a closed universe or of a one-life system, has become sterile and has no real answers to the awesome problems of our time.

Today, we face a decisive moment of choice. Human beings cannot by mere repudiation of an obsolete mode of thinking efface it entirely from their minds. Many people are muddled and fearful victims of the collective psychosis, and seem to be constantly in need of psychological reinforcement. The more they look back, like Lot's wife, the more they are in danger of being immobilized. The threshold of awakening is touched when mature souls search for spiritual wisdom and sense the reality of Mahatmas and their boundless compassion for the whole of humanity. When a person is profoundly affected by a preliminary vision of the quest for enlightenment, it is impossible to go back when the moment of choice has come. Initiates alone know what is the critical threshold for any individual or civilization. In recent years many souls have been confronted with a collective bewilderment that is a prelude to fateful choices. For some it is already too late. Others, unknown to themselves, when they least expect it, will find their way into the civilization of the future. All such choices involve complex chains of causation that are shrouded in the arcane mathematics of karma. All acts have their exact consequences and all thinking generates appropriate results. The degree of intensity is a function of the level of awareness, motivation and concentration. To think on universal lines is to initiate stronger currents than those generated from a sectarian or separative standpoint.

H.P. Blavatsky said:

> The co-disciples must be tuned by the guru as the strings of a lute (*vina*) each different from the others, yet each emitting sounds in harmony with all. Collectively they must form a keyboard answering in all its parts to thy lightest touch (the touch of the

Master). Thus their minds shall open for the harmonies
of Wisdom, to vibrate as knowledge through each and
all, resulting in effects pleasing to the presiding gods
(tutelary or patron-angels) and useful to the Lanoo. So
shall Wisdom be impressed for ever on their hearts and
the harmony of the law shall never be broken. . . . The
mind must remain blunt to all but the universal truths
in nature, lest the 'Doctrine of the Heart' should
become only the 'Doctrine of the Eye'.

The true chela is one who has no taste for the small talk of the
world, not owing to disinterest in individuals but because of caring
so deeply for all souls. Deaf to deceptive formulations of the
complexities of human existence, the chela can hold his strength
within, instead of being ceaselessly concerned to reform everyone
else. The prime concern is to secure a firm anchor within the
divine sphere of one's being, to stay aloof from turbulent currents,
so as to remain continually attuned to the sacred music of the
flute of Krishna, to the *filia vocis* within, the promptings of the
higher Self, the dictates of one's *Ishtaguru*. There are varying levels
of intensity to diverse modes of thinking. If the disciple is to
achieve the quantum jump to a totally new and initially painful
way of thinking, which is abstract and universal but wholly free,
this requires continuity of concentration to be established as a
stream of ideation and untrammelled awareness. Then it will be
possible to initiate far more potent consequences in a short span
of time than could be generated through muddled kamamanasic
thinking over a long period of time. This change of polarity and
scope of ideation is connected with the intensity and continuity
of the energy level of radiant matter. At higher levels there is an
increasing fusion of thought, feeling and volition. The deeper one
draws from the central source of noumenal energies in the
universe, the greater the potency of thought, feeling and will —
provided one protects this current by the power of silence and
true reticence. At one level this is sheer good taste; at another
level it demands absolute fidelity to the highest and most sacred.
If one can master this mode, one may work as nature works, in

silence and secrecy, from the depths of the soil wherein germinates the seed within the seed, slowly unfolding the humble acorn and the mighty oak.

Spiritual life involves taking a risk far greater than any other. One is risking the collapse of one's personal identity, not merely worldly conceptions of success and failure, but also the rooted identification with name and form and physical existence, with likes and dislikes, delusions and fears. To take that risk and plunge into the void requires real courage. This cannot come without a preliminary purificatory process of asking why one is afraid. One has to look at one's attachments and see them without illusion as far as possible. One has to grasp why yesterday's attachments, which seemed to be all-absorbing, are utterly meaningless today. An unfortunate soul gets trapped in the cycle of involvement for a lifetime, experiencing one disillusionment after another. A wiser soul soon sees to the core of the delusive process of externalizing the self. Herein lies the great enigma of the noetic variation among human beings, in terms not only of environment and heredity, but even more in the appreciation of the karma brought into this life, the karma shared with others and the karma engendered by oneself. To become capable of moral and spiritual courage, to see everything from the standpoint of the Ishwara within, means in practice that one is willing to work patiently, like a private in the army, without any access to the well-guarded plans of the Chief of Staff. What matters is doing the best one can and knows how. To master this mental posture is to come closer to the sacred orbit of the Brotherhood of Bodhisattvas. They can see every stumbling mountain climber, every little lamp, from the terrace of enlightenment. They instantaneously see what they call "the Tathagata light", the spirit of true devotion, abstention from fault-finding, and altruism in thought, word and deed.

A person so preoccupied with learning that he entertains no expectations for self, may suddenly receive the privilege of sharing glimpses of a universal vision, such as that which Krishna conferred upon Arjuna. Soul-wisdom cannot be construed in terms of any known symbols or visible tokens. True disciples are fortunate to live in an epoch when so many people have reached the terminus of an entire way of thinking, the salvationist mentality of looking for instant results and vicarious atonement. Over two thousand years this spiritual materialism sullied the pure teaching of Jesus Christ. In the last decade a lot has happened fast. Those who frantically sought quick results have been rapidly disillusioned. The great sifting of souls has enormously facilitated the emergence of the truly courageous, the self-selected pioneers who seek the good of the whole, and are willing to train as "fortune's favoured soldiers" in the ancient Army of the Voice. The keynote of universal brotherhood was already struck in the nineteenth century in the message of the Maha Chohan, who calmly declared: "He who does not feel competent to grasp the noble idea sufficiently to work for it, need not undertake a task too heavy for him." There need be no chastising of those who are not ready for the larger task, and it is too late in history to coax the weak to simulate the language of the strong. One of the paradoxes of our time is that those who cannot maintain continuity of consciousness even for a week preach spiritual tenets for their own psychological survival. But out of such will not come the forerunners of the coming civilization, the alchemical agents for the radical transformation of modes of thought and action. These rare souls define themselves in an unmistakable manner, by unconditionality of commitment, magnanimity of mind and reverence for all the spiritual teachers of humanity.

The idea of unconditionality lies at the core of the perennial philosophy of the great sages at all times, in all conditions and in all cultures. This is the identifying hallmark of the authenticity of every true intimation of *Theosophia*. *The Secret Doctrine* points to the unthinkable and the unspeakable in the accents of the *Mandukya Upanishad*. H.P. Blavatsky prefaced *The Secret Doctrine* by the Rig Vedic Hymn to Creation, wherein the highest beings suggest that they perchance know not the ultimate purpose of creation, showing the authentic agnosticism of the enlightened. When men have attained to gnosis, their profound agnosticism diffuses a peerless fragrance that touches the hearts of the humblest people. If one tries to move from any concept of the immense to a sense of infinity, it may seem as if one is coming closer to the unconditional, but no concept of immensity or infinity can capture the boundlessness of invisible space, eternal duration, perpetual motion or unmodified consciousness. One cannot ever bring to the level of expression, symbolization or conceptualization that which one can apprehend and experience at a deeper level, wherein the whole of one's being is alive and awake. When the deep calls to the deep, the ineffable awareness of the boundless cannot be intimated except through silence and stillness. This is profoundly fundamental to the entire universe and all consciousness, to God, law and man. It entails unending reverence for the unknown in every being, not just as a mode but as the central truth in all relationships. It alone gives one true freedom and complete openness in relation to the inexhaustible possibilities of the future. Those who vainly seek to limit the future to their impressionistic scenarios and linear projections will be supplanted by the tidal wave of feeling that arises from the abundant fullness of human hearts, the untrammelled ideation of human minds and the creative wills of immortal souls.

As the structures of the past atrophy and crumble, only that could replace them which would existentially reflect the inner truth of soul-evolution, the insights of monads that pierce the veil of forms. The inversions of the insecure, allowing moral pygmies to speculate upon spiritual giants, will have no sway in the civilization of the future. There will be a pervasive recognition of the logical impossibility for the lesser to judge the greater, and the sure sign of littleness is the tendency to convert beliefs into verdicts. The Aquarian Age will foster that openness in relation to the larger circle which will be a natural extension of the open texture of our primary relationships — with parents, teachers, siblings, so-called enemies and friends. There will be a more widespread acknowledgement that as veil upon veil may lift, there must remain veil upon veil behind. When the human race as a whole can afford to live with such mature awareness, it will be hospitable to the sort of spiritual and moral toughness that can cope fully with the accelerated pace of karmic precipitation. Many will readily grasp the elementary axiom of the mathematics of the soul that in order to comprehend an Adept or Mahatma, one must first devote a lifetime to true discipleship.

This is an immensely liberating prospect, when compared with the stifling spiritual limitations of the last century. H.P. Blavatsky had to undergo the pain of risking profanation in testifying to the existence of Mahatmas in the heyday of Victorian prejudice and conceit. The spoilt victims of centuries of sectarian stupidity, more skilled in image-crippling than in true devotion, were almost constitutionally incapable of understanding Mahatmas. Speaking of them was then a great sacrifice. This is fortunately no longer necessary, because those who need to participate in the clamour of pseudo-claims and shallow judgments are now confronted with an abundant supply of readily available gurus. This offers a considerable protection to the real work in the world of the Brotherhood of Bodhisattvas. During the 1975 cycle there is no more need to make any concessions to the weak in the West that were unknown in the East. This augurs well for the future of humanity. All over the globe, the paramount problem is one of renewing and maintaining the minimal standards of being truly human. Only those souls who already have a profound grasp of *sunyata* and *karuna*, the voidness of all and the fullness of compassion, will undergo the lifelong training of discipleship and awaken the *Bodhichitta*, the seed of the Bodhisattva. There is thus the immense gain that the mixing of incompatible vibrations may be mitigated in this century. At the widest level, universal good — *Agathon* — is the keynote of the epoch.

The religion of humanity is the central emphasis of the 1975 cycle. Those who are self-elected by their own meditations, by their generous natures, and by their cooperative acts, who are willing to become true disciples of the Mahatmas, will readily undergo the rigorous discipline and share the rich resources of the divine dialectic, *Buddhi Yoga*, mirroring the divine wisdom of Brahma Vach or *Theosophia*. They will ceaselessly attempt to draw the larger circle. There is no reason why breadth should be at the expense of depth. A new balancing between a much broader diffusion of the fundamental truths of "the golden links" and a much deeper penetration into the visible is now possible and will come to a full flowering by the end of the century. In the climactic rush of the closing years, there will be an unprecedented outpouring of creative energies and spiritual resources, as well as the closing of many doors, plunging into obscurity many protracted illusions of the past. The religion of humanity is the religion of the future, fusing the philosophy of perfectibility, the science of spirituality and the ethics of growth in global responsibility.

GANDHIAN TRUSTEESHIP

I. THE ART OF RENUNCIATION

The act of renunciation of everything is not a mere physical renunciation, but represents a second or new birth. It is a deliberate act, not done in ignorance. It is, therefore, a regeneration.
MAHATMA GANDHI

For India, the most critical issue involves the current rethinking of Mahatma Gandhi's philosophy. Gandhi said that soon after his death India would bypass and betray his ideas, but that thirty years later India would be compelled to restore them. Events have begun to validate his prophecy, and the trend will accelerate. . . . When India fully accepts that it cannot conceivably emulate Japan without harnessing its own indigenous values and providing new motivations, and when out of necessity its leadership recognizes that it can no longer inflate the token symbols of Gandhi or the facile slogans of socialism, she will be forced to ask more fundamental questions. Only then can the real social revolution emerge, which could have a strong radical base and also borrow from ancient traditions as well as modern movements. While it would be difficult to predict the changes themselves, they will require serious reassessment of Gandhi's questions relating to the quantum of goods needed for a meaningful and fulfilling way of life.
Parapolitics — Toward the City of Man

Mahatma Gandhi held that all human beings are implicitly responsible to God, the Family of Man and to themselves for their use and treatment of all goods, gifts and talents that fall within their domain. This is so because Nature and Man are alike upheld, suffused and regenerated by the Divine. There is a luminous spark of divine intelligence in the motion of the atom and in the eyes of every man and woman on earth. We incarnate our divinity when we deliberately and joyously nurture our abilities and assets for the sake of the larger good. In this sense, the finest exemplars of trusteeship are those who treat all possessions as though they were sacred or deeply precious beyond any worldly scale of valuation. Thus, it is only through daily moral choice and the meritorious use of resources that we sustain our inherited or acquired entitlements. For this reason, the very idea of ownership is misleading and, at root, a form of violence. It implies rights and privileges over Man and Nature that go beyond the bounds of human need — although not necessarily beyond the limits of human law and social custom. It obscures the generous bounty of Nature, which provides enough for all if each holds in trust only what he needs, without excess or exploitation.

Gandhi sensed that all our resources and possessions, at any level, are not merely fragments of the Divine but are also inherently mortal and mutable. The Divine in its active aspect is ceaselessly creative and ever fluid in form. By analogy, human needs and material circumstances alter even while cultural patterns and social customs purport to maintain temporal continuity through established traditions. Ownership, from this standpoint, is truly a costly and illusory attempt to ensure permanency and succession. It gives birth to unwarranted attachments and insupportable expectations. The selfish grasping for possessions of any kind not only violates the deeper purposes of our human odyssey but eventually breeds possessiveness and greed, exploitation and revenge. This appalling moral malaise leads to inordinate self-assertion and self-projection which can only yield distrust, sorrow and "loss of all". But when we attain the sacred mental posture of the trustee who regards all possessions as held in trust for the good of all, we can progressively approach the high spiritual state of mental renunciation. We can, in the Upanishadic phrase, "renounce and enjoy". It is only when we voluntarily relinquish our unnatural claims and consecrate ourselves to a higher purpose that we can freely enjoy what we have. Thus, self-satisfaction is a natural outcome of a generous perspective and a greater purity of heart. It is truly a function of the harmonious cultivation of our spiritual, mental and material resources. In Gandhian terms, guilt-free enjoyment is inseparable from ethical probity. The real issue, then, is not how much or how little we possess in the way of property or talent, but the reasons and motives behind their allocations and uses.

Gandhi approached the concept of trusteeship at four different levels. First of all, trusteeship, as the sole universalizable means of continuously redistributing wealth, could be seen as a corollary of the principle of non-violence and simultaneously assure the generation and intelligent use of wealth.

> No other theory is compatible with non-violence. In the non-violent method the wrongdoer compasses his own end, if he does not undo the wrong. For, either through Non-violent Non-co-operation he is made to see his error, or he finds himself completely isolated.
> "Theory of 'Trusteeship'"
> *Harijan*, December 16, 1939

Even if wealth could be coercively redistributed, the resulting greed and inexperience on the part of many and the resentment on the part of the dispossessed would lead to economic instability and rapid decline. More likely than not, it would lead to class war, anomic violence and widespread self-alienation. Trusteeship, however, encourages owners to see themselves as vigilant trustees of their accumulated wealth for the larger community without threatening them.

Secondly, Gandhi's practical psychological intuition allowed him to see that fear would prevent other means of economic distribution from succeeding in the long run. A fundamental change in the concepts of activity and courage is needed to overcome passivity and cowardice. Courage must be detached from violence, and creativity must be dislodged from the self-protective formulations of entrenched élites. This involves rooting new notions of noetic activity which are creative, playful and tolerant, and new notions of moral courage which are heroic, magnanimous and civil, in a search for universal self-transcendence. An individual must feel, both abstractly and concretely, a secure sense of joyous eros in fellowship, and a positive sense of solidarity with hapless human beings everywhere. He must feel at one with the victims of incomplete revolutions, with the understandably impatient and occasionally mistaken pioneers of great revolutions, and even more with those willing to defy every presumptuous criterion and form of authority which trespasses upon individuality.

The fearful man tyrannizes others: forced redistribution would bring fearful responses from owners, who would see their lives and futures threatened, and fearful masses would deal with excess wealth incompetently. For Gandhi, the ever-present possibility of social change must be approached from a position of truth and courage, whereas fear is weakness which leads to violence. Strength should not be mistaken for the modalities of violence, which are instruments of fear and always lead to varying degrees of self-destruction. Since strength rests on human dignity and respect, workers must approach exploitative capitalists from a position of self-respect based on the capital of labour, for "labour is as much capital as metal". To abolish fear and even failure itself requires a fundamental change in the social structure. The feasibility of this social transformation does not lie in denying the judgements of others, but rather in regarding them as partially relevant though in no sense compelling. Individuals can commit themselves to increasing their own capacity for self-transcendence of external criteria of differentiation, and thereby attain liberation from the self-perpetuating iniquities and horrors of the System.

> Therefore, workers, instead of regarding themselves as enemies of the rich, or regarding the rich as their natural enemies, should hold their labour in trust for those who are in need of it. This they can do only when,

instead of feeling so utterly helpless as they do, they
realize their importance in human economy and shed
their fear or distrust of the rich. Fear and distrust are
twin sisters born of weakness. When labour realizes its
strength it won't need to use any force against moneyed
people. It will simply command their attention and
respect.

"Letter to B. Srirangasayi"
The Hindu, October 11, 1934

Gandhi discerned the critical role acceptability plays in
legitimating a social order, and distinguished between a people's
tacit acceptance and active dislike of an economic regime. So long
as any society finds its socio-economic system acceptable, that
system will stand even if a militant minority detests it. But should
a significant number of individuals find it unacceptable, it is
shaken to its foundations, regardless of the complacency of
privileged élites.

Thirdly, Gandhi contended that the idea of trusteeship could
be put into practice non-violently, because it could be instituted
by degrees. When asked if such 'trustees' — individuals who
possessed wealth and yet saw themselves as stewards for society —
could be found in India in his day, he rejected the question as
strictly irrelevant to the theory, which can only be evaluated by
extensive testing over time.

At this point I may be asked as to how many
trustees of this type one can really find. As a matter of
fact, such a question should not arise at all. It is not
directly related to our theory. There may be just one
such trustee or there may be none at all. Why should
we worry about it? We should have faith that we can,
without violence or with so little violence that it can
hardly be called violence, create such a feeling among
the rich. We should act in that faith. That is sufficient
for us. We should demonstrate through our endeavour
that we can end economic disparity with the help of
non-violence. Only those who have no faith in

non-violence can ask how many trustees of this kind can be found.

"Answers to Questions, Gandhi Seva Sangh Meeting",
Brindaban, Harijan, June 3, 1939

Gandhi knew that he sought the widespread realization of a forgotten ideal, but he repudiated the conventional notion that an experiment is unworthy to be tried simply because it stems from an exacting ideal. Even if one argued that trusteeship was doomed to failure, it ran no greater risk than the conventional social proposals of the day. Committed to principles but flexible in policies, Gandhi saw no reason to neglect ideals and to institute social reforms from a defeatist standpoint. Such an approach only guaranteed that structural faults would be built into the new social order. Rather, he emphasized, it is better to move towards the ideal and make appropriate adjustments necessitated by the specific failures encountered in attempting to reach it. In doing so, principles would remain uncompromised and the possibility of improvement would always remain, whereas in a system which assumes cupidity and corruption in human nature, nothing encourages their eradication.

Gandhi not only had faith that it was possible for human beings to become trustees of their resources for the sake of all, but also that many in fact were already and had always been trustees. They are the preservers of culture and tradition, who show their ethical stance through countless daily acts of graciousness and concern for others. To treat man as man requires not so much the acceptance of the equal potentialities of all men, let alone the infinite potentialities of all men, but rather the acceptance of the unknown potentialities of all human beings. Given scarce resources and the limits of productivity and of taxable income, there are definitely limits to what the State can do, but is there any reason why voluntary associations should not be entrusted with the task of extending the avenues of opportunity available to the disinherited? The socialist could argue that by an indefinite extension of opportunities (not always requiring State action) and by changing not only the structure but the entire ethos and moral tone of society, new social values could slowly emerge and usher in an era in which men show mutual respect which is not based on skills and promotions, rank and status.

The minimal goal of basic economic equity is easily stated, yet it is the fundamental first stage for the uplift of the whole.

> Everybody should be able to get sufficient work to make the two ends meet. And, this ideal can be universally realized only if the means of production of elementary necessaries of life remain under the control of the masses. These should be freely available to all as God's air and water are, or ought to be; they should not be made a vehicle of traffic for the exploitation of others. Their monopolization by any country, nation or groups of persons would be unjust. The neglect of this simple principle is the cause of the destitution that we witness today, not only in this unhappy land, but other parts of the world, too.
>
> "Economic Constitution of India",
> *Young India*, November 15, 1928

The principle of trusteeship in its application to the equitable distribution of wealth, as well as to the non-violent socialist reformation it underpins, is practicable because it does not require everyone to undertake it all at once. Unlike most socialists who reason that they must seize the power of the State before instituting effective reforms, Gandhi held that enlightened individuals could initiate the process of divesting themselves of what is unnecessary while becoming true trustees of their own possessions.

> It is perfectly possible for an individual to adopt this way of life without having to wait for others to do so. And if an individual can observe a certain rule of conduct, it follows that a group of individuals can do likewise. It is necessary for me to emphasize the fact

that no one need wait for anyone else in order to adopt a right course. Men generally hesitate to make a beginning, if they feel that the objective cannot be had in its entirety. Such an attitude of mind is in reality a bar to progress.

"Equal Distribution",
Harijan, August 25, 1940

Once the barrier in consciousness is broken, the principle of trusteeship can be made to work by letting go of the demand for a mechanically equal distribution, something Gandhi doubted could ever be realized. Instead, he held to the revolutionary ideal of *equitable* distribution, which would not only be possible but necessary in the non-violent socialist State.

Should attempts to encourage the abandonment of exploitation through misappropriation of the means of production fail, trusteeship could be made to work through non-violent non-cooperation, wherein workers realize the capital worth and collective strength of their labour. Should it succeed, ideas which arise out of narrow acquisitive thinking would vanish because they were rooted in unacceptable and illusory assumptions.

If the trusteeship idea catches, philanthropy, as we know it, will disappear. . . . A trustee has no heir but the public.

"A Question",
Harijan, April 12, 1942

Gradually, statutory trusteeship could be introduced in which the duties of the trustee and the public could be formed. The trustee may serve so long as the people find his services beneficial. He may even designate his successor, but the people must confirm it. Should the State become involved, the trustee's power of appointment and the State's power of review will strike a balance in which the welfare of the people will be safeguarded.

Fourthly and finally, Gandhi believed that social conditions were ripe for imaginative applications of the principle of trusteeship. The collapse of Western imperialism, the spiritual and social poverty of fascism and totalitarianism, the psychological failure of capitalism, the moral bankruptcy of state socialism and the ideological inflexibility of communism all indicate an ineluctable if gradual movement towards a reconstitution of the social order which will compel some form of redistribution.

The limits to growth make themselves felt through the undermining of social virtues like trust and truthfulness, restraint and mutual acceptance, as well as a sense of fraternal obligation, all of which are essential to individual initiative in a contractual economic system. If such virtues are treated as public goods necessary to universal welfare, then unrestricted individualism faces noticeable limits, lest the social justification and viability of the whole system be destroyed. C.B. MacPherson went so far as to predict that the time will come when it will no longer be feasible to put acquisition ahead of spiritual values, and that national power will become a function not of market power but of moral stature. Although we have to confront scarcity, the emphasis on Hobbesian self-preservation alone is inadequate.

> The rich should ponder well as to what is their duty today. They who employ mercenaries to guard their wealth may find those very guardians turning on them. The moneyed classes have got to learn how to fight either with arms or with the weapons of non-violence. . . . I see coming the day of the rule of the poor, whether that rule be through force of arms or of non-violence.
>
> "Advice to the Rich",
> *Harijan*, February 1, 1942

Even though the war against poverty will take a long time to win, it is necessary for the State to adopt various measures to reduce the sharp economic inequalities that undermine the working of mass democracy, and to strengthen the organizing power of peasants, artisans, and industrial and clerical workers.

In addition to fiscal and monetary measures to reduce income ceilings, it would be desirable to assist wealthy landlords and industrialists in parting with portions of their wealth, property and earnings as public contributions towards specific local schemes and plans. The more the redistributive process can be extended beyond legal compulsion and political action, the more democracy is strengthened at the social level. The more the State can bring together representatives of richer and poorer groups, stronger and weaker sections of society, in planning local programs, the better it will be for all.

At this point the socialist's faith as well as his integrity are tested, and so are his ultimate premises. Does he believe in perfectibility or in original sin? If, like Condorcet, he believes that the historical process and the progress of humanity involve an increasing equality among nations, equality within nations and the perfectibility of man, how much emphasis does it put on human growth and perfectibility rather than on inherent flaws and weaknesses? If committed socialists are not imbued with atavistic or original sin, if they hold to a truly open view of human nature, then they could adopt a different parapolitical standpoint. (See *Parapolitics — Toward the City of Man,* Chapter 5, p. 89.) They could say that it is because they believe in the unknown possibilities of every human being that they are concerned to extend the idea of human excellence to a point where external social distinctions do not matter, but where trusteeship is honoured wherever it is witnessed in human beings.

Owing to his unshakeable conviction that violence can never produce permanent results, only Gandhi's modesty prevented him from asserting that his ethical solution would come to be seen as the only feasible alternative to wholesale misery and destruction, if not now, than in the foreseeable future. He deliberately avoided elaborating a complete system of statutory or voluntary trusteeship out of the conviction that structural and organizational details necessarily varied with the social and political context and with the personnel, whilst the essential core of the ideal was universally applicable. Thus he could gain a serious hearing from those who

would be most affected by the implementation of his proposals
without threatening them.

> I am not ashamed to own that many capitalists are
> friendly towards me and do not fear me. They know
> that I desire to end capitalism almost, if not quite,
> as much as the most advanced Socialist or even
> Communist. But our methods differ, our languages
> differ. My theory of 'trusteeship' is no make-shift,
> certainly no camouflage. I am confident that it will
> survive all theories.
>
> "Theory of 'Trusteeship'", *loc. cit.*

II. REGENERATION AND REBIRTH

Ideals must work in practice, otherwise they are not potent.
                                        MAHATMA GANDHI

Looking at Gandhian trusteeship more closely, we might ask
what it actually means to be a trustee. *A trustee is one who
self-consciously assumes responsibility for upholding, protecting
and putting to good use whatever he possesses, acquires or earns.* For
an individual to be a trustee in any meaningful sense implies that
he is self-governing and morally sensitive. He is acutely aware of
the unmet needs of others and, simultaneously, is capable of
controlling and transmuting his own appropriating tendencies.
He is deeply committed to cultivating his most generous feelings
and altruistic hopes for others while consciously and patiently
freeing himself from all recognized exploitative attitudes and
relationships. He strives to become self-regulating, reliable and
sacrificial. But he must become so in a courageous and intelligent
way. He must learn to think and feel altruistically. He must learn
by degrees the heart's etiquette — to speak, touch and act with
the utmost purity and solicitousness. He must become, by virtue

of self-training, very attentive to every resource at his disposal — both inner and outer. It is precisely because he sees his abilities and possessions as belonging to God, mankind or to future generations that he is eager to use them to the maximum. His posture towards his overall resources is therefore not one of a lazy or selfish indifference. He is not concerned with hoarding nor is he fearful of multiplying his gifts, talents and possessions. Like the good servant in the New Testament, he wishes to increase his meagre "talents", but not for his own sake, nor merely for his own family.

The best trustee is indeed someone who has attained an inward moral balance. He is serenely detached, magnanimous and imaginative. But his detachment is never cold or narrow. It is an expression of his unshakeable confidence in the ontological plenty of Nature and the inexhaustible resourcefulness of Man. His steadfastness and trustworthiness are principally due to this broader focus of concentration. Likewise, his motive is benevolent and self-sustaining because it is not mixed with the turgid waters of personal aggrandizement. Instead, he expresses a quality of love and appreciation for what he has that enhances its moral and practical value for others. He might even possess little, but his sense of when, where and how to use what he has increases its potential good a hundredfold.

If this conveys the invisible grandeur of the Gandhian trustee, then what steps can we take to become more like such sage-like trustees and less like small-minded appropriators? Gandhi might well suggest that our first steps should be the fruit of honest self-examination. Grandiose gestures about giving up external possessions and impulsive statements about our good intentions have little practical impact on our character. The initial step should be at the level of thought. We should think clearly and deeply about the principles of trust and trusteeship. What does trusteeship mean as an idea and as an ideal? What are its practical implications? And what would we have to give up for it to become a potent mantram in our lives? This form of reflection and self-questioning initiates a period of "mental gestation". It allows us to strengthen our understanding, dispel illusions and light the subtle fire of altruism.

Once we have grasped the principle of trusteeship at a rudimentary level — and recognized its radical implications for our personal lives and impersonal relationships — then we could commit ourselves wholeheartedly to the moral heroism of non-possession. Thus moral commitment would be fused with clarity of thought and psychological honesty. Clarity in relation to the ideal of non-possession is vital, as is firmness of resolve. Mentally, we must see where we are going — even though it be only the next step — and we must be unconditional if we hope to approximate the end in view. Otherwise, we will neither overcome nor transform the possessive attitudes that self-examination reveals. This is a fundamental theme in Gandhian thought. We must be courageous and unflinching in our efforts to fulfil our self-adopted vows. Only an unqualified resolve can generate the curve of growth necessary to negate and transcend our appropriating tendencies.

If wholeheartedness or total renunciation is the ideal, we might ask ourselves, do little renunciations count? Yes, so long as they are unconditional. If, for example, I promise myself to return all that I borrow, then this promise is binding in relation to my children, to people I like, to people I dislike and to those who rarely return what I lend them. This illustrates the principle that non-possession (*aparigraha*) presupposes a change of heart, not merely a change of intellectual viewpoint. To be genuine, the change of heart must come about non-violently through the *tapas* of a self-imposed discipline. This is why Gandhi encourages us to integrate unconditional commitment with both philosophical thought and mature self-honesty.

A second step towards instilling the spirit of trusteeship is taken when we simplify our wants. This is a pivotal point in Gandhi's concept of non-possession. If we want to make the most deliberate and compassionate use of our individual talents, gifts, faculties and skills, then we need to simplify our desires and wants. Gandhi insisted upon this minimal moral asceticism for the trustee because he saw that unrestrained wants waste our internal capital and channel our resources into selfish uses. Inordinate wants obscure perceptions both of basic needs and deeper human aspirations. They diminish our sense of dignity as self-governing agents and corrode our credibility with others. Furthermore, when the multiplication of possessive desires proceeds far enough, it leads to self-destruction. This is compellingly depicted in Tolstoy's short story "How Much Land Does a Man Need?", in which a petty landowner is undone by his unchecked desire for land and wealth. He is initially simple and good, but his wish to improve his lot in life is progressively corrupted by a swelling ambition to own and possess more. In the end, Tolstoy answers the question raised in the story's title by wryly stating that the only land we truly need is a grave six feet long by three feet wide.

We might ask ourselves what it means to simplify our wants or needs in a Gandhian manner. It would seem that we can simplify our lives in at least two primary senses. First of all, we can make a concerted effort to reduce the sheer number of encrusted desires and habit-patterns that vitiate our altruistic impulses and fond dreams for others. We self-consciously check the tendency of the aggressive and expansive self to acquire more at the expense of others. But secondly, we take care to do this discriminatingly. We must, like the smelter and the goldsmith, extract and refine the pure metal from the crude ore. We want not just less possessive desires but more benevolent ones. Furthermore, as we cleanse the energy of desire, we purify our imagination. When we gain control over imagination, we establish mind control and render ourselves capable of using all personal, financial and other resources skilfully. We are more earthed, so to speak. With minds unclouded by vain imaginings, we feel more in charge of ourselves and are more responsive to the needs of fellow human beings. Our feeling for what others may attain is gradually enriched, whilst our fantasies about what we hope to acquire wane. We eventually insert our resources into the expanding circle of human interdependence.

Two other factors contribute crucially to our becoming authentic trustees — *the art of silence* and *the ability to put trust in others.* Silence or "speech control" is a precondition for all moral and intellectual growth. A trustee must guard his speech if he is to uphold and extend the good. This is not secretiveness but healthy common sense. A trustee's intentions should be as pellucid as crystal and visible to all. But wisdom is needed in all relationships. Hence, a trustee gradually learns not to speak prematurely or out of turn. He fosters a refreshing candour and reserve in speech which enables him to initiate constructive activity in season. He views wise silence and worthy expression as golden keys to maximizing the appropriate use of resources. No one would entrust us with anything precious or worthwhile if we were known to be garrulous, profligate, promiscuous or indiscreet. Nor could we be credible to ourselves and others if our speech is compulsive.

If the ears are the gates of learning and the eyes the windows of the soul, the tongue is the key to the alchemical transmutation of resources and the freemasonry of benevolence. Thus, a benign and intelligent silence is the precursor of effective, beneficial action. It aids mind control and augments true wealth. For example, parents often discern certain admirable qualities in their own children and those of others. These qualities are frequently at a germinal stage. We notice them intuitively but only partially observe them at an empirical level. By a sage-like silence we can help these virtuous traits to grow and luxuriate, thus becoming serene and sacred trustees of the good. Without drawing premature attention to what we perceive, we are ready to acknowledge or welcome the child's unfolding abilities when it seems helpful or important to do so. This makes every man and woman a custodian of the good in others. This is a high responsibility assumable by the poorest and most destitute as well as by the wealthy. Whenever any one of us treasures the finest qualities and exemplary contributions of another, we add to the store of human good. This commonwealth grows unseen but yields great benefits to all. Its value is especially apparent when we help someone going through difficult times. To remind someone gently of the best in himself is to remind him of what is most salutary and what is relevant to the moment of death.

Finally, we strengthen our desire to act as trustees for the good when we imaginatively extend our trust and the sacred responsibility for our riches in relation to others. This is integral to Mahatma Gandhi's idea of trusteeship. But what is the obstacle? According to him, the root of the problem lies in a fearful refusal to relinquish attachments. We often fail to confer equal trust on others or fail to share responsibilities with others because we will not distance ourselves from our suspicions and mental images of them. This is noticeably true with respect to parents faced with granting their own and other children a wider circumference of choice. It seems that a detached love is the only cure because there is no growth unless we expand the circle of opportunity continually and appropriately. This is not always easy, and good results are certainly not automatic. To confer upon the untried or inexperienced that which we have so judiciously cultivated is no simple task. To retire, like the court musicians of Akbar, from the limelight at the right time is a sign of self-mastery, while avoiding the sorry humiliation of hanging on to offices and honours. Such renunciation calls for a great deal of thought and a definite degree of risk-taking, but at least the risks are on the side of the potential good in others.

If every man or woman has some innate recognition of the true and the good, enriched by active participation in a theatre of political interaction, then a collectivity of citizens is a mature moral community. It necessarily rests upon and reinforces social sympathy born of self-awareness and a shared consciousness of "the species nature", the common humanity and essential similarity, of individuals in diverse roles, situations and circumstances. With this wider perspective, it is possible to derive a viable conception of the common good or public welfare from the individual's pursuit of the good in the privileged company of other men and women. This humane pursuit requires a reasoned reflection upon oneself in relation to others and an imaginative empathy with an expanding circle of human fellowship. The germs of noetic change — hidden within the depths of human beings — can become the basis of communities, communes, conceptions of community, at several levels and in concentric circles, in a novel and more intentional sense than any known in recorded history. They serve as the seeds of a rich variety of modes of participation in the politics of perfectibility. An ideal community is as utopian as the ideal man or the ideal relationship. But every human being is constantly involved in some kind of correction from his external environment, so that he engages in criticism of others (often his own way of criticising and defining himself). Everyone can see through formal laws and coercive sanctions and recognize constructive alternatives among true friendships for an easier, more natural, trustful context in which one can free oneself and grow.

If this is what is involved in becoming better and abler trustees, then what concrete implications could trusteeship have in relation to day-to-day matters? In other words, if we wish to embody the quintessential principle of trusteeship more fully, how might it affect our attitude and response towards (i) property, (ii) money, (iii) time and (iv) skills?

Several points should be kept in mind when considering trusteeship and property. In the first place, most of us do not own property, but we all occupy, use and share it. As trustees we should make every effort to look upon all private and communal property with gratitude. We should be grateful for what we have and treat it with respect — whether it be our bodies, our books or the flowers in public parks and private gardens. This mental posture helps us to divest ourselves of the false modern expectation that there is always more, that everything is replaceable, and that there is always someone else available to tend, fix or clean our material possessions — whether a gardener or a doctor. When we treat all matter with respect, we develop an immense appreciation for those who willingly help in the physical upkeep of our homes and grounds. Those who perform this specialized familial and communal service are thereby less likely to fall prey to an often unarticulated resentment when they see our authentic gratitude and the meticulous care we take with all our possessions and resources.

What could it mean for us to be scrupulous trustees of our money? What attitude and conduct are compatible with the living ideal of trusteeship? Money is a means of meeting certain basic needs, and not an end in itself. It must be handled with the same degree of care that we exercise in relation to electricity. We should plan for its proper use so that it fits into the overall purpose and rhythm of our individual and collective lives. It works best when it is in its proper place, and it can be put to noble, mundane and ignoble uses. Balance is required and so are balance sheets. If we specify suitable uses for our funds — from donations to necessities — they can aid private and collective endeavours. Often our bad habits make it seem as though we lack money, and we seek to earn or grab more. This merely creates an unnatural strain. If, however, we study our spending patterns, tracing them back to their roots, we will frequently find the existence of an unacknowledged trait or hidden desire that needs to be transmuted. As we simplify our wants, establish good patterns and set clear priorities, we generate opportunities to build capital for a higher use. Wealth is not itself the source of vice. Its moral meaning depends entirely upon why we seek it, how we acquire it and how we use or pollute it.

Custodianship of time can confront needlessly possessive and demanding attitudes in relation to time. This appears to be especially true in relation to 'open time' or non-compulsory time. It is undoubtedly true of obligatory time as well. When we are at work or performing necessary responsibilities at home, how conscientiously do we use our time? Is it well thought out? Is it properly coordinated? Are we cheerfully open to unexpected needs? Do we somehow manage to dissipate time through several 'chat sessions' a day? More significantly, how high is our precise level of constant attentiveness? How often does someone have to repeat the same points to us? Time is, to some degree, a function of conscious attention to duty. The more attentive we are, the more we learn and the more helpful we are to others with our time. This is because, paradoxically, the more concerned we are to do our best with and for others, the more we forget ourselves. Our troubles and trials are largely forgotten when we shift our focus of awareness to a higher and more considerate level of human involvement.

How possessive are we about our leisure — limited though it may be? Do we insist that this 'free' time is 'my' time because well earned? We may be quite entitled to what we term our 'private time'. Private time is an elementary human need (although not to the *yogin*, for whom time is a continuous inward state called 'living in the eternal'). But, whilst we are entitled to leisure time, we must, as ethical trustees, be willing to use it well. Furthermore, our chaste or corrupt visualization and use of free time often tells us something about the colour and direction of our spiritual will. If, for example, we use our leisure time constructively, then, in fact, time is a friend and not an enemy — either to us or to others. We work with the critical points within time — called cyclic recurrences — to regenerate ourselves within the spacious transcendental realm of the timeless. If we are wholly unable to use voluntary time well, then we sadly diminish ourselves and rapidly subtract from our opportunities to add to the sum of good. *Adharma* inevitably invites destructive *Karma*, "for whatsoever a man soweth, that shall he also reap."

When we turn to individual skills, we can appreciate the full significance of trusteeship — its subtle power of reconciliation and its ineffable moral beauty. In what sense, we might ask, are our individual skills to be held in sacred trust for others? In what sense can we badly abuse our skills and even use them to exploit others? *The litmus test as to whether or not we are true trustees of our skills lies in our expectations of return for using them.* Our motivation and our expectations are generally interwoven. In the modern West, and increasingly in the modernizing East, skills and specified knowledge are felt to be convertible into personal success and personal status. We might suppose that we are too mature to fall for the 'lure of filthy lucre', the cancer of greed, the canker of soulless competition. However, we are often all too susceptible to self-deception in this regard. We are subject to the satanic temptation that our hard-earned skills should purchase some intangible reward — from spiritual salvation to public praise. If we receive no external acknowledgements, then we are almost certain to be insidiously tempted to retreat into the tortured world of self-pity and self-approbation. This is because the tenuous exercise of borrowed knowledge and routinized skills is inescapably bound up with a fragile and fugitive self-image. Our frail sense of self-regard is disastrously opposed to the Aquarian spirit of effortless renunciation and intelligent sacrifice.

In practice, our daily approximation to distant ideals will depend upon the extent to which a substantial number of individuals balance their timid concern with individual claims to freedom against a calm willingness to consider the moral claims of the larger community of mankind. Can even the most ingenious organization of industry be dynamized by the innate desire to serve, not merely the desire to be served, the readiness to hold in trust and not the urge to appropriate? Psychologically, the spontaneous commitment to serve a community selflessly may be a self-conscious development, but the primary impulse to serve others is as much rooted in the universal desire for self-expression as the familiar instinct of self-preservation. The noble impulse to serve others, first displayed in the family, could progressively develop into the Bodhisattvic vow to serve the community of souls. This rests upon the compelling assumption that as citizens mature into creative individuals, the very process of individuation requires the growing recognition of the just claims of other individuals and of concentric communities, as well as a deepening concern with self-transcendence and the pilgrimage of humanity.

There is indeed no external cure for egotism or pride in what we have accomplished — especially when we strive and hope to see that it has truly benefited others. It is only through pain and patience that we learn to enjoy giving freely without expectation. However, if we readily recognize that trusteeship is a form of social action (yajna) natural to man, then it can truly help us to release the exhilarating sense of soul-satisfaction and soul-emancipation taught by the Ishopanishad and exemplified by Mahatma Gandhi.

Our daily sacrifices merge into the mighty stream of *Adhiyajna* or cosmic sacrifice. Such ungrudging contributions cannot be measured and meted out in the meagre coinage of thank yous and material rewards. Voluntary sacrifice *(tapas)* releases its own incomparable spiritual elixir. The sacramental yearning to use everything wisely for the greater welfare of our Teachers and for all Humanity could progressively dissolve the noxious sense of 'mine' and 'thine'. The raging fires of rampant greed, insatiable craving and demonic possessiveness could gradually subside because there would be less and less fuel to sustain them. There would then arise, Phoenix-like, the incandescent spirit of love and longing for *Lokasangraha*, universal welfare, the ceaseless celebration of excellence and promise. Meanwhile, courageous pioneers could light up all over the globe the sacred fires of creativity, altruism and universal fellowship in the common cause of *Lokasangraha*, human solidarity and welfare, enlightenment and emancipation.

TRANSCENDENCE AND TRANSFORMATION

It is argued that 'the human mind cannot conceive an indivisible unit short of the annihilation of the idea with its subject'. This is an error, as the Pythagoreans have proved, and a number of Seers before them, although there is a special training for it, and although the profane mind can hardly grasp it. But there are such things as metamathematics *and* metageometry. *Even mathematics pure and simple proceed from the Universal to the particular, from the mathematical, hence* indivisible *Point, to solid figures. The teaching originated in India, and was taught in Europe by Pythagoras, who, throwing a veil over the Circle and the Point — which no living man can define except as incomprehensible abstractions — laid the origin of the differentiated Cosmic matter in the basic or horizontal line of the Triangle. Thus the latter became the earliest of geometrical figures.*

The Secret Doctrine, i 616

The rigorous discipline of meta-geometry is concerned with the indispensable philosophical ideas required to construct the entire system of the manifested universe out of a single boundless Source. That inexhaustible Source, seen as a pervasive principle in the cosmos, vitalizes all planes and spheres and ceaselessly acts upon all forms, objects and subjects. Metaphysics, when rendered metaphorically and by analogy with the axioms and postulates of geometry, takes on much more than a merely theoretical relationship to the simple points, lines and constructions that are the basic elements of geometry. What at one level may appear to be merely geometrical relations between these elements are, at a metaphysical level, vital elements of the cosmos as a living geometry in repose. This is the deeper meaning of the systematic study of Euclid's elements, and it is a fundamental reality which constitutes the noumenal world. Numbers also interpenetrate the phenomenal world of objects and the complex relationships between them. Numbers, in all their possible combinations, give structure and order in an evolutionary universe to the totality of all that exists. So it is possible, through a highly precise and disciplined consideration of geometrical ideas — in effect, the study of meta-geometry at a preliminary level — to move beyond geometry, as generally understood, towards a true Buddhic insight into the underlying shape of metaphysics.

Though a highly difficult discipline, this process is crucial to one who would awaken the metaphysical imagination. All knowledge arises because of the immense power of visualization. It draws freely upon familiar phenomena from the world of sense-perception, yet alters and modifies the sensory world. This process is exemplified by any artist, whether painter or sculptor, musician or mathematician. Likewise, the creative power of visualization is central to any true science. For this fertile power depends upon precise renderings of formal relations between ever more abstract notions. As an innate capacity of the immortal soul, this enormous power is given exercise and direction through the study of mathematics. It is this which makes the natural scientist capable, at one level, of performing notable and elaborate acts of abstraction. The natural sciences become capable of attaining a seeming stability in their operational concepts through the relationship of thought to number. And through systems of complex equations, theorems and models, some continuity of transmission in this body of knowledge is also achieved.

At the same time, the power of visualization is limited neither by what one may know of objects nor by what one may know of procedures in logic and mathematics. The power of visualization must spring from the deepest core of subjectivity in every human being. Each and every man and woman, every *Manasa*, privileged to carry the sacred fire of self-consciousness, is necessarily capable of mental creation that transcends the limits not only of the seen but of the known. Thus every human being can, through the power of mental abstraction, ascend into the unknown ground and invisible origin that lies behind the entire phenomenal realm of existence. It is thereby possible through the power of visualization for the individual to transcend significantly all existing knowledge encapsulated in any set of equations, theorems and models.

All human beings are more or less at ease in exercising this power in relation to various subjects and objects. Yet often the very ease with which human beings visualize becomes an actual limitation. Nowhere is this more true than in the twentieth century, when through the natural sciences we have inherited so many extraordinary analogies — linking, for example, the solar system and the atom. This bold insight, coming at the close of the nineteenth century, was both intriguing and confining. In a sense, it was the product of a system of thought which had become fortified and solidified through a narrow interpretation of the ideas of Newton, and so fast becoming an impediment. It took a rare scientist, Werner Heisenberg, to see that it was essential to break with the known ways in which people were visualizing the world, to overturn assumptions confined by an over-simplified view of motion, location and causality. In his attempt to visualize a new way to understand subatomic phenomena, Heisenberg introduced a fresh model of the migration of entities from one point in space to another. He did not mean that subatomic particles literally migrate from one point of space to another as a bird might fly from tree to tree. Instead, he depicted the migration or shift of subatomic particles in terms of certain types of transitions between different possible quantum states. In effect, he introduced a more abstract notion of space than that connected with ordinary Cartesian extension.

Every such remarkable exercise of the enormous power of visualization, whether in the natural sciences or elsewhere, can free the imagination from limiting past patterns. In a society where so much consciousness is concentrated on physical phenomena, virtually any effort to abstract from the phenomenal world will yield some degree of transcendence. What is striking in the case of Heisenberg, and others like him, is that they were able both to transcend the limits of their perceptual models and yet to maintain a continuity with previous thought. So, as soon as his colleagues began to grasp the difficult Uncertainty Principle which Heisenberg had introduced into their science, they began to expand upon it. In Japan, for example, Hideki Yukawa joined the ideas of uncertainty and relativity together to formulate the model of the meson, an entity representing the rest mass of the nuclear binding force.

From the standpoint of meta-psychology, every human being as a subject is capable of drawing from the infinite resources of universal ideation, *Akasha*. What some mathematicians refer to as mind-space is itself only one aspect of the infinite *Akasha*. The capacity of the human being to extend the range of possible thoughts in all sorts of ways not previously imagined is essentially an application of the power of visualization in this mind-space. Far more is indeed possible. Such divine ideas and metaphysical possibilities go well beyond the entire system of visible and invisible manifested relationships.

Since it is precisely this realm of the unmanifest that is the focus and root of Gupta Vidya, the true awakening of the spiritual aspects of the power of visualization depends upon the ability to maintain continuity of consciousness completely apart from any perception of differentiated subjects or objects. Hence, H.P. Blavatsky warned:

> Those unable to seize the difference between the monad — the Universal Unit — and the *Monads* or the manifested Unity, as also between the ever-hidden and the revealed LOGOS or the *Word*, ought never to meddle in philosophy, let alone the Esoteric Sciences.
>
> *Ibid.*, 614

And again:

> Draw a deep line in your thought between that ever-incognizable essence, and the, as invisible, yet

comprehensible Presence *(Mulaprakriti)*, or Schekinah, from *beyond and through which* vibrates the Sound of the *Verbum,* and from which evolve the numberless hierarchies of intelligent *Egos,* of conscious as of semi-conscious, *perceptive* and *apperceptive* Beings, whose essence is spiritual Force, whose Substance is the Elements and whose Bodies (when needed) are the *atoms.*

Ibid., 629

The fundamental idea which the student of Gupta Vidya must initially grasp is that we can never relate the One to the many unless we first recognize that the One is by its nature unconditioned, without attributes, and so without any relationship to anything else. There is an unbridgeable abyss separating that Unconditioned One or *Parabrahman* from the differentiated world of manifestation. We cannot, therefore, reduce the multiplicity of manifestation to a primordial or primeval unity simply by invoking TAT or *Parabrahman* — the absolute, attributeless One. Rather, we can at best, in the dawn of manvantaric manifestation, find that which mirrors the One within a primordial field. This then becomes what is sometimes called the Second One, or more commonly, the Unmanifested Logos. The Unmanifested Logos is not *Parabrahman,* but it does, in a transcendental way superior to all formulatable conceptions of relationship, mirror *Parabrahman.* Since *Parabrahman* is out of all relation to space and time, not only as they are ordinarily known to finite minds but also in reference to all possible limits known even to the most developed minds, the Unmanifested Logos may be treated as the First Cause.

If *Parabrahman* were an infinite ocean consisting of centres of inconceivable potentiality, it is as if one of those centres became the Unmanifested Logos, mirroring and reflecting the absolutely inexhaustible nature of the whole in relation to all subsequent stages of manifestation subordinate to that Logos understood as a cause. Even here, however, it is crucial not to overlook the abyss between TAT, the unconditioned, attributeless Absolute, and the

Unmanifested Logos. The degree to which an individual appreciates this truth of arcane metaphysics is the degree to which an individual is ready to apprehend a similar analogical relationship between the Unmanifested Logos and the manifested Logos. There is a conceptual abyss between these two, though it is neither so intense nor so vast, nor can it serve as a model, whereby one may reduce the gap between the Unmanifested Logos and *Parabrahman*. Abstract though it is, the cognitive leap from the realm of the Unmanifested Logos to that of the manifested Logos is a less stern test of the power of metaphysical visualization than the "awesome mystery of *Parabrahman*".

Put in another way, the cornerstone of a real comprehension of the ancient science of spirituality is a proper grasp of the difference between what are called the Universal Unit and the manifested Unity. There is a fundamental difference between the supreme, Cosmic Monad — the Pythagorean *Monas* — and the vast aggregated Host of all the monads that spring forth like rays from the original Logos. Though this cannot be understood outwardly, it must be made a stimulus to meditation. Between Non-Being and even the vastest concept of Being there is a fundamental difference. Only when a human being is able, through meditation, to create a degree of voidness in relation to all other beings, all subjects and all objects, can the real relationship between the Logos and the monads be grasped. It is necessary to negate all finite attributes, even of the subjective self, and come to something like a pure apprehension of 'I am' that is consubstantial with, and corresponds to, the cosmic 'I am' — the Logos in the cosmos. Having attained that preliminary threshold, one must go farther, entering into the realm of Non-Being without any possible reference to any possible concept, thought, form, event or object. This realm, beyond any differentiated field, is, of course, extremely difficult to describe. Mystics, poets and men of meditation have tried by analogy and correspondence to evoke in the minds of those who are drawn in this direction some sense of what it is possible to experience in the way of the ineffable in the realm of Non-Being.

What it even means to speak of experience in this sense is almost impossible to convey. One cannot reduce zero to one, or one to zero. It is impossible to state the relationship between the One without a second, in the phrase of the Upanishads, to all that follows from it by multiplication and duplication, by permutation and combination, in the realm of numbers. There is a fundamental incommensurability between No-Number and the world of numbers. When the Vedic sages spoke of the mysterious bond of Being in Non-Being, they did not refer to any ascertainable relationship. This truth must be apprehended, even in the early stages of the Path, for it is essential to the development of *Manas* through universalization. It is impossible for the mind to reach the plane of *Mahat* or the universal mind until it is willing to forego its addiction to finitizing tendencies. Put more mystically, one must learn to recognize the fundamental difference between the Soundless Sound, the unutterable unmanifested Sound or Logos, and that which is partially uttered or revealed and is sometimes characterized by the sacred syllable *AUM*. Without understanding this difference it is impossible to become a true apprentice to Adepts, Magicians and Initiates, and to commence the progressive transmutation of all life-atoms.

Unless a person can to some extent understand this at a preliminary level, making it the basis of abstraction and meditation, he or she should leave Gupta Vidya alone. For, a person ill prepared for Gupta Vidya will be in constant danger of dragging the Teachings downward, concretizing them either through images of language or of perception. The same point was made by Nicholas of Cusa, in saying that no one would be entitled to have a meaningful conception of God who has not thoroughly mastered the idea of infinity. Human beings do, it is true, have a natural attraction to the unknown — one might even say to the Unknowable — and to the divine. But very few are actually willing to take the trouble to make a fundamental break in cognition with the world of visible things. This is why Socrates said in *Phaedo* that many bear the emblems, but the Initiates are few. Few are ready to enter into the invisible world in which they must progressively ascend towards the realm of the Divine Darkness, the realm of the noumenal Reality.

If the manifested cosmos in its invisible form is difficult for ordinary human beings even to conceive, how much more difficult must it be for them to distinguish that invisible but manifested universe from the absolutely ideal universe of the unmanifest? Where the highest metaphysical discrimination requires the capacity to negate even *Mulaprakriti* if one would not do violence to the mystery of *Parabrahman,* most human beings are not even prepared to cognize, much less negate, those aspects of *prakriti* that lie immediately beyond the physical, visible plane. The visible solar system, for example, is nothing but a superficial appearance upon the waves of space. That space, however, is not a blank abstraction, but rather a sphere pervaded by the *Vaishvanara* fire on the invisible plane of objective consciousness. Though invisible to the naked eye, this magnetic solar fire is the pre-genetic basis in metaphysical substance of the objective solar world. The solar magnetic fire, which is omnipresent throughout the solar system, is itself an emanation from an even more ethereal plane — the realm of the radiant *Hiranyagarbha* or Golden Egg of the solar world. This, in turn, is a differentiation of the eternal germ on the plane of *sutratman* that exists in latency within the bosom of *Mulaprakriti.* The entire range of possibilities inherent in that eternal and all-potent germ gives way to the Golden Egg of the invisible astral realm, itself connected with the objective magnetic fire omnipresent within the solar system. All these gradations of the invisible world lie on what one might call the near side of the unmanifest, forming together the cosmic differentiations of *Mulaprakriti. Mulaprakriti* itself is nothing but a veil over *Parabrahman.* Meta-geometry provides a series of powerful aids in comprehending this fundamental distinction upon which so much depends in meditation, mysticism and magic. Meta-geometry is, in effect, an archetypal record of the Mysteries.

From the very beginning of Aeons — in time and
space in our Round and Globe — the Mysteries of

Nature (at any rate, those which it is lawful for our races to know) were recorded by the pupils of those same now invisible 'heavenly men', in geometrical figures and symbols. The keys thereto passed from one generation of 'wise men' to the other. Some of the symbols, thus passed from the east to the west, were brought therefrom by Pythagoras, who was not the inventor of his famous 'Triangle'. The latter figure, along with the plane cube and circle, are more eloquent and scientific descriptions of the order of the evolution of the Universe, spiritual and psychic, as well as physical, than volumes of descriptive Cosmogonies and revealed 'Geneses'.

Ibid., 612

The Pythagorean Triangle was derived from India. In the Pythagorean School it was the basis of understanding something fundamental about the elements of geometry, which are prior to both space and time. They are metaphysical principles, and to grasp them in their pure essence is to understand them in relation to metaphysical space. The first great idea in the series of meta-geometric glyphs is that of the mathematical point within the circle, representing the universal and absolute Deity. The point presupposes the boundless plane of existence, represented by the plane of the boundless circle, which gives rise out of its infinitude and incognizability to that which becomes the pre-genetic basis of all manifestation. That root is the Pythagorean *Monas* or Point, which emerges out of the Divine Darkness, initiates a series of transformations and then withdraws again into the bosom of the Divine Darkness from which it came. Simultaneously with the disappearance of the Point within the Circle of its origin, the Point is transformed into a line or diameter, and then the diameter becomes the cross. Such meta-geometric transformations are not intended to create a logical or empirical relationship between the unconditioned and the conditioned. Rather, they are meant to help individuals reach out in imagination, in consciousness and through meditation, to the unconditioned.

Next in the series of meta-geometric glyphs comes the hierogram, or equilateral triangle, within the circle. Moving from the absolute unity of the Divine Essence, exemplified by the plane of the boundless circle and the point which represents the universal and absolute Deity, one comes to the Pythagorean Triangle.

> What it really meant was the triune co-equal Nature of the first differentiated Substance, or the *consubstantiality* of the (manifested) Spirit, matter and the Universe — their 'Son', who proceeds from the Point (the real, esoteric LOGOS) or the Pythagorean MONAD. For the Greek *Monas* signifies 'Unity' in its primary sense.
>
> *Ibid.*, 614

This Triangle is the unmanifest production of the first Point within the Circle. The Point retires and merges back into the Circle

> after having emanated the first three points and connected them with lines, thus forming the first *noumenal* basis of the Second Triangle in the Manifested World.
>
> *Ibid.*

Once the primordial Point has radiated its triadic ray to form the equilateral triangle and then disappeared, the apex of that Triangle takes on a Logoic role in relation to the subsequent stages of manifestation.

> The Monad — only the emanation and reflection of the Point (Logos) in the phenomenal World — becomes, as the *apex* of the manifested equilateral triangle, the 'Father'. The left side or line is the *Duad*, the 'Mother', regarded as the evil, counteracting principle (Plutarch, *De Placitis Placitorum*); the right side represents the Son ('his Mother's husband' in *every*

> Cosmogony, as one with the *apex*); at the basic line is
> the Universal plane of productive Nature, unifying on
> the phenomenal plane Father-Mother-Son, as these were
> unified in the *apex*, in the supersensuous World. By
> mystic transmutation they became the Quaternary —
> the triangle became the *TETRAKTIS*.
>
> *Ibid.*

Thus, it is the reflection of the original Point within the Circle
which becomes, at a later stage, that which generates the
Pythagorean Triangle, whose base line serves as the point of
emanation for the countless hosts of gods, monads and atoms in
the manifested worlds.

These successive hierarchies of beings are represented within
the Pythagorean Triangle by the Pythagorean Decad, the set of
one, two, three and four points.

> It consists of *ten points* inscribed pyramid-like
> (from one to the last four) within its three lines, and it
> symbolizes the Universe in the famous Pythagorean
> Decad. The upper single dot is a Monad, and represents
> a Unit-Point, which is *the* Unity from whence all
> proceeds, and all is of the same essence with it.
> While the ten dots within the triangle represent the
> phenomenal world, the three sides of the equilateral
> triangle which enclose the pyramid of dots are the
> barriers of *noumenal* Matter, or Substance, that separate
> it from the world of Thought.
>
> *Ibid.*, 616

Within the Decad, the four points at the base indicate the
connection between the Triangle and the world of solid geometry.
The Triangle itself may be seen as a tetrahedron or pyramid,
transformable into the cube and then into the other five
Pythagorean or Platonic solids.

The Decad within the Triangle is sometimes referred
to as the Tetraktys, a mystical term having many meanings.

These ten points contain the potential of all manifestation, providing the basis for everything that is possible in the vast multiplicity of the universe. Everything is prefigured within the ten points.

> The *ten points* inscribed within that 'Pythagorean *triangle*' are worth all the theogonies and angelologies ever emanated from the theological brain. For he who interprets them — on their very face, and in the order given — will find in these seventeen points (the seven Mathematical Points hidden) the uninterrupted series of the genealogies from the first *Heavenly* to *terrestrial* man. And, as they give the order of Beings, so they reveal the order in which were evolved the Kosmos, our earth, and the primordial elements by which the latter was generated. Begotten in the invisible *Depths,* and in the womb of the same 'Mother' as its fellow-globes — he who will master the mysteries of our Earth, will have mastered those of all others.
>
> *Ibid.,* 612-613

To understand the seven hidden points, one should attend to the six small triangles that can be formed within the Decad surrounding its central point. Each of these triangles has a central point of its own, and in addition, the midpoint at the base represents a seventh hidden point. The alchemical significance of these hidden points relates to the creation, through Deity Yoga, of a permanent divine vesture or Buddha-body. Sometimes misleadingly and loosely called the permanent astral, this vesture is an exact replica of the inmost causal body of the perfected man. Certainly, a conception so central to mystical training cannot have a merely mechanical or external interpretation. Thus, the seven hidden points within the Pythagorean Decad must, like all meta-geometric conceptions, be understood in relation to the concept of metaphysical depth. In addition to length, breadth and thickness, which are accessible in the realm of sensory perception, there is depth.

Whatever the objective dimensions of an entity, they can yield no direct sense of the mystical meaning of depth. No merely visual representation, however subtle, can reveal the dimension of depth which has to do with *Mulaprakriti*, primordial root substance, the one element and force in the undifferentiated realm. *Mulaprakriti* is a paradigmatic plane upon which the Logoic constructions of meta-geometry arise. One cannot approach this realm through any kind of inductive process based upon phenomenal conceptions of length, breadth and thickness. Such a below-above approach to meta-geometry can yield only a useless collection of lifeless truisms. The real breadth, depth and points of meta-geometry are living abstractions that embody first on the unmanifest planes and then on the manifest the boundless potential of the Divine Darkness.

The cosmic creativity represented in the glyphs of meta-geometry is inseparable from the Fohatic force of the cosmos, the vast reservoir of energy latent in *Mulaprakriti*. Meta-geometric diagrams are capable of endless duplication through transformation, translation and reflection along the axes of metaphysical space. Thus, each of the infinite points in space is capable of becoming and generating all that is displayed in the Pythagorean Triangle. This universally distributed potency is a key to understanding the process of manifestation itself. It must not be conceived in terms of staccato movements or static images, but rather in terms of a series of Fohatic unfoldments of pre-cosmic divine ideation within *Mulaprakriti*. Finally, at the third stage this brings about the synthesis of the seven Logoi, the seven Sons of Light, and then it becomes the basis of the vast manifestations of the forces at work in invisible and visible Nature. The natural sciences, which seek at once to understand these forces in relation to the phenomenal realm and to transcend them, will never succeed if they remain content in tracing out mere shadows or ghosts of supersensuous matter in motion. Limiting their study to the effects of the activity of that primordial field, they cannot understand very much about perpetual eternal motion. Cut off conceptually from the primordial field of undifferentiated energy, they cannot reveal anything about the infinitudes of latent energy within *Parabrahman*, which have no reference to any period of manifestation.

Nevertheless, each individual human monad in its pilgrimage throughout the seven kingdoms of manifested Nature has an intimate connection to that primordial field. Each and every human being has a living link, through the seven Sons of Light, to the most potent of all realms — that of absolute negativeness. All the scintillas of manifested life emerging through the base line of the Pythagorean Triangle into active manifested existence are ensouled by the divine energies radiating from the noumenon of the seven states of undifferentiated cosmic substance. The divine Dhyani energies arise in that zero realm as the differentiated aspects of universal motion, the Great Breath.

> When Fohat is said to produce 'Seven Laya Centres', it means that for formative or creative purposes, the GREAT LAW (Theists may call it God) stops, or rather modifies its perpetual motion on seven invisible points within the area of the manifested Universe. *'The great Breath digs through Space seven holes into Laya to cause them to circumgyrate during Manvantara.'*
>
> Ibid., i 147

The endless spinning of these seven invisible points in seemingly empty space is supremely potent in relation to the entire manifested realm. This hebdomadic activity of the One Logos makes possible, within any manifested system, the capacity to visualize its eventual disintegration and decay. At the same time, within such a manifested system, it is also the basis of the possibility of ultimate transcendence. Krishna, the Logos in the cosmos and the God in man, creates all these worlds through the mysterious power of *maya*, causing them to revolve upon the universal wheel of time. Krishna, as the divine Avatar, exists in all the invisible interstices and points hidden in the phenomenal world. Through devotion to Krishna, each pilgrim soul can find the breadth of heart and the depth of understanding needed to realize a relationship with the Logos within. Far beyond even the loftiest conceptions of modern thought, this is the true aim of Gupta Vidya, the hidden science, and the final goal of meta-geometrical insight, deep meditation and inward transformation.

THE ZERO PRINCIPLE

Laya is what Science may call the Zero-point or line; the realm of absolute negativeness, or the one real absolute Force, the NOUMENON of the Seventh State of that which we ignorantly call and recognise as 'Force'; or again the Noumenon of Undifferentiated Cosmic Substance which is itself an unreachable and unknowable object to finite perception; the root and basis of all states of objectivity and subjectivity too; the neutral axis, not one of the many aspects, but its centre.

The Secret Doctrine, i 148

The arcane conception of *laya* and the modern notion of a neutral axis are applications of what might be called the zero principle. According to the *Stanzas of Dzyan*, the formation of a cosmos proceeds through a primordial set of seven *laya* centres, noumenal points in metaphysical space that mediate between the unmanifest and the manifest. From an 'objective' standpoint, a *laya* centre is a point of rarefied matter wherein all differentiation has ceased. Given the cosmogonic distinction between undifferentiated matter and differentiated matter, theoretically there must be a point at which differentiation commences and also a point at which differentiation ceases. This is sometimes called the zero point. Zero as a general concept originated among the Hindus and was transmitted through the Arabs into Europe in the fourth century. It is a natural accompaniment of the decimal system, also an invention of Hindu thinkers, since the one and the zero are metaphysical correlates of each other.

These fundamental conceptions exist within a broader philosophical framework which is metaphysical and postulates that the whole universe progressively emanates from a Divine Ground. This Ground is empty of all form, prior to all differentiation and is often designated by the term *shunyata*, meaning 'Voidness' or 'Emptiness'. Thus, in its first and foremost philosophic meaning, the zero principle refers to that No-Thing which is equally the maximal and universal potential of the cosmos. This is the primary paradox of the zero, which, as a glyph, portrays the maximum potential that can be confined within an irreducible minimum space. Ultimately, when speaking of zero one is speaking of a point. That is, the zero contracts to an invisible minute zero, which is no other than a metaphysical or mathematical point. Such a point, representing the limit of an abstract capacity to contain potentiality within minimal space, is a depiction on the conceptual plane of the realm of absolute negation. The crucial significance of these abstruse ideas is that space is more real than anything it contains. Invisible metaphysical space is more real than anything perceivable by any human being.

A second major aspect of the zero is that it encompasses everything. It represents that which is complete while at the same time it represents that which is No-Thing. This feature of completeness is also present in the idea of a sphere, a kind of three-dimensional zero, metaphorically represented in all those ancient myths that speak of the womb of space and the cosmic egg. All of these allude to the principle of plenitude, the plenum within the voidness of the egg or a sphere. Thus, in addition to the idea of maximal containment within a minimum of space, the zero also signifies the idea of self-sufficiency and all-completeness. A third significant aspect of the zero is that it abides in itself without any external reinforcement. It is without a source, *anupadaka*, parentless. It represents the anti-entropic principle; it is inherently indestructible and incapable of running down. As the zero is intrinsically capable of self-maintenance, it signifies that principle in Nature which is the basis of all paradigms of perpetual motion and also of instantaneous, telepathic communication throughout space.

Such intuitive ideas are very much in the air in our time — if not yet within the acknowledged sciences, at least within that penumbra of imaginative conceptions called science fiction.

Nonetheless, they are no more than a dim foreshadowing of those facts of Nature which are fully known, at every moment, to enlightened beings. Buddhas and Bodhisattvas continually experience metaphysical truths as tangible facts, whilst these same truths serve as tantalizing conceptions and imaginative ideals to ordinary human beings. The profound truths inherent in the zero principle will, for some time, stand as inaccessible ideals for modern science, primarily because they cannot be conclusively established by any known empirical methods, nor can they be comprehended in terms of any conventional framework of ideas which imposes arbitrary limitations upon the untapped capacities of human beings. Nevertheless, if one approaches the subject philosophically, one may discern that throughout Nature, in all material manifestation and in all differentiated forms of consciousness and energy, there must be points joining and separating distinct phases of differentiation. In a remarkable passage linking together conceptions crucial to the process of cosmic manifestation and the idea of *Nirvana* so central to the path towards enlightenment, H.P. Blavatsky declared:

> No world, as no heavenly body, could be con-
> structed on the objective plane, had not the Elements
> been sufficiently differentiated already from their
> primeval *Ilus*, resting in *Laya*. The latter term is a
> synonym of Nirvana. It is, in fact, the Nirvanic
> dissociation of all substances, merged after a life-cycle
> into the latency of their primary conditions. It is the
> luminous but bodiless shadow of the matter *that was,*
> the realm of negativeness — wherein lie latent during
> their period of rest the active Forces of the Universe.
>
> *Ibid.*, 140

The close connection between the familiar notion of a neutral centre or neutral axis and the recondite conception of *Nirvana* has many ramifications. It contains the seed of an explanation of why the attainment of *Nirvana* is relative to a particular *manvantara,* a fact crucial to the distinction between the paths of renunciation and liberation. It also parallels the proposition that *manvantara* and *pralaya* are equivalent to the three *gunas* existing in alternating states of equilibrium and disequilibrium. This, as Patanjali taught, is connected with the cognitive basis of the appearance or non-appearance of the illusion of a differentiated world and sequential time before the eye of the soul. *Laya* and *Nirvana* have to do with the noumenon of undifferentiated substance, which is also the noumenon of force, both inaccessible to finite perception. The zero principle points to that which is the root and basis of all states of objectivity and subjectivity. Thus, the zero is inseparable from the mysteries of *nitya pralaya* and *nitya swarga*, ceaseless dissolution and ceaseless instantaneous creation.

To apprehend the zero principle fully, to plumb its depths completely, is to realize the degree to which anything and everything is possible, and simultaneously to understand that nothing actual has any real bearing upon that sublime state. The system of spiritual self-discipline and ethical training leading towards such a realization requires rare virtues like *uparati* and *titiksha*. The aspirant must wholly renounce all external means and adventitious aids and must simultaneously perfect the power of contemplation and abjure all desires. No disciple can fully realize the zero principle unless he or she is ready to part with everything in the world. They must be prepared to cancel all the noise that arises out of the endless oscillations of the manifested pairs of opposites and so bring the mind to a supreme state of stillness. The realization of the zero means the transcendence of all opposites. This, in turn, means the attaining of a plane of consciousness which is prior to all pairs of opposites. Thus, the disciple may reach a plane of reality wherein all the subjective and objective existences created through the interplay of opposites are held in pure potential.

In this realm of metaphysical negation, the realm of the zero, there is, in the words of Nicholas of Cusa, a *coincidentia oppositorum*, a reconciliation of opposites. Life and death, the real and the unreal, all pairs of opposites, become one. This can be put in terms of the standpoint of the sage, for whom there is no difference between light and darkness, night and day, birth and death. He himself is like the sacred *lingam*, a pillar of light, endlessly and dynamically linking up the formless *arupa* worlds to the worlds of form, the hidden archetypal and noumenal realms of causation to the phenomenal regions of effects. Such an enlightened being can traverse the limits of consciousness from the most ethereal empyrean of pure potential to the most limiting sphere of reference within physical space and time. He can do this at will because he has already created the equivalent of the zero principle within his body, and this can only be done in the body because it had been done in the astral, and this in turn is possible only if it has been done in the subtler bodies ultimately reaching back to the *karana sharira*, even to the *augoeides.* The sage, in other words, has mastered the principle of untrammelled mobility and instantaneous transmission.

What is realized by the highest beings is inherent in the universe as a whole, and therefore has a vital reference to what all human beings may glimpse or touch at certain moments. It is possible to understand the zero principle in a simpler way as a neutral centre or a limiting point in relation to a given set of senses.

> Thus, imagine two consecutive planes of matter as already formed; each of these corresponding to an appropriate set of perceptive organs. We are forced to admit that between these two planes of matter an incessant circulation takes place; and if we follow the atoms and molecules of (say) the lower in their transformation upwards, these will come to a point where they pass altogether beyond the range of the faculties we are using on the lower plane. In fact, to us the matter of the lower plane there vanishes from our perception into nothing — or rather it passes on to the higher plane, and the state of matter corresponding to such a point of transition must certainly possess special and not readily discoverable properties.
>
> *Ibid.,* i 148

If one wants to see, one should see until one can no longer see. If one wants to hear, one should hear until one can no longer hear. And, similarly, with touch and taste and smell. A point comes, often recognized by people who are blind or handicapped in one or other of the senses, at which one actually goes beyond the known limit of the common sensory range. To learn to do this consciously is to learn to move from plane to plane. If neutral centres did not exist, there could be no possible connection or communication between two consecutive planes. They would remain separated by unfathomable abysses. Yet it is possible to move from plane to plane and to alter one's responsiveness to the limits that pertain to sensory fields. So too, one can alter limits that pertain to cognitive and conceptual fields. It is no wonder, then, that the range of mentality is so vast; the plane of mentality must contain the set of all possibilities that are made manifest on the more gross sensory planes. This plane is so immense that few human beings could even begin to think of the virtually infinite range of possibilities for human ideation and imagination, cognition and thought, consciousness and self-consciousness.

Before one can begin to understand the possibilities of universal self-consciousness, one must grasp in principle and at a simpler level what is logically involved in the transcendence of any pair of opposites. Take, for example, any two points and draw intersecting lines through them that meet at an apex. Then draw a third line horizontally connecting the two original points. In relation to these two points on the base line — which is analogous to substance — the apex represents that which enables one to transcend a particular field, which is represented by the enclosed triangle formed by the three points. This is a simple enough idea but it must be applied to those five pairs of opposites, cited by the Maha Chohan, which are so perplexing to human beings. To take the simplest, consider pain and pleasure. Most human beings are stuck in the basement of human evolution, wrestling with the pain-pleasure principle. Yet it is possible to overcome the oscillation of the two opposites and to move to a point of balance, indifference or neutralization between them. If one is really willing to think it out, one will be amazed to discover the degree to which one can neutralize one's propensity towards pleasurable sensations and thereby one's corresponding aversion to painful sensations.

Moving to the moral plane, the neutralization and transcendence of egotism and altruism is the toughest challenge for those high souls truly struggling in spiritual mountain climbing. As soon as these souls take birth, they are burdened with the obligation and the temptation of taking on the karma of others, the problem of wise non-interference. They are also stuck with the principle of self-assertion for the sake of self-preservation. Though a difficult dichotomy, this is, in principle, no different from any other pair of opposites. The ethical dichotomy, having to do with right and wrong, must be understood in terms of the metaphysical distinction between good and evil. These, in turn, have their application in all relationships, social, political and otherwise, which give rise to the dichotomy of liberty and despotism. It is possible, with each of these dichotomies, to find a mode of neutralization. One may take as a starting point the simplest mode of neutralization, which is to find the midpoint between the extremes. In Buddhist terms one should seek out the Middle Way. If one can discover a moderating principle within oneself, one may begin to moderate one's preoccupation with right or wrong, good or evil, pleasure or pain, one's tendency to dominate or to be submissive. By continually engaging in self-correction, guided by the principle of the Middle Way, one may avoid both pitfalls and extremes.

This teaching of Buddha is accessible to all human beings. It is always possible for anyone to slow down, to cut down, to moderate. But in doing so one must avoid any tendencies to become passive, escapist or vague. To fall into these traps is not to follow the Middle Way but merely to flee reality. Thus, while remaining fully engaged in the field of dharma, one must also learn to moderate. One should begin with an appreciation of the principle of the Middle Way — lying between the extremes of unedifying self-indulgence and equally unedifying self-mortification. Then through meditation one must go beyond this initial point of departure, taking advantage of the teaching of the Aryan eightfold path as a bridge between metaphysics and ethics. One must, in practice, come to experience through meditation neutral states. The entire cycle of the eightfold path, beginning in right views and concluding in right meditation, requires a continual process of formation and dissolution of perspectives and assumptions. Whatever one's present mode of perception of the Dharma, whatever one's present practice of the Dharma, one must be prepared both to affirm and negate this framework. Only so can one pass through a neutral condition to a renewed and regenerated understanding of the Dharma. Whilst this will be understood at first in terms of one's solemn perspective and strenuous actions, owing to the salvationist tendency to project the idea of a path outside oneself, in time there will dawn a sobering realization that in fact this process of formation and neutralization is occurring within one's faculties of perception, within the substance of one's vestures.

It is not easy to master this mature understanding of the Path, wherein there is no external travelling and the aspirant becomes one with the path itself. There is no room for haste or pretence. Rather, one should approach the task a day at a time. Those who attempt to jump ahead at the start, because they know nothing better, will quickly despair and abandon the Path. That opens up the even worse risk of making judgements about the Path and about those who authentically are attempting to follow it. Anyone finding himself or herself in this self-begotten predicament should immediately stop engaging in such self-destructive behaviour and try to make a fresh beginning. They should get back to the basics, find a different rhythm, follow it out each day and each week, learn to act incrementally as Nature does. Then they may discover that though the process of enlightenment and self-transcendence is slow, it is authentic. There will be moments of exhilaration and joy, moments of freedom and beautiful insight, as well as moments of pure love and true compassion. Above all, there will be moments of true selflessness when, in thinking of other beings, one reduces oneself to a zero. One's eventual goal must be to thread one's life together out of such moments, learning how, through daily meditation and right mental posture, one can be of service to humanity.

If this is the immediate and existential meaning of the teaching regarding transcendence as well as the significance of the zero principle, the ultimate metaphysical meaning of the idea lies in the unfathomable bosom of the unmanifest. The mysterious neutral axis within the cosmos and within man, around which coil the diverse powers of dual manifestation, is also a luminous thread leading to the core of the mystery of the individuality. By discovering the more and more abstract aspects of the zero within Nature and Man, one may draw closer and closer to the universal basis of spiritual immortality. All the hosts of spiritual monads on all the many planes of existence in the manifested cosmos derive from a single hebdomadic Logoic source. Preceding the differentiations of consciousness and form in the solar and terrestrial worlds, that fount of immortality radiates through seven centres from one eternity to another.

> The seven *Laya* centres are the seven Zero points, using the term Zero in the same sense that Chemists do, to indicate a point at which, in Esotericism, the scale of reckoning of differentiation begins. From the Centres — beyond which Esoteric philosophy allows us to perceive the dim metaphysical outlines of the 'Seven Sons' of Life and Light, the Seven Logoi of the Hermetic and all other philosophers — begins the differentiation of the elements which enter into the constitution of our Solar System.
>
> *Ibid.*, 138-139

At this level the degrees of plenitude, self-sufficiency and self-regeneration connected with the *laya* principle are so profound that they have no comprehensible analogue within human life. This is the realm of Initiates. Nevertheless, every human being, as an immortal ray of the Central Spiritual Sun, has the opportunity and privilege of meditating upon the idea of Fohat, which is an emanation of the Seven Sons of Light. Whatever plane of self-consciousness a being inhabits, it is always helpful to a group of monads held together by an irresistible ideal and an overarching transcendental vision of the good to come together and strengthen their collective capacity to reduce themselves to zeros in the service of their common ideal. Training in this magical power of transmission is the essential meaning of the Sangha. When people come together, truly forgetting themselves and united by the magnetic attraction of the good, they emulate and serve in some small measure the Teachers of Humanity, the great galaxy of Buddhas and Bodhisattvas.

The highest beings learn to do this ceaselessly, invoking the Fohatic principle which is present potentially at every point in space. Even at the level of ordinary, unenlightened human beings, it is possible to take advantage of the zero principle at some elementary level. The integrity of human nature itself assures that every human being can mirror the transcendental beneficence of the highest beings. Ultimately, all the potentiality of the zero, of *shunyata* or the void, is present throughout the plenum. The void is the plenum. All of Nature stands as an open invitation to every group of human beings to take conscious advantage of the Fohatic potential that exists everywhere throughout the body of Nature, but which is most powerful in the realm of ideation, the realm of *Mahat*, universal mind or Aether-*Akasha*. This is an invaluable lesson for any group of pilgrim souls to learn if they would constitute themselves true helpers of the servants of humanity in the coming decades and in the dawn of the Aquarian Age. In all relationships — in one's household, at work and in the greater society — one may participate in the unfoldment of the ascending cycle that will stretch right into the next century.

To ally oneself truly with other human beings on behalf of the cause of humanity is to touch upon a much greater richness in human nature than can ever be experienced otherwise. Apart from the activation of the germ of spiritual self-consciousness, human beings are mostly semi-conscious, unconscious in relation to themselves and the potential in humanity. Once one learns to neutralize the lower self to some degree, thus transcending the opposites at a preliminary level, one will immediately discover what a fruitful diversity there is within oneself, between any two human beings, much less amongst larger groups. One will begin to see the profound importance of the plane of mentality — the plane of intellection — which is broader in its scope than any other plane. One will also begin to grasp the grandeur and magnitude of the vast inheritance of all human beings over eighteen million years.

Access to the plane of *Chit* — the vast and inexhaustible realm of boundless possibilities — inevitably depends upon self-conscious assimilation of the Law of Sacrifice. Within the planes of manifest existence there is a continual giving and receiving between all atoms, monads and beings. One may view all of this in terms of a calculus that seeks to measure how much one is getting in relation to how much one is giving. But the arithmetic of the marketplace is not easily applied to human affairs; the moral calculus is tricky. It would be most unwise to perform this moral arithmetic inefficiently and on behalf of one's ego. When human beings edit, forget and fall prey to ingratitude, they generate a tragic inversion of the principles of karma and justice. They think that whatever good they experience is self-generated, whilst whatever is bad comes from outside. In the end this amounts to a denial of the compassion at the core of the cosmos. In effect, by becoming obsessed with personal ratios of giving and receiving, one cuts oneself off entirely from the well-spring of one's own true being. Instead of succumbing to such a tragic fate, it is far healthier and much more human to learn to enjoy giving generously and wisely at all times. By stepping outside the realm of petty calculation, one becomes a creative participant in the universal wisdom-sacrifice, the *jnana yajna*, of the cosmos.

Each breath is a sign of involvement in the Great Sacrifice. Each thought is itself a part of that sacrifice. How, then, can human beings impose some narrow view, whether egotistic or bilateral, upon the boundless stream of universal sacrifice? Instead of ensnaring oneself in the unnecessary tensions of a pseudo-sense of justice, which is merely a noisy mass of humbug that will leave at death, an ugly *rupa*, one should reduce oneself to a zero. No amount of self-inflation and fearful grasping, no adherence to concretized images of oneself and one's possessions — physical, mental or even spiritual — can contribute one iota to one's well-being as a soul. It is not prudence but folly that leads human beings to store up treasures in the realm of manifestation. From instant to instant the entire cosmos passes through a neutral point, a metaphysical zero point, and instantly and effortlessly it is regenerated in all its vastness. If the universe itself continually depends upon the mystery of All and Nothing within the Zero, there can be no greater wisdom for human beings than to cooperate self-consciously with the zero principle. Living from day to day and moment to moment in calm assurance of the ontologically boundless plenty of the Great Sacrifice, the neophyte can learn to rest upon the bosom of the infinite waters of Truth.

KARMA AND
TRANSMUTATION

*According to esoteric teachings there are seven primary,
and seven secondary 'creations'; the former being the Forces
self-evolving* from the one *causeless* FORCE; *the latter,
showing the manifested Universe emanating from the already
differentiated* divine *elements.*

*Esoterically, as well as exoterically, all the . . .
enumerated Creations stand for the (7) periods of Evolution,
whether after an 'Age' or a 'Day' of Brahmā. This is the
teaching* par excellence *of Occult Philosophy, which,
however, never uses the term 'creation', nor even that of
evolution, 'with regard to* primary "Creation":' *but calls all
such* forces 'the aspects *of the Causeless Force.'*

The Secret Doctrine, i 446

E ach individual is an essential if unequal participant in the
fourteen phases of evolution indicated in the Puranic
Teachings concerning the seven creations. All human
beings share in the most subtle and sublime spiritual resources
of the universe as well as in its more manifest and mundane
features. From the standpoint of mental growth and moral
learning, the foremost element of human self-existence is its
partial participation in the Mahatic self-transcendence of the
Kumaras. Through the fiery spark of universal self-consciousness,
every human being is sacrificially endowed with the priceless gift
of learning truth, the right perception of existing things, and the
capacity for Bodhisattvic action. Existing as the latent seed of
divine self-consciousness, it is an inseparable portion of the
impartite field of primordial Wisdom — *Dzyan* — which supports
and pervades the differentiated universe.

Divine Wisdom is at once the luminous awareness of its
origins lost in the ineffable Darkness and Silence as well as the

directing intelligence of the noumenal cosmos. As Brahmā-Mahat it is the architectonic wisdom of Karma mirrored in the Buddhic faculty in man. As Brahmā-Rudra it is one with the hosts of Manasa-Dhyanis, endowing human beings with the immense potential of its transcendental wisdom. In the devotional heart of every human being it is Ishwara, the *Ishtaguru*, the prototype and preceptor, the living light of the lost Word guiding the pilgrim-soul along the Path.

The awakening of wisdom is not the exclusive concern of human beings as distinguished from the other kingdoms of Nature. Rather, it is the common current carrying every centre of life forward through evolutionary cycles of transformation. Governed from within by the universal law of harmony and compassion, each phase of evolution and each kingdom of Nature elaborates and defines one of a series of indispensable stages of growth. Each affords its own array of opportunities and each is circumscribed by its own limiting laws. Poised between transcendental unity and mayavic differentiation, consciousness experiences a series of states distinguished by permutations of space, motion and duration. Through birth and death, through involvement and withdrawal, through affirmation and negation, the appropriate soil is prepared and the seeds of self-consciousness quickened so that they might germinate and flower into the fullness of time.

Viewed in this light, the present phase of human evolution may be seen as a period of mature awakening to universal responsibility. To the extent that human beings realize their inmost identity with the Kumaras and Bodhisattvas, they may perceive the solidarity of their being with all other souls and hence the universality of their obligation of compassion. To the extent that they are illuminated and energized by the transcendental wisdom of the Kumaras, they will find within themselves the skill and strength needed to meet the just demands of a life of joyous service to other beings. As the active awareness of the bond of Being hidden in Non-Being, Karma is the basis of a philosophic fusion of the concepts of human nature, obligation, potentiality and destiny. Encompassing all from Brahmā-Mahat to the tiniest atom, Karma is inseparable from the world-wielding spirit of Wisdom which creates, sustains and regenerates manifestation out of non-manifestation.

Karma is thus one of the most mysterious and at the same time one of the most practical themes. In the present cycle it is the sacred responsibility of those who have been fortunate to receive the teaching of karma to use the doctrine intelligently and patiently, so as to be able to communicate by example — which is the school of mankind — as well as by precept — which is the mode of service to one's fellow beings — those insights into karma which they have been privileged to garner. Buddhic intuition with regard to the operation of karma is indispensable to human beings who wish to gain noetic control over their lives and instruments so that they may remain attuned to the potent vibration of the 1975 Cycle. As the karmic station of humanity demands the integration of Buddhic awareness and Manasic deliberation, the cultivation of mindfulness through daily exercises in meditation is an essential starting-point in gaining insight into karma. The practical art of mindfulness can begin with attentiveness to extremely simple and elementary points of existence. For example, in a variety of Buddhist schools aspirants are encouraged to observe their mode of breathing. By counting breaths over a period of time and by observing the rhythms of outbreathing and inbreathing, one can become aware of the pauses involved in breathing — before an outbreath, after an outbreath, before an inbreath, and after an inbreath. Such attention to breathing is not, however, equivalent to mindfulness, but must be linked through contemplation to an understanding of inward processes in consciousness. Inbreathing is important in relation to the powers of assimilation, preservation and absorption. Outbreathing is important in discharging one's debts to the seven kingdoms of Nature and to all human beings, seen and unseen, with whom one interacts. Each opportunity to breathe outwards is an opportunity to either bless or curse life-atoms.

Every human being is a receptacle of life-atoms from billions of other beings, immersed in a constant circulation that passes in and out of every astral form. In and through these *shariras* or vestures there is a ceaseless movement in the ocean of life of classes of life-atoms, which themselves belong to the hebdomadic kingdoms and sub-kingdoms of Nature. Each entering and exiting life-atom experiences and retains the impress of the thought and feeling of the human being presiding over the ephemeral vesture. All of these kingdoms and classes of elementals have had an archetypal function in the history of cosmic and human evolution. By combining a firm if rudimentary grasp of the metaphysics of Gupta Vidya concerning the seven creations with a persistent attention to the elementary processes of life, one can acquire through mindfulness a minimal insight into the magical process of breathing, thinking, feeling and willing. Minimally, one can begin to see that crude empirical notions like good luck and bad luck, being accident-prone or fortunate, are inadequate to an understanding of the exactitude and precision of karma. Similarly, one may come to see that neither wishful or dreamy thinking nor mechanistic or reductionist assumptions can be adequate to comprehend or cope with the challenges of life.

The awakening of the divine creative potential within human nature through an apprehension of karma requires a blending of a macro-perspective with a micro-application. Human beings in the Aquarian Age are the cultural inheritors of a vast vision of the physical universe constituted out of billions upon billions of galaxies. Whilst they may have few opportunities to observe the galaxies, they have many opportunities to hear and read about them. The reality of galactic space is much more alive for modern man than it was for the masses of people living before the present century. Through planetariums, through books and through the mass media, millions of people have been able to gain a glimpse of the awesome reality of myriad stars. Through the excitement of mental and physical voyages of discovery, many children of the present century have gained some inkling of the place of the earth amidst the starry heavens. Through this macro-perspective which is the heritage of contemporary humanity, individuals everywhere have gained access to the vast purifying powers of space. At the same time, the capacity to make use of such knowledge in daily life requires a micro-approach, something of that sort of attention stressed with great integrity in the Buddhist tradition. Beginning with Gautama's enigmatic Flower Sermon, there is a subtle emphasis placed upon the mystery of the individual flower, the beauty of the particular petal, the intimations of the individual moment.

Something of the same spirit was exemplified in the long life of Albert Schweitzer, who, out of his enormous compassion and sacrifice, laboured from small beginnings until his dying day, serving the needs of the ailing and the distressed. Schweitzer thought that the central problem of modern civilization came down to its lack of a sense of the sacred, its lack of "reverence for life". Through this great mantram, his therapeutic legacy to humanity, Schweitzer drew attention to the need for compassion, intelligence and humility in every interaction with Nature or other human beings. Through reverence for the smallest things and empty spaces in life, reverence in human relationships and for the potentials in all human beings, the sense of the sacred can be restored. As Schweitzer said, "Truth has no special time of its own. Its hour is now — always." This is the micro-approach, through which in every single hour one can make a significant difference. If only one would see clearly, every moment can make a decisive contribution to the current of ideation that is the surest sovereign protection of each and every human soul.

There is an essential relationship between the degree of one's reverence for life and the degree of one's apprehension of the mystery of life itself. Understood causally, *it is the rate of vibration of one's ideational current which determines the degree of integration of one's macro-perspective and micro-approach to life.* Some understanding of this principle may be seen in contemporary science, which seeks to connect the laws governing the life and death of galaxies and stars with the laws of micro-physics governing the vibratory properties of particles and energy. The same tendency in modern thought is seen in attempts to connect even the somewhat mechanistic theories regarding brainwaves and neurological phenomena with the still rather crude notion of mental vibrations affecting feelings and behaviour. The awakening of Divine Wisdom and the establishment of true continuity of consciousness depend upon a clear insight into the relationship between ideation and the involvement of life in form. Gupta Vidya teaches that life precedes the first atom of form, and that its manifestation on the seven planes must be traced to the active Dhyani-energies on the plane of *Mahat*.

Beginning with the primordial self-evolution of *Mahat*, Divine Mind or the Spirit of the Universal Soul, from the One Causeless Force, the series of seven primary 'creations' traces out the differentiation of the divine elements of invisible Nature. From the aggregate of spiritual intelligences, the Dhyanis and Manus constituting the primordial Logos, the first manifested and creative power, issue the influences stirring the first breath of differentiation of the pre-cosmic elements in primordial *Akasha*. This is the passage from the chaotic pre-nebular period of cosmogony to the first stages of cosmic life, the fire-mist period, wherein atoms emerge from *laya*. Here the second hierarchy of Manus and Dhyanis arises, those who in turn will originate the realm of form or *rupa*. Thus, in the sevenfold primary creation, as well as in the sevenfold secondary or material and terrestrial creation, the differentiation of the primordial germ of life precedes the evolution of life and form. The laws governing the manifestation of life on the terrestrial globe mirror the laws governing the agitation of undifferentiated cosmic matter by *Mahat* or Divine Intelligence. Through a purely transcendental process, witnessed solely by the supra-divine intelligence of the Rudra-Kumaras,

> The Supreme Soul, the *all permeant* (Sarvaga) Substance of the World, having entered *(been drawn)* into matter (prakriti) and Spirit (purusha), *agitated* the *mutable and the immutable principles*, the season of Creation (manvantara) having arrived.
>
> *The Secret Doctrine,* i 451

Pointing to the pervasive and profound mystery of the relationship between ideation, life and form, H.P. Blavatsky intimates something of the connection between breath and vibration, and speaks hopefully of the approach of modern thought to the ancient mystery.

> ... the *absolutely eternal* universal motion, or vibration, that which is called in Esoteric language 'the GREAT BREATH', differentiates in the primordial, first manifested ATOM. More and more, as chemical and physical sciences progress, does this occult axiom find its corroboration in the world of knowledge: the scientific hypothesis, that even the simplest elements of matter are identical in nature and differ from each other only owing to the variety of the distributions of *atoms* in the molecule or speck of substance, or by the modes of its *atomic vibration*, gains every day more ground.
>
> *The Secret Doctrine,* i 455

The ability to sustain a current of ideation, or vibration, through mindfulness in the blending of a macro-perspective and micro-application is the mature fruit of meditation and self-correction nurtured over lifetimes. Continuity of consciousness is the result of continuity of striving rooted in knowledge of the laws of Karma. For the ordinary human being who does not remember much of the past ten years of the present life, speculative pseudo-knowledge and supposed information regarding past lives is neither reliable nor helpful. All genuine knowledge is self-knowledge and derives from the soul-powers of deliberation, discrimination and detachment. It requires the ability to look at the world of objects in relation to the subjectivity of the ray of light that comes from a single universal and transcendent source. Gradually, through self-devised efforts checked by Karma, one must deepen devotional reverence for life, progressively purifying the inner vestures and the mind through the negation of all identification with form. Entering the void, one must seek the archetypal perspective of the Rishis who witness the eternal dawn of manifestation with the words,

> 'There was neither day nor night, nor sky nor earth, nor darkness nor light, nor any other thing save only ONE, unapprehensible by intellect, or THAT which is Brahma and Pumis (Spirit) and Pradhana (crude matter)' *(Veda: 'Vishnu Purana Commentary');* or literally: 'One Pradhanika Brahma Spirit: THAT was.' The 'Pradhanika Brahma Spirit' is Mulaprakriti and Parabrahmam.
>
> *The Secret Doctrine,* i 445

Mulaprakriti is the veil of primordial matter, or pre-cosmic chaos upon TAT, the unthinkable and the unspeakable. This ever exists, whether there are manifestations of myriads upon myriads of galaxies and stars, or whether there is nothing in the Divine Darkness in boundless space and eternal duration in which the ceaseless motion of the potential breathing of the One breathes breathless. When the mind is raised to the apex of contemplation of non-manifestation, one voids the entire cosmos. When this is done again and again, then, like those who get used to the rarefied air of higher altitudes by climbing mountains, one's mental breathing changes. It becomes possible to return to the daily sphere of obligations with a freshness, sweetness and an afflatus of supernal light. The more one experiences this, the more the mystery deepens and the more one is grateful for breathing, and grateful for learning and living. To learn truth and to see life rightly are the prerogatives earned by those who under karma become *srotapattis,* entering the stream of search for Divine Wisdom.

Every aspirant at the portal of the Path should know that it is possible by meditation to go beyond the galaxies, to reawaken the lost Eye and to restore the lost Word. No human being should ever hesitate to dare — spiritual life demands daring and courage, the *virya* of authentic striving. In that sense, every human being should reach for the sky, and indeed go beyond the sky, and having done so should come down to the tip of the nose. Of the five ordinary senses, the sense of sight is the most extraordinary in that the horizon of vision is much greater than the parameters of the other four senses. For example, it is possible for any person of average eyesight to see the tip of the nose, but at the same time to see the sun ninety-three million miles away. Even the most rudimentary reflection upon the power of vision reveals the immense privilege that human beings enjoy in their power of sight. In many meditative exercises it is useful to start by bringing together both eyes in a focus at the tip of the nose. There will be some initial eye strain for those unaccustomed to the practice, and it should not be forced. Nor should one engage in this practice of focussing the organs of vision upon the organ of breath merely upon the physical plane without thinking of that which is beyond oneself and also within the heart.

Ultimately, the quest for the awakening of wisdom through meditation is the quest for the realization of TAT — That which is the boundless space beyond the cosmos and also present in every atom. It is in the eyes and at the ends of one's fingers, and also at the tip of the nose. It is everywhere and nowhere, transcending mind and the categories of thought. It is the ONE that is neither first nor last, but ALL. As H.P. Blavatsky suggested,

> It is on the right comprehension of this tenet in the Brahmanas and Puranas that hangs, we believe, the apple of discord between the three Vedantin Sects: the Advaita, Dwaita, and the Visishtadvaitas. The first arguing rightly that Parabrahmam, having no relation, as the absolute *all*, to the manifested world — the Infinite having no connection with the finite — can neither *will* nor *create;* that, therefore, Brahmā, Mahat, Iswara, or whatever name the creative power may be known by, creative gods and all, are simply an illusive aspect of Parabrahmam in the conception of the conceivers; while the other sects identify the impersonal Cause with the Creator, or Iswara.
>
> *Mahat* (or Maha-Buddhi) is, with the Vaishnavas, however, divine mind *in active operation,* or, as

Anaxagoras has it, 'an ordering and disposing mind,
which was the cause of all things'.

The Secret Doctrine, i 451

Sometimes the Absolute has been characterized as the
supremely passive unconscious, but this is merely an expression
because, strictly speaking it is neither conscious nor unconscious.
It ever is. Brahmā, Mahat and Ishwara are all references to the
creative principle in the cosmos. They afford different ways in
which to understand the non-relationality of the absolute abstract
Parabrahm. At the same time, however, if they are not anthropo-
morphized or concretized, they can provide a ladder of ideas for
use in meditation for those who wish to bridge the gap between
the knower and the known, and between the unknown and the
Unknowable.

For the human being who adopts the spiritual discipline of
meditation in earnest, it becomes enjoyable to undertake repeated
exercises in spiritual training, in mind-control and in mindfulness.
Through unwavering resolve and unremitting attention to details,
the *srotapatti* enters upon the arduous path of self-evolution which
leads ultimately to the unfoldment of the Third Eye. Under the
ever-watchful eye of Karma, which must be mirrored in the
disciple's own vigilance, the mysteries of the seven primary and
seven secondary creations must be unlocked from within. These
'creations' correspond with periods of cosmic and human
evolution, as well as with various modes of differentiation in the
rupa and *arupa* worlds, and the respective hierarchies of solar and
lunar Dhyanis which constitute the inner nature of man. This
process of awakening to the fourteen colours of the rainbow is
referred to in the Puranas as the Eighth Creation, concerning
which H.P. Blavatsky stated:

> The 'eighth creation' mentioned is no *Creation* at
> all; it is a *blind* again, for it refers to a purely mental
> process: the cognition of the 'ninth' creation, which, in
> its turn, is an effect, manifesting in the *secondary* of that

> which was a 'Creation' in the *Primary (Prakrita)* Creation. The *Eighth,* then, called *Anugraha* (the *Pratyaya-sarga* or the *intellectual* creation of the Sankhyas, explained in *Karika,* v. 46, p. 146), is 'that creation of which *we have a perception'* — in its esoteric aspect —and 'to which we give intellectual assent (Anugraha) in contradistinction to *organic creation.'*
>
> *The Secret Doctrine,* i 456

A relevant and accessible example of this process of voluntary Manasic self-evolution can be found in the practice of taking daily mantrams or seed-thoughts for meditation and application. In this practice depth will follow upon continuity and continuity will follow upon resolve. The aim is to employ potent ideas in order to blow away mental misconceptions which are bound up with the limitations of the lunar astral form. Human beings are liable to limit themselves through sense-perception, acquiring a foreshortened and angular view of who they are. Through the progressive negation of false limitations, it is possible to regenerate awareness of the sphere of light that surrounds every human being, and to sense the intimate and close connection between that sphere and the sphere of light that surrounds every animal, every object, even every globe and planet, ultimately even the sun and the entire starry universe.

To remove the scales from one's eyes, to dissolve the encrustations and petrification that block the inner currents of vision, is a matter of careful concentration, wherein one focusses upon the core, the mathematical central point, in metaphysical space. Metaphysical space is a homogeneous medium in which there are none of the relations between parts that are found in the differentiated world of ordinary sense-perception. There are regions wherein the familiar divisions of time have no meaning, and light-energy flows instantaneously. To learn to inhabit these regions self-consciously, one must develop conceptions of energy-fields very different from those encountered when, for example, one pushes a cart through the aisles of a supermarket. But if one cannot do the latter calmly and patiently, one cannot learn to do the former.

One must learn to go at a speed which is governed by the needs of many other beings, but also amidst the clutter of objects and the narrow corridors through which one must move with patience and humility, stopping at each counter until one finds what it is that can be used to feed one's child and family. Again, it is the micro-approach to daily obligations which is the basis for deepening the powers of concentration and meditation. Owing to the enormous elasticity of the mind, it is capable of tremendous expansion as well as intense focus, but its wings will be clipped if it is weak in the embodiment of dharma. To understand in any degree the ubiquity of TAT is simultaneously to realize one's obligation to every point of life and to find within oneself the resources required to fulfil one's dharma. Broadly considered, the Eighth Creation spoken of in the Puranas is the transmutation through meditation, devotion and action of the responsibilities of human existence.

> It is the correct perception of our relations to the whole range of 'gods' and especially of those we bear to the *Kumaras* — the so-called 'Ninth Creation' — which is in reality an aspect of or reflection of the sixth in our manvantara (the Vaivasvata). 'There is a *ninth*, the Kumara Creation, which is both primary and secondary', says *Vishnu Purana*, the oldest of such texts. 'The *Kumaras*', explains an *esoteric* text, 'are the Dhyanis, derived immediately from the supreme Principle, who reappear in the Vaivasvata Manu period, for the progress of mankind.'
>
> *The Secret Doctrine*, i 456

Behind the screen of what seems to be material objects there are myriads of *devas* and elementals, gods and demi-gods, but to see them requires the eye of Buddhic intuition. One has to break down the false screen which is imposed upon objects and creates the illusion of the furniture of the world, with all its tables and chairs, cabbages and kings. Behind all of these are whirling centres of energy revolving in ceaseless motion at tremendous and different rates, and some of them are fundamental particles connected with what is called anti-matter. They are capable of instantaneously affecting fields extending over millions of miles. To penetrate the false screen of the visual world of objects, which is false because entirely relative to sense-perception, it is necessary to seal up the eyes and the mouth, as was the tradition in the Mysteries. By closing the mouth, one shuts out the desire to manifest, and with that the perceptual screen. One is liable initially to experience a dizzy buzzing in the brain, the bees of scattered thoughts, but they can be wiped off as one would wipe a slate clean with an eraser. The mental screen can be cleaned by thinking of the Divine Dark. One must banish all thoughts, voiding the sense of self, voiding the illusion of objects, voiding the sense of time, of yesterday, today and tomorrow. One must void all the six points of perception — north, south, east, west, above and below — but this is difficult because one has to start from below and to reach above, and it then takes time to destroy the distinction between the above and the below. To do this one must travel so far within that what is within is without, and what is without is within.

As the discipline of mental renunciation matures, a vast range of possibilities will unfold before the eye of the soul. One will become extremely aware of 'gods', which are millions upon millions of *devas* and *devatas* called elementals and belonging to the different kingdoms of Nature — sylphs and salamanders, gnomes and undines — all of which are invisible to the physical eye but cluster and move together in extremely disciplined arrays. Many people have some vague sense of this, through their relationship to machines and to animals, but when one becomes directly aware of this invisible world, then it becomes possible to raise one's sights cosmically to the magnificent perspective wherefrom one can broadly view human karma over eighteen million years. This is a vast period of time, far beyond the conception of many of the greatest minds of the age, but it is the privileged perspective of the human being who sees himself or herself as an immortal soul and wants to enact this truth in daily life. It is a perspective based upon meditation and the conviction that every being is an immortal soul. It is tested through one's ability to perceive others as rays of one source of light, enacting the reality of the immortal soul in all the vicissitudes of life.

As this conviction deepens and ripens, one will begin to sense the privilege of breathing on earth and will recognize the gift of the Kumaras, the Dhyanis who lit up the spark of self-consciousness in every human being. In Puranic tradition the Kumaras are sages who live as long as Brahma, being created by him in the first *kalpa*. Esoterically, they are the progenitors of the true spiritual SELF, the hierarchy of the higher Prajapati under the guardianship of and headed by Rudra-Nilalohita, and *derived immediately from the supreme Principle*. Meditation upon the Kumaras is both potent and benedictory, and once truly touched, it will leave one silently absorbed in deep rapture for a significant period of time. But then one will recall the teaching about mindfulness, and go forth into the world combining refined karmic precision with authentic creativity in the performance of duty out of love and compassion. Practising balance, one will both reach with extreme humility to the highest conceivable meditation, and at the same time act in the world with the inner confidence that one can genuinely help other human beings.

Maintaining mindfulness, one can transmute work and home into sacred arenas for the elevation of life-atoms, and can discover in every circumstance of life the golden opportunity to render true service. Long before one can honour the true presence of the Kumaras within, and regain the lost Word and the lost Light, one must come to see that there is no karmic meaning in meditation apart from the desire to render service to all that lives. Long before one can gain any direct sense of the ways in which Nature is the ally, pupil and servant of the perfected human will, one must quicken through meditation gratitude and deep inner humility for the privilege of being able, as a human being, to do something constructive each and every day. However intermittent the effort, one can create a noetic current which extends through the seasons until the point is reached where one wins true self-respect for the first time by staying with something that one starts. Authentic self-respect comes from binding oneself to do something noble and worthwhile for the sake of the human race. It is the karmic consequence of mindfulness. Once established, it will gradually bring about a change in the tropism of the life-atoms of the vestures. Meanwhile, under karma, one will encounter the hosts of angry elementals impressed by one's own past errors, delusions and incompletions, which are now neglected and want to be indulged but should be ignored. If one holds fast to the heart-vibration and the central current of ideation, then these will go away, and one will become like a child living in a magical world.

Whispering to the *Ishtaguru* within, who is felt but not yet seen, and listening to the whispers of *Buddhi* to *Manas,* but without speaking about these matters to anyone else, one may begin to recover the child-state. There is a holy simplicity in being like a little child, and a tremendous protection from interference with one's inner life by ignoramuses in the world. In time, under karma, as one becomes wedded to a life of meditation, service and consecration, one will become prepared for the linking of the Eighth to the Ninth Creation, the union of *Manas* and *Buddhi* in the presence of the *Paramatman.*

> *Learn now that there is no cure for desire, no cure for the love of reward, no cure for the misery of longing, save in the fixing of the sight and hearing upon that which is invisible and soundless. Begin even now to practise it, and so a thousand serpents will be kept from your path. Live in the eternal.*
>
> *The operations of the actual laws of Karma are not to be studied until the disciple has reached the point at which they no longer affect himself. The initiate has a right to demand the secrets of nature and to know the rules which govern human life. He obtains this right by having escaped from the limits of nature and by having freed himself from the rules which govern human life. He has become a*

recognized portion of the divine element, and is no longer affected by that which is temporary. He then obtains a knowledge of the laws which govern temporary conditions. Therefore you who desire to understand the laws of Karma, attempt first to free yourself from these laws; and this can only be done by fixing your attention on that which is unaffected by those laws.

Light on the Path

THE FIRES OF CREATION

After the changeless (avikara) *immutable nature* (Essence, sadaikarupa) *had awakened and changed* (differentiated) *into* (a state of) *causality* (avayakta), *and from cause* (Karana) *had become its own discrete effect* (vyakta), *from invisible it became visible. The smallest of the small* (the most atomic of atoms, or aniyamsam aniyasam) *became one and the many* (ekanekarupa); *and producing the Universe produced also the Fourth Loka* (our Earth) *in the garland of the seven lotuses. The Achyuta then became the Chyuta.*

The Secret Doctrine, ii 46-47

The archetypal evolutionary process, moving from the *arupa* planes of the unmanifest into the sevenfold worlds of form, enshrines the sacred mystery of creativity, divine and human. Creation is the ceaseless action of concentrated will acting upon cosmic matter, calling forth the primordial Divine Light and Eternal Fire latent within it. The noumenal quality of the outcome depends upon the degree of abstraction of volition and visualization and the corresponding depth of potential energy that is released. Beginning with the incognizable and imperishable *Brahman,* Hindu cosmogony depicts the gestation by Brahmā of four bodies — *Ratri* (night), *Ahan* (day), *Sandhya* (evening twilight) and *Jyotsna* (dawn). Through Dhyana Yoga, the supreme absorption of thought into its inmost self, Brahmā proceeds to construct the manifold orders of beings ranging from the highest Asuras to the varied denizens of the differentiated worlds — Gods, Pitris and Mankind. These four orders of beings are essentially correlated with the seven Hierarchies, each of which has its own creative role and distinct modality in the invisible and visible worlds, and all of which are integrally present in the sevenfold constitution of man.

The oldest Aryan philosophy associates the three highest *arupa* groups with the Agnishwatha, the Solar Pitris or divine ancestors of humanity, and assigns their potency to the purely formless and invisible Fire of the Central Spiritual Sun. This primordial Fire, one and threefold, is metaphysically prior to the septenary fire of the manifested universe, just as pre-cosmic Fohat is but a potential creative power in the unmanifested universe, preceding the differentiation of the triple One into the many and the awakening of the active seven creative forces of Nature. Similarly, Kamadeva is the first conscious and all-embracing desire for universal good, as well as the primordial feeling of infinite tender compassion, love and mercy that arose in the consciousness of the creative One Force when it came into life and being as a Ray from the Absolute. According to the Vedic Sages, it is the sacred bond between entity and non-entity, pellucid *Manas* and pure *Atma-Buddhi*, before it is transformed into the magnetic attraction between forms. Thus the creative powers of the Agnishwatha *arupa* Hosts are already implicit in *Daiviprakriti*, the Light of the unmanifest Logos, itself the product of the purely noumenal impress of Divine Thought upon pre-cosmic Root Substance.

The Sons of Fire and Wisdom are the hidden root of spiritual humanity and endow Man with the sovereign afflatus of *Atma-Buddhi-Manas*. They originate every Fohatic potency in the human principles, each of which seems to act as a living force summoned by will and desire, through which the relatively subjective continuously affects the relatively objective. Gupta Vidya teaches that these Fire-devas, engendered through the body of *Ratri* or Night, and known variously as Agni-Rudras, Kumaras, Gandharvas and Adityas, are at once the entire host of perfected Rishis, Munis and Nirmanakayas from previous *manvantaras*, as well as the personified sacred fires of the most occult powers of Nature. They are Agni, the first son of Brahmā, his three descendants and their forty-five sons by Aditi-Daksha's daughters, forty-nine fires in all. As the Kumara-Makaras they are linked to Kamadeva, *Aja* and *Atma-bhu*, unborn and self-existent, and one with Agni. As virgin ascetics they direct the six *shaktis* of *Mahamaya*, synthesized by the seventh, *Daiviprakriti*, in the work of cyclic evolution, and endow nascent humanity with *Manas*, which is capable of reflecting the forty-nine fires through *Kriyashakti*. Through this magical power of concentrated imagination and will, capable of producing perceptible results out of the inherent energy of ideas, the Kumaras created, during the Third Root Race, the Sons of Will and Yoga. Creating first the Seed of Divine Knowledge and then the Host of ancestors of all the Arhats and Mahatmas of the succeeding Races, the self-conscious Monads of the Nirmanakayas of past *manvantaras* entered the sheaths they themselves had formed by *Kriyashakti*.

Although reduced to a distant echo and dim reflection by the corruptions of anthropomorphic religion, a classic example of *Kriyashakti* in exoteric scripture is the *Fiat Lux* of *Genesis* in the Old Testament. In the East there is a beautiful tradition, whereby as soon as anyone puts on a light in the evening, all inwardly salute that light and the privilege of being able to perceive and to use it. Even though many levels of reflection removed from the pristine Light of the Logos, which defies every effort to capture it in any equation, visible light inevitably inspires gratitude in human beings in need. No wonder great universities adopted as their motto mantramic affirmations like 'May we be illuminated,' echoing the ancient invocation of the *Katha Upanishad*. Any person privileged to enter the sacred soil of any place wherein lies the possibility of preparing for some level of illumination in the sciences and arts is thrice-blessed, for all of these may be traced to the original instruction of infant humanity by its Divine Teachers. Nevertheless, what is true of horses is even more true of men and women: you may take them to water but you can neither make them drink nor can you drink for them. To drink of the waters of wisdom requires even more willingness, cheerfulness and concentrated self-training than that evidently required to learn a musical instrument, to learn to paint or sculpt, or to learn to fashion out of the resources of nature foods and artifacts for the nourishment and benefit of others. All arts involve the essential ingredients of concentration and imagination, combined with care and precision to enable one person to do something worthwhile for others. They all intimate a central logic to creativity, whether in literature, thought or human relationships and communication. When this numinous ordering is absent or obscured, there is a wasteful production of deformed shadows which only serve to separate and estrange human beings from each other through misunderstanding, instead of assisting the communion of minds, the understanding of hearts and the cooperation of wills in the realm of constructive action.

The divine gift of *Kriyashakti* is potentially present in the will of every human being, but it lies latent and even, alas, atrophied owing to the neglect, misuse and abuse of creative faculties in past lives, all of which prevent the tapping of its energy and power. Nor can this condition be abruptly changed. Just as it would be irresponsible in the extreme to allow a child or a fool to play with explosives or to come near high voltage equipment, it would be indefensible to give an unready human being easy access to spiritual wisdom and divine theurgy. The sad consequence could only be moral and mental harm to oneself and others, damage to future incarnations or, at worst, the tragedy of soul-destruction. Yet, in the realm of spiritual knowledge there is a natural protection rather like that in the complex code languages of modern science where, as Einstein knew, fewer people than can be counted on one's fingers will truly understand the fundamental equations of the most advanced theories. If this is fortunate in such areas as nuclear physics, laser technology and genetics, how much more so in regard to spiritual knowledge. Even so, there is a wealth of teaching in the *Stanzas of Dzyan* concerning the hidden logic of birth and growth, especially in the accounts of the development of the seven Races, which is relevant to understanding the complex mystery of creativity locked in the principles of man. The vastitude of suggestions, clues, hints and bare intimations will suggest to the slightest spark of the intuition that these overlapping anti shifting frameworks can guide the aroused imagination towards the archetypal logic of Nature which reflects the primordial germ of thought in the Divine Mind. Initially, creativity seems to the enquirer to be a temporal sequence of successive states and distinct interactions between beings only because the enquirer's state of awareness is almost wholly conditioned by differentiation in space and time.

It is helpful to recognize three archetypal phases in abstract creativity. The first is represented as a changeless potentiality in bare space, the *avikara* condition of immutable Nature, or *sadaikarupa*. The second phase is represented as the awakening out of the first, through an initial imperceptible differentiation, of a state of potential causality, the *avayakta* stage. The third phase involves the interconnection of cause, or *karana*, with discrete effects — *vyakta*. This must not be understood in terms of typical sense-bound notions of visible causes and separate results since it has to do with the origination of the visible within the invisible. Yet it is that invisible, indiscrete and eternal potentiality which, in a sense, becomes its own discrete effect, the purely spiritual atom becoming the One and the many and producing thereby the manifested worlds, including the globes of our earth. Like Solomon's temple, the temple of truth is built by invisible hands; from the visible effects alone nothing significant can be inferred in reference to true creativity. Those who either do not use their eyes sufficiently to see the sky, or merely employ visual images as the sole basis for inferences about results, will involuntarily incarnate again and again, trapped in the *maya* of visible phenomena.

Progress in human thought and the advent of true creativity in human affairs require the powers of philosophic abstraction, prolonged concentration and noetic meditation. It is essential to enter the invisible realm of germinating seed ideas and, like the good gardener, to learn to work with and through Nature. Disinterested in visible results, which are but the flowers of yesterday, one must learn to wait patiently for the cyclic harvest, sustaining a lightness of heart, an ardent love for the soil and a joyous gratitude for the generosity of Nature. The good gardener is the paradigm of the wise man or woman confirmed in a perception of invisible reality, in which there is always both a boundless potential and the germinating seeds. Beginning on the noumenal plane, the series of causes has its representation on the invisible plane of abstract mathematical form, and also in the secret core of the orderly if gradual progression in the realm of the visible. This hidden logic of creativity, birth and growth from invisible seeds is mirrored in the wisdom of natural forms, such as in the ever-increasing concentric rings of trees. Anyone who has contemplated the rings of an ancient pine or mighty oak, and seen how the steady growth of Nature follows her own seasons without reference to the vagaries of human emotion, can begin to appreciate how the smallest of the small, the *aniyamsam aniyasam,* becomes the One and the many, *ekanekarupa.* There is an immediate connection between the *Atman* in and beyond all, and the most minute of the myriads of invisible atoms within every single living form.

The highest sees through the eyes of the lowest. Hence the Kriyashaktic power of creative imagination lies waiting to be aroused in every Manasic being, but this requires the uttermost refinement of faith, will and desire through *Buddhi Yoga.* In conveying the process whereby Brahmā constructs his four bodies by concentrating his mind into itself, and then 'thinks of himself' as the progenitor of the world, H.P. Blavatsky refers to this as *Kriyashakti.*

> This *thinking of oneself* as this, that, or the other, is the chief factor in the production of every kind of psychic or even physical phenomena. The words 'whosoever shall say to this mountain be thou removed and cast into the sea, and *shall not doubt* . . . that thing will come to pass,' are no vain words. Only the word 'faith' ought to be translated by WILL. Faith without Will is like a wind-mill without *wind,* barren of results.
> *The Secret Doctrine,* ii 59

True faith and spiritual will have nothing to do with blind acceptance or petty wilfulness bound by likes and dislikes. They point instead to mental control, concentrated determination and unbounded effortless confidence which can be brought together in a mystic marriage or fusion of the higher faculties. One must gain an intuitive understanding of why Kamadeva-Agni, the primordial fiery spirit of compassion, allegorically the son of Dharma (sacred moral duty and justice) and Shraddha (faith), carries the sign of Makara on his banner. Apart from the sublime motive of universal compassion, the faculties of the Higher Triad in man cannot awaken to self-conscious creativity. But once the current is touched, then, out of noetic love for universal good, out of deep feeling and intense thought upon a firm basis that is impersonal, controlled and calm, one can release a current of ideation that can heal and help, bless and guide, any human being receptive and responsive to the power of that current.

Once this point is reached, one is prepared to pursue the exacting theoretical and practical discipline of occult science. The classifications of the principles of Man and Nature into septenary sets take on a living immediacy beyond any merely intellectual notions regarding rainbows, musical scales, days of the week, or any of the other septenates known to the casual observer. As the factor number of the *manvantaras*, 7 is critical to the whole of manifestation and to all human progress. Divided into the 3 and the 4, it is representative of both the Hierarchies and the various Pitris from which the human principles are derived through the Logos or Word. Proceeding from the Circle of Divine Thought to its Diameter, the Word containing π and the inmost logic of the Hierarchies in its ineffable nature, indiscrete fire becomes liquid fire, giving rise to the myriad centres of life — the union of Thought and the Word. As 7 is the number of Union, 3 is that of Light and 4 that of Life. In the human principles the higher three are born from the fiery Agnishwatha Pitris, the Asuras born from *Ratri*, the body of Night of Brahmā. The fourfold human body of illusion is formed by the inferior hosts of Barhishad Pitris, born from *Sandhya*, the body of Twilight of Brahmā. Until the Fire-devas incarnate into the prepared forms of the mindless Third Root Race, the Atma-Buddhic Monads of incipient humanity cannot attain self-consciousness. As the *Stanzas* explain:

> *It is from the material Worlds that descend they, who fashion physical man at the new Manvantaras. They are inferior Lha (Spirits), possessed of a dual body (an astral within an ethereal form). They are the fashioners of our body of illusion. . . .*
>
> *Into the forms projected by the Lha (Pitris) the two letters (the Monad, called also 'the Double Dragon') descend from the spheres of expectation. But they are like a roof with no walls, nor pillars to rest upon. . . .*
>
> *Man needs four flames and three fires to become one on Earth, and he requires the essence of the forty-nine fires to be perfect. It is those who have deserted the Superior Spheres, the Gods of Will, who complete the Manu of illusion. For the 'Double Dragon' has no hold upon the mere form. It is like the breeze where there is no tree or branch to receive and harbour it. It cannot affect the form where there is no agent of transmission (Manas, 'Mind') and the form knows it not.*
>
> *In the highest worlds, the three are one, on Earth (at first) the one becomes two. They are like the two (side) lines of a triangle that has lost its bottom line — which is the third fire.*
>
> The Secret Doctrine, ii 57

Human perfection requires the self-conscious mastery of the forty-nine fires, that is, the full alchemical union of *Manas*, which reflects the forty-nine fires, with *Atma-Buddhi*. Beyond the simple spectrum and septenary scale, with its division between three primary and four secondary colours and tones, there is a far more intricate and intertwined matrix of light and sound. Just so, the full complexity of the fiery hebdomadic Heart of the Dhyan Chohanic body, the Agnishwathas, is mirrored in the human principles, and even in the physical heart with its three higher divisions and four lower cavities. Every effort to gain continuity of consciousness in thought, dispassionate strength of will and deeper compassion in feeling, when pursued over seven days, seven years or seven lives, has a direct bearing upon the inward awakening of the creative fires of the Higher Triad. Similarly, all fragmentation of consciousness, personal wilfulness and selfish motivation is a form of mental and spiritual illness requiring the self-administered medicine of conscience and contemplation. In fact, every therapeutic measure of health, such as temperature, blood pressure, pulse and respiration rate is but a visible analogue of inner conditions, just as the art of physical medicine is the transference to the visible plane, by invisible Adepts, of the therapeutics of spiritual wisdom, for the sake of relieving humanity of some of its mental and physical pain.

The restoration of the spiritual health of humanity requires a renewal of the integrity of the operation of the four flames and three fires. Essentially, every person is an indivisible unitary being. Though it is possible to distinguish thought, will and feeling (or head, hands and heart, at another level) for the sake of understanding, these are not separable in fact, any more than the circulations of blood, plasma and spinal fluid can be severed from each other in the living body without producing a corpse. Similarly, without the highest faculties or fires that are mirrored in the simplest aspects of human life and being, one cannot have an integrated unitary human nature. This is why *The Voice of the Silence* calls those who are not yet awakened to the integrity of creative spiritual consciousness the 'living dead'. Nevertheless, one may make an initial approach to the teaching of the correlation between *Atman, Buddhi* and *Manas,* Spirit, Soul and Mind in man, and the three modes of fire connected with the Hierarchies. According to the veiled parables of the Puranas:

> The 'Three Fires', Pavaka, Pavamana, and Suchi, who had forty-five sons, who, with their three fathers and their Father Agni, constitute the 49 fires. Pavamana (fire produced by friction) is the parent of the *fire of the Asuras;* Suchi (Solar fire) is the parent of the fire of the gods; and Pavaka (electric fire) is the father of the fire of the *Pitris.* Rut this is an explanation on the material and the terrestrial plane. The flames are

evanescent and only periodical; the fires — eternal in
their triple unity. They correspond to the *four* lower, and
the *three* higher human principles.

The Secret Doctrine, ii 57

Pavamana, the fire produced by friction, involves a
differentiation of substance, implying knowledge of comple-
mentarity and polarity in reference to the substances involved, as
well as persistence. On the physical plane, friction represents that
without which engines will not run, but also that because of which
they will not run forever. In theogony, friction is produced by
Visvakarman using the *pramantha*, or fire drill, and the swastika
to produce Agni amidst *maya*. Cosmically, the *Pavamana* fire is
correlated with soul, and is the parent of the fire of the Asuras.
Metaphysically, it means union between *Buddhi* and *Manas*, the
latter merging partially into and becoming part of the Atma-
Buddhic Monad. Physically, it relates to the creative spark or germ
that fructifies and generates the human being. Psychologically, it
points to the possibility through meditation of betrothing idea
and feeling, consecrating and invoking them together, and using
their offspring of thoughts, volitions and feelings in daily life.
Through repeated attempts one may refine this union of idea and
feeling, deepening it by abstraction meditation and imagination,
until it acquires a mystical depth, breadth and continuity. Mystically,
the *Tretagni* is obtained by the attrition of fire-sticks made of
Ashwatha wood, whose lengths equal the metre of the *Gayatri*.

Suchi, the solar fire, is 'the drinker of waters'. Cosmically, it
corresponds to Spirit, and it is the parent of the fire of the gods.
Typically, human beings are only able to touch this solar fire in
sushupti, which accounts for the serene beauty, purity and
defencelessness reflected in the face of someone in deep sleep. It
is the source of the ineffable and elusive radiance which mothers
and midwives sense at the overwhelming and unique moment of
birth of every baby, each of whom sounds the Word in some form.
In theogony the Gandharvas are the aggregate powers of the solar
fire and constitute its forces, and under their leader, Narada, they

teach the secrets of heaven to mortals. Mystically connected with
soma, and psychically with the *sushumna* solar ray prized by yogis,
they are spiritually and physically the noumenal and phenomenal
causes of sound. By making one's entire life revolve around one's
most noble ideals and aspirations on behalf of all humanity,
maintaining the impulse with a continuity that transforms
consciousness, one may make the higher aspects of the *Suchi* fire
a living reality. Filled with secret joy and happiness, and exempt
from the lunar waxing and waning of passion and animal instinct,
one can constantly show compassion to others not so privileged
as to be at all times eternally young and cheerful. Once it is
aroused as a spark in the core of the invisible heart, the *Anahata*
or indestructible centre, the solar fire will then burn as the
constant steady flame of an entire life, making it into a poem, a
song, even a symphony.

The *Pavaka* electric fire is connected with the latent
intelligence in every elemental atom. The eternal motion of the
Atman is mirrored at the level of maximum differentiation in the
unerring, instinctual motion and power of life in every single
atomic constituent of all forms, organisms, constructs and
kingdoms. Cosmically, electric fire correlates with the body, and
is the parent of the *Kavyavahana* fire of the Barhishad Pitris. It is
called electric fire because it can only work through a positive
and negative pole, such as the head and feet of a human being or
the north and south poles of the earth. These two centres act as
the storehouse, receptacle and liberators of cosmic and terrestrial
vital electricity. In the solar-selenic radiance of the *aurora borealis*
and *australis,* the Fohatic forces working at the poles display
characteristic qualities of *Akasha,* air and fire, that is, sound, touch
and light or colour. The mysterious magnetosphere of the earth,
with equatorial, ecliptic and tropical circles, contains a mystical
key to the primeval revelation of the Vedas to those Rishis who
first saw, then heard, the songs of their Fathers. Through the
influence of alchemical writers like Boehme, much was learnt
during the nineteenth century regarding electricity on the physical
plane, but as contemporary theories readily acknowledge, there

are many hidden aspects of what is called electricity, the essential nature of which is sensed but largely unknown. The ancients gave great importance to electricity in its relation to self-purification through self-magnetization. This has to do not merely with physical hygiene, but with all modes of pollution and cleanliness affecting the body, brain and heart. Many people instinctively feel a wish to bathe after various kinds of debasing encounters, but one cannot produce a metaphysically and karmically purifying result through physical means alone. Nevertheless, if the abstract is made the basis of the external, through meditation, then spiritual knowledge and devotion can purify one's nature from within without, from above below.

These sacred fires are the priceless inheritance of every human being but this inheritance must be claimed by each individually. The integrity of the universe and the evolutionary logic of creativity, birth and growth must be accepted and examined in each avenue of one's life before they can be discovered within one's higher nature. As the dual progeny of the Solar and Lunar Pitris, man must discover how to incarnate the solar in the lunar, raise Agni in *maya*, thus aiding the forward impulse of Manasic evolution. The lunar realm is not wholly and inherently inimical to man. Indeed, this could not be so except in some absurd Manichean scheme which totally divorces the sun from the moon. The new and full moons, the eclipses regulated by Rahu and Ketu, and the twenty-eight days of the lunar month, associated in one sense with the twenty-eight *nakshatrams* and in another with the twenty-eight stars of Makara, contain keys crucial to making the solar relevant to the lower lunar light. Without penetrating these mysteries to the core, enlightenment understood as the total consummation of wisdom in action remains inaccessible to a human being. In essence, this means disengaging the sense of self from Indu, the psycho-physical moon, and discovering the occult nature of Soma, the spiritual regent of the invisible moon, and the father, by Tara, of Budha — Wisdom.

According to the ancient allegory of the war in heaven, this mystical marriage symbolizes the rejection of anthropomorphic religion in favour of the pursuit of inner wisdom. From the exoteric standpoint, this rebellion implies a fall from divine grace, but esoterically it is the revolt of *Manas* against bondage to the lower, albeit ethereal, creative hosts born from the *rupa* bodies of Brahmā. The original and metaphysical 'fall', by which the Achyuta become Chyuta, refers to the initial and inevitable differentiation of the universal spiritual light of cosmic ideation. This is the Mahatic light incarnated by the Sons of Wisdom into humanity through the power of *Kriyashakti*. It is this same power, the spirit of Divine Wisdom in man, the Manasic spirit, which taught man the secret of creation on the Kriyashaktic plane and procreation on the earthly plane, which led him on the path towards self-conscious immortality. That this provoked the wrath and envy of those polluted by anthropomorphic self-worship can scarcely be blamed upon the Kumaras and Agnishwathas, the spiritual benefactors of intellectual humanity. Hence the so-called fall of Adam and Eve, the rebellion of spiritual intelligence against the inertia of matter, marks the turning point in the movement from consciousness to self-consciousness and then towards universal self-consciousness. The cloying dogmas of original sin and demonology are nothing but the sorry legacy of self-mutilation, self-murder and perverse ingratitude perpetrated by those who live as if they matter more than universal good. Atlantean sorcerers inverted and misused spiritual knowledge and power, proliferated excuses and sought to shed their karmic debts on others. In the end, however, they will be wholly eclipsed in their own ever-lengthening shadows as they walk away from the sun.

Spiritual growth depends upon the daily, hourly and constant practice of walking towards the sun. No matter how heavy and footsore the pilgrim through self-imposed karmic burdens from the past, it is always possible to take gentle steps towards the light, to thrill at the thought that others are doing the same, and to learn from them and love them as companions on the Path. As understood by philosophers like Kant and sages like Buddha, no one can force another to reverse the tendency towards inertia.

Hence Buddha regarded the production of a permanent change in the life of an individual human being as the highest magic. But this magical ignition of *Bodhichitta* involves the consent, cooperation and gratitude, the questioning and intensity, as well as the love, devotion and compassion of that human being in wanting to pass on and transcend the separative sense of self. Without a spark of these spiritual qualities, it is not possible to realize the justice and magnificence of human life. It is central to the entire teaching of Gupta Vidya that whilst metaphysical differentiation through consciousness is indispensable for there even to be self-consciousness, this is fundamentally different from the difficulty for a ray of spirit, when encased in matter, to rebel against inertia. There are many modes of inertia — spiritual inertia which is the refusal to climb, mental inertia which is the refusal to think, moral inertia which is the refusal to take a vow or make a resolve, psychic inertia which is a refusal to be awake and responsive to the rhythms of nature and the extraordinary gifts of human life. None of these can be blamed upon the metaphysical differentiation of consciousness, and the purported second fall itself marks the awakening of that questioning spirit which is the signature of humanity's divine origin and is essential to overcoming all inertia.

The ancients were masters of the art of self-questioning and interrogating Nature. They knew, as does every great scientist or artist, that if one knows how to ask, and how to wait, Nature will never refuse to speak. This is above all true in the realms of philosophic religion and spiritual enlightenment. From the start, the pilgrim who enters a period of probation must see the whole of human existence as a profound process of learning, loving and living. From that initial stance, maintained through a lifetime of suffering and growth, one can come to the greater beatitudes of the mystery of self-enlightenment, whereby one is prepared to enter the antechamber of the temple of spiritual initiation into the primordial and eternal Wisdom of the Mahatmas and the Bodhisattvas, the Teachers and Friends of the human race.

THE FORWARD IMPULSE

Each class of Creators endows man with what it has to give: the one builds his external form; the other gives him its essence, which later on becomes the Human Higher Self owing to the personal exertion of the individual. . . . Where there is no struggle, there is no merit. Humanity, 'of the Earth earthy', was not destined to be created by the angels of the first divine Breath: therefore they are said to have refused to do so, and man had to be formed by more material creators. . . . The first humanity . . . was a pale copy of its progenitors; too material, even in its ethereality, to be a hierarchy of gods; too spiritual and pure to be MEN, endowed as it is with every negative (Nirguna) perfection. Perfection, to be fully such, must be born out of imperfection, the incorruptible must grow out of the corruptible, having the latter as its vehicle and basis and contrast.

The Secret Doctrine, ii 95

Since the absolute reality is boundless and inexhaustible, no realized degree of perfection by beings in any world or system of worlds can be considered as the final terminus. In every theatre of spiritual evolution there are some beings who represent the serene fulfilment of the impulse to growth from a prior period of evolution. There will be many others who must still struggle towards maturation and perfection. There will also be a few who represent the forward impulse of spiritual evolution, moving far beyond any degree of realized perfection ever known before. Like bright stars radiating from invisible centres in space, their hearts are centred upon unmanifest eternal wisdom, which they transmit and transmute into fresh opportunities for growth for every struggling being around them. Self-luminous with theurgic wisdom and therapeutic compassion, these are the Agnishvatta Pitris, the Promethean *Asuras* who light up self-consciousness in human beings when the moment is right.

Before this sacred hour can strike, preparatory work must take place, guided by those intermediate hosts of fecund intelligences that represent realized degrees of perfection from the past. These are the efflorescent *Suras*, the pantheons of ethereal gods, who are mentally passive in relation to the possibilities of the future but still able to form and furnish the needed vestures of lower hosts of struggling monads. The substantial difference between the *Suras* and *Asuras* may be seen as the enormous difference between passive goodness or negative perfection, and the heroic capacity, which is quintessentially human, to take existing forms and inspire authentic spiritual creativity. All heroic strength arises out of this magical power of the majestic light of divine self-consciousness. It is the rare ability to see that which does not exist and the creative capacity to make real that which has never been realized before, but has ever subsisted in the latent realm of Eternal Ideation. This remarkable ability to bring the Unmanifest to bear upon the active realm of manifestation is the extraordinary gift of higher self- consciousness. It is the talismanic gift of creative courage that characterizes the Agnishvatta Pitris.

Self-consciousness enables them to become skilful transmitters of the divine light of supersensuous ether in a world of grossly differentiated matter. They have developed the infallible capacity to sift and select, to concentrate to the exclusion of other things, and the dialectical ability to analyse and reduce to basic elements what is otherwise nebulous and diffuse. These are distinct faculties that all human beings possess to some degree, but are rarely understood because rarely considered. All too often, people imagine that these potent faculties are to be used for making final judgements about the world, for fattening the predatory *kama rupa* and buttressing the insecure self. In reality, however, they exist solely for the sake of spiritual freedom. The seminal gifts of the Agnishvatta Pitris repose in the human mind for the sake of self-conscious mastery over the chaotic kingdom of inherited vestures.

Thus, any viable conception of perfectibility requires a

sensitive, scrupulous care for the undeniable imperfections of flawed materials in the lunar vestures. These may be vitally affected if a vigilant individual generates fresh patterns of thought or feeling that can work like alchemy. It is certainly possible to change the polarity and quality of the life-atoms in the vestures by increasing the porosity of the elementals that comprise them. This is a creative and courageous task, and it can be carried out only if one faces the facts. One must always scrutinize and settle one's karmic accounts. One must be ever willing to look honestly where one really stands in relation to the moment of death. One must see through and beyond entire realms of appearances and so take a moral stand based on general principles. One must derive their deeper meanings and apt applications within the sacred sphere of one's duty. In short, one must cultivate one's own garden of Eden or Gethsemane.

This Promethean stance in relation to one's own spiritual evolution is crucial to the entire Theosophical philosophy of growth. It is supported by the ancient teaching, which was intuited by Leibniz, that every monad has inherent within it the potency of All-Force. Given typically truncated views of human nature, this is seldom understood by most human beings. As Mahatma K.H. explained in the last century:

> The great difficulty... lies in the liability to form more or less incomplete mental conceptions of the working of the *one* element, of its inevitable presence in every imponderable atom, and its subsequent ceaseless and almost illimitable multiplication of new centres of activity without affecting in the least its own original quantity.

He then intimated that from the beginning of a long sequence of manvantaric cycles, centred on a single point in abstract Space, proceeding through the development of a series of globes replete with genera, species and classes of beings, there is no loss of the original force or life-essence during the protracted evolution of their derivatives.

> The force there is not transformed into something
> else ... but with each development of a new centre of
> activity from *within* itself multiplies *ad infinitum*
> without ever losing a particle of its nature in quantity
> or quality. Yet acquiring as it progresses something plus
> in its differentiation. This 'force' so-called shows itself
> truly indestructible but does *not* correlate and is *not*
> convertible ... but rather may be said to *grow* and
> *expand* into 'something else' while neither its own
> potentiality nor being are in the least affected by the
> transformation.

The extraordinary energy in the One Element, when correctly
understood in relation to a complex doctrine of emanation, is
capable of endless reproduction, expansion and innovation
without taking away anything from that which was in the
beginning. Since the ultimate ground of the One Element is
inherently boundless and beyond all perceptible limitation, the
entire process of differentiation leaves intact the whole potential
in the impartite essence of that which was in the beginning.

The poet's observation that in love, "to divide is not to take
away", is a profound intuition of a fundamental law of Nature
which applies to all its operations, from the formation of worlds
to the transformations of atoms. This supreme law of cosmic Eros
(Fohat) governs all the processes whereby the one Universal
Element differentiates to form manifest Nature, with its incredibly
complex diversity of systems. In this recondite doctrine of
recurring emanation there is a hidden continuity between that
which was potentially present at the beginning and that which
is fully developed at the end of any cycle. What is vital for
alert human beings to realize, and what was so crucial to the
Leibnizian doctrine, is that the monad contains within it this
potent force of growth and development. But this seminal force
cannot be separated from the whole, even in the name of spiritual

individuation. It is not merely appropriate to any particular monad, but is itself all-potent on the plane of the One Element. Naturally enough, this force must be intelligently applied to the vast spectrum of possibilities within which the individual monad has to confront its own perceptions and apperceptions. Applying this mind-boggling idea to the monadic wave, working from the *devas* right down to the critical mineral kingdom, and onward and upward to the highest perfected human being, one can see that there is an incredible range and at the same time an extraordinary continuity. Always and everywhere this supreme principle of growth is at work, sustaining a myriad of processes of unfoldment and development, reform and regeneration.

In terms of human principles, this ubiquitous force of growth is objectively correlative with the Atma-Buddhic monad, the uncompounded thinking element that is the very essence of higher *Manas*. *Manas* itself may be thought of as a flame from the fire of Mahat. In man this flame is surrounded by dense smoke. That which is all-potent on the higher planes is obscured on the lower planes by inferior forces. That which is an extremely refined vibration on the higher planes, capable there of self-maintenance and perpetual motion, will be eclipsed when inserted into a context of harsher and grosser vibrations. This accounts for the tremendous gap in human beings between what they can touch and experience in deep sleep and what they can express in waking life. To understand this it is necessary to gain a dynamic sense of balance between the activation, on the deeper plane of ideation, of the all-potent force, and the dialectical difficulties of realizing its fullness in everyday life. To tap the noumenal power of growth in the human monad is to draw away from the so-called attraction of the lower realm of desire and become irradiated by the light of *Atman*. One must not fall prey to any false sense of obligation to express one's deepest thoughts or attempt to convince others. That will only serve to ensure disappointment, and it will never contribute to any significant improvement in the human condition.

Here one may profit from the teachings of the *Tao Te Ching.*

Taoism emphasizes a cool appreciation of the eternal interplay of light and shadow, and also the importance of minimizing manifestation, expression and interference with others. To gain spiritual buoyancy in the realm of ideation, it is necessary to let go of that which weighs one down. This is not something that can be done all at once, but rather must be made a regular practice. As one contemporary philosopher puts it, one must initiate a "*samadhi* shift". Most individuals are so caught up in the fickle ego that they become tense and strained, like the child in Aesop's fable who caught the fox. Instead, one should appropriately pause and let go. If one is in a mad hurry to get somewhere and has a flat tire, one should not fret and fume, but pause to look around, shifting attention to that which has nothing to do with oneself. If nothing else, one can always look up at the sky, which, as Emerson said, is the great purifier. This is a kind of *samadhi* shift into a realm of ego-free experience. Once one has let go, released all tension, one can achieve much more and with much greater ease. One can begin to enjoy the world from a non-egocentric standpoint, seeing it through the eyes of children or old people, of strangers or friends. To see the world in ways that go beyond one's tyrannical ego is to restore, if only for a moment, some awareness of one's vast potential for growth and timely self-correction.

To sustain and make more continuous this noetic awareness, it is necessary to have a clear philosophical conception of the different modes of manifestation of the universal power of growth. All the animal and vegetable kingdoms possess this immense power of growth; indeed, they could not exist without it. Nevertheless, it exists in them in an instinctual mode quite different from that relevant to thinking beings, to moral agents and responsible choosers. Gupta Vidya expresses this constellation of skills in terms of sets of fires constituting the principles of Man and Nature.

Man needs four flames and three fires to become one
on Earth, and he requires the essence of the forty-nine fires

> *to be perfect. It is those who have deserted the Superior*
> *Spheres, the Gods of Will, who complete the Manu of illusion.*
> *For the 'Double Dragon' has no hold upon the mere form. It*
> *is like the breeze where there is no tree or branch to receive*
> *and harbour it. It cannot affect the form where there is no*
> *agent of transmission* (Manas, 'Mind') *and the form knows*
> *it not.*
>
> The Secret Doctrine, ii 57

Through this arcane doctrine of the three fires, the *Occult Catechism* expresses something of the extraordinary subtlety of the dynamic relationship between the higher and lower planes of existence. These three fires correspond to three sets of entities: gods, *Asuras* and human beings. In manifestation, however, there must be material ancestors or lunar Pitris before there can be cognitively self-conscious beings. These are responsible for the projection in ethereal matter of human beings in form. When they also have got the gifts that come from the higher classes of gods and *Asuras,* they become human beings in mind. The three fires are the solar fire of the gods, the electric fire of the Pitris, and the fire by friction of the *Asuras.* These three fires cannot be understood through mere physical analogies, but must be understood through deep meditation, through the subtle interplay of idea and image in the realm of creative imagination. Indeed, this alchemical process is itself intimately connected with the Hermetic awakening to self-conscious awareness of these three higher fires. Thus, it is difficult to convey the eternal light of the *Atman,* the sempiternal light of universal *Buddhi* or the supernal light of pure self-consciousness to contemporary human beings, in whom the three higher principles are merely an overbrooding presence.

In most human beings, *Manas* itself is only very partially incarnated, because all attention is given to the external sensory world, to eating and drinking, to the clamorous wants of the physical body, to getting and spending. People seem only too willing to become servants, sadly enslaved to the legions of lunar and sidereal elementals that occupy the lower quaternary. When human beings have thoughtlessly enlisted themselves in the service of these insatiable elementals — and making all their tortuous cerebration utilitarian, centred upon a furtive and shadowy personal ego — they cannot be given any meaningful conception of the real subjective life of the true man of meditation in whom *Atma, Buddhi* and higher *Manas* are fully active. It is no wonder that most human beings have some intense experience of higher conscious activity only in deep sleep or in *devachan*. In the latter condition, it is solely the presence of the solar element of *Manas* that makes it a positive state of perception for the disembodied monad. In deep sleep and *devachan*, the involuntary absence of the ego-centred lunar *manas* permits the activation of these higher powers of perception.

Clearly, the common difficulty in releasing the creative potential for growth lies in the absurd way so many people identify themselves wholly or largely with the shadowy psycho-physical vestures. This is, in fact, a direct inversion and costly misappropriation of the quintessential and defining principle of man — *Manas*. How one employs the creative mind in thinking of oneself is a potent talisman and, according to Shankara, the chief key to both bondage and liberation. In the wondrous cosmogony of the Puranas, Brahmā is said to create by thinking of himself as the father of the world. As H.P. Blavatsky noted,

> This *thinking of oneself* as this, that, or the other, is the chief factor in the production of every kind of psychic or even physical phenomena. The words 'whosoever shall say to this mountain be thou removed and cast into the sea, and *shall not doubt* . . . that thing will come to pass', are no vain words. Only the word 'faith' ought to be translated by WILL. Faith without Will is like a wind-mill without *wind* — barren of results.
>
> *Ibid.,* 59

The capacity to think constructively of oneself is intimately connected with the mysterious power of *Kriyashakti*, and is crucial to the gaining of self-conscious immortality. Without vainly attempting to pry into arcane mysteries, anyone may begin to draw upon this sovereign power through mystic meditation. One may take the sublime portrait of the Self-Governed Sage — associating it, if one wishes, with an actual statue or picture — and think of the resplendent qualities of the Silent Sage, adoring and apprehending them, assimilating them in one's heart and mind. Thus can one actively and deliberately undertake a subtle process of transformation in one's own astral sphere.

The true aim of this esoteric practice of self-transformation is to engender the priceless seed of *bodhichitta*, which in the bloom of enlightenment becomes the Self-Governed Sage. By meditating upon, by adoring, by even thinking of oneself in relation to the Self-Governed Sage — intensely, persistently and with unconditional will, heart and mind — one may gestate the embryonic Bodhisattva in oneself. So it is that in the Deity Yoga of Tibetan Buddhism, detailed rules for meditation and purification are given in relation to the meticulous consecration of the field, the mandala, the magnetic sphere and the central image upon which the rapturous meditation is based. All are integral parts of a systematic discipline which can only be helpful if used with the assured guidance of an accredited guru, with an authentic spiritual lineage (*Guruparampara*).

In Deity Yoga, or indeed in any such arduous practice, it is vitally important to understand at some level the abstruse notion of voidness, of omnipresent *Akashic* space. One must have the proven capacity, philosophically, to make real to oneself transcendental and absolute abstractions. As soon as one can do this, one becomes intensely aware of the tremendous richness, the unbounded potency, existing within metaphysical Space and also, therefore, within any enveloping matrix of ideation, even within one's own imperfect vestures. As one gains this sacred awareness, one will become effortlessly able to bring down the ineffable light of intense concentrated adoration. This is an extremely high and difficult practice, and certainly much too sacred to be spoken about. But if one truly thinks about it, and truly determines to do it for the highest motives, there is no looking back.

Until this point is reached, the neophyte must patiently engage in a long and arduous course of preparation, probation and purification, seeking to gain at least conceptual clarity with regard to the impersonal nature of inmost creativity. In ordinary speech the term 'creativity' is used much too loosely. In the context of spiritual life it has to do with compassionate meditation and metaphysical imagination. It is grounded in subjective realities that have nothing to do with anything external, though it may express itself in external ways. Spiritual creativity has to do with releasing the spiritual will, which is nothing less and nothing else than the light energy of the *Atman*. It is universal, cosmic, unmodified and formless. Spiritual will is totally free. It is omnipotent. But it is also so universal that, like the light-energy of the *Atman*, it can be tapped only with complete mental purification.

It is necessary to create vital points of contact in the lower *manas* with higher *Manas*, centres for smooth transmission within one's manasic field of the subliminal energies of *Buddhi* and *Atman*. This naturally implies a great deal of theurgic work upon oneself, virtually all of which must take place in reverential silence and noetic secrecy. Though the cosmic will may be compared to the rushing wind, and faith to a rustic windmill, nevertheless, when one thinks of spiritual will moving the windmill of human faith, one should not think of that will as blowing from outside. In reality, one is thinking here of a benevolent spiritual breath which is only experienced within the sanctum of indrawn consciousness, when there is a complete quiescence of physical and mental activity, coupled with a slowing down of the rate of breathing and a calm withdrawal of attention from the lesser vestures. Through deep study and daily meditation upon these seminal ideas, through honest self-examination and cheerful self-correction, one may gradually come to clarify, at least in one's habitual conceptions, one's misty apprehension of spiritual creativity.

The true treasure-house of all cosmic creativity is the supernal realm of *Akashic* ideation. Just as there are many modes of refinement and specialization of intelligence in the different Rounds and Races on this globe, there must be many more on other globes, not only in the Earth Chain, but in all the chains of planets throughout the solar system. There is an incredible wealth to all the iridescent patterns of ideation and activity within the solar system, not to mention even vaster spheres of existence. All these patterns and potentialities for the variegated expression of Divine Intelligence have a definite impact, through the diffused *Akasha*, upon the creative potential of human beings. Through the sacred gift of the Agnishvatta Pitris, all human beings can draw freely from the Akashic realm. Those who are hierophants consciously invoke the highest hierarchies, and know how to tap those energies so as to advance human good on this terrestrial plane.

This is an exact and definite knowledge, inseparable in its awesome mastery and timely expression from the heroic courage associated with the divine hosts of *Asuras*. It is a courage to go beyond known limits, a daring refusal to settle down, a Promethean urge to redeem the human condition. It is sometimes only experienced as a confused disaffection with the earthly realm of personal existence, but in its origins it is a consistent refusal to settle on any sacrosanct finalities, to consolidate any final conception of human good, human progress and human perfectibility. This invaluable gift of the *Asuras* is revolutionary in the highest sense. But it is a revolutionary urge that is accompanied by such potent and profound compassion for every living being that it can hardly be compared with modern, mythified revolutions. Terrestrial revolutions sometimes arise from the altruistic urges of a few, but these rapidly become inverted. They are not, therefore, real revolutions. True revolutions in human consciousness are those initiated by Buddha and earlier by Krishna; they represent a fundamental alteration in the horizon of human consciousness. They affect classes of souls who become capable of reflecting their regenerative spirit throughout a series of civilizations. Those who voluntarily participate in these

Copernican revolutions become courageous pioneers, true helpers consecrated to universal welfare *(Lokasangraha)*.

This is the highest spiritual and revolutionary urge in humanity, and its inmost essence may be likened to the fiery presence of the Dragon of Wisdom. Unlike the Double Dragon — whose breath cannot make any difference to the external world because of its immense distance from this plane — the Dragon of Wisdom, reposing in man as *Buddhi-Manas,* can effortlessly master this field of differentiated elements and imperfect instruments. It can provisionally accept them and partake of them, while at the same time freely acting in the midst of them, to create a current of mental purification and spiritual regeneration. From time immemorial this has been associated with Shiva, the *Mahayogin.* The symbolic wearing of sackcloth and ashes expresses the spiritual truth that human beings are capable of experiencing exalted modes of renunciation and transcendence, of *tapas* and penance, even in their toughest conditions. All beings can release a revolutionary courage that is capable of moving into the *Akashic* realm and eliciting from the *Akasha* the concept of a golden age, the kingdom of heaven, a new humanity.

DELIVERANCE FROM BONDAGE

Perhaps the most widespread and universal among the symbols, in the old astronomical systems, which have passed down the stream of time to our century . . . are the Cross and the Fire — the latter, the emblem of the Sun. The ancient Aryans had them both as the symbols of Agni. Whenever the ancient Hindu devotee desired to worship Agni . . . he arranged two pieces of wood in the form of a cross, and, by a peculiar whirling and friction obtained fire for his sacrifice. As a symbol, it is called Swastica, *and, as an instrument manufactured out of a sacred tree and in possession of every Brahmin, it is known as* Arani.

The Theosophist   H.P. BLAVATSKY

Throughout the immense pilgrimage of humanity, Avatars, Initiates and Adepts have recorded and also incarnated the spiritual meanings and initiatory potentials of sacred symbols and glyphs. Each evolutionary advance of the human race depends upon a timely recovery and fresh realization of the insights hidden within archaic records of arcane wisdom. Not only do symbols enshrine matrices of forces in visible and invisible Nature, pointing to the complex interpenetration of planes of substance and consciousness, but they also reach to the indestructible core of spiritual wisdom within every human being. Therein lies the pristine seed of immortality, waiting to be quickened to life by the blazing fires of purification and illumination. Every new turning of the Wheel of Law offers appropriate avenues for growth for all souls nestled in the cosmic vestures of the Logos. Under the watchful eye of Krishna-Buddha-Christos, each human soul has the golden opportunity to insert itself into the forward movement of human evolution. Through the power of spiritual reminiscence, through minor and major awakenings, each may find its place in the awesome Guruparampara chain that binds together all human souls. So vast has been the variegated diffusion of sacred symbols through space and time that every human being has myriad sources from which to sift and select, with reverence and devotion, in seeking an authentic reminiscence of the sacred purpose of human existence. There are few human beings on earth, for example, who are not familiar with the figure of Buddha. There are millions of copies of statues of Buddha, ranging from the massive Kamakura Buddha to small reproductions readily available to the humblest devotee. Whether one is privileged to see a majestic and monumental representation of Buddha in the ancient centres of Buddhist culture in Asia, or one cherishes a modest image of Buddha in one's own home, anyone can make it a focus of concentration and compassion. The vital question is, even if one makes this a daily practice, how may one evoke through it a summons to self-enlightenment?

In order to awaken true reminiscence through the aid of a symbol it would be helpful to associate a powerful idea with a pleasing image. For instance, if one were to associate the Kwan Yin Pledge with one's contemplation of the statue of Buddha, and at the same time deepen and concentrate all one's feelings of gratitude for everything that one has received in life, this would begin to give life to the symbol. By linking the idea of renunciation with a potent and sublime image — whether it be of Buddha, of Christ or of Krishna — one may gradually gain the ability to see one's life not merely in terms of past, present and future, but *sub specie aeternitatis*. When one comes to live consciously within the rays of compassionate light and ideation streaming forth from the enlightened Teachers of Humanity, one can augment the power to alter the patterns of association of one's ideas and images. Just as the seven colours of the rainbow give way to many subtle hues in Nature and on the painter's palette, so too the compassion of the Bodhisattvas unveils varied modes of attunement accessible to human souls. Like the visible sun, which provides light and nourishment to innumerable leaves extending over an enormous range of greenish tints, the Spiritual Sun radiates a continuous stream of spiritual sustenance capable of sustaining human beings in every circumstance. The chief barriers to receiving benediction from this constant illumination are lack of meditation upon the light, ingratitude for its warmth, and fear-ridden selfishness originating from a life lived in the darkness.

By associating the ideas of *Buddhi Yoga*, thanksgiving and renunciation, with the sacred image of Buddha, even though one may know little about the life of Gautama, one could begin to see through the shadows of limited and imperfect associations which bind the soul. By taking a symbolic image as the constant focus and repository of one's calm reflections, one can build fresh constellations of ideas capable of serving as a salutary guide to action in daily life. One may even restore the multi-dimensional quality of the mind, ready to contemplate universal themes and to translate them into apt applications. Gradually, one will overcome the propensity of the mind to be distracted, to move towards dichotomous thinking, towards proliferating foci of personal concern, and steadily reorient it towards wisdom.

Since all spiritual discernment is necessarily connected with ethical practice, the true test of learning is the ability to strengthen and mature one's concern for the welfare of others. There are in the world today innumerable individuals with intuitive powers and one must become a silent member of their hallowed ranks, quietly labouring to alleviate the misery of mankind. As one's meditation upon the sacred symbols of the Gupta Vidya deepens one will begin to discern, amidst the cacophony of worldly events, fruitful opportunities for effective service to others. What is wisdom in Shamballa is seldom seen as wisdom on earth, and though the potent seeds of the 1975 Cycle are burgeoning in the soil everywhere, this will not be evident to those who are entrapped in anxious self-concern. With the good earth groaning under the burden of personal greed, what may seem like oppressive karma to the personality is, in fact, from the standpoint of the soul, beneficent karma. The acute sense of alienation from life caused by this gap in consciousness can be overcome only by turning the mind around and redirecting it away from the constricting circle of the separative personality towards the luminous sphere of the immortal soul. It is essential to reach in consciousness to the core of the idea of renunciation, and this is impossible without eliminating every trace of greed from one's nature. Even the minutest residue of greed is incompatible with the pristine spirit of gratitude exemplified by the galaxy of Bodhisattvas. One must learn to test oneself daily, to scrutinize the quality of one's desires and dreams. Unfortunately, the capacity for constructive self-examination has been attenuated through neglect. The primal power of desire itself has been diffused and dispersed, leaving individuals incapable of true philosophic contemplation, a deep love of ideas. They find themselves subject to random and mindless associations of ideas, a desperate reaching out to delusive alternatives that are false solutions to the basic needs of their lives. Through this fragmentation the fires of mind and motivation have gradually waned, and the electric current of ideation has ebbed. Rather than vainly seeking what seem to be pleasing solutions to problems, one must make a strong effort to rekindle the fire of self-consciousness within oneself. Although no one can do this for another, each must do it for the sake of all, and every person has the enormous resources of Nature and the sacred teachings to aid the attempt.

The restoration of the vital connection between the embodied self and the higher mind, and true communion between mind and spirit, requires soul-reminiscence. The right use of memory is aided by the pervasive compassion of Nature, which refrains from burdening any soul with those memories of errors and mistakes in past lives which might prevent it from doing what it needs to do in this incarnation. Nature mercifully veils the unneeded details of the past. It is, therefore, an utter waste of time to daydream or speculate about past lives. Proper understanding of the deeds and misdeeds of previous incarnations can come with the exactitude of the mathematics of the soul, but this precision can never be gleaned from external sources. It must be sought from within, and the first step is to take full responsibility for one's moral nature. One must learn to draw from memory and from one's abilities only that which one can truly use for the good of all. One must discover and enrich those activities which one can do right. A proper beginning must be made upon the path of the six virtues, the steep path of the *paramitas*, which culminates in that sublime condition wherein one is constitutionally incapable of deviating from the right way. One can discern within oneself the enduring basis of that harmony which ultimately makes one stand without variableness or shadow of turning. To learn to stand like a steady flame burning on holy ground, one must emulate the regulated motion of the sun and the planets. One must become one-pointed through the power of vows repeatedly taken and constantly observed over lifetimes. The concentrated moral effort to enact the ethics taught by Krishna, Buddha and Christ is the meaningful attempt to mirror the metaphysical harmony at the root of invisible Nature.

> The Central Point, or the great central sun of the Kosmos, as the Kabalists call it, is the Deity. It is the point of intersection between the two great conflicting powers — the centripetal and centrifugal forces, which drive the planets into their elliptical orbits, that make them trace a cross in their paths through the Zodiac. These two terrible, though as yet hypothetical and imaginary powers, preserve harmony and keep the Universe in steady, unceasing motion; and the four bent points of the Swastica typify the revolution of the Earth upon its axis.
>
> *The Theosophist*   H.P. BLAVATSKY

As participants in a world marked by social decay and disorder, individuals must learn to accept universal responsibility for the general state of malaise, which is the result of past actions in previous lives. They must meditate upon what it is to be worthy of living in a human temple. The ethical integrity of the cosmos requires individuals to accept the consequences of their former deeds as made manifest in existing conditions. They must be willing to engage in the painful process of sifting the good from the bad, the wheat from the chaff, in all that they have brought from the past, and be prepared to embrace the fiery heat of *tapas* emanating from the central point in the swastika. It is through the expiatory power of Agni, the focus of life and light and heat in that central point, that individuals may remove the obscuring mass of illusions and delusions which beset humanity, crucified upon the cross of matter. Once the cleansing and purifying fire has accomplished the work of purgation, the crystalline ray of Spirit may vivify and fructify the matrix of matter, bringing with it the restoration of a true sense of purpose for human existence. Then the fiery light, acting as Lucifer, the Morning Star, will be felt as the illuminating power within the heart of every responsive individual. That which cannot be brought through the fires but must be cast off will, through the compassion of Nature, be used and refined by the lower kingdoms.

For the individual, the process of awakening soul-memories is similar to the sifting processes of Nature. The wise being is concerned only to remember that which can be used in the present and the future, because it has its roots beyond all time. Unwisdom consists in fancying something and mistaking it for knowledge or in confusing the lower psychic fantasy, containing mere shadows of forgotten truths, with authentic deliverances of Buddhic imagination. There is a sad tendency amongst those who have not properly meditated during life to drift into daydream as they approach the moment of death. If they have heard, at some level, of the doctrines of karma and reincarnation and of the existence of spiritual Teachers, they may be taken over by highly personalized fantasies regarding supposed relationships with those Teachers in past lives. Such delusions have nothing to do with soul-memory, but are ineffectual compensations for failures in the present life to approach the true Teachers through the inward path of meditation. Mistaking intellectual involvement with words and psychic involvement with images for the establishment of lasting connections in their inner natures, they cut off the possibility of spiritual contact with the Buddhas in future lives.

Actual contact with spiritual realities can never be the result of passive association of ideas, however originated psychologically, but is the natural consequence of selfless motivation maintained consciously. Yet, on the other hand, there is hardly a human being alive today who has not in past lives received the potent seed of the teachings. In moments of despair and despondency over the inevitable collapse of worldly delusions, and in times of distress at one's inability to aid the suffering of another, each has received gentle words of encouragement from the Servants of the Bodhisattvas. "Do not feel guilty. Do not seek to blame others. Life is full of pain but there is no need to be afraid. Each may seek right livelihood in the world and search for the Path." When in similar moments in the present life such memories stir in the soul, then one may begin to associate the idea of renunciation and purification with the vibration of the Teachers. This alchemical fusion is the beginning of spiritual maturation in the present life. It does not matter whether this takes place at the age of ten, thirty or sixty, for once one begins to put the Teachings to good use, then it becomes possible to discover better uses. Such is the Law. "The books say well, my brothers. Each man his prison makes", taught Gautama Buddha, and each may also unmake his prison. The primary need is for deep reflection upon the root ideas of renunciation and bondage. Since the world will not teach one how this is to be done, the spiritual teachings are brought again and again to orphan humanity through the compassion of Bodhisattvas.

Whether one understands it in terms of the image of the Ashwattha tree depicted in the *Bhagavad Gita* or in terms of the image of the deadly *upas* tree, the world binds the soul with coils upon coils of ignorance. Krishna taught that this tree must be cut asunder at the root with the sword of spiritual knowledge sharpened by devotion. Whilst one cannot hope to do this fully at one stroke in this life, for that would imply that one had done so many times in previous lives, it is still possible to make a sufficient dent in the world tree that one may find space and time in the rush of life for deep thought and meditation. Anyone with a modicum of courage, as the sword of wisdom cannot be wielded by those with fear, may set aside every rationalization, at least for a few moments, and engage in earnest thought upon universal ideas. From such efforts one will find the strength to be able to help others, whether it be to render aid to an old person who is dying or to give gentle words of encouragement to a small child that is crying, and from these sacrificial acts one can gain further strength to engage in meditation.

When one finds within oneself the power to help others, one simultaneously discovers the power to help oneself to grow spiritually. Thus the wheel of the Great Law is turned and the endless stream of learning moves towards the universal ocean of wisdom. Through silent obedience and humble obeisance to the voice of conscience, one gradually builds a bridge in consciousness linking the experience of the outward nature with the wisdom of the soul within. In a small way one can come to mirror the Mahatmas, the paradigmatic exemplars of learning who are eternally and effortlessly obedient to the Maha Guru and ceaselessly engaged in exploration for the sake of implementing the modes of the future races. As the Light of the Logos is ubiquitous throughout the universe and present in each soul, the fundamental requirements of learning and the essential opportunities for growth are universally the same for all beings. Krishna-Buddha-Christos is present everywhere and eternally available to all who turn inward towards the light. No soul enters or leaves this world without the aid of the Logos. The modes of instruction of the Brotherhood of Bodhisattvas have nothing to do with the superficial and obsolete methods of mass modern education; they reach into the hearts of human beings and give them that which will come back to them in times of need. Every soul is whispered into at the moment of birth and whenever one is in real difficulty one is helped. Once one begins to realize this, and is ready to see the universality of the impulse towards spiritual enlightenment, then one is naturally much less entranced by the delusions of the world tree. Through thought and meditation, through contemplation of sacred glyphs and symbols, one becomes oneself a glyph — the glyph of man thinking. This inward transformation and restoration of one's true estate as a son of the *Manasa* is the real meaning and holy purpose of the presence of Gupta Vidya in the world of woe.

For the sake of recollection, the glyph of man thinking may be represented diagrammatically by the figure of a cross surrounded by an aureole of lambent flames, with a bridge forming a connection to a base below, the whole like a glowing lamp upon a secure stand. The object of thought may be represented by the glyph of three triangles surrounding the points of a central triangle, which together form the figure of a hexagon in the centre. The two glyphs — of the thinker and of thought — must be associated and made concentric, even though their geometric representation in space requires that they be distinct. Contemplation will reveal that the stand of the lamp is not essential to the process of thinking, any more than the clothes of the body are essential to its biological functioning. Just so, the physical human body is not the thinking self. In order to appreciate man thinking, one must dwell upon the nature of the cross, the fire and its rays, the triad, and their mutual relations to each other. Concern with the lampstand, whether through positive or negative forms of attachment, only serves as a distraction from deep reflection upon the essential meaning of the glyph. Unfortunately, many people rarely rise above or even reach the level of the bridge linking the lampstand to the golden light.

Through mental and moral laziness, fear and inertia, they fall prey to delusions and fantasies preyed upon by those purveyors of pseudo-occult theories who masquerade under the name of hypnotists, depth psychologists and the like. These pedlars and their victims constitute a matrix of pollution stemming from misuse of the sacred. From the one side, practising a nefarious craft through the corruption of words, and from the other side, seeking to gain spiritual value through payment with worldly goods, the two may seem karmically to deserve each other. Here as in every case of pollution, one must not succumb to judgementalism. Certainly in the compassion of Agni, the fiery divine dragon of wisdom, there is a precise knowledge of the virtually infinite mathematical complexity involved in the karmic curves of purgation of individual souls, but this may not bejudged from outside. In a time of universal purification and renewal, nothing is wasted, and even as the sweeping fires burn away the excrescences of the past, there are always soul-lessons to mitigate the agony of those who have made themselves the victims of self-hatred. Even the burning of the dross releases resources for the lower kingdoms.

The mystery of man thinking has been obscured in the modern world by its crude conceptions of progress. The cosmos has always been a macro-electronic universe, and for the past eighteen million years mankind has been living in a macro-electronic age. Recent expansions of human capabilities and innovations of thought are only seemingly new. They are, in fact, rather superficial applications of fundamental principles long known and taught by the Adepts. The sense of collective scientific advance and discovery in the modern age is a permissible illusion, particularly amongst people who without such encouragement would be drawn back into the violent and self-destructive tendencies of medievalism. Yet although this idea of progress offers some hope for human advancement, its danger is that it could eclipse the underlying reality of universal humanity and the logic of human evolution, which has nothing to do with external tokens.

Anyone who has stopped to think about the nature of material progress soon realizes that the true amelioration of the human condition does not depend upon external inventions but rather upon an internal transformation in man. The Great Work, as it was called by the Renaissance alchemists, is far more demanding than any of its materialized representations in so-called exact science. The inward symbolic synthesis, the alchemical process of becoming a true glyph, moves through precise phases and stages, represented as dissolution, sublimation, condensation and coagulation. This is true not only for the individual but also for the entire human race.

An important aspect of this universal work of transformation is the drawing together and synthesizing of all the lines of good karma from the ancient sacred orders and the manifold symbol systems of antiquity. The self-conscious synthesis into the threefold path of the philosophy of perfection, the religion of responsibility, and the science of spirituality is a central task in the present cycle. Particular systems of glyphs and symbols, each of which has its own period of effectiveness, are being drawn together to provide the basis for soul-recollection for the maximum possible number of human beings. Heralding the progress of this restoration of the inheritance of humanity unto itself, H.P. Blavatsky spoke in the last century of the work of diligent students of the Mysteries:

> ... these students, though none of them has yet mastered all the 'seven keys' that open the great problem, have discovered enough to be able to say: There *was* a universal mystery-language, in which all the World Scriptures were written, from *Vedas* to 'Revelation', from the 'Book of the Dead' to the *Acts*. One of the keys, at any rate — the numerical and geometrical key to the Mystery Speech is now rescued; an ancient language, truly, which up to this time remained hidden, but the evidences of which abundantly exist, as may be proven by undeniable mathematical demonstrations.
>
> *Lucifer*   H.P. BLAVATSKY

In the present period the further recovery of the mystery language depends upon the willingness of individuals to engage in selfless and lifelong learning. Anyone who is willing to ponder calmly, with an immense feeling of gratitude to the Teachers, upon the heavens and the omnipresent Logos, can contribute to the restoration of the sacred glyph of man thinking. Those who are wise will pursue this solitary work with no thought of selfish reward or recognition. Nor will they allow themselves to be captivated by the spectacle of the collapsing old order based upon blood covenants and vengeance. They will not be caught in the doomsday extrapolation of the record of disasters precipitated by those caught in self-contempt engendered by their desecration of the sacred. Rather, like children, they will seek to discern hieroglyphs in the sky and in the human heart, and treasuring their vision in silence they will look for means to connect the good in themselves and others with the innumerable rays of good flooding in on all sides.

The time has come for a self-conscious restoration of awareness of the original programme of human evolution. That programme and its meaning for the future are intimated in the symbol of the bird of everlasting life mentioned in *The Voice of the Silence*. The future of human evolution is bound up with the guardian race of Hamsa, the qualification for which is *ahimsa* — total non-violence in thought, word, feeling and will — the absence of any trace of self-assertion or egotism. This is the sacred tribe of Bodhisattvas surrounding the pavilion of the Logos, ceaselessly engaged in learning the teaching of Hamsa through the power of reverence and devotion. They are the exemplars *par excellence* of the truth taught by Buddha that uttermost self-surrender and reverence are the only means to deliverance from bondage. Ceaselessly engaged in learning, they are the true recorders of the enactment of divine truth by the Logos in the cosmos. As the custodians of the archives of spiritual humanity, they recorded the original esoteric texts from which the entire plethora of exoteric religions are derived. Having realized within their own inner natures the rich meaning of the signature of the Logos in Nature, they have given out from time to time, in veiled allegory and parable, glyphs and symbols which may serve as a bridge and ladder in consciousness for those vigilant souls ready to tread the path leading towards initiation.

The deepest secrets of initiation have not been and indeed cannot be transmitted, but must be discovered by the disciple within the sanctuary of the soul. The timeless truths of divine nature are eternally enacted in the heart of the Ever-Living Human Banyan that is the core of humanity, and this enactment is intimated in the hoary tradition of the Puranas. Therein one finds the allegorical story of Vishvakarman, the Omnificent, the Vedic god who is the architect of the world and who sacrifices himself to himself, having offered up all the worlds in *sarvamedha* or universal sacrifice.

> ... his daughter *Yoga-Siddha* 'Spiritual consciousness', the wife of *Surya*, the Sun, complains to him of the too great effulgence of her husband; and Viswakarma, in his character of *Takshaka*, 'wood cutter and carpenter', placing the Sun upon his lathe cuts away a part of his brightness. Surya looks, after this, crowned with dark thorns instead of rays, and becomes Vikarttana ('shorn of his rays'). All these names are terms which were used by the candidates when going through the trials of Initiation. The Hierophant-Initiator personated Viswakarman; the father, and the general *artificer* of the gods (the adepts on earth), and the candidate — Surya, the Sun, who had to kill all his fiery passions and wear the crown of thorns *while crucifying his body* before he could rise and be re-born into a new life as the glorified 'Light of the World' — Christos.
>
> *Ibid.*

None but Mahatmas, perfect embodiments of the truth, are really capable of understanding the full meaning of the divine enactment of the Mysteries or the mysterious avataric descent of the Logos into the world. They alone are permitted to record the archives of the Teachings of Hamsa, and will permit no pseudo-esoteric packagings of the truth to persist. Every sincere and devoted individual who is willing to become an apprentice in the arduous art of transcendent concentration and selfless meditation upon universal good is invited to enter the orbit of the Mahatmas. If one reads the *Bhagavad Gita* carefully, one will discover that Krishna always is surrounded by Mahatmas. It is only the consciousness corrupted by materialization and externalization which would mistake the allegorical scenes of the Mahabharata War for events constrained by the limits of physical space. The true locus of events is a matrix of divine Logoic ideation surrounded by the fathomless waters of invisible space, wherein Mahatmas, in their *vamanas* or aerial cars of inconceivably refined subtle substance, surround the Logos. They alone can see the invisible form of Krishna, and therefore they alone can tell the tale. The geographical space and colourful scene surrounding Krishna on earth is a form of *maya* hiding the "invisible garment of God". Within the invisible form of the Avatar there resides a galaxy of Mahatmas. Seated in ceaseless meditation and constant adoration within the matrix of the body of the Logos, they constitute the constellations, indeed the entire universe of enlightenment. Nothing of this can be known by going from without within, but something of it may be gathered by the intuition through contemplating Buddhist *tankas* showing myriads of Bodhisattvas surrounding a central figure of the Buddha like an aura of wisdom-light.

Once this central fact of human evolution is widely grasped, it marks the end of recorded history with all its pretentious pseudo-esoteric and secular accounts of the meaning of human existence. When the glyph of man thinking is realized within to be identical with the matrix of the Logos surrounded by the galaxies of Bodhisattvas, it is no more possible to be taken in by the trumped up stories and packaged accounts of spiritual life promoted by the failures in human evolution. Stripped of illusions, nothing remains but to insert oneself by the power of one's own mystic meditation into the universal vision of Shamballa. This is the vision of the One Flame and its innumerable rays streaming forth, each of which is like a jewel in the Logoic form of Shiva-Krishna or Nataraja-Narayana. Every diamond-souled Mahatma is an eternal witness to this sacred truth, and no concession can be made to any lesser vision. It has long been known in Shamballa that the time would come when there could be no further accommodation either to the ill-intentioned or to the passive which would obstruct the inward spiritual growth of humanity. It has always been inevitable that at some point the fiery divine dragon of wisdom — the living Word of Truth — should burn away the obscuring dross of past error. This is a necessary preparation for the entry of the good gardeners of Nature, who will prepare the soil for the future Garden of Eden. Those who are so fortunate to earn under karma, through decades of striving, the golden privilege of thinking the right thoughts at the moment of death, may also be so fortunate as to reincarnate again in a human form at some point in time when they may hear of the actual presence on earth of a new humanity. To be worthy of the rare good karma of returning to the earth at this distant time, one must begin now to nurture the seed of the Buddha-nature through *Buddhi Yoga*, through gratitude and renunciation. Then one may hope to experience the immense thrill of being alive in those far-flung aeons when Men of Meditation, masters of the mathematics of service to humanity, will walk the earth openly and all human beings alike understand that the only purpose for being in a human form is to be a true servant to humanity.

Through understanding the real purpose of meditation upon sacred glyphs and symbols, which has to do with the inward invocation of the fires of self-purification and illumination through self-transcendence, one may come to appreciate the truth of what Hegel once said about history, that the dialectic must have its joke. In a sense, at this point in history the joke of the divine dialectic is the only significant fact in history. The dialectic is smiling the smile of the Buddha. It is playing the flute of Krishna. It is also seated in divine meditation like Shankara. The dialectic, at the same time, is accelerating the disintegration of the thought-forms and entities of the past for whom the hour has struck. There is an increasingly widespread recognition that the old order is nearing its end, and that the Aquarian task of self-regeneration has begun.

> *Lodging the purified inner powers in the Self, the witness, who is pure illumination, gaining steadfastness step by step, let him fix his vision on the fullness of the Eternal.*
> SHRI SHANKARACHARYA

MYTH AND REDEMPTION

Transcendent Beings move variously over the earth.
PLOTINUS

M ystics and seers perceive time as a limitation to be surmounted by meditation. It is an illusion produced by the succession of our states of consciousness. The stilling of the compulsive flow of thought allows the mystic to dissolve the illusory self. He rises to a plane of awareness that is timeless, relative to the restless mind trapped in the discontinuities of sense-perception. Medieval alchemists, like the ancient Hindus, taught that the rarefied realm of pure thought gives access to the sequence of human evolution as well as a coherent knowledge of the cosmic forces regulating its progress. They postulated a homogeneous realm of radiant matter pervading space, the *Akasha* or *Mysterium Magnum*, the universal medium upon which are impressed vast assemblages of thought-forms emanating from the Cosmic Mind, as well as the record of their interaction with human consciousness on earth. It is both the true source of creation and a permanent repository of everything created. The astral realm is composed of many layers and grades of subtle matter, from the most ethereal to that which is barely beyond the purview of the physical sense. At its highest level it is an Akashic potency reflecting the untrammelled ideation of the Divine Mind, whilst at its lowest it is the register of the selfish and chaotic emanations thrown off by human beings. The radical difference between these two poles suggests a firm basis for discriminating mythic imagination from mediumistic delusion, true vision from mere fantasy.

The subtler realm of the *Akasha* or celestial light is noetic in nature and accessible through the deepest contemplation. Access to this realm requires the complete withdrawal of consciousness from the seductive plane of sense-perception, wherein the limitations are greatest. Between this tangible plane of the senses and the heights of Akashic awareness lie the sub-regions of the astral light which can induce and inflame the most dire deception. This "red mid-region", as George William Russell (A.E.) called it, is a composite of unexpended animal desire, disintegrating shells discarded by immortal souls and odious thought-forms engendered by human fantasy. Matter on this plane is in a critical state, inherently unstable and turbid. Desires are quickened and pleasures intensified. The mystic must pass through this region speedily before succumbing to its temptations, symbolized in Tibetan texts by luxuriant blossoms beneath which lurk coiled serpents. The increasing prevalence of degenerate mediums and deluded mystics testifies to the nefarious influence of this region in inverting and perverting all higher aspirations. The perception of formless spiritual essences characterizes the creative imagination and is only gained by directing consciousness effortlessly beyond the plane of psychic distortion. This is the fruit of lifetimes of training involving mental purification and spiritual discipline.

Mythology and folklore not merely represent a recollection of extraordinary events, but also point to the plane of perception on which those events occur. If one cannot rise in consciousness to the reality of myth, then one is unable to interpret its symbols correctly. The mythic imagination does not deny the material world but rather includes it in a vaster cosmos wherein sense-perception is the least significant type of experience. The exploration of myth requires a radical transformation of consciousness. The mythic form never disintegrates but abides as a latent stimulus to creative imagination. Myth spontaneously appears without author or title, contrivance or calculation, as the universal Logos speaking through receptive individuals. Men and women may be visited by its numen in their dreams, insights and memories, but to live within its sanctuary requires a complete subjugation of the separative ego together with an increasing identification with the whole of Nature. The release of the mythic imagination results from the fusion of self-forgetfulness with heightened self-awareness.

However sublime the archetypal realm may be, greater mansions of being lie beyond it. Myth is a record of intelligences still tied to the former *rupa*. By its very nature it is an authentic but still imperfect account of an ultimately seamless and formless reality. The Spiritual Sun cannot be known through its creations, but must be directly experienced in meditation and then traced throughout the stream of its emanations. This beatific vision, comparable to the prisoner's direct gaze into the sun in Plato's allegory, distinguishes the self-governed Sage from the mystic.

> They tell in a sacred story of those the spirit took
> to itself who had the infinite vision. I never came nigh
> that infinitude, but because I sought for it I was often
> happy and content knowing it was all about me.
>
> *Song and Its Fountains*

The limitless vision exemplified by Maha Shiva, the Initiator of Initiates, seated on snowy Mount Kailas, is the apotheosis of the mythic imagination. It represents that terrace of enlightenment where the Mahatmas abide as shining mirrors to the creative ideation of the Cosmic Mind and also as prime agents in its perpetual activity. These demiurgic hierophants and mighty *yogins* turn the wheel of evolutionary law. Their mystic meditations release benevolent currents of noetic energy, which become compassionate conduits between divine and human worlds. They are sovereign masters of *Kriyashakti*, effortlessly creating forms from their pristine imagination. Such perfected beings are the source and subject of all great myths, although they themselves have long ago risen above the realm of forms. They are the elect of the human race and the unacknowledged authors of the pioneering arts, sciences and mythologies of mankind. Fragments of their divine wisdom are strewn in the fables of all cultures, differing only in the symbols and veils through which they disseminate eternal verities.

Celtic cosmogony had been spawned by ancient Druids and unknown Adepts aeons ago. In their hoary legends we find the traces of a lost erudition, an arcane cosmogony. The One gives birth to man, imaging within itself boundless fields of ineffable light which become more shadowy and dim as they recede further from the source. Through these fields rays of luminous intelligences shoot forth and fall from the celestial city to earth. The memory of that past always remains, and the fallen gods, the divine rays in human form, preserve the knowledge of that heavenly descent in fable and legend. In Ireland the central characters in this archetypal pilgrimage are the Tuatha De Danann, the gods who settled the sacred isle of Eire after subduing the gigantic races of the Fomorians. These chthonic forces are identifiable as the Atlantean remnants of antiquity, races who had become demonic and decadent through sorcery. The Tuatha De Danann who disarmed them were wise beings who had transformed themselves into immortal gods by magical devices, some of which were taught to the early Druids.

> They were pre-eminently magi become immortal by strength of will and knowledge. Superhuman in power and beauty, they raised themselves above nature; they played with the elements; they moved with ease in the air.
>
> *The Legends of Ancient Eire*

The Tuatha De Danann had risen to remarkable heights of wisdom and invulnerable strength in previous periods of evolution. They were distinct from the lesser gods who were Nature-spirits or secondary intelligences having little to do with the expanding frontiers of noetic consciousness.

The reign of the Tuatha De Danann was co-extensive with the legendary cycle of the Golden Age. This powerful vibration, A.E. felt, resonated more deeply than any other throughout the Irish countryside. Tir na Nog is the mystical name of the Land of the Immortals, embodying a state of sublime awareness and cheerful contentment which could be comprehended by children, mystical poets and those of humble heart and pure perception.

Romantic poets spoke in impassioned tones of the awful loveliness of a world lying just beyond the circumference of the terrene sphere. More than a vision, it was an assured prophecy concerning a future humanity which would establish wise sovereignty over itself and bring sweet concord to all of Nature.

> These mysteries, all that they led to, all that they promised for the spirit of man, are opening today for us in clear light, their fabulous distance lessens and we hail these kingly ideals with as intense a trust and with more joy, perhaps, than they did who were born in those purple hours because we are emerging from centuries indescribably meager and squalid in their thought, and every new revelation has for us the sweetness of sunlight to one after the tears and sorrow of a prison house.
>
> *The Fountains of Youth*

The withdrawal of the immortals from their earthly habitation at the close of the Golden Age was a prelude to a final flowering of the Celtic peoples. This period, called the Age of Heroes, records the fabulous exploits of the mystic warriors of the Red Branch like Cu Chulainn, Conall Cernach and Conchobar, who freely discoursed with their presiding deities. They were followed by the heroes of the Finn cycle: Finn MacCumhaill and the Fenians. Their stories have been recited through millennia and still inspire movements for social reform in contemporary Ireland. The Gaelic tales speak of the protecting hand the native gods extend over Eire, gods who have not passed away but merely retreated to crypts in the hills or secret sanctuaries far removed from human sight. There they await the new cycle, and with it the lost wisdom of the ages. The stirring of the mythic imagination is a premonition of that splendid resurgence, anticipated in the legends of far flung peoples as the return of the Adepts, Magi, *Hotris*, *Pirs* and Hierophants, Jivanmuktas and Jinas, Arhats and Bodhisattvas, Rishis and Mahatmas, culminating in the appearance of the Purna Avatar.

Belief in the coming of an Avatar was common among A.E.'s compatriots in the Theosophical Society at the end of the nineteenth century. Some years later A.E. found this faith transfigured in a dream in which he saw a divine hero returning to assist the Celtic race. So great was the intensity of this dream that his son is said to have approached him that night asking, "What was the light?" For A.E. nothing was more sacred than the coming of an Avatar, the descent of Deity into the world. The Avatar exemplifies the supreme consummation of the mystic's path, and extends the rainbow bridge between heaven and earth upon which the visionary becomes transfigured and beatified. From this crowning vision springs the compassionate concern to choose the burdens of earthly life for the sake of ameliorating human misery and advancing the cause of universal enlightenment.

A.E.'s *The Avatars* is an unparalleled portrait of a pair of celestial saviours. A futurist fantasy, it completes the allegory of *The Interpreters* at the close of which the small band of heroic and humane revolutionaries faces execution at the hands of the State, whilst the political fate of the nation is being decided in a general uprising. In *The Avatars* it transpires that the elitist State maintains its control in the cities but yields the rural areas to migratory groups who are harbingers of a new civilization. Their numbers steadily increase as a wave of spiritual regeneration sweeps across the countryside, but in the city spiritual hunger grows though material wants are satisfied. The Avatars appear in the countryside to kindle the mystical aspirations of the disinherited and to sow the seeds of a spiritual culture which can replace the shallow materialism of a morally defunct regime. The divine pair of Avatars, Aodh and Aoife, do not appear directly in the book. What is clearly intimated is the profound transformation in consciousness they initiate in a group of companions — an artist, a philosopher, a poet, a recluse (like Wordsworth's Solitary) and a few friends in a rocky retreat in western Ireland.

A.E. was as concerned with the descent of the gods as with the moral elevation of men, women and children. He sensed that only the spiritually vigilant could recognize and profit from the presence of an Avatar. The concept of the Avatar is one of the most recondite in the philosophy of religion. As Jesus declares in *The Gospel According to Thomas,*

> If the Flesh
> Came into Being for the sake
> Of the Spirit, that is
> A Mystery. But if
> The Spirit came into Being
> For the sake of the Body,
> That is a wondrous Miracle.
> How did such great wealth
> Make its home, I wonder,
> In such poverty?

He alludes to the mystery that Spirit should choose to become other than itself for the sake of that other — the body — a sacrificial act which cannot be understood in mundane terms. The Word made flesh is incomprehensible to atheists and cynics because it seems to be a supererogatory act of an intelligence greater than human. It is the sacred prerogative of enlightened beings who have wholly transcended the circle of delusion, decay and death, who have travelled beyond even the realm of ethereal forms into the infinitudes of undivided Being. According to Gupta Vidya, the great minds and hearts that attain to this exalted state are exempt from involuntary incarnation and may enjoy the blissful repose of *nirvana* or unconditioned consciousness. But there have always been those magnanimous souls who have renounced this sempiternal peace to return across the ocean of *samsara* to aid the afflicted in their desperate struggles for self-redemption. In performing this glorious renunciation, the Great Sacrifice (*mahayajna*), these Promethean spirits freely accept the severe limitations of those they have come to help. Their voluntary descent represents the immaculate ideal of unconditional love, unintelligible to those ensnared by the meretricious glamour of modern civilization.

The Avatar signifies the descent of Spirit into matter for the sake of the progressive elevation of all beings to the state of self-conscious godhood. Without the compassionate wisdom of Bodhisattvas and spiritual teachers, human evolution towards greater heights of self-mastery and moral solidarity would be thwarted, and the inward impulse of all souls to aspire upwards would be aborted. This is the deeper significance of the Promethean myth. Had not Prometheus sacrificed himself, the human race would have continued to be held back by Zeus. Threats to the spiritual survival of humanity were real possibilities at critical points in human evolution. The race of mankind may not have been destroyed physically, yet the timely sacrifices of great souls at decisive moments enabled entire communities to cast off their mental fetters and morbid fears and rejoice in the light and warmth of the Word made flesh. Such has been the sacred work of the Avatars that recorded history has celebrated, Saviours such as Krishna, Buddha and Christ. They come for all humanity to rekindle the flame of spiritual aspiration in responsive hearts.

The Avatar cannot be comprehended from below. By its very nature, such a rare exemplification can only be grasped by tapping the depths of universal love and impersonal wisdom it releases and incarnates. In this enlarged perspective, enlightenment is an ever-present possibility for each human soul. Were it not so, the unenlightened could neither contemplate the prospect nor consider the means to its attainment. Avatars have taught why every human being is dual in nature, at once demonic and divine. The latency of the immortal spark in the individual soul enshrines the seed of enlightenment, known as *bodhichitta*. To the mind entranced by the dichotomies of incarnated existence, the germinating spiritual seed appears twofold: as the ascent of the soul to the Divine and as the descent of the Divine into the world. Spiritual aspiration is the vessel through which a luminous intelligence may work for the welfare of all. As the pre-Socratics often repeated, the way up and the way down are the same. Each man is potentially, if distantly, a Buddha. Christhood is a divine archetype towards which all human growth aspires with differing degrees of self-consciousness. The extent to which a person has approached or is seeking this demonstrated ideal with uttermost devotion to the Avatar is his or her true measure as a human being.

There are myriad avenues for the Logos to incarnate in the world. Indeed, every pure act of sacrifice releases and spreads the Avatar-light. Each pain endured in the probationary effort to transcend oneself for the sake of others cleanses a channel through which higher energy may flow, and A.E.'s humanized and incomplete notion of the Avatar draws upon this deeper esoteric truth. *The Avatars* portrays them not as the angelic beings or accredited Paracletes celebrated in canonical texts, but rather as a highly evolved and enchantingly magnetic pair of human beings who show a serene self-validating assurance of their ineffable divinity and a supreme sense of fullness of truth, love and beauty. This is undoubtedly a restrictive rather than a revelatory use of the term 'Avatar', but it does serve to highlight the universal possibilities for human growth. Above all, A.E.'s Avatars seem to be apostles of a silent, subtle and non-violent revolution, who come to inspire folk wisdom in new directions, to establish fresh patterns of communion and celebration, and to serve as microcosmic models for the future:

> The purpose of an Avatar is to reveal the spiritual character of a race to itself.
>
> *The Avatars*

An Avatar always transmits some fundamental and forgotten truths to an entire epoch and initiates a new cycle of inner growth and human fellowship. The resounding vibration disseminated by the Avatar provides the essential keynote for the epoch he inaugurates. Thus Lord Krishna came to teach a philosophy of joyous and unbounded love to a humanity about to descend into the darkness of the Iron Age or Kali Yuga. A.E.'s Aodh and Aoife similarly seek to propagate the Golden Age vibration of Krishna amidst the impotence and desperation spawned by the soulless materialism of the modern State. They transmit the glad tidings of an emergent humanity conscious of its divine kinship with all of Nature. They transmute the everyday relationships between estranged human beings, kindling the sparks of magnanimous altruism, cheerful civility and thoughtful compassion to arise spontaneously as the basis of a spiritual culture, rooted in a shared reverence for the divine, foreshadowing the fecund promise of the global civilization of the dawning Aquarian age.

> By the presence of these two the days had been coloured with a rich wonder. . . . Then came stories of men and women raised above themselves in some transfiguration so that they saw each other in some shining way in dances which had been taught them by the mystic visitors. . . . In their enchantment they were god and goddess to each other.
>
> *Ibid.*

Most of the Avatar's work is indeed invisible and hidden. A.E.'s Avatars accomplish nothing stupendous on the physical plane, but we recognize them by their heart-warming and healing benediction, by the soul memories they have evoked, the social paradigms they have bequeathed, and by the many lives they have radically altered. They themselves appear and withdraw almost without trace. Their origins and destiny are shrouded, yet for those who briefly shared their supernal and veiled vision, the world is wholly transformed. They endow their ardent disciples with the strength and sensitivity needed to promulgate their joyous message of freedom and rebirth, by song and story, to those who are spiritually deprived. A.E. was aware that the gift of Divine Wisdom was so potent that the mysterious presence of one enlightened man and one enchanting woman could gently initiate a soul-revolution on a global scale. In this sense *The Avatars* was less a contrived fantasy than a controlled dramatization of the archetypal cycle of divine descent of the Verbum, invoked by the Fraternity of Sages, the Brotherhood of Bodhisattvas.

In the fourteenth century the Tibetan reformer Tsong-Kha-

Pa initiated a septenary centennial movement which would signal the spread of a seminal spiritual impulse during the last quarter of each forthcoming century. These impulsions would be focussed through the fervent sacrificial work of faithful emissaries of the Brotherhood, self-exiled from the fabled Sacred White Island. As a young man A.E. had witnessed the tidal wave initiated by H.P. Blavatsky and W.Q. Judge, and for the rest of his life he sought to prepare for the next great impulsion. He wrote in 1897:

> Avatars, kingly souls once on earth, and now returning again with the wisdom of a greater day and of the world spirit urgent within their wills. I seem to see this confused transition period or plan whereto all is tending; a true social state with divine dynasties and solar heroes at its head, like those who ruled Egypt in its mystic beginning. Already spirits with such imperial instincts begin to appear amongst us, laying a deeper foundation for the spiritual revolution. . . . We have become expectant.
>
> *On the March*

As the impulsion of the nineteenth century drew to a close, A.E. became increasingly concerned that careless speculation about Spiritual Teachers and Avatars was disproportionate to the willingness of students to assimilate and apply the priceless teachings as aids to self-transformation. In his essays on "Shadow and Substance" and "Self-Reliance", he warned that incessant talk on spiritual matters is useless and even harmful if 'the divine discipline' of the esoteric philosophy is not incarnated and instantiated in daily life. He counselled that the sad failures of many of his fellows lay in their selfish concern to use the magical powers of the immortal soul without having first grasped the unitary nature of the Self. The pupils must fit themselves to the Guru and not the other way around. Indeed, all feeble and presumptuous attempts to fashion a convenient image of the Guru would be the greatest barrier to finding one. A.E. knew that even access to an authentic Spiritual Teacher, rare in any age but unique in ours, was not arbitrary, but wholly dependent upon the well-tested efforts of the disciple. He recognized that the disciple was drawn to the Guru by a law of spiritual gravitation: spiritual qualities attract by magnetic affinity. Any person who has sufficiently developed the unmistakable marks of an unprejudiced mind, a pure heart and a deep love of divine wisdom will be naturally drawn to the shining exemplar of these excellences.

No one should seek a Spiritual Teacher for instant salvation. Masters come to train disciples in the intelligent service of humanity, not to relieve the burdens of those who refuse to exercise their own powers of noetic self-determination and selfless service. A.E. knew that one must earn discipleship and that this in itself is an arduous task. But he insisted that anything less might mean a disastrous fall into delusive presumption which could prevent the aspirant from ever finding or being accepted by wise Teachers. He recognized that though access to them is never easy, it is aided by devoted study and honest practice of their sacred teachings. "As a man thinks, so shall he be." The power to pursue and incarnate spiritual ideals is coeval with the soul's assumption of a human form. One's thought and ideation determine one's destiny. They constitute both the cause of imprisonment and the means of liberation from the darkness of ignorance and servitude.

> 'What a man thinks, that he is: That is the old secret.' In this self-conception lies the secret of life, the way of escape and return. We have imagined ourselves into littleness, darkness and feebleness. We must imagine ourselves into greatness.
>
> *The Renewal of Youth*

For this compelling reason, the earliest Avatar in recorded history, Lord Krishna, descended amidst humanity on the eve of Kali Yuga, the Iron Age, to extol the spiritual attributes of the silent sage. In the second discourse of the *Bhagavad Gita*, he gives Arjuna the classic portrait of an enlightened being, confirmed in spiritual self-knowledge, a master of *Buddhi Yoga*, fusing *jnana* and *bhakti*, wisdom in action and effortless renunciation of the fruits, *svadharma* or self-chosen duty and *anasakti yagna*, sacrificial self-denial.

> When, O Partha, a man puts away all the desires that arise in the mind, and reposes in the Self, rejoicing in the Self alone, he is spoken of as a man of steadfast wisdom (*sthitaprajna*).
>
> He whose mind is unperturbed by suffering, who is untouched by the allurement of happiness, from whom passion (*raga*), fear (*bhaya*) and anger (*krodha*) have fallen away, he is called a *muni*, a man established in meditation.
>
> Whosoever, without selfish attachment on any side, neither rejoices nor repels when meeting anything favourable or unfavourable, his wisdom (*prajna*) is firmly set.
>
> *Bhagavad Gita*, II.55-57

Contemplation of such golden excellences (*deity yoga*) by anyone mired in abject despair can lighten the mind and confer upon it the pattern of its own pathway to deliverance. A.E. knew that discriminating the devotional essence of spirituality from its deceptive simulacrum was a vital prerequisite for progressive enlightenment. *The Avatars* sought to give the aroma of the perfected soul 'a local habitation and a name', thereby testifying to the ever-present perfectibility of all souls, who ardently seek the Kingdom of Heaven even upon a desolate and desecrated earth, Shamballa in Myalba, *nirvana* in *samsara*, the dawning of the golden age of Kronos in the deceptive Age of Zeus.

*   *   *   *   *

AUM

> To You, O Krishna, who upheld of yore
> The holy Vedas, who bore all the worlds
> Upon Your holy Self, who raised this Earth,
> Who slew the demon, tricked Bali, then
> Destroyed the Kshatriyas, and overcame

Pulasti's child, who brandished high the plough,
Spread kindness far and wide, and last of all
Exterminated barbarous hosts — to You
Who acted thus in ten most different roles,
O Krishna, now I give my heart's delight
Of joyous lowly adoration here!

Gitagovinda   JAYADEVA

THE GAYATRI INVOCATION

Aum bhur bhuvah svah
tatsaviturvarenyam bhargo devasya dhimahi
dhiyo yo nah prachodayat. Om.

AUM. IN ALL THREE WORLDS — TERRESTRIAL, ASTRAL, AND CELESTIAL — MAY WE MEDITATE UPON THE SPLENDOUR OF THAT DIVINE SUN WHO ILLUMINATES ALL. MAY ITS GOLDEN LIGHT NOURISH OUR UNDERSTANDING AND GUIDE US ON OUR JOURNEY TO ITS SACRED SEAT. OM.

It is a very ancient and sacred teaching that the Gayatri, corresponding to Vach, consecrating the Light of the Logos in Sound, should only be invoked on behalf of universal welfare. In general, all those who have any attraction to spiritual ideas must cleanse their hearts and strengthen those feelings in them that are truly universal and limitless, even though they may not know in advance what limitless love is. They must be willing to move towards unconditional and boundless love. They must refuse to consolidate partial loves and blinding hates and especially those shadows of love which contribute to human sorrow and deception. In affirming true love they must show spiritual courage and kindle the light of daring in the heart. The more one attempts this, the more one can keep moving. There is no way in which one could really grow without repeatedly assisting in the disintegration of a limited equilibrium which worked at one time. Either one does it, or it will be done to one. If it is done from outside, it may happen slowly, but when it comes, one may collapse. Whereas, if one does it consciously, refusing to consolidate even the finest traits or the glittering simulacra of virtue, if one is willing again and again to take stock and rebuild one's self-conception, the more one will have a chance of bringing closer the inmost urges that are in line with the highly potent spiritual invocation of the Gayatri mantram, and of negating the familiar and latent elements of conditionality in one's nature.

In many old cultures wisdom is often shown in cooperating with the seasons of Nature and the cycles of time. Individuals may make some sort of inward affirmation of benevolence towards all that lives. If one simply enjoys the thought of being a friend to every living being, one could make discoveries about oneself and about the correction of habits, and then one can take stock like a craftsman. One can discern certain patterns and link them up to causes that are recognizable in certain mental states and thought-patterns. One may then counteract them, but in the process of doing this, one must recognize that it cannot be accomplished all at once. At the surface level people do not self-consciously mature in the manner in which everything in nature grows, giving time sufficient scope to do its own healing magic. Therefore impatience arises with impetuosity as the stimulus, resulting in inertia and defeatism. This is the loud assertion of mortality, and even those who have heard the sacred teaching of immortality may still bring to it something of the intensity and the frenetic nature of mortality. This is implicit in the human condition, the translation downwards from the higher to the lower, from the immortal to the mortal, from eternal Duration to the language of Time. One has to penetrate these categories and see that in the indivisible hidden moment there is a mirroring of boundless Duration, that within the invisible atom there is boundless Space. This is the metaphysical basis of the Gayatri invocation to the Spiritual Sun. To be able to use this daily and especially in reference to human relationships, in reference to all one's obligations, in reference to one's dharmas and karmas, requires great wisdom.

One must truly feel compassion for that in all human beings which represents inertia, stultification, coldness, disintegration and death. The major obstacles to growth, producing a stony and indifferent heart, are ignorance combined with inertia — *tamas* — leading to a repeated persistence in a restricted view of the world. One of the asymmetrical characteristics of the universe is that individuals can expand without limit, but personalities cannot contract without limit. One may contract to a point where one might even enjoy contraction, where one becomes habituated to the dingy, the cloudy, the chaotic and the claustrophobic. This is the sense in which many people, habituated to self-torture and self-torment, find that they cannot attach meaning to any language, and cannot give credibility to themselves with reference to the sacred. They may know the noblest teachings, but they bring to them a facile sort of analytical familiarity and a stale routine in their response. A point comes when they become cold, when the psychic fire has burnt itself out and the cool waters of wisdom wash over dead ashes.

This has analogies with what goes on in the astronomer's universe. When a planet goes sufficiently far away from the sun — and there is a decisive difference between the parabolic movement of some bodies and the elliptical movement of others — it cannot keep pace at a certain level of intense, rapid, whirling motion around the powerful, incandescent centre. Then a point is reached when one of these bodies in its slow movement is expelled, going further and further away from the solar centre. It becomes cold because it enters into a state which must eventually culminate in a kind of disintegration or death, a tragic fulfilment of Nature's laws. There is an analogy between what takes place in reference to matter in the galaxies and what takes place within the solar system of the human form. The *Atman* is like the sun in the Gayatri mantram, and all the other principles are like planets or comets in relation to it. It is possible that a person, though familiar at some level with a sacred teaching, especially the idea of immortality, may be constantly translating downwards in terms of what is dark and sombre. The person may after a point experience something comparable to an extreme coldness, an amazing lack of any spiritual vitality. Sometimes this can combine with an extraordinary versatility in acting out roles in the world, an atavistic skill in mimetics.

The origin of this may be sought in one of two ways. Either in another life the person, having made considerable spiritual progress, may have been stymied and halted because of some deep-seated fear, pride or selfishness, and therefore there was a damage to the astral form which must reoccur in life after life until it is met by commensurate compassion, self-conquest and self-modification. But the person does not know this, though somewhere deep down he or she senses it. Or, it is the result of the gravity effect exercised by the sum-total of human weaknesses, stagnation and inertia upon anyone who, by the Light of the Logos, by the power of thought and the purity of sacred speech, tries, in the words of St. Paul, to "Come out from among them and be ye separate." This is not easy. It is precisely when one tries to stand apart, as Arjuna found in the first chapter of the *Bhagavad Gita*, that one becomes acutely self-righteous because the weak can work through the virtues of the strong. One of the greatest causes, metaphysically, for the collective brake that eventually must work at individual levels as well, is self-righteousness. This is why the ancient teaching is: "Do not fancy you can stand aside from the bad man or the foolish man. They are yourself, though in a less degree than your friend or your master. . . . Therefore, remember that the soiled garment you shrink from today may have been yours yesterday, may be yours tomorrow." One cannot feel any different, any better than any being that is alive. Out of the very harshness of judgement or the ignorant attempt to separate oneself from even a Hitler, one will actually draw to oneself shadows of spiritual pride. To invoke the Gayatri mantram is truly to bid farewell to all self-righteousness. Self-righteousness is the illusory source of self-preservation — or what looks like it in the short run — but which in the long run is a barrier that sunders one from the whole of life.

The Voice of the Silence says, "Give up thy life, if thou would'st live." All the great Teachers have spoken in terms of eternal life *versus* what is thought to be life but which is really selfishness. One either lives in the immortal individuality that focusses the life of the universal *or* within the prison-house of the persona. A fundamental choice is involved in the Gayatri invocation and this is very much connected with the evolutionary processes of Nature.

Physiologically, life is a losing race against death; every moment everyone is dying. Why, then, is there life in the physical body? Why is there homeostasis? Why is there resistance to the ocean of life and to all the forces of disintegration? This has to do with the power of cohesion, which involves the mind and its wakefulness. It involves the heart and its rhythms. But it also involves the spiritual will, an act of faith in one's purposefulness and in the meaningfulness of one's existence, in one's relevance to the human condition. To be able to find meaning and relevance from the largest standpoint, as in the Gayatri mantram, is from the beginning and also daily to say good-bye to ordinary conceptions of terrestrial life.

No doubt a person who intones the Gayatri mantram will participate in the world, will go through the duties of life, will enter into relationships that involve sharing the concerns of others with all their limitations. In this very process a pilgrim may lose the thread and become forgetful, rather like a visitor to Plato's cave, unable to penetrate through the cacophony of sounds in the dark den where the shadows have acquired exaggerated significance, unable to stand apart from the false language of success and failure, honour and dishonour, of human beings who entertain worldly perspectives. This is precisely the risk that is taken by every pilgrim who consciously incarnates for a high and holy purpose. At the same time, one must recognize that in the process of incarnation one is going to forget. In that sense, as Plato taught, the whole of life is involved with the basic problem of remembering and forgetting. How much one forgets depends upon what one cares for and chooses to remember. What one remembers at a deep level must be instructive to the levels at which one may forget. Human beings need a variety of aids, such as writing down what is true and good and beautiful, what is enduring and unconditional. Connecting ideas with events in nature, with the rhythms and cycles of day and night, of sleeping and waking, with the various seven-year cycles in life as well as the seven-day week, one may begin to discover analogies and correspondences. It is as if one is constantly cooperating with the eternal memory of Nature (enshrined in the Spiritual Sun) and always overcoming, amidst the inevitable forgetfulness, the danger of forgetting what is important. Hence the daily invocation of the Gayatri.

Wise disciples periodically renew the vow that they first took, continually summoning the golden moment of original awakening. If one thinks of the truest, most beautiful moment in one's life, when something was so real that one's whole being responded, it can be summoned repeatedly by the power of thought if one is not falsely convinced that it belongs to the past. Past and present have nothing to do with that which gives reality in consciousness to an idea. The individual must endow it with a sense of reality through the energy of meditation. Human beings become prisoners of the process of change and forget that the very capacity to endow reality springs from the timeless Self in man, and its pristine light of divine wisdom. The archetypal example of this may be found in the life of Buddha. Even so great a being as Gautama Buddha knew before he took birth that to incarnate means to participate in the ignorance, pain and delusion of the world. It is also to risk much. It is said that Buddha, having attained enlightenment and pondering the Bodhisattva path, looked upon the world and thought, "All human beings are like lotuses in a pond. There are those human beings, alas, very many, who, even if I remain in the world to show them the way to enlightenment, to the Spiritual Sun, will not listen. They are mired in maya and so much enjoy it that they are like lotuses still caught in the wet earth at the bottom of the pond, unable to rise to the light of the sun. There are human beings who are already like lotuses that have moved to the surface of the waters, opening out to the light of the sun, and who do not need me because they are able to bloom on their own. Why, then, do I have to remain in a body? For the sake of those, whoever they be, who are struggling in *maya* but wish and will to reach upwards. They need the assurance that they can do it. And for these I shall remain." Thus the AUM is enacted in word and deed.

It is indeed possible to preserve an extraordinary, cool, wise, detached, discriminating and beautifully proportioned sense of purpose to one's life. The point of this compelling myth about Buddha is that when, as Gautama, he goes through all his trials before his supreme enlightenment, when he encounters *Mahamaya*, the great tempter Mara, one of the temptations is — and it is also one of the temptations of Christ — the charge that his work will be irrelevant, that he will not succeed. Such pre-vision puts one on the plane which is above success and failure, enabling one to grasp the central logic of an incarnation. The Bodhisattva vow is voluntary, but because it is recorded in time, it can only do so much and no more to mitigate the sum of human misery. If there is a sufficiently long period of evolution and a sufficient number of souls, as well as many hazards and repeated failures over many lives, something like this must be true. Therefore, the wish of the Bodhisattva to come to the world is merely to make some small difference to the earthly scene. But what is small relative to numbers may be very great when seen in terms of time. The potent impulse released by a Buddha or a Christ twenty-five hundred or two thousand years ago is alive today and will reverberate thousands of years from now. It has a vertical dimension as well as lateral influence. It is a vibration that can be repeatedly picked up, and if it is picked up by some individuals here and there who are totally seized with it and transform themselves, then they in turn become very powerful magnets for other souls to do the same, all tapping the supreme source of strength, the Spiritual Sun.

So mysterious, then, are the currents of Karma that much of what is called living is only on the surface of existence. It is perceived in terms of years and months and days, but this has application not even to the astral but to the physical form most of the time. It does not reveal the immortal saga of the soul, its immemorial pilgrimage through space and time, linked up to myriads of souls. One's conception of life must become so different, so universal, that in relation to that larger life one can consecrate a lesser life, but not the other way around. To become ensnared in the small, in one's micro-conception of living, is to deny oneself an openness to a larger concept of life. One can test this every day and night. Negate each day and intone the Gayatri mantram before going to sleep. Repeat it as many times as one can, clearly and silently, and see if one can wake up with the mantram as one's first thought. Do this again and again through the week to see if one really can carry the vibration through deep sleep. To be able to do this is to know what it means to overcome the barriers between lives, the illusion of *devachan*, the debris of *kama loka*, to cut through the *mahamaya*. To be unable to do it simply means that there is a great deal in oneself that is disconnected between the highest and the lowest. Instead of wallowing in a state of despair or panic, one should persist.

The Gayatri invocation is an infallible means to self-transcendence. Sometimes one cannot use it as well as at other times, but even if it is not the first thought on waking, one can keep reminders for oneself. It is eventually possible to train the memory cells in every single part of each vesture, all of which have their own mode of registration, enlisting them all in the service of one's highest motivation rooted in a universal plane of creative ideation. If one partakes of daily meditation, experiencing a sense of Duration, then one can repeatedly transcend the boundaries of time and its compression into secondary causes and effects. One can let go every psychic preoccupation with external relations in visible space, and develop a deeper, noetic sense of what it is to live inwardly. Daily, replenished by the cool stream of insight that flows from the Spiritual Sun, one may actualize the Gayatri mantram with a deep resolve that will endure without wavering, releasing a mighty current of unacknowledged but incalculable benefit for the entire human family and indeed for all living beings.

* * * * * * *

Feeling, while going about, that he is a wave of the ocean of Self: while sitting, that he is a bead strung on the thread of universal consciousness: while perceiving objects of sense, that he is realizing himself by perceiving the Self: and, while sleeping, that he is drowned in the ocean of bliss; — he who inwardly constant, spends his whole life thus is, among all men, the real seeker of liberation.

All this world, consisting of name and form, is only the particular manifestation (vyashti) of the universal Substance (viraj); it moves and knows all objects by virtue of the primal life (mukhya-prana) that inspires it. This Self like the sun, is neither the doer nor the enjoyer. Thus, directly realizing, does he that is full of knowledge and realization live his life, through incessant contemplation of the Supreme Self.

Just as the one sun, independent of other objects, yet, by virtue of reflection in several waters, becomes many and has the same stability or motion as the medium reflecting it; so does the Supreme Self seem to be affected by properties by virtue of its reflection of all beings, high and low, but, when clearly realized, shines unaffected by those properties.

The Supreme Self has three aspects, namely, the full, the self and the not-self, the first being the unconditioned Self, the second being that which is conditioned by the consciousness, and the third being a mere reflection, in the same way as space has three aspects in respect of water, namely, that which is inside and outside of the water, that which is conterminous with water, and that which is reflected therein. When the conditioned self is merged in the unconditioned, then the condition together with its consequences vanishes altogether.

SHANKARACHARYA

NIRVANA AND SAMSARA

All life is either a conscious and deliberate, or a furtive, half-hearted and indirect acknowledgement of the Absolute. It is the One Law, the One Life, the one Force of all Forces, the One Element that is the source of all elements, and as the One Being it is the source of all being. It is the One that is alone, unaffected and untouched by manifestation, by space, time and motion, by mind and matter. It is omnipresent in every point of space, in every second of time, in every thought or feeling, however foolish, of every being and in every breath. It is everywhere. It can be excluded from nothing, and yet it is no-thing. It is within everything. It is outside everything. It is beyond everything. It is everything and nothing. It is TAT, and TAT is SAT, the truest of all that is true, the most real of all that is real. It is *Chit*, and it is beyond all consciousness, even beyond the power of conceiving or being conscious, because it is beyond all objects of thought, and it is beyond all subjects who think. It is beyond the process of thinking itself, which pertains to the realm of the manifest and which is often dead before it ever comes to be visible.

It is the source of all that is creative and yet it is unconfined and indifferent to all creations, to every leaf that withers, to every human being that dies, to every soul that goes into *avitchi*. None of these affect the Absolute. And yet, it is all compassion. It is the power that gives life to good and evil, to death and birth, to everything that happens, to everything that confines and everything that frees. But it is still beyond all these things and therefore it is called THAT or IT. Only the IT in us can reach out to the IT in THAT, and therefore the *mahavakyam* of the Great Sages: *Tat Tvam Asi* — That Thou Art. The emphasis at one level for the meditative mystic is THAT which is transcendent, whilst at another level it is Thou which transcends all specific acts of longing, looking and searching. This shows obeisance and reverence to every parent, every teacher, and to all the lineages of all the sages, wise men, and awakened ones. So magical is this reverence that it dignifies a human being, making him more human, and divinizes him in the act of veneration to all those greater than himself, to all those beyond him who have trodden the same path and become signposts. They have left footprints, and in myriad ways shown to the homeless wanderer the way back to the only home he searches for, and which, when he finds it, he finds he never left it. Life is a return to where one started, and therefore all of life is a meditation on the Absolute.

The moment this meditation, which must be as ceaseless as breathing, is translated into a set of finite acts, forms, fruits and seeds — even the best — something is lost. More is lost than saved in the telling, even in the sharing. It is unshareable, and is the source of all that is to be shared. Therefore the wise recognize that there is nothing more beautiful in the *Mahamaya*, in the realm of the unreal where relativity supervenes, than the supreme veil that shrouds the majesty of the Absolute. Not just the rare astronomer, but many a humble sea captain and many an ordinary person has had the privilege of seeing the nimbus of the solar corona during an eclipse of the sun. Having seen something so overwhelmingly beautiful, they understand that everything seen and known about the physical sun is but a dim, paltry veil upon the glory of the Invisible Sun.

Its radiance is even more overwhelming in the Divine Darkness which illuminates and gives intelligence to the whole of life and every atom. It is the sanctuary of the highest beings in the whole of evolution. The Lords of Light belonging to the primordial seven rays — ever motionless like the Absolute within the moving wheel of time — give forth the most potent thing conceivable in manifestation. These are the myriads upon myriads of nucleoli that are indestructible like the Absolute, sprung from within the secret, sacred heart of the Spiritual Sun, making a dark embrasure into the hidden Darkness. This dark veil upon that which is eternally hidden can be recognized only by going within, by averting one's gaze from everything that is outside, including most of oneself, and by persisting in the darkness of the cave in the heart. Moving fearlessly like a spiritual mountain climber, one must experience intense horrors that bring one close to the most tragic beings in the worst possible states of the hell of loneliness, self-hatred and self-destruction. At the same time one will see even there the compassion of the greatest and wisest beings, who are far greater than any conceivable god, because they are Sages and *yogins*. They raised the fundamental questions aeons ago, answered them, and remained simple witnesses, by their breathing, to that ever-present, invisible lineage of inexhaustible divine wisdom, which makes the earth what it is and certainly saves it from much worse than ever faces it.

The light of the Invisible Sun lends whatever beauty, truth and meaning there is to human life and to the lives of all beings, so powerful and potent is it. Though one can see and sense this even on the physical plane, most people fail to think about it. Instead of drenching in the external, coarse, visible sunlight, which the wise find suffocating, one should sit in the shade as birds and animals do, and as human beings do when they remain simple and full of love for the soil on which they walk. Then when closing one's eyes, whether at mid-day or at night after one has fulfilled one's duties of the day, one should turn homeward within and think of the ineffable, invisible glory hidden behind the veil of the visible, the mask of manifestation, ever celebrating the One without a second, the One and only existence. Then one may recognize the unbelievable solidarity of the greatest beings conceivable in manifestation who are of one mind, one heart, one breath. They have no identity apart from the whole, and where they are hierarchies that maintain this universe in motion, individuality only belongs to them in groups. Where they are Mahatmas, enlightened beings, they have totally destroyed the root of individuality at the highest level in *Mahat* and in their subtlest vesture, let alone in name and form that belong to the evanescent body. That mystery beyond the radiant veil is invoked in the Gayatri:

UNVEIL, OH THOU WHO GIVEST SUSTENANCE TO THE
UNIVERSE, FROM WHOM ALL PROCEED, TO WHOM ALL MUST

RETURN, THAT FACE OF THE TRUE SUN, NOW HIDDEN BY A
VASE OF GOLDEN LIGHT, THAT WE MAY SEE THE TRUTH, AND
DO OUR WHOLE DUTY, ON OUR JOURNEY TO THY SACRED SEAT.

That radiant veil of supple, noumenal, light — too sacred to
be spoken of aloud — is the light of understanding and inner
illumination, the light that lighteth up the soul of every man.
When one invokes it on behalf of universal good, consciously
and deliberately, one fulfills one's mission as a human being,
consecrating one's life and breathing through adoration and
veneration until these enter into the breathing of all the vestures
and vehicles. This devotion brings one closer to the greatest Beings
in the entire system, enabling one to enjoy — through their eyes,
their minds, and their hearts — the pure perception of the
ultimate hidden meaning behind the whole wheel of time, the
whole cycle of manifestation, the whole of *samsara*. One can even
come to appreciate and enjoy in the *Maya*, the *Mahamaya* — the
priceless opportunity extended from the divine ground for infinite
learning to an overwhelming, boundless array of elementals
and beings in all kingdoms of Nature, including the human, so
that there is a ceaseless onward march towards the universal
enlightenment of everything that lives and breathes.

This consummation far transcends all worlds, systems and
paths, and far surpasses the imaginative capacity of human beings.
The wise characterize it as 'the endless end.' The ending of
manifestation is lost in that realm where all endings and all
beginnings have dissolved. One can gain an intimation of this
supernal state with the help of sacred words in sacred scriptures,
especially ones made alive by those who know, using them as aids
to refine, train, purify and clarify one's heart. The heart is more
important than the head. The clarification of the heart and the
feeling nature requires a purging of every wish other than the
wish that all may thrive and flourish. Cleansing the mind means
getting at the root of all the clusters of pseudo-thoughts that have
been given artificial life by a kind of ghoulish mental blood
transfusion. They are mental corpses, creating a kind of *kamaloka*

and fattening the *kamarupa*. One must let them go and dispel them until they are dissolved and do not lodge anywhere. Then one can open what Shakespeare calls "the book and volume in the brain" beyond and behind the bonfire of cremated thoughts. As one enters its hidden spaces, one comes closer to the pulse of divine thought and ceaseless divine ideation, and begins to see that which underlies all thoughts, that which transcends all conceptions and conditions of embodied and disembodied consciousness. It is so free that it is inconceivable within the mortal mind and finite consciousness. It is so rich and magnificent that once one begins to get a taste of it, one wants nothing else.

When it becomes the most natural thing in the world to enjoy mystic meditation, one is always seeking every opportunity to get back to that fundamental current of ideation. Everything else is merely a veil, distracting and concealing, falsifying, and often alas, tragically inverting the truth of the Oneness of all life. Therefore many sages speak about there being only one true human being in any solar system in any period of manifestation. All seemingly separate human beings are merely atoms within that one being. The immensity of this can be understood by thinking of the billions of cells in the human body, that virtual universe or cosmos which each soul carries on the physiological plane. Yet, most people are not aware of it most of the time, and are merely leaning back upon nature's cycles, trusting to Nature's compassionate toil in keeping the vast cosmic computer working. To be able to insert oneself into the unity of Nature and human life consciously and deliberately, and to do it joyously and with total consecration, self-abandonment and self-abnegation at the root, destroys at the source all thought which gives rise to false and delusive desire, which can only trap one in time, making one captive to bondage, illusion and delusion.

Therefore, one meditates upon karmalessness by honoring the one universal, unknowable, ever mysterious Law of Karma, cleaving to that which is at the core of it, beyond all definition and articulation. In the memorable words of the *Light of Asia*, "the heart of things is sweet." There is bliss at the core of the cosmic process.

There is love and compassion, and therefore one can rejoice — amidst a world of ignorance, darkness and mortality — that the immortal prevails, that light persists, and that goodness ever triumphs at the end of the pilgrimage of the immortal soul. To raise one's sights and see beyond all lesser perspectives is to relativate and make absurd the mimicry of the mind working through the mimicry of human speech. The chattering of monkeys and crows is more beautiful and meaningful than the chattering of human beings who have, often unaware, desecrated that divine estate.

Now, if the Absolute is logically beyond all and cannot have any relationships whatsoever, this is merely a correlate of the ontological fact that there is nothing else but the Absolute. It has no parts, so there can be no relations between parts of the Absolute. Nor can one treat worlds as parts of the Absolute, because that would be to fail to understand homogeneous Spirit-Matter. It would be a failure to understand the nature of that ultimate divine field in which there is a potentiality of universes. The Absolute must transcend anything and everything that is confined within the logic of worlds and systems, let alone the little worlds of little human lives. Consequently, all true learners know that all questioning is self-questioning. Instead of becoming complicated and indirect, they learn consciously to commune with that which is boundless, the Rootless Root within themselves. Once they begin to do this, much starts to happen. They suddenly become courageous, solitary and free, effortlessly able to gain self-mastery over their field. At the same time, they are ever receptive to the music of the spheres, to the flute of Krishna, to the majestic heartbeat of the universe, to the majestic F note of nature, to what the ocean is saying by not saying it, what the sky is breathing inaudibly, and what true fire and true water — the true elements — are speaking. Then one is grateful to all those beings, whether they be birds or poets, that bear witness to the rich, magnificent, melodious language of invisible Nature, which is a ceaseless celebration of *Sat-Chit-Ananda* — truth, intelligence and joy fused forever in a sacred Three-in-One at the heart of the Absolute.

Only the highest Dhyanis can directly reflect the divine thought and ideation of the Universal Mind, of which only a small portion, called *Mahat,* becomes the mind of a cosmos during a period of manifestation. Those who understand this will begin to learn from and listen to everyone who knows more than themselves. On that inner journey, they will also have the courage within themselves to prostrate before, to seek avidly, and to move towards the exalted, invisible Enlighteners and Teachers of the human family. They will see them all as parts of one immense Tree, and try to get to the invisible sap and roots of that invisible Tree. They will try to see the crown of that Tree which is like the crown over the head of every human being. The *Atman* is above the body, and the *Atman* is below the body. The *Atman* is within in the secret, sacred, spiritual heart of every being. The *Atman* also is ceaselessly within the Golden Egg of the cosmos that is mirrored in the pristine, golden Aura around every being that breathes. It is most sublimely present in the Divine Host that descended eighteen-and-three-quarter million years ago into the human form. It is silent throughout mundane life, though it whispers in deep sleep. It speaks more strongly in deep and regular meditations, and, in those who begin to become wise and enlightened at any level, it becomes a *chitkala,* the infallible Voice that guides, speaks, opens the eyes, opens the doors of the senses, and goes beyond them. It gives one myriad gifts, enabling one to see beyond the cycles of time and the confines of space. It enables one to experience closeness to what is so seemingly far off in physical space-time. It gives one the ever present companionship of the entire assembly of the Gods, and the sages higher than the gods, but also all those true beings who have learned to walk in the ways shown by the sages and blessed by the Gods. This is an eternal undertaking in which the language of separation makes no sense. To talk of the *I,* even the *I-am-I,* the I that is immortal, is an absurd illusion. The notion of the I falls away, and all language becomes merely the working of the elements or *gunas,* the forces of Nature using all bodies as vehicles for the great enlightenment of all life.

At the highest level *Sat-Chit-Ananda*, the Three-in-One, is a much richer and more profound representation of the essentially nameless ground of all being and non-being than the 'Absolute', which is, as a philosophical term, scarcely two hundred years old. There is even more abundant meaning in the truly ancient Sanskrit term *Parabrahman* — that which is beyond all Brahmās and all periods of manifestations, that from which all the Brahmās come. The lower mind falsely thinks that the moment one points to something beyond, one is belittling what is below. On the contrary, to speak of *Parabrahman* is to give beauty to all the Brahmās, because they come out of *Brahman*. There can be as many personal gods as one wishes, in as many systems, as long as one sees, like the peasant, that they all come from that which is beyond all definition and limit. True philosophical negation — of form, colour and limitation — is endless affirmation of the sort shown by humble souls like Carlyle or Whitman, who spoke of accepting life, accepting the universe, accepting everything that comes, and rejoicing in it.

The challenge is to learn to see life now the way one will see it at the moment of death, lest in life one become a traitor to one's true self. Where one cannot understand, one must be as patient as the mountains and the rocks, waiting to learn the meaning of a particular moment or event, even if it takes all one's life. This demands trust in the integrity of the universe, trust in the divine, trust in its supreme and total infallible mathematical exactitude. When this trust is real, the words of the sages become real: there is not a single accident, not a single misshapen day; there is not a misfortune or mishap that is unnecessary to the evolution of the soul, and which one cannot courageously understand. Instead of seeing a tiny portion of the curve, one could see the larger extensions of the vast infinite series of chains that must surely bridge what existed billions and millions of years ago and what exists now. The universe has integrity not just in terms of spatial extension, but it has an even deeper integrity, like a tree, through time. There is nothing now which is not connected with all that existed before. In the age of computers when literally billions of operations are involved in running the simplest program, to presume that the integrity of life cannot be understood could only be a symptom of soul sickness and pathetic perversity. In fact, it is much worse. It is evidence of a secret alliance to the legions of darkness — power maniacs, traducers and desecrators of the sacred — pacts souls have made in other lives, which they keep secret, but which work constantly through weaknesses making them terrified that they will be rejected by the universe.

They are right. The universe rejects everything that comes in the way of the whole. The part must always give way to the whole, and those who are self-separated from the noble stream of life are the enemies of humanity and of all life. Yet, even they are given a function by Nature and the gods. They become the scavengers of manifestation. But those who seek to be part of the grand stream and cooperate with it consciously must learn to be like the gentle birds and the beasts all around, like the gods ceaselessly engaged in sacrifice, like the sages ever celebrating the joyous light of the *Atman*, and like the best beings of every age who have shown the way of soul strength and unpretentious compassion. Separating themselves from the mass of sick elementals masquerading as human beings, they become attentive to the Voice, the Soundless Sound, meditating upon the exalted Three-in-One hidden in *Parabrahman* itself. *Sat-Chit-Ananda* is one way of characterizing it. The three Logoi is another. They correspond exactly to that which is not just the Logos of the entire system, but also of every human being — the *Atman*, which is the *Paramatman* in its cosmic sense, and the *Atman* ruling over each and all. This is the true meaning of the light of the *Atman* called *Buddhi*, which is the light of understanding and the beauty of concentrated thought. From *dharana* through *dhyana* the soul readies itself for absorption through *samadhi* into the Absolute, into the *Atman*, which exactly mirrors in its eternal motion the light essence of the *Parabrahman*. Unaffected by time, it is the only source of dynamism in this universe, which makes its continuous maintenance possible as Vishnu, its perpetual destruction and regeneration possible as Shiva, and its ceaseless creation possible as Brahmā. These are all only three names of the same Supreme Godhead, too sacred to be spoken of unless one has earned the right to do so by giving one's whole life to it and cooperating utterly with that Divine, as all the mystics have shown.

At the same time, one must not mistake the *correspondence* in the human constitution to the highest in the Divine for *identity*. What is below is only a small portion of what at the cosmic level precedes and antedates, as well as succeeds and goes beyond, the vastest periods of time and grandest arenas of space. Therefore the outstanding way of understanding this, as pointed out in the *Mahabharata* by the great Rishi Sanatsujata — Dakshinamurti, the Initiator of Initiates, who is again the custodian of this moment of global civilization — is that meditation is silence, meditation is the AUM, meditation is *Brahman, Brahman* is the AUM, and *Brahman* is silence. Whether one thinks of the AUM or of silence, or of *Brahman*, or indeed of true meditation, all of these are the same. Everything in life leads to that same Unit Source, which means meditation must go beyond all divisions, comparisons and contrasts. Those who have the courage to revere the richer life hidden in Nature know that the whole of the invisible Himalayas is in the human heart, and that the invisible Ganges flows through the human body. Right there, within oneself, are the invisible beauties of Nature which bring one closer to the wise. They do not lie in the realm of the visible, which is only a theatre of trial, temptation and of deception. Therefore the AUM represents the forever concealed. Every representation of it points to that which is unrepresentable, concealed within the heart of the Absolute. When it spreads its light it becomes that which binds the whole, the Three becoming the Four, which was honoured by disciples of Pythagoras as the holiest of holies, the *Tetraktys*, the Three-in-One which cements the whole.

To see this is to see that meditation upon the Absolute is a recovery of the Lost Word. It is becoming worthy of the Word, becoming capable of seeing the hidden Sound behind all sounds, the hidden Word behind all the revealed words of all the scriptures. It is the unutterable and the unuttered Word — because its utterance is only possible among Initiates within the Mysteries after myriad lives of discipline and preparation. Any human being at any time can get an inkling of the triad within, and there are millions of triads within. But, they all have ultimately their root in a supreme Triad that has never incarnated in a human being, because it is in the immortal direct Ray from the Absolute. That is the highest teaching hidden in all the sacred books. The Unit Ray, which does not divide, is the AUM. Therefore the wise unify and integrate, healing and overcoming all splits and fragmentations, and they go beyond all words and concepts, all pairs of eyes, all forms, and all names. Meditation means a continual enjoyment of transcending the multiplicity of names and forms and getting only to that One which is honored above all, and to which one pays total homage and makes one's whole life an act of obeisance.

Never is that Word in manifestation without men of the Word, custodians of the Word, true Gurus. Though they may work in myriad ways through all life, through all the elements of Nature, and through all beings, above all they remain in themselves obedient servants of the Hierophantic Host that serves the One and Only, Supreme in Eternity and in time, which is the hidden meaning of the doctrine of the *Purna Avatar*. That direct Ray is the most potent gift that a human being has, but it is only when one transcends all that is indirect and lesser — by painful degrees burning out everything that comes in the way — that one comes any closer to the direct Ray of divine perception and illumination. In it one begins to experience the thrill of communion leading to union, becoming ultimately a constant fact of ever present unity with the cosmic Three-in-One. That is the highest teaching ever given, and it can only become real if one can practice seeing that AUM in the *Atman* all around. One must refuse to use the eyes or the ears, let alone the tongue, except to see and hear and speak of That. Naturally, if one is going to do it all the time, it will have to be done quietly, even inaudibly, without coming in the way of other people and their fickle ties and their false attractions. One has got to see it amidst everything in the realm of the manifest and within in every being. This is a slow and painful education, because if one leaves out a single being on earth, this will come and haunt one for lives. No being can be excluded. This learning, then, becomes a kind of practice of all inclusiveness in thinking and feeling, and it only becomes authentic and honest by the divine discipline of self-consecration, regular purgation and purification of the mind and the heart. Like a child learning to lisp, one must practice the language of the Silence, the language of the Divine, which is the forgotten language of the soul, so that one can hear it in deep sleep, recognize it in dreams, use it in meditation and in the anterooms of preparation for the Mysteries, thereby becoming a true listener to the highest expressions of that Voice which is the eternal religion of humanity, the *Sanatana Dharma*.

One cannot really do this without voiding everything that is lesser, and one cannot do this once and for all. One does it repeatedly, just as one does not eat or bathe for all time, but eats and bathes every day. Every day one must cleanse, purify and nourish the body, and, which is the key to health, one must eliminate all that is unnecessary. Similarly, everything in the mind and heart that is on a lesser plane in one's thoughts, words, feelings and reactions to the world must be eliminated. Otherwise, one cannot begin to be worthy of the presence of the enlightened, the illuminated Instructors of humanity who are ever present, but whose presence — even if one were right there next to them — would never mean anything to the soul if one's whole being was not consecrated. That is why the alchemists speak of the mystic marriage in which one is wedded forever by the most sacred and indissoluble vow of all vows. It does not matter in what form one makes this vow, for it is the intensity and authenticity of it that will bind one to the entire golden chain. The truer and more constant one is, the more irrevocably one binds oneself in consciousness to the brotherhood of all beings and the working of the one great Law. The ceaseless harmonizing and equilibration of all life atoms in all kingdoms is going on invisibly in manifestation all the time, but it is too subtle and too illusive to be understood by the lower mind and the finite heart. It can only be understood by the cosmic heart and the cosmic mind, which means one must attune one's small heart and small mind to the great heart of humanity, the greater heart of all true disciples, and the measureless heart of Adepts and Initiates, which will bring one closer to the singular secret heart of the Absolute in the form of the Ishvara, the Supreme.

Real meditation on the Absolute, then, releases everything that is true and good, everything that is light giving and beautiful, everything that is lasting and honest, everything that works compatibly with the good of all in one's life. Even if there are only three or four things one could select out of the myriad mass of one's life, if they are authentic, the very act of selection teaches one how to learn and lisp the language of recognition. One will begin to draw out from one's hidden resources a lot that could never otherwise emerge, because of the beastly and treacherous alliances one has made to so much that is so false, so wicked and so horrible. Taken from the dregs of the astral light and the depths of *kamaloka,* and made into what one thinks one is, this poison takes people almost to the point where the thread is cut and one becomes a leaky jar. But even the worst of cases can be redeemed by invoking the Light of all lights, by invoking the compassion of the lineages, and making not just what people make all the time — a new start — but making a more fundamental beginning in using all one's energy towards the only thing that makes life worth living. This invocation will work infallibly, gradually healing the heart and mind, and slowly removing from the vestures all the scars, such as those depicted in many a painting of many a disciple, even though these portraits are feeble attempts to reveal the mysterious inner process of alchemy and self-transformation. At the moment of death one will still be able to lay the finest and the purest of the best in oneself at the feet of the Guru — while the entire house is burning, so to speak. This act of consecration only becomes real when one actually begins to bring it to the level of touch, taste and the physical body, when one feels that every atom is sacred, that nothing is one's own, but everything is borrowed. Misuse of this consecration would be fatal and indeed at a certain point of evolution would be final, so one needs the courage to move against the grain, to come out and be separate, in the words of St. Paul. But this is not something to talk about, because that will only destroy the work. The key is actually to do it repeatedly until one can respect oneself. In essence that work is the divinization through self-magnetization of the *Atman* in every atom — in the fingers and eyes, in the forehead, in the tongue, in the lungs, even in the liver and spleen, everywhere. Indeed, what can be more sacred than the generative principle, reaching from above the head through the sacred organs to the soles of one's feet, because man is meant to create and to emanate, but out of the deepest sense of the sacred, and he is meant to produce thoughts that can become potent and beautiful blessings and benedictions to all that lives.

Because this is such a vast and magnificent enterprise, once one really gets serious and reaches a certain foothill, one begins to recognize myriads of beings who already are there, some of whom are stuck but others of whom are pointing the way ahead. Then one begins to see what is real, totally hidden behind the so-called real world in which one had lived before. People therefore naturally find, as all the Mahatmas have, that the sovereign mode of *Buddhi Yoga* is total surrender of the will, called *ishvarapranidana* by Patanjali — total surrender and total devotion. That alone is what brings one closer to understanding the mysterious eleventh chapter of the *Bhagavad Gita* — *Vishvarupa Darshana Yoga*, The Yoga of the Vision of the Cosmic Form — which precedes the twelfth chapter on *Bhakti Yoga*, The Yoga of Devotion, and follows the magnificent ninth and tenth chapters — The Yoga of the Sovereign Science and the Sovereign Secret and the Yoga of Divine Excellences. But these chapters can never be understood until one has actually mastered the teachings in the first six chapters, which is why reading them only arouses soul memories, but does not instruct the mind. Before the soul can be instructed, the mind has to be totally put aside.

In the fifteenth chapter, The Yoga of the Supreme Spirit, Krishna declares:

> Since I transcend the perishable and am also higher than the imperishable, I am therefore extolled in this world and in the Vedas as the Supreme Being — *Purushottama.* He who thus, undeluded, knows Me as *Purushottama,* knowing all, worships Me with his whole nature.

That is the ultimate secret about the Absolute. Behind all persons there is one supreme *Uttama Purusha.* Otherwise this universe would have no logic to it. That is what is too sacred and too wonderful ever to be caught by human beings in any known representations of the God idea. The homage of the Sages alone is entitled to sing and speak at this highest level. Those human beings are wise who have so far transcended the realm of opinion and auto-generation, at the lower level of reaction, that they have totally become, in Gandhi's words, Zero, a cipher, floating on the ocean of Divine Truth. They therefore experience within the sanctuary of the heart the joy of the discovery that the object and the subject of meditation are ultimately one. Can it be any less than the whole of the cosmos? Can the meditator be any other than the *Uttama Purusha?* Can everything else that one sees in the realm of the many, be anything else than a mirroring? That is why the wise speak of the Self-Existent meditating upon itself. Below that, everything else is mayavic. Enlightened Beings are those who have fully mastered and recognized the truth of *dukkha,* the pain of living and of humanity. They see *nirvana* in *samsara* and inwardly experience the secret joy of the divine smile behind the divine dance that is ceaselessly working, in ways that transcend the reckoning and opinions of human minds, for universal uplift — *sarvodaya,* for *lokasangraha* — the welfare of all, for universal good — *tò àgathón* — and the universal enlightenment of the entire human race and of all that lives and breathes.

So potent is this teaching on Meditation on the Absolute that, if devoted disciples genuinely try to use it in the coming months and years, it will give them a strong foundation which then can set a pattern in their lives that will become meaningful and sacred. Everyone can benefit from this teaching and all can participate in it. Quality is more important than quantity in this meditation, though quality does depend upon persistence and continuity in the attempt. It does not matter so much whether these disciples spend time together, for although this can help, it is also often a hindrance. The true Brotherhood they seek is eternally established in the Heart of the Logos, which is the *fons et origo* of all enlightenment and Enlightened Beings. Turning inward towards the light of the *Paramatman,* they will discover the only true joy allotted to intrepid pilgrim souls, which is the joy of moving towards that one True Light of their being through universal selfless service. Then, their highest meditations and noblest deeds, their deepest thoughts and finest feelings, will serve as living seeds and points of contact, not just among themselves, but really with the whole of humanity for the sake of the greater good of all.

KALKI MAITREYA

*Starting upon the long journey immaculate; descending
more and more into sinful matter, and having connected
himself with every atom in manifested* Space — the
Pilgrim, *having struggled through and suffered in every form
of life and being, is only at the bottom of the valley of matter,
and half through his cycle, when he has identified himself
with collective Humanity. This,* he has made in his own
image. *In order to progress upwards and homewards, the
'God' has now to ascend the weary uphill path of the
Golgotha   of
Life. It is the martyrdom of self-conscious existence. Like
Vishvakarman he has to sacrifice* himself to himself *in order
to redeem all creatures, to resurrect from the many into the*
One Life. *Then he ascends into heaven indeed; where,
plunged into the incomprehensible absolute Being and Bliss
of Paranirvana, he reigns unconditionally, and whence he
will redescend again at the next 'coming', which one portion
of humanity expects in its dead-letter sense as the* second
advent *and the other as the last 'Kalki Avatar'.*

The Secret Doctrine, i 268

> *If any one among you thinks that he*
> *Is wise in this age,*
> *Let him become a fool*
> *That he may become wise.*
> *For the wisdom of this world*
> *Is folly before God.*
>
> *I Corinthians* 3:18-19

Everyone who has the priceless privilege to enter the ancient
Path to the Divine Mysteries is the recipient of a sacred
trust. It can be transmitted only through a life of
unremitting sacrifice and striving for the sake of universal
enlightenment. Entry into the far-flung orbit of the Avatar may

be seen as an approach, even if unintentional, to the antechamber or the threshold of the inward spiritual Path leading to the true Mysteries. A few fortunate souls are able to avail themselves of the sacred teachings concerning the *hiranyagarbha*, the golden sphere of the Cosmic Egg, the *brahmanda*, and its mirroring in the immortal individuality of human souls. It is the basis of the sutratmic thread, the luminous link binding together all the incarnations of the pilgrim-soul and the divine vesture within which is gestated the possibility of spiritual birth into self-conscious immortality. It is the hallowed vessel within which the eternal seed of divine humanity is sown and fructified, the pristine medium of the potent current flowing between the higher Triad overbrooding man and the Logos in the cosmos.

The initial self-awakening in the earnest seeker for wisdom is the starting-point of the 'longest journey', the arduous Path pointing not merely to individual enlightenment, which is an extremely sublimated form of exalted selfishness, but even more to ultimate reunion and total identification with the Self of all, the Logos in the Cosmos and the God in Man. The true life of the indwelling Spirit in Man and Nature is a life of eternal Wisdom-Sacrifice, *jnana yajna*, ceaselessly enacted on each plane of being and in all worlds of differentiated subjects and objects. The spiritual seeker is invited to participate self-consciously in this primordial Sacrifice, *adhiyajna*, through self-purification and self-correction, mystic meditation and joyous initiation into the realm of cosmic ideation. In order to do this effectively, it is essential to withdraw allegiance to the outer shell of the composite personality. One must separate entirely one's sense of being from the epiphenomenal activity of the external form with an assumed name, the *namarupa*.

Like the Self-governed Sage in the second discourse of the *Bhagavad Gita*, one must withdraw all the powers of perception and conception from the outer organs and objects, reconsecrating them for a noumenal task within the inmost chamber of contemplation. This withdrawal is certainly not a selfish retreat into what *The Voice of the Silence* calls "the carapace of selfhood".

Rather, it is the complete realization of contentment in the universal Self alone, within the omnipresent *paramatman*, the unmanifest source of all creativity, inward illumination and spiritual self-regeneration. When the soul withdraws into the inmost Holy of Holies, the sacred ark of the Mystery Fires, it becomes as "an everlasting lode-star, that beams the brighter in the heavens the darker here on earth grows the night."

Ever and always, from its distant dawn down to the present historical moment, the spiritual pilgrimage of Humanity has been presided over by the highest and holiest of beings, the sacrificial servers of Arghyanath, the mysterious Lord of Libations, the chief custodian of the sacred Mysteries. Arghya Varsha is the Land of Libations or the sanctuary of divine Hierophants, which stretches from Mount Kailas to the Shamo Desert. This is the spiritual home and birthplace of Io, the mother of physical humanity. It is also the real Argos, the fountain-head of the ancient lineages of divine dynasties of King-Initiates. Mount Meru, the navel of the world and the abode of Mahavishnu and Mahashiva, is the magnetic centre of the preservative and regenerative forces in the invisible cosmos. It is the Sacred Lha — the sanctuary of those whose destiny is to last from the commencement to the ending of the *manvantara* during each Round. It is the dwelling-place of the last divine mortal chosen as the *sishtha* or sacred germ for the future seed of humanity. It is also the spiritual realm from which the divine descent of Kalki Maitreya takes place.

All spiritual life on earth is encompassed in the Religion of Humanity, the sacrificial service of the Spirit of Divine Truth, SAT, and Absolute Compassion, *mahakaruna*. Perpetually sweeping away everything that is moribund and morbid in human nature, all the incrustations of falsehood and mummery stifling the human soul, the eternal Lord of the Mysteries, Dakshinamurti, Hari-Hara, the True Saviour of Humanity and the Good Gardener of Nature, guides and nurtures with perfect gnosis and divine impartiality the potent seeds of human futurity, including all, excluding none except the self-excluded. Every sacred tradition revolves around the seminal utterances, the abounding grace and magnanimous benediction of God-men, all of whom are accredited reflections of Him who was in the beginning, the Ancient of Days and the Initiator of Initiates. Those who comprehend this central truth in their hearts and minds, to whatever degree, are able to come closer in consciousness to the Supreme Source of Divine Wisdom, to Brahma Vach.

Such souls are readily willing to purify themselves, practise the quintessential ethics of the immemorial Teachings, meditate on the metaphysics which lies at the basis of true theurgy, and elevate themselves with deep, unconditional devotion to *lokasangraha*, the welfare of the whole world. Unfortunately, there are also those who, inherently incapable of resonating to the anti-élitist and universal keynote of the timeless Teachings, compensate for their own insecurities and failures by attempting to limit access to the *Philosophia Perennis*. That is why it is so vital to the present epoch and the future of humanity that no motive even a shadow less than a sincere, all-absorbing desire to serve the universal enlightenment of all beings should concern any seeker of wisdom. Nothing less will do, and nothing else will work as a substitute or stimulus. Lord Krishna stated in the *Bhagavad Gita* that "in whatever way men approach Me, in that way do I accept them". As the Qur'an teaches, there are as many ways to God as there are breaths of the children of men. There is room for each and all under the mighty banyan Tree of Divine Wisdom, the Tree of Immortality and Life Eternal.

Gupta Vidya takes its starting-point and also attains its summit in the same transcendental and absolute Divine Ground, THAT (TAT) which is beyond all differentiations of spirit and matter, all dimensions of space and time, all rates and quanta of motion. This is the Divine Darkness, the Supreme Silence or *maunam* which is the eternal source of both light and sound. The archetypal mode of pristine creativity at the basis of the cosmos and Man lies hidden in the mystery of the Soundless Sound, the Eternal AUM throughout the ages. The Sacred Word, Vach, the Verbum, is the original and enduring vibration in *Akasha* behind the myriad reverberations that bring into being myriad worlds and vast hosts of sentient creatures belonging to all the seven kingdoms of Nature. The living presence of the sound in the silence is the invisible and inaudible core of every monad, divine and human, solar and lunar. As the sound in the light and the light in the sound, it is the fecund source of all the supernal and sublunar, celestial and terrestrial, manifestations of embodied intelligence and concentrated wisdom, for all these are the sacred progeny of the sublime Vach.

In its subtlest and highest meaning, this is realized in its fullness by that unseen tribe of casteless and classless Magi, the Sages and Seers, the Initiators and Instructors, of the elect of all peoples and societies, cultures and civilizations. It is impossible to draw closer to Them without rediscovering and rebecoming the Sacred Word that is the Rootless Root of all immortal monads, all souls who are like multi-hued rays of the hidden Spiritual Sun. Through the Word, one recovers one's true stature as one's own master and inner god, attuning oneself to the currents of divine ideation that flow forth from the primal source, the *fons et origo* of each and all. Every form of partisanship and partiality, all concern for the lesser self, every element in oneself that is bound up with the part and does not flow with the whole, must be let go. Anything less leaves one unworthy of the great gift of the *Manasa*, the priceless potency of pure self-consciousness, the supreme inheritance of the whole of the human family. This is the true spirit in which one must and can prepare to draw closer to the sacred threshold of the Holy of Holies, the adytum of the Mysteries, in which one may be reborn and reclaim one's divine birthright. Thus one may relearn how to live in that light and sound which suffuses, sustains and regenerates the human tabernacle of the self-realized, self-existent godhead.

One must come to comprehend fully the complex set of solar and lunar forces in the cosmos as in the human constitution. One must thereby learn to pay one's deep debt of gratitude to all the elements and principles, essences and hosts, that have created the varied vestures of the divine monad and the hallowed temple of the human form. Inevitably, this means repaying unacknowledged debts and engaging in wise self-correction and alchemical transmutation. To re-become the Egg, to live in it self-consciously and continuously, one must reduce oneself to a zero. Then one may come into the presence of the pristine flame within the forty-nine fires, the all-presence which is no-thing, the ever unmanifest ground of all Nature and Humanity. Thus one may constitute oneself an authentic co-worker with Nature, a true servant of Humanity, a silent worshipper of the Divine in all its noumenal radiations. This is the meaning of daily self-purification (*tapas*), self-surrender (*bhakti*) and self-sacrifice (*yajna*), the abiding basis of intuitive (Buddhic) perception and noetic action.

There is certainly nothing wrong in the creative use of pure reason, the consistent application of the principle of *ratio* in the service of the progressive understanding of divine ideas and symbols. How else would it be possible to perceive and apprehend, much less engage in constructive self-correction in relation to errors and omissions? If one is going to be an authentic devotee of Divine Wisdom, then one must certainly be prepared to think, and to think deeply, about every aspect of human life, including birth and death, decay and sickness, illusion and delusion. Naturally, such concentrated reflection must be accompanied by the profoundest feelings of universal gratitude towards all Teachers, magnanimity to all beings and effortless, unconstrained compassion. The finest feelings are the inevitable concomitants of any abiding realization of SAT, the truth in all things. The highest understanding and the deepest love are inseparably interwoven in genuine meditation upon abstract glyphs and concrete symbols of the diffusion of the divine Life-Force in the cosmos and in all Humanity.

Everything has its dharma, which can be described from the standpoint of the lower kingdoms as the laws of Nature, and which works in the animal kingdom with the unerring precision of instinct. For the self-conscious human monad, however, deliberation, choice and commitment constitute the appropriate terms of discourse within which to formulate human obligation, duty and destiny. *Svadharma*, which is one's self-chosen, self-renewed and self-exemplified duty, that which is due from each individual to the whole of Nature and Humanity, is not a personal possession or a private, cloistered arena. Since each soul is self-conscious to some degree, dharma becomes the *svadharma* of each, *sui generis*, unique, incomparable and inalienable, that which none can delegate or transfer to another. At the same time, since all human selves are essentially rays of the Self of all, and as all human beings are like limbs in the collective, composite organism of Vaivasvata Manu or Adam Kadmon, *svadharma* cannot be construed in exclusively separatist terms or individualistic language.

Any person can only individuate truly to the extent to which he or she can universalize consciousness, and *svadharma* has to be understood in the context of the universal dharma of the human family in any age or epoch. *Svadharma* is the deft application of dharma to the karmic conditions of the moment in any situation, with its limits, parameters and possibilities. The *Bhagavad Gita* (III.35) affirms: "Better is one's own duty, though imperfectly done, than the duty of another well done. Better is death in doing one's own duty *(svadharma)*; the duty of another brings danger." The perverse refusal or pathetic inability to translate dharma into the appropriate thought and action in the present moment is indeed *adharma*, unrighteousness, the source of all sordid confusion and culpable wrongdoing, as well as moral backsliding. No doubt, none can, without the self-validating universal vision of the Adept, judge the duty of another. This makes it all the more vital that each and every one enacts *svadharma* with the modicum of courage needed to act on one's deepest convictions and fullest understanding. Given the inevitability of falling short of these time and again, it is an elementary requirement of the Golden Rule to show genuine tolerance and empathy for the frailties of others.

Conflicts between individuals, groups, societies and nations are all too often the outgrowth of militant self-righteousness and fearful intolerance, whilst reflecting abysmal lack of clarity or fidelity in regard to one's own *svadharma*. Human beings exist today in the most spiritually straitened or diminished circumstances. They are mentally diminished in an age of immense proliferation of information; they are psychically diminished at a time when there is an involuntary recognition of universal interdependence, at least in the economic and ecological spheres; they are emotionally diminished in a generation which has received a succession of emotional shocks in regard to human depravity, duplicity and cruelty; they are even physically diminished in an era of mass consumption and compulsive multiplication of wants; above all, they are spiritually impoverished in an age of unprecedented access to the world's sacred texts and spiritual manuals. And yet, at rare moments of harmonic convergence of human hopes and desperate longings for a safer and saner world, there are poignant tokens and gestures of suppressed feelings of universal solidarity in distress, even a collective outpouring of cries and appeals for the visible appearance of a Secret Saviour, a New Revelation, the Day of Final Reckoning or Divine Judgement, and a new Elysium on a new earth.

As pilgrim-souls, all human beings are essentially integral parts of a single monadic stream of evolution on a vast collective spiritual odyssey, the limits and contours of which cannot be conceived by ordinary temporal consciousness. Each and every individual is inescapably involved in a set of composite vestures which reflect the complex karma of a long history of thought and conduct, in a world which each one's karma has inexorably determined to be suitable for spiritual self-correction and further progress or retardation, according to one's willingness to learn and unlearn. Owing to deep-rooted ignorance, lack of mental clarity and moral resolution, age-old proclivities and persisting habits formed in this life, much of one's involuntary involvement in the world's malaise can become inverted and deflected. As a result, all too many weak-willed persons exacerbate and intensely react to much that is unnecessary, behaving like moral serfs with mindless and slavish tendencies, entangling themselves in messes of their own making. They are terrified to assume the burden of responsibility for themselves and others. Since all true learning requires patient assimilation and skilful practice, mere theoretical knowledge and mechanical techniques cannot reverse this tropism, let alone the strange infatuation with the insufferable pride in spiritual failure.

If one thinks seriously in terms of the striking metaphors of *The Voice of the Silence*, seeing oneself and others as immaculate rays of light with opaque clay material on the outer surface, no amount of scrutiny of the dense covering can release any insight into light-energy. One must show the courage to turn aside from externals and look within the seeming darkness. Since 'inner' and 'outer', 'within' and 'without', are relative terms, one will in no time discover that one's initial notions of what is within will be displaced by deeper awareness. The very postulation of the spiritual Path to self-enlightenment implies that one must begin where one is, rather than waiting for others before making a start in self-scrutiny. So one must retire in secret to converse with the imprisoned soul, to consider the plight of the greater self one has pushed aside into the abyss of non-being, leaving oneself in a sorry state of self-alienation, impotence and bondage to delusion. The more one contemplates one's role as a callous jailer of one's own better self, the more one will notice the complicity of others, with all their compulsive verbiage and mediocre rationalizations, in the profanation of the sacred and in the downward path of self-destruction. This wretched condition is due to cowardly neglect and diabolical abuse in the past. In the realm of the sacred, even neglect is a form of abuse and every abuse is an act of perfidy and self-betrayal.

The only way out is to acknowledge one's forgotten pact with the legions of the demoniac and to proceed to ask for a permanent divorce. One must show that one is in earnest by invoking the Holy Light and the Holy Power of the imprisoned Christos. One must seriously strive to meditate upon the Spiritual Sun, the most potent of all healers, and upon Agathon, Universal Good. It does not matter that one's conception of *dhyana* or deep meditation, and one's ability to initiate and sustain it, are woefully inadequate, muddled and pitiable. Like ghee drawn from heated butter, practice clarifies, chanting aloud helps, and the act of abject self-surrender may itself be converted into the posture of redemptive humility. As one works persistently and patiently to establish a more intimate relation with one's imprisoned splendour, one's exiled *alter ego,* Pollux, the banished brother of Castor, one's frail conceptions of meditative stillness and one's feeble attempts at sustained practice will undergo change. The temple of the tortured body can be cleansed and purified, even now, as with the daily act of taking a shower. At this stage it helps enormously to take a brief holiday from one's sordid self-preoccupation, and to reflect upon human souls in distress.

One simple form of preliminary meditation is known in the Tibetan tradition as 'taking and giving'. This consists of consciously and imaginatively breathing in the sufferings and sins of others, their self-suffocating distress and immeasurable ignorance, which are like black rays of pollution, and breathing out white rays of hope and faith, love and charity, fellowship and compassion. Done repeatedly, especially before a deep sleep of innocence, it can help on waking up to think about benevolent breathing before going out into the world. It would now help to intensify and deepen this daily practice by calming the mind and making a bold attempt to develop the power of clear visualization, whether of the boundless sky or of omnipresent space, of the fathomless ocean of life or of the subterranean streams of life-giving elixirs in the Himalayan mountain ranges, of pure white light or the rainbow bridge between the earth and the empyrean, of the evening star or the midnight sun, of the radiant hosts of enlightened Buddhas and compassionate Bodhisattvas seated around the central figure of the healing Maitreya Buddha, as in many a Tibetan *tanka,* or even of the all-conquering Rider on the White Horse (Kalki) of the *Book of Revelation* of St. John of Patmos.

Vishnu-Soshios-Lakshminarayana leads the Legions of Light and the toilers of Maitreya, unseen by all who would be blinded by the radiant vision, joyously greeted by myriads of perceptive souls in the silence of their grateful hearts, rural exemplars of Himalayan patience, supremely confident that Truth will triumph in the fullness of days; that the armies of Belial and Moloch and the host of lesser demonic chiefs will be frustrated in their designs to set up a global robotocracy and to convert this entire planet into a necropolis of the damned; that the meek shall yet inherit the earth; and the decisive victory of Shamballa will light up the Mystery Fires in hallowed places, in groves of good goblins and wizened gremlins, in the humble huts and haunts of innocent fools and inspired children, revelling in sacred chants and hymnodies of divine rhapsody. In the words of the mystic Hallaj, "Now, brightly blazing forth, Truth's luminary hath driven out of sight each flickering, lesser light." In the incantatory, initiatory language of *The Voice of the Silence,*

> . . . the *Dhyana* gate is like an alabaster vase, white and transparent; within there burns a steady golden fire, the flame of *Prajna* that radiates from *Atma.* . . . Behold! thou hast become the Light, thou hast become the Sound, thou art thy Master and thy God.

It is foretold in the ancient Puranas that Kalki will come not once, but over and over again, each time the world passes through another catastrophic cycle of precipitous decline in righteousness and the earth groans with its insupportable burden of demonic cacophony and spiritual barrenness. It now seems to many tortured souls that our own epoch, in the most barbaric of centuries in recent recorded history, is marked and mauled by the most appalling and pervasive desecration of the Holy of Holies, in thought and speech, emotion and action, in so-called religious sanctuaries, in the chancelleries and capitals of nations, in secular forums, in schools and in streets, in divided homes and blood-stained battlefields, in the mass media and on the lips of pseudo-sophisticates, in the perverted minds and poisonous hearts of well-disguised "murderers of souls", in the moral plagues sweeping the countryside as well as the drug-infested cities, let alone the massive corruption in the reeking corridors of power and paper money, in the citadels of selfish leaders and in the marketplaces of the demoralized and the doomed.

So long as the heavy karma of the desecration of the Holy of Holies remains as a sinister albatross casting its nefarious shadow over the stormy sea of *samsara*, so long will the Kalki function be a paramount concern and inescapable facet of the mysterious work of all Divine Incarnations, spiritual reformers and World-Teachers, who are both light-bringers and fire-bringers. Yet, awful and execrable as this profanation of the sacred is in its impact upon the astral light, Nature's 'infinite negative', it is not the entire truth about the contemporary epoch or indeed about any century or civilization, including even the Atlanteans five million years ago. If, as ancient Sages hint, the real difficulty extends back about eleven million years ago, there still reverberates in the *Akasha* the golden vibration inscribed in the 'antique heart' of mankind over eighteen and three-quarter million years ago, in the dawn of human self-consciousness.

Five thousand years ago, on the eve of the commencement of Kali Yuga, Lord Krishna struck the sacred keynote of *svadharma, nishkama karma* and *jnana yajna,* of self-chosen duty, disinterestedness and wisdom-sacrifice, in an age of accelerated change, wherein there is *varnashankara,* the confounding of all the social orders. There is no reliable clue in the world of externals to the inward journey and spiritual growth of the human soul; there are no institutionalized guarantees for human progress whilst Karma-Nemesis does its necessary work of destruction of old modes and codes in the midst of universal social chaos and psychological disintegration. This was also the deeper meaning of the Mahabharata War, wherein to look behind to the annals of historical memory was to be lost.

Now, more than ever before, as courageous individuals gain the clarity of philosophic insight (*vijnana*), rooted in deep meditation (*dhyana*), they can reconnect themselves with the primordial vibration of the Mysteries, "the eternal thought in the eternal mind", the authentic source of the abundant creative potentials in themselves and in all Humanity. The irreversible tidal wave of the present historical moment will sweep away many of the relics and monuments of moribund traditions and the monstrosities of modern, so-called civilization. Divine Wisdom is immensely vaster and much more ancient than can remotely be sensed within the perspectives of present-day humanity. It is inconceivable that anything can stand in its way, that even the accumulated sins and crimes of fallen sorcerers and their myriad vampirized victims can resist the mighty onrush of the New Cycle, which, working mostly in the realm of *Akasha*, acts as a potent alchemical solvent in the astral light and in the inmost consciousness of hosts of souls, both embodied and awaiting incarnation. It would be a costly illusion for any group of monads, for any religious sect or social coterie, for any nation or continent, to transfer its own sense of doom to the whole of the human family, or to imagine that any power on earth can resist the rising tide of the progressive enlightenment of the humanity of the future.

In a very real sense, all human souls are always exiles in this world, but this is poignantly true of so many in a time of colossal karmic precipitation, widespread sifting between the 'quick' and the 'dead', and the dawning of a new global civilization, rising phoenix-like out of the ashes of the older orders. Porphyry's profound words on self-exile have a peculiar appositeness to our age:

> We resemble those who enter into or depart from a foreign region, not only because we are banished from our intimate associates, but in consequence of dwelling in a foreign land, we are filled with barbaric passions, and manners and legal institutes, and to all these have a great propensity. Hence, he who wishes to return to his proper kindred and associates should not only with alacrity begin the journey, but, in order that he may be properly received, should meditate upon how he may divest himself of everything of a foreign nature which he has assumed, and should recall to his memory such things as he has forgotten, and without which he cannot

be admitted by his kindred and friends. After the same manner, also, it is necessary, if we intend to return to things which are truly our own, that we should divest ourselves of everything of a mortal nature which we have assumed, together with an adhering affection towards it, and which is the cause of our descent; and that we should excite our recollection of that blessed and eternal essence, and should hasten our return to the nature which is without colour and without quality, earnestly endeavouring to accomplish two things: one, that we may cast aside everything material and mortal; but the other, that we may properly return, and be again conversant with our true kindred, ascending to them in a way contrary to that in which we descended hither.

All the outward forms and manifestations that constitute the clutter and outworn furniture of physical existence and psychic fantasy obscure and suppress the spiritual intuitions and intimations in human consciousness. By becoming caught up in the region of ephemera, true inward perception, Buddhic awareness, is blocked. Authentic depth perception is a perception of essences, a laser-like clarity in regard to primary causes, a bringing together of the centripetal, concentrated ideation of *Manas* and the centrifugal, expansive empathy of *Buddhi,* until there emerges a radiation of *Buddhi-Manas-Taijasi* which can flow downward and illumine the brain, the heart and the sensorium. As a human being learns to live progressively and increasingly in the divine egg of *Sat-Chit-Ananda,* a deeper sense of being, of ideation and eros, is awakened in all the vestures; there is a clarification and purification of all perception, and the awakening of an eye for essentials, the eye of transcendental synthesis fusing the standpoints of eternity and time. To light up the promise and possibility of such a radical reorientation of human consciousness in as many souls as possible is the awesome task and the noble prospect of the Aquarian Age, as well as the humanity and civilization of the future.

There is no learning, no acquisition of Divine Wisdom, no

spiritual enlightenment without a life consecrated by sacrifice. The true mark of the authentic member of the Army of the Voice is instantaneous responsiveness to the law of sacrifice, without reservation, let or hindrance. The willingness to suffer and sacrifice separates the Lords of Light from the legions of darkness, the right-hand Path from the left-hand, the Sage from the sorcerer. We would all gladly suffer for those we love, like the mother for her newborn child. Much more is needed: to suffer for all others means to become a compassionator and creator of beneficent ideation, a theurgist who breathes benevolently and effortlessly radiates streams of light-energy and selfless love. A familiar line from Edwin Markham's poem is often cited: "But Love and I had the wit to win", pointing to the vital connection between readiness and ripeness, love and wisdom, rooted in self-knowledge. Wisdom penetrates and clarifies; love expands and includes, it does not expel and exclude. As more and more sensitive souls come to grasp fully that everyone is an integral part of a whole, which is now enacting a decisive drama that involves the Mysteries and cannot be understood in less than cosmic terms, profound currents of magnetic love-energy may be released that can act in and through many an unseen actor on the contemporary scene.

Mahavishnu, whilst reclining upon Shesha (the cosmic serpent eating its tail, floating upon the crystalline waters of Aditi-*Akasha*, noumenal Space in Eternal Duration), emanates this entire cosmos and yet remains in supreme repose. Kalahansa is the Swan of Everlasting and also the Eternal Saviour in the realm of Time. The Purna Avatar is fully incarnated on earth as the decisive determinant of the destinies of all monads, in the context of all karmic sum-totals displayed on the cosmic computer of *Mahat*, and yet he stands apart from all manifestation, with a mere *amsha* or fragment of his divine splendour ensouling the fullest possible embodiment in the materials of contemporary humanity. As Kalki, he is the manvantaric harbinger of the Day of Reckoning for each and all; as Maitreya, he is linked with Hermes-Mercury as the Avatar of unconditional love and universal mercy.

As the anonymous author of a French work on the Tarot and

Hermeticism prophesied in 1967:

> Since it is a question of the work of the fusion of revelation and knowledge, of spirituality and intellectuality, it is a matter throughout of the fusion of the Avatar principle with the Buddha principle. . . . On the historical plane the Maitreya Buddha and the Kalki Avatar will be one. . . . He will not merely teach the way of salvation, but he will advance the course of this way; he will not be solely a witness of the divine and spiritual world, but he will make human beings into authentic witnesses of this world; he will not simply explain the profound meaning of revelation, but he will bring human beings themselves to attain to the illuminating experience of revelation . . . bringing human beings to first-hand experience of the source itself of all revelation ever received from above by mankind, as also of all essential truth ever conceived by mankind. . . .
>
> It will not be popularity and general acclaim which will characterize the work of the Avatar, but rather the fusion of spirituality and intellectuality, no matter whether this pleases or not. . . . He will be the guide in the transformation of potential schizophrenic madness into the wisdom of the harmony of the two worlds and of their experience. He will be the example and living model of realization of the Arcanum which occupies us. . . . Logic becomes transformed into formal logic — passing through the intermediary stage of 'organic logic' — into 'moral logic'. . . . His intellectuality — his 'horse's head' — will be moved solely by revelation from above. Like the horse, it will be directed by the Rider. This is the Arcanum at work on the historical plane.

Almost forty years earlier, in his *Heart of Asia*, Nicholas Roerich, the mystic painter and explorer, conveyed the esoteric teaching he received in trans-Himalayan monasteries concerning the work of Kalki Maitreya before the end of the twentieth century:

> It is predicted that the manifestations of Maitreya shall come after the wars. But the final war shall be for the cause of the True Teaching. But each one rising up against Shamballa shall be stricken in all his works. And the waves shall wash away his dwellings. And even a dog shall not answer to his call. No clouds but lightning shall he see on the final night. And the fiery messenger shall rise up on pillars of Light. The Teaching indicates that each warrior of Shamballa shall be named the Invincible. The Lord Himself hastens. And his banner is already above the mountains. Thy Pasture shall reach the Promised Land. When thou tendest thy flocks, dost thou not hear the voices of the stones? These are the toilers of Maitreya, who make ready for thee the treasures.

OM

APPENDICES

APPENDICES

PSYCHIC AND NOETIC ACTION

. . . I made man just and right,
Sufficient to have stood, though free to fall,
Such I created all th' ethereal powers
And spirits, both them who stood and them who fail'd,
Truly, they stood who stood, and fell who fell . . .

MILTON

. . . The assumption that the mind is a real being, *which can be acted upon by the brain, and which can act on the body through the brain, is the only one compatible with all the facts of experience.*

Elements of Physiological Psychology   GEORGE T. LADD

I

A new influence, a breath, a sound — "as of a rushing mighty wind" — has suddenly swept over a few Theosophical heads. An idea, vague at first, grew in time into a very definite form, and now seems to be working very busily in the minds of some of our members. It is this: if we would make converts the few ex-occult teachings, which are destined to see the light of publicity, should be made, henceforward, *more subservient to, if not entirely at one with modern science.* It is urged that the so-called *esoteric** (or *late* esoteric) cosmogony, anthropology, ethnology, geology — psychology and, foremost of all, metaphysics — having been adapted into making obeisance to modern (hence *materialistic)* thought, should never henceforth be allowed to contradict (not *openly,* at all events) "scientific philosophy." The latter, we suppose, means the fundamental and

---

* We say "so-called," because nothing of what has been given out publicly or in print can any longer be termed esoteric.

accepted views of the great German schools, or of Mr. Herbert Spencer and some other English stars of lesser magnitude; and not only these, but also the deductions that may be drawn from them by their more or less instructed disciples.

A large undertaking this, truly; and one, moreover, in perfect conformity with the policy of the medieval Casuists, who distorted truth and even suppressed it, if it clashed with *divine Revelation*. Useless to say that we decline the compromise. It is quite possible — nay, probable and almost unavoidable — that "the mistakes made" in the rendering of such abstruse metaphysical tenets as those contained in Eastern Occultism, should be "frequent and often important." But then all such have to be traced back to the interpreters, not to the system itself. They have to be corrected on the authority of the same Doctrine, checked by the teachings grown on the rich and steady soil of *Gupta Vidya*, not by the speculations that blossom forth today, to die tomorrow — on the shifting sands of modern scientific guesswork, especially in all that relates to psychology and mental phenomena. Holding to our motto, "There is no religion higher than truth," we refuse most decidedly to pander to *physical* science. Yet, we may say this: If the so-called *exact* sciences limited their activity only to the physical realm of nature; if they concerned themselves strictly with surgery, chemistry — up to its legitimate boundaries, and with physiology — so far as the latter relates to the structure of our corporeal frame, then the Occultists would be the first to seek help in modern sciences, however many their blunders and mistakes. But once that over-stepping material Nature the physiologists of the modern "animalistic"* school pretend to

---

* "Animalism" is quite an appropriate word to use (whoever invented it) as a contrast to Mr. Tylor's term "animism", which he applied to all the *"Lower* Races" of mankind who believe the soul a distinct entity. He finds that the words *psyche, pneuma, animus, spiritus,* etc., all belong to the same cycle of superstition in "the lower stages of culture," Professor A. Bain dubbing all these distinctions, moreover, as a "plurality of souls" and a "double materialism". This is the more curious as the learned author of "Mind and Body" speaks as disparagingly of Darwin's "materialism" in *Zoonomia,* wherein the founder of modern Evolution defines the word *idea* as "contracting a motion, or configuration of the fibres which constitute the immediate organ of Sense" ("Mind and Body," p. 190, Note).

meddle with, and deliver *ex cathedra dicta* on, the higher functions and phenomena of the mind, saying that a careful analysis brings them to a firm conviction that no more than the animal is man a *free-agent,* far less a responsible one — then the Occultist has a far greater right than the average modern "Idealist" to protest. And the Occultist asserts that no materialist — a prejudiced and one-sided witness at best — can claim any authority in the question of mental physiology, or that which is now called by him the *physiology of the soul.* No such noun can be applied to the word "soul," unless, indeed, by soul only the lower, *psychic* mind is meant, or that which develops in man (proportionally with the perfection of his brain) into *intellect,* and in the animal into a *higher* instinct. But since the great Charles Darwin taught that "our *ideas* are animal motions of the organ of sense" everything becomes possible to the modern physiologist.

Thus, to the great distress of our scientifically inclined Fellows, it is once more *Lucifer's* duty to show how far we are at loggerheads with exact science, or shall we say, how far the conclusions of that science are drifting away from truth and fact. By "science" we mean, of course, the majority of the men of science; the best minority, we are happy to say, is on our side, at least as far as free-will in man and the immateriality of the mind are concerned. The study of the "Physiology" of the Soul, of the Will in man and of his *higher Consciousness* from the standpoint of genius and its manifesting faculties, can never be summarized into a system of general ideas represented by brief formulae; no more than the *psychology of material nature* can have its manifold mysteries solved by the mere analysis of its physical phenomena. *There is no special organ of will,* any more than there is a *physical basis* for the activities of self-consciousness.

> If the question is pressed as to the *physical basis* for the activities of self-consciousness, no answer can be given or suggested. . . . From its very nature, that marvelous verifying *actus* of mind in which it recognizes the states as its own, can have no analogous or

corresponding material substratum. It is impossible to specify any physiological process representing this unifying *actus*; it is even impossible to imagine how the description of any such process could be brought into intelligible relation with this unique mental power.[*]

Thus, the whole conclave of psycho-physiologists may be challenged to correctly define Consciousness, and they are sure to fail, because Self-consciousness belongs alone to man and proceeds from the SELF, the higher Manas. Only, whereas the psychic element (or *Kama-manas*)[†] is common to both the animal and the human being — the far higher degree of its development in the latter resting merely on the greater perfection and sensitiveness of his cerebral cells — no physiologist, not even the cleverest, will ever be able to solve the mystery of the human mind, in its highest spiritual manifestation, or in its dual aspect of the *psychic* and the *noetic* (or the *manasic*),[‡] or even to comprehend the intricacies of the former on the purely material plane — unless he knows something of, and is prepared to admit the presence of this dual element. This means that he would have to admit a lower (animal), and a higher (or divine) mind in man, or what is known in Occultism as the "personal" and the "impersonal" *Egos*. For, between the *psychic* and the *noetic*, between the *Personality* and the *Individuality*, there exists the same abyss as between a "Jack the Ripper," and a holy Buddha. Unless the physiologist accepts all this, we say, he will ever be led into a quagmire. We intend to prove it.

As all know, the great majority of our learned "Didymi" reject the idea of free-will. Now this question is a problem that has

[*] *Physiological Psychology*, etc., p. 545, by George T. Ladd, Professor of Philosophy in Yale University.

[†] Or what the Kabalists call *Nephesh*, the "breath of life."

[‡] The Sanskrit word *Manas* (Mind) is used by us in preference to the Greek *Nous* (noetic) because the latter word having been so imperfectly understood in philosophy, suggests no definite meaning.

occupied the minds of thinkers for ages; every school of thought having taken it up in turn and left it as far from solution as ever. And yet, placed as it is in the foremost ranks of philosophical quandaries, the modern "psycho-physiologists" claim in the coolest and most bumptious way to have cut the Gordian knot for ever. For them the feeling of personal free agency is an error, an illusion, "the collective hallucination of mankind." This conviction starts from the principle that no mental activity is possible without a brain, and that there can be no brain without a body. As the latter is, moreover, subject to the general laws of a material world where all is based on necessity, and where there is no spontaneity, our modern psycho-physiologist has *nolens volens* to repudiate any self-spontaneity in human action. Here we have, for instance, a Lausanne professor of physiology, A. A. Herzen, to whom the claim of free-will in man appears as the most *unscientific* absurdity. Says this oracle: —

> In the boundless physical and chemical laboratory that surrounds man, organic life represents quite an unimportant group of phenomena; and amongst the latter, the place occupied by life having reached to the stage of consciousness, is so minute that it is absurd to exclude man from the sphere of action of a general law, in order to allow in him the existence of a subjective spontaneity or a free will standing outside of that law.
> *Psychophysiologie Générale*

For the Occultist who knows the difference between the psychic and the noetic elements in man, this is pure trash, notwithstanding its sound scientific basis. For when the author puts the question — if psychic phenomena do not represent the results of an action of a molecular character whither then does motion disappear after reaching the sensory centers? — we answer that we never denied the fact. But what has this to do with a free will? That every phenomenon in the visible Universe has its genesis in motion, is an old axiom in Occultism; nor do we doubt that the psycho-physiologist would place himself at logger-heads with the whole conclave of exact scientists were he to allow the idea that at a given moment a whole series of physical phenomena may disappear in the vacuum. Therefore, when the author of the work cited maintains that the said force does not disappear upon reaching the highest nervous centers, but that it is forthwith transformed into another series, *viz.*, that of psychic manifestations, into thought, feeling, and consciousness, just as this same psychic force when applied to produce some work of a physical (*e.g.*, muscular) character gets transformed into the latter — Occultism supports him, for it is the first to say that all psychic activity, from its lowest to its highest manifestations is "nothing but — motion."

Yes; it *is* MOTION; but not all "molecular" motion, as the writer means us to infer. Motion as the GREAT BREATH (*vide* "Secret Doctrine," vol. i, *sub voce*) — *ergo* "*sound*" *at the same time* — is the substratum of Kosmic-Motion. It is beginningless and endless, the one *eternal life*, the basis and genesis of the subjective and the objective universe; for LIFE (or Be-ness) is the *fons et origo* of existence or being. But molecular motion is the lowest and most material of its finite manifestations. And if the general law of the conservation of energy leads modern science to the conclusion that psychic activity only represents a special form of motion, this same law, guiding the Occultists, leads them also to the same conviction — and to something else besides, which psycho-physiology leaves entirely out of all consideration. If the latter has discovered only in this century that psychic (we say even spiritual) action is subject to the same general and immutable laws of motion as any other phenomenon manifested in the objective realm of Kosmos, and that in both the organic and the *inorganic* (?) worlds every manifestation, whether conscious or un-conscious, represents but the result of a collectivity of causes, then in Occult philosophy this represents merely the A,B,C, of its science. "All the world is the *Swara; Swara* is the Spirit itself" — the ONE LIFE or *motion*, say the old books of Hindu Occult philosophy. "The proper translation of the word *Swara* is the *current of the life wave*," says the author of "Nature's Finer

Forces,"* and he goes on to explain: —

> It is that wavy motion which is the cause of the evolution of cosmic undifferentiated matter into the differentiated universe. . . . From whence does this motion come? This motion is the spirit itself. The word *atma* (universal soul) used in the book *(vide infra)*, itself carries the idea of eternal motion, coming as it does from the root, AT, or eternal motion; and it may be significantly remarked, that the root AT is connected with, is in fact simply another form of, the roots AH, breath, and AS, being. All these roots have for their origin the sound produced by the breath of animals (living beings). . . . The primeval current of the life-wave is then the same which assumes in man the form of inspiratory and expiratory motion of the lungs, and this is the all-pervading source of the evolution and involution of the universe. . . .

So much about *motion* and the "conservation of energy" from old *books on magic* written and taught ages before the birth of inductive and exact modern science. For what does the latter say more than these books in speaking, for instance, about animal *mechanism*, when it says: —

> From the visible atom to the celestial body lost in space, *everything is subject to motion* . . . kept at a definite

* *The Theosophist*, Feb. 1888, p. 275, by Rama Prasad, President of the *Meerut Theosophical Society*. As the Occult book cited by him says: "It is the *swara* that has given form to the *first accumulations of the divisions* of the universe; the *Swara* causes evolution and involution; the *Swara* is God, or more properly the *Great Power* itself *(Maheswara)*. The *Swara* is the manifestation of the impression on matter of that power which in man is known to us as *the power which knows itself* (mental and *psychic* consciousness). It is to be understood that the action of this power never ceases. . . . It is unchangeable existence" — and this is the "Motion" of the Scientists and the universal *Breath of Life* of the Occultists.

distance one from the other, in proportion to the
motion which animates them, the molecules present
constant relations, which they lose only by the
addition or the subtraction of a certain quantity of
motion.*

But Occultism says more than this. While making of motion
on *the material plane* and of the conservation of energy, two
fundamental laws, or rather two aspects of the same omnipresent
law — *Swara*, it denies point blank that these have anything to
do with the *free will* of man which belongs to quite a different
plane. The author of "Psychophysiologie Générale," treating of
his *discovery* that psychic action is but motion, and the result of a
collectivity causes — remarks that as it is so, there cannot be any
further discussion upon spontaneity — in the sense of any native
internal proneness created by the human organism; and adds that
the above puts an end to all claim for *free will!* The Occultist denies
the conclusion. The actual fact of man's psychic (we say *manasic*
or noetic) *individuality* is a sufficient warrant against the
assumption; for in the case of this conclusion being correct, or
being indeed, as the author expresses it, the *collective hallucination
of the whole mankind throughout the ages*, there would be an end
also to psychic individuality.

Now by "psychic" individuality we mean that self-determining
power which enables man to override circumstances. Place half a
dozen animals of the same species under the same circumstances,
and their actions while not identical, will be closely similar; place
half a dozen men under the same circumstances and their actions
will be as different as their characters, *i.e.*, their *psychic individuality*.

But if instead of "psychic" we call it the higher Self-conscious
Will, then having been shown by the science of psycho-physiology
itself that *will has no special organ*, how will the materialists connect
it with "molecular" motion at all? As Professor George T. Ladd says:

* *"Animal Mechanism," a treatise on terrestrial and aerial locomotion.* By E.J.
Marey, Professor at the College of France, and Member of the Academy of
Medicine.

The phenomena of human consciousness must be regarded as activities of some other form of Real Being than the moving molecules of the brain. They require a subject or ground which is in its nature unlike the phosphorized fats of the central masses, the aggregated nerve-fibres of nerve-cells of the cerebral cortex. This Real Being thus manifested immediately to itself in the phenomena of consciousness, and indirectly to others through the bodily changes, is the *Mind (manas).* To it the mental phenomena are to be attributed as showing what it *is* by what it *does.* The so-called mental 'faculties' are only the *modes of the behavior* in consciousness of this real being. We actually find, by the only method available, that this real being called Mind believes in certain perpetually recurring modes: therefore, we attribute to it certain faculties. . . . Mental faculties are not entities that have an existence of themselves. . . . They are the modes of the behavior in consciousness of the mind. And the very nature of the classifying acts which lead to their being distinguished, is explicable only upon the assumption that *a Real being called Mind exists,* and is to be distinguished from the real beings known as the physical molecules of the brain's nervous mass."*

And having shown that we have to regard consciousness *as a unit* (another occult proposition) the author adds:

We conclude, then, from the previous considerations: *the subject of all the states of consciousness is a real unit-being, called Mind; which is of non-material nature, and acts and develops according to laws of its own, but is specially correlated with certain material molecules and masses forming the substance of the Brain."†*

---

* The higher *manas* or "Ego" (*Kshetrajna*) is the "Silent Spectator", and the voluntary "sacrificial victim": the lower manas, its representative — a tyrannical despot, truly.

† *Elements of Physiological Psychology.* A treatise of the activities and nature of the mind, from the Physical and Experimental Point of View, pp. 606 and 613.

This "Mind" is *manas,* or rather its lower reflection, which whenever it disconnects itself, for the time being, with *kama,* becomes the guide of the highest mental faculties, and is the organ of the free will in physical man. Therefore, this assumption of the newest psychophysiology is uncalled for, and the apparent impossibility of reconciling the existence of free will with the law of the conservation of energy is — a pure fallacy. This was well shown in the "Scientific Letters" of "Elpay" in a criticism of the work. But to prove it finally and set the whole question definitely at rest, does not even require so high an interference (high for us, at any rate) as the Occult laws, but simply a little common sense. Let us analyse the question dispassionately.

It is postulated by one man, presumably a scientist, that because "psychic action is found subject to the general and immutable laws of motion, there is, therefore, *no free will in man."* The "analytical method of exact sciences" has demonstrated it, and materialistic scientists have decreed to "pass the resolution" that the fact should be so accepted by their followers. But there are other and far greater scientists who thought differently. For instance, Sir William Lawrence, the eminent surgeon, declared in his lectures* that: —

> The philosophical doctrine of the soul, and its separate existence, has nothing to do with this physiological question, but rests on a species of proof altogether different. These sublime dogmas could never have been brought to light by the labours of the anatomist and physiologist. An immaterial and spiritual being could not have been discovered amid the blood and filth of the dissecting room.

Now, let us examine on the testimony of the materialist how this universal solvent called the "analytical method" is applied in

---

* W. Lawrence, *Lectures on Comparative Anatomy, Physiology, Zoology, and the Natural History of Man,* 8 vo. London, 1848, p. 6.

this special case. The author of the *Psychophysiologie* decomposes psychic activity into its compound elements, traces them back to motion, and, failing to find in them the slightest trace of free will or spontaneity, jumps at the conclusion that the latter have no existence in general; nor are they to be found in that psychic activity which he has just decomposed. "Are not the fallacy and error of such an unscientific proceeding self-evident?" asks his critic; and then argues very correctly that: —

> At this rate, and starting from the standpoint of this analytical method, one would have an equal right to deny every phenomenon in nature from first to last. For, do not sound and light, heat and electricity, like all other chemical processes, once decomposed into their respective elements, lead the experimenter back to the same motion, wherein All the peculiarities of the given elements disappear leaving behind them only 'the vibrations of molecules'? But does it necessarily follow that for all that, heat, light, electricity — are but illusions instead of the actual manifestations of the peculiarities of our real world? Such peculiarities are not, of course, to be found in compound elements, simply because we cannot expect that a part should contain, from first to last, the properties of the whole. What should we say of a chemist, who, having decomposed water into its compounds, hydrogen and oxygen, without finding in them the special characteristics of water, would maintain that such did not exist at all nor could they be found in water? What of an antiquary who upon examining distributed type and finding no sense in every separate letter, should assert that there was no such thing as sense to be found in any printed document? And does not the author of "Psychophysiology" act just in this way when he denies the existence of free-will or self-spontaneity in man, on the grounds that this distinctive faculty of the highest psychic activity is absent from those compounded elements which he has analysed?

Most undeniably no separate piece of brick, of wood, or iron, each of which has once been a part of a building now in ruins, can be expected to preserve the smallest trace of the architecture of that building — in the hands of the chemist, at any rate; though it would in those of a *psychometer,* a faculty by the bye, which demonstrates far more powerfully the law of the conservation of energy than any physical science does, and shows it acting as much in the subjective or psychic worlds as on the objective and material planes. The genesis of sound, on this plane, has to be traced back to the same motion, and the same correlation of forces is at play during the phenomenon as in the case of every other manifestation. Shall the physicist, then, who decomposes sound into its compound element of vibrations and fails to find in them any harmony or special melody, deny the existence of the latter? And does not this prove that the analytical method having to deal exclusively with the elements, and nothing to do with their *combinations,* leads the physicist to talks very glibly about motion, vibration, and what not, and to make him entirely lose sight of the *harmony produced by certain combinations of that motion* or the "harmony of vibrations"? Criticism, then, is right in accusing Materialistic psycho-physiology of neglecting these all-important distinctions; in maintaining that if a careful observation of facts is a duty in the simplest physical phenomena, how much more should it be so when applied to such complex and important questions as psychic force and faculties? And yet in most cases all such essential differences are overlooked, and the analytical method is applied in a most arbitrary and prejudiced way. What wonder, then, if, in carrying back psychic action to its basic elements of motion, the psycho-physiologist depriving it during the process of all its essential characteristics, should destroy it; and having destroyed it, it only stands to reason that he is unable to find that which exists in it no longer. He forgets, in short, or rather purposely ignores the fact, that though, like all other phenomena on the material plane, psychic manifestations *must* be related in their final analysis to the world of vibration (*"sound" being the substratum of universal Akasa*), yet, in their origin, they belong *to a different and a higher World of* HARMONY. Elpay has a few severe sentences against the assumptions of those he calls "physico-biologists" which are worthy of note.

> Unconscious of their error, the psycho-physiologists identify the compound elements of psychic activity with that activity itself: hence the conclusion from the standpoint of the analytical method, that the highest, distinctive specialty of the human soul — free-will, spontaneity — is an illusion, and no psychic reality. But as we have just shown, such identification not only has nothing in common with exact science, but is simply impermissible, as it clashes with all the fundamental laws of logic, in consequence of which all these so-called physico-biological deductions emanating from the said identification vanish into thin air. Thus to trace psychic action primarily to motion, means in no way to prove the 'illusion of free-will.' And, as in the case of water, whose specific qualities cannot be deprived of their reality although they are not to be found in its compound gases, so with regard to the specific property of psychic action: its spontaneity cannot be refused to psychic reality, though this property is not contained in those finite elements into which the psycho-physiologist dismembers the activity in question under his mental scalpel.

This method is "a distinctive feature of modern science in its endeavor to satisfy inquiry into the *nature* of the objects of its investigation by a detailed description of their *development*," says G. T. Ladd. And the author of *The Elements of Physiological Psychology* adds: —

> The universal process of 'Becoming' has been almost personified and deified so as to make it the true ground of all finite and concrete existence. . . . The attempt is made to refer all the so-called development

of the mind to the evolution of the substance of the brain, under purely physical and mechanical causes. This attempt, then, denies that any real unit-being called the Mind needs to be assumed as undergoing a process of development according to laws of its own. . . . On the other hand, all attempts to account for the orderly increase in complexity and comprehensiveness of the mental phenomena by tracing the physical evolution of the brain are wholly unsatisfactory to many minds. We have no hesitation in classing ourselves among this number. Those facts of experience which show a correspondence in the order of the development of the body and the mind, and even a certain necessary dependence of the latter upon the former, are, of course, to be admitted; but they are equally compatible with another view of the mind's development. This other view has the additional advantages that it makes room for many other facts of experience which are very difficult of reconciliation with any materialistic theory. On the whole, *the history of each individual's experiences is such as requires the assumption that a real unit-being (a Mind) is undergoing a process of development, in relation to the changing condition or evolution of the brain, and yet in accordance with a nature and laws of its own* (p. 616).

How closely this last "assumption" of science approaches the teachings of the Occult philosophy will be shown in Part II of this article. Meanwhile, we may close with an answer to the latest materialistic fallacy, which may be summarized in a few words. As every psychic action has for its substratum the nervous elements whose existence it postulates, and outside which it cannot act; as the activity of the nervous elements are only molecular motion, there is therefore no need to invent a special and psychic Force for the explanation of our brain work. *Free Will would force* Science to postulate an invisible *Free-Willer,* a creator of that special Force.

We agree: "not the slightest need," of a creator of "that special" or any other Force. Nor has any one ever claimed such an absurdity. But between *creating* and *guiding*, there is a difference, and the latter implies in no way any creation of the energy of motion, or, indeed, of any special energy. *Psychic* mind (in contradistinction to manasic or noetic mind) only transforms this energy of the "unit-being" according to "a nature and laws of its own" — to use Ladd's felicitous expression. The "unit-being" creates nothing but only causes a natural correlation in accordance with both the physical laws and *laws of its own;* having to use the Force, it guides its direction, choosing the paths along which it will proceed, and stimulating it to action. And, as its activity is *sui generis* and independent, it carries this energy from this world of disharmony into its own sphere of harmony. Were it not *independent* it could not do so. As it is, the freedom of man's will is beyond doubt or cavil. Therefore, as already observed, there no question of creation, but simply of *guidance.* Because the sailor at the wheel does not create the steam in the engine, shall we say that he does not direct the vessel?

And, because we refuse to accept the fallacies of some psycho-physiologists as the *last* word of science, do we furnish thereby a new proof that free-will is an *hallucination?* We deride the *animalistic* idea. How far more scientific and logical, besides being as poetical as it is grand, is the teaching in the *Kathopanishad,* which, in a beautiful and descriptive metaphor, says that: "The senses are the horses, body is the chariot, mind *(kama-manas)* is the reins, and intellect *(or free-will)* the charioteer." Verily, there is more exact science in the less important of the *Upanishads,* composed thousands of years ago, than in all the materialistic ravings of modern "physico-biology" and "psychophysiology" put together!

II

. . . The knowledge of the past, present, and future, is embodied in Kshetrajna (the 'Self ').

Occult Axioms

Having explained in what particulars, and why, as Occultists, we disagree with materialistic physiological psychology, we may now proceed to point out the difference between psychic and noetic mental functions, the noetic not being recognized by official science.

Moreover, we, Theosophists, understand the terms "psychic" and "psychism" somewhat differently from the average public, science, and even theology, the latter giving it a significance which both science and Theosophy reject, and the public in general remaining with a very hazy conception of what is really meant by the terms. For many, there is little, if any, difference between "psychic" and "psychological", both words relating in some way to the *human* soul. Some modern metaphysicians have wisely agreed to disconnect the word Mind (*pneuma*) from Soul (*psyche*), the one being the rational, spiritual part, the other — *psyche* — the living principle in man, the breath that *animates* him (from *anima*, soul). Yet, if this is so, how in this case refuse a soul to *animals?* These are, no less than man, informed with the same principle of sentient life, the *nephesh* of the 2nd chapter of *Genesis*. The Soul is by no means the Mind, nor can an idiot, bereft of the latter, be called a "soul-less" being. To describe, as the physiologists do, the human Soul in its relations to senses and appetites, desires and passions, common to man and the brute, and then endow it with God-like intellect, with spiritual and rational faculties which can take their source but in a *super-sensible* world — is to throw for ever the veil of an impenetrable mystery over the subject. Yet in modern science, "psychology" and "psychism" relate only to conditions of the nervous system, mental phenomena being traced solely to molecular action. The higher *noetic* character of the Mind-Principle is entirely ignored, and even rejected, as a "superstition" by both physiologists and psychologists. Psychology, in fact, has become a synonym in many cases for the science of psychiatry. Therefore, students of Theosophy being compelled to differ from all these, have adopted the doctrine that underlies the time-honored philosophies of the East. What it is, may be found further on.

To better understand the foregoing arguments and those which follow, the reader is asked to turn to the editorial in the September *Lucifer* ("The Dual Aspect of Wisdom," p. 3), and acquaint himself with the *double aspect* of that which is termed by St. James in his Third Epistle at once — the *devilish, terrestrial* wisdom and the "wisdom from above." In another editorial, "Kosmic Mind" (April, 1890), it is also stated, that the ancient Hindus endowed every cell in the human body with consciousness, giving each the name of a God or Goddess. Speaking of atoms in the name of science and philosophy, Professor Ladd calls them in his work *"supersensible beings."* Occultism regards every atom* as an "independent entity" and every cell as a "conscious unit." It explains that no sooner do such atoms group to form cells, than the latter become endowed with consciousness, each of its own kind, and with *free-will to act* within the limits of law. Nor are we entirely deprived of scientific evidence for such statements as the two above-named editorials well prove. More than one learned physiologist of the golden minority, in our own day, moreover, is rapidly coming to the conviction, that memory has no seat, no special organ of its own in the human brain, but that it has *seats* in every organ of the body.

"No good ground exists for speaking of any special organ, or seat of memory," writes Professor G. T. Ladd. "Every organ, indeed, every area, and every limit of the nervous system has its own memory" (p. 553 loc. cit.).

The seat of memory, then, is assuredly neither here nor there, but everywhere throughout the human body. To locate its organ in the brain is to limit and dwarf the Universal Mind and its

---

* One of the names of Brahmā is *anu* or "atom".

countless Rays (the *Manasaputra*) which inform every rational mortal. As we write for Theosophists, first of all, we care little for the psychophobian prejudices of the Materialists who may read this and sniff contemptuously at the mention of "Universal Mind" and the Higher *noetic* souls of men. But, what *is* memory, we ask. "Both presentation of sense and image of memory, are transitory phases of consciousness," we are answered. But what is Consciousness itself? — we ask again. "*We cannot define Consciousness,*" Professor Ladd tells us.* Thus, that which we are asked to do by physiological psychology is, to content ourselves with converting the various states of Consciousness by other people's private and unverifiable hypotheses; and this, on "questions of cerebral physiology *where experts and novices are alike ignorant,*" to use the pointed remark of the said author. Hypothesis for hypothesis, then, we may as well hold to the teachings of our Seers, as to the conjectures of those who deny both such Seers and their wisdom. The more so, as we are told by the same honest man of science, that "if metaphysics and ethics cannot properly dictate their facts and conclusions to the science of physiological psychology... in turn this science cannot properly dictate to metaphysics and ethics the conclusions which they shall draw from facts of Consciousness, by giving out its myths and fables in the garb of well ascertained history of the cerebral processes" (p. 544).

Now, since the metaphysics of Occult physiology and psychology postulate within mortal man an immortal entity, "divine mind," or *Nous*, whose pale and too often distorted reflection is that which we call "Mind" and intellect in men — virtually an entity apart from the former during the period of incarnation — we say that the two sources of "memory" are in these two "principles." These two we distinguish as the Higher *Manas* (Mind or Ego), and the *Kama-Manas, i.e.,* the rational, but earthly or physical intellect of man, incased in, and bound by, matter, therefore subject to the influence of the latter: the all-

---

* *Elements of Physiological Psychology*

conscious SELF, that which reincarnates periodically — verily the WORD made flesh! — and which is always the same, while its reflected "Double," changing with every new incarnation and personality, is, therefore, conscious but for a life-period. The latter "principle" is the *Lower* Self, or that, which manifesting through our *organic* system, acting on this plane of illusion, imagines itself the *Ego Sum,* and thus falls into what Buddhist philosophy brands as the "heresy of separateness." The former, we term INDIVIDUALITY, the latter *Personality.* From the first proceeds all the *noetic* element, from the second, the *psychic, i.e.,* "terrestrial wisdom" at best, as it is influenced by all the chaotic stimuli of the human or rather *animal passions* of the living body.

The "Higher EGO" cannot act directly on the body, as its consciousness belongs to quite another plane and planes of ideation: the "lower" *Self* does: and its action and behavior *depend on its free will and choice* as to whether it will gravitate more towards its parent ("the Father in Heaven") or the "animal" which it informs, the man of flesh. The "Higher Ego," as part of the essence of the UNIVERSAL MIND, is unconditionally omniscient on its own plane, and only potentially so in our terrestrial sphere, as it has to act solely through its *alter ego* — the Personal Self. Now, although the former is the vehicle of all knowledge of the past, the present, and the future, and although it is from this fountain-head that its "double" catches occasional glimpses of that which is beyond the senses of man, and transmits them to certain brain cells (unknown to science in their function), thus making of man a *Seer,* a soothsayer, and a prophet; yet the memory of bygone events — especially of the earth earthy — has its seat in the Personal Ego alone. No memory of a purely daily-life function, of a physical, egotistical, or of a lower mental nature — such as, *e.g.,* eating and drinking, enjoying personal sensual pleasures, transacting business to the detriment of one's neighbor, etc., etc., has ought to do with the "Higher" Mind or EGO. Nor has it any direct dealings on this physical plane with either our brain or our heart — for these two are the organs of a power higher than the *Personality* — but only with our passional organs, such as the liver, the stomach, the spleen, etc. Thus it only stands to reason that the memory of such-like events must be first awakened in that organ which was the first to induce the action remembered afterwards, and conveyed it to our "sense-thought," which is entirely *distinct from the "supersensuous" thought.* It is only the higher forms of the latter, the *superconscious* mental experience, that can correlate with the cerebral and cardiac centres. The memories of physical and *selfish* (or personal) deeds, on the other hand, together with the mental experiences of a terrestrial nature, and of earthly biological functions, can, of necessity, only be correlated with the molecular constitution of various *Kamic* organs, and the "dynamic associations" of the elements of the nervous system in each particular organ.

Therefore, when Professor Ladd, after showing that every element of the nervous system has a memory of its own, adds: — "This view belongs to the very essence of every theory which considers conscious mental reproduction as only one form or phase of the biological fact of organic memory" — he must include among such theories the Occult teaching. For no Occultist could express such teaching more correctly than the Professor, who says, in winding up his argument: "We might properly speak, then, of the memory of the end-organ of vision or of hearing, of the memory of the spinal cord and of the different so-called 'centres' of reflex action belonging to the chords of the memory of the medulla oblongata, the cerebellum, etc." This is the essence of Occult teaching — even in the Tantra works. Indeed, every organ in our body *has its own memory*. For if it is endowed with a consciousness "of its own kind," every cell must of necessity have also a memory of its own kind, as likewise its own *psychic* and *noetic* action. Responding to the touch of both a physical and a *metaphysical* Force,* the impulse given by the *psychic* (or psycho-molecular) Force will act from *without* within; while that of the *noetic* (shall we call it Spiritual-dynamical?) Force works *from*

---

* We fondly trust this very *unscientific* term will throw no "Animalist" into hysterics *beyond* recovery.

within without. For, as our body is the covering of the inner "principles," soul, mind, life, etc., so the molecule or the cell is the body in which dwell its "principles," the (to our sense and comprehension) immaterial atoms which compose that cell. The cell's activity and behavior are determined by its being propelled either inwardly or outwardly, by the noetic or the psychic Force, the former having no relation to the *physical* cells proper. Therefore, while the latter act under the unavoidable law of the conservation and correlation of physical energy, the atoms — being psycho-spiritual, not *physical units — act under laws of their own,* just as Professor Ladd's "Unit-Being," which is our "Mind-Ego," does, in his very philosophical and scientific hypothesis. Every human organ and each cell in the latter has a key-board of its own, like that of a piano, only that it registers and emits sensations instead of sounds. Every key contains the potentiality of good or bad, of producing harmony or disharmony. This depends on the impulse given and the combinations produced; on the force of the touch of the artist at work, a "double-faced Unity," indeed. And it is the action of this or the other "Face" of the Unity that determines the nature and the dynamic character of the manifested phenomena as a resulting action, and this whether they be physical or mental. For the whole of man is guided by this double-faced Entity. If the impulse comes from the "Wisdom above," the Force applied being noetic or spiritual, the results will be actions worthy of the divine propeller; if from the "terrestrial, devilish wisdom" (psychic power), man's activities will be selfish, based solely on the exigencies of his physical, hence animal, nature. The above may sound to the average reader as pure nonsense; but every Theosophist must understand when told that there are *Manasic* as well as *Kamic* organs in him, although the cells of his body answer to both physical and spiritual impulses.

Verily that body, so desecrated by Materialism and man himself, is the temple of the Holy Grail, the *Adytum* of the grandest, nay, of all, the mysteries of nature in our solar universe. That body is an Æolian harp, chorded with two sets of strings, one made of pure silver, the other of catgut. When the breath from the divine Fiat brushes softly over the former, man becomes like unto *his* God — but the other set feels it not. It needs the breeze of a strong terrestrial wind, impregnated with animal effluvia, to set its animal chords vibrating. It is the function of the physical, lower mind to act upon the physical organs and their cells; but, it is the higher mind *alone* which can influence the atoms interacting in those cells, which interaction is alone capable of exciting the brain, *via the spinal "centre" cord*, to a mental representation of spiritual ideas far beyond any objects on this material plane. The phenomena of divine consciousness have to be regarded as activities of our mind on another and a higher plane, working through something less substantial than the moving molecules of the brain. They cannot be explained as the simple resultant of the cerebral physiological process, as indeed the latter only condition them or give them a final form for purposes of concrete manifestation. Occultism teaches that the liver and the spleen-cells are the most subservient to the action of our "personal" mind, the heart being the organ *par excellence* through which the "Higher" Ego acts — through the Lower Self.

Nor can the visions or memory of purely terrestrial events be transmitted directly through the mental perceptions of the brain — the direct recipient of the impressions of the heart. All such recollections have to be first stimulated by and awakened in the organs which were the originators, as already stated, of the various causes that led to the results, or, the direct recipients and participators of the latter. In other words, if what is called "association of *ideas*" has much to do with the awakening of memory, the mutual interaction and consistent inter-relation between the personal "Mind-Entity" and the organ of the human body have far more so. A hungry stomach evokes the vision of a past banquet, because its action is reflected and repeated in the *personal mind.* But even before the memory of the personal Self radiates the vision from the tablets wherein are stored the experiences of one's daily life — even to the minutest details — the memory of the stomach has already evoked the same. And so with all the organs of the body. It is they which originate according to their animal needs and desires the electro-vital sparks that illuminate the field of consciousness in the Lower Ego; and it is these sparks which in their turn awaken to function the reminiscences in it. The whole human body is, as said, a vast sounding board, in which each cell bears a long record of impressions connected with its parent organ, and each cell has a memory and a consciousness of its kind, or call it instinct if you will. These impressions are, according to the nature of the organ, physical, psychic, or mental, as they relate to this or another plane. They may be called "states of consciousness" only for the want of a better expression — as there are states of instinctual, mental, and purely abstract, or spiritual consciousness. If we trace all such "psychic" actions to brain-work, it is only because in that mansion called the human body the brain is the front-door, and the only one which opens out into Space. All the others are inner doors, openings in the private building, through which travel incessantly the transmitting agents of memory and sensation. The clearness, the vividness, and intensity of these depend on the state of health and the organic soundness of the transmitters. But their reality, in the sense of trueness or correctness, is due to the "principle" they originate from, and the preponderance in the Lower *Manas* of the *noetic* or of the phrenic (*"Kamic,"* terrestrial) element.

For, as Occultism teaches, if the Higher Mind-Entity — the permanent and the immortal — is of the divine homogeneous essence of "Alaya-Akasa,"* or Mahat, — its reflection, the Personal Mind, is, as a temporary "Principle," of the Substance of the Astral Light. As a pure ray of the "Son of the Universal Mind," it could perform no functions in the body, and would remain powerless over the turbulent organs of Matter. Thus, while its inner constitution is Manasic, its "body," or rather functioning essence, is heterogeneous, and leavened with the Astral Light, the lowest element of Ether. It is a part of the mission of the Manasic Ray, to get gradually rid of the blind, deceptive element which, though it makes of it an active spiritual entity on this plane, still brings it

---

* Another name for the Universal Mind.

into so close contact with matter as to entirely becloud its divine nature and stultify its intuitions.

This leads us to see the difference between the pure noetic and the terrestrial psychic visions of seership and mediumship. The former can be obtained by one of two means; *(a)* on the condition of paralysing at will the *memory* and the instinctual, independent action of all the material organs and even cells in the body of flesh, an act which, once that the light of the Higher Ego has consumed and subjected for ever the passional nature of the personal, lower Ego, is easy, but requires an adept; and *(b)* of being a reincarnation of one, who, in a previous birth, had attained through extreme purity of life and efforts in the right direction almost to a *Yogi*-state of holiness and saintship. There is also a third possibility of reaching in mystic visions the plane of the higher Manas; but it is only occasional and does not depend on the will of the Seer, but on the extreme weakness and exhaustion of the material body through illness and suffering. The Seeress of Prevorst was an instance of the latter case; and Jacob Boehme of our second category. In all other cases of abnormal seership, of so-called clairaudience, clairvoyance and trances, it is simply — *mediumship.*

Now what is a medium? The term medium, when not applied simply to things and objects, is supposed to be a person through whom the action of another person or being is either manifested or transmitted. Spiritualists believing in communications with disembodied spirits, and that these can manifest through, or impress sensitiveness to transmit "messages" from them, regard mediumship as a blessing and a great privilege. We Theosophists, on the other hand, who do not believe in the "communion of spirits" as Spiritualists do, regard the gift as one of the most dangerous of abnormal nervous diseases. A medium is simply one in whose personal Ego, or terrestrial mind, *(psyche)*, the percentage of "astral" light so preponderates as to impregnate with it their whole physical constitution. Every organ and cell thereby is attuned, so to speak, and subjected to an enormous and abnormal tension. The mind is ever on the plane of, and quite immersed in, that deceptive light whose *soul* is divine, but whose body — the light waves on the lower planes, infernal; for they are but the black and disfigured reflections of the earth's memories. The untrained eye of the poor sensitive cannot pierce the dark mist, the dense fog of the terrestrial emanations, to see beyond in the radiant field of the eternal truths. His vision is out of focus. His senses, accustomed from his birth, like those of a native of the London slums, to stench and filth, to the unnatural distortions of sights and images tossed on the kaleidoscopic waves of the astral plane — are unable to discern the true from the false. And thus, the pale soulless corpses moving in the trackless fields of "Kama loka," appear to him the living images of the "dear departed" ones; the broken echoes of once human voices, passing through his mind, suggest to him well co-ordinated phrases, which he repeats, in ignorance that their final form and polish were received in the innermost depths of his own brain-factory. And hence the sight and the hearing of that which if seen in its true nature would have struck the medium's heart cold with horror, now fills him with a sense of beatitude and confidence. He really believes that the immeasurable vistas displayed before him are the real spiritual world, the abode of the blessed disembodied angels.

We describe the broad main features and facts of medium-ship, there being no room in such an article for exceptional cases. We maintain — having unfortunately passed at one period of life *personally* through such experiences — that on the whole, mediumship is most dangerous; and *psychic* experiences when accepted indiscriminately lead only to honestly deceiving others, because the medium is the first self-deceived victim. Moreover, a too close association with the "Old Terrestrial Serpent" is infectious. The odic and magnetic currents of the Astral Light often incite to murder, drunkenness, immorality, and, as Eliphas Lévi expresses it, the not altogether pure natures "can be driven headlong by the blind forces set in motion in the *Light*" — by the errors and sins imposed on its waves.

And this is how the great Mage of the XIXth century corroborates the foregoing when speaking of the Astral Light: —

We have said that to acquire magical power, two things are necessary: to disengage the will from all servitude, and to exercise it in control.

The sovereign will (of the adept) is represented in our symbols by the woman who crushes the serpent's head, and by the resplendent angel who represses the dragon, and holds him under his foot and spear; the great magical agent, the dual current of light, the living and astral *fire* of the earth, has been represented in the ancient theogonies by the serpent with the head of a bull, a ram, or a dog. It is the double serpent of the *caduceus*, it is the Old Serpent of *Genesis*, but it is also the *brazen serpent of Moses* entwined around the *tau*, that is to say, the generative *lingha*. It is also the goat of the witch-sabbath, and the Baphomet of the Templars; it is the *Hylé* of the Gnostics; it is the double-tailed serpent which forms the legs of the solar cock of the Abraxas: finally, it is the Devil of M. Eudes de Mirville. But in very fact it is the blind force which souls (*i.e.*, the lower *Manas* or Nephesh) have to conquer to liberate themselves from the bonds of the earth; for if their will does not free 'them from this *fatal attraction*, they will be absorbed in the current by the force which has produced them, and *will return to the central and eternal fire*.'*

The "central and eternal fire" is that disintegrating Force, that gradually consumes and burns out the *Kama-rupa*, or "personality," in the Kama-loka, whither it goes after death. And verily, the Mediums are attracted by the astral light, it is the direct cause of their personal "souls" being absorbed "by the force which has produced" their terrestrial elements. And, therefore, as the same Occultist tells us: —

All the magical operations consist in freeing one's self from the coils of the Ancient Serpent; then to place

---

* *Dogme et Rituel de la Haute Magie,* quoted in *Isis Unveiled.*

the foot on its head, and lead it according to the operator's will. 'I will give unto thee,' says the Serpent, in the Gospel myth, 'all the kingdoms of the earth, if thou wilt fall down and worship me.' The initiated should reply to him, 'I will not fall down, but thou shalt crouch at my feet; thou wilt give me nothing, but I will make use of thee and take whatever I wish. For *I am thy Lord and Master!*'

And as such, the *Personal Ego,* becoming at one with its divine parent, shares in the immortality of the latter. Otherwise . . .

Enough, however. Blessed is he who has acquainted himself with the dual powers at work in the ASTRAL Light; thrice blessed he who has learned to discern the *Noetic* from the *Psychic* action of the "Double-Faced" God in him, and who knows the potency of his own Spirit — or "Soul Dynamics."

Lucifer, October & November 1890   H. P. BLAVATSKY

THE ETERNAL PILGRIM AND THE VOICE DIVINE*

*Come unto Me, all ye that labor and are heavy-laden,
and I will give you rest.*

THE VOICE: Blistered are thy feet, O Pilgrim! parched are thy lips with thirst! From what far-off climes hailest thou? Who put this heavy burden on thy stooping back? Across what trackless deserts hast thou come?

THE ETERNAL PILGRIM: Whosoever the Voice is, be thou my guide and light. So tired am I of my long journeyings that I have well-nigh forgotten whence I set out. I have roamed over regions of whose features I have now no more recollection than the cuckoo has of its eggs. Times many and unnumbered have I passed with such heavy burdens, but none relieved me of my load. There is darkness behind, there is darkness before and darkness all around. Wherever I turn Despair stares me in the face. When I think that help is at hand, and when I eagerly ply my steps forward, I find that my path, though a little changed, is always one of thorns, woes and fatigue. O Voice! Know that I am the twin brother of sorrow; but there is something within my innermost WITHIN that oft-times tells me that I am the heir of Eternal Bliss. Oh! For one to lead me to my HOME!

THE VOICE: Fear not, pain-wedded wanderer, thou art not the only one who is in search of rest. Millions upon millions like thee are panting to reach their goal, now driven here, now whirled away there, lost and bewildered, not knowing where to go, upon

---

* This spiritual dialogue from an unspecified source was sent by W.Q. Judge as a gift to the Lodges of the Theosophical Society. The essay was dedicated "to all on the PATH in token of love".

what road to walk. Heir to the Kingdom of Heaven, rightfully and in the long run thine own, thy purity of mind and thy strong will shall carry thee safely on. There was a time when thou livedst with, nay thou wast the *Nitya Vastu*, that Thing-in-itself, unclogged with the many garments of flesh which thou hast now and again worn. Thy separation has cost thee dear, and thy habits, the consequence of thy past deeds, which have made of thee an exotic in strange lands, stand an insuperable barrier in thy upward path.

THE PILGRIM: Teach me then, O Voice, my WHAT, my WHENCE, and my WHITHER.

THE VOICE: Just say what is there before thine eyes.

THE PILGRIM: I see nothing but bare Space.

THE VOICE: Ah! That is thy illusion; it is not bare; it is the ever-living source from which flow forth the fleeting forms which, times out of mind, thou hast borne with thee. A time there was when thou wast one with it. So long wast thou safe. This is the soil divine from which spring forth trees big with sweet and bitter fruits. When the trees wither and are no more, new ones from the seeds let fall on the eager soil are but a question of time.

Turn thine eyes from north to south, from east to west, from the zenith to the nadir, from the sun to the stars, thou shalt see nothing but forms, name-bearing forms dotting what thou callest empty space all over. It is the body of the unknown X which human mind can never discern. Above Time, its greatest attribute is that IT is Attributeless. I cannot name it otherwise than as expressing what each one has to realize within himself in his moments of deepest calm, in his self-oblivious *Svanubhava* when the outward world sleeping gives full play to the Divinity within. It is the nirvanic sleep when the Limited merges into the Unlimited. In those moments, O Pilgrim, when thou enterest within thyself, then hast thou a chance of knowing who thou art.

Cease thy wanderings after the unreal, free thy mind from those baits which fetter thy Divine Self to finite things, shut thine ears to those siren voices which drag thy mind in a thousand and one directions, and thou shalt be one with HIM who fills all space. Thou halt a body, so weak and so easily preyed upon by what mortals call PAST, PRESENT, and FUTURE, a body which varies with Time, ever subject to appearance and disappearance, to Birth and Death, whilst this Space is the ever-living robe of the Eternal Self. This boundless, seeming Void is saturated with thought, invisible, ineffable wingless phoenixes, ever dying, ever living, of waves upon waves of Humanity that have come and gone from the Mayavic theater of Life.

Not a man came to sentient life, but asked himself for what purpose did he exist. From the beginning of Kosmos — if ever it had a beginning — man has been attempting to solve this knotty, all-absorbing, many-sided question. Its solutions seem as many and as numerous as there are human heads. The riddle is betwixt Man and his God, the Fathomable and the Unfathomable; the former, with intellect beyond arithmetic, unable to grasp the One mighty INTELLECT, which thrills through the stone, the tree, the insect, the animal, the man, the whole solar system, nay, through each and every atom so minute as the billionth part of an inch. *Anor aniyan Mahato mahiyan* [smaller than the small, greater than the great]. Like the lotus which opens its great rose-colored petals on the tank to the golden sun at dawn, the minutest fraction of the Divine unbosoms itself to the First Integer. The Hidden and the Manifest, the Noumenon and the Phenomenon, are but the two aspects of THE ONE. During the long process of purification which each undergoes in cyclic eons of TIME, the Divine AIM is unbroken Progress.

So long as the Phoenix Thought is used for noble super-sensuous purposes, the spark of the Undying Flame wafteth thee through the mazes of Life, subtle or gross. Every Progress has a beginning, its uninterrupted march upwards and onwards, the spiritual Himavats towering upon Himavats of still higher, purer altitudes, till Thought itself at such grand heights is dazed, and poor man holds his temples in his hands, shuts his eyes and banishes speech from his mouth, to reach the Final Goal. To scale such heights is then thy mission. How can the Boundless be made to rest in the Confined? As the whole Universe has evolved from a single Parabrahmic Point into its present vastness, even so its present vastness will, after its period of activity, be involved to the same mysterious Point. Man, the phenomenal phase of the Universal Mind, has within him the essence of the same Point which is able to expand likewise to systems as many as the grains of sand on the seashore.

To man, to Humanity in the aggregate, is given the all-reaching privilege, by retreating within his inmost INMOST, to offer his homage to the steady Light, and by his most transcendental soaring and constant meditation, to become that Light. To know the Truth is to become Truth. O *man*, divine man, lord of the great and small, the real and unreal, the eternal and the fleeting, thou temple of Jerusalem, thou hast depths of consciousness within thee. Here I do not mean the man of flesh who carries like a snail his house of clay upon him, but the Real Man: a Power, a Glory, a Divinity, aye, the truest Truth, the Supreme Self itself. It only needs that the blind of Ignorance should be removed to be one with Nature and Nature's laws. A hooded hawk is powerless to seize its prey.

The human mind ever longs to know its origin and its destiny. In this arduous struggle man sometimes launches into the Sea of Despair, and for this very reason, Oh Wanderer of Worlds, benevolent hearts throbbing in sympathy with human miseries, once their own, are ever ready to extend fellowship to those who are anxious to advance. They are MERCY itself on earth. What shall I say of these MAN-GODS who, filled with universal love, are ever on the lookout to help weary pilgrims like thee, who, tired of the trials of life, the heritage of the Body, are ready to take a leap into the abysmal pit of Darkness and Death?

That there is the perishable man and that therefore there must be his counterpart, the imperishable *Atman*, can never be doubted, inasmuch as Nature, the most faithful and unswerving observer of Harmony in her Laws, has evolved all beings in pairs.

Look, there are the dualities of light and darkness, happiness and woe, good and evil. In this twofold rule of Nature, that which is good, that which is light, everything in short that has not the taint of the transitory upon it, will guide your barque of life safe into the haven of Nirvana.

MOKSHA is cessation from Birth and Death. It is the ladder which leads man heavenwards. Hence thy efforts should be devoted rather towards shaking off the trammels of the Flesh with a view to idealize the Real, realize the Ideal, than towards any motive which is founded in selfishness.

Do not question the existence of Life until thou art in the folds of thy Spirit. For regaining Self-consciousness, as the part and parcel of the Great Perfection; for the grander appreciation of the THAT; for thy higher advancement — perfection wanting to be perfected; for the realization of *Sat-Chit-Ananda* in the envelope of matter, as a demonstrable proof that Spirit has the power of endowing the former with its divinities; but above all for the Bliss of that Eternal Knowledge which no words and no thoughts can fitly describe, hast thou chosen this self-imposed task of Life. This MYSTERY is a "Beyond all Beyonds."

Each one's mission is best known to himself. He is the be-all and end-all of his own experiences, and is guided by his own Karmic foretastes. The one drawback to the regeneration of the world is that each man, having his own Eternal God within himself, goes to another to ask where his God is. How can the mirror reflect itself? He whose God is not within him cannot find HIM *without* him. In the Karmic picture gallery there are philosophers and fools, the godly and the godless, a very medley of contraries, but, with self-reawakening, a diapason of the most seraphic music fills the vaults of heaven.

The eternal *Sat* is ever the same in all phases of manifestation; good and bad alike to it are the same; each is so to his own weal or woe. Said the great Vaivasvata to Sri Shankaracharya — The sun withholds not his rays from the Holy Ganga, nor from the foul cesspool. Bear in mind suffering purifies, as gold is refined by fire.

"Know, will, dare, and keep silence," for Silence is Heaven's own Virtue.

THE PILGRIM: Voice Divine, teach me how to reach the POINT whence radiates the Kosmic effulgence, the one White Ray of variegated colors.

THE VOICE: First and foremost, if thou art ready to revisit thy native shores, hear what the Voice of the Silence constantly whispers in the ears of man: "Empty thyself, and I will fill thee."

Earthbound and spellbound, thou Temple of the Invisible Deity, thy mortal walls are under the battering-ram of Time. The Shrine, the heirloom of Mother Earth who reared it, is truly hers, but the God within — who art thyself — is above and beyond decay. Therefore if thou wishest to be one with the Universal, cast off thy limitations that thy coming Progress may be commensurate with thy present living. With thoughts of the world thou art finite, above them thou art infinite.

The Supreme Point cannot be conceived by what mortals call Thought, the product of the brain loom. But to you is given the Key which unlocks the Gates of Gold; it is not found in mere cerebration. To make myself clear to thee, I shall call that which is beyond thought — the key which ushers man into the regions of the One Pure Life — META-THOUGHT, or Intuition. Free from man-made blendings, it gives an insight into that supernatural knowledge which is the Quintessence of Life. To gain this META-THOUGHT thy mind should be wholly free from those ties which bind it to the Earth. When the Ocean, attracted by the hot Sun, becomes transformed into humid atmosphere, it leaves its saltness behind and sails to the skies in buoyant clouds. Shorn of thy earthly impediments, O Wanderer, thy flight will be both easy and speedy. When thy mind ceases to get its nourishment from the outer world, *Samadhi* is at hand, and this state is accomplished when thy senses, whose slave so long thou wast, are in their turn brought under subjection.

The next point upon which thou cannot be warned too

much is the paramount importance to Humanity of that Law of Nature which no aspirant can safely overrule, and which requires him to be at one with her methods in all his longings after the Divine. This means that thou, in wishing thy Bliss, must not only do thy utmost for the removal of that mass of evil under which thy brethren groan, but must ever study without the least thought of self to seek their salvation in thine own. A real Savior thou, if but a single vice fall to thy moral sword.

This Space which thou seest as vacant has within it that Ineffable Principle of the ONE which is to Space what that is to thy physical eye. This inscrutable Principle is Space permeable through Space. It is both Within-without and Without-within. From time immemorial man's thoughts have been brooding in Space. Humanities after humanities have come and gone, and they have left therein undying shadows of their thoughts.

In this Earth man is a Farmer sowing seeds of his deeds after the plough of his Thoughts. Pilgrim in mortal coils, know that Thought is the beginning and end of this world. Tenuous as Tenuity itself, this wielder of the fate of worlds and their contents gives birth to all Upadhis that ever spring up in the passing phantasmagoria. Therefore, to free thy back from its heavy load, O thou self in search of Self, try to attune thy thoughts with Nature's Harmony. TO THINK IS TO BE. Thou art now in sad trouble because of the mad crowd of past thoughts that deceived thee like so many mirages on the horizon of Maya. Misdirected thoughts and a thirst after things as perishable as the hands that made them are at the bottom of all thy irksome pilgrimages.

Thought is the father of deeds; hence, every day, every hour, every minute, need I say every second, sit thou in judgment over thyself, and concentrate thy mind upon the one POINT from which thou hast wandered. By evil thoughts came the troubles of Life. With the Single Thought of the Highest their end is near at hand. If the mind is to be retrieved from its wild and aimless rush after short-lived emotions, it should be made to center upon its Pivot, by a process akin to that by which a schoolboy flying his kite winds up its thread upon the reel.

The owner of a mind absorbed in useless passing concerns of the world finds himself in the same state as the wealthy man who, having staked his all in great speculations, is unable, notwithstanding all his riches, to meet an unexpected heavy call. Like the burning-glass, all the movements of the mind should be focused upon the Primordial Law, so that its love of vanities may be consumed by its spiritual rays.

The Universe from one end to the other is a chained whole, and the Waves of Life which pulsate through its length and breadth from the Sun, the central source of mortal life, the faint reflection of the spiritual one which energizes it, are fraught with psychic power, the vehicle of human thoughts which do good or evil as the varied circumstances of daily existence may dictate, producing births which end in death as soon as their mission of Life is accomplished.

Now imagine such waves circling round each Upadhi, and think that Life as such is from the Eternal Fount whence proceeds everything that to mankind is Absolute Truth and Absolute Knowledge, which latter means that CALM SERENE in which the knower, knowledge, and the thing known are unified. This is *Tripti*, the supreme Bliss gained by the seeker after many processes of purification.

If the slightest effort is made by one Upadhi either in thought, word or deed to upset its neighbor — for the all are in ONE, and the ONE is in all — the whole organization of the Man is thrown into confusion. Thus, if the Upadhi A runs counter to the psychic and life-giving currents undulating round H, the necessary result is that these two will not only throw themselves into confusion, but even the union prevailing between the intermediate ones will be equally disturbed.

Nature and Nature's laws sweep along with these Upadhis in Space, and when one of them aids her original Design, which is constant upward Progress — on psychic and spiritual planes — it is no longer subject to limitations, and feels the Essence within, which had first quickened it into Life. On this basis, those great readers of Nature, Souls sublime, who in past lives have gained all human experiences and make it their felicity to work for men, as undying oracles of God, proclaim the everlasting truth that the mischief done to one is mischief done to all, and that the good of one is the good of all. A stone thrown into still water with its ever increasing circles will show thee the force of what I mean. The Wise Ones of Earth send forth their good wishes to Humanity by their all-powerful magnetic will. Beware of evil thoughts, for their record is everlasting in Heaven. No man while pursuing his own way of life should by his thoughts do wrong to another. A fervent thought sent round for the well-being of Humanity is worth more than kingdoms. The Great Souls rule the world by their holy thoughts and aspirations, while the edicts of kings are in force but for a day. In all ages and in all climes the keynote of the Sage has been, "Do good and be good."

Remember that the Universe exists in two planes, the physical and the spiritual, both being strictly complementary; the one to the other, as fire produces heat, and heat, fire. What tongue can tell the smallest Secret of Physical Nature? There is Soul in a blade of grass, and even in a dumb stone. Listen to what Pushpadanta, a Hindu poet, said of God, in his *Mahimna* [*stava*]:

> For one Brahmā Kalpa, Saraswati (Minerva) sang thy glories, O Shambhu, God of Heavens, on a paper of the size of the Earth's dimensions, with the pen of Kalpataru dipped in the ink-horn of the Ocean, and yet but a few of thy virtues were done justice to.

The immovable rock, the ever-flowing river, the busy ant are the dwelling adyta of the Holy One. Everything that exists has its own spiritual hiding-place to which it retires day and night. If this be the physical view of the Universe, its spiritual is past human speech. Here the Universe is an equilateral triangle, one of its sides being Universal Justice, another Universal Love, joined together with the basic line of Universal Harmony. The equipoise of the scales of Nature's justice makes manifest the millionth part of a grain of unrighteousness. Far from having favorites, her loyal sons are chastened with the same impartiality as those who disobey her. Justice is the axis upon which unceasingly turns the spiritual Universe, governed by the sun benign of Universal Love.

In Justice, Love, and Harmony there is a Life that knows no Death; in injustice, hatred and discord there is that which induces Death in Life. There is no sin greater than that of ill will towards others, and no virtue higher than good will towards all. These are the watchwords of Salvation by self, a Salvation which says as long as there is a single soul writhing in pain, the wise man's mind shall strive to relieve it.

True Salvation is collective, it is never for one. It covers humanity with its blissful folds. The Salvation which is for one is but an inn, a momentary resting-place before the journey is resumed. Pray therefore, nay, ardently desire that thou mayest rise with all, and that Humanity's rise may be thine own.

Aspire! Aspire! Aspire! Thy message is Peace, and as such I give it thee. So help thee thy Higher Self. Thine be the Deathless Joy. AUM.

Blessed be Humanity, doubly blessed those who bless it by noble deeds. SHANTI.

*   *   *

As the Voice ceased, the heavy load fell from the Pilgrim's back to the ground. A sudden flash, and the Eternal Pilgrim knew that the Voice he had heard had come to him from the HOLY OF THE HOLIES of his own Heart — the lotus throne of Narayana, wherein Being, Thought, and Bliss are indissolubly one.

WILLIAM Q. JUDGE

PILGRIMAGE IN INDIA*

A FRAGMENTARY TALE

Twice before have I seen these silent temples standing by the rolling flood of sacred Ganges. They have not changed, but in me what changes have occurred! And yet that cannot be, for the I changeth not, but only the veil wrapped about, is either torn away or more closely and thickly folded round to the disguising of the reality. It is now seven months since I began to use the privilege of listening to Kunala. Each time before, that I came to see him, implacable fate drove me back. It was Karma, the just law, which compels when we would not, that prevented me. Had I faltered then and returned to the life then even so far in the past, my fate in this incarnation would have been sealed — and he would have said nothing. Why? Happy was I that I knew the silence would have not indicated in him any loss of interest in my welfare, but only that the same Karma prevented interference.

Very soon after first seeing him I felt that he was not what he appeared exteriorly to be. Then the feeling grew into a belief within a short time so strong that four or five times I thought of throwing myself at his feet and begging him to reveal himself to me. But I thought that was useless, as I knew that I was quite

---

*In the month of December he arrived at Benares, on what he hoped would be his last pilgrimage. As much as I am able to decipher of this curious manuscript, written in a mixture of Tamil — the South Indian language — with Marathi, which, as you know, is entirely dissimilar, shows that he had made many pilgrimages to India's sacred places. . . . As he must long ago have risen above the flowery chains of even the Vedas, we cannot really tell for what reason these journeys were made. Although, as you know, I have long had possession of these papers, the time had not until now seemed ripe to give them out. He had, when I received them, already long passed away from these busy scenes to those far busier, and now I give you liberty to print the fragmentary tale.

W.Q. Judge

impure and could not be trusted with that secret. If I remained silent I thought that he would confide to me whenever he found me worthy of it. I thought he must be some great Hindu Adept who had assumed that illusory form. But there this difficulty arose, for I knew that he received letters from various relatives in different parts, and this would compel him to practice the illusion all over the globe, for some of those relatives were in other countries, where he had been too.

Various explanations suggested themselves to me. I was right in my original conception of Kunala that he is some great Indian Adept. . . .

I always thought of retiring from this world and giving myself up to devotion. To Kunala I often expressed this intention, so that I might study this philosophy, which alone can make man happy in this world. But then he usually asked me what I would do *there* alone? . . . If I really wanted to gain my object I should have to work in the form in and through which I had met so many good men and himself also, and when the Higher Ones, whom I dare not mention by any other names, were satisfied with me they themselves would call me away from the busy world and teach me in private. . . . He said once to me: "One of our Brothers has told me that as you are so much after me I had better tell you once for all that I have no right to give you any information about them, but if you go on asking Hindus you meet what they know about the matter you might hear of them, and one of those Higher Ones may perhaps throw himself in your way without your knowing him, and will tell you what you should do.". . .

I then asked one or two of my own countrymen, and one of them said he had seen two or three such men, but that they were not quite what he thought to be 'Raja Yogis.' He also said he had heard of a man who had appeared several times in Benares, but that nobody knew where he lived. . . . I never lost the firm confidence that Adepts do live in India and can still be found among us. No doubt too there are a few in other countries, else why had Kunala been to them. . . .

The next day came X to see us. He never speaks of himself,

but as 'this body.' He told me that he had first been in the body of a Fakir, who, upon having his hand disabled by a shot he received while he passed the fortress of Bhurtpore, had to change his body and choose another, the one he was now in. A child of about seven years of age was dying at that time, and so, before the complete physical death, this Fakir had entered the body and afterwards used it as his own. He is, therefore, doubly not what he seems to be. As a Fakir he had studied Yoga science for 65 years, but that study having been arrested at the time he was disabled, leaving him unequal to the task he had to perform, he had to choose this other one. In his present body he is 53 years, and consequently the inner X is 118 years old. In the night I heard him talking with Kunala, and found that each had the same Guru, who himself is a very great Adept, whose age is 300 years, although in appearance he seems to be only 40. He will in a few centuries enter the body of a *Kshatriya*, and do some great deeds for India, but the time had not yet come.

Yesterday I went with Kunala to look at the vast and curious temples left here by our forefathers. Some are in ruins, and others only showing the waste of time. What a difference between my appreciation of these buildings now, with Kunala to point out meanings I never saw, and that which I had when I saw them upon my first pilgrimage, made so many years ago with my father. . . . *

Yesterday, just after sunset, while Kunala and X were talking, Kunala suddenly seemed to go into an unusual condition, and about ten minutes afterwards a large quantity of malwa flowers fell upon us from the ceiling. . . .

---

* It is apparent that he had often been before to the holy city of Benares, and had merely seen it as a place of pilgrimage for the religious. Then, in his sight, those famous temples were only temples. But now he found, under the instruction of Kunala, that every really ancient building in the whole collection had been constructed with the view to putting into imperishable stone, the symbols of a very ancient religion. . . . There were many Adepts then well known to the rulers and to the people. They were not yet driven by inexorable fate to places remote from civilization, but lived in the temples, and while not holding temporal power, they exercised a moral sway which was far greater than any sovereignty of earth. . . . These Adepts, some of them here and there

When I was there and after I had finished my work and was preparing to return here, a wandering Fakir met me and asked if he could find from me the proper road to Karli. I directed him, and he then put to me some questions that looked as if he knew what had been my business; he also had a very significant look upon his face, and several of his questions were apparently directed to getting me to tell him a few things Kunala had told me just before leaving Benares with an injunction of secrecy. The questions did not on the face show that, but were in the nature of inquiries regarding such matters, that if I had not been careful, I would have violated the injunction. He then left me saying: "You do not know me but we may see each other." I got back last night and saw only X, to whom I related the incident with the Fakir, and he said that, "it was none other than Kunala himself using that Fakir's body who had said those things, and if you were to see that Fakir again he would not remember you and would not be able to repeat his questions, as he was for the time being taken possession of for the purpose, by Kunala, who often performs such things." I then asked him if in that case Kunala had really entered the Fakir's body, as I have a strange reluctance toward asking Kunala such questions, and X replied that if I meant to ask if he had really and in fact entered the Fakir's person, the answer was no, but that if I meant to ask if Kunala had overcome that Fakir's senses, substituting his own, the answer was, yes: leaving me to make my own conclusions.

I was fortunate enough yesterday to be shown the process pursued in either entering an empty body, or in using one which has its own occupant. I found that in both cases it was the same, and the information was also conveyed that a Bhut goes through

being really themselves Maha Rajas, caused the temples to be built in forms, and with such symbolic ornaments, that future races might decipher doctrines from them. . . . The ideas underneath symbols do not alter, no matter what might be the language, and symbols are clear immortally, because they are founded in nature itself. In respect to this part of the matter, Kunala informed him that the language used then was not Sanscrit, but a far older one now altogether unknown in the world. W. Q. J.

just the same road in taking command of the body or senses of those unfortunate women of my country who sometimes are possessed by them. And the Bhut also sometimes gets into possession of a part only of the obsessed person's body, such as an arm or a hand, and this they do by influencing that part of the brain that has relation with that arm or hand; in the same way with the tongue and other organs of speech. With any person but Kunala I would not have allowed my own body to be made use of for the experiment. But I felt perfectly safe, that he would not only let me in again, but also that he would not permit any stranger, man or gandharva, to come in after him. . . .

The feeling was that I had suddenly stepped out into freedom. He was beside me and at first I thought he had but begun. But he directed me to look, and there on the mat I saw my body, apparently unconscious. As I looked, the body of myself opened its eyes and arose. It was then superior to me, for Kunala's informing power moved and directed it. It seemed to even speak to me. Around it, attracted to it by those magnetic influences, wavered and moved astral shapes, that vainly tried to whisper in the ear or to enter by the same road. In vain! They seemed to be pressed away by the air or surroundings of Kunala. Turning to look at him, and expecting to see him in a state of samadhi, he was smiling as if nothing, or at the very most, but a part, of his power had been taken away. Another instant and I was again myself, the mat felt cool to my touch, the bhuts were gone, and Kunala bade me rise.

He has told me to go to the mountains of — — where — — and — — usually live, and that even if I were not to see anybody the first time, the magnetized air in which they live would do me much good. They do not generally stop in one place, but always shift from one place to another. They, however, all meet together on certain days of the year in a certain place near Bhadrinath, in the northern part of India. He reminded me that as India's sons are becoming more and more wicked, those adepts have gradually been retiring more and more toward the north, to the Himalaya mountains. Of what a great consequence is it for me to be always with Kunala. And now X tells me this same thing that I have always felt. . . . All my hopes and future plans are therefore centred in him. My journey therefore to upcountry has done me one good, that of strengthening my belief, which is the chief foundation on which the grand structure is to be built.

As I was walking past the end of Ramalinga's compound holding a small lamp of European make, and while there was no wind, the light there several times fell low. I could not account for it. Both Kunala and X were far away. But in another moment, the light suddenly went out altogether, and as I stopped, the voice of revered Kunala, who I supposed was many miles away, spoke to me, and I found him standing there. For one hour we talked; and he gave me good advice, although I had not asked it — thus it is always that when I go fearlessly forward and ask for nothing I get help at an actual critical moment — he then blessed me and went away. Nor could I dare to look in what direction. In that conversation, I spoke of the light going down and wanted an explanation, but he said I had nothing to do with it.

I then said I wanted to know, as I could explain it in two ways, *viz*: 1st, that he did it himself, or 2d, that someone else did it for him. He replied, that even if it were done by somebody else, *no Yogi will do a thing unless he sees the desire in another Yogi's mind.* The significance of this drove out of my mind all wish to know *who* did it, whether himself, or an elemental or another person, for it is of more importance for me to know even a part of the laws governing such a thing, than it is to know who puts those laws into operation. Even some blind concatenation of nature might put such natural forces in effect in accordance with the same laws, so that a knowledge that nature did it would be no knowledge of any consequence.

I have always felt and still feel strongly that I have already once studied this sacred philosophy with Kunala. . . . This must have been a fact, or else how to account for the feelings created in me when I first met him, although no special or remarkable circumstances were connected with that event. All my hopes and plans are centred in him, and nothing in the world can shake my confidence in him especially when several of my Brahmin acquaintances tell me the same things without previous consultation.

I went to the great festival of Durga yesterday, and spent nearly the whole day looking in the vast crowd of men, women, children and mendicants for some of Kunala's friends, for he once told me never to be sure that they were not near me, but I found none who seemed to answer my ideas. As I stood by the ghat at the river side thinking that perhaps I was left alone to try my patience, an old and apparently very decrepit Vairagin plucked my sleeve and said: "Never expect to see anyone, but always be ready to answer if they speak to you; it is not wise to peer outside of yourself for the great followers of Vasudeva: look rather within.". . .

Very wearying indeed in a bodily sense was the work of last week and especially of last evening, and upon lying down on my mat last night after continuing work far into the night I fell quickly sound asleep. I had been sleeping some hour or two when with a start I awoke to find myself in perfect solitude and only the horrid howling of the jackals in the jungle to disturb me. The moon was brightly shining. . . . Finding that sleep had departed, I began again on those palm leaves. Just after I had begun, a tap arrested my attention and I opened the door. Overjoyed was I then to see Kunala standing there, once more unexpectedly.

"Put on your turban and come with me", he said and turned away. . . . He walked out into the jungle and turned into an unfrequented path. The jackals seemed to recede into the distance; now and then in the mango trees overhead, the flying foxes rustled here and there, while I could distinctly hear the singular creeping noise made by a startled snake as it drew itself hurriedly away over the leaves. . . . He at last came to a spot that seemed bare of trees, and bending down, seemed to press his hand into the grass. I then saw that a trap door or entrance to a stairway very curiously contrived, was there. Stairs went down into the earth. He went down and I could but follow. The door closed behind me, yet it was not dark. Plenty of light was there, but where it came from I cared not then nor can I now tell. It reminded me of our old weird tales told us in youth of pilgrims going down to the land of the Devas where, although no sun was seen, there was plenty of light.

At the bottom of the stairs was a passage. Here I saw people but they did not speak to me and appeared not to even see me although their eyes were directed at me. Kunala said nothing but walked on to the end, where there was a room in which were many men looking as grand as he does. . . .

Once more I got out into the passage, but never to my knowledge went up those steps, and in a moment more was I again at my door. It was as I left it, and on the table I found the palm leaves as I dropped them, except that beside them was a note in Kunala's hand, which read: "Nilakant — strive not yet to think too deeply on those things you have just seen. Let the lessons sink deep into your heart, and they will have their own fruition." . . .

Once more I was to be blessed by another visit with Kunala to some of his friends whom I revere and who will I hope bless me too. When everyone had quieted down he told me to go with him to the sea which was not far away. We walked for about three quarters of an hour by the seashore, and then entered as if into the sea. At first a slight fear came into me, but I saw that a path seemed to be there, although water was all around us. He in front and I following, we went for about seven minutes, when we came to a small island; on it was a building and on top of that a triangular light. From the sea shore, the island would seem like an isolated spot covered all over by green bushes. There is only one entrance to go inside. And no one can find it out unless the occupant wishes the seeker to find the way. On the island we had to go round about for some space before we came in front of the actual building. There is a little garden in front and there was sitting another friend of Kunala with the same expression of the eyes as he has. I also recognized him as one of those who was in the room underground. Kunala seated himself and I stood before them. We stayed an hour and saw a portion of the place. . . .

I have been going over that message I received just after returning from the underground room, about not thinking yet too deeply upon what I saw there, but to let the lessons sink deep into my heart. Can it be true — must it not indeed be true — that we have periods in our development when rest must be taken for the physical brain in order to give it time as a much less comprehensive machine than these English college professors say it is, to assimilate what it has received, while at the same time the real brain — as we might say, the spiritual brain — is carrying on as busily as ever all the trains of thought cut off from the head. Of course this is contrary to this modern science we hear so much about now as about to be introduced into all Asia, but it is perfectly consistent for me.

The Path   D.K. MAVALANKAR
June, July 1886

WORLD PERIODS

A striking illustration of the uniformities of Nature is brought out by the first glance at the occult doctrine in reference to the development of man on the earth. The outline of the design is the same as the outline of the more comprehensive design covering the whole chain of worlds. The inner details of this world, as regards its units of construction, are the same as the inner details of the larger organism of which this world itself is a unit. That is to say, the development of humanity on this earth is accomplished by means of successive waves of development which correspond to the successive worlds in the great planetary chain. The great tide of human life, be it remembered — for that has been already set forth — sweeps round the whole circle of worlds in successive waves. These primary growths of humanity may be conveniently spoken of as rounds. We must not forget that the individual units, constituting each round in turn, are identically the same as regards their higher principles, that is, that the individualities on the earth during round one come back again after completing their travels round the whole series of worlds and constitute round two, and so on. But the point to which special attention should be drawn here is that the individual unit, having arrived at any given planet of the series in the course of any given round, does not merely touch that planet and pass on to the next. Before passing on, he has to live through a series of races on that planet. And this fact suggests the outline of the fabric which will presently develop itself in the reader's mind, and exhibit that similarity of design on the part of the one world as compared with the whole series, to which attention has already been drawn. As the complete scheme of Nature that we belong to is worked out by means of a series of rounds sweeping through all the worlds, so the development of humanity on each world is worked out by a series of races developed within the limits of each world in turn.

It is time now to make the working of this law clearer by coming to the actual figures which have to do with the evolution of our doctrine. It would have been premature to begin with them, but as soon as the idea of a system of worlds in a chain, and of life evolution on each through a series of rebirths, is satisfactorily grasped, the further examination of the laws at work will be greatly facilitated by precise reference to the actual number of worlds and the actual number of rounds and races required to accomplish the whole purpose of the system. For the whole duration of the system is as certainly limited in time, be it remembered, as the life of a single man. Probably *not* limited to any definite number of years set irrevocably from the commencement, but that which has a beginning progresses onward towards an end. The life of a man, leaving accidents quite out of the account, is a terminable period, and the life of a world system leads up to a final consummation. The vast periods of time, concerned in the life of a world system, dazzle the imagination as a rule, but still they are measurable; they are divisible into sub-periods of various kinds, and these have a definite number.

By what prophetic instinct Shakespeare pitched upon seven as the number which suited his fantastic classification of the ages of man, is a question with which we need not be much concerned; but certain it is that he could not have made a more felicitous choice. In periods of sevens the evolution of the races of man may be traced, and the actual number of the objective worlds which constitute our system, and of which the earth is one, is seven also. Remember, the occult scientists know this as a fact, just as the physical scientists know for a fact that the spectrum consists of seven colours, and the musical scale of seven tones. There are seven kingdoms of Nature, not three, as modern science has imperfectly classified them. Man belongs to a kingdom distinctly separate from that of the animals, including beings in a higher state of organization than that which manhood has familiarized us with as yet; and below the mineral kingdom there are three others, which science in the West knows nothing about; but this branch of the subject may be set aside for the present. It is mentioned merely to show the regular operation of the septenary law in Nature.

Man — returning to the kingdom we are most interested in — is evolved in a series of rounds (progressions round the series of worlds), and seven of these rounds have to be accomplished before the destinies of our system are worked out. The round which is at present going on is the fourth. There are considerations of the utmost possible interest connected with precise knowledge on these points, because each round is, as it were, specially allotted to the predominance of one of the seven principles in man, and in the regular order of their upward gradation.

An individual unit, arriving on a planet for the first time in the course of a round, has to work through seven races on that planet before he passes on to the next, and each of those races occupies the earth for a long time. Our old-fashioned speculations about time and eternity, suggested by the misty religious systems of the West, have brought on a curious habit of mind in connection with problems bearing on the actual duration of such periods. We can talk glibly of eternity, and, going to the other end of the scale, we are not shocked by a few thousand years, but directly years are numbered with precision in groups which lie in intervening regions of thought, illogical Western theologians are apt to regard such numbering as nonsense. Now, we at present living on this earth — the great bulk of humanity, that is to say, for there are exceptional cases to be considered later — are now going through the fifth race of our present fourth round. And yet the evolution of that fifth race began about a million of years ago. Will the reader, in consideration of the fact that the present cosmogony does not profess to work with eternity, nerve himself to deal with estimates that do concern themselves with millions of years, and even count such millions by considerable numbers?

Each race of the seven which go to make up a round — *i.e.* which are evolved on the earth in succession during its occupation by the great wave of humanity passing round the planetary chain — is itself subject to subdivision. Were this not the case, the active existences of each human unit would be indeed few and far between. Within the limits of each race there are seven subdivisional races, and again within the limits of each subdivision there are seven branch races. Through all these races, roughly speaking, each individual human unit must pass during his stay on earth, each time he arrives there, on a round of progress through the planetary system. On reflection, this necessity should not appal the mind so much as a hypothesis which would provide for fewer incarnations. For, however many lives each individual unit may pass through while on earth during a round, be their numbers few or many, he cannot pass on until the time comes for the round-wave to sweep forward. Even by the calculation already foreshadowed, it will be seen that the time spent by each individual unit in physical life can only be a small fraction of the whole time he has to get through between his arrival on earth and his departure for the next planet. The larger part of the time — as we reckon duration of time — is obviously, therefore, spent in those subjective conditions of existence which belong to the "World of Effects," or spiritual earth attached to the physical earth, on which our objective existence is passed.

The nature of existence on the spiritual earth must be considered *pari passu* with the nature of that passed on the physical earth, and dealt with in the above enumeration of race incarnations. We must never forget that between each physical existence the individual unit passes through a period of existence in the corresponding spiritual world. And it is because the conditions of that existence are defined by the use that has been made of the opportunities in the next, preceding physical existence, that the spiritual earth is often spoken of in occult writing as the world of effects. The earth itself is its corresponding world of causes.

That which passes naturally into the world of effects after an incarnation in the world of causes is the individual unit or spiritual monad; but the personality just dissolved passes there with it, to an extent dependent on the qualifications of such personality — on the use, that is to say, which the person in question has made of his opportunities in life. The period to be spent in the world of effects — enormously longer in each case than the life which has paved the way for existence there — corresponds to the "hereafter" or heaven of ordinary theology. The narrow purview of ordinary religious conceptions deals merely with one spiritual life and its consequences in the life to come. Theology conceives that the entity concerned had its beginning in this physical life, and that the ensuing spiritual life will never stop. And this pair of existences, which is shown by the elements of occult science, that we are now unfolding, to constitute a part only of the entity's experience during its connection with a branch race which is one of seven belonging to a subdivisional race, itself one of seven belonging to a main race, itself one of seven belonging to the occupation of earth by one of the seven round-waves of humanity which have each to occupy it in turn before its functions in Nature are concluded — this microscopic molecule of the whole structure is what common theology treats as *more* than the whole, for it is supposed to cover eternity.

The reader must here be warned against one conclusion to which the above explanations — perfectly accurate as far as they go, but not yet covering the whole ground — might lead him. He will *not* get at the exact number of lives an individual entity has to lead on the earth in the course of its occupation by one round, if he merely raises seven to its third power. If one existence only were passed in each branch race the total number would obviously be 343, but each life descends at least twice into objectivity in the same branch — each monad, in other words, incarnates twice in each branch race. Again, there is a curious cyclic law which operates to augment the total number of incarnations beyond 686. Each subdivisional race has a certain extra vitality at its climax, which leads it to throw off an additional offshoot race at that point in its progress, and again another offshoot race is developed at the end of the subdivisional race by its dying momentum, so to speak. Through these races the whole tide of human life passes, and the result is that the actual normal number of incarnations for each monad is not far short of 800. Within relatively narrow limits it is a variable number, but the bearings of that fact may be considered later on.

The methodical law which carries each and every individual human entity through the vast evolutionary process thus sketched out, is in no way incompatible with that liability to fall away into abnormal destinies or ultimate annihilation which menaces the *personal* entities of people who cultivate very ignoble affinities. The distribution of the seven principles at death shows that clearly enough, but viewed in the light of these further explanations about evolution, the situation may be better realized. The permanent entity is that which lives through the whole series of lives, not only through the races belonging to the present round-wave on earth, but also through those of other round-waves and other worlds. Broadly speaking it may, in due time, though at some inconceivably distant future, as measured in years, recover a recollection of all those lives, which will seem as days in the past to us. But the astral dross, cast off at each passage into the world of effects, has a more or less independent existence of its own, quite separate from that of the spiritual entity from which it has just been disunited.

The natural history of this astral remnant is a problem of much interest and importance; but a methodical continuation of the whole subject will require us in the first instance to endeavour to realize the destiny of the higher and more durable spiritual Ego, and before going into that inquiry there is a good deal more to be said about the development of the objective races.

Esoteric science, though interesting itself mainly with matters generally regarded as appertaining to religion, would not be the complete comprehensive and trustworthy system that it is, if it failed to bring all the facts of earth life into harmony with its doctrines. It would have been little able to search out and ascertain the manner in which the human race has evolved through eons of time and series of planets, if it had not been in a position to ascertain also, as the smaller inquiry is included in the greater, the manner in which the wave of humanity with which we are now concerned has been developed on this earth. The faculties, in short, which enable adepts to read the mysteries of other worlds, and of other states of existence, are in no way unequal to the task of travelling back along the life-current of this globe. It follows that while the brief record of a few thousand years is all that our so-called universal history can deal with, the earth history, which forms a department of esoteric knowledge, goes back to the incidents of the fourth race, which preceded ours, and to those of the third race, which preceded that. It goes back still further indeed, but the second and first races did not develop anything that could be called civilization, and of them therefore there is less to be said than of their successors. The third and fourth did — strange as it may seem to some modern readers to contemplate the notion of civilization on the earth several millions of years ago.

Where are its traces? they will ask. How could the civilization with which Europe has now endowed mankind, pass away so completely that any future inhabitants of the earth could ever be ignorant that it once existed? How then can we conceive the idea that any similar civilization can have vanished, leaving no records for us?

The answer lies in the regular routine of planetary life, which goes on *pari passu* with the life of its inhabitants. The periods of the great root races are divided from each other by great convulsions of Nature, and by great geological changes. Europe was not in existence as a continent at the time the fourth race flourished. The continent on which the fourth race lived was not in existence at the time the third race flourished, and neither of the continents which were the great vortices of the civilizations of these two races are in existence now. Seven great continental cataclysms occur during the occupation of the earth by the human life-wave for one round-period. Each race is cut off in this way at its appointed time, some survivors remaining in parts of the world, not the proper home of their race; but these, invariably in such cases, exhibiting a tendency to decay, and relapsing into barbarism with more or less rapidity.

The proper home of the fourth race, which directly preceded our own, was that continent of which some memory has been preserved even in exoteric literature — the lost Atlantis. But the great island, the destruction of which is spoken of by Plato, was really but the last remnant of the continent. "In the Eocene age," I am told, "even in its very first part, the great cycle of the fourth race men, the Atlanteans, had already reached its highest point, and the great continent, the father of nearly all the present continents, showed the first symptoms of sinking — a process that occupied it down to 11,446 years ago, when its last island, that, translating its vernacular name, we may call with propriety Poseidonis, went down with a crash.

"Lemuria" (a former continent stretching southwards from India across what is now the Indian Ocean, but connected with Atlantis, for Africa was not then in existence) "should no more be confounded with the Atlantis continent than Europe with America. Both sank and were drowned, with their high civilizations and 'gods'; yet between the two catastrophes a period of about 700,000 years elapsed, Lemuria flourishing and ending her career just about that lapse of time before the early part of the Eocene age, since its race was the third. Behold the relics of that once great nation in some of the flat-headed aborigines of your Australia."

It is a mistake on the part of a recent writer on Atlantis to people India and Egypt with the colonies of that continent, but of that more anon.

"Why should not your geologists," asks my revered Mahatma teacher, "bear in mind that under the continents explored and fathomed by them, in the bowels of which they have found the Eocene age, and forced it to deliver them its secrets, there may be hidden deep in the fathomless, or rather unfathomed ocean beds, other and far older continents whose strata have never been geologically explored; and that they may some day upset entirely their present theories? Why not admit that our present continents have, like Lemuria and Atlantis, been several times already submerged, and had the time to reappear again, and bear their new groups of mankind and civilization; and that at the first great geological upheaval at the next cataclysm, in the series of periodical cataclysms that occur from the beginning to the end of every round, our already autopsized continents will go down, and the Lemurias and Atlantises come up again?

"Of course the fourth race had its periods of the highest civilization." (The letter from which I am now quoting was written in answer to a series of questions I put.) "Greek, and Roman, and even Egyptian civilizations are nothing compared to the civilizations that began with the third race. Those of the second race were not savages, but they could not be called civilized.

"Greeks and Romans were small sub-races, and Egyptians part and parcel of our own Caucasian stock. Look at the latter, and at India. Having reached the highest civilization, and, what is more, *learning*, both went down; Egypt, as a distinct sub-race, disappearing entirely (her Copts are but a hybrid remnant); India, as one of the first and most powerful offshoots of the mother race, and composed of a number of sub-races, lasting to these times, and struggling to take once more her place in history some day. That history catches but a few stray, hazy glimpses of Egypt some 12,000 years back, when, having already reached the apex of its cycle thousands of years before, the latter had begun to go down.

"The Chaldees were at the apex of their occult fame before what you term the Bronze Age. We hold — but then what warrant can you give the world that we are right? — that far greater civilizations than our own have risen and decayed. It is not enough to say, as some of your modern writers do, that an extinct civilization existed before Rome and Athens were founded. We affirm that a series of civilizations existed before as well as after the glacial period, that they existed upon various points of the globe, reached the apex of glory, and died. Every trace and memory had been lost of the Assyrian and Phoenician civilizations, until discoveries began to be made a few years ago. And now they open a new, though not by far one of the earliest pages in the history of mankind. And yet how far back to those civilizations go in comparison with the oldest, and even then history is slow to accept. Archaeology has sufficiently demonstrated that the memory of man runs back vastly further than history has been willing to accept, and the sacred records of once mighty nations, preserved by their heirs, are still more worthy of trust. We speak of civilizations of the ante-glacial period, and not only in the minds of the vulgar and the profane, but even in the opinion of the highly-learned geologist, the claim sounds preposterous. What would you say then to our affirmation that the Chinese — I now speak of the inland, the true Chinamen, not of the hybrid mixture between the fourth and fifth races now occupying the throne — the aborigines who belong in their unallied nationality wholly to the highest and last branch of the fourth race, reached their highest civilization when the fifth had hardly appeared in Asia. When was it? Calculate. The group of islands discovered by Nordenskiöld of the *Vega* was found strewn with fossils of horses, sheep, oxen, *etc.,* among gigantic bones of elephants, mammoths, rhinoceroses, and other monsters belonging to periods when man, says your science, had not yet made his appearance on earth. How came horses and sheep to be found in company with the huge antediluvians?

"The region now locked in the fetters of eternal winter, uninhabited by man — that most fragile of animals — will very soon be proved to have had not only a tropical climate, something your science knows and does not dispute, but having been likewise the seat of one of the most ancient civilizations of the fourth race, whose highest relics we now find in the degenerate Chinaman, and whose lowest are hopelessly (for the profane scientist) intermixed with the remnants of the third. I told you before that the highest people now on earth (spiritually) belong to the first sub-race of the fifth root race, and those are the Aryan Asiatics, the highest race (physical intellectuality) is the last sub-race of the fifth — yourselves, the white conquerors. The majority of mankind belongs to the seventh sub-race of the fourth root race — the above-mentioned Chinamen and their offshoots and branchlets (Malayans, Mongolians, Tibetans, Javanese, *etc., etc.)* —

with remnants of other sub-races of the fourth and the seventh sub-race of the third race. All these fallen, degraded semblances of humanity are the direct lineal descendants of highly civilized nations, neither the names nor memory of which have survived, except in such books as 'Populvuh,' the sacred book of the Guatemalans, and a few others unknown to science."

I had inquired was there any way of accounting for what seems the curious rush of human progress within the last two thousand years as compared with the relatively stagnant condition of the fourth-round people up to the beginning of modern progress. This question it was that elicited the explanations quoted above, and also the following remarks in regard to the recent "rush of human progress."

"The latter end of a very important cycle. Each round, each race, as every sub-race, has its great and its smaller cycles on every planet that mankind passes through. Our fourth-round humanity has its one great cycle, and so have its races and sub-races. 'The curious rush' is due to the double effect of the former — the beginning of its downward course — and of the latter (the small cycle of your sub-race) running on to its apex. Remember, you belong to the fifth race, yet you are but a western sub-race. Notwithstanding your efforts, what you call civilization is confined only to the latter and its offshoots in America. Radiating around, its deceptive light may seem to throw its rays on a greater distance than it does in reality. There is no rush in China, and of Japan you make but a caricature.

"A student of occultism ought not to speak of the stagnant condition of the fourth-round people, since history knows next to nothing of that condition, 'up to the beginning of modern progress,' of other nations but the Western. What do you know of America, for instance, before the invasion of that country by the Spaniards? Less than two centuries prior to the arrival of Cortez there was great a rush towards progress among the sub-races of Peru and Mexico as there is now in Europe and the United States. Their sub-race ended in nearly total annihilation through causes generated by itself. We may speak only of the 'stagnant' condition into which, following the law of development, growth, maturity and decline every race and sub-race falls during the transition periods. It is that latter condition your universal history is acquainted with, while it remains superbly ignorant of the condition even India was in some ten centuries back. Your sub-races are now running toward the apex of their respective cycles, and that history goes no further back that the periods of decline of a few other sub-races belonging most of them to the preceding fourth race."

I had asked to what epoch Atlantis belonged, and whether the cataclysm by which it was destroyed came in an appointed place in the progress of evolution, corresponding for the development of races to the obscuration of planets. The answer was: —

"To the Miocene times. Everything comes in its appointed time and place in the evolution of rounds, otherwise it would be impossible for the best seer to calculate the exact hour and year when such cataclysms great and small have to occur. All an adept could do would be to predict an approximate time, whereas now events that result in great geological changes may be predicted with as mathematical a certainty as eclipses and other revolutions in space. The sinking of Atlantis (the group of continents and isles) began during the Miocene period — as certain of your continents are now observed to be gradually sinking — and it culminated first in the final disappearance of the largest continent, an event coincident with the elevation of the Alps, and second, with that of the last of the fair islands mentioned by Plato. The Egyptian priests of Saïs told his ancestor, Solon that Atlantis (i.e. the only remaining large island) had perished 9000 years before their time. This was not a fancy date, since they had for millenniums preserved most carefully their records. But then, as I say, they spoke but of the Poseidonis, and would not reveal even to the great Greek legislator their secret chronology. As there are no geological reasons for doubting, but, on the contrary, a mass of evidence for accepting the tradition, science has finally accepted the existence of the great continent and archipelago, and thus vindicated the truth of one more 'fable.'

"The approach of every new obscuration is always signalled by cataclysms of either fire or water. But, apart from this, every root race has to be cut in two, so to say, by either one or the other. Thus, having reached the apex of its development and glory, the fourth race — the Atlanteans — were destroyed by water; you find now but their degenerate fallen remnants, whose sub-races, nevertheless, each of them, has its palmy days of glory and relative greatness. What they are now, you will be some day, the law of cycles being one and immutable. When your race, the fifth, will have reached its zenith of physical intellectuality, and developed its highest civilization (remember the difference we make between material and spiritual civilizations), unable to go any higher in its own cycle, its progress towards absolute evil will be arrested (as its predecessors, the Lemurians and the Atlanteans, the men of the third and fourth races, were arrested in their progress towards the same) by one of such cataclysmic changes, its great civilization destroyed, and all the sub-races of that race will be found going down their respective cycles, after a short period of glory and learning. See the remnants of the Atlanteans, the old Greeks and Romans (the modern belong to the fifth race). See how great and how short, how evanescent were their days of fame and glory. For they were but sub-races of the seven offshoots of the root race.* No mother race, any more than her sub-races and offshoots, is allowed by the one reigning law to trespass upon the prerogatives of the race or sub-race that will follow it; least of all to encroach upon the knowledge and powers in store for its successor."

The "progress towards absolute evil," arrested by the cataclysms of each race in turn, sets in with the acquisition, by means of ordinary intellectual research and scientific advancement, of those powers over Nature which accrue even now in adeptship from the premature development of higher faculties than those we ordinarily employ. I have spoken slightly of these

---

* Branches of the subdivisions, according to the nomenclature I have adopted previously.

powers in a preceding chapter, when endeavouring to describe our esoteric teachers; to describe them minutely would lead me into a long digression on occult phenomena. It is enough to say that they are such as cannot but be dangerous to society generally, and provocative of all manner of crimes which would utterly defy detection, if possessed by persons capable of regarding them as anything else but a profoundly sacred trust. Now some of these powers are simply the practical application of obscure forces of Nature, susceptible of discovery in the course of ordinary scientific progress. Such progress had been accomplished by the Atlanteans. The worldly men of science in that race had learned the secrets of the disintegration and reintegration of matter, which few but practical spiritualists as yet know to be possible, and of control over the elementals, by means of which that and other even more portentous phenomena can be produced. Such powers in the hands of persons willing to use them for merely selfish and unscrupulous ends must not only be productive of social disaster, but also for the persons who hold them, of progress in the direction of that evilly spiritual exaltation which is a far more terrible result than suffering and inconvenience in this world. Thus it is, when physical intellect, unguarded by elevated morality, runs over into the proper region of spiritual advancement, that the natural law provides for its violent repression. The contingency will be better understood when we come to deal with the general destinies towards which humanity is tending.

The principle under which the various races of man as they develop are controlled collectively by the cyclic law, however they may individually exercise the free will they unquestionably possess, is thus very plainly asserted. For people who have never regarded human affairs as covering more than the very short period with which history deals, the course of events will perhaps, as a rule, exhibit no cyclic character, but rather a chequered progress, hastened sometimes by great men and fortunate circumstances, sometimes retarded by war, bigotry, or intervals of intellectual sterility, but moving continually onwards in the long account, at one rate of speed or another.

As the esoteric view of the matter, fortified by the wide range of observation which occult science is enabled to take, has an altogether opposite tendency, it seems worth while to conclude these explanations with an extract from a distinguished author, quite unconnected with the occult world, who nevertheless, from a close observation of the mere historical record, pronounces himself decisively in favour of the theory of cycles. In his "History of the Intellectual Development of Europe" Dr. J.W. Draper writes as follows: —

> We are, as we often say, the creatures of circumstances. In that expression there is a higher philosophy than might at first sight appear.... From this more accurate point of view we should therefore consider the course of these events, recognizing the principle that the affairs of men pass forward in a determinate way, expanding and unfolding themselves. And hence we see that the things of which we have spoken as though they were matters of choice, were in reality forced upon their apparent authors by the necessity of the times. But in truth they should be considered as the presentation of a certain phase of life which nations in their onward course sooner or later assume. To the individual, how well we know that a sober moderation of action, an appropriate gravity of demeanour, belong to the mature period of life, change from the wanton wilfulness of youth, which may be ushered in, or its beginning marked by, many accidental incidents; in one perhaps by domestic bereavements, in another by the loss of fortune, in a third by ill-health. We are correct enough in imputing to such trials the change of character; but we never deceive ourselves by supposing that it would have failed to take place had those incidents not occurred. There runs an irresistible destiny in the midst of all these vicissitudes....
>
> There are analogies between the life of a nation and that of an individual, who, though he may be in one respect the maker of his own fortunes, for happiness

or for misery, for good or for evil, though he remains
here or goes there, as his inclinations prompt, though
he does this or abstains from that, as he chooses, is
nevertheless held fast by an inexorable fate — a fate
which brought him into the world involuntarily, as far
as he was concerned, which presses him forward
through a definite career, the stages of which are
absolutely invariable — infancy, childhood, youth,
maturity, old age, with all their characteristic actions
and passions —and which removes him from the scene
at the appointed time, in most cases against his will.
So also it is with nations; the voluntary is only the
outward semblance, covering, but hardly hiding, the
pre-determined. Over the events of life we may have
control, but none whatsoever over the law of its
progress. There is a geometry that applies to nations an
equation of their curve of advance. That no mortal man
can touch.

Esoteric Buddhism   A. P. SINNETT

THE RENEWAL OF YOUTH

I

I am a part of all that I have met;
Yet all experience is an arch wherethro'
Gleams that untravel'd world . . .
. . . . . . Come, my friends,
'Tis not too late to seek a newer world.

ULYSSES

Humanity is no longer the child it was at the beginning of the world. The spirit which prompted by some divine intent, flung itself long ago into a vague, nebulous, drifting nature, though it has endured through many periods of youth, maturity, and age, has yet had its own transformations. Its gay, wonderful childhood gave way, as cycle after cycle coiled itself into slumber, to more definite purposes, and now it is old and burdened with experiences. It is not an age that quenches its fire, but it will not renew again the activities which gave it wisdom. And so it comes that men pause with a feeling which they translate into weariness of life before the accustomed joys and purposes of their race. They wonder at the spell which induced their fathers to plot and execute deeds which seem to them to have no more meaning than a whirl of dust. But their fathers had this weariness also and concealed it from each other in fear, for it meant the laying aside of the sceptre, the toppling over of empires, the chilling of the household warmth, and all for a voice whose inner significance revealed itself but to one or two among myriads. The spirit has hardly emerged from the childhood with which nature clothes it afresh at every new birth, when the disparity between the garment and the wearer becomes manifest: the little tissue of joys and dreams woven about it is found inadequate for shelter: it trembles exposed to the winds blowing out of the unknown. We linger at twilight with some companion, still glad, contented,

and in tune with the nature which fills the orchards with blossom
and sprays the hedges with dewy blooms. The laughing lips give
utterance to wishes — ours until that moment. Then the spirit,
without warning, suddenly falls into immeasurable age: a sphinx-
like face looks at us: our lips answer, but far from the region of
elemental being we inhabit, they syllable in shadowy sound, out
of old usage, the response, speaking of a love and a hope which
we know have vanished from us for evermore. So hour by hour
the scourge of the infinite drives us out of every nook and corner
of life we find pleasant. And this always takes place when all is
fashioned to our liking: then into our dream strides the wielder
of the lightning: we get glimpses of a world beyond us thronged
with mighty, exultant beings: our own deeds become infinitesimal
to us: the colors of our imagination, once so shining, grow pale
as the living lights of God glow upon them. We find a little honey
in the heart which we make sweeter for some one, and then
another Lover, whose forms are legion, sighs to us out of its
multitudinous being: we know that the old love is gone. There is
a sweetness in song or in the cunning re-imaging of the beauty
we see; but the Magician of the Beautiful whispers to us of his
art, how we were with him when he laid the foundations of the
world, and the song is unfinished, the fingers grow listless. As we
receive these intimations of age our very sins become negative:
we are still pleased if a voice praises us, but we grow lethargic in
enterprises where the spur to activity is fame or the acclamation
of men. At some point in the past we may have struggled mightily
for the sweet incense which men offer to a towering personality;
but the infinite is for ever within man: we sighed for other worlds
and found that to be saluted as victor by men did not mean
acceptance by the gods.

But the placing of an invisible finger upon our lips when
we would speak, the heart-throb of warning where we would love,
that we grow contemptuous of the prizes of life, does not mean
that the spirit has ceased from its labors, that the high-built beauty
of the spheres is to topple mistily into chaos, as a mighty temple
in the desert sinks into the sand, watched only by a few barbarians

too feeble to renew its ancient pomp and the ritual of its once shining congregations. Before we, who were the bright children of the dawn, may return as the twilight race into the silence, our purpose must be achieved, we have to assume mastery over that nature which now overwhelms us, driving into the Fire-fold the flocks of stars and wandering fires. Does it seem very vast and far away? Do you sigh at the long, long time? Or does it appear hopeless to you who perhaps return with trembling feet evening after evening from a little labor? But it is behind all these things that the renewal takes place, when love and grief are dead; when they loosen their hold on the spirit and it sinks back into itself, looking out on the pitiful plight of those who, like it, are the weary inheritors of so great destinies: then a tenderness which is the most profound quality of its being springs up like the outraying of the dawn, and if in that mood it would plan or execute it knows no weariness, for it is nourished from the First Fountain. As for these feeble children of the once glorious spirits of the dawn, only a vast hope can arouse them from so vast a despair, for the fire will not invigorate them for the repetition of petty deeds but only for the eternal enterprise, the war in heaven, that conflict between Titan and Zeus which is part of the never-ending struggle of the human spirit to assert its supremacy over nature. We, who he crushed by this mountain nature piled above us, must arise again, unite to storm the heavens and sit on the seats of the mighty.

II

We speak out of too petty a spirit to each other; the true poems, said Whitman:

> Bring none to his or to her terminus or to be content
> and full,
> Whom they take they take into space to behold the
> birth of stars, to learn one of the meanings,
> To launch off with absolute faith, to sweep through the
> ceaseless rings and never be quiet again.

Here is inspiration — the voice of the soul. Every word which really inspires is spoken as if the Golden Age had never passed. The great teachers ignore the personal identity and speak to the eternal pilgrim. Too often the form or surface far removed from beauty makes us falter, and we speak to that form and the soul is not stirred. But an equal temper arouses it. To whoever hails in it the lover, the hero, the magician, it will respond, but not to him who accosts it in the name and style of its outer self. How often do we not long to break through the veils which divide us from some one, but custom, convention, or a fear of being misunderstood prevent us, and so the moment passes whose heat might have burned through every barrier. Out with it — out with it, the hidden heart, the love that is voiceless, the secret tender germ of an infinite forgiveness. That speaks to the heart. That pierces through many a vesture of the Soul. Our companion struggles in some labyrinth of passion. We help him, we, think, with ethic and moralities. Ah, very well they are; well to know and to keep, but wherefore? For their own sake? No, but that the King may arise in his beauty. We write that in letters, in books, but to the face of the fallen who brings back remembrance? Who calls him by his secret name? Let a man but feel for what high cause is his battle, for what is his cyclic labor, and a warrior who is invincible fights for him and he draws upon divine powers. Our attitude to man and to nature, expressed or not, has something of the effect of ritual, of evocation. As our aspiration so is our inspiration. We believe in life universal, in a brotherhood which links the elements to man, and makes the glow-worm feel far off something of the rapture of the seraph hosts. Then we go out into the living world, and what influences pour through us! We are "at league with the stones of the field." The winds of the world blow radiantly upon us as in the early time. We feel wrapt about with love, with an infinite tenderness that caresses us. Alone in our rooms as we ponder, what sudden abysses of light open within us! The Gods are so much nearer than we dreamed. We rise up intoxicated with the thought, and reel out seeking an equal companionship under the great night and the stars.

Let us get near to realities. We read too much. We think of that which is "the goal, the Comforter, the Lord, the Witness, the resting-place, the asylum, and the Friend." Is it by any of these dear and familiar names? The soul of the modern mystic is becoming a mere hoarding-place for uncomely theories. He creates an uncouth symbolism, and blinds his soul within with names drawn from the Kabala or ancient Sanskrit, and makes alien to himself the intimate powers of his spirit, things which in truth are more his than the beatings of his heart. Could we not speak of them in our own tongue, and the language of today will be as sacred as any of the past. From the Golden One, the child of the divine, comes a voice to its shadow. It is stranger to our world, aloof from our ambitions, with a destiny not here to be fulfilled. It says: "You are of dust while I am robed in opalescent airs. You dwell in houses of clay, I in a temple not made by hands. I will not go with thee, but thou must come with me." And not alone is the form of the divine aloof but the spirit behind the form. It is called the Goal truly, but it has no ending. It is the Comforter, but it waves away our joys and hopes like the angel with the flaming sword. Though it is the Resting-place, it stirs to all heroic strife, to outgoing, to conquest. It is the Friend indeed, but it will not yield to our desires. Is it this strange, unfathomable self we think to know, and awaken to, by what is written, or by study of it as so many planes of consciousness? But in vain we store the upper chambers of the mind with such quaint furniture of thought. No archangel makes his abode therein. They abide only in the shining. No wonder that the Gods do not incarnate. We cannot say we do pay reverence to these awful powers. We repulse the living truth by our doubts and reasonings. We would compel the Gods to fall in with our petty philosophy rather than trust in the heavenly guidance. Ah, to think of it, those dread deities, the divine Fires, to be so enslaved! We have not comprehended the meaning of the voice which cried "Prepare ye the way of the Lord," or this, "Lift up your heads, O ye gates. Be ye lifted up, ye everlasting doors, and the King of Glory shall come in." Nothing that we read is useful unless it calls up living things in the soul. To read a mystic book truly is to invoke the powers. If they do not rise up plumed and radiant, the apparitions of spiritual things, then is our labor barren. We only encumber the mind with useless symbols. They knew better ways long ago. "Master of the Green-waving Planisphere, . . . Lord of the Azure Expanse, . . . it is thus we invoke," cried the magicians of old.

And us, let us invoke them with joy, let us call upon them with love, the Light we hail, or the Divine Darkness we worship with silent breath. That silence cries aloud to the Gods. Then they will approach us. Then we may learn that speech of many colors, for they will not speak in our mortal tongue; they will not answer to the names of men. Their names are rainbow glories. Yet these are mysteries, and they cannot be reasoned out or argued over. We cannot speak truly of them from report, or description, or from what another has written. A relation to the thing in itself alone is our warrant, and this means we must set aside our intellectual self-sufficiency and await guidance. It will surely come to those who wait in trust, a glow, a heat in the heart announcing the awakening of the Fire. And, as it blows with its mystic breath into the brain, there is a hurtling of visions, a brilliance of lights, a sound as of great waters vibrant and musical in their flowing, and murmurs from a single yet multitudinous being. In such a mood, when the far becomes near, the strange familiar, and the infinite possible, he wrote from whose words we get the inspiration:

> To launch off with absolute faith, to sweep
> through the ceaseless rings and never be quiet again.

Such a faith and such an unrest be ours: faith which is mistrust of the visible; unrest which is full of a hidden surety and reliance. We, when we fall into pleasant places, rest and dream our strength away. Before every enterprise and adventure of the soul we calculate in fear our power to do. But remember, "Oh, disciple, in thy work for thy brother thou hast many allies; in the winds, in the air, in all the voices of the silent shore." These are the far-wandered powers of our own nature, and they turn again home at our need. We came out of the Great Mother-Life for the purposes of soul. Are her darlings forgotten where they darkly wander and strive? Never. Are not the lives of all her heroes proof? Though they seem to stand alone the eternal Mother keeps watch on them, and voices far away and unknown to them before arise in passionate defense, and hearts beat warm to help them. Aye, if we could look within we would see vast nature stirred on their behalf, and institutions shaken, until the truth they fight for triumphs, and they pass, and a wake of glory ever widening behind them trails down the ocean of the years.

Thus the warrior within us works, or, if we choose to phrase it so, it is the action of the spiritual will. Shall we not, then, trust in it and face the unknown, defiant and fearless of its dangers. Though we seem to go alone to the high, the lonely, the pure, we need not despair. Let no one bring to this task the mood of the martyr or of one who thinks he sacrifices something. Yet let all who will come. Let them enter the path, facing all things in life and death with a mood at once gay and reverent, as beseems those who are immortal — who are children today, but whose hands tomorrow may grasp the sceptre, sitting down with the Gods as equals and companions. "What a man thinks, that he is: that is the old secret." In this self-conception lies the secret of life, the way of escape and return. We have imagined ourselves into littleness, darkness, and feebleness. We must imagine ourselves into greatness. "If thou wilt not equal thyself to God thou canst not understand God. The like is only intelligible by the like." In some moment of more complete imagination the thought-born may go forth and look on the ancient Beauty. So it was in the mysteries long ago, and may well be today. The poor dead shadow was laid to sleep, forgotten in its darkness, as the fiery power, mounting from heart to head, went forth in radiance. Not then did it rest, nor ought we. The dim worlds dropped behind it, the lights of earth disappeared as it neared the heights of the immortals. There was One seated on a throne, One dark and bright with ethereal glory. It arose in greeting. The radiant figure laid its head against the breast which grew suddenly golden, and Father and Son vanished in that which has no place or name.

III

Who are exiles? as for me
Where beneath the diamond dome
Lies the light on hills or tree
There my palace is and home.

We are outcasts from Deity, therefore we defame the place of our exile. But who is there may set apart his destiny from the earth which bore him? I am one of those who would bring back the old reverence for the Mother, the magic, the love. I think, metaphysician, you have gone astray. You would seek within yourself for the fountain of life. Yes, there is the true, the only light. But do not dream it will lead you farther away from the earth, but rather deeper into its heart. By it you are nourished with those living waters you would drink. You are yet in the womb and unborn, and the Mother breathes for you the diviner airs. Dart out your farthest ray of thought to the original, and yet you have not found a new path of your own. Your ray is still enclosed in the parent ray, and only on the sidereal streams are you borne to the freedom of the deep, to the sacred stars whose distance maddens, and to the lonely Light of Lights.

Let us, therefore, accept the conditions and address ourselves with wonder, with awe, with love, as we well may, to that being in whom we move. I abate no jot of those vaster hopes, yet I would pursue that ardent aspiration, content as to here and today. I do not believe in a nature red with tooth and claw. If indeed she appears so terrible to any it is because they themselves have armed her. Again, behind the anger of the Gods there is a love. Are the rocks barren? Lay your brow against them and learn what memories they keep. Is the brown earth unbeautiful? Yet lie on the breast of the Mother and you shall be aureoled with the dews of faery. The earth is the entrance to the Halls of Twilight. What emanations are those that make radiant the dark woods of pine! Round every leaf and tree and over all the mountains wave the fiery tresses of that hidden sun which is the soul of the earth and parent of your soul. But we think of these things no longer. Like the prodigal we have wandered far from our home, but no more return. We idly pass or wait as strangers in the halls our spirit built.

> Sad or fain no more to live?
> I have pressed the lips of pain
> With the kisses lovers give
> Ransomed ancient powers again.

I would raise this shrinking soul to a universal acceptance. What! does it aspire to the All, and yet deny by its revolt and inner test the justice of Law? From sorrow we take no less and no more than from our joys. If the one reveals to the soul the mode by which the power overflows and fills it here, the other indicates to it the unalterable will which checks excess and leads it on to true proportion and its own ancestral ideal. Yet men seem for ever to fly from their destiny of inevitable beauty; because of delay the power invites and lures no longer but goes out into the highways with a hand of iron. We look back cheerfully enough upon those old trials out of which we have passed; but we have gleaned only an aftermath of wisdom, and missed the full harvest if the will has not risen royally at the moment in unison with the will of the Immortal, even though it comes rolled round with terror and suffering and strikes at the heart of clay.

Through all these things, in doubt, despair, poverty, sick, feeble, or baffled, we have yet to learn reliance. *"I will not leave thee or forsake thee"* are the words of the most ancient spirit to the spark wandering in the immensity of its own being. This high courage brings with it a vision. It sees the true intent in all circumstance out of which its own emerges to meet it. Before it the blackness melts into forms of beauty, and back of all illusions is seen the old enchanter tenderly smiling, the dark, hidden Father enveloping his children.

All things have their compensations. For what is absent here there is always, if we seek, a nobler presence about us.

> Captive, see what stars give light
> In the hidden heart of clay:
> At their radiance dark and bright
> Fades the dreamy King of Day.

We complain of conditions, but this very imperfection it is which urges us to arise and seek for the Isles of the Immortals. What we lack recalls the fullness. The soul has seen a brighter day than this and a sun which never sets. Hence the retrospect: "Thou hast been in Eden, the garden of God; every precious stone was thy covering, the sardius, topaz, and the diamond, the beryl, the onyx, the jasper, the sapphire, emerald. . . . Thou was upon the holy mountain of God; thou hast walked up and down in the midst of the stones of fire." We would point out these radiant avenues of return; but sometimes we feel in our hearts that we sound but cockney voices as guides amid the ancient temples, the cyclopean crypts sanctified by the mysteries. To be intelligible we replace the opalescent shining by the terms of the scientist, and we prate of occult physiology in the same breath with the Most High. Yet when the soul has the divine vision it knows not it has a body. Let it remember, and the breath of glory kindles it no more; it is once again a captive. After all it does not make the mysteries clearer to speak in physical terms and do violence to our intuitions. If we ever use these centres, as fires we shall see them, or they shall well up within us as fountains of potent sound. We may satisfy people's minds with a sense correspondence, and their souls may yet hold aloof. We shall only inspire by the magic of a superior beauty. Yet this too has its dangers. "Thou hast corrupted thy wisdom by reason of thy brightness," continues the seer. If we follow too much the elusive beauty of form we will miss the spirit. The last secrets are for those who translate vision into being. Does the glory fade away before you? Say truly in your heart, "I care not. I will wear the robes I am endowed with today."

You are already become beautiful, being beyond desire and free.

> Night and day no more eclipse
> Friendly eyes that on us shine,
> Speech from old familiar lips.
> Playmates of a youth divine.

To childhood once again. We must regain the lost state. But it is to the giant and spiritual childhood of the young immortals we must return, when into their dear and translucent souls first fell the rays of the father-beings. The men of old were intimates of wind and wave and playmates of many a brightness long since forgotten. The rapture of the fire was their rest; their out-going was still consciously through universal being. By darkened images we may figure something vaguely akin, as when in rare moments under the stars the big dreamy heart of childhood is pervaded with quiet and brimmed full with love. Dear children of the world, so tired today — so weary seeking after the light. Would you recover strength and immortal vigour? Not one star alone, your star, shall shed its happy light upon you, but the All you must adore. Something intimate, secret, unspeakable, akin to thee, will emerge silently, insensibly, and ally itself with thee as thou gatherest thyself from the four quarters of the earth. We shall go back to the world of the dawn, but to a brighter light than that which opened up this wondrous story of the cycles. The forms of elder years will reappear in our vision, the father-beings once again. So we shall grow at home amid these grandeurs, and with that All-Presence about us may cry in our hearts, "At last is our meeting, Immortal. O starry one, now is our rest!"

> Come away, oh, come away;
> We will quench the heart's desire
> Past the gateways of the day
> In the rapture of the fire.

The Irish Theosophist　　　　　　　　　　　GEORGE WILLIAM RUSSELL
August - October 1895, June 1897

THE SEVEN STAGES
OF COGNITION

The Sage Vasishtha said: O Sinless Rama, attend now to the sevenfold stages of cognition, knowing which, you will no more plunge into the mire of ignorance. Disputants are apt to speak of many more stages of *Yoga* meditation, but I hold these seven to be sufficient for the attainment of the chief good or ultimate emancipation.

Knowledge is understanding and consists of acquaintance with these seven stages only, but emancipation from transmigration is the object of knowledge and transcends such acquaintance, while knowledge of truth is ultimate emancipation itself. These three terms are synonymous, since the living being who knows the truth is freed from transmigration and thereby attains ultimate emancipation.

The grounds of knowledge are comprised first of the desire of becoming good; then comes discretion, followed by purity of mind, the third stage in the acquisition of knowledge.

The fourth is self-reliance as the true refuge; worldly indifference is the fifth. Sixth is the power of abstraction; and the final stage of knowledge is universalization of all in the One.

Emancipation lies at the end of these and is attained without difficulty after them. Attend now to the definitions of these steps, as I shall explain them unto you.

First is the desire of goodness — *subhechha* — springing from disinterest in mundane affairs, and consisting in the thought, "Why do I sit idle? I must come to know the *Shastras* in the company of good men."

The second is discretion — *vicharana* — which arises from association with wise and good men, study of the *Shastras*, and habitual aversion to worldliness; it consists in an inclination to good conduct and the doing of all sorts of good acts.

The third — *tanumanasa* — is subduing the mind and restraining it from sensual enjoyments; it is produced by the former qualities of desire for goodness and discretion.

The fourth is self-reliance, and dependence upon the Divine Spirit as the true refuge of the soul — *sattapatti;* it is attained by means of the three previous qualities.

The fifth is worldly indifference — *asansakti* — and is shown by detachment from all earthly concerns and the society of men; it arises from the previous quadruple internal delight.

By practise of these fivefold virtues, and by their attendant feelings of satisfaction and inward delight, a man is freed from his thoughts and cares of all internal and external objects.

Then comes the power of penetration into the abstract meanings of things — *padarthabhava* — the sixth step in the attainment of true knowledge, fostered by one's own exertions and the guidance of others in search of truth.

Continual practice of these six qualifications, indifference to divergences of religions, and reduction of them all to knowledge of the one true deity of nature, is universalization — *Turiyagati.*

It pertains to the nature of the living liberation of the man who beholds all things in one and the same light. Above this is the state of that glorious light itself, which is attained by the disembodied soul.

Those fortunate men, 0 Rama, who have arrived at the seventh stage of knowledge, are great minds who delight in the light of their souls, and have reached to their highest state of humanity.

The living liberated ones are not plunged in the waters of pleasure and sorrow, but remain calm and unmoved in both states; they are at liberty to perform or disdain the duties of their conditions and positions in society.

These men, being roused from their deep meditation by intruders, betake themselves to their secular duties like men awakening from slumber.

Being suffused by the inward delight of their souls, they

feel no pleasure in the delights of the world, just as men immersed in sound sleep can feel no delight at the dalliance of beauties about them.

These seven stages of knowledge are known only to wise and thoughtful men, not to beasts, brutes and immobile entities. They are unknown to barbarians and others with barbarous minds and dispositions.

But any being who has attained to these stages of knowledge, whether beast or barbarian, embodied being or disembodied spirit, has undoubtedly obtained emancipation.

Knowledge severs the bonds of ignorance, and by loosening them produces the emancipation of our souls. It is the sole cause of removing the fallacy of the appearance of water in the mirage and similar errors.

Those who, being freed from ignorance, have not yet arrived at the ultimate perfection of disembodied liberation, have still secured the salvation of their souls by entering these stages of knowledge in their embodied state during their lifetime.

Some have passed all these stages, others two or three; some have passed the six grades, while a few have attained to the seventh state all at once.

Some have gone over three stages, others have attained the last; some have passed four stages, and some no more than one or two.

There are some who have advanced only a quarter, or half, or three-fourths of a stage. Some have passed over four quarters and a half, and some six and a half.

Common people of this earth know nothing of these travellers in the paths of knowledge, but remain blind, as though their eyes were dazzled by some planetary light, or eclipsed by its shadow.

Those wise men are compared to conquering kings, who stand victorious on these seven grounds of knowledge. The celestial elephants are as nothing beside them, and mighty warriors must bend their heads before them.

Those great minds that are victors on these grounds of knowledge are worthy of utmost veneration, as they are the conquerors of the enemies of their hearts and senses. Their rightful station is high above that of mere emperors and rulers, both in this world and in the next, both in their embodied and disembodied liberation.

Yoga Vasishtha Maharamayana
Utpatti Khanda, CXVIII

THE BROTHERHOOD
OF HUMANITY

The doctrine we promulgate being the only true one, must — supported by such evidence as we are preparing to give — become ultimately triumphant, like every other truth. Yet it is absolutely necessary to inculcate it gradually; enforcing its theories (unimpeachable facts for those who know) with direct inference, deduced from and corroborated by, the evidence furnished by modern exact science. That is why Col. H.S. Olcott, who works but to revive Buddhism, may be regarded as one who labours in the true path of Theosophy, far more than any other man who chooses as his goal the gratification of his own ardent aspirations for occult knowledge. Buddhism, stripped of its superstition, is eternal truth; and he who strives for the latter is striving for Theosophia, divine wisdom, which is a synonym of truth. For our doctrines to practically react on the so-called moral code, or the ideas of truthfulness, purity, self-denial, charity, etc., we have to preach and popularize a knowledge of Theosophy. It is not the individual and determined purpose of attaining Nirvana — the culmination of all knowledge and absolute wisdom, which is after all only an exalted and glorious selfishness — but the self-sacrificing pursuit of the best means to lead on the right path our neighbour, to cause to benefit by it as many of our fellow creatures as we possibly can, which constitutes the true Theosophist.

The intellectual portion of mankind seems to be fast dividing into two classes: the one unconsciously preparing for itself long periods of temporary annihilation or states of non-consciousness, owing to the deliberate surrender of intellect and its imprisonment in the narrow grooves of bigotry and superstition — a process which cannot fail to lead to the utter deformation of the intellectual principle; the other unrestrainedly indulging its animal propensities with the deliberate intention of submitting to annihilation pure and simple, in case of failure, and to millenniums of degradation after physical dissolution. Those intellectual classes reacting upon the ignorant masses — which they attract, and which look up to them as noble and fit examples to be followed — degrade and morally ruin those they ought to protect and guide. Between degrading superstition and still more degrading brutal materialism, the White Dove of Truth has hardly room whereon to rest her weary unwelcome feet.

It is time that Theosophy should enter the arena. The sons of Theosophists are more likely to become in their turn Theosophists than anything else. No messenger of the truth, no prophet has ever achieved during his lifetime a complete triumph — not even Buddha. The Theosophical Society was chosen as the cornerstone, the foundation of the future religions of humanity. To achieve the proposed object, a greater, wiser, and especially a more benevolent intermingling of the high and the low, the alpha and the omega of society, was determined upon. The white race must be the first to stretch out the hand of fellowship to the dark nations, to call the poor despised 'nigger' brother. This prospect may not smile for all, but he is no Theosophist who objects to this principle. In view of the ever-increasing triumph and at the same time misuse, of free thought and liberty (the universal reign of Satan, Eliphas Levi would have called it), how is the combative natural instinct of man to be restrained from inflicting hitherto unheard-of cruelties and enormities, tyranny, injustice, if not through the soothing influence of Brotherhood, and of the practical application of Buddha's esoteric doctrines? For everyone knows that total emancipation from the authority of the one all-pervading power, or law — called God by the priests, Buddha, Divine Wisdom and enlightenment, or Theosophy, by the philosophers of all ages — means also the emancipation from that of human law. Once unfettered, delivered from their dead-weight of dogmatism, interpretations, personal names, anthropomorphic conceptions, and salaried priests, the fundamental doctrines of all religions will be proved identical in their esoteric meaning. Osiris, Krishna,

Buddha, Christ, will be shown as different means for one and the same royal highway of final bliss — Nirvana. Mystical Christianity teaches *self*-redemption through one's own seventh principle, the liberated Paramatma, called by the one Christ, by others Buddha; this is equivalent to regeneration, or rebirth in spirit, and it therefore expounds just the same truth as the Nirvana of Buddhism. All of us have to get rid of our own Ego, the illusory, apparent self, to recognize our true Self, in a transcendental divine life. But if we would not be selfish we must strive to make other people see that truth, and recognize the reality of the transcendental Self, the Buddha, the Christ, or God of every preacher. This is why even exoteric Buddhism is the surest path to lead men toward the one esoteric truth.

As we find the world now, whether Christian, Mussulman, or Pagan, justice is disregarded, and honour and mercy are both flung to the winds. In a word, how — since the main objects of the Theosophical Society are misinterpreted by those who are most willing to serve us personally — are we to deal with the rest of mankind? With that curse known as 'the struggle for life' which is the real and most prolific parent of most woes and sorrows, and all crimes? Why has that struggle become almost the universal scheme of the universe? We answer: because no religion, with the exception of Buddhism, has taught a practical contempt for this earthly life; while each of them, always with that one solitary exception, has through its hells and damnations inculcated the greatest dread of death. Therefore do we find that struggle for life raging most fiercely in Christian countries, most prevalent in Europe and America. It weakens in the Pagan lands, and is nearly unknown among Buddhist populations. In China during famine, and where the masses are most ignorant of their own or of any religion, it was remarked that those mothers who devoured their children belonged to localities where there were the most Christian missionaries to be found; where there were none and the Bonzes alone had the field, the population died with the utmost indifference. Teach the people to see that life on this earth, even the happiest, is but a burden and an illusion; that it is but our own Karma, the cause producing the effect, that is our own judge — our saviour in future lives — and the great struggle for life will soon lose its intensity. There are no penitentiaries in Buddhist lands, and crime is nearly unknown among the Buddhist Tibetans. The world in general, and Christendom especially, left for two thousand years to the *regime* of a personal God, as well as to its political and social systems based on that idea, has now proved a failure.

If the Theosophists say: "We have nothing to do with all this; the lower classes and the inferior races (those of India, for instance, in the conception of the British) cannot concern us, and must manage as they can," what becomes of our fine professions of benevolence, philanthropy, reform, etc.? Are those professions a mockery? And if a mockery, can ours be the true path? Shall we devote ourselves to teaching a few Europeans — fed on the fat of the land, many of them loaded with the gifts of blind fortune — the rationale of bell ringing, of cup-growing, of the spiritual telephone, and astral body formation, and leave the teeming millions of the ignorant, of the poor and oppressed, to take care of themselves, and of their hereafter, as best they know how? Never! perish rather the Theosophical Society with both its hapless Founders, than that we should permit it to become no better than an academy of magic, and a hall of Occultism! That we, the devoted followers of that spirit incarnate of absolute self sacrifice, of philanthropy, divine kindness, as of all the highest virtues attainable on this earth of sorrow, the man of men, Gautama Buddha, should ever allow the Theosophical Society to represent the embodiment of selfishness, the refuge of the few, with no thought in them for the many, is a strange idea, my brothers! Among the few glimpses obtained by Europeans of Tibet and its mystical hierarchy of perfect Lamas there was one which was correctly understood and described. The incarnations of the Bodhisattva Padmapani or Avalokitesvara, of Tsongkhapa, and that of Amitabha, relinquished at their death the attainment of Buddhahood, *i.e.* the *summum bonum* of bliss, and of individual personal felicity, that they might be born again and again for the benefit of mankind. In other words, that they might be again and again subjected to misery, imprisonment in flesh and all the sorrows of life provided that they, by such a self sacrifice, repeated throughout long and weary centuries, might become the means of securing salvation and bliss in the hereafter for a handful of men chosen among but one of the many planetary races of mankind. And it is we, the humble disciples of the perfect Lamas who are expected to allow the Theosophical Society to drop its noblest title, that of the Brotherhood of Humanity, to become a simple school of Psychology. No! no! our brothers, you have been labouring under the mistake too long already. Let us understand each other. He who does not feel competent to grasp the noble idea sufficiently to work for it, need not undertake a task too heavy for him. But there is hardly a Theosophist in the whole Society unable to effectually help it by correcting erroneous impressions of outsiders, if not by actually propagating the ideas himself. Oh! for noble and unselfish men to help us effectually in that divine task! All our knowledge, past and present, would not be sufficient to repay them.

Having explained our views and aspirations, I have but a few words more to add. To be true, religion and philosophy must offer the solution of every problem. That the world is in such a bad condition, morally, is a conclusive evidence that none of its religions and philosophies — those of the civilized races less than any other — have ever possessed the TRUTH. The right and logical explanations on the subject of the problems of the great dual principles, right and wrong, good and evil, liberty and despotism, pain and pleasure, egotism and altruism, are as impossible to them now as they were 1880 years ago. They are as far from the solution as they ever were; but to these problems there must be somewhere a consistent solution, and if our doctrines will show their competence to offer it, then the world will be the first to confess that *ours* must be the true philosophy, the true religion, the true light, which gives truth and nothing but the TRUTH.

1880   THE MAHA CHOHAN

GLOSSARY

abhyasa	Constant practice; exertion
Adhiyajna	Primordial sacrifice; region of sacrifice
Aditi	Vedic name for *Mulaprakriti*; the abstract aspect of *Parabrahman*, though both manifested and unknowable
Agnishwatha Pitris	*Also* Solar Pitris. A class of dhyanis who lit up the principle of manas in the third race; our solar ancestors
ahankara	Egoism; the sense of 'I', self-identity
Akasha	Space, universal solvent, spiritual substance, the *upadhi* of Divine Thought
Alaya	Universal Soul; identical with *Akasha* in its mystic sense, and with *Mulaprakriti* in its essence, as it is the basis or root of all things
Amitabha	Cosmic Buddha, the "Boundless Age," the Dhyani Buddha of Gautama Buddha
ananda	Bliss, joy
Anima Mundi	The seven-fold Universal Soul and material source of all life, the divine essence which permeates, animates and informs all, the essence of seven planes of sentience, consciousness and differentiation; *Alaya*
antaskarana	The bridge between the lower mind (head) and the higher mind (heart), between the divine Ego and the personal soul of man
anu	Atom; point
Anupadaka	Parent-less, self-existing
Ashwatha	Sacred tree used to kindle the sacrificial fire: the Bo tree; the Tree of Knowledge, *ficus religiosa*
asuras	Class of celestial beings born from the breath—*Asu*—of Brahmā-Prajapati; the spiritual and divine ancestors of Manasic humanity
Atma	The Universal Spirit, the divine Monad, the seventh Principle in the septenary constitution of man; the Supreme Soul
Atman	SELF; divine breath; the universal Self
AUM	The sacred syllable, eternal vibration
avidya	Fundamental ignorance, any failure to discern the truth
Barhishad Pitris	*Also* Lunar Pitris. Lunar Gods, those who evolved astral prototypes of the human form; called in India the Fathers, "Pitris" or the lunar ancestors, and subdivided into seven classes or hierarchies

bhakti	Devotion
Bodhi	Wisdom
bodhichitta	*Lit.* 'seed of enlightenment'; embryo of spiritual man
Bodhisattva	*Lit.* 'he whose essence *(sattva)* has become Wisdom *(Bodhi)*'; enlightened being who remains in *samsara* to serve and help humanity
Book of Dzyan, The	*Also* 'The Stanzas of Dzyan'. An ancient, esoteric text written in an unknown language upon which *The Secret Doctrine* and *The Voice of the Silence* are based; *see* Dzyan
Brahmā	The creative Logos; the creator of the manifest universe in the Indian pantheon, the first of the Trimurti (three forms) of Brahmā, Vishnu and Shiva (creator, sustainer and destroyer/regenerator) existing periodically in manifestation then returning to *pralaya* (dissolving into non-manifestation) at the end of this cycle
Brahma	*Also Brahman.* The impersonal, supreme and incognizable principle of the universe; the Ultimate Reality; the attributeless Absolute
Brahma Vach	Divine wisdom; divine speech
Buddhi	Intellection, intuitive discernment, direct perception, resolute conviction, wisdom; the Universal Soul; the spiritual soul in man (the sixth principle), vehicle of *Atman;* divine discernment; Universal Intelligence
chakra	Wheel, discus; cycle; sphere; plexus or nerve center
chela	Disciple, especially the initiated disciple
chit	Thought, ideation, intellect
chitta	Consciousness; sometimes used generically for 'mind'
daimon	Inner voice of conscience and intuition; an aspect of the human soul
Daiviprakriti	Divine Nature; primordial, homogeneous light; the Light of the Logos
dana	Charity; the act of giving; alms-giving; generosity in thought, word and deed; the first *paramita*
deva	God, celestial being, resplendent deity
devachan	A post-mortem state of heavenly bliss wherein the Ego assimilates and enjoys the fruition of the good karma and harvest of the universal thought and intuition of the last life
Dhamma, the	*See* dharma
dharana	Concentration; steadiness in focus; mental firmness
dharma	Duty, moral law; social and personal morality; natural law, natural obligation; teaching, essence

Dhyan Chohan	*Lit.* 'Lord of Light'; one of the the highest gods; *pl.* the primordial divine intelligences and agents of divine law through which *Mahat* manifests and guides the Kosmos
dhyana	Contemplation, meditation; state of abstraction; the fifth *paramita*
Dhyani	Divine embodiment of ideation; man of meditation
Dzyan	*Lit.* 'To reform one's self by meditation and knowledge'; *see* The Book of Dzyan
Ego, the higher	SELF; the consciousness in man of "I am I" or the feeling of "I-am-ship"; Esoteric philosophy teaches the existence of two Egos in man, the mortal or personal, and the Higher, the Divine and the Impersonal, calling the former "personality" and the latter "Individuality."
Eros	The third personage of the Hellenic primordial trinity of Ouranos, Gaea and Eros; the abstract and universally beneficent creative force in nature, degraded by later attributions; *see also kama*
Fohat	The active (male) potency of the *Sakti* (female power) in nature; Higher Eros or *Kamadeva*, the essence of cosmic force or electricity; *Daiviprakriti;* the link between spirit and matter
gnosis	Spiritual, sacred Knowledge; the technical term used by the schools of religious philosophy before and during early Christianity
Great Breath	Symbolizing eternal ceaseless Motion; the One Life, eternal yet periodic in its regular manifestations; Absolute, omnipresent Consciousness
Grihastha Ashrama	The householder stage of life
guna	Propensity; quality; constituent
Gupta Vidya	Secret Wisdom, highest knowledge
guru	Venerable teacher; religious preceptor; spiritual teacher
Guruparampara	Sacred lineage of teachers
Hatha yoga	The practice of the lower form of Yoga, in which physical means for purposes of spiritual development are used; the opposite of Raja Yoga
Hermes-Thot	(Often written Hermes-Thoth) The archetype of Initiators; the God of Wisdom with the Ancients, who, according to Plato, whether as the Egyptian god Thot or the Greek god Hermes, 'discovered number, geometry, astronomy and letters'
Hiranyagarbha	The radiant or golden egg or womb; esoterically, the luminous 'fire mist' or ethereal stuff from which the universe was formed
Hotri	A priest who recites the hymns from the Rig Veda, and makes oblations to the fire

Ishtaguru	One's chosen teacher
Ishwara	The sovereign Lord; the omnipresent Spirit; the controller of maya
Itchashakti	The divine power of the will; one of the seven powers in nature and the human being
jiva	Life, life-essence; individual soul; the Monad or *Atma-Buddhi;* Life as the Absolute
jnana	Wisdom; knowledge
jnana yajna	Wisdom-sacrifice
Kali Yuga	The dark age; the fourth age; the iron age that began in 3102 B.C.
kalpa	Cosmic cycle, day of Brahmā
kama	Desire, attraction, passion; cleaving to existence; creative impetus and longing; *see also* Eros
kama manas	The desire mind, the lower *Manas* or human animal soul, the reflection of the higher *Manas*
kamaloka	The semi-material plane, to us subjective and invisible, where the disembodied "personalities" or human astral remains gradually disintegrate
kamarupa	The form of desire; the assemblage of cravings
karana	Instrument of action; basis of causation
karana sharira	The causal body; the inmost sheath
karma	Act, action; the law of ethical equilibrium
Krishna	The eighth Avatar of Vishnu
Kriyashakti	Creative imagination; a cosmic and human power
kshetra	Field, soil; portion of space; sphere of action; Nature
Kwan Yin	The female logos, the "Mother of Mercy"
lanoo	A disciple; *see also* chela
laya	Absorption, dissolution, repose; resting place; motionless point, still center; zero point
linga sharira	Astral body, aerial vesture, prototypal, vital body; *eidolon;* doppelgänger
Logos	The 'Verbum'; the 'Word'; the manifested Deity, the outward expression of the ever-concealed Cause
loka	Abode, circumscribed place; world, sphere; plane
Lunar Pitris	*See* Barhishad Pitris
Madhyamika	The "middle way" school of Buddhism
Maha Chohan	The chief of a spiritual Hierarchy, or of a school of Occultism; the head of the trans-Himalayan mystics

mahamanvantara	The manifestation of cosmos from *mahapralaya;* outbreathing of the Great Breath
Mahat	The first principle of universal intelligence and consciousness; the primal basis of individuation; cosmic ideation; the cosmic Mind behind manifested Nature and the great hebdomadal Heart of all humanity
Mahatma	Great soul; exalted exemplar of self-mastery and human perfection
Manas	Mind; the faculty of cognition, choice and self-awareness
Manasa	"The efflux of the divine mind"; the divine sons of Brahmā-Viraj, identical with the Kumara, the Manasaputra, and are identified with the human "Egos"
Manasaputras	The sons of (universal) Mind; human "Egos"; spiritual individuality of each human being
manvantara	Cosmic cycle of manifestation
maya	Illusion, appearance; the cosmic power behind phenomenal existence
moksha	Deliverance, emancipation
Monad	The Unity, the One; the unified triad (*Atma-Buddhi-Manas*), or the duad (*Atma-Buddhi*); the immortal part of man
Mulaprakriti	Root Nature; undifferentiated primordial substance; unmanifested matrix of all forms
Nadabrahman	Transcendental Sound or Vibrations; the Unmanifested Logos; *also Sabdabrahman*
namarupa	The fourth link in the chain of twelve *nidanas; nama* or mind, and *rupa* or form; *see nidana*
nidana	The twelve links in the chain of dependent origination, a concatenation of causes and effects; the cycle of birth, life, death and rebirth
nirguna	Without attributes; devoid of relations and qualities; unmodified; unbound
Nirguna Brahman	Brahma without attributes; Brahma (neuter); *see nirguna*
nirvana	Unalloyed bliss; the entire 'blowing out' of separateness; absolute consciousness
nitya pralaya	One of four kinds of *pralaya,* the stage of chronic change and dissolution, of growth and decay; the constant and imperceptible changes undergone by the atoms which last as long as a *mahamanvantara,* a whole age of Brahmā
nous	A Platonic term for the Higher *Manas* or Soul; Spirit as distinct from animal soul or psyche; divine consciousness or mind in man
OM	The mystic monosyllable; the soundless sound; the Word
OM TAT SAT	The triple designation of *Brahman*

para	*Lit.* 'beyond' or 'above'
Parabrahman	Supreme *Brahman;* the attributeless Absolute
Paramartha	Absolute existence and universal self-consciousness
paramitas	Transcendental virtues that lead to enlightenment
philos	Love, usually distinguished from love in any passionate sense, but rather as in love of brother or love of philosophy; in *philo-sophia,* love of wisdom
Philosophia Perennis	The perennial philosophy; the source of all true religions and philosophies; sometimes equated with the Secret Doctrine
Pitris	The ancestors or creators of mankind, of seven classes, three incorporeal *(arupa),* and four corporeal; *see* Solar Pitris and Lunar Pitris
prajna	A synonym of *Mahat,* the Universal Mind; the capacity for perception; Consciousness; wisdom; the sixth *paramita*
prakriti	Nature in general; spiritual nature, as distinct from *purusha,* Spirit; together the two primeval aspects of the One Unknown Deity
pralaya	A period of obscuration or repose—planetary, cosmic or universal—the opposite of *manvantara*
prana	Life-Principle; the breath of life
Pranava	The sacred Word, OM
Purusha	Spirit; the primeval man; the supreme being; the animating principle in all beings
Raja Yoga	System of developing spiritual powers through union with the Supreme Spirit; regulation and concentration of thought
rajas	One of the three *gunas* which constitute the qualities or divisions of matter; activity and change
Ṛg Veda, Rig Veda	The first and most important of the four Vedas; recorded in Occultism as having been delivered by great sages on Lake Manasarovar beyond the Himalayas
Root Race	The human Race has been compared to a tree—the main stem may be compared to the Root-Race, its larger limbs to seven Sub-Races
Saguna Brahman	With attributes and all perfections; Brahman
samadhi	*Lit.* 'self-possession'; the highest state of yoga; ecstatic meditation; supreme self-control
samsara	Conditionality, as contrasted with *nirvana;* realm of becoming, in contrast to Being; birth and death; conditioned existence; illusion
Sanatana Dharma	The eternal doctrine; the perennial philosophy; immemorial codes

Sangha, the	Order of monks; assembly; community; preservers, transmitters and teachers of the dharma
SAT	The ever-present Reality, absoluteness, Be-ness
Sat-Chit-Ananda	Abstract reality, consciousness and bliss
sattva	One of the three *gunas* which constitute the qualities or divisions of matter; the quality of goodness or purity; *see gunas*
satya	Supreme truth
shakti	The feminine, active creative forces in nature, mirrored in the seven forces in man
Shankaracharya	The great religious teacher and legendary reformer of India, the founder of Advaita Vedanta philosophy; *also* Shankara
sharira	Body
shila	Harmony in action; virtue, morality; an internally enforced ethical outlook; the second *paramita*
Shiva	Third god of the Hindu *Trimurti* Brahma-Vishnu-Shiva; in his character of Destroyer, he destroys only to regenerate on a higher plane
Solar Pitris	*See* Agnishwatha Pitris
Sophia	Wisdom; the female Logos of the Gnostics; the Universal Mind
Sophrosyne	Ancient Greek concept of self-control, restraint, soundness of mind, prudence and temperance
srotapatti	One who has entered the stream leading to enlightenment
sthula sharira	In metaphysics, the physical body
sunyata	'Void' or 'nothingness', but not a mere negation: the ineffable non-dual Reality that transcends all limitations and dualities, including *nirvana* and *samsara*
suras	Gods, *devas*
sushupti	Deep sleep consciousness
sutratman	Thread soul; reincarnating individuality
svadharma	One's own duty; natural calling; self-chosen responsibility
svasamvedana	*Lit.* the 'reflection which analyses itself'; *see paramartha*
swaraj	Freedom; self-rule, disciplined rule from within; political independence
tamas	The lowest of the three *gunas* which constitute the qualities or divisions of matter; the quality of darkness, foulness, inertia, and ignorance
tanha	The thirst for life; desire to live; clinging to life on this earth which causes rebirth or reincarnation; *also trishna*

tapas	Moral fervor; self-suffering; specific austerities and prolonged contemplation; that which burns up impurities
TAT	*Lit.* 'That'; *Brahman;* beyond the three worlds; the pre-existent
tattva	Truth, reality; principle, essence
Tathagata	Nature of a Buddha; one who has followed in the steps of his predecessors
tathata	Real nature, ultimate nature; attributelessness
Tetraktys	The sacred Quaternion; the Number of numbers; the Source of Nature; manifest Deity; the creative principle, represented by the triangle containing ten points in four rows, symbolizing the creative triad, the manifesting tetrad and the basic integers $(1 + 2 + 3 + 4 = 10)$, as well as the point (1), line (2), figure (triangle, 3) and solid (tetrahedron, 4)
Theosophia	"Divine Wisdom", the substratum of truth and knowledge which underlies the universe, from which of all the great world-religions and philosophies were derived; pure divine ethics. While *Theosophia* cannot be put entirely in words, Theosophy is what can be expressed at this time.
Theosophy	The maximal expression of *Theosophia* at this time in history; See *Theosophia*
Thot-Hermes	*See* Hermes-Thot
trishna	*Lit.* 'thirst' or 'craving', the cause of suffering; *also tanha*
Tsong-Kha-Pa	1357-1419 A.D. The 'model of virtue': Tibetan Buddhist founder of a new reformed order, the Gelugpa, to which all Dalai Lamas belong; stated by H.P. Blavatsky to have initiated a Seven Century Plan to infuse the Wisdom current into Western consciousness through various agents of the Society of Sages
turiya	Spiritual wakefulness; the fourth or highest state of the soul
upadhi	Basis; the vehicle, carrier or bearer of something less material than itself
Upanishads	Esoteric doctrines; interpretations of the Vedas by the methods of Vedanta
upaya	*Lit.* 'skill in means' or 'skilful device', the means by which difficult teachings are made comprehensible to persons of differing mental capacities
vahan	vehicle
Vak	From *vach, vacha:* voice, word, speech
Vedas	The most ancient and sacred Sanskrit works: the *Rig, Atharva, Sama, Yajur Vedas;* from the root *vid* 'to know' or 'divine knowledge'
Verbum	The Word; the manifested Deity, the outward expression of the ever-concealed Cause; *see* Logos

viraga	Detachment; indifference to pleasure and pain, illusion conquered, truth alone perceived; in certain trans-Himalayan schools, an additional *paramita* inserted as the fourth in the series
virya	Energy directed towards truth; vigour; courage; the fourth *paramita*
Word, the	*See* Verbum
Yang	The masculine active principle in nature that in Chinese cosmology is exhibited in light, heat, or dryness
Yin	The feminine passive principle in nature that in Chinese cosmology is exhibited in darkness, cold, or wetness
yoga	Unswerving concentration; fusion, integration; union with the divine; skill in action
yogin	Practitioner of yoga; proficient in yoga
Zarathustra	*Lit.* 'the star who sacrifices to the Sun'; the founder of Zoroastrianism; a title which some traditions give to thirteen Magus-Teachers

BIBLIOGRAPHY

Arnold, Sir Edwin. *The Light of Asia.* David McKay Co.,
  Philadelphia 1932.

Bellamy, Edward. *The Religion of Solidarity.* Concord Grove
  Press, Santa Barbara 1977. Originally published
  in 1874.

Blavatsky, Helena Petrovna. *Isis Unveiled.* Theosophy Co., Los
  Angeles 1982. Originally published in 1877.

———— *The Key To Theosophy.* Theosophy Co., Los Angeles 1987.
  Originally published in 1889.

———— *Lucifer,* 1887-1890. H.P. Blavatsky and Mabel Collins,
  London.

———— *The Secret Doctrine.* Theosophy Co., Los Angeles 1947.
  Originally published in 1888.

———— *Theosophical Articles, Vols. I - III.* Theosophy Co., Los
  Angeles 1981. Originally published in 1886-96.

———— *The Theosophical Glossary.* Theosophy Co., Los Angeles
  1973. Originally published in 1892.

———— *Transactions of the Blavatsky Lodge.* Theosophy Co., Los
  Angeles 1987. Originally published in
  1890-91.

———— *The Voice of the Silence.* Concord Grove Press, Santa
  Barbara 1989. Originally published in 1889.

Collins, Mabel. *The Gates of Gold.* Concord Grove Press, Santa
  Barbara 1982. Combined volume: *Through the
  Gates of Gold* (1887) and *Light on the Path* (1885).

Crosbie, Robert. *The Friendly Philosopher.* Theosophy Co., Los
  Angeles 1934.

———— *The Language of the Soul.* Concord Grove Press, Santa
  Barbara 1982. Originally published in 1919.

Iyer, Raghavan, ed. *In the Beginning (Zohar)*. Concord Grove Press, Santa Barbara 1979.

────── *The Golden Verses of Pythagoras*. Concord Grove Press, Santa Barbara 1980.

────── *The Gospel According to Thomas*. Concord Grove Press, Santa Barbara 1976.

────── *Hermes*, 1975 - 1989. Concord Grove Press, Santa Barbara.

────── *Return to Shiva (Yoga Vasishtha)*. Concord Grove Press, Santa Barbara 1977.

────── *Tao Te Ching*. Concord Grove Press, Santa Barbara 1978.

────── *The Jewel in the Lotus*. Concord Grove Press, Santa Barbara 1983.

Judge, William Quan. *The Bhagavad Gita: The Book of Devotion*. Theosophy Co., Los Angeles 1971. Originally published in 1890.

────── *"Forum" Answers by William Q. Judge*. Theosophy Co., Los Angeles 1982. Originally published 1889-96.

────── *The Ocean of Theosophy*. Theosophy Co., Los Angeles 1962. Originally published in 1893.

────── *Theosophical Articles*. Theosophy Co., Los Angeles 1980.

Mavalankar, Damodar K. *The Service of Humanity*. Concord Grove Press, Santa Barbara 1982. Originally published in 1884.

Patanjali. *Yoga Aphorisms*. Theosophy Co., Los Angeles 1951.

Plato. *The Banquet*. Translation by P.B. Shelley, Concord Grove Press, Santa Barbara 1981.

Plotinus. *The Enneads*. Translation by S. Mackenna. Faber and Faber, London 1966.

Russell, George William. *The Descent of the Gods, The Mystical Writings of A.E.* Ed. by Raghavan and Nandini Iyer. Colin Smythe, London 1983.

Shankar, Bhavani. *The Doctrine of the Bhagavad Gita.* Concord
    Grove Press, Santa Barbara 1984. Originally
    published in 1966.

Shankaracharya, Shri. Shankara's *Crest-Jewel of Discrimination:*
    Timeless Teachings on Nonduality — The Viveka-
    chudamani. Translated by Christopher
    Isherwood and Swami Prabhavananda. Vedanta
    Press, UK 1978.

Taimni, I.K. *The Gayatri.* The Theosophical Publishing House,
    Madras 1974.

Wadia, B.P. *The Grihastha Ashrama.* Concord Grove Press,
    Santa Barbara, 1981. Originally published in
    1941.

——— *The Law of Sacrifice.* Concord Grove Press, Santa Barbara,
    1981. Originally published in 1961.

INDEX

cyclical rhythm in every human life which is related to the mystery of numbers and the mathematics of collective cycles · 302

Cyclopean eye belongs to the subtler vestures which antedate the emergence of the physical form with its familiar organs · 217

Daiviprakriti · 23, 66, 94, 167, 254, 309, 317, 591, 592

Daiviprakriti is Vach in its *madhyama* form · 65

Dakshinamurti · 17, 19, 57, 104, 476

Dakshinamurti, Hymn to · 207

Dakshinamurti, the eternal Lord of the Mysteries · 672

Dakshinamurti, the Initiator of Initiates · 19, 45, 57, 476

Dakshinamurti, the Initiator of Initiates, who is again the custodian of this moment of global civilization · 663

darshana, every, corresponds with a familiar state of mind of the seeker, a legitimate and verifiable mode of cognition which makes sense of the world and the self at some level · 392

darshanas · 392, 397, 407, 408

darshanas or paradigmatic standpoints, shedding light from different angles on noumenal and phenomenal realities · 388

darshanas, sometimes called the six schools of Indian philosophy · 391

Darwin's thought leaves life to languish as a statistical accident, a blind offspring of a philosophy that is itself blind to the potency of ideation · 313

Dawn of manifestation and the Twilight of the onset of *Pralaya* are not to be thought of as two points of sequential time separated by vast intervals · 382

Days and Nights of Brahmā, *manvantara* and *pralaya* · 7

death, moment of, is the completion of a cycle of fulfilment of earthly duties and spiritual exercises · 211

deliverance, for Patanjali, can only come through *abhyasa*, assiduous practice, and *vairagya*, dispassionate detachment · 424

demonic qualities, resulting in spiritual inertia, are the product of misuse in previous lives · 237

descent of Spirit into matter, the spiritual and physiological processes are strictly coordinate during the · 219

despair, nature cannot negate, without human assistance · 33

detached, only when one fulfils all one's familiar obligations in many spheres can one become truly, free to contemplate and free to go beyond the claims of the world · 165

devachan is a period of rest and assimilation between lives · 11

devachan, basis of the popular mythology of heaven · 11

Devas · 4

devas and *devatas* · 112, 586

devas and *devatas*, echoed in mythic allusions to sylphs, salamanders, undines and gnomes, are all references to elementals · 145

devas, man can neither propitiate nor command the · 148

devotion arose out of that feeling, and became the first and foremost motor in his nature · 485

devotion to the invisible prototype that is the Guru is signified by the higher line in the symbol of Aquarius · 75

devotion, from *de votum*, 'to dedicate by a vow' · 78

dharana · 438, 443, 446, 449, 662

Dharana is full concentration, the focussing of consciousness on a particular point · 445

dharma · 87, 115, 236, 311, 322, 337, 352, 391 - 397, 498, 568, 585, 675, 676

dharma and *shraddha*, moral necessity and spiritual conviction · 317

Mysterium Magnum, the universal medium upon which are impressed vast assemblages of thought-forms emanating from the Cosmic Mind · 631

Mystery Schools · 47, 478, 485

Mystical Christianity teaches *self*-redemption through one's own seventh principle, the liberated Paramatma, called by the one Christ, by others Buddha · 773

Mythology and folklore not merely represent a recollection of extraordinary events, but also point to the plane of perception on which those events occur · 632

Nada Brahman · 495

Nada Brahman, the cosmic sound · 290

nadabrahman, the Divine Resonance and perpetual motion of absolute Spirit · 441

namarupa · 303, 492, 671

names (and words) are either BENEFICENT *or* MALEFICENT; *they are, in a certain sense, either venomous or health-giving* · 295

nastika or heterodox schools of Indian thought · 388

nation's spiritual decline accompanies its material ascent · 48

Nature affords individuals innumerable occasions for the clarification and purification of perception and intention · 86

Nature cannot negate despair without human assistance · 33

Nature, a servant of Adepts but a teacher to everyone else · 258

Nature, ceaseless activity in, is at all times constructive, requiring the disintegration and rebuilding of structures, expressing beauty in every one of the seasons · 286

nature, unseen tablets of, are a vast reservoir of enigmatic glyphs and symbols and eternal verities · 18

negation of all limited states of consciousness equivalent to affirmation of universal life and absolute freedom · 339

negation of form essential to the realization of ideals · 346

negations of false continuity of consciousness are vital opportunities to awaken to a deeper continuity in consciousness · 346

Nemesis was not a goddess originally, but rather a moral feeling which stood as the barrier to evil and immorality · 322

New Cycle, working mostly in the realm of *Akasha,* acts as a potent alchemical solvent in the astral light and in the inmost consciousness of hosts of souls · 682

Nirguna Brahman · 377, 378, 379

Nirguna Brahman, the attributeless Absolute, generating the possibility of universal mind, which in turn becomes Mahat, the cosmic mind of a particular system · 378

nirodha · 413, 447, 448

nirodha, a condition of balance · 79

nirodha, restraint, cessation or interception · 446

nishkama karma · 681

nishkama karma or disinterested action · 400

niyamas · 441

niyamas, the five binding observances constituting the positive dimension of ethical probity · 439

niyamas, the observances · 438

Noble (Arya) Path · 356

noetic and psychic action, the difference between seeing from within without and seeing only from outside · 91

Noetic awakening presupposes that one learns to take nothing for granted · 209

noetic magic, a summoning from latency to active potency of arcane knowledge that was originally impressed in the imperishable soul-memory of all humanity · 46

parasitic and derivative existence through restrictively conceptualizing consciousness, which itself is essentially as unbounded as the sky · 363

particle physics · 47, 89

particulars to universals, tracing is as crucial to art as to psychology · 5

Pashyanti Vach, coexistent with the Logos and inseparable from its own highest self-awareness · 65

pasts and futures, in principle possible for there to be beings in the universe who can see all · 517

Patanjali · 79, 259, 317, 409 - 451, 458, 459, 468, 565, 667

Patanjali set out the Taraka Raja Yoga system, linking transcendental and self-luminous wisdom (*taraka*) with the alchemy of mental transformation · 401

Patanjali, founder of Yoga school · 392

Path · ix, 60, 99, 113, 149, 154, 181 - 185, 197, 284, 358, 427, 478, 508, 514, 553, 569, 575, 581, 589, 602, 622, 670 - 671, 737

path begins and ends outside the lower self · 331

Path of Renunciation · 176, 178, 180

Path of true spiritual self-consciousness commences at that crucial point where one is ready to live in and through diverse beings · 174

Path of Woe · 280, 513

Path of Woe, mental woe for all souls trapped in the abject wretchedness of living death · 180

Path, right-hand · 684

Path, the, ever exists; not something invented or first propounded by Gautama Buddha · 357

patterns of Nature, capacity to discern, is the prerequisite for enlisting the forces of Nature on behalf of human designs · 98

peak experiences · 37

peak experiences, without developing spiritual and mental insight, one cannot comprehend the scope and range of possible · 229

perfectibility · 233, 488, 525, 535, 542, 614, 643

perfectibility, any viable conception of, requires a sensitive, scrupulous care for the undeniable imperfections of flawed materials in the lunar vestures · 605

personal identity has no continuity whatsoever except through repetition of signs and sounds, and no intrinsic validity except through passive acquiescence · 177

personality, merely a tool or instrument and in itself of no consequence other than as a transient vesture of the Immortal Soul · 331

pervasive principle of continuity in the cosmic order and in human nature · 229

Philosophia Perennis · 3, 11, 351, 673

philosophic fusion of science and religion, of *vidya* and *dharma*, is essential to the structure of the Aquarian civilization of the future · 87

philosophic religion · 603

Philosophy does not resolve the ultimate questions, even though it brings great clarity to cognition · 409

philosophy ends where realization begins, in Sankhya as in Vedanta · 409

philosophy of human perfectibility · 3

physical form, every point in the, each life-atom, is shot through with reflected Mahabuddhi, the latent power of self-consciousness · 112

physical plane, everything on the, is not only isomorphic, but also isodynamic with something on a higher plane · 276

physics and chemistry have partially revealed the complex matrix of differentiations of the ATOM, as they apply to the lowest planes · 92

pilgrim soul, every, is eternally impelled from within by an immortal longing for reunion with its essential nature, its transcendent source · 151

NOTES

NOTES

NOTES

NOTES

NOTES

NOTES

NOTES

NOTES

NOTES